Muirheads Trawlers, Ltd., Edinburgh.

W. H. Burn, St. Andrews.

T. Devlin, junr., Newhaven, N.B.

Fraserburgh & North of Scotland Steam Trawling Co., Ltd., Fraserburgh.

Balgownie S. T. Co., Aberdeen.

Bookless Brothers, Aberdeen.

The Walker S.T. Co., Aberdeen.

The Wetherley S.T. Co., Aberdeen

United Steam Fishing Co., Ltd., Aberdeen.

D. J. McKinnon & Son, Dundee.

Boston Deep Sea Fishing & Ice Co., Ltd.

Vve. Christiaens, A. Bourgain & Cie., Boulogne s/mer.

Gaston Vallée, Rouen, France.

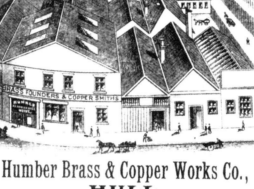

Nat. Tel. : 1552.   Telegrams : Gameful, Hull.

Humber Brass & Copper Works Co., HULL.

BRASSFOUNDERS, COPPERSMITHS, ELECTRICAL ENGINEERS, PLUMBERS, METAL MERCHANTS.

Manufacturers of every description of SHIP'S BRASS WORK

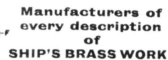

Wheel Valves,
Gland Cocks,
Plug Cocks,
Bath and Lavatory Cocks,
Steam and Water Fittings,
Tallow Cups,
Steam Whistles,
Sight Feed Lubricators.

All kinds of Brass Castings to Order.

John Duncan, Son & Co., Liverpool.

J. Marr & Son, Ltd., Fleetwood.

Wyre S. T. Co., Ltd., Fleetwood.

The Heron Steam Trawler Co., Ltd., Swansea

Castle Steam Trawlers, Ltd., Swansea.

Southern S. T. Co., Milford Haven.

Neale & West, Cardiff and Milford Haven.

Western S. T. Co., Ltd., Bristol.

O. T. OLSEN, NAUTICAL INSTRUMENT MAKER, GRIMSBY.

BRITISH
STEAM
TRAWLERS

FROM DEVELOPMENT TO DEMISE

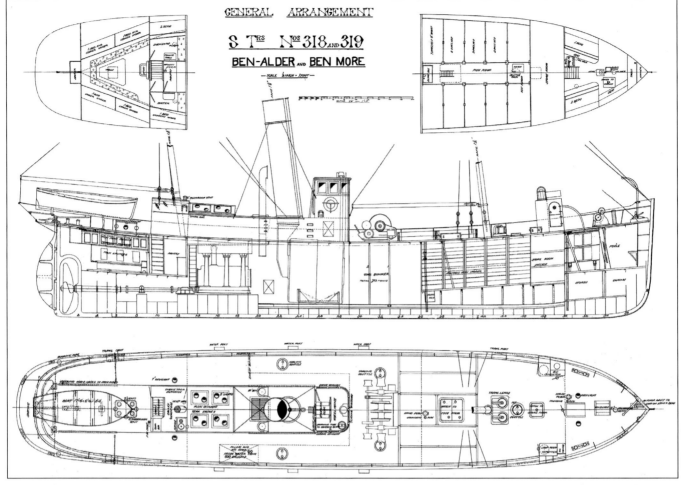

Plan 1: Steam trawlers **Ben Alder** (A.16) and **Ben More** (A.82), which were built by Hall, Russell in 1899 and owned by Richard Irvin & Sons, North Shields. **Ben Alder** was sold to the Holbech Steam Trawler Company, Scarborough in 1914 and requisitioned as a boom defence vessel in June 1915. Returned to owners in 1919. **Ben More** was lost on 23rd December 1911 after running ashore at Whitelink Bay, Inverallochy, with no loss of life. Note 'trawling ports' fitted prior to the usual gallows.

The coloured end papers are courtesy Olsen's Fisherman's Nautical Almanack 1910.

© Donald Smith and Black Dwarf Publications 2016
Designed by Alan Kittridge and Neil Parkhouse
British Library Cataloguing-in-Publication Data.
A catalogue record for this book is available from the British Library

ISBN: 9781903599 23 5

Black Dwarf Lightmoor Publications Ltd
Unit 144B, Lydney Trading Estate, Harbour Road, Lydney, Gloucestershire GL15 5EJ
Black Dwarf Publications is an imprint of Black Dwarf Lightmoor Publications Ltd
www.lightmoor.co.uk
Printed in Poland
www.lfbookservices.co.uk

BRITISH
STEAM
TRAWLERS

FROM DEVELOPMENT TO DEMISE

Painting 1: The Aberdeen steam liner **Fernbank (**A.910) from a painting by A. Harwood. Launched in 1907 as the steam trawler **Loch Kildonan** (A.163 – 115ft x 22ft x 12ft 6ins, 211g) by Hall Russell's for the White Star Steam Fishing Co. Ltd, Aberdeen. She was requisitioned as a minesweeper in August 1914 and returned in 1919. In 1920 she was sold to the Montrose Steam Fishing Co. Ltd and renamed **River Annan** (ME.249). She returned to Aberdeen in August 1922 as **Fernbank (**A.910), owned by the Stephen Fishing Co. Ltd who converted her for lining. She was bombed and sunk by German aircraft 12 miles NW of Mygganaes Light, Faeroes on 16th November 1941, with the loss of four of her crew.

Donald Smith

LEFT: A cutaway view of a typical steam trawler by Laurence Dunn and used as an advertisement by Hall, Russell & Co. of Aberdeen.

BELOW: Plan 2: Built by A. Hall, Aberdeen in 1917 as *Captain Pollen*, Yard No. 536, 275 tons, for A.V. Cole of Cheltenham. Requisitioned in December 1917 as a minesweeper, she was returned to her owners in 1919 and sold to Belgium as *Prevoyance Sociale*. Bought by the North Star Steam Fishing Company Ltd, Aberdeen in 1935 and renamed *Avonglen* (A.383). Requisitioned in August 1940 as a port examination vessel but later converted to a hospital tender. Returned to owners in August 1946. Scrapped at Granton 1959.

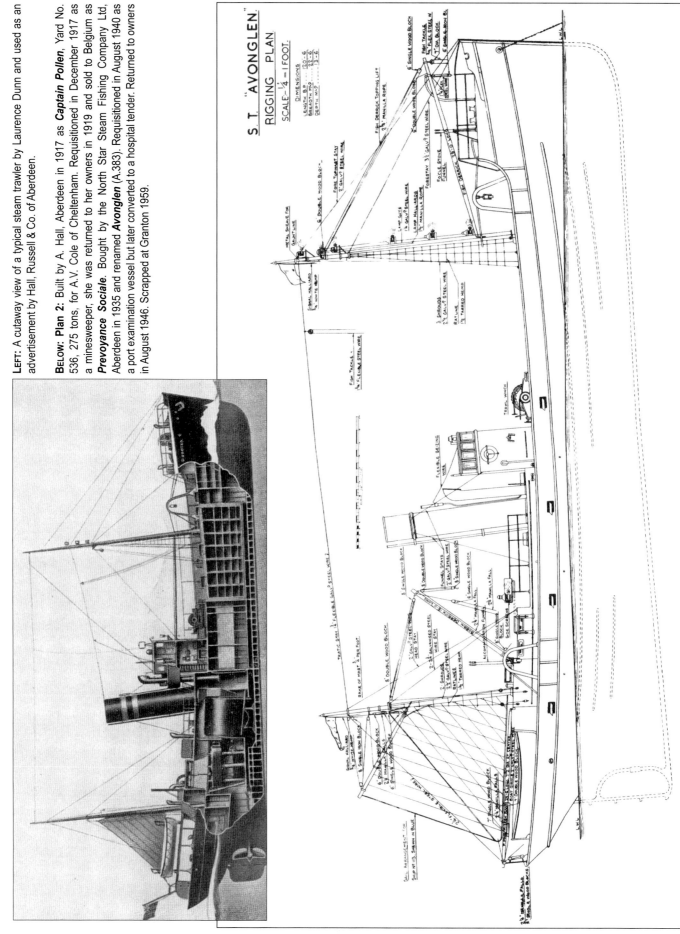

CONTENTS

ABBREVIATIONS

All dimensions are in feet = **ft** and inches = **ins**

OA = overall length. **BP** = length between perpendiculars. **WL** = waterline.

G = gross tons. **N** = nett tons. **IHP** = indicated horse power. **NHP** = nominal horse power. **S** = stroke.

DF = direction finding. **RT** = radio transmission. **WT** = wireless telegraphy. **FW** = fresh water. **WC** = water closet (toilet).

AA = anti-aircraft. **APV** = armed patrol vessel. **A/S** = anti submarine. **BDV** = boom defence vessel. **LCT** = landing craft tank

MAS = motor anti-submarine boat. **MFV** = motor fishing vessel. **M/S** = minesweeper.

A/A = anti aircraft. **BT** = bomb throwing. **D/C** = depth charge. **H/A** = high angle. **L/A** = low angle. **Q/F** = quick firing.

PREFACE

When I began researching this book back in the late 1960s, the internet was unknown and research was far more labour intensive, involving much letter writing and personally visiting many sources. Now, thankfully, information can be more readily accessed by way of the world wide web and the information world seems to have shrunk, or is just more accessible. My passion for the steam trawler stems from childhood. I grew up in Aberdeen, in Old Torry to be precise, where I was surrounded by the trawlermen and their vessels. From my primary school class room, I would watch them in the navigation channel which lead to the grey North Sea. In the 1960s, I served in RAF Marine Craft and one of my postings was to 1104 Marine Craft Unit, Bridlington, where I came in close contact with the Distant Water trawlers out of Hull and Grimsby. For a time we serviced our launches at Hull, on the slips at the western end of St. Andrew's Dock, where our 63ft wooden craft were overshadowed by these large trawlers. St. Andrew's Dock during this period was a mecca for the steam trawler enthusiast, being packed with ships. Some were unloading their catches on the 'wet' side of the dock, while others were laid as many as three deep along the 'dry' side, being repaired, re-fuelled and taking on ice and stores, ready to return to sea. As a modelmaker, I was disappointed that there was no really accurate detailed drawings commercially available for these ships, so I would spend my lunch breaks in the trawler companies' offices searching out information. From the Manager of the St. Andrew's Steam Fishing Co., I received my first genuine builders GA (General Arrangement) drawing of the 1936-built *St. Cathan* and her sisters. This plan was to be the catalyst which motivated me to write this book. As this work has taken over forty years to complete, many who gave encouragement and help have passed on. Not only have the people gone, so too have the ships, the yards that produced them and almost all the owners who managed them. So many records were destroyed over the years, by well meaning individuals in the name of 'rationalisation', that much invaluable information has been lost forever. Research can be difficult enough, living here in the north of Scotland and this was not helped by the powers that be moving all the Custom House Registers down to Cardiff. Where, as formerly, a great deal of research could be done in one afternoon (at no cost), nowadays, one is totally dependant on the good nature of the staff of the Registrar of Shipping to answer queries, in between carrying out their normal duties.

I am deeply indebted to the following for their assistance and for their patience over this period.

My wife Mary, who has suffered my obsessions since the first day we met, for without her help and understanding, this book would never have been finished. I am grateful to Norman Willis, of Hull, who spent most of his life as a radio officer on the Distant Water ships and also to Marcus Brockman, and his late, lovely wife Doreen, who sadly wound up the family business of C.D. Holmes of Hull in the 1970s. The company had been marine engineers since 1868, long before the evolution of the steam trawler, and had taken over the shipbuilding interests of Cook, Welton & Gemmell in April 1963. Stan Byatt was the company manager during the 1970s and I cannot thank him enough for all his help with supplying drawings, specifications and photographs, etc. Help from Cochranes was freely given by Ian Johnson and, ironically, some of his letters from 1976, are stamped 'In receivership', another sad end to a famous yard. The staff at Smith's Dock, Middlesborough, Richards Ironworks and other shipyards also provided masses of information

From my home town of Aberdeen, Douglas Paul of Hall, Russells and Sandy Curle of John Lewis both helped immensely with supplying drawings and technical answers; sadly these yards are no more. Another dear friend and a stalwart figure of Aberdeen's waterfront was the late Bill Ritchie. Bill was, for many years, the senior harbour pilot and one of his many jobs was to take most of the new trawlers out on sea trials. His wealth of knowledge on Aberdeen-built trawlers can never be bettered. Other close friends, whose encouragement over the years I must acknowledge, are the late George Coull, who strove to preserve the history of Aberdeen's trawling trade, and Donald Leiper, one of the old school of ships' draughtsmen, who worked for Hall, Russell's and the Naval Contracts Drawing Office of Canadian Vickers.

I should like to thank the many staff at all the libraries and museums throughout the UK, who so willingly gave of their time. My special thanks must go to Miss Isobel Deans of Aberdeen Public Library; Rosalyn Rennie from Aberdeen City Archives; Arthur Credland of the Town Docks Museum, Hull; Dr Ian Harrison and his staff at the National Fishing Heritage Centre at Grimsby; and the librarians of the Old Torry Research Station at Aberdeen. Thanks are also long overdue to Ted Wilson, John Lambert, Peter Brady, Parry Watson, Jim Wood and the late Edward Paget Tomlinson.

Thanks are due to many firms (some now defunct) who supplied information about their products: Robertsons of Fleetwood; the Marconi Company; Donkin & Co.; Schat and Welin davit companies; and the old Great Grimsby Coal, Salt & Ice Company, to name but a few. Among the many trawler owners who assisted, my special thanks go to Richard Irvin's of Aberdeen, along with companies such as Boston Deep Sea Fisheries (originally the Boston Deep Sea Fishing & Ice Co. Ltd), Marr & Sons, Boyd Line Ltd, Thomas Hamlings, Iago Steam Trawling Co. Ltd and Kingston Steam Trawling Co. Ltd (I have given their pre-amalgamation names).

To the many people who have so willingly supplied photographs, I am indeed grateful and to others whose pictures may appear here without their consent, I offer my sincere apologies, as often it is impossible to trace the original source of a photograph. My thanks also to Steve Farrow for allowing me to use his excellent trawler paintings.

Finally, thanks also go to Pat O'Driscoll, my very good friend the late Phil Thomas, who goaded me for the past four decades to get the book finished, and to Dr Charles Waine for his never ending patience.

Donald Smith
Whitehills, 2016

Steam trawler industry advertising

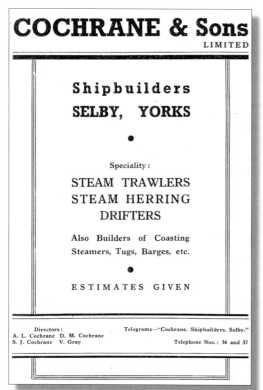

COCHRANE & Sons
LIMITED

Shipbuilders
SELBY, YORKS

•

Speciality :

STEAM TRAWLERS
STEAM HERRING
DRIFTERS

Also Builders of Coasting
Steamers, Tugs, Barges, etc.

•

ESTIMATES GIVEN

Directors :
A. L. Cochrane D. M. Cochrane
S. J. Cochrane V. Gray

Telegrams—"Cochrane, Shipbuilders, Selby."

Telephone Nos. : 36 and 37

Modern Vessels by LEWIS

The LEWIS Yard posseses facilities for :
• The complete construction of vessels ready for sea.
• Construction and installation of reciprocating steam engines up to 3,000 H.P.
• Hull repairs and private electric slipway.
• Diesel and steam engine and boiler repairs.
• Steam trawl and cargo winches and windlasses.
• Scottish shipbuilding traditions, and skilled workmen and engineers.

THE MODERN FACILITIES of the LEWIS SHIPYARD and marine engine works, Aberdeen, are now available for the construction and repair of VESSELS of all kinds for Coastal and Fishing Use (up to 280 feet).

JOHN LEWIS & SONS, LTD.
GRAMS :-
'BOILER' ABERDEEN **ABERDEEN** TELEPHONE 7000
6 LINES

Since 1856
we have manufactured
WINDLASSES and CAPSTANS
which have been recognised as the standard for the world. Simplicity, strength, power and efficiency has gained us a reputation which is second to none

For your new vessels specify
EMERSON WALKER

EMERSON WALKER LIMITED
DUNSTON, GATESHEAD-ON-TYNE, 11
Works Telephone Nos.: Dunston 84257-8-9   Telegraphic Address : "Nestor, Gateshead"
London Agent : WATTS, FINCHAM (1932) LTD.
2 GREAT WINCHESTER STREET, E.C.2   Telephone : London Wall 5216

CHARLES D. HOLMES & Co., Ltd.
Hull Engineering Works,
HULL.

Registered Office :
ALFRED STREET.

Telegrams : COMPOUND.
Telephones : 6353 } Central.
6435 }

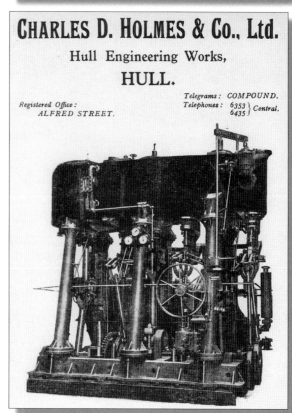

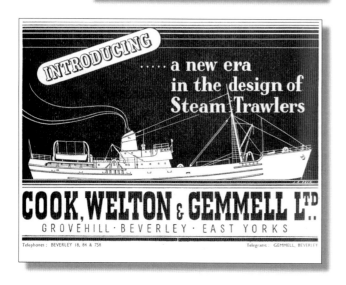

INTRODUCING
..... a new era
in the design of
Steam Trawlers

COOK, WELTON & GEMMELL LTD.
GROVEHILL · BEVERLEY · EAST YORKS
Telephones : BEVERLEY 18, 84 & 758   Telegrams : GEMMELL, BEVERLEY

Steam trawler development 1890-1950

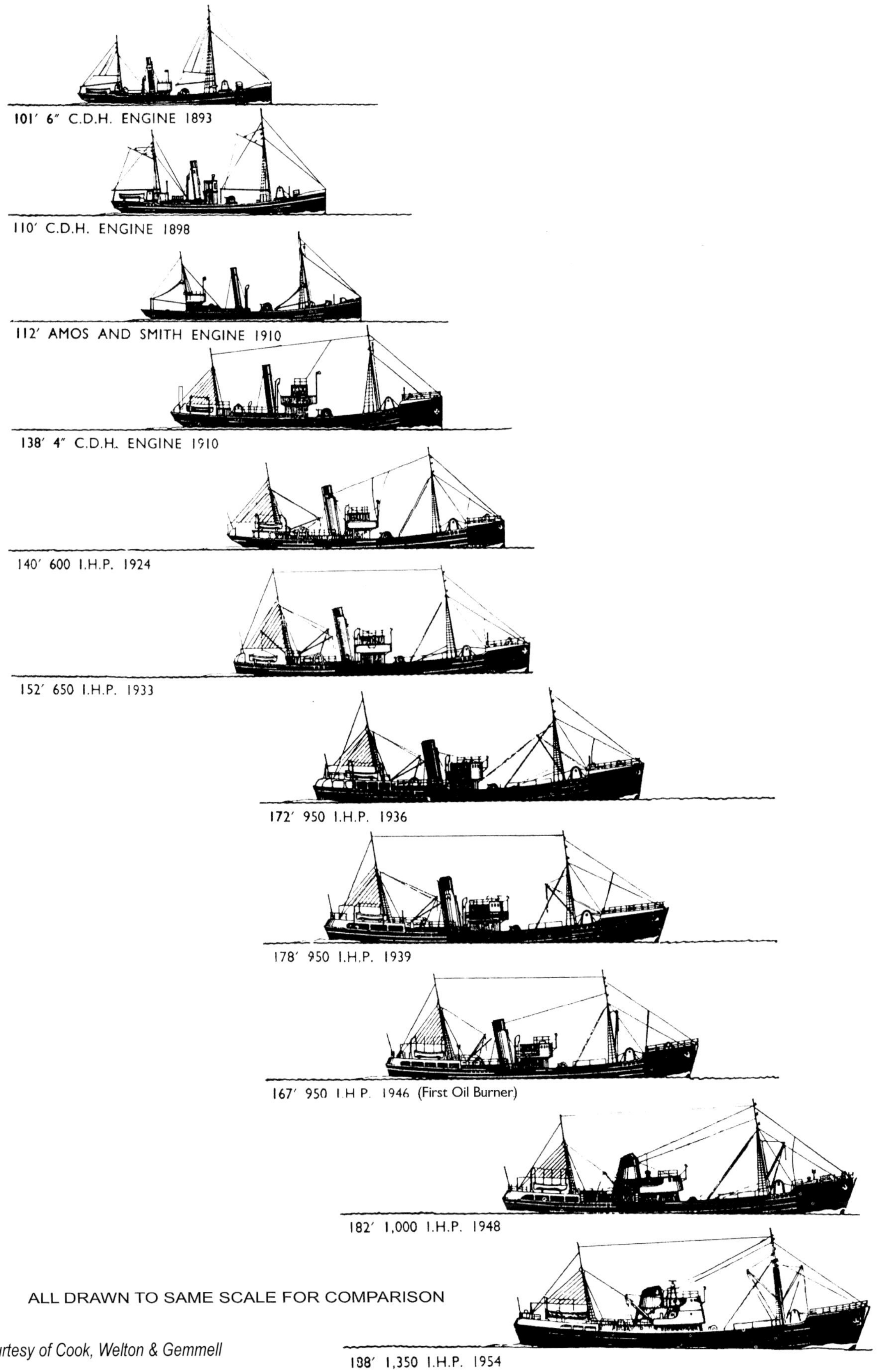

101' 6" C.D.H. ENGINE 1893

110' C.D.H. ENGINE 1898

112' AMOS AND SMITH ENGINE 1910

138' 4" C.D.H. ENGINE 1910

140' 600 I.H.P. 1924

152' 650 I.H.P. 1933

172' 950 I.H.P. 1936

178' 950 I.H.P. 1939

167' 950 I.H.P. 1946 (First Oil Burner)

182' 1,000 I.H.P. 1948

ALL DRAWN TO SAME SCALE FOR COMPARISON

Fig. 0: *Courtesy of Cook, Welton & Gemmell*

138' 1,350 I.H.P. 1954

Schematic drawing of a steam trawler

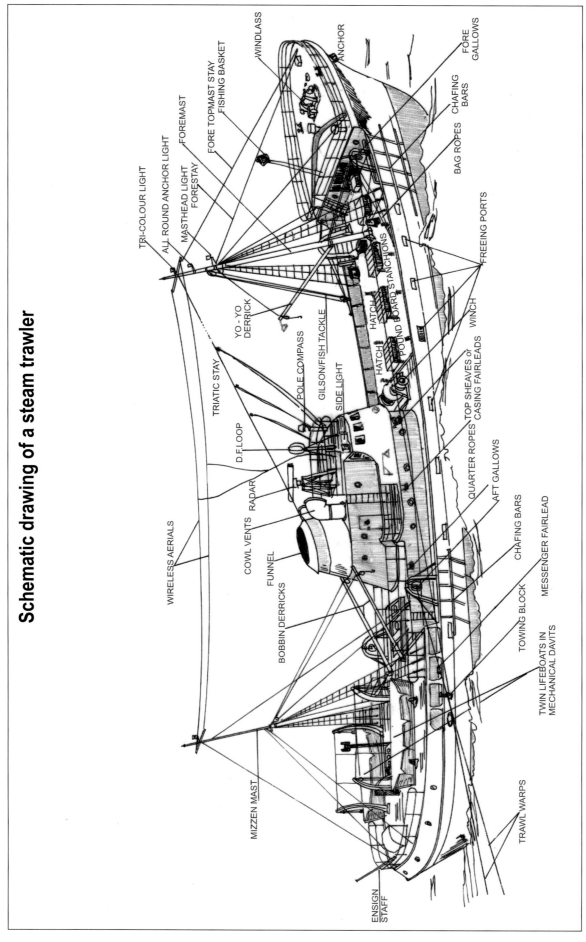

Fig. 1: Schematic of a Distant Water steam trawler.

Chapter 1: INTRODUCTION

For want of water they drank water,
when there was plenty of water, they drank beer
TRAWLERMAN'S RIDDLE.

This is primarily a study of the development of British built and owned commercial steam trawlers, rather than a treatise on the trawling industry. It includes some trawlers built in UK yards for foreign owners, as their design played an intrinsic part in the greater picture. Likewise, I have included two classes built in Germany for UK owners, plus details of steam liners, drifter/trawlers and fish carriers. When dealing with military trawlers, I have mainly included drawings of those based on mercantile types. The history of the steam trawler is obviously wholly linked to the requirements of the industry and owners alike but apart from touching, where necessary, on the commercial side, I have endeavoured, as far as possible, to keep to the main theme. To save repetition, overall length and gross tons are given, unless otherwise stated.

ORIGINS OF STEAM TRAWLING

The steam trawler evolved from the sailing smacks and indeed the early ships, apart from a woodbine funnel (named after Wills 'Woodbines', a very thin cigarette) and an inefficient steam engine, were almost identical in both outline and rig. The first steamers were actually Long Liners and, although built of iron, they frequented the same grounds as their sailing counterparts and even used the same well system to keep the catch fresh. As fleeting formed a large part of the Humber operations, it was a logical progression to replace the sailing trawlers with steamers and huge fleets of these ships worked the North Sea. Of course, not all the trawlers worked together in fleets; indeed, the majority were termed 'single boaters' and instead of working under an 'Admiral', their skippers were free to find fish wherever they could.

The Scottish sector of the industry never adopted the fleeting system. One of the drawbacks of the steam trawler was its cost. The early second hand paddle tug/trawlers cost at least double that of a new sailing smack. This brought about the demise of the skipper/owner, with most new steam trawlers being built for larger companies, with directors and shareholders, few of whom ever even went aboard their ships, let alone got their feet wet. The steam trawler, with four times the catching power of the smack, turned the Victorian sail fishing industry into the highly commercial operation that the financiers came to expect. If one compares the lines of these early vessels, they are mirror images of their sailing counterparts and even the 115ft 'Strath' Class trawlers show basically the same underwater shape as the cod smacks.

The owners have always been regarded as villains and crooks by the trawlermen. In many cases I am sure this was true but it is possibly a little unfair to tar them all with the same brush. One should remember that, without the hard bitten attitudes and huge financial commitments of these men, few, if any, of the large fleets would have existed. Trawling has always been a gamble; for some it paid off handsomely but for the majority, it merely gave them a tenuous living, with death always looking over their shoulder.

TYPES OF FISH CAUGHT

Demersal Fish: These are the true deep sea fish that live on the bottom of the sea, comprising two main types, round and flat fish, and are the trawlers' principal catch.

Round Fish:

Cod	Inhabits the northern waters, notably the north of Britain, Iceland and Newfoundland. Cod was the primary catch of Hull and Grimsby Distant Water ships.
Ling	Inhabits northern waters, west of Scotland and Ireland, and north towards Iceland and Newfoundland.
Haddock	Inhabits northern waters. Nearly half the total catch is caught in the North Sea, the remainder from the White Sea to the Bay of Biscay. The Haddock was the major catch of Aberdeen, Granton and Grimsby Near Water trawlers.
Whiting	Found in great numbers in the North Sea, it is more coastal than the Cod or Haddock and was a favourite with Near Water trawlers.
Hake	Most of the catch is caught to the south west of Ireland and north west of Scotland. Also found off Morocco and in the Bay of Biscay. Hake was the main catch for Fleetwood's Middle Water ships.

Flat Fish:

Sole	A shallow water fish, common in the Irish Sea.
Plaice	Inhabits northern waters, all round Britain and Iceland.
Flounder	Inhabits estuaries in the North Sea and Baltic.
Halibut	Inhabits northern waters. It attains a large size, six feet or more.
Turbot	Not very abundant, inhabits the deeper parts of the North Sea.

TERRITORIAL FISHING LIMITS

Britain banned trawling within a three mile limit all round her coasts. This territorial limit, laid down by the International Law of the Sea, was originally the maximum range of shore based cannon. One exception was the 1,400 square mile area of the Moray Firth, the traditional inshore grounds of the Scottish 'line' fishermen. When steam trawlers began to encroach on these grounds, often destroying the 'long lines' as they lay on the seabed, tempers flared and the Moray Firth became a battlefield. In 1889, Bye Law 10 of the Herring Fishery (Scotland) Act closed the entire area inside a line drawn from Rattray Head to Duncansby Head to UK trawlers. Unfortunately, there was a loop hole in the law, which allowed foreign trawlers to work up to the old territorial three mile limit and the English owners took full advantage of this by registering their ships on the Continent, giving rise to the terms 'Hull Belgians' and 'Grimsby Norwegians'. This misuse of the law was quite legal providing one crew member was a foreign national but it only inflamed the situation. A failed attempt in 1905 to apply the Scottish Law to foreigners eventually led to the 1909 Act, which prohibited landing any fish caught in the Moray Firth

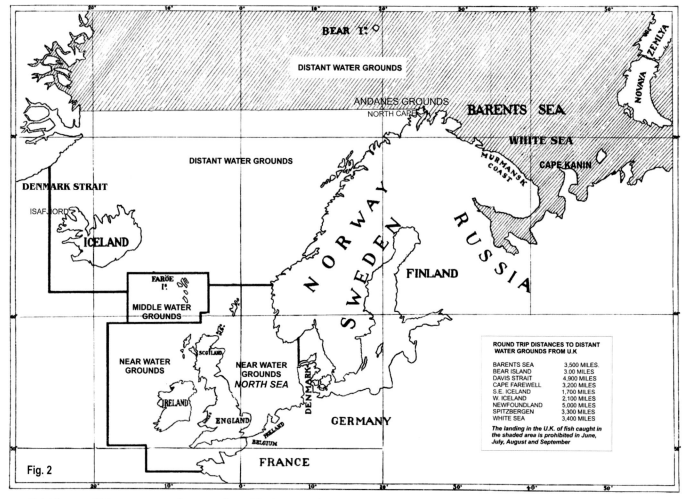

Fig. 2

ROUND TRIP DISTANCES TO DISTANT
WATER GROUNDS FROM U.K

BARENTS SEA	3,500 MILES.
BEAR ISLAND	3.00 MILES
DAVIS STRAIT	4,900 MILES
CAPE FAREWELL	3,200 MILES
S.E. ICELAND	1,700 MILES
W. ICELAND	2,100 MILES
NEWFOUNDLAND	5,000 MILES
SPITZBERGEN	3,300 MILES
WHITE SEA	3,400 MILES

The landing in the U.K. of fish caught in the shaded area is prohibited in June, July, August and September

at a British port. This was yet another unenforceable Act, as unless actually caught 'poaching', the trawlers would insist that they had been nowhere near the Moray Firth and when it became too difficult in Britain, they would land their catches on the Continent. This 'poaching' continued until the First World War, when most of the British trawlers were requisitioned for Naval service. Iceland and the Faeroes were also complaining, as far back as 1890, that their waters were being stripped of fish by British steam trawlers. This was the start of the very first 'Cod War' in 1893 and the outcome was the insistence of a 13 mile limit. This, of course, was hotly disputed by our politicians but an agreement was eventually reached with Iceland in 1896, which allowed our trawlers to seek shelter in the fjords, providing all their gear was lashed and stowed; in return, we would not fish east of a line drawn from Illunypa to Thornodesker.

FISHING NUMBERS

In 1868, the Customs & Excise decreed that every commercial fishing vessel be allotted its own unique identification mark. Every vessel had to show a port of registry, followed by a number, not difficult to achieve one would think, until they complicated things by giving fishing vessels three separate classes within the regulations:

1st Class To include all steamers and other boats of 15 gross tons and upwards. Port letters and numbers to be 18ins high and 2½ins wide, positioned 3-4ins below the gunwale. Funnel letters and numbers of a conspicuous size and positioned 12ins below the top. Port letters after number.

2nd Class To include all steamers and other boats of less than 15 gross tons, or of 18ft. keel and upwards. Letters to be 10ins high by 1¾ins wide. Port letters after number.

3rd Class To include all boats under 18ft keel, other than those navigated by oars only and marked in accordance with Section 176 of the Customs Consolidation Act 1876. Letters to be 6ins high by ¾ins wide. Port letters before number.

The port registration letters are generally the first and last letter of the port, making Grimsby GY, Montrose ME, Fleetwood FD and so on. Unfortunately, not all ports are so identified. Aberdeen vessels only carry the letter A, for reasons unknown as the letters AN have never been allotted. Hull is shown only as H, because Hartlepool HL, was registered before Hull; Littlehampton carries the LN letters rather than London with LO; North Shields vessels carry the SN registration rather than NS, which was given to North Sunderland (Seahouses); and Oban is OB rather than ON. **Fig. 3** shows the register in 1948 but since then, many ports have stopped fishing and been removed from the registry. Others have been grouped together under one main centre, such as Ayr, which now shows the BA registration for Ballantrae. These names and numbers were to be painted in white oil colour on a black background. The same letters and numbers were also to be painted on each side of the mainsail, immediately above

PORT DISTINGUISHING LETTERS FOR BRITISH FISHING VESSELS 1948

A	ABERDEEN	CK	COLCHESTER	GR	GLOUCESTER	NN	NEWHAVEN	SU	SOUTHAMPTON
AA	ALLOA	CL	CARLISLE	GW	GLASGOW	OB	OBAN	SY	STORNOWAY
AB	ABERYSTWYTH	CN	CAMPBLETOWN	GY	GRIMSBY	P	PORTSMOUTH	TH	TEIGNMOUTH
AD	ARDROSSAN	CO	CARNARVON	H	HULL	PD	PETERHEAD	TO	TRURO
AH	ARBROATH	CS	COWES	HL	HARTLEPOOL	PE	POOLE	TT	TARBERT
AR	AYR	CT	CASTLETOWN	IE	IRVINE	PEH	PERTH	UL	ULLAPOOL
B	BELFAST	CY	CASTLE BAY	IH	IPSWICH	PGW	PT.GLASGOW	W	WATERFORD
BA	BALLANTRAE	D	DUBLIN	INS	INVERNESS	PH	PLYMOUTH	WA	WHITEHAVEN
BCK	BUCKIE	DE	DUNDEE	K	KIRKWALL	PN	PRESTON	WD	WEXFORD
BD	BIDEFORD	DH	DARTMOUTH	KY	KIRKALDY	PW	PADSTOW	WH	WEYMOUTH
BE	BARNSTAPLE	DO	DOUGLAS	LH	LEITH	PZ	PENZANCE	WI	WISBECH
BF	BANFF	DR	DOVER	LI	LITTLEHAMPTON	R	RAMSGATE	WK	WICK
BH	BLYTH	DS	DUNFRIES	LK	LERWICK	RO	ROTHESAY	WN	WIGTOWN
BK	BERWICK	E	EXETER	LL	LIVERPOOL	RR	ROCHESTER	WO	WORKINGTON
BL	BRISTOL	F	FAVERSHAM	LO	LONDON	RX	RYE	WY	WHITBY
BM	BRIXHAM	FD	FLEETWOOD	LR	LANCASTER	SA	SWANSEA	YH	YARMOUTH
BN	BOSTON	FE	FOLKESTONE	LT	LOWESTOFT	SD	SUNDERLAND		
BRD	BROADFORD	FH	FALMOUTH	LY	LONDONDERRY	SE	SALCOMBE		
BU	BURNTISLAND	FR	FRASERBURGH	M	MILFORD	SH	SCARBOROUGH		
BW	BARROW	FY	FOWEY	ME	MONTROSE	SM	SHOREHAM		
C	CORK	GE	GOOLE	MH	MIDDLESBROUGH	SN	N. SHIELDS		
CA	CARDIGAN	GH	GRANGEMOUTH	ML	METHIL	SR	STRANRAER		
CF	CARDIFF	GK	GREENOCK	N	NEWRY	SS	ST.IVES		
CH	CHESTER	GN	GRANTON	NE	NEWCASTLE	SSS	S.SHIELDS		

Fig. 3: Port distinguishing letters.

the close reef points. Painted on white sails in black and black sails in white, and on sails of intermediate colours in black or white as may be decided by the authority (Articles 5-10 of the regulations).

The steam trawler, evolved, flourished and died within one person's life span. The motor powered side trawler lived on for a while after the demise of her steam driven sisters but, all too soon, they likewise disappeared from the scene. Along with the ships went the trawlermen, a breed of men skilled in the ways of the sea; men who had also jumped to this nation's defence through two world wars. How many of today's generation have ever seen a steam trawler and, if so, was it a Distant Water, a Middle Water, or a North Sea ship? To the inexperienced eye, trawlers all looked the same. Rusty, smelly and work-weary. They scarcely warranted a second glance. Few people, when on holiday, would get up at some godforsaken hour just to visit the nearest fish market when the trawlers were being unloaded. Not for them the windy, smelly, slippery quaysides, such as Grimsby's 'Pneumonia Jetty', Hull's St. Andrew's Dock or Fleetwood's Fish Dock. My own home of Aberdeen was perhaps more fortunate, being a holiday resort in its own right but the port's battered old steam trawlers of the fifties did little to enthral the casual observer. This is a great shame, as no ships were ever worked harder than the steam trawler. The large trawlers that thrived in the high northern latitudes of the White Sea and Bear Island, had only the permanent semi-darkness of the polar night for company. They probed the stormy waters of Greenland, steamed to the North Cape of Norway and then north again to Spitsbergen. The smaller vessels struggled to make a living in the North Sea, while others worked the west coast Hake grounds of St. Kilda. Middle Water ships went north to the Faeroes and some as far south as the west coast of South Africa. The pattern of work was the same. Steam to the grounds, work like men possessed, them steam full speed for market. Two days at home, then back out again. The ships were tough and the men even tougher, often dubbed unfairly 'two day millionaires'.

SIZES OF SHIPS

Roughly speaking, trawlers can be divided into three main groups, based on their size, which somewhat governs their areas of operation. This grouping was a gradual progression as ships grew in size, for in the early days, even the smallest ships could be found at Iceland. Coaling problems were overcome by carrying extra bags on deck and replenishing stocks at northern ports *en route*. The smallest of the group are the Near Water ships, ranging from 80 to 120ft in length and from 90 to 150 gross tons. They worked the North and Irish Sea grounds, with trips of between five to ten days duration. Speed was around 8 knots and catch capacity was 12 to 40 tons. Next came the Middle Water class that frequented the Faeroes grounds, with occasional trips to Iceland, the North Cape of Norway and even Greenland. Their voyages lasted from thirteen to sixteen days. Their length was between 120-140ft, speed 10-12 knots, 180-450 gross tons, with a hold capacity of between 60 to 110 tons. The largest type were the undisputed queens of the

STEAM TRAWLER CAPACITIES FOR ICE, COAL & FRESH WATER

LENGTH FEET	FRESH WATER TONS	ICE TONS	BUNKERS TONS	DAILY COAL CONSUMPTION TONS
117	12	25	120	8.9
120	15	35	120-160	9-10
125	18	50	170-190	10-12
130	20	60	190-220	12-14
140	25	70-75	230-250	14-16
160	45	75-80	300-320	20-22
120	60	80-85	350-400	24-26

Distant Water fleet. They measured between 140ft and 200ft, 450 to 850 gross tons, with a speed of 11 to 16 knots. They worked far into the high northern latitudes, with trip times of twenty to twenty-eight days and they could catch around 270 tons of fish.

As the trawlers grew in size, they were able to venture further afield. With the opening up of Distant Water grounds, problems arose with bunker capacity and preservation of the catch on the longer trips. The first was overcome on the larger ships by filling the after fish-room with coal, which was used up *en route* to the grounds, the compartment being scrubbed out thoroughly before fishing commenced. Some smaller ships had to supplement this with sacks of coal on deck and these would be used first. The Fleetwood ships would put into Broad Bay on the Isle of Lewis, where this deck cargo would be emptied into the main bunkers before heading out for Iceland. On the homeward leg, they would have to bunker at Stornoway. The problem of catch condition was solved by stowing the fish in ice, which if kept at a steady temperature would keep the catch reasonably fresh for up to eighteen days. Initially, this ice was brought across from Norway and Sweden in sailing vessels, and stored in warehouses, ready for use. This method worked well enough with the small early fleets but, as the industry progressed, a more productive source of supply was required. This increased demand was met by the setting up of ice making factories at the major fishing ports. This man-made ice emerged as large frozen blocks, which could be kept in cold storage until required. As these blocks were too large to fit through a trawler's small ice room hatch, they had to be crushed before the vessel could take on her quota of ice for the trip. In the early 1930s, attempts at freezing fish at sea were undertaken. Although relatively successful, they were halted by the outbreak of war and were never really pursued until the emergence of the stern trawler in the late 1950s.

The steam trawler, although somewhat standardised by the 1900s, continued to develop. By the outbreak of the First World War, wireless equipment was gradually finding its way into the fishing fleet, proving an invaluable asset to both safety and navigation. Ships were fitted mostly with receivers but key vessels would have been supplied with a transmitter. The trawler became an indispensable part of our nation's defence during this period. There was suddenly a huge demand for naval trawlers and the Admiralty commissioned scores of 'Strath', 'Castle' and 'Mersey' types, which were based on proven mercantile designs. After the war, these ships entered the fishing fleets. The trawler designers continued to improve the vessels throughout the inter war period. Liver oil boilers were fitted to Distant Water ships, superheated steam was standard on new ships, and the exhaust turbine gave much greater power and fuel economy. One eternal problem faced by trawler designers was that the owners had only two requirements regarding speed – 'fast' and 'faster'. Around this time, Lever Brothers took delivery of their Bremerhaven built 'Northern' sisters, which set new standards for size, speed and crew comfort. Of course, there was a limit to the overall size of ships. This was determined by the period of time that the catch would keep fresh in ice, normally around seventeen days. This factor more than any other governed the average duration of the trip. Coupled to the fuel consumption, this gave the designers a feel for the machinery and fishroom spaces. The crew would be the minimum necessary to efficiently work the side trawl and

process the catch once it was aboard. The designers added just enough space fore and aft for accommodation. Add to these a boiler casing, funnel and wheelhouse, and one has the simple basic formula for trawler size.

With the outbreak of hostilities in 1939, the Royal Navy once again turned to the trawler fleets for both ships and men. However, the country desperately needed a steady supply of fish to supplement the strict rationing of other foodstuffs, caused by the German U-boat offensive but very few seaworthy ships were left for this task. Again, the Admiralty ordered various commercial designs to be built as minesweepers, anti-submarine and armed patrol trawlers. These were the 'Round Table', 'Fish', 'Hills' and 'Military' classes. In addition, the Royal Navy's own 'Bassett' Class was updated as the 'Tree', 'Dance', 'Shakespearian' and 'Isles' classes. All these new ships retained the trusted triple expansion engine, scotch marine type boilers and coal firing.

This conflict took a very heavy toll in resources and the patrol service in fact lost more men and ships than did either the Merchant Navy, or their Royal overseers. Their bones are scattered all round the globe, from Namsos in Norway, all along the route of the dreaded Russian convoys from Stornoway to Murmansk, and to the frozen Kola Inlet. They lie along the eastern seaboard of America, across the cruel seas of the Atlantic Ocean, through the warm waters of the Mediterranean and to the far tip of South Africa. Many lie closer to home, off the beaches of Dunkirk, in the Channel, the Irish Sea and all along the very coasts that in happier times would have been a welcome landfall.

When peace came eventually, the industry was quick to react. New larger ships were ordered to replenish the fleets, and ex-naval commercial trawlers were purchased and hastily converted for fishing duties. This was a period of prosperity for both owners and crews alike, with record trips being landed at all the main centres. On the Distant Water grounds, it was a time of 'dip and ill'. The fish were there for the taking, the stocks having increased ten fold during the war period. Unfortunately, the lessons of history are never learned and the stocks of fish slowly succumbed to the catching power of the fleet. Once again, the trawlermen had to search for the elusive shoals. To make matters worse, our traditional fishing grounds were being denied us, as Iceland and Norway imposed new territorial limits. The Near Water grounds of the Faeroes followed and, as the 1960s drew to a close, it was obvious that the writing was on the wall for our Distant Water steam sidewinders. They were relegated to the wild waters of Bear Island, the Barents Sea and to Spitzbergen, Greenland and the Grand Banks off Newfoundland. Landmarks such as Mount Misery and Cape Farewell were as well known to our Distant Water trawlermen, as was the Spurn Lightship at the mouth of the River Humber.

Escalating fuel oil prices were yet another factor for the decline of the British steam trawler. Most of the large vessels had been converted from coal firing in the late 1940s. When one considers that the average annual coal consumption was between 1,500 and 2,000 tons per ship, it is not difficult to see why. Only the smaller Near Water ships still sailed with their stokeholds full as, owing to their age, it was not considered worthwhile spending money on upgrading them. The price of coal had also increased dramatically during this period, whilst with the closure of most of the mines, the coal had to be transported to the ports, thus adding even more to the cost. By the late 1950s, the Distant Water ships were the last of the line, as by this time almost all the Near Water steam trawlers had been replaced by motor ships. They were technologically as far removed from the old paddle trawlers as the Apollo spacecraft was from the Wright brothers bi-plane. Oil fuel had replaced coal, central heating was provided throughout the ships, PA systems and piped music were commonplace, and their wheelhouses were equipped with every available electronic gadget for navigation and fish finding. These were the undisputed queens of steam trawler design, the culmination of a lifetime's study by naval architects, that produced some of the finest ships that ever followed the Northern Trawl; 200ft triple deckers, with graceful clipper stems, well balanced cruiser sterns, streamlined superstructures and well capable of steaming at over 15 knots through Arctic seas. Their designs were no longer merely a stretched version of an earlier build, they were tank tested, under all weather conditions, to ensure their utmost suitability for the demanding work that lay ahead of them.

The final twenty years of the steam trawler were dogged by problems of access to traditional fishing grounds, lack of investment by the Near Water sector, escalating fuel costs and a lack of government support. Eventually, a 'Scrap and Build Scheme' was introduced but it came too late for the steam trawler, as by then they were being replaced by motor powered ships. Alas, no more do we have a requirement for such ships. Even supposing we did, the trawler building yards have all gone. An industry that once gave full employment to thousands of both skilled and semi-skilled workers has been made so 'lean and mean' by successive governments that only a handful of workers remain and theirs is an uncertain future. Once, the steam trawler was supreme. An observer could stand on any headland around our coasts and, without a doubt, trawlers could be seen either at work just outside the limit, or steaming past, on their way to or returning from their fishing grounds. From an embryo collection of some dozen or so ships in 1882, the fleet expanded rapidly, to the extent that, by 1910, our steam trawler numbers had grown to around 1,660 ships, with the five major centres being Grimsby with 506 steamers, Hull with 447, Aberdeen with 231, Granton with 84 and Fleetwood with 71. Grimsby, alone, was taking delivery of almost 100 new trawlers annually after 1900 and if one adds in the other ports, the output from our building yards must have been very prolific indeed.

TRAWLERMEN

Trawlermen had to endure the privations of life on the fishing grounds, working sometimes for days on end without rest, in the hostile Arctic Sea. Washed around the open deck while labouring in the pounds, or in the fishroom, they worked a minimum of sixteen hours a day like automatons, struggling to clear the decks of fish. These men were the last of the hunters, paid by results. Most trawlermen were stoical fatalists, who would gamble their very lives to bring home a catch, often only to see the fruits of their labours sold for fish meal, or dumped overboard during times of a glut. There was no room in the trawling trade for failures, or shirkers. Every man had to be as good as the next, both as a seaman and a fisherman. Their lives depended on their hard won skills and courage. As a unit, they were secure in the knowledge that, when danger struck, every man would do his duty to the full. Perhaps not

in the Nelsonian tradition but certainly in that of the brotherhood of the sea. Some trawlermen were deeply religious, others not so but, whatever their beliefs, when fishing God was all around. The skipper was God, the mate a Demi-God, and accidents and death were consequently Acts of God. They were mostly family men, with wives and children living with the constant dread of maybe never seeing them again. These families were segregated from the normal shore workers, living as they did in close knit communities and seldom venturing outside their immediate neighbourhood. Life was a constant struggle. The women eked out their small allowances, collected every Friday from the dock offices, supplementing this whenever possible by part-time work, either in the fish houses or at home braiding trawl nets. They saw their men folk for two days between trips and even this prime time had often to be shared with his shipmates in the pubs and clubs. Time ashore was precious to the trawlerman. For the lucky ones, they were two day tycoons, their pockets soon emptied, as their heads filled with booze. A few short hours in which to forget the last trip but also to remember lost comrades and their ships, which would never again follow the Northern Trawl.

Shore folk thought the trawlermen rough and uncouth, with far too much money to spend. Such were the misguided notions of people who live sheltered lives, whose menfolk worked shifts in the local factory, or in a nine to five job in the town. These people had no conception what the job of a trawlerman entailed, neither did they really care, just so long as fish was good, cheap and readily available. Make no mistake, our trawlermen were the poorest paid of all British workers and other writers more capable than I am have proved this to be fact. One should remember, a trawlerman spent twenty four hours a day away from home, working in some of the most hostile environments on the planet. Conditions were more extreme than even our offshore workers of today could ever imagine – no air conditioned luxury aboard a steam trawler, no catering company serving up *cordon-bleu* food in airy dining rooms, no working 'twelve on, twelve off' shifts and, certainly, no two or three weeks off (on full pay) between trips. The trawlerman had no 'Conditions of Service' and very little trade union support. He was, to the very last, a casual worker, signing off at the end of each trip. He had no guarantee of getting another ship and only exceptional men would be permitted to sail with a skipper on a regular basis. He had no pre-determined annual sick leave allotment, no sick pay and definitely no redundancy when he lost his job. For his spell ashore between trips, he was unpaid. If he wanted a trip off to take the wife and kids on holiday, he depended on landing a good trip beforehand, or it was disappointment all round and he went back to sea instead. Should his vessel founder and he be among the lucky survivors, his wages stopped. The owners reckoned that he was not working, so – no work, no pay! There was no redundancy or golden handshakes when he retired (either forcibly or otherwise), as the Department of Health & Social Security rules laid down that, to qualify, he had to have worked a minimum of two years for the same employer. This rule meant that a fisherman had to serve on the same ship for the unbroken period of two years, an impossible situation when one bears in mind that these trawlermen were always employed on a casual trip to trip basis, so there was no way he could satisfy the rules.

The skippers and mates fared better. They did not (until the early 1960s), receive a regular basic wage; instead they were paid on a share of the value of the catch. This was usually on the net value, after all the other costs of the trip had been deducted. Sometimes they would receive agreed bonuses in the form of one per cent of the gross earnings. Admittedly, some of the top (or 'Don') skippers earned vast amounts of money but the insecurity was ever present. There were always more skippers than ships, so the pressures of staying in the top earning league were immense. In order to bring home a catch, some skippers were not averse to doing a bit of poaching on the side. If this ploy paid off, then all so well and good but, if caught, then the repercussions were very expensive indeed. But even the best skipper had little better terms of employment than the men, bearing in mind that the rules for redundancy payments also applied to them, although as they were very high earners, they should have been well able to provide for themselves on retirement.

Notwithstanding the high cost in men's lives, trawlers are costly to build and operate. As in most industries, they must show a good return, otherwise the investors pull their money out and companies go to the wall. It is very easy to generalise and say that all businesses carry an element of financial risk but none more so than the trawl fishing industry. Big profits can be made but in order to make them, even bigger risks have to be taken, and any skipper who cuts and runs when the weather begins to blow up soon finds himself out of work. To help make this profit, trawlers have to fish in all but the severest weather, a fact which is foremost in the designers mind when he plans the vessel. Trawlers on the whole were the finest sea ships afloat, a credit to both builders and designers alike.

And the answer to the trawlerman's riddle – when 'laying off' (wanting water), waiting for the tide to flood so as to allow the trawler to enter the lockpits or cross the harbour bar, they had to drink ship's water. But when there was plenty of water over the bar or the lockpit sills, they could enter port, go ashore and drink beer.

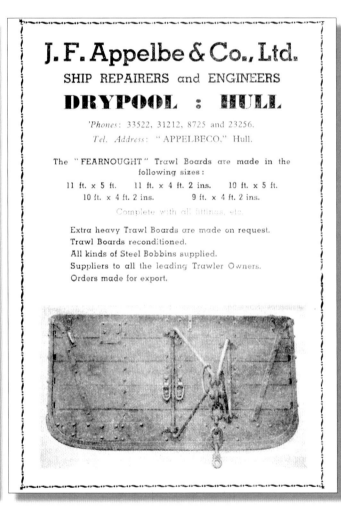

Chapter 2: TRAWLS AND TRAWLING GEAR

The sailing trawler and early steam trawlers fished with the Beam Trawl, using one trawl warp from either a hand/steam capstan or single barrelled winch (**Fig. 5**). The winch used wire instead of rope for the trawl warp. With the introduction of the Otter or Granton trawl, two warps were used from a twin barrelled steam winch.

THE BEAM TRAWL

The beam trawl been in almost constant use since 1377, when the Commons complained to King Edward III about a new secretly contrived instrument called a 'wondychroun' (**Fig. 6 inset**). The original drawing of this net *'which caught a great many small fishes to the destruction of the fisheries'*, was found on the back of an old State Paper. Throughout the 16th and 17th centuries, use of this Beam Trawl was still illegal. Sheriffs Officers periodically rounded up recalcitrant trawlermen and burned all their gear. In spite of these laws and ensuing public outcry, the use of the trawl could not be stamped out. (**Fig. 6**) shows a flat, purse shaped triangular net, its mouth kept open by a heavy wooden trawl beam. In our case this is supported at either end by Trawl Heads or Irons (**Fig. 7,** *overleaf*) but often these are replaced by large rollers.

These wooden beams were of massive construction, often up to 2.5ft in circumference, by 30 to 50ft in length. They were normally constructed from ash, elm, or beech, built up and scarphed together. East Anglian trawlers used a much shorter beam than the Brixham smacks, as they maintained that conditions on the Dogger Bank tended to close the mouths of the larger trawls. The downside to the Beam Trawl was the beam itself. If over 50ft long, they would sag in the middle and close up the mouth of the net. This problem was overcome with the introduction of the Otter Trawl.

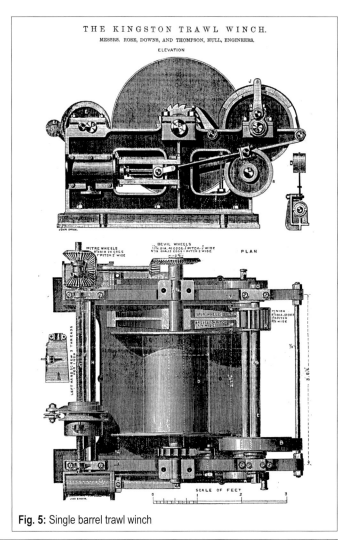

THE KINGSTON TRAWL WINCH.
MESSRS. ROSE, DOWNS, AND THOMPSON, HULL, ENGINEERS.

Fig. 5: Single barrel trawl winch

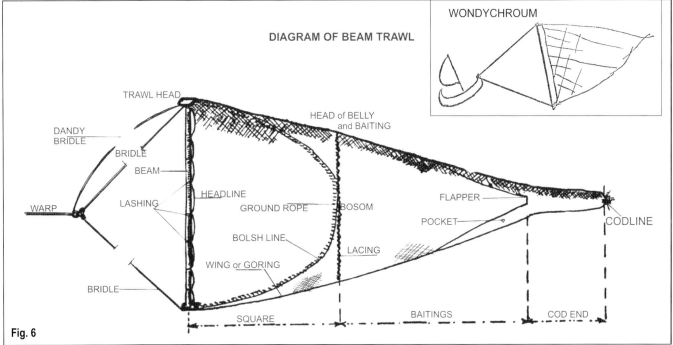

DIAGRAM OF BEAM TRAWL

WONDYCHROUM

Fig. 6

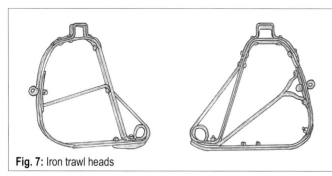

Fig. 7: Iron trawl heads

THE OTTER TRAWL

This type of trawl net is one of the most efficient and important means of catching bottom feeding fish. In 1894, Skipper Normandale of Scarborough devised a revolutionary new method of keeping the mouth of the net open. He used two wooden boards; one on each wing. These boards were rigged so as to shear away from the angle of tow, in the same way that a rowing boat will shear away from the side of her parent vessel if the towing line is made fast to the forward thwart, instead of to the painter ring fixed in the eyes of the boat. As with many new innovations, these otter boards refused to behave as he intended and when towing in a strong cross tide, the net tied itself in knots. During these trials, a single towing warp had been used, as the Beam trawl winch had only a single drum. A twin barrelled winch was designed, allowing the trawler to shoot two warps, one to each board, and the problem was solved. Although these otter boards got their name from Skipper Normandale's trawler the **Otter** (SH.70 – an iron vessel built at South Shields in 1888), they were in fact modified from an Irish method of fishing for pike and trout in the local Loughs. Here we are faced with a small conundrum, for north of the border at Granton, the development of this trawl commercially was attributed to a Mr Scott (hence the term 'Granton trawl'), although he maintained that the method had been in use on yachts since the 1880s.

With the early Otter or Granton trawls, the otter boards, or 'doors', were connected directly to the wings of the net by way of butterfly couplings. In the later types, such as the French or 'Vigneron Dahl' trawl, the boards are some distance from the net and connected to it by wire bridles and the large 'Dhan-Leno Bobbins'. The head rope of the net is kept up by a series of spherical floats and the basic shape of the net follows closely that of the Beam Trawl. The Granton or Otter trawl may thus be divided into the following sections: cod end; belly; baitings; square; lower wings; top wings; and floppa.

Cod End: This last piece is the holding area where the trapped fish end up. It is

Photo. 1: Dhan Leno bobbin and butterfly with small rubber ground rope bobbins used for middle water fishing.

an oblong shape, braided with doubled twine for strength, and forms part of the belly and baitings section of the trawl net. At the extreme tail end of the cod end, a 4 to 5 fathom length of manila rope of between 1.5ft and 2ft diameter is rove through the meshes to enable the cod end knot to be tied off. This is a special quick release knot, that discharges the catch when the net is hauled aboard. Protection for this part of the net from the ravages of the sea bed is by way of 'false bellies'. These are old sections of net, around six in number, that are fastened to the underside of the cod end, with each one overlapping its neighbour. Further protection from chafing is provided by cow hides, which are split lengthways and fixed to the underside of the net; one piece was sufficient for the North Sea trawls, whereas the trawls used on the Distant Water grounds would require up to four such hides.

Square: As the name describes, it is a large section of net up to 25ft long when used on the Arctic grounds.

Lower Wings: Two in number, braided as identical pairs and forming the lower leading edge of the trawl. They are oblong in shape, with the widest part attached to the belly section of the net. Their other sides link up with the square and top wing sections.

Top Wings: Again braided in pairs, they form the upper leading edge of the trawl net, connected to the lower wings and ends of the square. The forward edges of the top wings are connected to the headline which, along with its floats, is in turn fixed to the middle of the square.

Floppa: This forms one of the most important parts of the net and acts as a form of non-return section that closes up and prevents the catch escaping from the trawl during hauling. Floppas are not usually found on the trawls of Distant Water ships, as these deep sea trawls have extended lengths of belly and baitings braided in. This enables these ships to haul the trawl and bring the catch aboard in stages or 'bags', as often the weight of the catch would be in excess of the safe working load of the gear.

The 'Ground Rope' is protected in its advance over the sea bed by large rolling bobbins, made originally from timber but later from metal. Latter day ground ropes were constructed using rubber discs over flexible steel wire. It was found that the later ground ropes were much more economical than the earlier types, but they still required to be fitted with armoured steel bobbins, interspaced along their length. These bobbins were made in standard sizes, from 14ins to 22ins diameter and around 12ins in width, with a central hole some 2ins diameter for the ground rope to be rove through. If the trawler was after 'Flats' (Plaice or Sole), tickler chains would be rigged. These stretch across the mouth of the net and being shorter than the ground rope, they move ahead of it, churning up the bottom and stirring up the recumbent fish. Without chains, the net would pass harmlessly over the fish. Such was the design of this net that it was reckoned to be a fourfold improvement over the Beam trawl. As previously mentioned, at the wings of the net, are to be found the Dhan Lenos (**Photo. 1**). In the early days these were wooden posts, 3ft long by about 4ins square, which helped keep the sides of the net upright. The name once again appears to have come from the French 'Guindineau' ('guinder'- the verb 'to hoist'). Up to the end of the First World War, the design of the trawl net had advanced very little. The basic shape was almost identical to that of the early beam trawls, only larger and with no attempt being made to streamline the net. In the early 1920s, the industry became increasingly concerned about high running costs. The price of coal kept escalating and even with many owners also being shareholders in coal mines, it was impossible to reduce this principal cost. Coal was consumed at a rate of between 7 to 12 tons per day, depending on the size of the trawler, so a way had to be found of utilising the available power more efficiently. An approach was made to Mr H.S. Rowton, an expert in minesweeping gear. After some three years work, he completely redesigned the trawl net and produced a paper entitled *Science Versus Power in relation to The Otter Trawl Net, or How The Power Cost of Trawlers Can Be Reduced*. He discovered that the normal form of net, made up of square sections, caused an unnecessary drag on the towing vessel. The net, which he agreed was a most cunning and effective device for catching fish, represented one of the most glaring examples of the extravagant use of steam power and a total absence of scientific construction. In simple terms he meant that when the flat net took up its towed conical shape, many of the side meshes would close up tight and increase the load on both the warps and the towing vessel. He completely redesigned the net, calling it The British Stream Line Trawl, and issued the following specification:

1. Every curve conforming to the natural law of free suspension.
2. Accurate braiding of the net to correctly fit these curves.
3. Total elimination of surplus meshes or slack net at the Selvedges.
4. Every mesh, irrespective of size, carrying equal pressure and open to the same angles.
5. Maximum release of internal water pressure.
6. Complete control over the construction of the 'flow' of the wings.
7. Accurate design of the Wings, Square, Belly, Baitings and Cod End.
8. Reduced ground friction and damage to the lower portions of the net.
9. Increased elevation at the mouth of the net.
10. Correct relationship of design between the Head Rope, Foot Rope and Selvedges, and the spread of the trawl boards.
11. Correct relationship of design between the different sections of the net and the curves of the lines forming the outer and inner boundaries of the net.
12. The first Otter Trawl Net ever designed in the history of the Trawling industry, in which the Head Line, Foot Rope, Selvedges, the different sections and every mesh forming the net, conform to the 'Law of Suspension', and every mesh carries the same pressure and is open to the same angle of spread – when the net is fishing (**Fig. 8**).

The new net was constructed under a special licence, issued to

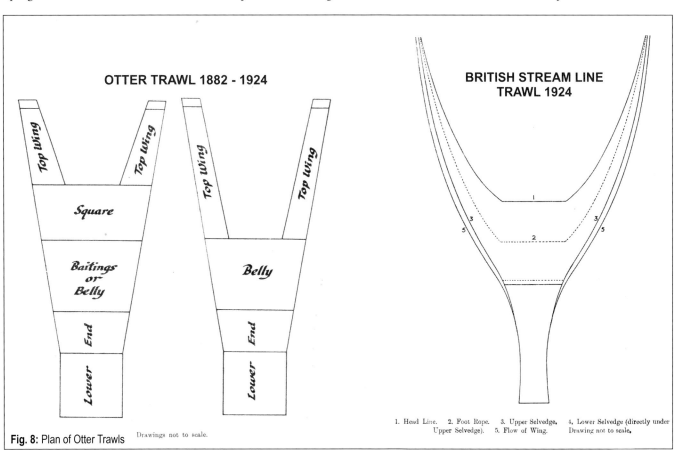

OTTER TRAWL 1882 - 1924

Top wing   Top wing   Top wing   Top wing

Square

Baitings or Belly   Belly

Lower End   Lower End

Fig. 8: Plan of Otter Trawls   Drawings not to scale.

BRITISH STREAM LINE TRAWL 1924

1. Head Line.   2. Foot Rope.   3. Upper Selvedge.   4. Lower Selvedge (directly under Upper Selvedge).   5. Flow of Wing.   Drawing not to scale.

the net makers by the parent company and had to be braided to their exact specifications. Potential customers for the trawl had to first apply for a licence to use the net and also fill in a company specification form, stating the type of vessel that they intended to fit out. On acceptance by the company, the trawl owner was issued a 'Right of User' certificate, for which he had to pay an annual royalty of £52 per vessel, payable half yearly in advance. Whether or not the owners were convinced about the merits of this new net, I have been unable to ascertain but I feel sure that the extra £52 per ship per year would have been looked at very closely indeed. Nevertheless, it shows that the industry was not standing still and was always on the lookout for increased productivity.

A much greater advance in the catching power of the trawl came about when Bridles were introduced in the 1930s, between the Dhan Lenos and the otter boards, as they allowed a wider area to be swept by the trawl (**Fig. 9**). Although somewhat of a nuisance when manhandling the gear alongside, it was estimated that up to 50% more fish were caught by using 100ft bridles, as opposed to having the boards attached directly to the net. As time progressed, the ships grew in size, running and building costs escalated, and crews grew bigger in order to work these larger trawlers. Consequently, trawlers have to catch more fish in the same fishing time. To enable them to do this, the gear has grown larger and more efficient but equally more cumbersome. One important feature of the net is mesh size. This is regulated by international agreement, in order to conserve fish stocks. Mesh size in UK waters is policed by the Fishery Protection Service (FPS) and the Scottish Fishery Protection Service, whose vessels are referred to as 'gunboats' or 'watchers'. Naval ships engaged on FPS duty carry a funnel badge of a pennant with yellow and blue quarters.

SHOOTING AND HAULING

On arrival at the chosen fishing ground, a fish basket is hoisted on the forestay to denote that the vessel is engaged in trawling. At night, the trawler displays a tri-coloured fishing light at her masthead. This red, white and green light is the international signal for a fishing vessel on the grounds, and is additional to her normal steaming and working lights. When the skipper decides to 'Shoot away', he turns his vessel beam on to wind and sea, so that she will be blown away from the gear as it is streamed. In the unlikely situation of there being no wind, he must use his rudder and engines to keep the angle of the trawl correct. The gear is always shot over the starboard side, unless the gear has been damaged, when he would shoot the port side gear. This would allow the deck crew time to repair or replace the damaged starboard trawl whilst continuing fishing. During the latter years of the side trawler, when the accommodation for the crew had been moved aft out of the fo'c'sle, the port side gallows could not be fitted and vessels were compelled to handle the gear on the starboard side only. The cod end, with its heavy protective cow hides, is first over the side, heaved up and dropped into the sea from the 'yo-yo', boom on the foremast. The telly of the net is dragged over after it and the heavy bobbins are lifted over the rail by means of the 'Gilson' tackle fixed at the foremast head. The winch men release their brakes and the wire Bridles are hauled off the drums until the doors can be shackled on. Then the otter boards go over. It

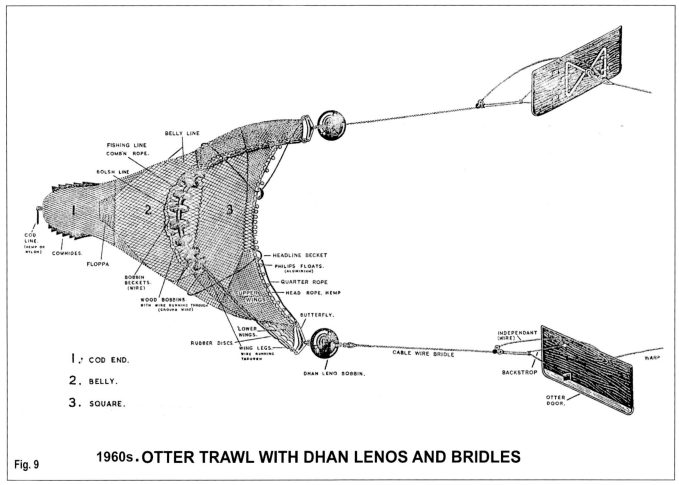

1. COD END.
2. BELLY.
3. SQUARE.

Fig. 9   **1960s. OTTER TRAWL WITH DHAN LENOS AND BRIDLES**

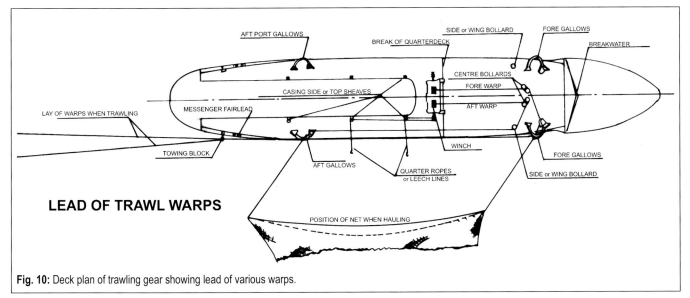

LEAD OF TRAWL WARPS

Fig. 10: Deck plan of trawling gear showing lead of various warps.

is imperative that these Boards or Doors are not allowed to drift together and wrap the warps round each other. To prevent this happening, the skipper rings down for full speed, thus streaming the gear away from the ship like a huge drogue. When the required length of warps have been run off and the winch brakes locked up, they must be clamped in the towing block down aft, otherwise the vessel will be unmanoeuvrable whilst towing. A messenger wire, complete with hook, is skilfully thrown over the warps and led aft, from where it passes to the warping drums of the winch by way of lead blocks on the ship's casing. As this messenger wire is hauled in, the two trawl warps are drawn together at the hinged towing block, hanging from the vessel's rail at the quarters. Once both warps are secured in the block, the messenger wire is cast off and the trawler settles down to tow her gear. The vessel will tow at about 4 knots, head to wind, until the skipper decides to haul. During towing, the deck crew are hard at work gutting the catch, so as to clear the decks for the next haul. This procedure in fine weather looks and sounds deceptively simple, and when the work is done by an efficient crew, there is no teamwork to beat it but trawling is a highly dangerous occupation, normally undertaken in the fiercest of weathers, when all the rules of good seamanship state that a vessel should never be allowed to fall off

beam on to wind and sea. The low freeboard of trawlers allows huge quantities of water to be shipped over the rails and wash over the sodden frozen men working on her exposed open deck. Wires under terrific strain, like the trawl warps, settle any obstacle of flesh and bone that gets in their way, instantly, by amputation. Missing digits are the hallmark of the trawlerman's calling and are accepted without fuss. Trawl fishing, traditionally, had the highest accident and mortality rate of any industry. This includes coal mining, quarrying and the modern offshore oil industry.

When he decides to haul the net, the skipper again turns the ship beam on to wind and sea, with the gear laying out to starboard. Standing well forward of the towing block, one of the hands knocks out the locking pin from the block with a large heavy spanner kept for the purpose. The free warps spring away from the ship, thrumming through the water, and the heavy iron towing block crashes violently against the ship's side. The winch man, having previously opened the drain cocks to release the condensate from the cylinders, starts up the winch and slips the port clutch, thus engaging the barrel for the fore-warp. He hauls in the fore-warp until satisfied that the gear will come in all square and the starboard clutch is then engaged. The winch rattles and rumbles like a labouring express train as it hauls in the heavy gear. As the

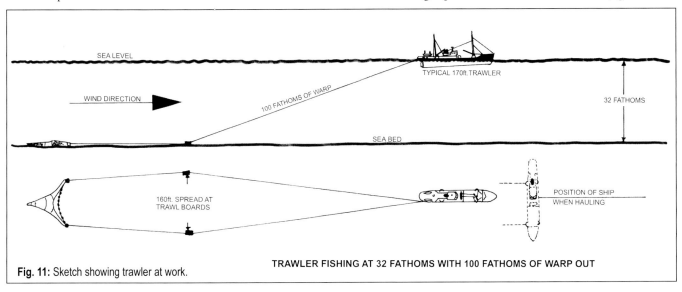

Fig. 11: Sketch showing trawler at work.

TRAWLER FISHING AT 32 FATHOMS WITH 100 FATHOMS OF WARP OUT

Photo. 2a: Manhandling the bobbins over the rail, looking forward. Note the aft trawl warp between the men's legs and the size of the ground rope bobbins. The wire bridle can be seen at the right of the picture leading aft to the gallows, from where it will be attached to the Otter Board.

Photo. 2b: 'Blocking Up'. The messenger hook has pulled the warps together so they can be fixed into the towing block. Note the messenger wire passing round the messenger sheave and leading to the starboard warping drum on the trawl winch.

Photo. 2c: Large bag of fish coming alongside. The fore quarter rope can be seen passing outboard from the casing top sheaves and the forward Otter Board is hanging in its chains. Note also the storm handrails on the casing side.

Photo. 2d: Hooking the chains onto the forward trawl board – fingers beware! Note the size of the hanging block.

warps come in, they have to be guided onto the winch drums otherwise one turn will ride over its neighbour, with disastrous results at shooting time. This procedure is known as 'Riding On', a backbreaking job with a manual system, but much improved when the automatic spooling gear was introduced in the 1920s. As if by magic, at the first turn of the winch, hordes of screaming gulls appear from a seemingly empty sky and their raucous cries mingle with the rumble of the steam winch and the squeal of sheaves under load; the winch is their dinner bell and they come to dine.

In fine weather, the after door is hauled up first but should the weather be foul, then the fore door leads, bringing the vessel's head further up into the wind. As the doors come up, sling chains are passed round their brackets and hooked onto the gallows, the warps are eased up and the doors allowed to hang by their chains, thus taking their weight off the warps. The 'G' links (or shackles)

are unclipped from the doors and the warps hove on until the Dhan Lenos come into the gallows, when the winch brakes are screwed on and the clutches unshipped. The after quarter rope is then taken by the boatswain and deckhand to the winch, and the fore quarter rope taken to the winch by the third hand, and spare

Photo. 2e: Trawl board/door close up, with the 'G' link passing over the sheave. Note the square headed shackle pin; this was tightened using a 3ft long open ended spanner with serrated jaws, known as the 'laughing crocodile'. The Bar in top left hand corner is the gallows stay from forecastle head.

Photo. 2f: Mate hooking the bag becket onto the lower fish tackle/Gilson block; note the aft trawl warp passing round the wing bollard. The two thick items of rigging at the right of the shrouds are the bag ropes, which prevent the full cod end swinging across the ship when she rolls.

hand. These quarter ropes are hauled in until the bosom of the net is brought to the top of the ships rail and dropped on deck, when the after end is made secure. All hands then man the trawl and heave up in unison as the vessel dips to the sea and bring the cod end alongside.

A becket is passed round the the cod end, hooked onto the fish tackle and hove up by the winch, until the bag swings inboard against the bag ropes. The mate releases the cod end knot and the catch falls onto the deck. The gear is made ready again, repairs are carried out as expeditiously as conditions allow and the gear is shot again. A trawler only makes money when the net is on the

bottom. This description is for a single 'bag' of fish. If the catch is large, then the cod end is brought aboard in two or three lifts. The fish has then to be gutted, washed and packed below. It is the boatswain's duty to see that the catch is properly washed and cleaned, and it is the mate's responsibility to ensure that the fish are properly stowed and iced below in the fish room. The job of the fishroom men, although sheltered somewhat from the elements, is no sinecure. To them falls the unrelenting task of breaking down the heap of crushed ice that has welded itself into a frozen wall. This ice is then shovelled onto the fish as they are packed away on the shelf boards ready for market. In order for the catch to reach port in a marketable condition, the fishroom temperature was kept at 31 degrees Fahrenheit. Unless the greatest of care was taken with the stowage of the fish, they would inevitably deteriorate and be fit only for fish meal, the end result being that the crew, after three weeks away, would 'settle below the red line' (in debt). When the trawler lands her catch, it still remains the Mate's responsibility and in order to present the fish attractively, both by size and quality, he will give the landing squad foreman a small 'backhander'. The men who discharge the fish are called 'Bobbers' at Hull, 'Lumpers' at Grimsby and Fleetwood, and 'Porters' at Aberdeen.

N°s 257 & 8
OFFSETS

FERGUSON BROS.
(PORT-GLASGOW) LTD
SHIPBUILDERS & ENGINEERS

Nº of Section	Waterlines 2'-0"	4'-0"	6'-0"	8'-0"	10'-0"	12'-0"	13'-6"	Main Dk ½ Breadth	Knuckle ½ Breadth	Rail ½ Breadth	Rail Heights	F'cle ½ Breadth	Diagonal	Buttocks 2'-0"	4'-0"	6'-0"	8'-0"
A.P.																	
0			Aft Perpendicular				3'-1¼"	6'-8"	7'-9½"	8'-6"	17'-8½"			13'-1½"	13'-9¼"	14'-5½"	15'-9¾"
½	-3¾"	5½"	8½"	1'-4"	2'-10"	5'-7¼"	8'-0"	8'-11"	9'-5"	9'-8¼"	17'-3¾"		3'-1"	9'-1"	10'-10½"	12'-2½"	13'-6"
1	1'-2"	2'-0"	3'-0½"	4'-6½"	6'-6½"	8'-6¾"	9'-8½"	10'-0"	10'-3"	10'-4½"	17'-0¼"		5'-9"	4'-0"	7'-3¾"	9'-5¼"	11'-4¾"
2	4'-1⅜"	6'-3¼"	7'-11½"	9'-3½"	10'-2"	10'-8½"	10'-11¼"	10'-11¾"	11'-0"	11'-0¾"	16'-8¾"		9'-8½"	4"	1'-10"	3'-8¼"	6'-0½"
3	7'-3½"	9'-6¾"	10'-7"	11'-0¾"	11'-3"	11'-3¾"	11'-3½"	11'-3½"		11'-2¼"	16'-6¾"		12'-1¾"	1" Below.	6¼"	1'-3½"	2'-5¼"
4	8'-11½"	10'-11"	11'-5"	11'-6"	11'-6"	11'-5½"	11'-5"	11'-5"		11'-3"	16'-6"		13'-3½"	1" Above	5¾"	10¾"	1'-6¼"
5	9'-2"	11'-1"	11'-6"	11'-6"	11'-6"	11'-5½"	11'-5"	11'-5"		11'-3"	16'-6"		13'-5¼"				
6	8'-3½"	10'-9¾"	11'-4"	11'-5	11'-5"	11'-4¾"	11'-4¼"	11'-4"		11'-2¾"	16'-8½"		13'-2¾"	8"	1'-0½"	1'-5¼"	1'-10½"
7	6'-5½"	9'-7¾"	10'-7¾"	10'-11¾"	11'-1¼"	11'-2"	11'-2"	11'-1¾"		11'-1¼"	17'-3½"		12'-2½"	11¾"	1'-4½"	1'-10¼"	2'-7¾"
8	4'-1½"	6'-11½"	8'-3¼"	9'-0"	9'-6¼"	9'-11"	10'-2"	10'-4¾"		10'-9"	18'-3½"	10'-11½"	10'-1"	1'-3¾"	1'-11"	3'-1"	5'-5½"
9	1'-6½"	3'-2¾"	4'-1¼"	4'-9¼"	5'-4½"	5'-11¼"	6'-5½"	7'-7"		8'-8½"	19'-10¾"	9'-6"	6'-0¾"	2'-4"	5'-8½"	12'-2"	18'-1"
9½	-2½"	1'-2½"	1'-9½"	2'-2¾"	2'-6¾"	2'-11½"	3'-3¼"	4'-4¾"		5'-6½"	20'-10½"	6'-6½"	3'-2¾"	6'-10½"	16'-7"	21'-10"	
10			Fore	Perpendicular							22'-0"						

DIMENSIONS :- 140'-0" B.P. × 23'-0" MLD × 13'-6" MLD TO MAIN DECK.
MAIN DECK AT SIDE IS PARALLEL 3'-0" BELOW RAIL.
F'CLE DECK AT SIDE IS PARALLEL 2'-0" ABOVE RAIL.
BEAM CAMBER 6" ON MAIN DECK ½ BREADTH.
SECTIONS ARE SPACED 14'-0" APART, HALF SECTIONS 7'-0" APART.
Nº 0 SECTION IS ON A.P., Nº 10 SECTION IS ON F.P.
RISE OF FLOOR 2'-3". DROOP OF KEEL 3'-0".
KEEL & STEM 7½" × 1⅛" BULB PLATE. RUDDER POST 5¾ × 3¼. PROPELLER POST 6" × 5¼".
FRAME SPACING 21½" THROUGHOUT.
FORECASTLE FRONT ON FRAME Nº 66.
ALL HEIGHTS ARE GIVEN ABOVE BASE LINE.

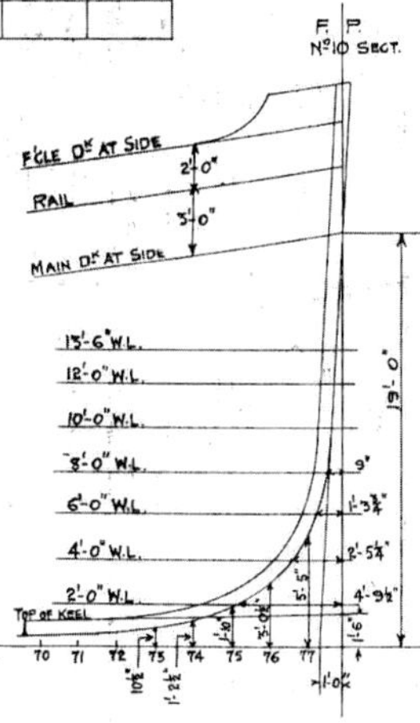

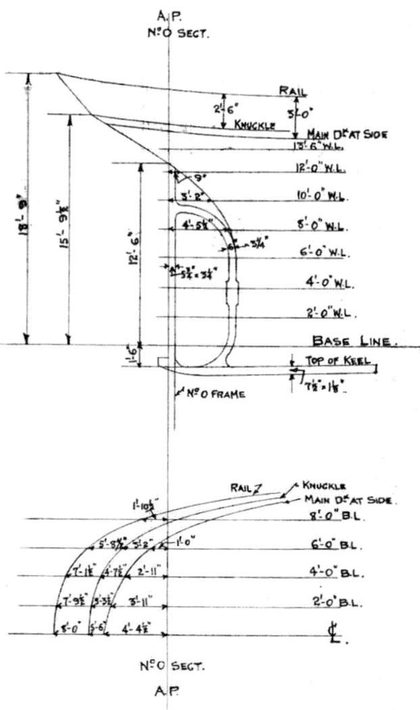

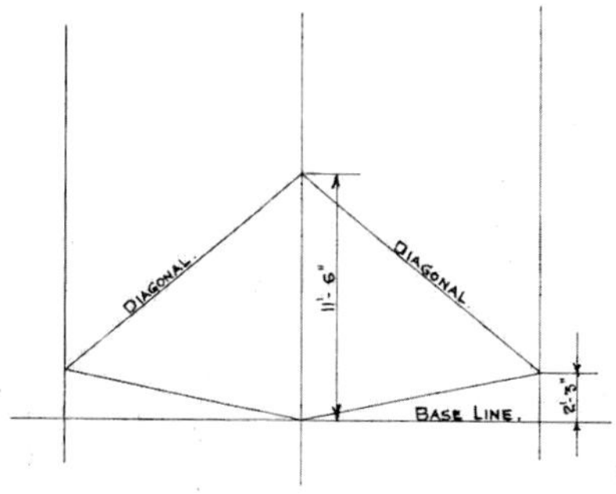

DRAWING Nº 14.
DRAWN BY H.D.
DATE 22-11-19.

Plan 3: Table of offsets for ***Hornbill*** and ***Nuthatch***.

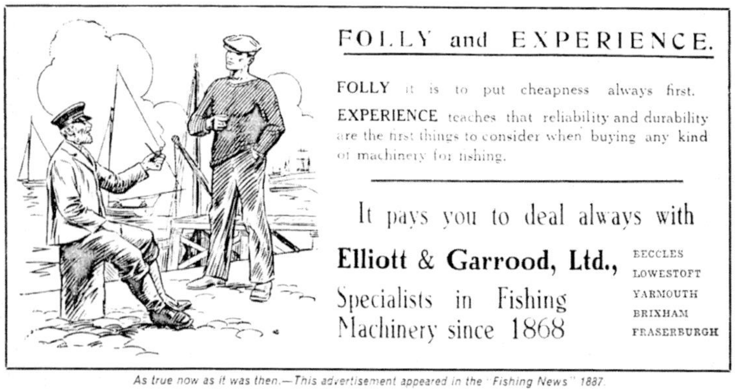

As true now as it was then.—This advertisement appeared in the "Fishing News" 1887.

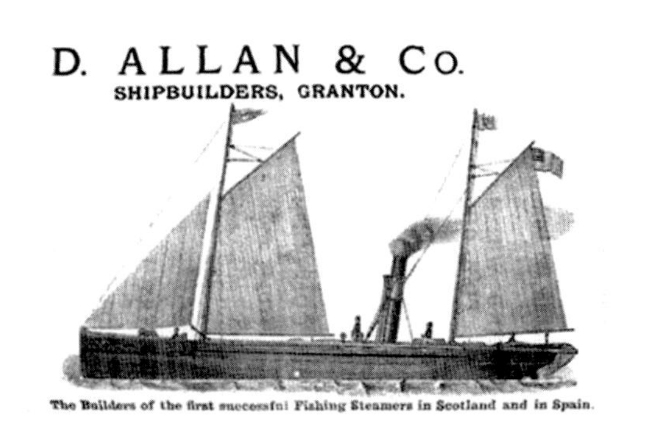

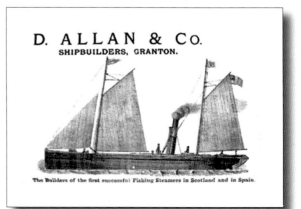

Chapter 3: DESIGN AND CONSTRUCTION

When an owner required a new ship, he would have many meetings with prospective builders. He would be looking for the best design to suit his requirements, which would hopefully steal a march on his competitors, the best price and, finally, guaranteed delivery times. In order to simplify this process, many owners had developed good working relationships with 'preferred' shipyards, who knew exactly what was required and were up to date with all advances in design, machinery and outfit. Steam trawlers were built both for strength and speed but their design was not as simple as it first appears. Most deep sea vessels leave harbour and arrive at their destination in the same state of trim, because as their bunkers are emptied, water ballast is taken on to compensate if necessary. A trawler on the other hand, leaves port fully laden with fuel, ice, fresh water and stores for the fishing grounds, which could be over a thousand miles away. *En route*, she uses up her fuel and some feed water. Should she encounter bad weather on the way, then more fuel will be used, so the longer the 'run off' (outward journey), the more unstable she becomes. Once on the grounds, she must replace the weight of fuel consumed by a corresponding weight of fish caught. Bad weather on the grounds can see her burning up more valuable fuel without catching any fish to compensate. Added to this, if she is working the Arctic grounds in winter, she will collect ice and this will further compromise her stability. Even when she is filling her fishrooms with fish, her longitudinal centre of gravity is changing due to the fishrooms being forward of 'midships and when steaming home after a long trip she is down by the head. Should she again meet with bad weather, she could well arrive home in a tender condition. To survive and work under these conditions, the steam trawler had, of necessity, to be as sturdily built as possible. To this end, the scantlings were normally from 10 to 20 per cent in excess of Lloyds' requirements for a cargo vessel of the same size.

EARLY DESIGN CRITERIA

In 1907, one of Lloyd's Register's surveyors in Bordeaux was disturbed by the lack of a regulative system for determining the relationship between trawler length and moulded depth. He carried out a study of the problem and published his results in various professional papers, and a book entitled *Chalutiers a Vapeur: Formule Servant a Determiner Leurs Dimensions*. This work originated from a request by an important French trawling company, for him to supply guideline dimensions for a proposed 150ft trawler, *Baliene*. On studying the relative dimensions of the only other two trawlers of this size, he was puzzled by the fact that their moulded depth was identical to that of the much favoured but smaller 115ft British trawlers of the time. He turned at once to the *Freeboard Tables*, as published by the Board of Trade for Cargo Steamers, for clarification but they confused him even further by stating the following dimensions:

Length of Cargo ship	115ft	Moulded depth = 9ft 7ins
	150ft	Moulded depth = 12ft 6ins
	156ft	Moulded depth = 13ft

After numerous studies of trawler trials reports, he eventually arrived at the conclusion that, for a vessel of a given length, her other dimensions were standardised by the experience of the builders (he seems to have neglected the fact that the majority of British trawler builders were already highly specialised in the design of fishing vessels). It took him quite some time, however, to discover that a trawler was in fact completely different from a cargo ship. The latter was designed to a deadweight criteria – a measurement that figured very little in the design of trawlers. He found that a cargo vessel was designed to carry a fixed cargo capacity, with respect to varying draught and freeboard measurements; this in essence was borne out by the BoT Freeboard Rules. The trawler, on the other hand, was designed with a good turn of speed, coupled to excellent sea keeping abilities and the need for a stable working platform when beam on to the wind and sea. What he did discover was that only when a trawler's length reached 208ft did it start to correspond to the moulded depth of a cargo vessel. He states in his book:

'If experience seems to have confirmed that there exists for steam trawlers a certain relation between the length and the under deck tonnage, careful observation has led me to conclude that in the case of the trawlers which have been proved to give the most successful results, there exists a much closer co-relation as regards length, beam, rise of floor, and moulded depth, and that with certain co-efficient of fineness, varying within narrow limits, this co-relation could be embodied in an empiric formula which would allow steam trawlers to maintain their own characteristics, whatever their length, until the limit of 208ft. was reached, when the moulded depth given by the formula is blended with the standard moulded depth as per freeboard tables of the British Board of Trade for cargo steamers of the same length.'

His formula for setting out these dimensions was:

$$\frac{b + c}{L} = \frac{c}{2b} = \frac{r}{c} = 0.005\,(708 - L)$$

with a standard under-deck tonnage equal to $0.66\,L\,b\,(c - 1)$.

L = length of vessel measured on load from the fore side of the stem to the aft side of the after post (bp – between perpendiculars)
b = the extreme breadth measured to the outside of the plating
c = moulded depth
r = rise of floor.

'If the formula is not absolutely correct' concludes Monsieur Van der Cruyce, *'it offers, nevertheless, the advantage of giving dimensions, good in themselves, and which, therefore, will be a valuable auxiliary to ship owners and shipbuilders.'* He put his formula to the test by designing the *Baliene* but was so unsure of his results that he sent them to a high ranking English Naval Architect who, after careful deliberation, pronounced them to be accurate, so the then *'biggest steam trawler in the world'* was ordered in June 1906. She was followed by two other large French-built trawlers, *Nordcaper* in July 1907 and *Beluga* in February 1908 – each 150ft bp x 15ft x 13ft 7ins.

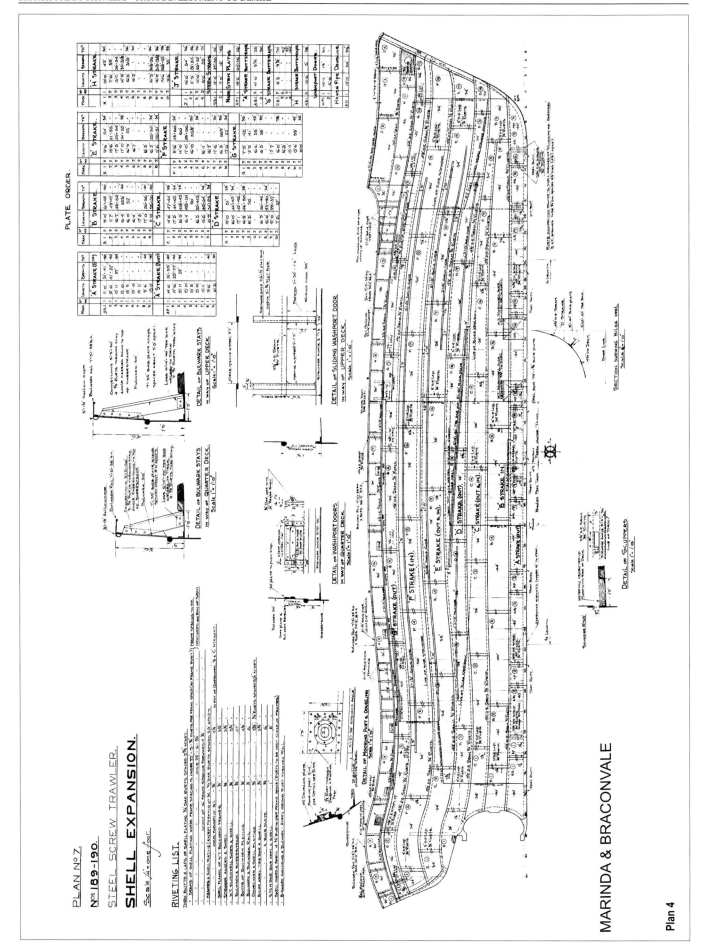

MARINDA & BRACONVALE

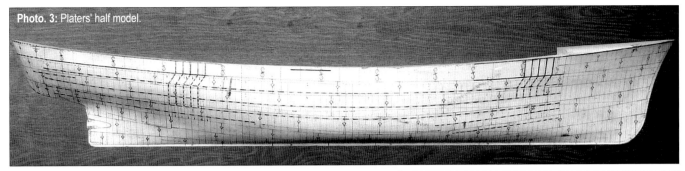

Photo. 3: Platers' half model.

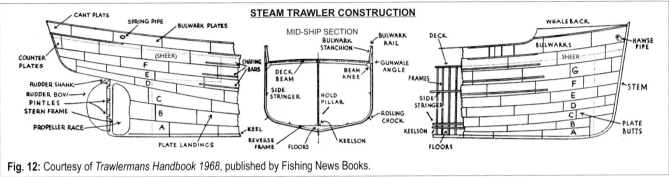

STEAM TRAWLER CONSTRUCTION

Fig. 12: Courtesy of *Trawlermans Handbook 1968*, published by Fishing News Books.

By now, the reader will have gathered that, as the ships developed, designers strove for more speed coupled to greater stability. This is evident more in the Distant Water ships but had a 'knock on effect' in their smaller sisters. Fishroom capacity, within a set hull length, was of paramount importance to the owners and, by the late 1950s, deep water steam trawlers could be roughly classified as follows:

Length BP	Fishroom (cu.ft)	IHP	Laden Speed (knots)
168.0ft	13,000	875	12
175.0ft	15,000	1,050	13
180.0ft	16,000	1,100	$13^1/_4$
185.0ft	17,000	1,350	$13^3/_4$

PLANS AND DRAWINGS

To construct a steam trawler many hundreds of drawings are required, detailing every component of the ship. Within the drawing office were ship, steelwork, electrical and engineering draughtsmen, all backed up by a team of tracers who converted the pencil drawings into ink masters for reproduction. Every shipyard had their own drawing style, some producing a very basic 'General Arrangement' (GA), while others were highly detailed. These latter examples of the draughtsman's skill were true works of art and will never be replicated by computer aided draughting. When the draughtsman prepared the hull drawings and Table of Offsets (**Plan 3**) for a ship, it was necessary for him to undertake three items – a plate lines body plan, a half block model and a shell expansion drawing. The plate lines body plan (which showed the width of the plates at each frame) was started with the plating information obtained from the midship section drawing, which gave the width of the midship plates. The plate lines were extended in a fair curve, narrowing as they reached the ends of the vessel. At the same time, a highly skilled joiner prepared the half hull model. This was either painted matt white, or varnished and screwed to a backing board. This board was marked out with the hull profile and frame spacings (**Photo. 3**). The model was then fitted with a

right angled sliding bridge, allowing the draughtsman to transfer the frame lines onto it.

Although it was usual to draw all the lines on the model in black, some shipyards drew the frame lines in red, which helped to differentiate between bulkheads, tank top and deck lines. On the plate lines plan, the horizontal plate seams were drawn in and once these were reasonably fair, they were transferred to the model by paper 'girthing strips', moved very carefully along the frame lines, thus giving the horizontal plate runs. These lines were then joined vertically to give the length of each plate and were then transferred to the plate lines drawing, giving the locations of the plate butts. Finally, when every thing looked fair, all this information was transferred to the Shell Expansion drawing (**Plan 4**).

To fully understand shipyard drawings, it is necessary to establish exactly what one is looking at. Sometimes a GA drawing will show either the outboard profile, or a longitudinal section through the centre line, or even a mixture of both. The detail can be confusing and this side view must be read in conjunction with the various plan views, in order to fully understand where everything is positioned within the hull. Lines plans too have their pitfalls, as the stations or cross sections do not always tie in with bulkhead positions and waterlines bear no resemblance to the decks. This is where difficulties arise when taking builders drawings as gospel. Shipyard drawings should always be cross-checked in order to clarify whether or not the GA actually shows the vessel in 'as fitted' condition. Some yard drawings have an amendment panel, which shows when and by whom these were incorporated in the actual design. This is a great help, as it gives a clear indication as to how far advanced the projected design was at that date. The drawings in this book have been mostly redrawn from old originals and I have restricted them to GAs, lines plans, Shell Expansions, mid-ship sections and sail/rigging plans, and for anyone wanting to build a full size hull, I have included Tables of Offsets. This table was converted by the 'Loftsman' into full size drawings on the drawing loft floor, from which frame shapes could be lifted and wooden moulds made for fabrication.

Photo. 4a: Showing a rivetting forge with foot operated bellows and hand riveters swinging their hammers. Below deck would be the 'holder on', who held the 'dolly' which formed the inside head of the rivet. The iron rivets were heated by the 'furnace man' until red hot. They were then removed with tongs and thrown to the 'rivet catcher', who can be seen placing them in position.

CONSTRUCTION

Iron and steel trawlers were all built to basically the same set of rules. Right through the era of steam trawling, Bar Keels were used, both for strength and to give the ships directional stability. Initially, trawlers were all rivetted, with 'in' and 'out' strakes and with the vertical plate butts overlapped, as in standard shipbuilding practice (**Fig. 12**). Some builders used either single or double buttstraps on the sheerstrake and garboards, whilst the bulwarks were normally flush rivetted, with single buttstraps. The shell plating was rivetted to the frames, which were joggled and caulked in the way of watertight bulkheads, water tanks, etc. A typical steam trawler would have four or five such bulkheads (these can be seen in the GA diagrams).

Thomas Watson a well known Naval Architect, wrote:

'All who have to do with the design, building, and maintenance and repairs of ships are aware that the use of rivets as the principal means for the connection of parts in ship structures, has many disadvantages.'

In his many papers, he stated that, *'rivetting was very time consuming, difficult, and tied up a large force of skilled labour.'* Maintenance was difficult and costly. The rivetted plates would slip and the vessels start to leak. In fact, rivetting had very little favouring it and was only used because there was nothing else available at the time. The three photographs presented here (**4a, b & c**) show building in progress at Cochrane's yard.

A rivetting gang usually consisted of four men: the heater, the catcher, the holder on and the riveter (in some squads, the catcher doubled up as the holder on, with two riveters). The rivets would be heated in a perforated tin until white hot by means of a portable hearth (or cooker). This was fired by either coke or coal, with air induced under pressure to speed up the process. In the early days, this was supplied by bellows but later an air supply was piped to the hearth. The heated rivet was thrown to the catcher, often some 15 to 20 feet away. It was then placed in the prepared hole and the holder on applied pressure with his dolly while the riveter beat the red hot rivet into a closing head. Often these men worked in pairs on the external stage, beating the rivet rhythmically in turn with long slender hammers. They had a variety of these hammers, each specially weighted for different sizes of rivets. The wooden hammer shafts had an innate elasticity which was often improved by paring them down. These men were classed as semi-skilled and often worked on piece work. A good hand riveter could close around 300 rivets a day but when the pneumatic hammers came into use, this went up to nearer 1,000. Working conditions were very unhealthy, with men subjected to the incessant noise of

rivets being hammered up. Not only did this noise make it hard for the yard to keep men, it also led to complaints from outside, by people living in close proximity to the shipyards. The rivetting method was costly and the extra steel used, plus the rivets, added considerably to the finished weight of the ship. With every extra ton added, one less ton of cargo could be carried, thus cutting the profit margin for the owners. The rivet holes themselves offered lines of relative weakness when compared to the surrounding plates, and the raised laps in the plating caused extra drag and increased fuel consumption. It was estimated that 15 to 20% more steel was required in a rivetted ship as opposed to a welded one. Time and motion studies also proved that for a welding job that took 18.5 hours, the same job would take 47.2 hours using rivets.

When electric welding came into use, trawlers pioneered the welding techniques that later became standard practice. It was first used to affix the external cope irons and beltings to the hull, as they were a constant source of leaks when rivetted. Next, the strake of plating above the waterline was welded, as it too was a trouble spot, caused by the hammering it got from the trawl doors as they came up. As time progressed, more and more of the structure was welded but, to my knowledge, there was never a steam trawler built by a British yard that was all welded, despite the fact that hammer welding has been known for thousands of years.

Photo's 4b & c: Showing various stages in construction, from framing up, fitting shell plating and bulkheads, to laying steel decks and construction of the superstructure. Openings for the fishroom hatches can be seen, along with the step up to the quarterdeck. **Photo. 4b** (left) is Yard No. 1328 *Rinovia* (GY.527) taken on 29th May 1947, while **Photo. 4c** (below) is of Yard No. 1211 *Le Royal* on 4th December 1941.

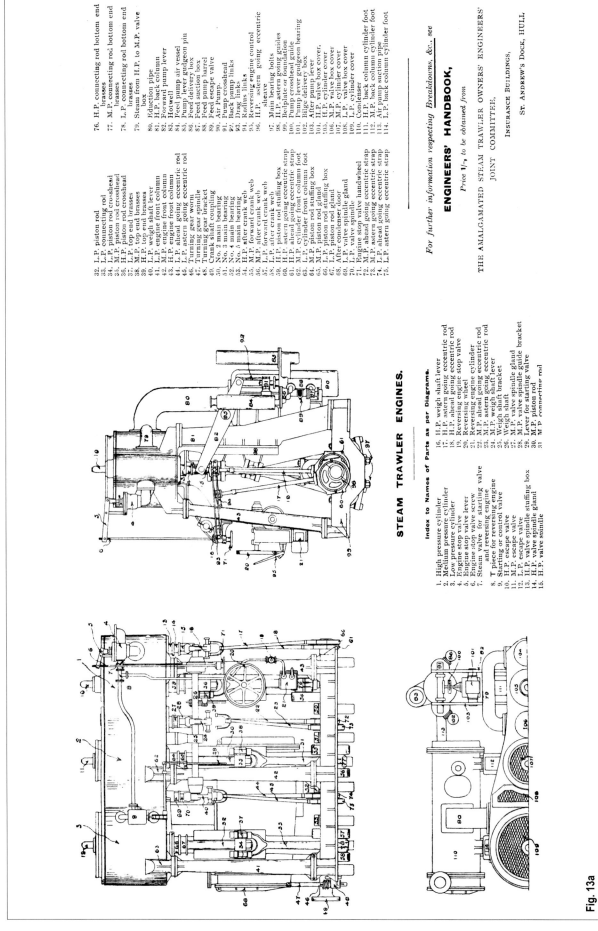

STEAM TRAWLER ENGINES.

Index to Names of Parts as per Diagrams.

1. High pressure cylinder
2. Medium pressure cylinder
3. Low pressure cylinder
4. Engine stop valve
5. Engine stop valve lever
6. Engine stop valve screw
7. Steam valve for starting valve and reversing engine
8. T piece for reversing engine
9. Starting or control valve
10. H.P. escape valve
11. M.P. escape valve
12. L.P. escape valve
13. H.P. valve spindle stuffing box
14. H.P. valve spindle gland
15. H.P. valve spindle

16. H.P. weigh shaft lever
17. H.P. astern going eccentric rod
18. H.P. ahead going eccentric rod
19. Reversing engine stop valve
20. Reversing wheel
21. Reversing engine cylinder
22. M.P. ahead going eccentric rod
23. M.P. astern going eccentric rod
24. M.P. weigh shaft lever
25. Weigh shaft bracket
26. Weigh shaft
27. M.P. valve spindle gland
28. M.P. valve spindle guide bracket
29. Lever for starting valve
30. M.P. piston rod
31. M.P. connecting rod

32. L.P. piston rod
33. L.P. connecting rod
34. M.P. piston rod crosshead
35. M.P. piston rod crosshead
36. H.P. piston rod crosshead
37. L.P. top end brasses
38. M.P. top end brasses
39. H.P. top end brasses
40. L.P. weigh shaft lever
41. L.P. engine front column
42. M.P. engine front column
43. H.P. engine front column
44. L.P. ahead going eccentric rod
45. L.P. astern going eccentric rod
46. Turning gear worm
47. Turning gear spindle
48. Turning gear bracket
49. Crank shaft coupling
50. No. 2 main bearing
51. No. 3 main bearing
52. No. 4 main bearing
53. No. 5 main bearing
54. H.P. after crank web
55. M.P. forward crank web
56. M.P. after crank web
57. L.P. forward crank web
58. L.P. after crank web
59. H.P. piston rod stuffing box
60. H.P. astern going eccentric strap
61. H.P. ahead going eccentric strap
62. M.P. cylinder front column foot
63. M.P. cylinder front column foot
64. M.P. piston rod stuffing box
65. M.P. piston rod gland
66. L.P. piston rod stuffing box
67. L.P. piston rod gland
68. After condenser door
69. L.P. valve spindle gland
70. L.P. valve spindle
71. Engine stop valve handwheel
72. M.P. ahead going eccentric strap
73. M.P. astern going eccentric strap
74. L.P. ahead going eccentric strap
75. L.P. astern going eccentric strap

76. H.P. connecting rod bottom end brasses
77. M.P. connecting rod bottom end brasses
78. L.P. connecting rod bottom end brasses
79. Steam from H.P. to M.P. valve box
80. Eduction pipe
81. H.P. back column
82. Forward pump lever
83. Hotwell
84. Feed pump air vessel
85. Pump lever gudgeon pin
86. Feed delivery box
87. Feed suction box
88. Feed pump barrel
89. Feed escape valve
90. Air Pump.
91. Pump crosshead
92. Back pump links
93. Drag links
94. Radius links
95. Reversing engine control
96. H.P. astern going eccentric sheave
97. Main bearing bolts
98. H.P. astern going guides
99. Bedplate or foundation
100. Pump crosshead guide
101. Pump lever gudgeon bearing
102. Bilge delivery box
103. After pump lever
104. H.P. valve box cover.
105. H.P. cylinder cover
106. H.P. valve box cover
107. M.P. cylinder cover
108. L.P. valve box cover
109. L.P. cylinder cover
110. Condenser
111. H.P. back column cylinder foot
112. M.P. back column cylinder foot
113. Air pump suction pipe
114. L.P. back column cylinder foot

For further information respecting Breakdowns, &c., see

ENGINEERS' HANDBOOK,

Price 1/-, to be obtained from

THE AMALGAMATED STEAM TRAWLER OWNERS' ENGINEERS'
JOINT COMMITTEE,

INSURANCE BUILDINGS,

ST. ANDREW'S DOCK, HULL.

Fig. 13a

STEAM TRAWLER ENGINE.
(Back View.)

WITH WROUGHT IRON (OR STEEL) CONDENSER.

STEAM TRAWLER ENGINE, 500 INDICATED HORSE POWER,
WITH ORDINARY CAST IRON CONDENSER. (Front View.)

Photo. 5: Set of Triple Expansion trawler engines by Smith's Dock Ltd.

Electric arc welding was patented by Wilde as early as 1865. The first mention of gas welding appears in 1887, when Thomas Fletcher invented a system of blowpipes, using a mixture of either hydrogen or coal gas and oxygen. In 1900, the French discovered that by mixing oxygen and acetylene, a flame could be the basis of oxy-acetylene welding.

TRAWLER ENGINES AND BOILERS

To avoid repetition, all engines referred to through this book are of the Triple Expansion, Surface Condensing type unless otherwise noted (**Fig. 13a** and **Photo. 5**). Engine dimensions are given as cylinder diameters in inches x stroke in inches. The standard boiler fitted to steam trawlers was the 'Scotch' cylindrical return tube type (**Fig. 13b**). Some boilers were fitted with superheaters. A 'U'

shaped superheater tube was fitted in each smoke tube, with the open ends bolted to headers in the smokebox. By passing saturated steam from the boiler through these tubes, a small degree of superheat is obtained. With reciprocating engines, superheated steam would not be used until the engines were fully warmed up and arrangements were made to use saturated steam until the trawler was underway.

Trawler furnaces were either at the aft or fore end of the boiler, giving rise to the terms 'fore side' and 'aft side' jobs. With the latter type, coal had to be moved from the cross bunkers the extra length of the boiler, so these were not as popular as the 'fore side jobs'. The easy way to tell which firing method was used was by the position of the stokehold cowl vents: ahead of the funnel on a 'foresider' and behind the funnel on an 'aft sider'.

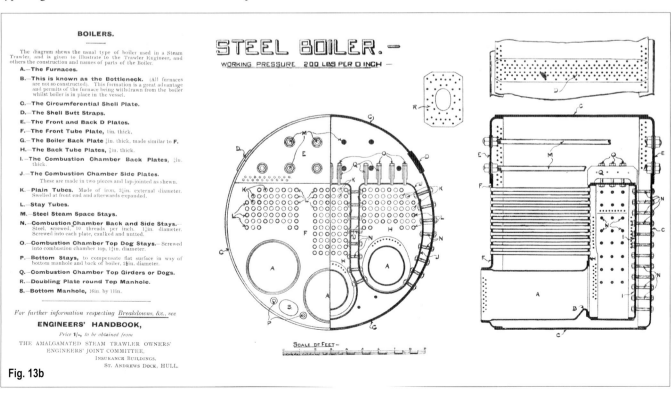

BOILERS.

The diagram shews the usual type of boiler used in a Steam Trawler, and is given to illustrate to the Trawler Engineer, and others the construction and names of parts of the Boiler.

A.—The Furnaces.

B.—This is known as the Bottleneck. (All furnaces are not so constructed). This formation is a great advantage and permits of the furnace being withdrawn from the boiler whilst boiler is in place in the vessel.

C.—The Circumferential Shell Plate.

D.—The Shell Butt Straps.

E.—The Front and Back D Plates.

F.—The Front Tube Plate, ⅝in. thick.

G.—The Boiler Back Plate ⅝in. thick, made similar to **F.**

H.—The Back Tube Plates, ½in. thick.

I.—The Combustion Chamber Back Plates, ⅝in. thick.

J.—The Combustion Chamber Side Plates. These are made in two pieces and lap-jointed as shewn.

K.—Plain Tubes. Made of iron, 3¼in. external diameter. Swelled at front end and afterwards expanded.

L.—Stay Tubes.

M.—Steel Steam Space Stays.

N.—Combustion Chamber Back and Side Stays.— Steel, screwed, 10 threads per inch, 1⅛in. diameter. Screwed into each plate, caulked and nutted.

O.—Combustion Chamber Top Dog Stays.— Screwed into combustion chamber top, 1¼in. diameter.

P.—Bottom Stays, to compensate flat surface in way of bottom manhole and back of boiler, 2¼in. diameter.

Q.—Combustion Chamber Top Girders or Dogs.

R.—Doubling Plate round Top Manhole.

S.—Bottom Manhole, 16in. by 11in.

For further information respecting Breakdowns, &c., see

ENGINEERS' HANDBOOK,

Price **1/-** *to be obtained from*

THE AMALGAMATED STEAM TRAWLER OWNERS'
ENGINEERS' JOINT COMMITTEE,
INSURANCE BUILDINGS,
ST. ANDREWS DOCK, HULL.

STEEL BOILER.—
WORKING PRESSURE 200 LBS PER ☐ INCH —

SCALE OF FEET

Fig. 13b

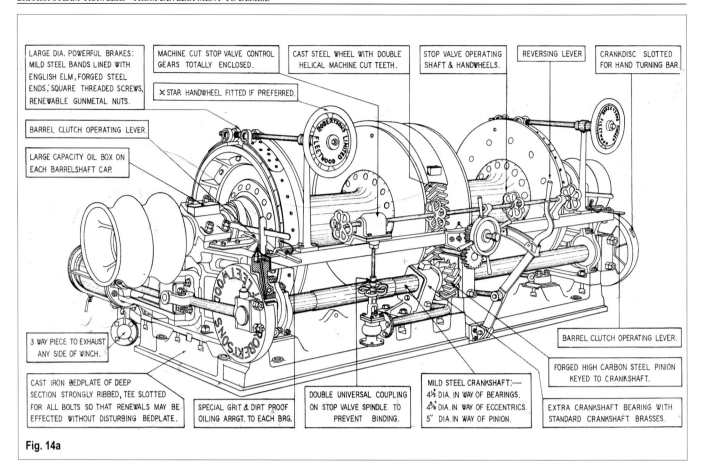

LARGE DIA. POWERFUL BRAKES: MILD STEEL BANDS LINED WITH ENGLISH ELM, FORGED STEEL ENDS, SQUARE THREADED SCREWS, RENEWABLE GUNMETAL NUTS.

MACHINE CUT STOP VALVE CONTROL GEARS TOTALLY ENCLOSED.

CAST STEEL WHEEL WITH DOUBLE HELICAL MACHINE CUT TEETH.

STOP VALVE OPERATING SHAFT & HANDWHEELS.

REVERSING LEVER

CRANKDISC SLOTTED FOR HAND TURNING BAR.

STAR HANDWHEEL FITTED IF PREFERRED.

BARREL CLUTCH OPERATING LEVER.

LARGE CAPACITY OIL BOX ON EACH BARRELSHAFT CAP.

3 WAY PIECE TO EXHAUST ANY SIDE OF WINCH.

CAST IRON BEDPLATE OF DEEP SECTION STRONGLY RIBBED, TEE SLOTTED FOR ALL BOLTS SO THAT RENEWALS MAY BE EFFECTED WITHOUT DISTURBING BEDPLATE.

SPECIAL GRIT & DIRT PROOF OILING ARRGT. TO EACH BRG.

DOUBLE UNIVERSAL COUPLING ON STOP VALVE SPINDLE TO PREVENT BINDING.

MILD STEEL CRANKSHAFT:— 4½ DIA. IN WAY OF BEARINGS. 4⅝ DIA. IN WAY OF ECCENTRICS. 5" DIA. IN WAY OF PINION.

BARREL CLUTCH OPERATING LEVER.

FORGED HIGH CARBON STEEL PINION KEYED TO CRANKSHAFT.

EXTRA CRANKSHAFT BEARING WITH STANDARD CRANKSHAFT BRASSES.

Fig. 14a

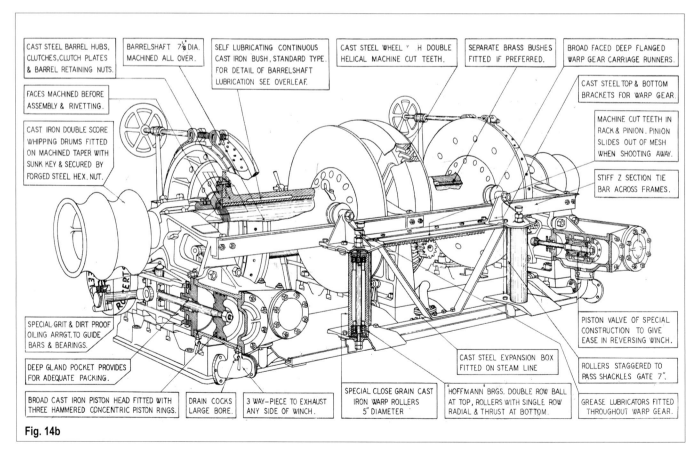

CAST STEEL BARREL HUBS, CLUTCHES, CLUTCH PLATES & BARREL RETAINING NUTS.

BARRELSHAFT 7⅛ DIA. MACHINED ALL OVER.

SELF LUBRICATING CONTINUOUS CAST IRON BUSH, STANDARD TYPE. FOR DETAIL OF BARRELSHAFT LUBRICATION SEE OVERLEAF.

CAST STEEL WHEEL WITH DOUBLE HELICAL MACHINE CUT TEETH.

SEPARATE BRASS BUSHES FITTED IF PREFERRED.

BROAD FACED DEEP FLANGED WARP GEAR CARRIAGE RUNNERS.

FACES MACHINED BEFORE ASSEMBLY & RIVETTING.

CAST STEEL TOP & BOTTOM BRACKETS FOR WARP GEAR.

CAST IRON DOUBLE SCORE WHIPPING DRUMS FITTED ON MACHINED TAPER WITH SUNK KEY & SECURED BY FORGED STEEL HEX. NUT.

MACHINE CUT TEETH IN RACK & PINION. PINION SLIDES OUT OF MESH WHEN SHOOTING AWAY.

STIFF Z SECTION TIE BAR ACROSS FRAMES.

SPECIAL GRIT & DIRT PROOF OILING ARRGT. TO GUIDE BARS & BEARINGS.

DEEP GLAND POCKET PROVIDES FOR ADEQUATE PACKING.

BROAD CAST IRON PISTON HEAD FITTED WITH THREE HAMMERED CONCENTRIC PISTON RINGS.

DRAIN COCKS LARGE BORE.

3 WAY-PIECE TO EXHAUST ANY SIDE OF WINCH.

SPECIAL CLOSE GRAIN CAST IRON WARP ROLLERS 5" DIAMETER

HOFFMANN BRGS. DOUBLE ROW BALL AT TOP, ROLLERS WITH SINGLE ROW RADIAL & THRUST AT BOTTOM.

CAST STEEL EXPANSION BOX FITTED ON STEAM LINE

PISTON VALVE OF SPECIAL CONSTRUCTION TO GIVE EASE IN REVERSING WINCH.

ROLLERS STAGGERED TO PASS SHACKLES GATE 7".

GREASE LUBRICATORS FITTED THROUGHOUT WARP GEAR.

Fig. 14b

Chapter 4: TRAWLER DECK FITTINGS AND DETAILS

Under this heading will be found the specialised fittings common to the steam powered side trawler.

THE TRAWL WINCH

One of the most prominent and important pieces of equipment aboard a steam trawler is her winch. It is situated immediately forward of the superstructure, within earshot of the wheelhouse, except on the early beam trawlers where their single barrel winches were abaft the foremast. On the larger trawlers it stands at the break of the quarterdeck. This step up of around 12ins effectively raises the vessel's freeboard, increases her buoyancy and forms a breakwater, which helps to stop offal, small fish and loose gear being swept aft. The steam trawl winch is a massive affair, weighing from 8 to 20 tons and is securely bolted down to the deck. It stands around shoulder height and consists of two large drums for the towing warps, and a warping drum at either end of the main shaft, for handling the falls from the Gilson and yo-yo derricks. The winchmen, one operating each drum or side, must have a clear view of the centre and side bollards, and the fore and aft gallows, in order that they can follow all operations safely. Great skill was necessary to operate the winch efficiently when the ship was pitching and rolling in heavy weather – trawling did not stop until the weather was such that it was impossible for men to keep the deck. They had to be ready to ease the warps quickly if they came fast, or the ship would be pulled over, whilst imagine the disastrous results if they tried to pull the three-quarter ton trawl doors through the gallows block.

The modern trawl winch evolved from the capstan, first manually, then steam powered. From George Bidder's patent winch fitted to his trawling smack *Bertha*, through the single barrelled type fitted to the early steam beamers, on to the small double barrel 'Strath' and Elliot & Garrood winches necessary for working the Otter Trawls of the North Sea ships, and finally to the huge 'Bear Island', 'Andanes' and 'Newfoundland' winches fitted to the later oil burners.

The main design criteria for steam trawl winches was that they must be capable, when hauling, of:

- Exercising a pull of about 10 tons at 200ft per minute.
- Stalling and easing back should a submerged object foul the net.
- Maintaining the tension on the trawl warps to keep the mouth of the net open and off the seabed.

The power necessary to fulfil these requirements is around 200ihp.

The general arrangement perspectives of a typical steam winch, taken from Robertson's 1933 catalogue, shows all the features. Points of interest are the drain cocks, which allow the condensate or cold water to be blown from the cylinders prior to starting up. The operator had to run the winch up slowly after being shut down, otherwise this water residue would cause the pistons to 'hydraulic', blowing the gland packing seals, thus rendering the winch temporarily inoperative. Another important feature is the Warp Guide Roller system, or Spooling Gear. This carriage arrangement traverses the front of the barrels, ensuring that the trawl warp reels in cleanly, with no riding turns that could jam up when shooting away. Before the introduction of automatic spooling, this task was controlled by a spoked wheel at the rear of the winch, the operation being commonly known as 'riding on' (yet another of the many backbreaking jobs aboard a trawler). By

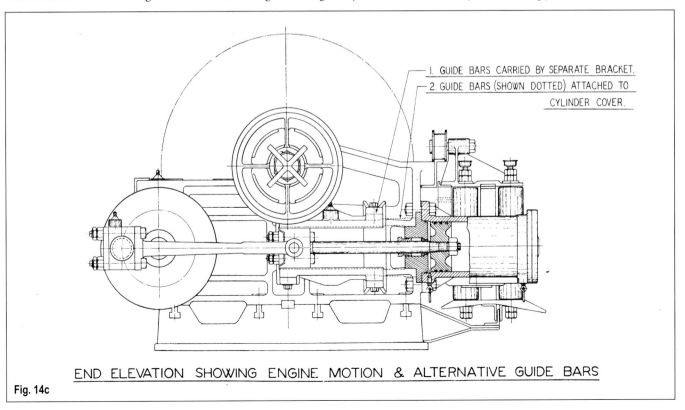

1. GUIDE BARS CARRIED BY SEPARATE BRACKET.
2. GUIDE BARS (SHOWN DOTTED) ATTACHED TO CYLINDER COVER.

END ELEVATION SHOWING ENGINE MOTION & ALTERNATIVE GUIDE BARS

Fig. 14c

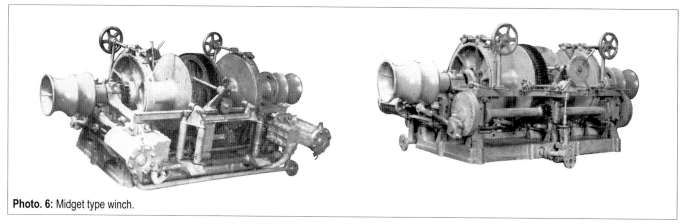

Photo. 6: Midget type winch.

Photo. 7: Drifter type winch.

far the tallest features of the trawl winch are the Brake Bands and their hand wheels. These bands are long steel straps which encircle the brake drums, being tightened by a horizontal steel rod. This rod has both a right and left handed thread cut into it, which fits corresponding nuts on the bands. The bands themselves were lined with either English elm, or *lignum vitae* shoes. Copious amounts of seawater or cods livers were often applied to keep them from overheating and catching fire. (**Fig. 14, a, b & c**)

Steam winches ranged from capacities of 250 fathoms of 2.5ins circumference warp on each drum, with power of up to 300bhp. They are driven externally, either by two powerful single cylinder, double acting engines fitted to the main frames, having cylinders from 6ins diameter and 10ins stroke, up to 10ins diameter with 13ins stroke, and either slide or piston valves; or by compound twin cylinder engines of 6ins by 11ins diameter and 13ins stroke. Both types had an easily accessible, slip eccentric, double-link reversing gear. The main gearing had either square cut teeth or the more efficient helical cut type, as supplied by Robertsons and the Strath Engineering Co.

Names synonymous with steam trawl winches were:

ROBERTSONS of Fleetwood. One of the country's leading manufacturers of trawl winches since the early 1900s. They had a wide range of designs to suit all sizes of vessel and depths of water, namely:

• 'Midget' trawl winch, 6ins diameter by 10ins stroke, with slide valves and 200 fathoms of 2.5ins circular warp on each barrel (**Photo. 6**). This winch is very similar to the 'Strath' type winch.

• 'Drifter' trawl winch, 7.5ins diameter by 12ins stroke, with slide valves, 350 fathoms of 2.5ins warp on each barrel (**Photo. 7**).

• 'Iceland' type, 9ins diameter by 14ins stroke and slide valve cylinders. 500 to 1,500 fathoms of $2^5/8$ins warp (**Photo. 8**).

• 'Bear Island' winch, 9ins diameter by 14ins stroke, fitted with piston valves and a choice of hand or fully automatic spooling gear. 1,200 fathoms of 3ins circular warp (**Photo. 9**).

• 'Andanes' types, 9ins diameter by 14ins stroke, piston valves to both cylinders, automatic spooling gear, automatic drain cocks and fully enclosed gearbox. 1,200 to 1,500 fathoms, up to 3ins warp (**Photo. 10**). There was also another winch of this type, with larger 10ins diameter by 15ins stroke cylinders.

• 'Newfoundland', an exceptionally powerful winch, with 10ins diameter by 14ins stroke cylinders, piston valves, totally enclosed gearbox, mechanical lubrication and a second motion shaft. The latter allowed for two separate whipping drums outside the main

Photo. 8: Iceland winch.

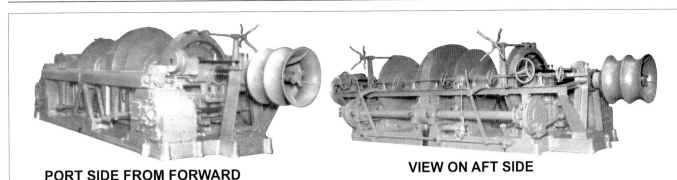

PORT SIDE FROM FORWARD

VIEW ON AFT SIDE

Photo. 9: Bear Island winch.

Photo. 10: Andanes winch.

frames. The main difference between this design and the rest was in the positioning of the cylinders. They were fitted between the main barbells, rather than on the outside frames. This arrangement kept the main crankshaft quite short. 1,200 fathoms of 3ins circular warp.

There was another famous winch made by the company – the 'Arctic' Class. This machine was powered by a high speed, vertical, three cylinder steam engine, of either 6.5ins diameter by 6ins stroke, or 8ins diameter by 7ins stroke, housed in its own compartment below the wheelhouse. This location afforded complete protection from the elements. The engine itself was totally enclosed, with forced lubrication, which alleviated much time consuming servicing. The winch itself was driven by an output shaft, fitted with an oil-immersed, totally enclosed, worm gear and had a capacity of from 1,000 to 1,500 fathoms of either $2\frac{5}{8}$ins or 3ins warp on each barrel. The cost of this winch was originally around £1,300 in 1940 (**Photo. 11**).

CHARLES D. HOLMES of Hull. Although better known for their

engines, this company produced an excellent series of winch types, under the brand name 'Triton' (**Photo. 12**). These included:

• Type 'A'. Some 12ft 7ins wide, 8ins bore by 13ins stroke, slide valve cylinders and a capacity of 700 fathoms of 2.75ins warp on each barrel.

• Type 'B'. 13ft 3ins wide, with 8ins bore and 13ins stroke. 840 fathoms of 2.75ins trawl warp.

• Type 'C'. 14ft 3ins wide, cylinders of 8ins bore and 13ins stroke, capacity 1,050 fathoms of 2.75ins warp.

• Type 'M'. Although the same width as the 'C', the main barrels were 3ins wider, which allowed them to carry 1,100 fathoms of 2.75ins warp.

For ease of manufacture, these four winches all used the same cylinder castings. The next four types all had compound twin cylinder engines:

• Type 'D'. 13ft 9ins wide overall, with 6ins by 11ins bore and 13ins stroke, each barrel carrying 840 fathoms of 2.75ins warp.

• Type 'E'. This winch was 12ins wider than its predecessorbut used the same cylinder castings and had a capacity of 1,050 fathoms of 2.75ins warp on each barrel.

• Type 'F'. Some 15ft 1ins wide and again it used the same set of cylinder castings as the previous model but had the larger capacity of 1,090 fathoms of 2.75ins warp.

• Type 'G'. Larger again at 15ft 9ins wide overall, with cylinders of 6ins by 12ins bore and 13ins stroke, and a capacity of 1,230 fathoms of 2.75ins warp.

• Type 'H'. Some 13ft 3ins wide, with similar cylinders to the 'A' type but with a capacity of 840 fathoms of 2.75ins warp.

• Type 'I'. A midget of a winch, only 9ft 9ins wide, with 7ins

Photo. 11: Arctic type winch.

Photo. 12: Triton winch.

diameter and 12ins stroke, The barrels each carried 390 fathoms of 2.75ins trawl warp.

The latter two winches were fitted with a second motion shaft, which gave both a double, and a single whipping drum outboard of the frames.

• Type 'J'. Another small winch, 11ft 7ins wide, holding some 518 fathoms of 2.75ins warp and cylinders of 8ins diameter by 12ins stroke.

• Type 'K'. Another tiddler, 9ft 7ins wide, with 8ins diameter by 12ins stroke cylinders and a capacity of 400 fathoms of 2.75ins warp.

• Type 'L'. A heavier duty winch, some 15ft 3ins overall, having cylinders of 9ins diameter by 14ins stroke and a capacity of 1,230 fathoms of 2.75ins warp.

CLARKE CHAPMAN (Photo.13). This well known manufacturer of cargo winches, windlasses and other marine equipment, also produced their own model of steam trawl winch. This was a large deep water winch, of conventional design, having a second motion shaft fitted with a single light duty whipping drum, which complimented the double whipping drums on the main shaft. Reversing gear was of the double eccentric link-motion, with a counterbalanced reversing lever. Automatic spooling gear was fitted, along with screw operated brake gear to each barrel. No barrel capacities are available but from the company's brochure illustration, 12,000 to15,000 fathoms would seem appropriate. The company supplied two models, one with totally enclosed working parts, and the other with only basic guards and the latter

Photo. 13: Clarke Chapman winch.

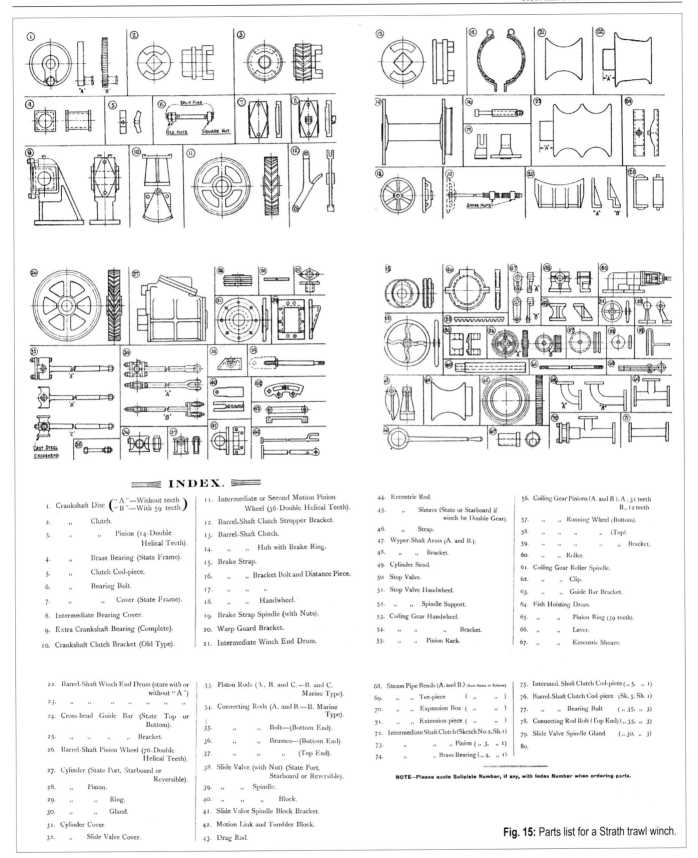

Fig. 15: Parts list for a Strath trawl winch.

shows square cut gearing as favoured by the makers.

STRATH ENGINEERING WORKS, Aberdeen. The Aberdeen owners favoured locally made winches of the 'Strath' type. This made sound sense, as carriage costs were minimal, and shore based servicing and repair facilities were close at hand, ensuring a very short 'down time' should any require attention. Although the company was a prolific manufacturer, I have only been able to trace one of their small pamphlets. This is an abridged specification and illustrated parts list. which gives a good impression of all the main winch parts (**Fig. 15**).

Photo. 14: Showing centre bollards. One of the pound board stanchions can be seen on the right of the picture. Note the guard rails around the bollards and large greasing points on top of the sheaves.

Photo. 15: Showing early type of bollards on a Smith's Dock 'fleeter', with the long run of warp up to the hanging block. The crew are packing the fish into boxes ready for transfer to the 'Carrier'.

ELLIOTT & GARROOD LTD of Beccles, in Suffolk, was another company better known, possibly, for its steam engines and steam capstans, the latter under the 'Beccles' trademark. They also constructed their own trawl winches, mainly smaller North Sea types which were fitted to local dual purpose drifter/trawlers. My manufacturer's drawing shows a steam trawl winch, some 9ft 1ins wide, with cylinders of 6ins diameter by 10ins stroke. Slip eccentric reversing gear is fitted and the brake bands are shown on the inner flanges of the barrels (they were normally attached to the outer flanges). Again, no capacities are shown but a possible maximum of 450 fathoms per drum would appear about right.

Trawl winches were also supplied by specialist chandlers such as the famous GREAT GRIMSBY COAL, SALT, & TANNING CO LTD. This well known firm could completely outfit a steam trawler (see Appendix 2), with offices and workshops at all the main fishing centres. In the 1920s, they supplied a Distant Water steam winch, classed as the new 'H' type, with a capacity of 1,200 fathoms of

2.5ins warp per barrel. The cylinders were some 8.5ins diameter by 14ins stroke, with slip eccentric reversing gear and the spooling gear was hand operated.

One variation to the trawl winch was in the use of twin steam capstans fitted to Scottish steam drifters during hasty trawling conversions. The second capstan was bolted down abreast the vessel's original, forming what was, in effect, a second winch barrel. These makeshift conversions were a common sight in 1921, when the fishermen of the Moray Firth were faced with poverty brought about by the failure of the winter herring fishing. To further rub salt into their wounds, the fleet was tied up over the summer months because of a coal strike. It is small wonder that this illegal trawling within the confines of the Moray Firth was tried as a last resort.

CENTRE BOLLARDS

These are placed either side of the fore mast and consist of heavy cast frames with double rollers. A protective handrail is usually

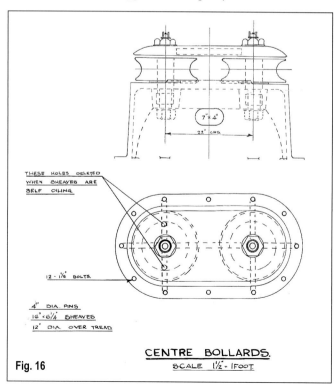

Fig. 16   CENTRE BOLLARDS.
SCALE 1½" = 1FOOT

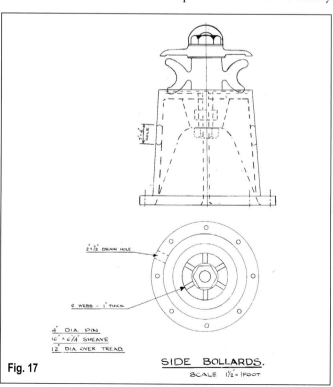

Fig. 17   SIDE BOLLARDS.
SCALE 1½" = 1FOOT

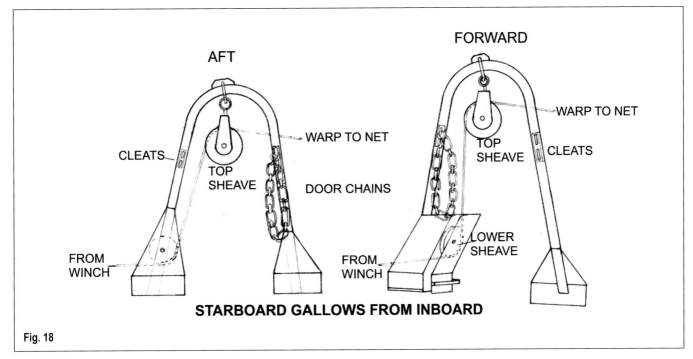

AFT

FORWARD

WARP TO NET

CLEATS

TOP SHEAVE

WARP TO NET

CLEATS

TOP SHEAVE

DOOR CHAINS

LOWER SHEAVE

FROM WINCH

FROM WINCH

STARBOARD GALLOWS FROM INBOARD

Fig. 18

fitted round their top. These fairleads take the trawl warps from the winch to the Wing Bollards (**Fig. 16 and Photo. 14**).

SIDE OR WING BOLLARDS

These are fitted either abreast the main bollards or abeam of the trawl winch, depending on whether the former are fitted ahead or behind the mast. They are similar in design to the main bollards but have only a single sheave. Their function is to lead the after warps to their respective gallows (**Fig. 17 and Photo. 15**). Although of immense strength, these bollards have been known to shatter in conditions of extreme cold (conditions well known to Distant Water trawlermen).

GALLOWS

These inverted horse shoe erections, above all, identify the vessel as a side trawler. These fittings are not carried by either Drifters or Liners. The fore gallows are usually bolted down to the steel sub deck immediately abreast of the foremast and the after gallows can be found abeam of the galley or the engine room casing. Both pairs incline outwards in order to bring the hanging block over the rail (**Fig. 18 and Photo. 16**).

Although most steam sidewinders were fitted with gallows on both sides, some of the very early ships and 'fleeters' only carried them on the port side, possibly a throw back from beam trawling days. Other explanations were that 'fleeters' carried their boat on the starboard side of the foredeck, and also some early vessels were fitted with left handed screws. These very early steam trawlers were often fitted with 'patent bulwark rollers', or 'trawl ports', instead of gallows frames (**Plan No.16 of** *Strathdon*). From these trawl ports the gallows evolved, first as upright steel posts, then as 'gibbet' type davits (the origin of the name) and finally on to the inverted 'U' form. These gallows frames are formed from strong steel channel section or 'H' bar, attached to the steel deck by plate webs and knees, and further supported at their crowns by rod stays. For the fore gallows, these stays are fixed to the foremast and to the break of the whaleback. Where no whaleback is fitted,

these stays are either bolted or rivetted at the waterways, or to the casing of the fo'c'sle companionway. The stays for the after gallows are fixed fore and aft to the waterway or steel side deck and the crown stays are attached to the casing or galley top. At the base of each gallows frame can be found the 'gallows frame sheave'. On the fore gallows, it is either built in to the base of the after leg or bolted separately to the deck under the centre of the frame. No

Photo. 16: Starboard forward gallows showing hanging block and fixed gallows block with rod stay. Note the chains for securing the trawl board.

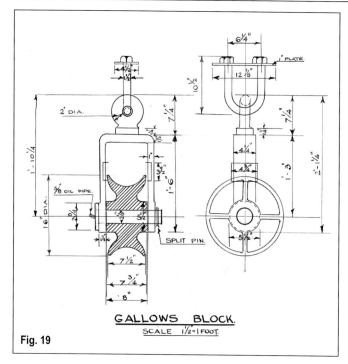

Fig. 19

GALLOWS BLOCK.
SCALE ½" = 1 FOOT.

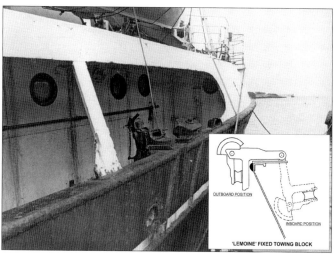

Photo. 17: Lemoine' type towing block (inboard position) with diverter/messenger sheave fitted behind. This safer and more efficient type of towing block was introduced in the late 1950s.

matter what system is used, this sheave must be in a fair leading line with the centre rollers. The after gallows frame sheave is fitted into the base of the foreleg. Bolted to the crown of the gallows is the 'norman', which is a bracket for the 'hanging block' or 'gallows frame block' (**Fig. 19**).

TOWING BLOCKS

(**Fig. 20**) These are basically heavy hinged clasps, used to clamp the two trawl warps together when towing. This is necessary for manoeuvrability, and to prevent the warps fouling the screw propeller. They are attached to the vessel's quarters by means of a short chain fixed to the ship's rail. The blocks themselves are fabricated from iron or steel, about one inch thick and of a special hardness so as not to chafe the warps. Their design is such that, at hauling time,

Photo. 18: Hand Capstan typical of its time with all gearing exposed.

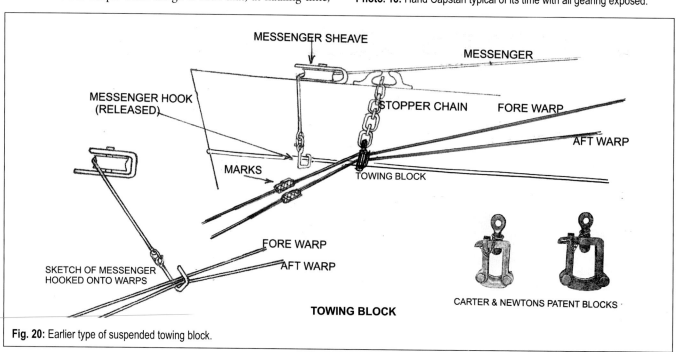

Fig. 20: Earlier type of suspended towing block.

40

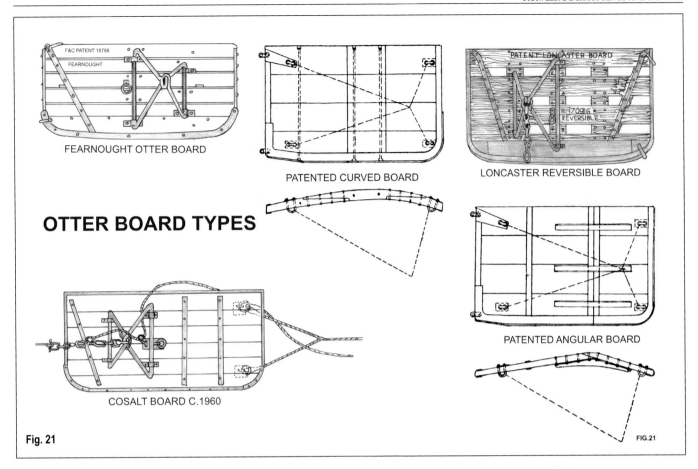

FEARNOUGHT OTTER BOARD

PATENTED CURVED BOARD

LONCASTER REVERSIBLE BOARD

OTTER BOARD TYPES

PATENTED ANGULAR BOARD

COSALT BOARD C.1960

Fig. 21

FIG.21

the 'block key' is knocked out by a sharp blow to the underside and the block opens, releasing the warps, which then separate. Great care must be exercised when 'knocking out', as the strain on the block is considerable and can be thrown backwards with tremendous force. The crew member responsible for this operation must always be on the forward side of the block for safety. After the gear is shot away, the warps on leaving the gallows blocks are brought together using a messenger hook and wire, before being clamped in the towing block. This messenger wire leads through the top sheaves on the casing to the whipping drum on the winch. These suspended towing blocks were replaced in the 1950s with the 'Lemoine' type (**Photo. 17**). The beam trawler *Strathdon* had a similar but quite different set up. No gallows were needed before the advent of the Otter Trawl, so the single warp passed round the centre rollers and out though the trawl ports in the ship's side. A 'dandy score' or roller fairlead was fitted on the quarters for the trawl warp. This arrangement was similar to that of a sailing trawler but the steam winch had replaced the hand operated capstan (**Photo. 18**).

TRAWL DOORS OR OTTER BOARDS

Trawl doors or otter boards which keep the mouth of the net open are constructed from stout timber strengthened by steel diagonal straps, 'H' or 'U' section steel ties and a heavy iron shoe. Their sizes ranged from 8 to 11ins in length and from 4 to 6ins deep, weighing between 7 and 15cwt. As an example, a 150ft trawler would use boards of 7ft 6ins by 4ft 6ins, working an Otter Trawl with a 70ft to 80ft head rope. Four such boards are carried immediately ready for use, stowed between the gallows and the rail. Spare boards are carried, lashed to either the casing side or under the whaleback. As with the net, these boards have evolved from the simple affairs shown in the early photographs, through to the high performance boards of the late 1950s. The Germans have always been great innovators and, as far back as the 1920s, Dr Oertz designed his *'patent Otter Board of curved form'*. This design apparently reduced the drag factor, with a resulting saving in coal. As mentioned previously, trawl boards had to be designed and constructed to rigid standards in order to minimise damage to

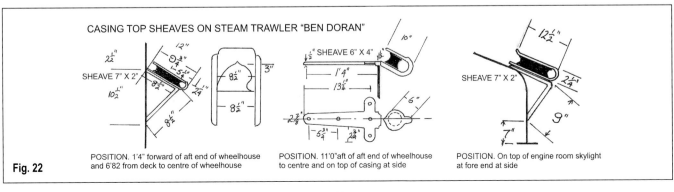

CASING TOP SHEAVES ON STEAM TRAWLER "BEN DORAN"

SHEAVE 7" X 2"

SHEAVE 6" X 4"

SHEAVE 7" X 2"

POSITION. 1'4" forward of aft end of wheelhouse and 6'82 from deck to centre of wheelhouse

POSITION. 11'0"aft of aft end of wheelhouse to centre and on top of casing at side

POSITION. On top of engine room skylight at fore end at side

Fig. 22

underwater cables. The foremast derrick (yo-yo boom) was used to lift these heavy boards but prior to these being fitted, tackles were rigged from the masthead (**Fig. 21**).

TRAWL NET STOWAGE

This was normally stowed below when not in use but when 'running off' or steaming to the fishing grounds, the net is made ready for use and lashed along the inside of the bulwarks. A common feature of the Aberdeen ships was the trawl net hanging on the funnel.

CASING FAIRLEADS OR TOP SHEAVES

(**Fig. 22**) These are fitted either side of the casing and are used for leading the falls of the after bobbin derrick and the messenger wire from the towing block, to the whipping drums on the winch.

GILSONS

(Pronounced with a soft 'G'). To assist with the handling of their heavy gear, trawlers are fitted with a derrick, or yo-yo boom on the foremast and either single or twin 'bobbin' derricks on the casing aft. The latter are used to hoist the spare trawl doors into position when changing over and to lift the bunt bobbins of the net over the rail. The fore Gilson tackle is rove through a heavy masthead block and is used for handling most of the fishing gear on the foredeck. The fore derrick is a most vital piece of equipment, as without it, lifting the cod end outboard would be a gargantuan task. The cod end is exceptionally heavy, especially when 'dressed' with cow hides which prevent the net chafing through on the sea bed.

TRAWLER DECKS

These are generally of steel plate, either welded or rivetted. On most ships, with the exception of the Admiralty-built trawlers, they were wood sheathed. This took the form of 5ins by 3ins Douglas fir, pitch pine or Oregon pine bolted to the steel deck, with the bolt heads countersunk and capped with wooden dowels. In the way of the boiler room and the winch base, the decks are further strengthened with chequer plate or cement. Cement

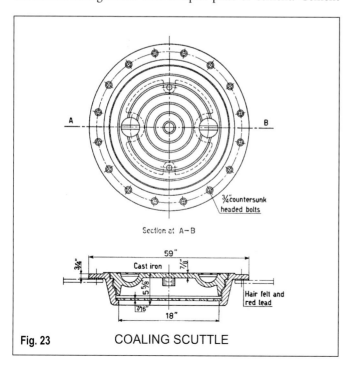

¾"countersunk headed bolts

Section at A–B

59"
Cast iron
¾"
⅞"
5⅝"
⅞₁₆"
Hair felt and red lead
⁷⁄₁₆"
18"

Fig. 23   COALING SCUTTLE

waterways were fitted around the maindeck margins and on the larger trawlers, this was often flushed over with hinged, perforated steel plates. Steam liners had a raised wooden platform on the port side abreast the foremast, for shooting and hauling the long lines. This working stage was covered in rough coir matting which gave a good grip to the men's sea boots. On the coal burners, numerous circular openings were cut into the decks over the bunker spaces. A noticeable feature common to all steam trawlers were the sections of steel chequer plate bolted both sides of the casing at main deck level over the boiler. These allowed the boiler to be lifted in at the fitting out berth after the decks had been laid.

COALING SCUTTLES.

(**Fig. 23**) These are fitted with screw in, cast iron bunker lids, bedded down with grease or tallow. A favourite ploy of trawlermen when trying to buy extra shore time was to throw these lids into the dock. In Aberdeen, these covers could be ten deep on occasion and brought forth some choice expletives from the local dredger crews. Oil burners on the other hand had no such scuttles and filling valves were fitted into recesses on the casing side for bunker replenishment.

The foredeck is the part of the main deck lying forward of the winch or quarter deck and it is pierced by numerous hatches. On the fore side of the foremast can usually be found an ice room hatch and a smaller hatch to the net store. On the German-built 'Northerns' of 1936, the latter space was quite cavernous and could also be reached by means of a scuttle in the forward crew space. Between the mast and the quarterdeck, trawlers have a set of fishroom hatches. All hatches have raised steel coamings, with 3ins thick hatch boards running athwartships. When battened down, these hatches are further covered by tarpaulin covers or cowhides, secured by bars and wedges into cleats in the coamings. On the last large oil burners, these hatches were fitted with insulated steel hatch covers, pierced by a small circular access hatch, and were removed by the 'bobbers', 'lumpers' or porters when discharging the catch. The foredeck is divided up into sections by the pounds. These segregate the deck, stopping the catch when it is being processed from sliding around and being damaged as the vessel works in the seaway. These divisions are formed by removable wooden 'pound boards', approximately 1.5ins thick by 9ins wide, and are interchangeable wherever possible. They are slotted three or four deep into wooden or steel channel section stanchions or sockets, securely bolted or welded to the steel deck. These necessary divisions received many kicks and curses from the weary deckhands as, heavily clad, they stumbled and worked on the slippery heaving decks. As a compensation, they made welcome working seats for men who had spent upwards of eighteen hours in the pounds with gutting knife and heading iron. Men so fatigued that actions became automatic, as their brains shut down from sheer physical exhaustion.

FREEING PORTS/SCUTTLES

Another important feature in trawler design was the necessity to quickly drain off any heavy sea that came aboard. With regard to these, it was generally considered that these should be equal in area to not less than 15% of the bulwark area. This was to ensure a rapid clearance of sea water and this figure was a considerable increase on the common figure of between 3% and 6%. The 15%

Photo. 19: Double barrel steam anchor windlass and cable stoppers. Note the rigging screws which form part of the 'devil's claw' type chain stopper and the flush fitting anchor shackle pin.

recommended is based on the desirability of clearing water from the trawler's deck through ports on one side during the period of half a roll, approximately three and a half seconds.

WHALEBACKS

These were a standard fit on most of the trawlers over 120ft in length and were retro-fitted to even the smaller trawlers in later years. This whaleback or 'turtleback' had a well rounded form for shedding green water as it came over the bows. Yet another common form was the flat-topped fo'c'sle head, such as fitted to Smith's Dock-built 'Castles'. Whatever the shape, at maindeck level they were either left open or enclosed by a watertight bulkhead. The whaleback forms both a shelter for the deck crew and an easily accessible store for ready use gear. On some ships, the crew were actually housed directly under this deck, whilst on others, their accommodation was in a 'fo'c'sle' below maindeck level. Standard fittings on the whaleback comprised a substantial 'V' shaped, angled 'breakwater' or 'spurnwater', which prevented most of the solid water as it came over the bows from crashing down onto the men working in the pounds. An 'escape' hatch was often fitted immediately behind the breakwater. Fixed or drop type stanchions were fitted all round this raised deck, complete with

either rod or chain rails. These guardrails were very susceptible to damage, which resulted in the peculiar twisted headrails seen on many photographs.

WINDLASS, CABLE STOPPERS AND ANCHORS

These were either carried on the whaleback or on the maindeck below, as can be seen from the drawings. In basic form, it was a single gypsy, hand operated affair but, on the larger ships, powerful steam windlasses were the order of the day. Manufacturers such as Gemmell & Frow and Clarke Chapman were the main suppliers of these winches. Steam windlasses were powered by twin cylinder, horizontal, non-reversing engines, fitted with single or double cable lifters (or gypsies) and external warping drums (**Photo. 19**). Brakes would be of the screw down band type and, on the larger ships, these were steam operated. Owing to their very exposed position, windlasses were normally protected by canvas covers securely lashed in place. Many of the larger trawlers, such as *Lancella* and her sisters, in addition to their main steam windlass, carried a hand windlass for mooring purposes, whilst the large German-built ships were fitted with wire reels for their mooring warps.

Single or double hawsepipes were fitted, depending on the size of the vessel. Aboard the older, smaller ships without whalebacks,

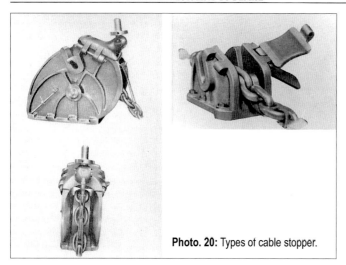

Photo. 20: Types of cable stopper.

these were simple oval 'hawse holes' cut into the forward bulwarks, and fitted with cast iron lips. When whalebacks were fitted to these older ships, the layout remained virtually unchanged, with the anchor being unshackled from the cable, stowed under the whaleback and the hawse holes plugged when at sea. Another variation was to move the windlass onto the whaleback, retaining the original hawse holes but linking them to the new deck with short pipes. With this arrangement, the stocked type anchors were left shackled to the cable and lashed down on the whaleback, ready for use. These ships had their guardrails fitted with either drop down stanchions or quick release chains and fixed stanchions. The anchors carried on the early ships were of the 'Fisherman' or 'Admiralty' pattern. Chain stoppers, if carried, were of the simple sliding plate type.

As the trawlers increased in size, whalebacks were written into the specifications and proper hawse pipes were fitted. These later ships had anchor pockets or recesses built in to the ship's side for the stowage of stockless or close stowing anchors of the Hall or Byers type. The last large steamers, such as the German-built *Coldstreamer* and *Lord Beatty*, were fitted with deck type anchor pockets. With these, no hawse pipes were necessary as can be seen from the plans. Whilst on the subject of anchors, the Distant Water trawlermen, when running in to the fjords for shelter, would rig up a 'snow' anchor. The port anchor cable would be hove up from the chain locker and broken at the second shackle. The outboard end of this cable was then shackled to the port trawl warp and the chain cable hove back onto the winch. This system allowed the ship to anchor in the deep water of the fjords, where blizzards would strike without warning, obliterating any landmarks. The advantages of these emergency anchors could well be appreciated on the pre-radar ships.

Plate type cable stoppers were still common but self holding bowstoppers with hinged clamps were supplied after 1950 (**Photo. 20**). From the windlass, the chain cable passed through the spurling pipe to the chain locker below. These, along with the hawse pipes, often passed through the crew's quarters, proving a constant source of discomfort to the occupants. The pipes were normally plugged with quick setting cement to prevent the ingress of sea water. These chain cable plugs were wrenched free when the anchor was dropped. As well as the stopper, a short length of fixed chain with a two pronged hook or devil's claw was fitted to the cable.

SANITARY ARRANGEMENTS

Toilet facilities aboard early trawlers were little better than crude – only a very slight improvement on the 'bucket and chuck it' variety. In fact, aboard some Aberdeen ships, crews often preferred to squat over the counter in fine weather, using the mizzen crutch as a 'straining bar'. In bad weather, they would use a shovel in the stokehold, disposing of their spoil in the boiler furnace. Other ships had slightly more acceptable toilets; some even had wooden seats. On the smaller ships, these toilets were built in alongside the fo'c'sle companionway or, alternatively, as small hooded compartments either side of the open foredeck. The Humber 'Hansom Cab' type trawlers often had their sanitary accommodation built in under the wings of the wheelhouse verandah, as on *Viceroy*. The position changed with the introduction of whalebacks on the Deep Water ships, where the toilets were built into the whaleback (*Lord Melchett*). To say that these affairs were uncomfortable was an understatement. The one way valves often seized up, so that when the ship dipped to a sea, the unfortunate occupant was forcibly ejected by freezing sea water. Some ships did have the luxury of a steel bath filled with cold water from a bucket and heated with an open steam pipe. It was not until the mid 1930s that the crews of the Distant Water ships were treated to better sanitary conditions and, regrettably, it was the German builders that led the way with the large 'Northern' boats. The drawing of Lewis's *Cape Cleveland* of 1949 shows heated tiled washrooms, drying rooms, WCs and even a bath. By the mid 1950s, when the crews were relinquishing the wet fo'c'sles for better quarters aft, steam heated washrooms with showers were the norm. Although these 'luxuries' were praised by the owners, the crew had scant regard for these advances. The ships were single skinned, with no insulation, so these washplaces were cold at the best of times but in freezing conditions the insides would be covered in ice and the water supply was turned off. Even as drying rooms they were next to useless. When heated the air would fill with condensation and the gear would be just as wet when removed as it was when hung up to dry. Also, fresh water was limited and had to be used sparingly.

SUPERSTRUCTURES, CASINGS AND 'AFT SIDE AND FORESIDE JOBS'

Construction was generally of flush steel plate, rivetted to butt straps and angle frames, though later welding replaced rivetting. Internal steel decks were often covered with either a layer of cement and loose wooden duckboards, or wood decking. External finishes ranged from all over brown to a beautiful grained effect, with the undersides of verandas and wheelhouse tops being painted white.

Much variation was found in the design of these structures, although they all followed the same basic shape of a long narrow casing, with a bridge perched on top. This bridge was initially an open structure, placed at the after end, behind the funnel as in *Strathdon*, and *Viceroy*. Dubbed 'Hansom Cabs', they found great favour with the Humber owners who operated large numbers of 'fleeters'. The design was a direct descendant of the sailing trawler, with the skipper standing at the tiller and conning the ship from aft, where he could keep an eye on the warp. Later, when the bridge moved forward of the funnel, it remained completely open to the elements and contained only the most basic of navigational aids – a wheel, compass and voice pipe to the engineroom or possibly an engine room telegraph. To offer a small degree of protection,

No. 971

OVERHEAD COMPASS

For trawlers, etc. Transparent compass with card graduated degrees and ¼ points on underside. Windproof oil lamp which can be unshipped from inside wheelhouse, and electric light. Brass binnacle finished grey. 6″ card 8″ bowl. 14″ dia. over flange. Weight 28 lbs. Corrector spheres supplied at extra cost.

Fig. 24: Simpson & Lawrence inverted trawler compass.

canvas dodgers were often fitted to shelter the occupants from the worst of the weather, as aboard the *Kirkton*. The standard form of enclosed wheelhouse came with or without a verandah. These verandahs had wood sheathed steel decks and were supported by steel webs or knees. They were surrounded by a wood capped rail, either open or sometimes covered in rope netting, as on *Reptonian*, or they were completely plated in. These early wheelhouses contained few creature comforts and very little in the way of fish finding or navigational equipment. The floor was covered in either coir matting or duckboards. The draughty railway carriage type windows were raised and lowered by a perforated leather strap, the holes of which located over a brass button fixed below the frame. If wood panelled, then vertical tongue and groove boarding was normal. The main steering compass was the inverted type fitted outside on the roof and read internally (**Fig. 24**).

On the Distant Water ships, a pole compass was fixed either to the front of the wheelhouse or to the forward verandah, where it was relatively free from magnetic influences. An exception to this position was on some of the ex-Second World War 'Military' Class ships, where it was fitted to the starboard side of the wheelhouse (**Photo. 88**). By the mid 1930s, the size of the ships had increased dramatically and the wheelhouse accommodation had grown apace. This larger square standing structure housed the wheelhouse proper, still with the inverted steering compass and with a dedicated compartment to the rear of the after bulkhead housing the steam steering gear. Attached to this compartment were the wireless cabin and chartroom. These cabins were usually panelled in either mahogany or teak and fitted with settees and bunks for the occupants, with the latter serving as the skipper's day cabin when on the grounds. The first trawlers to be seen with a three deck superstructure were the large Bremerhaven-built 'Northern' boats. These ships were a great improvement, offering much improved living quarters for the skipper and radio operator. Our own builders did not construct this type of superstructure until the late 1940s and early 1950s – *Northern Jewel*, *Lancella*, etc. These later wheelhouses contained a vast array of navigational and electronic fish finding equipment. The old poorly sealed windows were replaced by modern Beclawat types, with the fixed forward facing windows fitted with 'Kent Clear View' revolving screens. These were most effective, clearing the water by centrifugal force. When compared to the early cramped wheelhouses, they were as big as football pitches in the eyes of some writers – '*when on the bridge of a modern trawler, the skipper travels in first class luxury*'. A small bonus indeed, when referring to men '*who went to hell and back again for nowt*'. The compartment at the forward end of the casing on maindeck level served a number of functions. Normally it held the skipper's cabin/chartroom, with often the only entrance a wooden ladder from the wheelhouse above. Natural light came from circular ports and an escape port of some 16ins diameter was fitted to the forward bulkhead. When radio receivers were initially fitted to the smaller trawlers, they were often shoe-horned into the skipper's berth, as no other space was deemed suitable. On many Aberdeen trawlers, this space was often used as the lamp room, store room and even liver boilers when fitted. On Cook, Welton & Gemmell's *Bempton*, this compartment was a dedicated wireless room, as her wheelhouse was aft. On some of Crampins'

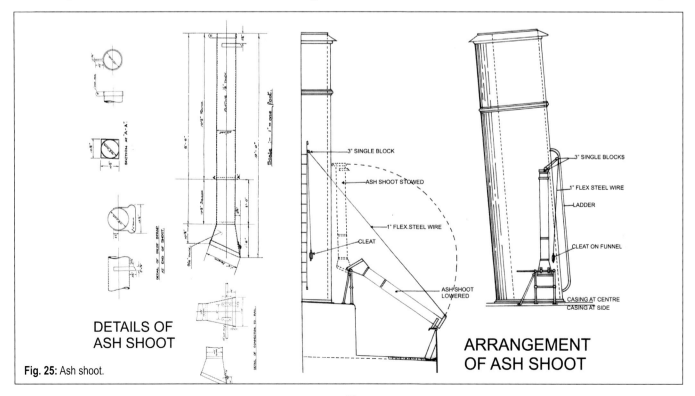

DETAILS OF ASH SHOOT

3″ SINGLE BLOCK

ASH SHOOT STOWED

1″ FLEX. STEEL WIRE

CLEAT

ASH SHOOT LOWERED

3″ SINGLE BLOCKS

1″ FLEX STEEL WIRE

LADDER

CLEAT ON FUNNEL

CASING AT CENTRE
CASING AT SIDE

ARRANGEMENT OF ASH SHOOT

Fig. 25: Ash shoot.

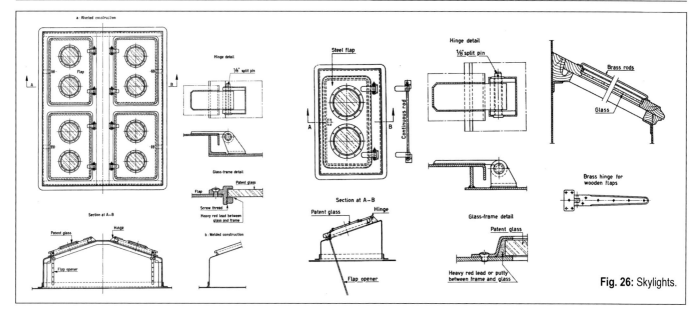

Fig. 26: Skylights.

ships that were fitted with the 'Arctic' type winch, the steam winch engine was housed here. With the triple decked superstructures of the German-built trawlers, this forward section of the casing was fitted out as accommodation for twelve deck hands, complete with *en-suite* WC. No such luxury for the hands aboard our home-built ships, with this space reserved for the mates, engineers and cooks.

CASING

This was the term given to the trawler's superstructure, originating from the simple boiler casing covers fitted to the very first steamers. For the most part, it was just that, giving necessary height to the machinery spaces but with accommodation being fitted in at either end. With the majority of trawlers classed as 'fore siders', the stokehold ventilators were in front of the funnel, whilst with 'aft siders', the opposite was the case but this type of ship was unpopular with the firemen as, once the wing bunkers had been emptied, coal had to shifted from the cross bunker, down the side of the boiler to the furnace. As very few steam trawlers were ever fitted with forced draught ventilation, these large vents had their cowls protruding above the top of the wheelhouse in order to receive an unrestricted airflow. They could be revolved so as to make the best use of wind direction, either by means of a rack and pinion arrangement fitted near their base, operated by a control rod in the stokehold below, or by just manually turning them and locking them in position by way of a thumb screw. They were fitted with either hinged or sliding ash doors, which were used to remove the buckets of waste ashes from the boiler room ready for dumping over the side – this was yet another of the dangerous practices to be found aboard steam trawlers.

ASH SHOOTS

These were found on the larger ships after 1930 (**Fig. 25**) and were fitted to the storm rail on the casing top abreast the funnel. They were bell-mouthed, hollow, square or round hinged tubes. When not in use, they were stowed against the funnel and were raised and lowered by a single whip tackle. Between the stokehold vents could be found the fiddley grating, which gave some small measure of natural daylight and released the hot air from the stokehold. They stood about 9ins high, with an open grid of round bars and hinged plate storm covers.

FUNNELS

As the plans and photographs show, they came in all shapes and sizes, from tall 'Woodbines' (*i.e.* cigarette shaped) to streamlined, as found on the last oil burners. In all but a few cases, the funnels were raked in harmony with the vessel's masts. Later they were faired into the streamlined superstructures and contained drying rooms. The older slender funnels were set up with stays to the casing top. Because the funnels expanded when hot, these were never tight, otherwise buckling would occur. The most distinctive thing about funnels were their markings. Every owner had his own distinctive house style, often with shields, flags, crowns and other heraldic devices. Unfortunately, by the end of the steam trawler age, most, if not all, of the smaller firms had disappeared or merged and trawlers were less colourful. They retained their original colours for a short time, before discarding them in favour of bland utilitarian styles. Companies themselves even changed their colours occasionally. Behind the funnel, some trawlers, such as *Gava*, carried small egg timer-shaped liver boilers, which drew steam from the main boiler. The resulting oil would be drawn off into 40 gallon drums, that were lashed down aft until the vessel made port.

ENGINE ROOM SKYLIGHTS

One of the more dominant features of the casing top, they often supplied the only daylight to the machinery space. On very early trawlers this would have been constructed from timber but, by the 1890s, steel had replaced wood. No matter what material the builders used, their design varied little throughout their history, namely a pitched roof with from four to eight opening lights. They were either full width of the casing, faired into its sides, or they sat in the middle with a walkway on each side. The lights could be opened and closed by a screwed rod and, in heavy weather, they were battened down using heavy dog clips, or screw down hasps (**Fig. 26**).

Further aft was the raised roof of the galley. This carried a small skylight, which was almost always of wood, with one or two square lights. This roof was pierced by two funnels, one for the galley itself, the other for the heating stove in the aft cabin. These funnels took the distinctive 'H' form, necessary to prevent the ingress of water or, alternatively, were fitted with hinged cowls.

In addition, the mizzen mast usually passed through the roof, being stepped on the galley floor below, whilst some earlier ships carried a couple of harness casks on the galley roof, which held the supply of salt beef. The galley itself is the most important domestic compartment aboard a trawler and, from its confines, the cook produces three square meals per day, bakes fresh bread on every second day and ensures that a never ending supply of 'trawler tea' is always to hand. All this from a coal fired range, operated in all weather conditions, including some that had to be experienced to be believed. The galley was a small compartment, with no room for modern gadgets. A single cold water tap was the norm on older ships but with the later vessels came hot water, whilst even a potato peeler was fitted in the Lewis-built **Red Rose** and **Red Hackle**. The trawler cook's domain was equipped with the barest essentials of a coal box, small wooden cupboard and a tiled floor but, given the simplest of ingredients, he could perform miracles and fish, when freshly caught and cooked, could never be surpassed. A good cook was a necessity, a bad one a disaster.

On the smaller Aberdeen trawlers with their shorter trips, fresh bread was only baked occasionally and by the most dedicated cooks. A supply of fresh bread was taken on board at the outset of the trip and was supplemented by local 'rowies' or 'butteries'. These had a high fat content, allowing them to be stored for long periods without turning stale and were the staple diet of fishermen. Even today they are a firm favourite in the north east of Scotland and are relatively unknown outside the area.

BOAT DECKS

These often formed an extension from the galley roof but, on some ships, they were fitted over the main engine room skylight. They were usually wood sheathed over the accommodation but bare steel under the boats. Sometimes these boat deck extensions took the form of light open spar decks supported on steel angles and tie plates. In all cases where deck fittings were employed, they were: 1. Bolted to the steel sub-deck; 2. Bolted to wooden deck seats, which in turn were bolted to the steel deck; 3. Bolted to fabricated steel deck stools, which were either bolted or welded to the steel deck. Distant Water ships had their mizzen masts stepped on the boat deck in steel fabricated deck sockets, with the standing rigging set up in line with the outer edge of the steel galley casing below. A companionway from the accommodation below led up to the boat deck, allowing the men to reach the wheelhouse without using the maindeck when changing watches. It also served as a direct escape route to the lifeboats. The emergency hand operated steering gear was also situated on this deck, either in the open or enclosed in a small house, as with **Lord Alexander**.

ESCAPE TRUNKS AND PORTS

These were fitted as per Board of Trade regulations. Escape from below deck usually meant climbing a vertical ladder and exiting above deck, either through a 16ins escape port fitted at the rear of a square skylight casing or by a watertight hatch. Escape from the officers quarters below the wheelhouse on main deck level was through circular escape ports fitted into the casing.

LIFE SAVING EQUIPMENT

Small trawlers were generally equipped with one 16ft or 18ft 'C' Class wooden lifeboat, either transom sterned or double-ended

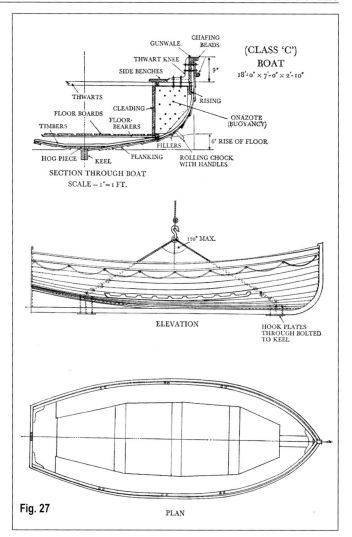

Fig. 27

(Fig. 27). This was carried on chocks or pedestals fitted aft between the galley and the taffrail or on top of the casing, or on the foredeck as with the 'fleeters' (**Fig. 26b**). On many Aberdeen trawlers, this vital piece of life saving equipment was a regular 'pandora's box'. It provided a very convenient storage space for unwanted bits of gear, along with a variety of broken fish boxes, potatoes, sacks of coal, 'creepers' for recovering lost lines, odd sea boots and oilskin frocks, etc. Somewhere among this collection of debris were the oars, bung and bailers, sufficient to prove to the Ministry of Transport or Board of Trade inspector that it was indeed a lifeboat. On the Distant Water ships, these boats were treated with greater respect, being fitted with wooden or canvas protective covers. These Arctic ships, with their correspondingly bigger crews, carried larger boats than their Near Water counterparts. Generally of double ended design, each boat was capable of holding the vessel's full crew, should one of the boats be damaged or be impossible to launch. Later, glass reinforced plastic (GRP) boats were fitted.

CARLEY FLOATS AND WOODEN LIFERAFTS

These were fitted on special racks abaft the funnel or lashed down onto the upper after gallows stays either side of the galley and sometimes lashed to the mizzen shrouds. Along with the wooden boats, they were eventually replaced by modern inflatable rubber rafts, stored at first in canvas valises, then in wooden boxes and finally in GRP containers. It was a sad reflection on modern

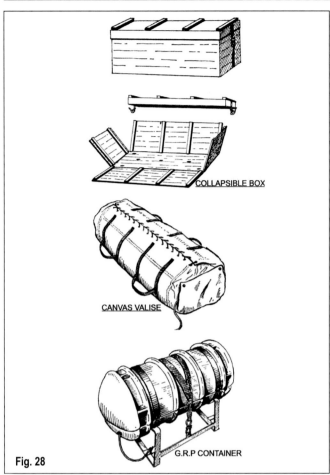

COLLAPSIBLE BOX

CANVAS VALISE

G.R.P CONTAINER

Fig. 28

society that too often these vital pieces of life saving gear were vandalised by shore junkies, who would remove the morphine from the medical kits to satisfy their addiction (**Fig. 28**).

LIFEBUOYS OR LIFEBELTS

Quantity and types as laid down in the rules were fixed at various points around the trawler and fitted with either lifelines, calcium carbide flares or electric lights. The former ignited when the seawater reached the chemical and the latter when they inverted on entering the water.

SMOKE MASK

Another piece of life saving gear found aboard the larger trawlers. This was stowed in a red painted wooden box on the upper deck or casing top and occasionally on the roof of the wheelhouse. Its function was to enable a crew member to enter a smoke logged compartment to carry out fire fighting or rescues. It consisted of a length of canvas hose some 1.5ins diameter, with a clear face mask at one end and a funnel at the other. In use, the funnel was hung in the open, allowing the wearer to have a supply of fresh air on demand.

LIFEBOAT LAUNCHING GEAR

There were various methods of launching the trawler's boat or boats, the earliest and possibly the simplest being the mizzen boom. When required the boom would be topped up to around 45 degrees, and used to swing the boat outboard, as on the *Mount Keen* (**Fig. 28**). On ships where the boat was carried over the engine room skylight, it would be launched using the bobbin derrick or

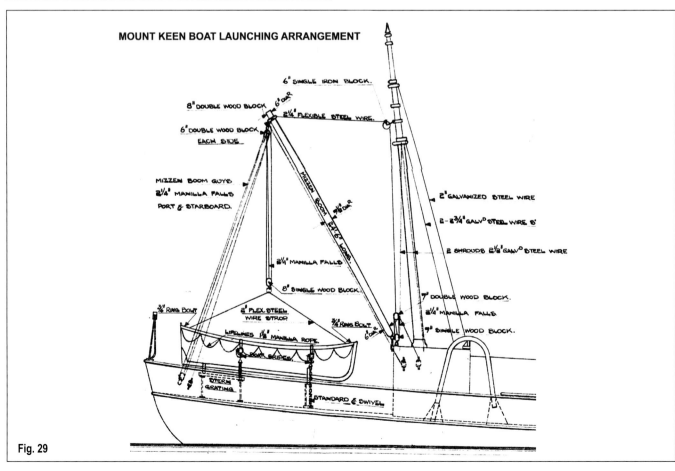

MOUNT KEEN BOAT LAUNCHING ARRANGEMENT

Fig. 29

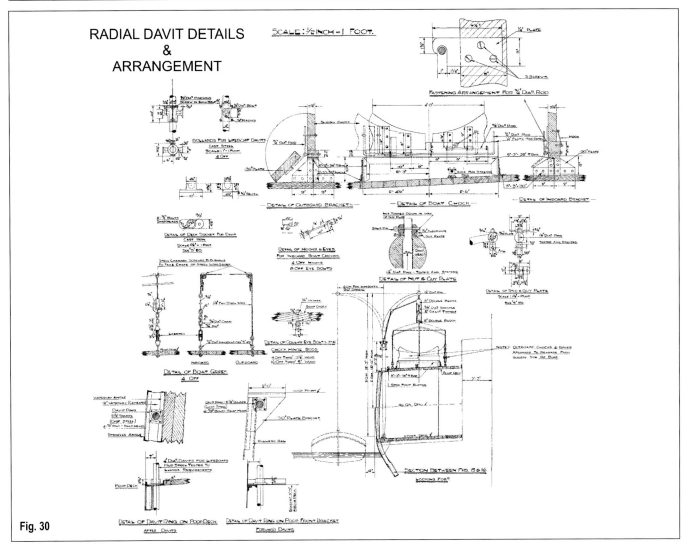

RADIAL DAVIT DETAILS
&
ARRANGEMENT

SCALE : ½ INCH = 1 FOOT.

Fig. 30

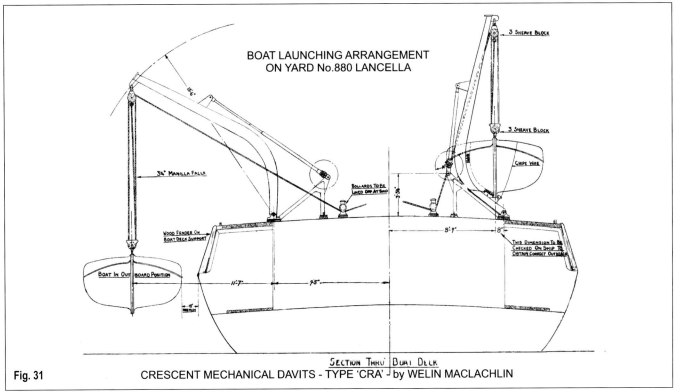

BOAT LAUNCHING ARRANGEMENT
ON YARD No.880 LANCELLA

Fig. 31   CRESCENT MECHANICAL DAVITS - TYPE 'CRA' - by WELIN MACLACHLIN

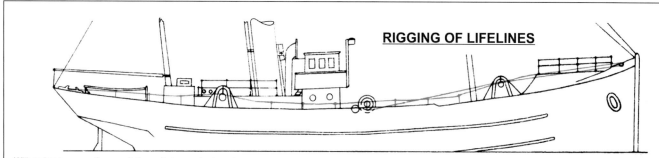

RIGGING OF LIFELINES

With a view to preventing men falling or being washed overboard when the vessel is on passage or hove to at sea, the following precautions MUST BE STRICTLY OBSERVED. Trawl warps or lifelines of wire rope should be carried forward through the fairleads on each bow, then brought aft through the hanging blocks of the gallows and through the fairleads on each quarter, and shackled together and hove taught. Frapping lines being used in the waist of the vessel (and elsewhere if required) in order to bowse the warp down to about 18" to 24" above the rail.

Fig. 32

manhandled over as the vessel dipped her rail. On larger trawlers fitted with double boats, these were provided with radial davits (**Fig. 29**) although a photograph of the trawler *Coquet* (H.831) shows an unusual arrangement of a single boat behind the galley and a set of radial davits on the starboard rail. By the late 1940s, trawlers were leaving the builders with gravity davits of either Welin McLachlan crescent type or Schatt pattern (**Fig. 30**). With the advent of inflatable rafts, many of the Distant Water ships had their boats reduced to one. This was fitted on the centre line along with a single arm davit but, finally, even this boat was removed in favour of enclosed rubber rafts. There is little doubt as to the immense benefits offered by these rafts over the open wooden lifeboats, when used in freezing Arctic conditions. The removal of the double boats and their davits also helped prevent the build up of ice on the boat decks but from a purely aesthetic point of view, the ships had lost their balance of form.

LIFELINES

These were to be rigged during bad weather when there was a danger to the crew on deck. Laid down in the Merchant Shipping Act (Fishing Vessels) 1903 and Board of Trade rules, they were also insisted on by the insurers. This requirement also arose from the number of fishermen falling overboard from 'fleeters'. The practice of stacking empty fish boxes along the side decks interfered with free passage and forced the men to walk over the top of them (**Fig. 32**).

STEERING GEAR

Trawler steering gears ranged from the most basic hand tillers, to highly sophisticated electric/hydraulic systems. The very early steam powered beam trawlers were steered with a tiller but, as the ships grew in size, 'chain and drum' steering gear became standard. In its basic form, it comprised of a spoked wheel fixed to a chain drum or barrel, round which the steering chains passed. From here the chains ran under duckboards, through sheaves in the sides and dropped down to other sheaves just above deck level. After passing round these second sheaves, the chains ran in either open topped channels or pipes along the casing, then aft to another pair of lead blocks near the quarters, finally to the rudder head or quadrant. On some vessels, heavy coil springs were fitted as tensioners or shock absorbers near the tiller head. This method

Fig. 33

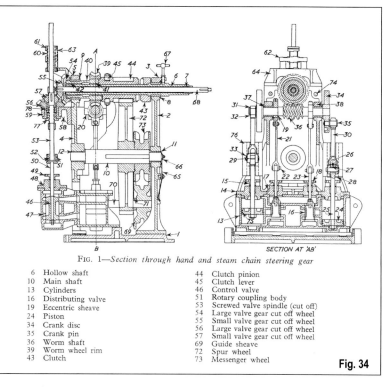

FIG. 1—*Section through hand and steam chain steering gear*

6	Hollow shaft	44	Clutch pinion
10	Main shaft	45	Clutch lever
13	Cylinders	46	Control valve
16	Distributing valve	51	Rotary coupling body
19	Eccentric sheave	53	Screwed valve spindle (cut off)
24	Piston	54	Large valve gear cut off wheel
34	Crank disc	55	Small valve gear cut off wheel
35	Crank pin	56	Large valve gear cut off wheel
36	Worm shaft	57	Small valve gear cut off wheel
39	Worm wheel rim	69	Guide sheave
43	Clutch	72	Spur wheel
		73	Messenger wheel

Fig. 34

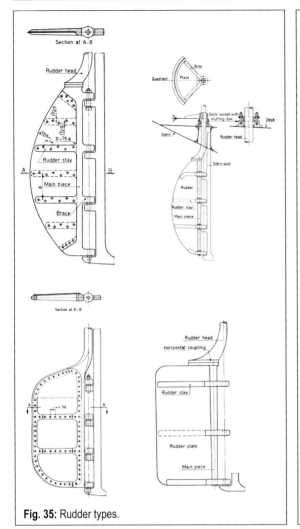

Fig. 35: Rudder types.

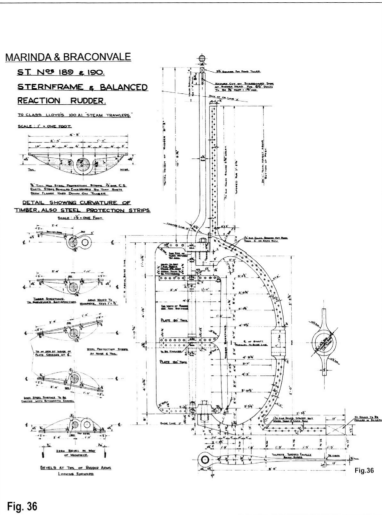

Fig. 36

of trawler steering was to remain until the very end of the era and it took twenty-six full turns of the wheel to put the rudder hard over from port to starboard. There were variations on the design, with some ships carrying reversed tiller arms, whilst others had the 'dead' lengths of chain in the channels replaced by either rods or special section links but, in all cases, a spare tiller arm was carried for emergency use. On the larger trawlers, 'steam and hand' steering gear was specified. This gear was housed in a special compartment at the rear of the wheelhouse, protected from the elements yet readily accessible for maintenance. Manufacturers associated with these gears were Donkins, C.D. Holmes and Gemmell & Frow (**Fig. 33**). This gear still relied on rods and chains to transmit the power to the rudder. The Distant Water ships, from the late 1940s on, were equipped with either 'steam/hydraulic' or 'electro/hydraulic' systems (**Fig. 34**). This gear was housed in the tiller flat and coupled to the ship's wheel by small bore hydraulic pressure piping. This powerful type of unit dispensed with the tedious winding of the large diameter steering wheel and a smaller power assisted wheel was fitted in front of the main wheel. It was normal practice to switch over from power to hand operation immediately the ship had cleared land and was running off. Immaterial of whatever type of main steering gear was fitted, a set of emergency hand gear was carried, usually on the boatdeck or in the tiller flat.

RUDDERS

(**Fig. 35**) The early wooden rudders were invariably oak, some 3ins thick at the leading edge, tapering to 2ins at the trailing edge, complete with iron straps, gudgeons and pintles. The next development was the 'single plate' rudder or 'barn door' type, as was specified for J. Duthies *Trawfisk*, Yard No. 456:

'The rudder to be of single plate type, with arms shrunk and keyed to the post, and stops forged on. Rudder head to be 4.5ins diameter, to have four portable pintles. Top pintles to be fitted with locking head to prevent rudder lifting. Stuffing box of cast iron to be made adjustable and fitted with wedge shaped keys, and lignum vitae chocks. A strong wrought iron yoke to be fitted and keyed to the rudder head, and as a further precaution, the boss of the yoke to be heated and shrunk onto the rudder head. Adjustable chains with long links to be fitted to the yoke.'

As trawlers developed, they were fitted with more efficient hyrodynamic rudders. Common were the double plate streamlined types made by the Oertz Company (*St. Cathan*, *Nectan*, etc) and these could be either fully or semi-balanced. The Balanced Reaction Rudder Co. of 22 Billeter Street, London, produced their own patented rudder form, as on **Mount Keen** and **Marinda** (**Fig. 36**). Sometimes a ship could lose her rudder and would require assistance. Trawler skippers would, on occasion, rig a jury rudder

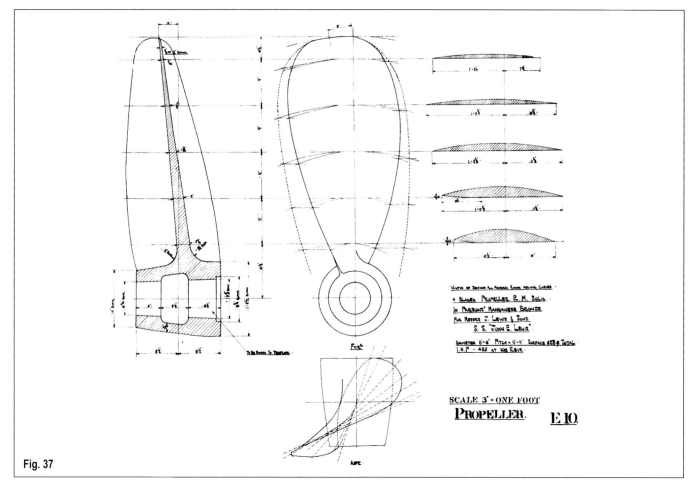

Fig. 37

from any handy material such as spare trawl/otter boards.

PROPELLERS

(**Fig. 37**) The very early steam trawlers were fitted with two bladed screws, as this form was reckoned to reduce the drag when under sail. Later, four bladed propellers became standard. They were right handed and usually made from cast iron, although some later ships had manganese bronze propellers. Occasionally these propellers were painted white, which enabled the shore gang to spot any flaws or cracks when the vessel was on the slip for repairs or survey. Lloyd's instructions to Surveyors, No. 148 of 1927 states:

'The screw shaft is to be drawn at intervals of not more than three years in the cases of shafts fitted with continuous liners, and of shafts fitted with approved glands or other approved appliances at their after ends to permit them being efficiently lubricated. In the cases of other screw shafts, they should be drawn at intervals of not more than two years (On the application of the owners, the Committee will be prepared to give consideration to the circumstances of any special case).'

Few, if any, trawlers ever carried a spare propeller but I remember in the 1950s the disused Old Torry Free churchyard being full of spare trawler propellers.

MASTS AND RIGGING

Trawlers normally carried two masts, a foremast and a mizzen. The mainmast disappeared in the 1870s, when the remaining three masted luggers were reduced to two masts. All trawler masts, whether of wood or steel, are raked, around 1.5ins per foot for the fore and slightly more for the mizzen. With the exception of drifter/liners, masts are fixed and cannot be lowered. The foremast is set up either with deadeyes and lanyards, or patent rigging screws. The mast is further supported by stays running forward to the fo'c'sle head; these comprise the forestay and the topmast stay, plus port and starboard jumper stays (a glance at the rigging plans will clarify the arrangement). A triangular jib and loose footed foresail were carried on the older trawlers but these went out of use in the 1930s. By the late 1950s, when the stability effects of icing had been calculated, trawlers were fitted with tripod foremasts which noticeably reduced the amount of standing rigging. The mizzen mast was fitted with three shrouds a side, plus forestays. These shrouds were set up using sheaves as an alternative to screws and deadeyes. Mizzen sails were either gaff or jib-headed and their primary function was to help keep the ship's head up to wind. When tripod foremasts were introduced, the mizzen masts were often replaced with thin tubular wireless masts fitted to the aft side of the funnel or funnel casing.

TRIATIC STAY. This was a strong wire span which ran from a point at the head of the foremast to a similar point on the mizzen (occasionally it ran to the funnel top band). This stay was equipped with gin blocks and tackles rigged over the fishroom hatches for discharging the catch. Canvas ventilation chutes were also rigged from this stay, for inducing fresh air to the holds.

WIRELESS AERIALS. These were rigged between the masts and were fitted with all necessary insulators and lead-ins to the superstructure. At either end they were fitted with halliards and downhauls, reeved through single blocks at the masthead. These aerials were lowered to the deck out of harm's way when the ship was under the coal shoots. It was the radio operator's first duty to check that they had been reset before the ship put to sea.

NAVIGATION LIGHTS

In addition to the masthead lights described above, a trawler carried green, starboard and red port steaming lights. These were constructed so as to show an unbroken light over an arc of the horizon of ten compass points and fixed so as to throw the coloured light from dead ahead to two points abaft the beam on either side of the ship. These lights were fitted with inboard screens, projecting far enough forward so as to prevent the light being seen across the bow. A white stern light was fitted, covering a horizontal arc of 12 degrees, where possible to be on the same level as the side lights.

ANCHOR LIGHTS. A vessel under 150ft in length, when at anchor, was required to show an all round white light, placed forward where it could best be seen, at a height not exceeding 20ft above the hull. This light should show an unbroken beam visible all round the horizon, for a distance of at least one mile. A vessel over 150ft carried this forward white light at a height of not less than 20ft and not exceeding 40ft above the hull, plus another such light at or near the stern, not less than 15ft lower than the forward light.

OIL LAMPS. Until new regulations came into force in late 1969-70, all trawlers had to carry a duplicate set of oil lamps for emergency use when there was a power failure. After this date, the alternative set could be electric. This measure was adopted as a means of reducing the amount of rigging carried on trawlers, as it attracted a fast build up of ice high above the vessel's centre of gravity. Prior to electric lighting on trawlers, oil and acetylene lamps were in common use, the former for navigation and the latter as working lights.

FISHING LIGHTS. In addition to the usual steaming lights described, a trawler, when fishing, must also show a tri-colour light (or lantern) on the foremast. This displayed a white light from dead ahead to two points on either bow, a green light, and a red light showing from two points on either bow to two points abaft the beam on the starboard and port sides respectively. Additionally, an all round white light should be shown, at not less than 6ft or more than 12ft below the tri-colour fishing light (this was normally the vessel's anchor light). Should the trawl be foul on the bottom and the vessel stopped, the vessel shall exhibit an additional white light, at least 3ft below the anchor light and at least 5ft away from it in the direction of her gear. There was another set of fishing lights used on the Distant Water ships – the 'Andanes' lights, so called after the Norwegian grounds where they were initially used. These were two all-round white lights, set one above the other on the wheelhouse top to warn other vessels to keep their distance. One or both could be switched on to indicate that the ship was either shooting away or hauling its gear.

MORSE LAMP. This was fitted on the wheelhouse top showing an all-round white light and was operated by the radio officer. Another light carried on most Deep Water ships was a 'searchlight', which was also on the wheelhouse roof.

DECK OR WORKING LIGHTS. A trawler working during the hours of darkness (these were almost constant on the Arctic grounds) was illuminated like a small town. The men lived and worked within their own pool of light, isolated from the world of inky blackness all around them. Bulkhead lights were fitted overhead, at intervals all round the casing and below the bridge overhang, behind the winch (**Fig. 38**). Bulkhead and conical type floodlights were also fixed to the wheelhouse front, shining downwards onto the foredeck. A shrouded floodlight was affixed to the end of the yo-yo or fish derrick on the foremast, fitted so as to always point vertically downwards no matter the angle of the spar, and a similar fixed type was often fitted above the Gilson block on the mast.

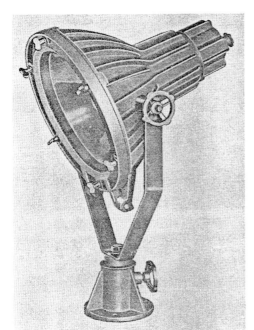
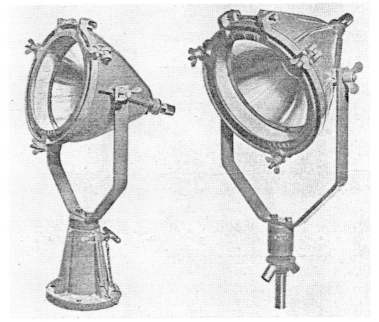

DECK LIGHTS BY Telford, Grier & MacKay & Co Ltd Glasgow

Fig. 38

Bulkhead lights were fitted to the fo'c'sle bulkhead and often these were supplemented by deck floodlights fixed to the rails above. Deck floodlights were fitted in hinged brackets to the wheelhouse verandah and to the boat deck aft for illuminating the side decks. Another fixed light was also fitted above the towing block on the boat deck overhang. On ships without boat decks, this would either be carried on a stanchion fitted in a socket on the rail or alternatively on the casing, if this ran far enough aft. The earlier oil or acetylene working lights were strung along a wire span over the foredeck. These suspended lights swung about, causing dangerous areas of shadow when the vessel moved in a seaway and they were supplemented by lanterns hung on stanchions on the mainrail.

POLE COMPASS

This was a common feature on Distant Water ships, normally fitted at the front of the wheelhouse well away from magnetic interference. It provided an accurate compass, free from any magnetic influences which would arise from the steel superstructure. All the fittings, including the rod stays, were of non ferrous metal. They were fitted with pole steps to enable the compass to be read and compared with the steering compass on the wheelhouse roof. This feature is shown on many of the plans and can be also identified from the photographs.

RULES FOR FISHING NUMBERS

These were laid down under the Sea Fisheries Acts of 1868 and 1883, along with Part IV of the Merchant Shipping Act, 1894. Under these rules, steam trawlers are deemed to be of the 'First Class' and, as such, must exhibit:

'Registration numbers shall be painted in Black or White as the Board of Trade may direct.
The letters shall precede the number.
The letters and number shall be placed on each bow of the vessel three or four inches below the gunwale.
Steamers shall in addition carry the letters and numbers on each quarter, and on the funnel, twelve inches from the top, of a conspicuous size, and as fast as possible, on the foremost part of the circumference.
The letters on the hulls to be 18ins high, and 2½ ins in breadth.
In all cases a space equal to one-third of the height of the letters, shall be left between every two letters, and every two figures forming the number, and the letters shall be separated from the numbers by twice the same space.'

Some of the early trawlers also carried these fishing numbers on their mizzen sails, in this case:

'The same letters and numbers to be painted in white oil colour on each side of the centre cloth of the sail, and in such a manner as to be plainly visible.'

This accounts for the majority of trawler fittings. For more in depth information, the reader should study the appendices.

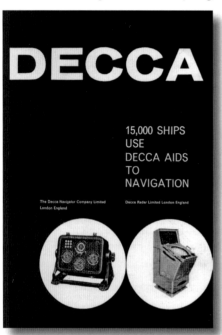

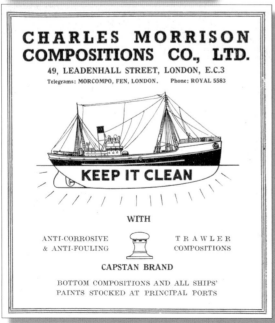
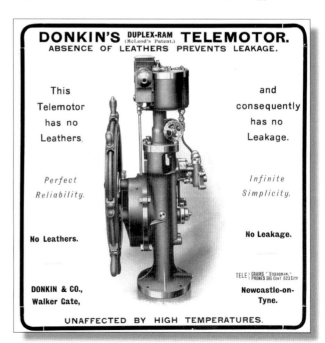

Chapter 5: THE PIONEERS 1860-1880

Probably the earliest mentions of steam powered fishing vessels being constructed, was in 1853-4, for the Manchester, Sheffield & Lincolnshire Railway. The order comprised of seven sailing smacks and two steam long liners, *John Ellis* and *Thomas Dennison*, all to be built and sailed from Grimsby.

Also around this time, Messrs J. & M.W. Ruthven of Granton built the steam powered water-jet fishing vessel *Enterprise* (90ft bp x 15ft, 47n). She had a cylindrical boiler and two pairs of oscillating cylinders, with vertical crankshafts driving a centrifugal pump 7ft in diameter. This drew in water forward and exhausted through 10ins diameter crescent shaped nozzles, which could be pointed in any direction, including downwards to hold the vessel stationary. The idea appears to have been to avoid the fouled nets experienced by paddle trawlers. She was tested by the Deep Sea Fishing Association of Scotland and on trials did 8 knots on about 5lbs of coal per ihp. Unfortunately, she seems to have been a failure and finished her days as a yacht on the Wicklow coast.

The port of Grimsby up till this time was virtually unknown in commercial fishing circles. It had a small local fleet of sailing smacks, which as far back as the 15th century fished the Distant Waters off Iceland. These boats could only supply the local markets, as there was no provision for keeping the fish fresh after it had been landed. These long-lining smacks were around 40ft to 50ft long, heavily built of oak and elm. Practically the whole of the midship section of these craft was used to keep the catch alive. The vessels' sides were perforated in order to give a constant flow of seawater through the hold or fish well, in which the fish were kept swimming about until the smack reached her market. This of course was the origin of the term 'well smack'. In those days, live fish were welcome but dead fish had no commercial value. This dead catch was usually sold off as stocker bait and the money that it made was shared out among the smack boys, two or three of whom sailed on every boat.

The only smack owner to accept the railway company's incentives was a Mr Howard from Manningtree in Essex. He moved his family and his six sailing smacks north to Grimsby. This was the beginning of the trawling industry at the Lincolnshire port, an industry in which Grimsby was to lead the world until the final demise of the British deepwater trawler in the late 1970s. The term 'trawler' appears to be a derivation of the French word '*trauler*', which literally translated means 'to draw hither and thither' – an apt description of the fishing method employed by these vessels. True, the experiment with steam was not very successful, such that within a short time the vessels had their engines, boilers, and propellers removed, and they reverted to sailing smacks. This lack of success was due to a number of factors, the first being the fishermen's aversion to change. Another factor was that trained engineers were unwilling to put to sea on a fishing vessel, the engines of which were none too reliable. Fishermen also complained that the beat of the propeller frightened the fish and that the smell of the engine oil tainted the catch. It was also reported that, in comparison to the sailing smack, the power driven vessel was noisy and uncomfortable to live aboard – although conditions aboard the smacks could hardly be called homely! Building costs were far higher for a steamer as against

those for a smack and whereas builders would construct a sailing vessel 'on spec', they were unwilling to gamble on finding a buyer for a steamer. Attitudes would change of course as the distance to the grounds increased, sail would then not prove to be quite so reliable in catching a market, as would her steam counterpart.

A steam powered vessel was first used for trawling in 1858, when the *Corkscrew*, an iron steamer built at Blackwall, sailed from Grimsby. She was powered by a 50hp engine and her fishing gear consisted of port and starboard beam trawls. She made one or two trips to the fishing ground but fish at this time were plentiful and cheap, and the wind power necessary to drive the smack cost the owner nothing. Coal for the vessel on the other hand cost the princely sum of 10s a ton (50p), so the vessel was laid up. She was later purchased by Messrs Bailey & Leetham, lengthened and renamed *Jutland*. She was still in the register at Hull in 1862.

In 1866, two vessels, *Cormoran* and *Heron*, were ordered from Randolph, Elder & Co., Govan (later to become the Fairfield Shipbuilding & Engineering Co. Ltd); both were laid down as steam trawlers. In the 1860s, another two steam auxiliaries were launched, *Sequel* and *Tubal Cain*. The former tried her luck at several Humber and Yorkshire ports, and was finally voted a failure for the same reasons as *Corkscrew*. The *Tubal Cain*, was the brainchild of Frederick Rushworth, who, after serving his apprenticeship, soon rose to being a smack owner. In 1870, he conceived the notion of owning a steam powered, line fishing boat. A determined man and one not easily swayed once his mind was made up, he placed an order for a steam fishing smack with the well known Hull builder William Willory Dawson. The specifications laid down that she would be constructed of iron throughout (77ft x 20ft x 10ft). The ship had to have a compartment that could be used as an engineroom.

The vessel was built in 1870 at Dawson's yard but, as this shipyard on the outskirts of Hull had no water frontage for the launch, the ship was actually constructed in sections. These were transported through the city, re-assembled on the river bank and there launched. *Tubal Cain* (GY.288) was an iron vessel when the remainder of Grimsby's fleet were all of wooden construction. She seemed to be a great success as a long liner, fishing the Dogger Bank as well as off the Faeroes and Iceland. Being a well smack she always delivered her catches in prime condition. In the 1880s, a screw propeller and shaft were fitted in her vacant race and she was equipped with a vertical steam engine and boiler.

Her first records as a steamer were not encouraging, due in the main to the unsuitability of the engine. This had been acquired second hand and lacked the power necessary, so Rushworth made arrangements for the fitting of a larger compound engine. To house the new engine would mean lengthening the ship by some 12ft but this turned out to be easier than it first seemed, bearing in mind that the vessel was originally built in sections. She was re-engined at the close of 1884 by Messrs Charles D. Holmes of Hull. Year after year, the arrival of *Tubal Cain* with her catches of supreme cod and halibut were important events at the fish dock. This vessel materially shortened the distance between the Humber and Faeroe and Iceland. Soon a company was formed to build and operate a fleet of steam longliners from Grimsby. This was Moody & Kelly, with their ships known locally as the ABC fleet by the reason of the nomenclature of the vessels names: *Arctic*, *Baltic*, *Celtic* and *Doric*, all in alphabetical order and suffixed by 'ic'.

Tubal Cain soldiered on, and proved to be, in Aberdeen slang, 'a fishy boat', making a good return for Rushworth. She finally met her end in the North Sea on 3rd August 1898, off Flamborough Head, where she sank after being in a collision with the Newcastle registered *Admiral Nelson*. By a strange coincidence, on 3rd August 1906, her namesake, *Tubal Cain* (GY.88) Yard No. 784, built in 1905 at North Shields for Messrs J. Rushworth & R. Atkinson, made the national press. Her crew were presented with silver medals and diplomas by the King of Norway after rescuing the crew of the stricken Norwegian barque *Ailsa*. It was in August yet again that the second *Tubal Cain* met her end. This was on 7th August 1914, when she was sunk by gunfire by the *Kaiser Wilhelm* some 50 miles WNW from Staalberg Huk, Iceland.

NORTH SHIELDS PADDLE TRAWLERS.

It was not, however, until early November 1877 that steam trawlers appeared to be a practical proposition. William Purdy of North Shields fitted out the wooden paddle tug *Messenger* with trawling gear and, ignoring the ridicule of his fellow fishermen, put her to sea. Her first catch sold for the sum of £7 10s; she picked a towing fee of £5 and, in a little less than 24 hours, she grossed £12 10s. Her conversion costs from tug to trawler were some £20, an outlay which would soon be cleared if she continued in the same vein. Scorn turned to admiration among the locals. Here was a way of putting the redundant tugs back to sea and, within a few months, all the inshore grounds of the North East coast were crowded with these vessels. Tugs had long been associated with the fishing industry. They towed the herring luggers and trawling smacks to sea during adverse weather conditions and towed them home again with their valuable catches if the wind dropped. In those days, it was imperative to get the catches to market quickly, as ice was seldom if ever carried on the smacks, and herring and trawl caught fish deteriorated very rapidly. Having thus 'taken steam', the fly smacksmen thought it only fair game to drop their trawls over the side for a quick tow on the way in, often taking good catches in this manner.

This encroachment of the traditional inshore grounds by these 'steam trawlers' was met with fierce opposition from the line fishermen. These mechanical scavengers were ruining their local grounds and stealing the inshore men's livelihood:

'The trawler, of course, has long been the piscatorial scapegoat, reviled by the inshore line fishermen with an energy which is usually in inverse ratio to that with which they pursue their own calling, and condemned with scant ceremony by the amateur naturalist and public at large ...' E. W. Holt 1895 (Holt was a well known and respected English biologist)

This anger was much fiercer in Scotland as the local fishermen were unaccustomed to trawling. The fishers cried out for a stop to be put to '*The ravages of these trawling monsters of the deep*'. At a heated meeting in Aberdeen, the chairman, Mr Esslemont, told the aggrieved deputation of fishermen: '*Men the only advice that I can give you is go and do likewise. The sooner you are into steam the better*'. Ironically, the most ardent and outspoken critic of the

steam trawler at this meeting was Thomas Walker, who was later to become one of the port's leading trawler owners, his vessels, prefixed by 'Star', were well known and respected ships. When referring to this anti-trawling campaign, it is worth remembering that had these old tugs been designed with the power and seaworthiness needed for trawling, they would have been able to fish farther afield, well away from the inshore grounds. But, by then most of those decrepit old tugs were scarcely even seaworthy.

'Many of our readers must be acquainted with those that are to be seen on the Tyne, they are a round bodied style of craft, with bluff ended clinker built hulls, which may have been modelled on the old GOOLE BILLY BOY. The machinery in them is much in keeping with their outward appearance. The wonder is that these vessels could do the work assigned to them in their best days, and now these are long past. It is an even greater wonder how they hold together the way they do. Such craft as these dare not venture on long voyages but keep trawling about inshore, and the consequence is that the line fishermen are afraid to shoot their lines, for instead of taking fish, they are likely to find that a trawl has been foul of them and done perhaps £3 or £4 worth of damage ...' THE ENGINEER, July 27th 1883

Unseaworthy or not, the steam trawler had come to stay and, by July 1878, over 900 tons of fish had been landed at North Shields by the port's fleet of fifty-three steam paddle trawlers. The owners thoughts were now turning to more efficient vessels, purpose designed for the rigours of trawling.

EARLY STEAM TRAWLERS.

To picture the first vessels designed as steam trawlers we must go back to 1867, when George Bidder of Dartmouth in South Devon launched the 49ft vessel *Thistle* (**Plan 5A**). She was followed in 1868 by *Florence* (**Plan 5B**). These two vessels were altogether considered to be too small for the heavy task of towing a heavy beam trawl and were consequently scrapped. The next vessel to be constructed by this able engineer, was the 66ft *Bertha* (**Plan 5C**). She was launched at Dartmouth in 1870 and proceeded under sail to the Tyne, where she was fitted with engines by Robert Stevenson & Co. These engines were of the simple jet condensing type, with a pair of 15ins cylinders and a multi tube boiler giving her a top speed under power of 11 knots. The engines also drove the wire hawser winding drum, a piece of equipment considered so important by her designers that they took out a patent on it. They hoped that she would prove a great success but, alas, she was again too small, with insufficient space for either fish or crew. Another drawback with *Bertha* was her exposed screw propeller, which constantly severed the trawl warps. After several abortive trips she was cut down to a sailing smack. *Bertha*'s engines were later fitted in *Edith* (**Plan 5D**), built at Dartmouth in 1872. Bidder's latest vessel was fitted with a lifting propeller designed to eliminate any damage to the trawl warp. Yet another innovation was her steam capstan. This appears to be the first of its type fitted in a trawler and formed the model for all future North Sea capstans. *Edith* was considered by many to be the perfect trawler and after working off the west coast of England for a period, she transferred to the North Sea, where she was employed as a carrier for the Lowestoft fleet. Unfortunately for *Edith*, this fish carrying

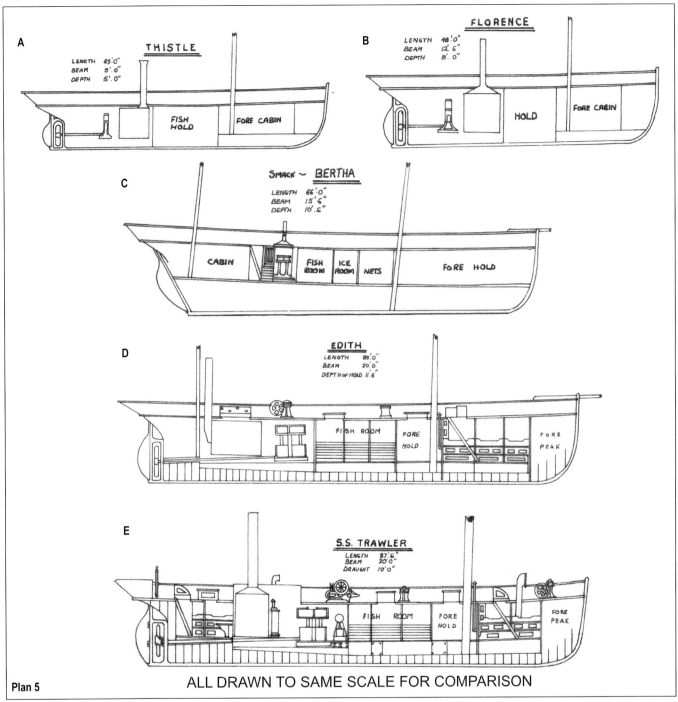

A
THISTLE
LENGTH 45'.0"
BEAM 9'.0"
DEPTH 5'.0"

FISH HOLD   FORE CABIN

B
FLORENCE
LENGTH 48'.0"
BEAM 12'.6"
DEPTH 8'.0"

HOLD   FORE CABIN

C
SMACK ~ **BERTHA**
LENGTH 66'.0"
BEAM 15'.6"
DEPTH 10'.6"

CABIN   FISH ROOM   ICE ROOM   NETS   FORE HOLD

D
EDITH
LENGTH 85'.0"
BEAM 20'.0"
DEPTH of HOLD 11'.6"

FISH ROOM   FORE HOLD   FORE PEAK

E
S.S. TRAWLER
LENGTH 87'.6"
BEAM 20'.0"
DRAUGHT 10'.0"

FISH ROOM   FORE HOLD   FORE PEAK

Plan 5   ALL DRAWN TO SAME SCALE FOR COMPARISON

trade in the North Sea was a closed shop. On her trips from the fleet to London, she proved that she could carry the equivalent of six sailing cutters but the merchants would only allow her two shares out of every ten and consequently she was taken off her station. Even with the fitting of the lifting screw, it was impossible to work the vessel in strong tide ways, as the trawl warp still fouled the propeller. It was not until a Mr Griffiths and a Mr Lake devised the 'Griffiths Patent Encased Propeller' was it practicable to fish in most weathers. These early vessels built by Bidder are recognised as the world's first steam trawlers. They were shown to an industry brought up and steeped in tradition, and slow to adopt change. They were voted as failures in both operating costs and fishing methods. In retrospect, it would seem that they were too far in advance of their time.

Not unnaturally, it was only a few years before the interest in the construction of steam powered fishing vessels moved north of the border. In 1876, J. McKenzie of Leith launched *Waterwich*, a small steam powered drifter/liner. She was sold to Ireland after an unsuccessful season off the north of Scotland and not attracting very much enthusiasm in fishing circles. She was not completely forgotten, however, and in 1881 the firm's successors, J. Cran, launched the steamers *Venture*, *Puffin* and *Dunlin*. These were wooden vessels, copper fastened and built to Lloyds' special survey. They were dandy rigged, with a lowering foremast in order to pursue the herring fishery. The crew were accommodated in the usual fo'c'sle, fitted with a coal fired bogey stove for both cooking and heating. An iron bulkhead coated with non-conducting cement divided the engine and boiler space from the fish hold.

The '*engine driver and his mate*' were accommodated in a small cabin down aft. (It is interesting to note that until quite late on, the Scottish fishermen acquired their engineers from the railways and hence they were termed 'drivers'). The engines working at 90psi were of the inverted compound, surface condensing type and steam was supplied by an upright tubular boiler. The engines were controlled from either on deck or in the engine room, an arrangement that was very useful when fishing or when entering the small awkward harbours on the Scottish coast. These vessels achieved quite steady speeds of around 8.5knots. *Dunlin* and *Puffin* were also fitted with steam capstans directly driven from the engine and used when hauling drift nets.

In 1877, the firm of William Allan & Co. of Leith (later of Granton) launched *Pioneer*, a steam powered wooden fishing vessel designed for net and line fishing off the Shetlands. Powered by a 10hp engine which drove her at 6 knots, she apparently answered her purpose well. Unfortunately, her crew were unable to operate her then complicated machinery and, like many of her predecessors, she proved costly to her owners. Allan's next vessel, *Onward* (60ft x 16ft x 7ft 6ins, 40n, 80nhp with a top speed of 8knots), also failed commercially. She had a long rather full body, hollow garboards, bow full above the waterline and hollow below, a short run aft and a rounded stern. She was fitted with high pressure engines, which due to their faulty construction were a constant source of trouble. So much so in fact, that her owners were unable to secure a crew brave or foolish enough to take her to sea. Allan's, however, were not to be discouraged and their next vessel was a successful combination of their former failures. *Mamelina I*, built from the same lines as *Onward* but fitted with surface condensing compound engines, was the company's first successful screw fishing boat. She was built to the order of Mercader & Sons of San Sebastian, who were so impressed with her performance that they ordered a further two vessels to the same design, *Mameline II* and

Mameline III. Allans also built a further three of these steamers for a subsidiary of Mercader's, who operated in the Canary Isles. The superb sea keeping characteristics of Allan's steamers is shown in the following extract:

'I had just finished delivering the cargo at St. Annes Bay, and was leaving, when I got a telegram to come full speed back to Kingston to carry government dispatches. I arrived there at 6.30am the next morning and, after a detention of two and a half hours taking coal, water and stores, was sent off to this place Bermuda, with news of Colley's death and the Cape Despatch, with orders to stop the troopship **Orontes** *with the 99th Regiment, and send them to the Cape. HMS* **Phoenix** *had been dispatched from a place 86 miles nearer Bermuda, 28 hours previously. I had strong headwinds the first two days; when I met a heavy NW gale. Knowing the importance of the mission entrusted to me, and the capabilities of the vessel, I kept on, although it blew with hurricane force at times, and the crew complained that I was trying to drown them. I arrived safely on the morning of the fifth day the distance being 1,130 miles. I got here just in time to stop the* **Orontes**, *as she was due to leave 2 hours after I arrived. HMS* **Phoenix**, *did not arrive until 24 hours after I did, she being hove to for 36 hours.* (Bermuda, SS *Sea Queen*, 11th March 1881)

Sea Queen was a small wooden inter island steamer, built to the same design as Allan's fishing vessels.

The first steam trawlers to be built by Allan & Co. in the early 1880s were *Granton* (**Plan 6**) and *Gannet*, the former's slightly smaller sister. Both were built of wood. *Granton's* fuel consumption worked out at some three tons per day, plus she was fitted with a donkey boiler and steam winch. Both these vessels were carvel built, of larch planking over oak frames, with excellent seaworthy lines, designed to be swift enough for a speedy

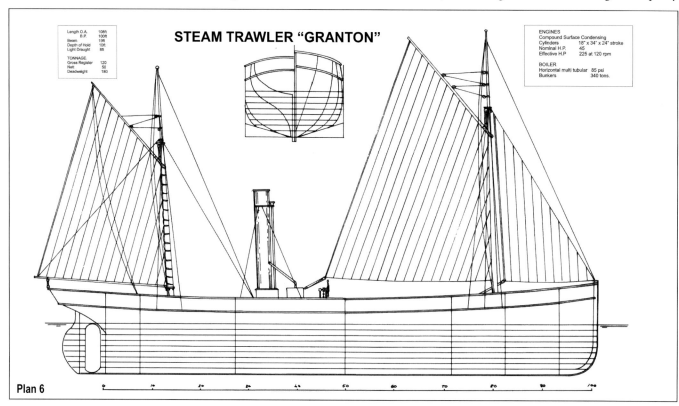

STEAM TRAWLER "GRANTON"

Length O.A.	108ft
B.P.	100ft
Beam	19ft
Depth of Hold	10ft
Light Draught	8ft
TONNAGE	
Gross Register	120
Nett	50
Deadweight	180

ENGINES	
Compound Surface Condensing	
Cylinders	18" x 34" x 24" stroke
Nominal H.P.	45
Effective H.P	225 at 120 rpm
BOILER	
Horizontal multi tubular	85 psi
Bunkers	340 tons.

Plan 6

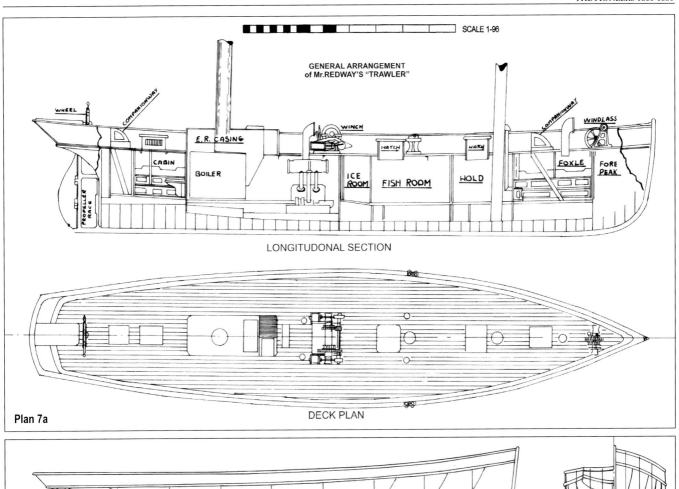

SCALE 1-96

GENERAL ARRANGEMENT
of Mr.REDWAY'S "TRAWLER"

LONGITUDONAL SECTION

DECK PLAN

Plan 7a

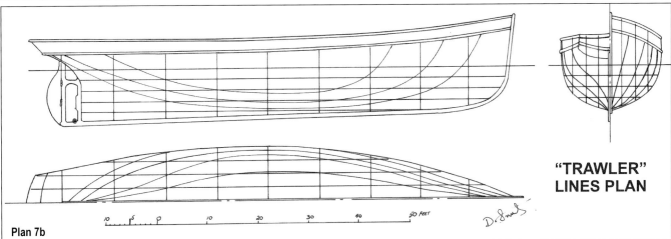

"TRAWLER"
LINES PLAN

Plan 7b

return from the grounds, plus a good carrying capacity. They had moderately sharp vertical stems, curved fore foots, with 'V' shaped forward frames and their finely formed runs terminated in well balanced elliptical counter sterns. They were flush-decked, and ketch-rigged with vertically cut foresail, mainsail and mizzen. A deckhouse was positioned aft of the mainmast, similar in shape and function to the cabin house found aboard American fishing schooners. This was necessary to increase the headroom in the cabin below. Steering was by rod and chain, with the open wheel placed amidships. A steam winch was fitted for handling the trawl gear. These highly successful ships were the first steam powered screw trawlers to operate north of the border and were to be the forerunners of the Forth's trawling fleet. The following newspaper account in the *Edinburgh Scotsman* of 2nd July 1881, describing the opening of the new Edinburgh Dock, goes on to state:

'A branch of the shipbuilding industry which came into being a few years ago ,is the building of wooden steam trawling vessels. Messrs Allan & Co., who may be said to be the inventors of this class of vessel, have now removed from Leith to larger premises in Granton, and their ground has been taken over by Messrs. Ramage and Fergusson. The first of these vessels was launched in 1877 and since that date four more of a similar construction have been launched and others are in progress. While some of these vessels were for the home trade, others have gone all over the world. These trawlers have quite revolutionised the fishing industry, and have financially proved most successful.'

Allan's were subsequently awarded two special prizes at the International Fisheries Exhibition in London, in addition to the Gold Medal for the excellence of their 'models'.

In 1878, Henry Hird Foster of Scarborough took delivery

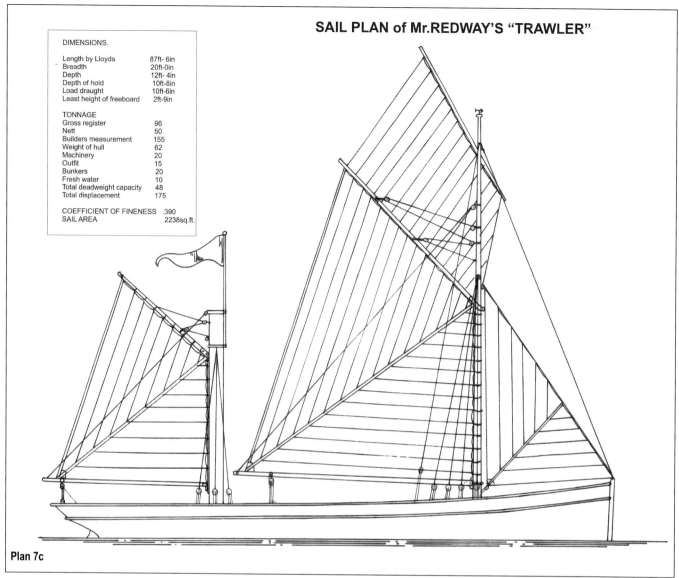

SAIL PLAN of Mr.REDWAY'S "TRAWLER"

DIMENSIONS.

Length by Lloyds	87ft- 6in
Breadth	20ft-0in
Depth	12ft- 4in
Depth of hold	10ft-8in
Load draught	10ft-6in
Least height of freeboard	2ft-9in

TONNAGE

Gross register	96
Nett	50
Builders measurement	155
Weight of hull	62
Machinery	20
Outfit	15
Bunkers	20
Fresh water	10
Total deadweight capacity	48
Total displacement	175

COEFFICIENT OF FINENESS	.390
SAIL AREA	2238sq.ft.

Plan 7c

of *Cormorant*, a 62ft screw steam yacht, which was fitted out with a beam trawl some 33.5ft across the mouth and 46ft long. Constructed of iron at Preston in Lancashire by Richard Smith, she was fitted with a set of their compound steam engines.

Yet another steam trawling pioneer was W. E. Redway of Milford Haven, who was constructing steam trawlers for the Irish Deep Sea Fisheries in the early 1880s. One of these vessels was appropriately called *Trawler* (**Plans 7a, b & c**), which had characteristics common to most of Redway's vessels. Their engines were of the compound type (12ins, 24ins x 24ins), with an intermediate receiver giving 120ihp. Steam was supplied by an ordinary return flue type steel boiler. The vessels shown are dandy rigged, no bowsprit being fitted. The mizzen was hoisted on an iron jackstay fixed to the after side of the funnel – an arrangement which brought forth many contemptuous remarks from the older fishermen. This novel rig was apparently successful, as the trawlers attained a fair speed under sail alone and coupled with their fine lines, proved themselves to be excellent sea boats. The deck layout is typical for the period, with the anchor windlass well forward; aft of this is the large cowl type ventilator for the fo'c'sle and aft again is the forward companion hood way. Immediately forward of the foremast is the fo'c'sle stove pipe and on the aft side of the mast is the hatchway for the fore hold/

warp room. Next is the main fishroom hatch and on the deck centre line is the fixed towpost or 'dummy'. A single barrel trawl winch is placed amidships over the engine room and further aft is the boiler room side casing and funnel housing. Aft of this casing is the cabin skylight, the after companionway and hand steering gear. This latter was an unusual feature of these vessels, as smacksmen preferred the tiller steering, which they maintained gave them a better feel of the boat. I imagine that the steering gear fitted to these boats would have been either the Werner Patent, or the standard worm and yoke type. In contrast to her outboard profile, below deck she resembled the latter day true steam trawler, with a fo'c'sle for the hands; fore hold; shelved fishroom and ice room. The propelling machinery differs from the later steam trawlers, as the boiler was fitted abaft her engine. The after cabin was fitted with four bunks and a folding table. There is no galley shown on the plan but at this period food was probably prepared in the fo'c'sle and carried aft at mealtimes, No coal bunkers are shown; coal would either be carried in the wings or in the ice room, with the ice being stored in the fishroom. The feed water for the boiler and fresh water for drinking may have been stored in double bottom tanks or in a fore peak tank. From the foregoing one can appreciate the vast amount of thought that Redway put into his design, so much so that his small vessels were

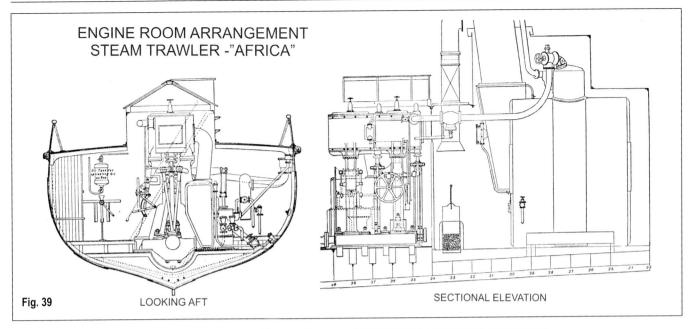

ENGINE ROOM ARRANGEMENT
STEAM TRAWLER -"AFRICA"

Fig. 39   LOOKING AFT   SECTIONAL ELEVATION

classed 90A at Lloyds. The main characteristics of his vessels were to be embodied in nearly all future steam trawler designs. Little was heard of these vessels after their launch and the last reports said that they were carrying out extensive experiments on all the older grounds in the North Sea. They opened up new grounds, including the English and St. George's channels. Nothing was ever recorded as to either their success or failure and it would be interesting to hear of their ultimate end.

It was around this time in 1883, that a steam trawler was built with an upper deck of corrugated iron. The vessel appeared to be a one off. She was *Africa* (**Fig. 39**), built by Sir W. Armstrong Mitchell & Co. Ltd, for Nelson & Donkin of Newcastle. She was built to Lloyds 100 A1 (100ft bp x 20ft x 10ft), with engines supplied by Ross & Duncan of the Whitefield Works in Glasgow.

The port of Swansea never featured as a major trawling centre; nevertheless, in 1883, the small iron beam trawler *Stag* (SA.23, Official No. 78443) began work here. Shed was built and engined by Jon Payne of Bristol (57ft 3ins x 12ft, 40.97g), with a 95nhp steam engine (**Photo. 21**). I suspect that the photograph was taken later in her life, as she features a fully enclosed wheelhouse. These early 'Hansom Cabs' were mostly fitted with open bridges. Unfortunately little else is known about this vessel.

FLEETING AND FISH CARRIERS

As early as the 1840s, the fleets of smacks from Barking in Essex were boxing their catches at sea and combining them to send to Billingsgate by fast sailing cutters. The method of transferring the catch from the trawler to the carrier, or 'boarding' as it was termed, was one of the most dangerous ever to be used in the UK fishing industry. Few of the smacksmen could swim and even those who could stood little chance of survival in the North Sea, dressed as they were in heavy oilskins and heavy leather thigh boots. Boats would be smashed to pieces as they lay alongside the carrier, or overturned whilst 'dropping down', heavily laden with boxes of fish from the trawling smacks. The trawlers would drop their boats upwind of the carrier and these small over-laden 14ft to 16ft vessels, under the command of the mate, would drop down alongside the carrier as best they could, where they would discharge their trunks of fish. Meantime, the parent trawlers would work their way to leeward of the carrier ready to pick up their boats. This complex operation was controlled by an 'Admiral', whose signals told the skippers when and where to fish, and when to offload their catch to the carrier. The Admirals' boat usually took up position immediately downwind of the carrier, from where he could oversee the complete operation. The skippers of the steam carriers often wasted much time and coal in trying to find the fleet, which used to move around a fair bit seeking the most prolific grounds. This problem was solved in 1913, when Hellyer's fleet from Hull first used wireless for direction and position finding, with their mark boat *Columbia* (H.42) and the trawlers *Bardolph* (H.296), and *Caliban* (H.76). Communications were scheduled for five minutes before every hour and radio enthusiasts ashore, who wandered off the BBC wavelength, would be puzzled by the language as the vessels arranged their rendezvous. The carrying trade to Billingsgate ended in 1936 and no more would 'Old Father' Thames resound to the deep notes of the carriers steam sirens, as they groped their way up river in a thick fog:

'In season and out of season, in fair weather and foul,

Photo. 21: The iron trawler *Stag*; note the capstan ahead of the foremast.

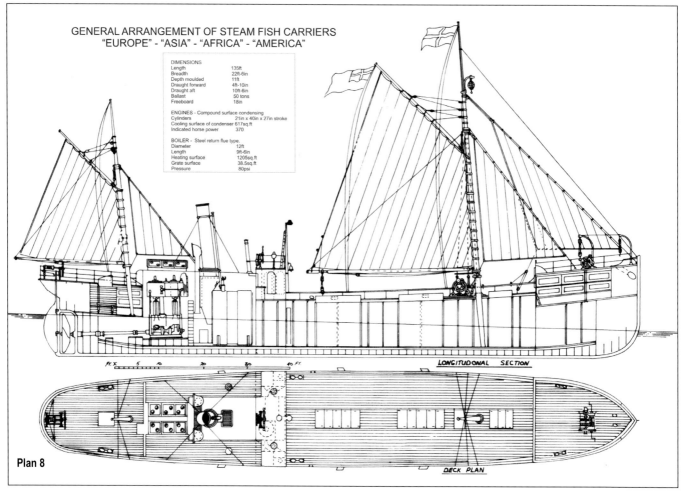

GENERAL ARRANGEMENT OF STEAM FISH CARRIERS
"EUROPE" - "ASIA" - "AFRICA" - "AMERICA"

DIMENSIONS
Length   135ft
Breadth   22ft-6in
Depth moulded   11ft
Draught forward   4ft-10in
Draught aft   10ft-6in
Ballast   50 tons
Freeboard   18in

ENGINES - Compound surface condensing
Cylinders   21in x 40in x 27in stroke
Cooling surface of condenser   617sq.ft
Indicated horse power   370

BOILER - Steel return flue type.
Diameter   12ft
Length   9ft-6in
Heating surface   1205sq.ft
Grate surface   38.5sq.ft
Pressure   80psi

LONGITUDONAL SECTION

Plan 8

DECK PLAN

away from all that is dear to him, fed on hard biscuit and salt junk, snatching sleep when he can, paid at a rate incommensurate with the risks and suffering he undergoes, and removed from his chance of satisfying his most innocent and legitimate passions, the poor fleeter leads a life, which for severity, can only be compared with that of a man undergoing penal servitude for crime.' THE ENGINEER, July 1884

The Fisheries Exhibition of 1883 did much to enlighten the fishing industry about the development of the steam trawler and fish carrier. Owners and merchants were by now convinced of their viability, and the many conferences and seminars held during the exhibition sparked the formation of steam trawler fleets, with their attendant carriers. The steam carrier, although not a trawler in the true sense of the word, forms an important part of their history. The use of steam carriers evolved from the days of the sailing cutters that raced to London with the fleet's catch. These fleets of sailing smacks, such as Hewett & Co's Short Blue Fleet and the Columbia Fleet of the North Sea Trawling Co. were totally dependant on the speedy sailing cutters for the conveyance of their fish to the main market at Billingsgate. This system was forced upon fishermen by the fleet owners, so the smacks could be more profitably engaged. Originally, the first smack to run out of food and water would hoist the appropriate signal and collect the fish from her consorts. The cutters' task was no sinecure, and there has scarcely been a better example of determination and fine seamanship in a heavily laden boat. The following facts and figures were disclosed at one of the many conferences held at the above exhibition:

'According to statistics collected by the Duke of Edinburgh, the total weight of fish consumed annually in Britain is 615,000 tons. This represents in monetary terms around £7,380,000 and in addition, £2,332,605 worth of fish is imported from abroad. Last year (1882), 143,000 tons of fish were dispatched to London, of which 118,977 tons passed through Billingsgate. Of this quantity, 76,578 tons were sent by land and 42,399 tons by sea. The great advantage of railway over steamboat carriage, is quick transit; but this is not always gained, and when it is, may be too dearly paid for.'

The railway carriage of fish in the 1880s was a rather haphazard affair, delivery erratic and freight charges high. The average charge for fish carriage from Yorkshire to London was between 25s and 30s a ton. From Scotland and Ireland, things were much worse. It is not difficult to understand why the merchants and trawl owners should focus their attentions on the steam carrier, endeavouring to reduce transport costs and provide a reliable service. In the same discussion, Mr Sayer, who was connected with Billingsgate Market, stated:

'The carriage of Mackerel from Ireland was 10s per box or £5 per ton when brought from the English coast by rail, but steamers had been put on for bringing Mackerel from the West coast of Ireland

Photo. 22: Steam Carrier **Australia**, note the open bridge and large winch abaft the foremast. The funnel is black with the company logo of a red cross on a white flag.

and Skibbereen to the London markets, and this fish was actually sold for less that the cost of the railway carriage alone.'

The steam carrier did much to regulate and speed up this trade, as the steam engine was hardly affected by headwinds. The first mention of steam carriers being constructed was in 1865, when *Lord Alfred Paget* and *Hallett* were launched at Stockton-on-Tees for Robert Hewett of Barking – named after two of the company's directors. Both were iron screw steamers (120ft x 21ft, 186g). They were apparently driven at exceptional speeds for the time, by two-cylinder engines which were heavy on coal. They were followed by the larger more advanced *Wellesley* and *Frost* in 1866 but they were still coal gobblers. These vessels were designed to load some 3,900 boxes of fish, interspersed with ice. The company went on to own no less than fourteen such vessels. One of their fleet, *The Major*, was used as a test bed for various innovations and she has the honour of being the first British fishing vessel to be fitted with a refrigeration plant. However, it did not prove very successful, so she reverted back to the old ice method of preserving the catch.

Typical of these steam carriers were the vessels designed and built by Earles of Hull, namely Yard No. 229 *Europe*, No. 230 *Asia*, No. 231 *Africa* and No. 232 *America* (H.1284 – lost after a collision in the Humber in 1897), all built for the Hull Steam Fishing & Ice Company Ltd in 1880. Having a Lloyd's classification of 100A1 (**Plan 8**), they were a far cry from Bidders' *Edith*. Aft there is a raised quarterdeck for the officers and a fo'c'sle forward for the deck crew.

The principal features of Yard No. 247 *Australia*, launched in March 1882 (**Photo. 22**), were a speed during acceptance trials of 10.8 knots and a fuel consumption of between 8 and 9 tons in 24 hours. Externally, these vessels differed little from later steam

trawlers, with an open bridge forward of the tall funnel, a pole compass, engine room skylight and large twin cowl stokehold vents. The emergency steering gear aft was also in keeping with her larger successors.

'These steam carriers have a cargo capacity of between 3,000 and 3,500 trunks of fish, each box or trunk holding from 80 to 90 lbs. The amount of ice carried in order to preserve this fish varies from 10 tons in Winter, to 25 to 30 tons in Summer. The crew as a rule numbers twelve men all told, four of these being in the engine room, and the remaining eight on deck and in the galley. The deck gang is composed of the Captain, Mate, and Bosun, and four Seamen, while the cooking is done by another of the men who is usually called a Steward.' BULLETIN OF THE U.S. FISHERIES COMMISSION, 1888

The fish carrier was held in high esteem by the merchants of the period and several vessels were built to the same design. They seemed to be wonderful sea-boats, driving through gales that held up the larger steamers of the time. Famous among them were *Pelican* and *Gannet* (the latter not to be confused with the wooden vessel of the same name built by Allans on the Forth), *Albatross* and *Cormorant*, which kept almost railway-like regularity between the North Sea grounds and London.

Back in 1878, the Great Grimsby Ice Company, had three iron screw cutters built at Middlesborough. These were *Precursor*, *Dispatch* and *Celebrity* (all 130ft x 21ft x 10.5ft, 190 tons; 50nhp). The company commissioned a fourth vessel, *Velocity*, and this was launched from the yard of Messrs Railton & Dixon on 10th June 1879. In 1880, the Great Northern Steamship Fishing Co. Ltd of Hull ordered four steam carriers from Murdoch & Murray of Port

Photo. 23: The fish carrier *Progress*; note the enclosed wheelhouse with flying bridge Gallows were fitted to the port side only, as they would impede the loading of fish from the small boats. Her colours are grey hull and a black topped white funnel, with yellow flag and red fish motif.

Glasgow. These were *Progress, Onward, Vigilant* and *Speedwell* (all 130ft x 21ft x 11ft). Their engines, by Muir & Houston of Glasgow, were of the compound surface condensing type, of 20ins, 40ins x 27ins stroke. The last of the quartet, *Speedwell*, went down the ways on 25th May 1880. Another fish carrier, named *Progress* (H.475), was built at Leith in 1899 (145ft loa, 273g), for the Great Northern Steamship Fishing Co. Ltd (**Photo. 23**). She was sunk on 3rd May 1915, by a time bomb set by the crew of a German submarine, some 160 miles east-north-east of Spurn Point.

This Hull company also owned a further two steam carriers, *Eastward* (144 tons) built by Earles in 1882 and *Colonel Smith* built at Blackwall in 1884.

By far the largest steam fishing vessels of the 1890s were the carriers *New Zealand*, and *Hornsea*, both built by Cook, Welton & Gemmell of Hull for the Hull Steam Fishing & Ice Co. Ltd. The *New Zealand* (H.413) of 1898 (146ft 7ins x 22ft 6ins x 10ft 8ins, 290g) was driven by engines of 50nhp built by Amos & Smith, as was *Hornsea* (H.485) of 1899 (148ft 7ins x 22ft 8ins x 11ft 2ins, 305g). These two ships were the most powerful additions to the Humber fleet before the turn of the century.

The system of 'fleeting' or 'boxing' as it was known on the Humber was to continue up to the 1930s, supported by the Great Northern Steamship Fishing Co. Ltd; the Red Cross Fleet and the Gamecock Fleet. This last mentioned fleet, as late as 1921 ordered two steam carriers from Fergusson Brothers, Port Glasgow. These were *Hornbill* and *Nuthatch* (140ft x 23ft), and are possibly worth a closer study (**Plan 9**). On the fo'c'sle head they carried a twin barrelled, hand operated anchor windlass by Emmerson & Walker of Gateshead. The crew's fo'c'sle, on a slightly lower level than the main deck, slept eight hands, the only comfort being the small bogey stove set against the aft bulkhead.

Conditions in this cramped space were not improved by the chain pipes passing through the cabin table and the hawse pipes for the anchor cable— both of which would have been a constant source of leaks in anything but the calmest weather. The large flush main deck was pierced by the usual hatches for ice, coal and fish, with a spare propeller and shaft carried on the fore-deck. Although no gallows are shown on the plan, the ships were fitted with a 'Stockton' double barrelled trawl winch. These winches, supplied by Rogers & Co. Ltd of Stockton on Tyne, were of the vertical twin cylinder type, as opposed to the more normal horizontal design. Oak samson posts were fitted to the rails, in order to facilitate the mooring of the fleeter's boats when discharging their boxes of fish. The superstructures of these vessels had a rather cluttered appearance, with their tall wheel houses above both the captain's quarters and the galley. A wireless cabin was fitted immediately abaft the tall funnel; this was completely self contained with sleeping accommodation provided. A light spar deck was fitted over the engine room casing. This platform carried a spare stockless anchor, water cask and the ship's boat, which was mounted athwartship on sliding chocks. Aft of the engine casing is a store room with the door offset to port. The door on the starboard side leads to the engine room and after cabin. The cabin houses the crew's mess room and two small cabins for the engineer and mate. The exhaust gases from the messroom stove passed up through the hollow mizzen mast, instead of through the more usual stove pipe. Masts were fitted with topmasts to carry the wireless aerials. Overall, the standard of accommodation was high and the vessels, with their fine runs and flared bows, would have been excellent fast sea boats

Another yard building steam carriers was Mackie & Thomson of Govan, who built the sister ships *Macbeth* (H.869 – **Photo. 24**)

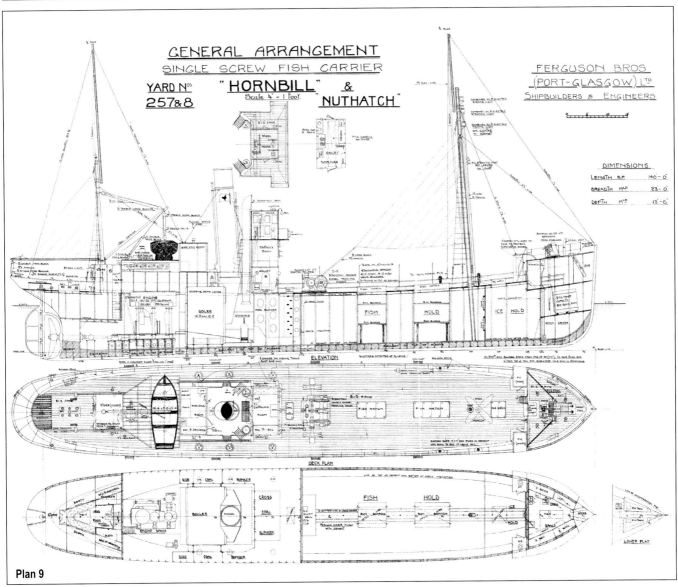

Plan 9

Photo. 24: The steam carrier *Macbeth*. She shows all the characteristics of later steam trawlers, with her port side gallows and trawl winch arrangement. Note the forecastle; her lifeboat is carried in radial davits abaft her funnel giving her a clear deck aft. She is seen here in early Hellyer colours, of black hull, brown superstructure and a yellow black topped funnel with white 'H' on a blue flag.

Photo. 25: *Desdemona*, a typical early fleeter with open bridge, port side gallows and small boat stowed against the starboard bulwarks. Note the spare otter boards stowed against the casing and the same Hellyer colours as *Macbeth*.

and *Macduff* (H.894) for Hellyer's of Hull in 1906. Both ships were requisitioned in the First World War, *Macbeth* in October 1914 as a minesweeper, armed with a 12pdr, and a 3pdr gun; she was returned in 1919. Her sister also served as a minesweeper from June 1915 until 1919, when she was sold to Grimsby as *Macduff* (GY.771), owned by the Bunch Steam Fishing Co. They sold her in November 1926 to S. Melmuish, who in turn sold her to the Macduff Steam Fishing Co. in October 1934. She went to the breakers in September 1937. As well as the carriers, Hellyer's also ordered four steam fleeters from the Govan yard. They were Yard No's 70-73: *Angus* (H.895), *Sebastian* (H.888), *Cassio* (H.889)and *Desdemona* (H.904 – **Photo. 25**). *Angus* was reported missing on 17th November 1913, no trace being found, and *Sebastian* disappeared without trace on or around 22nd

May 1915. *Desdemona* went missing, with no survivors, around 3rd December 1913 and *Cassio* was sunk on 24th July 1915, by gunfire from a German submarine in the Atlantic, some 123 miles off Hoy Head, in the Orkneys.

Other firms using fish carriers included the Great Yarmouth Steam Carrying Co. Ltd of London, who had four ships built, one of which was *Endeavour* (123ft x by 21ft x 11ft 6ins, 200g). They achieved a speed of 12 knots from engines developing only 55nhp. A more unusual vessel was the twin screw carrier *Arabian* (126ft x 22ft x 9ft 6ins), built for work on the west coast of Scotland by Murray Brothers of Dumbarton. She was driven by a patent triple expansion engine divided between the two shafts, having the high and intermediate pressure cylinders on one shaft and a second high and the low pressure cylinder on the other, using 150psi.

Chapter 6: THE EARLY YEARS 1880-1900

The 1880s were a period of great technological advance. Victorian industry was at its height and the fishing industry became increasingly more alert to the advantages of steam power. Shipbuilders turned their attentions to supplying the trawl owners with new tonnage. The demand rose to such proportions that iron, wooden and steel trawlers were constructed and launched from the most unlikely sites. Some firms built only one or two vessels, whereas others launched ship after ship, each new vessel superior in design to its predecessor. Firms that specialised in steam trawler construction became well known names within the industry. The year 1881 saw the formation of the Grimsby & North Sea Steam Trawling Co. Ltd, the principal shareholders being Messrs Cook, Mackrill, W. Moody and J. Alward. They decided to build a steam trawler which would also serve as a carrier to the sailing fleets during the summer months. This they hoped would help to offset the heavy fuel costs of 11s a ton. They realised that one of the main difficulties would be making a screw propeller efficient enough to tow the heavy trawl. Earles of Hull were consulted and they agreed that the normal type of screw would be useless to the venture. They became interested in the problem and designed an efficient screw propeller for the vessel. So it came about that, during the closing months of 1881, the Grimsby company placed an order for two steam trawlers. One was to be built by Earles and the other across the Humber at Charlton's of Grimsby. The purchase price for these ships worked out at £3,800 for the Hull vessel and £3,500 for the Grimsby-built one. Their design was unambitious, based mainly on the sailing smacks of the period. They were to be 86ft long, fitted with vertical engines and a tall funnel. The only distinguishing feature between the two craft was that the Hull-built ship would be fitted with a bridge, for conning the vessel.

Zodiac (GY.828 – **Plans 10a & b**), the first name chosen, was given to the Hull-built ship, whilst *Aries* (GY.832) was the second ship, built at Charlton's yard. The Grimsby & North Sea Steam Fishing Co. Ltd had agreed that, should the operation prove

successful, they would build a fleet of steam trawlers, each bearing a name from the signs of the Zodiac. The start of 1882 saw both ships putting to sea, heralding a new era for the Humber fishing industry. *Zodiac* and its first sign, *Aries*, caught about four times as much as a sailing smack. They could work during calms, thus fishing more efficiently than the sailing trawlers, and they were able to work the smaller and rougher grounds previously untouched. Another important consideration was that they could land their catches in prime condition, thus ensuring a good market price. All these salient points were not missed by the smack owners, who had previously scorned the 'steam kettles'. Soon steam trawling companies sprang up in Grimsby, Boston and Hull, with North and South Shields, Granton, Leith and Aberdeen following closely behind. Over on the west coast, trawling stations opened up at Glasgow, Fleetwood and Milford Haven, and many smaller ports also succumbed to the age of the steam trawler. Orders for steam trawlers were placed whereever they could be built. The initial building cost for *Zodiac* was to be £4,000 but this was reduced by £200 as a goodwill gesture by Earles. Apparently, this shipyard was never too busy to listen to the owners' recommendations and, if the latter are to be believed, the builders appeared to show a greater interest in the venture than those who actually put forward the capital. Earles were well repaid for this small act of goodwill, for few firms contributed as much to the building of steam trawlers in the years that followed the tiny pioneer. *Zodiac* was a flush decked, iron screw trawler, with a standard fo'c'sle for the hands. Aft of this was the forward fish room and separating this from the main fish room was the ice room. This ice room measured 7ft fore and aft, extending the full width of the vessel, and was sealed by patent air tight doors. The ice carried varied from 8 tons in winter to 15 tons in summer. Between the main fish room and the engine room was the main bunker space, forming a good insulation between boiler and fish rooms. Engines were compound fed from a single drum steel return tube boiler. The trials speed of the ships was 9

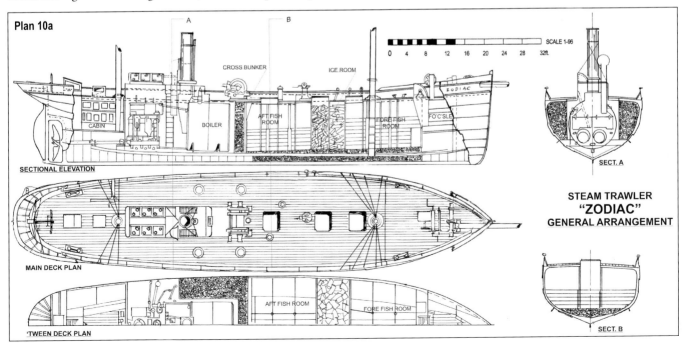

Plan 10a

SCALE 1·96

0 4 8 12 16 20 24 28 32ft.

CROSS BUNKER

ICE ROOM

ZODIAC

CABIN BOILER AFT FISH ROOM FORE FISH ROOM FO'C'SLE

SECTIONAL ELEVATION

SECT. A

MAIN DECK PLAN

STEAM TRAWLER
"ZODIAC"
GENERAL ARRANGEMENT

AFT FISH ROOM FORE FISH ROOM

'TWEEN DECK PLAN

SECT. B

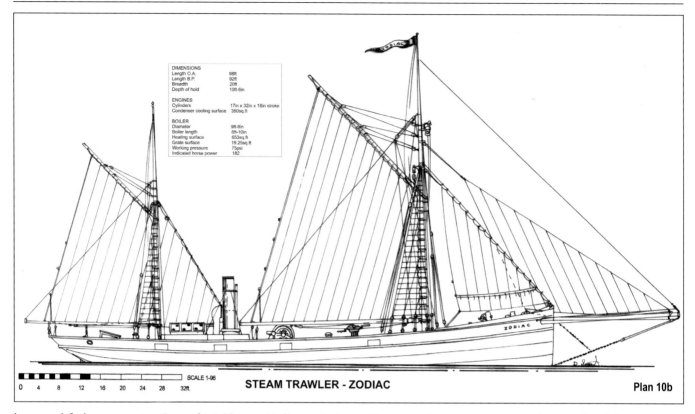

DIMENSIONS
Length O.A.   98ft
Length B.P.   92ft
Breadth   20ft
Depth of hold   10ft-6in

ENGINES
Cylinders   17in x 32in x 18in stroke
Condenser cooling surface 350sq.ft

BOILER
Diameter   9ft-8in
Boiler length   8ft-10in
Heating surface   653sq.ft
Grate surface   19.25sq.ft
Working pressure   75psi
Indicated horse power   182

SCALE 1-96
0 4 8 12 16 20 24 28 32ft.

STEAM TRAWLER - ZODIAC

Plan 10b

knots and fuel consumption 4 tons for 24 hours. *Zodiac* worked from Grimsby until she went missing on 25th September 1889. Her successor, GY.151, of 149 tons, was built of iron at Govan in 1890 for S.J. Green and D. James of St. Dogmaels, Cardigan. She lasted somewhat longer than her predecessor, being hired by the Admiralty from 1918 until the close of hostilities in 1919 and was owned by W. Mould in 1920. She had five owners during her fishing days, finally ending up at Lowestoft.

Zodiac and *Aries* had scarcely completed their maiden trips before orders were placed for *Cancer* (GY.890) and *Leo* (GY.896) both built by Charlton's of Grimsby. These were at sea by the end of 1882. The Grimsby & North Sea Steam Fishing Co. Ltd's next two ships built by Earles were *Taurus* (GY.883) and *Gemini* (GY.885) – both seven feet longer than their predecessors – and so the fleet grew until *Zodiac* and the twelve signs were complete. The fears of anyone who reckoned on thirteen being an unlucky number were soon dispelled. By 1901, *Taurus*, *Gemini*, *Cancer* and *Leo* had been sold to Norwegian owners. *Leo* returned to her home port in 1902 as GY.1225, only to be sold soon afterwards to France. *Taurus* and *Gemini* returned to their original owners, the Grimsby & North Sea Steam Fishing Co. Ltd, as GY.136 and GY.137 respectively. In April 1915, *Taurus* went to George Craig and others of Aberdeen, as A.655. She was lost on 26th June 1917 in the North Sea, after hitting a mine. In 1914, *Gemini* was cut down to a coal lighter but resumed fishing again in October 1918, when she was purchased by the Brent Steam Fishing Co. Ltd; her name was changed to *Bedouin* (GY.1217). This work-weary vessel finally went to the breakers in June 1924 and, at the ripe old age of forty-one, was the last of her clan. The specifications for *Taurus* and *Gemini* were supplied by Earles to the United States Fish Commission and were printed in their bulletin of 1888. I quote these in the appendix to provide an accurate description of trawlers of the time.

The costs of running a steam trawler were detailed in print:

'A steam trawler such as described, would cost from £4,000 to £4,500, which was about three times as much as a first-class sailing trawler would cost. Then a steamer was more expensive to run. In the first place, she must have three more men, of the class, too, that receive high pay, then there are the repairs to machinery, coal, oil, etc, which together amount to quite a sum. As an offset to this, a steamer will stock from twice to three times as much as a sailing trawler. ENGINEERING, *10th August 1883*

To begin with, these early steam trawlers fished with a single beam trawl, which was more substantial than those of the sailing smack. Skipper W. Browning of *Leo* discovered that the steam trawler wore out its fishing gear much faster than a smack. Numerous trawls were also lost on the rougher grounds frequented by the steamers, giving a substantial loss of fishing time. On one of these occasions, after returning with a meagre catch and a smashed trawl, Browning audaciously asked the owners to fit his vessel with two trawls, which could be used alternately with one always in reserve. Reluctantly, the owners agreed and skipper Browning was able to reduce his time at sea and still land full catches. The one major factor predominant throughout the history of trawl fishing is that, when the trawl is not on the bottom, the vessels are not earning money and this one fact alone was the key element in the design of better gear and more efficient ships. There could have been little or no rest aboard *Leo*, for immediately the decks were cleared of fish, they would begin hauling once more. In spite of the men's grumbles, spare gear was to become standard outfit for all future steam and motor trawlers.

In 1889, Mackie & Thomson of Govan launched Yard No's 5 and 6, the steam long liners *Aquarius* (GY 214) and *Capricornus* (GY.215) (101ft 3ins x 20ft 7ins x 12ft, 164g), both engined by

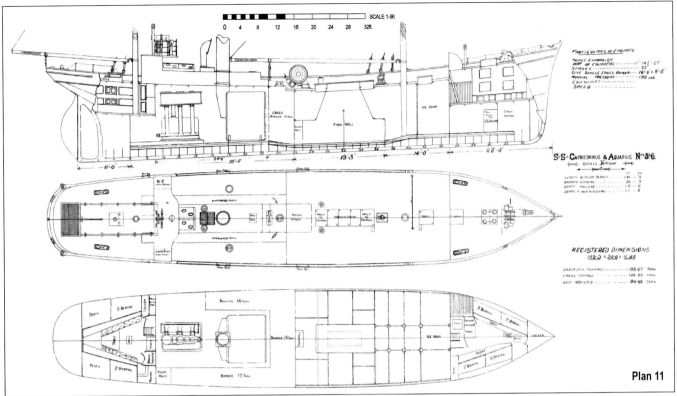

Plan 11

Messrs Muir & Houston and owned by the Grimsby & North Sea Steam Fishing Co. Ltd. The former vessel differed from her sister, being fitted with a patent well, operated by a centrifugal pump. This enabled the vessel's fish hold to be dried out between trips. It was in these two ships, along with *Perseus* in 1891, that James Alward sailed to pioneer the Icelandic trawling grounds. The round trip of some 2,000 miles meant a steaming time of 10 to 12 days. This, coupled with an actual fishing time of say 5 to 6 days, meant that bunkers in the region of 80 tons had to be carried. *Aquarius* was lost in 1904. In December 1899, *Capricornus* was sold to France as *St. George* and was lost in 1907 (**Plan 11**). Later, in 1891, Mackie & Thomson built four iron 'fleeters' for the Great Grimsby & East Coast Steam Fishing Co. Ltd. They were *Umbria* (GY.420), *Utopia (*GY.415), *Columbia* (GY.430) and *Dalmatia* (GY.435 – **Plan 12**, *overleaf*), Yard No's 42, 43, 44 and 45 (100ft 6ins x 20ft 6ins x 10ft 7ins, 121n, all fitted with a 70nhp engine). They bunkered 55 tons of coal, which gave them a duration of around ten days, and a fresh water supply of 500 gallons, or a little over two tons, which would last the fifteen man crew about the same time. The plan shows a typical beam trawler with the bridge aft of the funnel. The main deck steps up forward, to give headroom in the eight man crew's cabin below. The after living space has tiny separate cabins for the master and engineer. The only strange items shown on the plan are the passageways running outboard of the fish room, as they terminate at either end at a watertight bulkhead. It is difficult to see what purpose they serve, unless they were used for transferring the ice to the hold. Their deck plan shows a single barrelled trawl winch in front of the casing, with the single warp guide roller placed centrally between the trawling ports in the bulwarks and a squared off counter stern.

Under the bridge wings are the lamp room to starboard and a WC to port. The galley is entered by doors on either side of the casing, with the engine room and after accommodation entrances on the aft end. A spiral stair leads down to the cabin and a straight stairway serves the machinery space. There appears to be little room either side of the boiler, so firing must have entailed dragging coal from the cross bunker through the wing bunkers, once they were empty. *Umbria* was later sold to Devon fish merchant Pike Ward, and later again, in October 1904, to Norwegian owners. She returned to Grimsby in October 1906, as GY.193, belonging to the Grimsby Union Steam Fishing Co. Ltd. They kept her until 1908, when she was sold to Denmark; she finally became the Icelandic trawler *Freyr*. *Utopia* served her original owners until May 1899, when she also was sold to Denmark and later to Icelandic owners. *Columbia* was transferred to Blyth in March 1912 and went missing, presumed lost with all hands, around 12th September 1916. The last of the quartet, *Dalmatia*, also went to Blyth in 1912. In 1892, the yard built the following eight steel 'fleeters', all 100ft 2ins oa x 20ft 6ins x 10ft 6ins, 142g. They were: Yard No. 82 *Cashmere* for the United Kingdom Steam Trawling Co. Ltd of London; No. 84 *Brent*; No .85 *Marec*; No. 87 *Coot*; No. 89 *Ibis*; No. 90 *Eider* (later A. 75) and No. 92 *Grebe*, all for William Hamilton of Port Glasgow. Yard No. 86 *Collingwood* was registered at Boston but owned by W. Ingram of London; No. 88 *Stromo* was owned by the White Star Steam Fishing Co. Ltd, Grimsby.

On the north bank of the River Humber in Hull, one of the first owners to go into steam was George Beeching, who commissioned his first purpose built steam trawler, *Irrawaddy* (H.1479), from Cook, Welton & Gemmell in 1885. Mr Pickering, later of Pickering & Haldane's Steam Trawling Co. Ltd, soon followed. He ordered the steam trawlers *Romulus*, *Remus*, *Lark* and *Linnett*. The former pair were ordered from Andrew Cochrane's shipyard at Grovehill, Beverley and were the first steam trawlers built by this company, as Ship No's 11 and 12, with *Romulus* (H.1483 – **Photo. 26**) delivered on 1st March 1886, closely followed by *Remus* (H.1487).

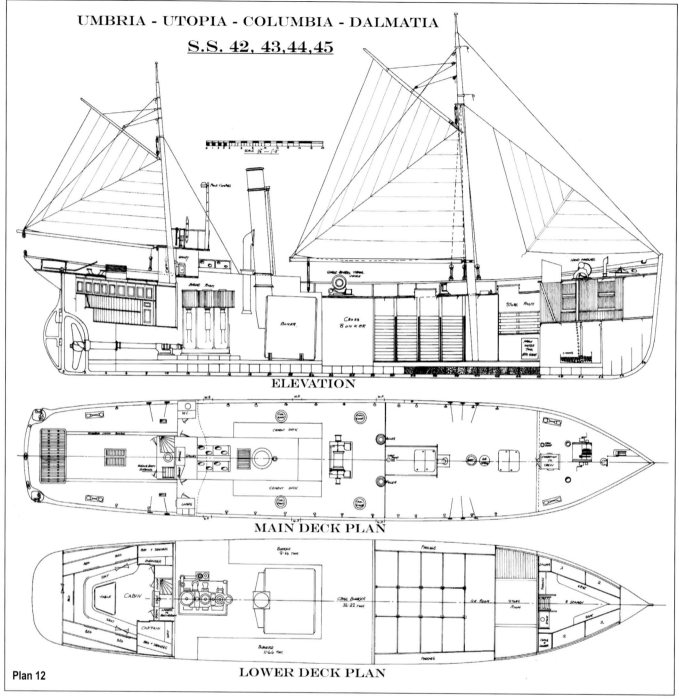

UMBRIA - UTOPIA - COLUMBIA - DALMATIA
S.S. 42, 43, 44, 45

ELEVATION

MAIN DECK PLAN

Plan 12

LOWER DECK PLAN

This yard was to become second to none in the construction of trawlers, sending some 204 vessels sideways into the water by the end of the 19th century. The other two ships, *Lark* and *Linnett* (90ft x 20ft 4ins x 11ft 8ins) were constructed on the River Hull by Cook, Welton & Gemmell as Ship No's 12 and 13, with engines by C.D. Holmes. The first steam trawler built by this company was Yard No. 9, *Irrawaddy* (H.1479 – 100ft x 20ft, 45nhp). She was completed in December 1885 for George Beeching & Thomas Kelsall of Hull. In 1889, she was sold to the British Steam Fishing Co. Ltd, Hull, who sold her to Aberdeen owner Thomas Stephen as A.313 in April 1910. She was sold again in April 1914, to J.N. Sanne of Uddevalla, Sweden, who renamed her *Albatross*; she was scrapped in 1923.

Unfortunately, Cochrane's launch of their first steam trawler was not as well covered in the press as the occasion might have merited. Other builders launching similar vessels received much more glowing reports in the shipping press. The *Marine Engineer* of 1885, simply stated:

'ROMULUS, *On December 24th Messrs. Cochrane & Co. launched from their shipyard at Grovehill, Beverley, a steam trawler for Messrs. Pickering & Haldane of Hull. The ceremony of naming the vessel was performed by Miss Cochrane. The* ROMULUS, *is the first of four steam trawlers now building for Messrs. Pickering & Haldane. Her principal dimensions are – Length of Keel, 105ft., Breadth, 20ft., Depth, 12ft. The vessel is built with a raked stem, quarterdeck and a fo'c'sle. She is to be fitted with a patent windlass, worked by a messenger chain from*

Photo. 26: Steam trawler *Romulus* in later life. Note her clipper stem and early type of gallows. She has a black hull and brown superstructure and her black topped red funnel bears Pickering & Haldanes motif of a white rectangle, with a blue St. Andrew's cross, inside which are the letters P H & Co in red.

Photo. 27: *Remus* when owned in Newhaven. Note her twin lifeboats, canvas dodger around the open bridge and her square trawl board.lashed to the shrouds. She carries a full set of sails and the bulwark step up indicates a raise quarterdeck.

Photo. 28: *Kirton*, showing single arm 'gibbet' type gallows ahead of her foremast and large trawl boards. Note the hinged side light screens. No bobbin derrick is fitted but she has a tackle from the mizzen mast which would assist with hoisting the Otter Board over the rail.

the steam winch. Her engines are to be supplied by Charles D. Holmes & Co. of Hull, and are Compound Surface Condensing, 45 Nominal Horse Power.'

Romulus (H.1483) was later bought by J. Marr & Son in 1910 and, by 1913, was registered at Fleetwood as FD.128. Eight years later, they in turn sold the vessel to Nelson Blow in Grimsby (GY.146), who kept her for a couple of years before she went to the Bristol Sand & Gravel Co. who converted her into a dredger.

There was another *Remus* built by Oswald Mordaunt at Woolston and launched on 10th March 1888 for Messrs Bensuade & Co. of Newhaven as NN.35. A picture taken after 1896 shows her fitted with primitive otter boards, although no gallows are shown (**Photo. 27**). She is a tough looking little vessel (109ft x 20ft x 10ft), with an open bridge and only a weather cloth to shelter the skipper and helmsman. Another early Hull trawler (although built north of the border) was *Spider* (H.914), from Scott of Bowling as Yard No. 71 in 1888 for Knowles & Robbins.

It was around this time, in 1886, that the Boston Deep Sea Fishing & Ice Co. Ltd placed its first order for a steam trawler with Cochranes. This was Yard No. 15 *Kirton* (BN.188 – 92ft 3ins x 21ft x 10ft 9ins, 125g), engined by C.D. Holmes. **Photo. 28** shows her in later life when rigged with otter boards. No gallows are evident but vertical towing posts can be seen. The forward ones are braced from the turtle backed houses at the break of the fo'c'sle and the aft pair are braced from the casing. The forecastle is flush with the rail, giving her a sleek appearance, and her wheelhouse is forward of the funnel. I would think that originally she had on open bridge similar to that of *Remus*. Boston Deep Sea Fishing & Ice Co. Ltd sold her to Granton owners Thomas Devlin in 1907, as GN.42. In 1909, she ran ashore in St. Cyrus Bay but her crew were rescued by lifeboat and she was later refloated. She was requisitioned in May 1916 as a boom defence vessel and was returned to Devlin's

in 1919. In June that year, she was sold to W. High, Dundee and sold again the following year to G. Ampetakiotis, Glasgow, who renamed her *Gleaner*, registered at Vathy. In 1930, she was sold to A. Demetriades, Glasgow, who converted her into the salvage vessel *Triton* (125g); she went for scrapping in 1937.

Throughout the country in the 1880s, the steam trawler building programme gathered momentum. On 17th September 1880, there took place the launch of **Sea Queen**, built especially for steam trawling. She was a vessel of some 83 tons (90ft x 16ft 6ins x 8ft 4ins, 130nhp), engined by Muir & Houston and gave a trials speed of 10 knots. Another small trawler, *James Jackson* (60ft x 14ft. x 8ft 2ins) was launched from the Hesketh Shipyard, South Shields on 2nd August 1882. Built for Mr Jackson, she was powered by a vertical engine with twin 21ins diameter cylinders.

STEAM TUGS AS TRAWLERS.

Paddle and screw tugs were also being built around this time, to swell the ranks of the embryo trawler fleets. These later tugs were far removed from the older wooden vessels that had pioneered the Tyne trawling industry. Most were iron or steel vessels, designed specifically for towing and trawling work. One such vessel was *Constance* (SH.21 – 120ft x 20ft x 10ft 6ins), an iron paddle trawler launched at South Shields on 31st August 1882 to the order of W.H. Shawcross of Scarborough. Fitted with side lever engines rated at 40nhp, she was in fact the last such trawler to work from the port and was wrecked on 22nd March 1910 near Hartlepool.

Scarborough was about the only Yorkshire port to take advantage of the paddle tug/trawler combination. Essentially a holiday resort for the industrial Midlands, pleasure boat trips rated highly among its many amenities and, at the height of the season, the waterfront would be thronged with holidaymakers all clamouring for pleasure trips to Whitby, Filey Brigg, Flamborough Head (with its famous lighthouse) or to Bridlington. In winter, the tugs went back to

RIGHT: **Photo. 29:** The paddle trawler *Dunrobin* at Scarborough circa 1900; note her beam trawl and derricks. She was built as a tug at Cardiff in 1876 for Jacob Jenkins but was later sold to Belfast owner J. Douglas. After going ashore at Ballyhalbert, Co. Down in 1894, she was declared a wreck but was salvaged and rebuilt the following year as a trawler, in which guise she was bought by George Adamason of Scarborough. She was finally lost after going ashore again in 1908.

BELOW: **Photo. 30:** Steam tug/trawler *Dragon*. Note her trawl gallows and winch. Although rigged for trawling, she still has her original towing arrangement.

trawling. Some continued fishing from Scarborough but many also fished out of Hull. At its height in 1882, the Scarborough paddle trawler fleet had twenty-seven vessels on the register, most of which had been bought second hand for between £2,000 and £3,000. This was quite expensive when one considers the building costs for new purpose built steam screw trawlers ten years later was only around £3,500. The Britannia Steam Fishing Co. of Scarborough took delivery of the iron paddler *Clyde* (120ft x 20ft x 10ft 6ins) in September 1882 from Howard's of Newcastle. Her engines by Hepples were of the side lever type, with 38ins and 58ins cylinders. This vessel was to be the forerunner of a fleet of ships intended for fishing on the Dogger Bank, whilst in the summer months, she was to be redeployed on excursion work. One cannot but wonder how they disguised the stale smell of fish.

Dragon (FH.216 – 114ft x 20ft 1ins x 10ft 5ins, 168g) was yet

another example of the early tug/trawler combination, launched in 1883 and owned by the Falmouth Fishery Company (**Photo. 30**).

Another dual purpose, or perhaps triple purpose vessel launched around this time was the iron screw steamer *Advance*, built by the Commercial Graving Dock, Cardiff in August 1882. She was owned by W.&H.R. Strong and intended for towing and trawl fishing. She also had some passenger accommodation and was issued with a Board of Trade passenger certificate. Her engines were supplied by the Tyneside Engine Works, Bute Dock, Cardiff. This was Strong's second vessel and it appears that she was the first screw tug ever to work out of that port.

It was a year earlier, in 1891, that Fleetwood received its first steam trawler. This was *Lark* (FD.120 – 99ft long), built at Middlesborough by R. Dixon & Co. for Moody & Kelly of Grimsby and powered by an engine supplied by the North East Marine Engineering Co. Ltd, of Sunderland. *Lark* apparently gave good service to the Lancashire port before being sold to Burma. She was scrapped in 1936. This Grimsby company also sent their ABC fleet round to work out of Fleetwood, presumably converting them from their original long liner configuration to that of a trawler. Another company showing interest in the steam trawler was Kelsall Bros & Beeching, with their Gamecock Fleet. They built up a fleet of some thirty-two trawlers between 1891 and 1897, with such vessels as *Burmah* (FD.148 – 110ft, 110g), built by Edwards Brothers at North Shields in 1892 and quite large for the time. In 1897, she went to Hull as H.86, fishing from that port until she went for scrap in 1924. Her fishing career was interrupted from October

1914 until November 1919, when she was requisitioned as a minesweeper. Other ships of the Gamecock Fleet at this time were *Bovic* (FD.143), which also went to Hull in 1897 as H.51 and was requisitioned as a minesweeper in November 1914. She sank after a collision off Souter Point on 5th August 1917. *Grouse* (FD.169) went to Hull in 1897 as H.100 and was called up for minesweeping duties in the First World War, eventually going to the breakers in 1928. As can be seen, most of the Gamecock Fleet transferred to Hull around 1897, where they fished as 'fleeters' or 'boxers', as opposed to the single boaters that worked from other ports.

The Doughty Museum at Grimsby has the builder's model of the steam trawler *Chillian* (GY 564 – 115ft x 20ft 6ins x 10ft 8ins, **Photo. 31**). She appears to have been a transitional vessel, rigged for both beam and otter trawling. She was built for the Co-operative Box & Fish Carrying Co. Ltd, Grimsby by Edwards of North Shields and was typical of the trawlers of the period, with her flying bridge abaft the funnel, and her full suit of fore and aft sails complete with fore staysail and jib. These ships were commonly known as 'Hansom Cabs', after a type of horse-drawn carriage where the driver sat behind the passenger compartment. She was launched by Miss E. Alward on 23rd December 1893. Her maiden trip commenced early in 1894, landing some 180 boxes of haddock, 300 score of cod, 60 boxes of plaice and some other species. Alas her working life was soon over when, on Sunday 8th April 1894, she went aground on Filey Brigg, subsequently becoming a total loss. One feature of the model is the outfit of both beam and otter trawls, and this would appear to be the first model ever built showing the new type of otter boards for the net which were only developed in that year. It is doubtful whether she ever fished with the new gear, as she only carries a single barrel trawl winch, which would have been unsuitable for the task, although gallows are in evidence.

TRAWLING

Before continuing this somewhat statistical trip through steam trawler history, let us digress for a short while and take a trip to the North Sea grounds on a steam trawler of the 1880s. Our vessel is the iron screw ketch *Sybil* (**Plan 12** – 105ft x 21ft 8ins x 10ft 2ins),

built by the Norfolk Co. of Hull in 1883 for Brocklebank & Co., London. She was powered by a two cylinder compound engine (17.5ins, 34ins x 24ins) by Wood Bros. of Sowerby Bridge. Her layout is typical of the period, with the only refinement being the crews bunks, which are fitted with sliding doors:

'When the hour comes to turn in, the trawlerman casts himself in full rig upon the hard boards of his bunk, and shrouding himself with a homely rug, sinks uncoaxed into a profound slumber. Callously indifferent to the rules of ventilation or hygiene, he closes his sliding doors, and, so to speak, seals himself hermetically into sleep. THE ENGINEER, *July 1884*

Our small crew comprises, skipper, mate, second and third hands, deckie, cook and two engineers. We sail mid morning for the North Sea trawling grounds, having steamed some 50 miles by evening. The beam trawl is shot in about ten fathoms, with no success, so we lash up and steam to a position around 120 miles off the Humber, where we are to spend the next two weeks. The gear that we are using is the beam trawl. This was usually shot over the port side of the vessel, whereas the later otter trawl was normally shot over the starboard side first, as the transverse thrust from the right handed propeller helped keep it clear of the gear. Shooting and hauling goes on continuously and during the time when the net is on the bottom, the deck gang are fully employed gutting, cleaning and stowing the catch below in the hold, ready for the next haul. Free time is unknown aboard a trawler when she is on the grounds and even when the fishing is slack, there are nets to be repaired. At sea, a trawlerman is exposed to long periods of hard physical labour in often extreme weather conditions, soaked to the skin, swept off their feet and rolled around the decks like rag dolls as sea after sea sweeps their small vessels. They are starved of sleep and fortified by a diet that even hardened convicts would call 'criminal'. Meat has to be towed astern to remove most of the salt content before being cooked. This and heavy suety puddings helped stave off hunger aboard a North Sea trawler of the 1800s. But even with these conditions, the life on board a single boater like *Sybil* was eminently superior to that aboard a 'fleeting' or 'boxing' trawler. The single boater enjoys at least two nights ashore out of twelve, whereas the 'fleeter' spends eight weeks afloat at a stretch.

The trawl was hauled at dawn on the third day, after towing most of the night. It broke surface, full to bursting point – a conservative estimate was around 60 baskets or 2 tons. Alas, this load was too much for our repeatedly repaired net and as it was being hoisted over the rail, it split wide open and over £40 worth of prime fish disappeared back into its natural element, providing a ready feast for the multitude of screaming gulls that appear from an empty sky immediately the trawl is hauled. After ten days fishing and the ice being all used up, the skipper heads for home. On the way in we pass other trawlers coming out; our skipper says, "*they're coming out to go home, we're going home to come out again*". The bunkers being low, he decides to make for Grimsby. Here the catch will be transferred into boxes, before being sold

Photo. 31: Model of *Chillian*. Note the two types of trawling gear. She has a raised bulwark at the break of the quarterdeck. She is a typical 'Hansom Cab', with open bridge, pole compass and hinged side light screens. Note her port side gallows and otter boards.

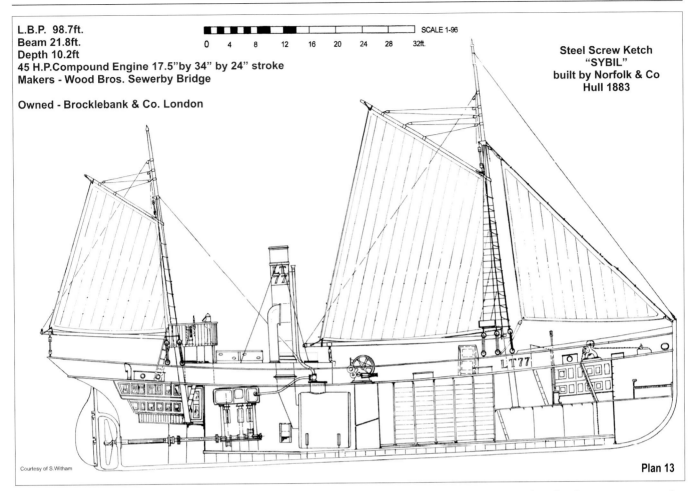

L.B.P. 98.7ft.
Beam 21.8ft.
Depth 10.2ft
45 H.P.Compound Engine 17.5"by 34" by 24" stroke
Makers - Wood Bros. Sewerby Bridge

Owned - Brocklebank & Co. London

SCALE 1-96
0 4 8 12 16 20 24 28 32ft.

Steel Screw Ketch
"SYBIL"
built by Norfolk & Co
Hull 1883

Courtesy of S.Witham

Plan 13

by dutch auction on the pontoon – the old Grimsby fish market. These sales are normally held between nine and ten o' clock every morning. Organised chaos ensues as the buyers hurry from one salesman to another, at the traditional cries of "*Turbot buyers, Cod buyers, Haddock buyers, and Lemon Sole buyers*". When the catch has been sold, we shift berth to take on coal, ice and stores ready for the next trip.

In 1894, *Sybil* was renamed *Bonito* but she was lost in the North Sea later that year.

ABERDEEN'S EARLY STEAM TRAWLERS

As the 1880s progressed, more owners were changing to steam. Minor almost unknown fishing ports, such as my hometown of Aberdeen, were transformed into flourishing trawling centres. The birth of the 'Granite City's' trawl industry took place in 1882, when a group of local businessmen formed a syndicate to purchase a steam trawler. These men comprised Robert Bowman, Robert Brown, John Barclay, Andrew Craig, Alex and George Collie, F. Henderson, John Matthews, William Morrison, William Pyper and William Smith. After their fruitless efforts to purchase a suitable vessel on the Clyde, they looked further afield and eventually found the object of their search in Ireland. *Toiler*, a wooden paddle tug built by Messrs Altringham & Co. on the Tyne, was eventually purchased from R. Tedcastle of Dublin for £1,550. The Irish crew were retained for the passage to Aberdeen and her engineer, J. O'Connor, was so attached to his charge that he decided to stay on with the ship. Her passage to Aberdeen was uneventful, passing through the Caledonian Canal, thereby

avoiding the dreaded Pentland Firth. After fitting out as a trawler, she sailed on her maiden trip on 22nd March, attempting one 'drag' in Aberdeen Bay. The resulting draught of fishes was by no means miraculous but it was large enough to warrant distribution among her owners and their friends. The following day, *Toiler* went fishing in earnest and returned to port with three boxes of haddock, which fetched the somewhat modest sum of £1 17s. Notwithstanding the preliminary difficulties experienced by the crew in operating the trawl gear, *Toiler* realised over £200 from her first month's trips. All this was before the days of the three mile limit, so no doubt she fished pretty close to the shore during her working up period. (This limit was traditionally the maximum range of a cannon ball and laid down by the International Law of the Seas.) The total for her first half year's operations amounted to £1,772 2s, out of which, after all expenses had been settled, left a surplus of £769 4s. The owners received 100% on the capital investment and the sum of £524 4s was divided amongst the crew as follows: Willian Watson (skipper) £127 18s 9d; James Harris (first fisherman) £100 6s 8d; Alexander Ross (second fisherman) £80 15s 9d; J. O'Connor (engineer) £88 8s 3d; John Irvine and Thomas Wilson (firemen) £63 8s 4d each. Alas this happy state of affairs was not to last for very long for the old clincher built vessel and repairs were inevitable. The final outcome was that after a thorough overhaul, the vessel landed up £1,000 in debt and the owners were more than willing to part with her. *Toiler* had made her point. Not only was she Aberdeen's first successful steam trawler, she inaugurated a new method of fish selling – by auction, which until that time was unknown in the city. She was sold for

£700 and finally met her end in the Moray Firth, on 31st March 1887, when she sank after fracturing a discharge pipe. She had left Aberdeen on 28th March but had to shelter from the weather in Fraserburgh the next day. Sailing again the following day, she ran into a severe NE gale off the Orkneys and was forced to run before it. The seas by this time were sweeping over the little ship, her boiler fires were swamped and she was taking a lot of water on board. Eventually dismasted, her exhausted seven man crew were rescued by the trawler *Royal Duke*, owned by Robert Brown of Aberdeen but registered at North Shields. *Toiler*'s oak trawl beam was later dragged up by her successor *North Star* and was taken to Hillhead, the residence of William Pyper, who had been the driving force behind the venture. Apparently, the first screw trawler came to the port in 1883. She was *Pioneer*, an ex-Scarborough vessel, although she did not appear in the registers for very long.

The first steam trawlers to be built at Aberdeen were *North Star* (A.393) and *Gypsy* (A.612 – both 105ft x 19ft x 10ft 4ins). *North Star* was launched from John Duthie's shipyard on 18th September 1883 and the builder's half model reputed to be of this vessel showed a very hybrid design. It had the elliptical counter stern of an iron or steel vessel, yet the hollow garboards common to sailing 'Fifies' and 'Zulus'. *Gypsy* was launched on the same day but one hour later. Their compound surface condensing engines (19ins, 38ins x 27ins, 60nhp) by Hall, Russells gave 14 knots (builder's launch report) and on sea trials, *Gypsy* ran at 12 knots over the measured mile. These two vessels were specially built for trawling and could remain at sea for up to ten days by curing their catch on board if necessary. *North Star*'s trawling trials were undertaken in the company of another eight trawlers from the Forth and Tyne, and the two owners, Messrs Pyper and Leslie, were well pleased with the experiment. Had the experiment failed, then the two ships could have been rapidly converted to their designed secondary role as screw tugs. From 29th September 1883 until May 1891, *North Star* landed fish to the total of £4,659. She was sold to Cardiff owners in August 1902. *Gypsy*, built for Messrs George Leslie & Co., was chartered by the government immediately after completion and was to remain in Aberdeen harbour until required for active service. With this commission duly executed, *Gypsy* was discharged and her owners handsomely reimbursed. This, needless to say, was a far more rewarding catch than she ever made trawling. Aberdeen's trawling fleet was growing steadily, backed up by steam drifters and long liners. Still in the background there remained a few paddle tug/trawlers, by now very work weary and finding it difficult to compete profitably with the screw vessels. One such vessel was *Bonito* (A.93 – 85ft x 19ft 4ins x 10ft 1in, 18n), built of iron at South Shields in 1878, with engines of 98ihp, and purchased from the Thames by Daniel Mearns and Thomas Walker. Her first skipper, Crombie, was later to become the harbourmaster at Aberdeen. The vessel appeared to be quite successful as a trawler but was regretfully lost one mile north of the River Ythan off Newburgh, on 20th December 1894. She was then only sixteen years old and relatively young for an iron vessel. By the time of her loss, however, her owners had convinced some of their friends as to the merits of the steam trawling industry.

There were of course many other converted screw and paddle tugs working out of Aberdeen in the 1880s. Two of the better known vessels were *Ben Ledi* (A.847 – 90ft x 18ft 6ins x 10ft 2ins) and *Coastguard* (A.619). The former was an iron paddle tug

built by Hall, Russells in 1878, for J.E. Gibb of Middlesex. She was purchased in 1883 by George Davidson (coal merchant) and managed by J. Newton of Aberdeen. *Coastguard* (78ft x 17ft 3ins x 9ft 3ins, 80g) was a wooden paddle tug built at Willington in 1876. She was bought from W. Dodds of South Shields in 1883 by Peter Johnstone, Nigg, Aberdeen and managed by William Meff & Co., who were later to become one of the port's leading managers of fishing vessels.

Subsequently, in 1884, John Fleming ordered *Gleneagles* (135ft 9ins x 23ft 2ins x 11ft 9ins, 207g) from Hall, Russells as Yard No. 238. This was their first venture into this field but proved to be the start of a trawler building programme that was to place the yard at the forefront of the industry. The vessel herself was quite large for the time, with one iron deck and four watertight bulkheads. She was fitted with a Menzies single barrel trawl winch and compound engines (22ins, 42ins x 27ins stroke). Built under special survey to Lloyds 100A1, she was launched on 24th May 1884. Although her principal design was that of a deep sea trawler, fish carrier and general cargo boat, she also had a Board of Trade passenger certificate. If and when the opportunity presented itself, she could be readily adapted for towing, lighterage or salvage duties and her large bunker capacity gave her a more extended range than other trawlers of the time. Her outfit included a full set of fore and aft sails, and a pair of beam trawls. On the homeward leg of her trials trip, when under the command of Captain James Grant, she rendered assistance to a small two man fishing boat that was anxious to reach port before the onset of darkness. After towing her for about two miles, the tow rope parted and, according to newspaper reports, *Gleneagles* rescued the crew and left the boat to sink. Little is known of her short fishing career, as in 1885 she was converted into a passenger ferry for Malta service.

Early in 1885, Thomas Walker had *St. Clement* (A.70 – 115ft 3ins x 21ft 1in x 11ft 1in, 165g) built by Hall, Russells as Yard No. 240. She was to become the standard size for Aberdeen's Near Water fleet until the demise of the steam sidewinder, known locally as 'scratchers'. In addition to forming the nucleus of the later Walker Steam Trawling Co. fleet, she was the first recorded steam trawler to be fitted with a refrigeration plant. This Type 'B' unit was supplied by J.&E. Hall of Dartford in Kent, at a cost of £450 and appeared to work well. It was, however, removed a few years later, as the Aberdeen ships only fished the Near Waters of the North Sea and the average trip duration did not warrant forfeiting the valuable fishroom space taken up by the equipment. *St. Clement* was sold in 1901 to the Stirling Boiler Co., Edinburgh, who fitted her with one of their 200psi square boilers. They converted her to a yacht/demonstration vessel and claimed a speed of 15-16 knots without additional coal consumption. In 1905, *St. Clement* was purchased by Vickers, Sons & Maxim Ltd, who used her as a tug with Barrow-on-Furness as her port of registry. In 1912, she was sold to France as *Pilote V*, operating as a tender for Dunkirk Pilots. Subsequently, she lay in Alexandra Dock, Hull from January 1919, when she arrived for repairs, until 1922 when the harbour authorities put her up for sale to clear unpaid berthing fees. She was bought by G.W. Pogson for £515 and joined the Grimsby fleet as *Pilote 5* (GY.104) on 15th December 1922. She was later fitted with another new boiler which gave her a speed of 10.5 knots. In May 1925, she was sold to Spanish owners S. Aldegandis. In 1931, she was owned by Angel Portalis of Santander as *Cantabro*

No. I and in 1933 she went to Valencia as *Kakau*, still registered as a fishing vessel. In early 1939, she was sunk in the harbour at Valencia but was re-floated in September 1940 and returned to fishing. She was finally lost off Corunna on 23rd November 1944.

Walkers next ships were *Star of Peace* (A.69) and *Star of the East*, costing around £3,000 each. Within a decade, the firm had a further eight new trawlers built by the Aberdeen yards of Hall, Russell, and John Duthie (Torry). From these handful of vessels, the Walker Steam Trawling Co. and their famous 'Stars' were to shine throughout the long history of the Granite City's trawling trade.

On 2nd October 1888, Alexander Hall of Aberdeen received their first order for a steam trawler, from Thomas Walker. *Maggie Walker* (A.259), Yard No. 329 (95ft bp x 20ft x 10ft 3ins, 117g), had a set of compound engines, supplied by the builders, of 50nhp. She cost £3,525, the breakdown of which was as follows:

Hull and steam winch £2,005 11s 11d

Engine £1,107 16s 9d

Boiler ....£ 411 13s 9d

Total building costs of £3,525 2s 5d gave a loss of £185 2s 5d on the contract.

Their next steam trawler was Yard No. 334 *St. Fotin* (A.392 – 100ft bp x 20ft 6ins x 10ft 6ins, 141g), also for Thomas Walker. She was slightly larger with a 58nhp compound engine, which was bought second hand for £650, having been removed from *St. Olaf* of Aberdeen. Halls made another loss with this vessel as the breakdown shows:

Hull...............................£2,276 13s

Engine and winch............£ 986 5s 10d

Boiler..............................£ 476. 11s 7d

Total building cost was £3,739 10s 5d, with the purchase price being £3,270, making a loss of £469 10s 5d. She was renamed *The Rose* in 1906 and operated as a tug for W.J. Guy of Cardiff but sank after a collision later that year. All these early steam trawlers would have initially been fitted with single barrel trawl winches and trawling ports in the bulwarks.

DUNDEE SHIPYARDS

South of Aberdeen at Dundee, on 3rd November 1885, two steam trawlers went down the ways of the Caledon Yard owned at that time by W.B. Thompson of Glasgow and Dundee. These two ships were Yard No. 76 *Lamberton* (95ft x 19ft x 10ft), with compound surface condensing engines (17ins, 34ins x 16ins stroke), and Yard No. 72, *Bonito* (A.93 – 90ft x 20ft x 9ft), with engines of (10.5ins, 15 ins, 27ins x 16ins stroke). Both ship's engines were rated at 78nhp:

The engines of the **Bonito**, *are the first to be made in Dundee of the Triple Expansion Type, and present several novel features not found in the ordinary two cylinder engine, nor in the ordinary three crank triple expansion engine. Designed and built by Mr. Thompson at the Tay foundry, they display a remarkable simplicity of construction, having no less than 40 fewer journals to attend to and lubricate, than is usual. The valve motion of each cylinder, is wrought off a single eccentric, in place of the double eccentric and link motion usually fitted.* MARINE ENGINEER *1885*

Both ships ran trials together in order to determine the comparative merits of their propelling machinery. Before leaving the dock, both bunkered 30cwt of Newcastle household coal. This was carefully weighed into sacks for use when raising steam and running trials. In close company, from the mouth of the Tay, the vessels steamed to the North Carr Beacon, from there to St. Andrews and back to Dundee, and all the while detailed measurements were taken to compare the two power units. The ihp of *Lamberton*, with a steam pressure of 90psi, was 155 at 65rpm and the coal consumption 24.5cwt, from laying the fires to the end of the trials. *Bonito*, with steam at 115psi, developed 123ihp at 104 revolutions, and consumed 21.25 cwts. of coal over the same period. Both trawlers were rigged as 'fore and aft schooners', carrying enough canvas to run under sail alone if needs be. Although they were fitted out specifically for beam trawling and their main fish rooms had divisions for both fish and ice, they were also fitted with towing hooks and rails. A steam winch was fitted abaft the foremast, providing the necessary power for gear hauling, with a hand windlass forward for the anchor. A teak companionway led down to the crew's accommodation in the fo'c'sle, whilst a cabin aft housed the skipper, mate and engineer. The steering gear fitted over the boiler casing. Built to the highest Lloyd's classification and equipped to Board of Trade regulations. *Lamberton* went to Berwick on Tweed, although she was owned by the General Steam Fishing Co. Ltd of Granton and registered as GN.24. *Bonito* went to the Lowestoft Steam Fishing & Carrying Co. There was an even earlier screw trawler *Bonito* (SN.1168), which arrived at North Shields in 1881 and was the first such vessel to work from the port. Built originally at South Shields as a screw tug and later converted for trawling, she moved to Aberdeen in 1884 as A.93 owned by Thomas Walker but was lost by stranding at Newburgh on 20th December that year. The local lifeboat attempted to rescue her seven man crew and returned to the vessel hoping to salvage her with the assistance of the tug *Fairweather*. The weather deteriorated and *Bonito*'s crew had to be finally brought ashore by Collieston Life Saving Apparatus.

These were not the first steam trawlers to be built by Thompson's. Their very first steam trawler was *Snowdrop* (DE.587 – 96ft x 20ft x 9ft, 44nhp), owned by W.H. Burn of Dundee. She was an iron screw steamer and, on trials on 29th April 1885, she attained 11 knots. Another of their early vessels of 1886 was Yard No. 75 *Dalhousie* (90ft, 89g), built for W.B. Thompson. She was an iron vessel, later going to Scarborough as *Dalhousie* (SH.72) and owned by G. Alderson-Smith in 1910. The company's last and largest British steam fishing vessel was Yard No. 78 *Jubilee*, a carrier to the order of the Great Northern Steamship Fishing Co. Ltd of Hull in 1887.

The neighbouring Panmure Yard of Dundee Shipbuilders launched their first steam powered fishing vessel in 1896. She was the small 40 ton *Marie* for France, with 25nhp compound engines. Their next steamer in 1897 was *Largo Bay* (KY.575 – 130g/40nhp) for the Bay Fishing Co., Anstruther. By 1901, she was owned in Aberdeen by J.A. Harrow, as *Largo Bay* (A.372), later going to the North Star Fishing Co. Ltd. She was sunk by gunfire from an enemy U-boat on 12th April 1917, about 30 miles NE of Peterhead. She had a sister ship, *Curlew* (DE.91), built for the Tay Steam Line Fishing Co. Ltd the same year. She came to Aberdeen in September 1903 as A.906, owned by A.W. Ritchie of Ferry Road, Torry. Later, in 1907, skipper J. King took her over.

She was lost while entering Aberdeen in a SW gale on 3rd February 1922. All her crew were rescued by breeches buoy but she became a total loss. In 1898, the Panmure Yard launched five steam liners for Grimsby owners, of which the first four were: *Nellie Bruce* (GY.494) and *Conisbro' Castle* (GY.533) for the Crampin Steam Fishing Co. Ltd, Grimsby; and *Honoria* (GY.693) and *Hilaria* (GY.698) for the Rushworth Steam Trawling Co. Ltd. They were all sister ships (112ft, 180g, 60nhp) and were fitted with wells for keeping the catch alive until it reached market. The fifth vessel was *Magic* (GY.586 – 108ft, 160n, 57nhp), built for the Atlantic Steam Fishing Co. Ltd, Grimsby. The company's largest pre-1900 trawler/liner was *Balmoral Castle* (GY.530 – 125ft, 269g, 540ihp), launched in 1899 for the Castle Line Steam Fishing Co. Ltd, Grimsby. In June 1908, she was sold to Holland but returned to Grimsby the following year as *Friesland* (GY.459), owned by A. South. In 1914, she went to a group of local owners and on 12th May 1921, she sank some 25 miles off the mouth of the Humber.

FORTH SHIPYARDS

On 13th June 1885, the forerunner of a fleet of steam trawlers for the Pioneer Steam Fishing Co. Ltd, South Shields, was launched from the yard of Marr Brothers of Leith. *Pioneer* was a wooden trawler 74ft long overall. After her launch, she was towed to North Shields for her machinery to be installed. A somewhat larger wooden steam trawler, *Degrave I* (110ft x 20ft 6ins x 9ft 6ins), was launched a month previously by Allans of Granton, with engines by Hutson & Corbett of 35nhp. She was one of the first steam trawlers to be built for Ostende owners, a port that in future years was to have many trawlers built in the UK. Another Forth shipbuilder, J. McKenzie of Leith, launched the wooden steamer *Evelyn* (67ft x 17ft x 8ft 6in) for Messrs Hawthorn & Clarke of Leith; engined by Cranns, she was designed for deep sea net and line fishing. From the foregoing, one tends to assume that the builders on the Firth of Forth concentrated solely on wooden vessels. This of course is untrue.

In 1883, Hawthorn & Co. of Leith, launched the screw trawlers *Bruce* (GN.10) and *Wallace* (GN.12), part of an order for four iron steam trawlers for the General Steam Fishing Co. Ltd, Granton, the other vessels being *Buccleugh* (GN.6) and *Roseberry* (GN.8).

'The late Mr R.W. Duff of Fetteresso, Member of Parliament for Banffshire, wrote a letter to the newspapers pointing out that, in his opinion, the time had come for the introduction of steam in the catching of fish and to further evince his interest in the matter, he started a company at Granton called the General Steam Fishing Company Ltd. This company is still in existence. It has had its ups and downs but at present it is still to the fore. The irony of fate was notably exemplified in Mr Duff's subsequent attitude on fishery affairs, for both in and out of the House of Commons, he was one of the bitterest opponents of trawling, and took part in advocating the closing of the Moray Firth, which has fomented so much angry controversy.' PEOPLES JOURNAL *1903*

The company's first four vessels measured 92ft x 18ft x 9ft 6ins, 102g, with compound surface condensing engines developing 32nhp, at 70psi. Another two of their early trawlers were constructed of iron by Scott of Bowling, as Yard No's 85 and 86,

in 1891: *Breadalbane* (GN.32) and *Athole* (GN.35). By 1895, the port of Granton had some nineteen steam trawlers on the register. Yet another Forth-built steam trawler of 1883 was *Jane Buchan* (102ft x 20ft x 10ft, 40nhp). She was launched by William Jarvis of Anstruther for Inverbervie owners.

HUMBER SHIPYARDS

The demand for steam trawlers was increasing steadily and, by the start of the 1890s, Cochrane & Cooper at Beverley had launched twenty-one such vessels. These included yard No. 23 *Rob Roy* (H.91 – 105ft 7ins x 20ft 7ins x 10ft 9ins) for Pickering & Haldane's Steam Trawling Co. Ltd; they sold her in 1905 to R. Turnbull of Hartlepool as HL.80 and she foundered some seven years later in the North Sea. Other vessels included two well boats, No's 26 and 27 *Azalea* (GY.199) and *Begonia* (GY.210), for the North Eastern Steam Fishing Co. Ltd, Grimsby, with their engines supplied by C.D. Holmes. The former met her end in June 1897 after running ashore at Stroma, whereas her sister lasted until March 1908, when she too became a total loss after going ashore on the Pig & Sow Rocks near Blyth. Two larger vessels of 1886 were No's 13 and 14, *New Zealand* (117ft x 22ft x 11ft 2ins) and *Canada* (H.1) for the Hull Steam Fishing & Ice Co. Ltd. Laid down as fish carriers, they were much larger than the trawlers of the period. *New Zealand* finished as a coaster for HM Government and her sister worked as a carrier until sold and converted to a coaster by Guernsey owners W.&S. Henval.

The other famous Yorkshire yard of Cook, Welton & Gemmell were busy building steam trawlers from their shipyard at Hull; the company operated from Hull until moving to the Grovehill shipyard at Beverley – Andrew Cochrane's old yard. The year of 1890 marked the turning point for the firm, when for the first time, more than twelve trawlers were completed in any one year. In the years between 1884 and 1900, the company finished a total of 221 steam trawlers. The yard's first such vessel and, incidentally, the first steam trawler to sail out of Hull, was Yard No. 3 of 1885, *Magneta* (H.1447 – 95ft 7ins x 20ft 4ins x 9ft 5ins), for Francis & Thomas Ross Ltd, Hull. Quite a small vessel, engined by C.D. Holmes (16ins, 30ins x 22ins), she was lost on 24th January 1908 off Scarborough. In 1889, the company launched their first vessel fitted with a triple expansion engine, No. 36 *Torfrida* (106ft x 19ft 5ins x 11ft, 126g). Her engines by C. D. Holmes were 14ins, 22ins, 36ins x 22ins stroke, developing 75nhp at 150psi. She was followed by *Undine* (GY.204), an iron well boat for the Grimsby Union Steam Fishing Co. Ltd.

The steam powered fishing vessel was fast finding favour throughout the whole of the fishing community. These tough little ships, built for both speed and seaworthiness, were held in high regard by skippers. It was said around the early 1880s that '*No seriously minded fish merchant should be without one*'. It was possibly after hearing these words that, in 1891, Joseph Marr ordered his first steam trawler from Cochrane & Cooper at Beverley, aptly named *Marrs*, Yard No. 59 (100.8ft x 20.5ft x 11ft, 153.7g) with engines by C.D. Holmes. Her sister ships were *Kittiwake* and *Cormorant*, for Pickering & Haldane's Steam Trawling Co. Ltd, and *Ampere* for Francis & Thomas Ross Ltd. *Marrs* (H.172) transferred to Fleetwood in 1898 as FD.31. She was sold in 1919 to France, renamed *Le Barre* and sank after a collision in 1921. *Kittiwake* (H.149) transferred to Deep Sea Trawlers Ltd of

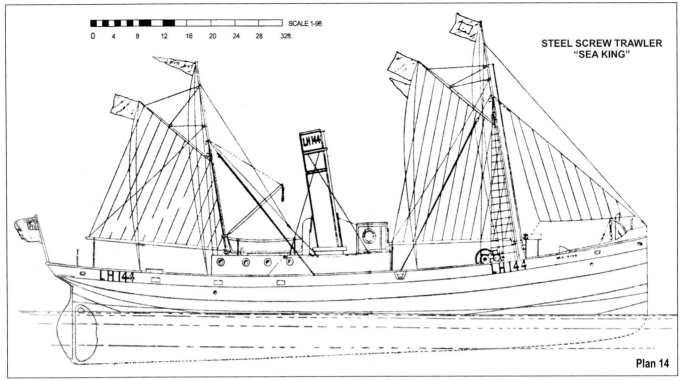

SCALE 1-96
0 4 8 12 16 20 24 28 32ft.

STEEL SCREW TRAWLER
"SEA KING"

Plan 14

Fleetwood in 1907 as FD.146. They sold her to Patons of Glasgow in 1909, who renumbered her GW.24. Two years later she went to Aberdeen as A.469. By 1919 she had gone south to Lowestoft owners W. Mullender as LT.378, who sold her to C. Duttant in 1926. She ended her days fishing for E. Hellings of Milford Haven as M.87, going to the breakers in 1933. Her sister **Cormorant** (H.156) was sold to the Port of Blyth Steam Fishing & Ice Co. Ltd in 1911 as BH.81. She was purchased by A. Smith and others at Grimsby in 1915 and renamed **Niblick** (GY.520). By 1918, she was under H. Wood of Grimsby's colours, eventually going for scrap in 1924. **Ampere** (H.169) was sold to Consolidated Fisheries Ltd of Lowestoft in 1925 as LT.184, going to the breakers in 1938.

The launch reports were also changing in favour of the steam trawler. No longer were they terse paragraphs in the shipping columns as the following extract shows:

*'The **Sea King** LH.144, [Plan.14] which was launched during the month of May, from the shipbuilding yard of Messrs. Cumming and Ellis, Inverkeithing, is of the following dimensions: Length 112ft; Breadth 21ft; Depth 11ft; and is fitted with Triple Expansion engines which indicated on her official trial slightly over 520HP. As will be seen from the illustrations, she is Ketch rigged, with a clear unbroken deck line right fore and aft, giving the greatest possible facility for handling the trawl nets, and also for passing the fish into the hold situated forward, and separated from the crews quarters by a commodious ice hold. A fresh water tank is also fitted forward to be used as a supplementary feed to the main boiler, as well as a ballast tank for trimming the vessel, whilst aft is fitted a large ballast tank, used for adjusting the trim of the vessel as the fish hold is filled and emptied. A large Humber steam winch, having double cylinders 7inches by 12inches, has been supplied by Messrs. Clarke, Chapman & Co, and this is placed forward of the main hatch, where it can be utilised for the discharge of the cargo. All other appliances about*

the decks are of the most modern and improved description. The accommodation for the crew is also on a more elaborate scale than obtains in ordinary trawlers. The after part of the vessel is fitted up for the Captain, Officers, etc. The Captain and Engineer are berthed in separate state rooms, whilst the remainder of the after part is arranged as a saloon with two berths on either side. This saloon is handsomely fitted up in solid, polished wainscot oak, with panels of floral lincrusta tastefully tinted and picked out in suitable colours, the ceiling being painted in flat white, with tinted beam moulding. A handsome tiled fireplace is also fitted in the forward part, with ornamental and bevel edged mirrors. A sofa of the best crimson American leather is fitted all round the saloon, and all the other furnishings are in keeping with the parts already detailed. Access to the saloon is obtained by a commodious entrance formed by the extension of the engine and boiler casings. Forward of the engine and boiler space is the fish hold, suitably fitted up for the storage of fish; also a large ice hold, for the purpose of preservation when required. In the forepart of the vessel are berthed the deckhands, this place being neatly fitted up with berths, seats, lockers etc., and also with a large stove of the most modern description. The engine power has exceeded the guarantee, and has proved itself capable of propelling the vessel at a mean speed of 12.5 knots per hour, making her one of, if not the fastest trawler in the world.' MARINE ENGINEER 1893

LATER ABERDEEN TRAWLERS.

In Aberdeen, Hall, Russells were responsible for some notably fine vessels in the 1890s, such as **Belcher** and **Bendigo**, **North Briton** and **North American**, **John Brown**, **Strathdon** and **Strathtay**. **Bendigo**, Yard No. 274, and **Belcher**, Yard No. 278, were built for John Wilson, South Shields in 1893, at a cost of £3,850 each and registered as SS.13 and SS.15 respectively. Both vessels were fitted with a patent Menzies special trawling winch. In April 1901, both these ships went home to Aberdeen as A.338, and A.341, owned

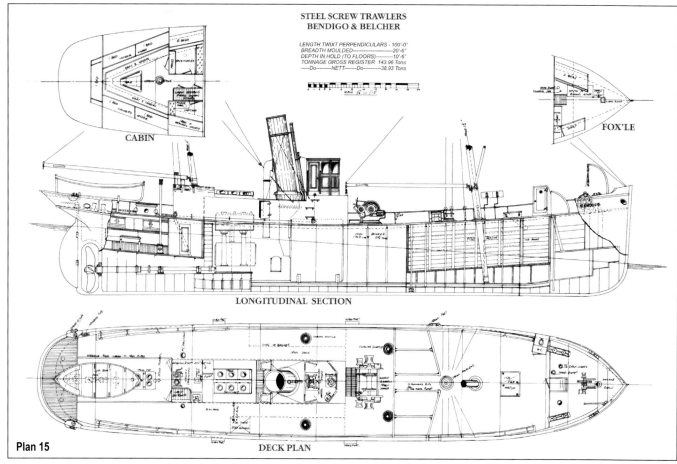

STEEL SCREW TRAWLERS
BENDIGO & BELCHER

LENGTH TWIXT PERPENDICULARS - 100'-0"
BREADTH MOULDED-----------------20'-6"
DEPTH IN HOLD (TO FLOORS)----------10'-6"
TONNAGE GROSS REGISTER 143.96 Tons
----Do--------NETT-----Do------- 38.93 Tons

CABIN

FOX'LE

LONGITUDINAL SECTION

Plan 15

DECK PLAN

by Peter Johnstone & Co. Ltd, Aberdeen. *Bendigo* (**Plan 15**) was owned in 1910 by W. Lyle, & W. Carlie, Leith as GN.2. *Belcher* met her end on 4th September 1903, when she ran ashore just north of Collieston with no loss of life. The mate was later charged with negligent seamanship at Aberdeen Sheriff Court and the wreck was sold for £3 10s to a Leeds salvage firm – an ignominious end for a fine early trawler.

The builder's drawing of *Bendigo* shows a small flush decked beam trawler (100ft x 20ft 6ins x 10ft 6ins, 144g). The main deck is unsheathed, which must have made it very slippery when awash with fish slime. Right in the eyes of the ship is a small raised anchor deck, a hand anchor windlass and a davit for handling the fisherman type anchor. Immediately abaft the windlass is the central companionway leading down to the crew's fo'c'sle. This tiny compartment is fitted with only two bunks; these are shared with shelves for lamps and small gear. The deck is pierced by two hatches leading down to the chain locker and the bosun's store, with the chain pipe passing up through the forward part of the fo'c'sle. On the main deck to port is a WC (quite an innovation aboard such a vessel in the 1890s). A joint fish room and ice room hatch is placed amidships between the companionway and the foremast, with a portable shoot fitted for filling the ice room. A single barrel steam trawl winch is positioned in front of the casing, with the trawl warp leading forward to the central roller fairlead, thence out through either the port or starboard trawl ports in the bulwarks. A portable hand bilge pump, and a sounding pipe is fitted. The casing has a small wooden panelled wheelhouse at its forward end, entered via three steps fitted to the casing side. This housed the hand steering gear, binnacle and engine room telegraph. Although

the *Bendigo* plan does not show a compass on the wheelhouse top, that of her sister does. She was an 'aft side job', with doors fitted to either side of the casing for ash removal. The engine room skylight sits on the casing top above her 50nhp compound engines. The cost of this machinery could be broken down as follows: Boiler, £54; Feed water heater, £7; Air, feed and bilge pumps, £198; and engines £1,276. Entrance to the engine room is through the galley at the after end of the casing and down a stairway on the port side. The steel galley floor is cemented over, a coal fired range sits against the aft bulkhead, the heel of of the mizzen mast sits alongside a small hand operated fresh water pump and a coal box is fitted to starboard. The aft cabin is entered through a 'stable' door on the starboard aft face of the casing, then down a stairway to a small lobby with a door into the skipper's berth and another leading into the after cabin. To port is another small two berth cabin for the engineers and the main cabin is fitted with five berths, padded bench seats with lockers under, a triangular table where all the crew took their meals and a coal fired bogey stove for heating. On deck, she is fitted with a single 16ft double ended ship's boat. Her bulwark stays are of round bar section rather than the later bulb plate type and her masts are set up with deadeyes and lanyards. Her foremast is fitted with a fish derrick.

North Briton (PD.487), owned by W.H. Leask, Aberdeen, and *North American* (PD.485), managed by William Pyper of Aberdeen and owned by J.G.A. Stephen & W. McKenzie of Peterhead, were two very small steam liners built by the yard in 1894, as No's 279 and 280, at a cost of £2,850 each (a sailing trawler would have cost about £560 around this time). They measured 86ft x 19ft x 9ft 3ins and were powered by compound engines of 40nhp. In view

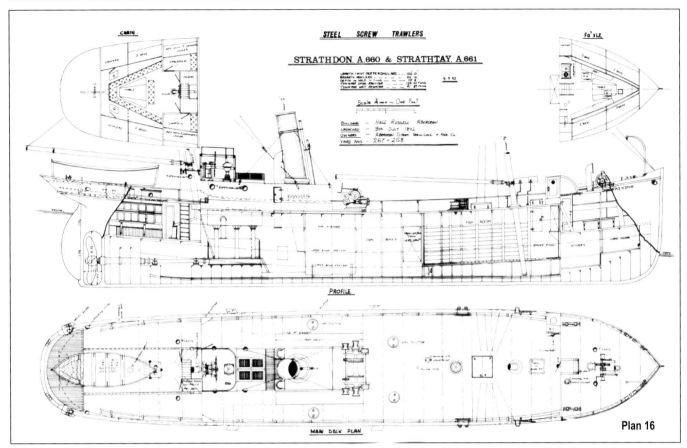

of their size (and port of registry), it seems probable that they were not a success as liners but they were able to be easily converted to trawlers or herring drifters – the builder's cost book shows an entry for '*alterations and additions for converting boats into trawlers as well as line fishers, £140 each*'. Their layout was similar to the above trawlers but there was no accommodation forward, only a store with a WC to starboard. On deck they had separate ice and fish room hatches, the former so placed that it could be used as a rope room hatch when working drift nets. Only three coal bunker lids are shown and the ship's boat is transom sterned. The wheelhouse is very drifter-like, with a door on the port side leading on to the casing but the most interesting feature of all on the drawing is the small hand hole to the safety valve immediately outside this door. *John Brown* (A.744 – 102ft x 21ft 6ins x 11ft) was the first vessel

Painting 2: A.661 *Strathtay* from a painting by the Aberdeen artist A. Harwood, showing crudely painted aft otter board.

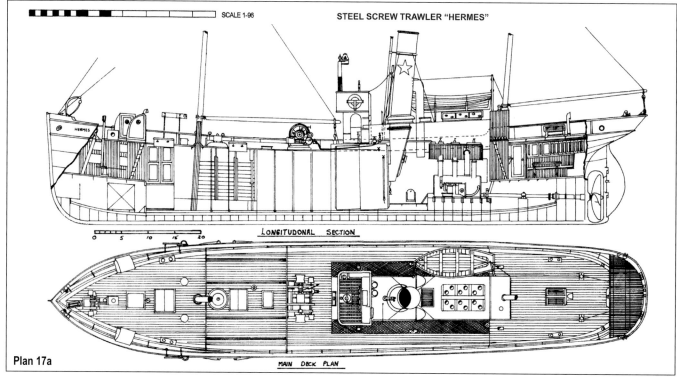

SCALE 1-96

STEEL SCREW TRAWLER "HERMES"

LONGITUDONAL SECTION

MAIN DECK PLAN

Plan 17a

to be ordered for the Aberdeen Steam Trawling & Fishing Co. Ltd on 15th December 1893. Named after the firm's manager, she cost £4,200, with triple expansion surface condensing engines of 14ins, 18ins, 30ins x 21ins stroke. She was a flush decked 'aft sider' and her drawing differs little from that of *Bendigo*, with the exception of a separate hatch for the ice room.

Strathdon (A.660) and *Strathtay* (A.661 – **Plan 16**) were the company's next two ships from Hall, Russell and, like *John Brown*, they were originally rigged as beam trawlers. Although built as 'Hansom Cabs', their open bridges were soon closed in and the well known local marine artist A. Harwood painted *Strathtay* with the later wheelhouse. I had the opportunity of viewing this

painting at an exhibition and someone had crudely added an otter board hanging over her port quarter but no gallows are evident.

The builder's drawing shows trawling ports cut into the bulwarks (otter boards could have been handled by means of a tackle set up from the masthead). *Strathtay* disappeared without trace in a severe gale off the Shetlands in 1900 and only recently has the true position of her wreck been established. Fifteen steam trawlers from Hull and Aberdeen were lost in the vicinity of Sumburgh Head on the night of 14th February 1900. One of these vessels was observed in difficulties under the lee of Horse Isle off Scatness. This was believed to be *Albatross* of Hull, as a lifebuoy bearing her name was later found on the foreshore but it

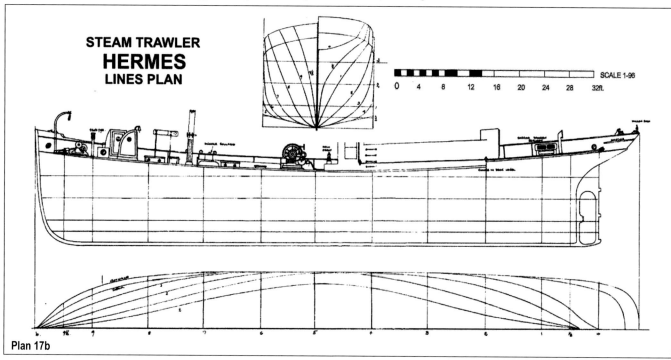

STEAM TRAWLER
HERMES
LINES PLAN

SCALE 1-96

0   4   8   12   16   20   24   28   32ft.

Plan 17b

Plan 18

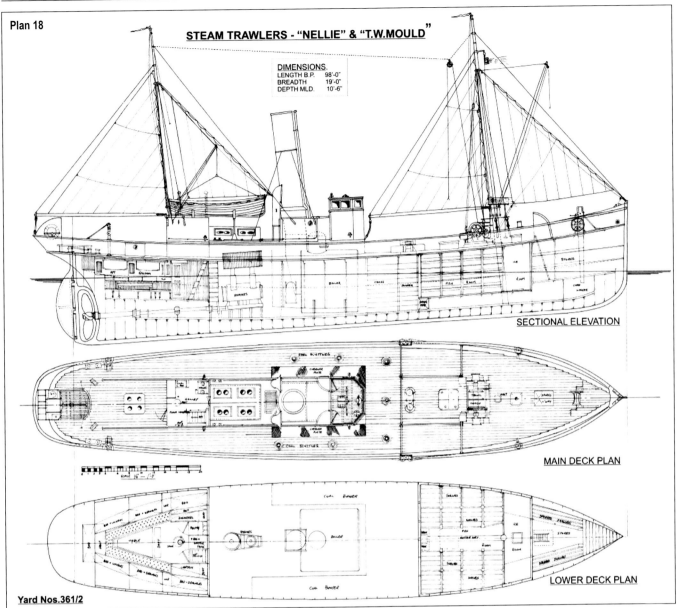

STEAM TRAWLERS - "NELLIE" & "T.W.MOULD"

DIMENSIONS.
LENGTH B.P.   98'-0"
BREADTH   19'-0"
DEPTH MLD.   10'-6"

SECTIONAL ELEVATION

MAIN DECK PLAN

LOWER DECK PLAN

Yard Nos.361/2

was not until 1977, when a builder's plate was salvaged, that the wreck was most certainly identified as *Strathtay* (A.661), the only Hall, Russell trawler to be built in 1891 and lost at that time. The other Hull trawlers lost were *Bermuda* (H.296), *Cyprus* (H.198), *Deerhound* (H.81), *Falcon* (H.321) and *Indian Empire* (H.369). This was indeed a black night in trawler history, when around 150 men were lost – a high price to pay but one that was to be dearly paid time after time, as men worked their ships in what could only be described as the world's most extreme occupation.

In March 1894, Alexander Hall of Aberdeen launched their largest and most powerful steam trawler to date. *Hermes* (H.200), Yard No. 357 (104ft bp x 20ft 5ins x 11ft 3ins), was built for the Anglo Norwegian Steam Fishing Co. Ltd, Hull (**Plan 17a & b**). It was constructed of mild steel in excess of Lloyd's highest class. The drawing of the vessel (drawn the opposite way to normal) shows a schooner rigged beam trawler, with a quarterdeck and a casing over the boiler and engines. A galley was fitted below the bridge and on deck she has a heavy duty single barrel trawl winch, with Sudron's patent revolving trawl ports and dandy scores aft. She followed the normal practice of having her ice and fish

rooms as one, and fitted out with pound and shelf boards. Her engines (12ins, 19ins, 32.25ins x 24.5ins stroke) were fitted with fully adjustable double bar type valve gear. The HP valve was a piston type with floating rings, while the IP and LP valves were the normal single ported type. The high and intermediate cylinders were fitted with Ramsbottom rings and the low pressure cylinder with Elliot's rings. The boiler measured 11ft 6ins diameter by 10ft long and was fitted with Purves Patent ribbed furnaces. There were two separate combustion chambers with rounded tops, stiffened with 'T' section iron girders. The boiler had a working pressure of 160psi, a total heating surface of 1150 sq. ft and a grate area of 40.25 sq. ft. The auxiliary machinery included feed heating installation, a Worthington pump, an ejector and a Kirkcaldy's fresh water evaporator. On trials the engines developed 413.3ihp at 10.5 knots.

Launch days at Aberdeen were always a social occasion, with the families of all the shipyard workers present. The youngest apprentice was usually sent to purchase the necessary bottle of 'christening wine' and I have it on good account that the vintage of the bottle that smashed against the ships stem was, more often

Painting 3: *Gloxinia*, showing a wheelhouse in place of the original open bridge and pole compass. COURTESY S. FARROW

than not, of a rather dubious nature – being the product of smaller almost unknown vineyards with vaguely familiar sounding local names. The launches at the John Duthies Yard in Torry were even more of an event. Greyhope Road, the main coast road that ran in front of the yard, was closed to all vehicular traffic and portable skids or launching ways were rigged up, connecting those of the shipyard to their corresponding sets on the foreshore. This spot was little more that a small patch of sand about the size of a council house front garden, affectionately known locally as 'the Sannies'.

SOUTH OF THE BORDER

In 1898, R.&W. Hawthorn Leslie & Co. Ltd of Hebburn on Tyne launched two sister ships, Yard No's 361 and 362 – *Nellie* (SN.254) for George Stephenson, North Shields, and *T.W. Mould* (SN.255) for Robert Mould, North Shields (**Plan 18**).

They were small perky looking ships (98ft bp x 19ft x 10ft 6ins, 109g), with compound engines of 39nhp. The original coloured shipyard drawing shows a simple early otter board type trawler. The double barrel trawl winch is tucked up close to the foremast, with a set of triple trawl rollers on the centre line. No gallows are fitted, the warps passing out through ports in the bulwarks and over towing posts aft, and they are rigged for working the gear from either side. These after posts were used in conjunction with a tackle at the mast head, for handling the heavy otter boards when shooting and hauling. The casing is very low for a trawler, only about a foot higher than the bulwarks, but there is a higher boiler casing, carrying the funnel, with the forward end scalloped at either side to allow entry into the wheelhouse. This small compartment has the bare necessities of wheel, compass and telegraph. The hand steering gear is connected to the rudder head by chains and rods, and to put the wheel hard over from port to starboard required twenty-six turns. A single ship's boat sits on cradles, with its aft end on top of the galley and the other over the

skylight. On each side of the wheelhouse and galley can be seen the top sheaves for the messenger wires. On the flush main deck there is a small hand windlass, set between two wooden knightheads, which are further supported by two iron or steel straps running forward. Aft of this is the forward companionway leading down to the net store. A watertight bulkhead separates this from the ice room, with its small access hatch on deck. No forward deck bollards are shown but mooring posts are fitted on the bulwarks in line with this hatch. A larger hatch just behind the winch leads to the fish room, fitted out with pounds and shelves for the catch. For their size these trawlers had considerable bunker capacity. The after accommodation was entered through the starboard side of the galley and down a wooden stairway. It was here that the small crew of seven men lived, rested and took their meals when at sea. The WC was fitted in the poop house and shared with the lamp room. The two nicely raked masts are set up with deadeyes and lanyards and a 24ft fish derrick is fitted to the foremast. Between the masts is what appears to be a chain span, with a gin block and tackle for discharging the catch. *Nellie* was captured on April Fool's day 1915, by a German submarine while fishing some 35 mile NE by E of the River Tyne. The crew escaped in the trawler's boat but the ship herself was sunk by enemy scuttling charges. Her sister was sunk by a mine on 1st December 1915, some 30 miles off the River Tyne; there were no survivors.

This yard only built two more steam trawlers, both in 1898, as Yard No's 363 and 365: *Rhodesia* (SN.258) and *Valentia* both for Richard Irvin & Sons Ltd, North Shields.

Another north east of England shipyard also making a name for itself around this time was the North Shields firm of Edwards Brothers. They became Smiths Dock Co. Ltd in 1899 and later moved to Middlesborough, building many first class steam trawlers and drifters, for which they received the following awards: Silver medal in 1894 at the Exposition Universelle D'Anvers and a

Highest award 1898 at the Bergen Fisheries Exhibition. In 1895, the yard launched the screw beam trawler *Lythie* (FD.140 – 105ft) and, in 1896, they built five 'Flower' Class steam trawlers for the Southern Trawling Co. Ltd, Waterford, who were actually based at Milford Haven: *Fuschia* (M.127), *Gloxinia* (M.126), *Ixia* (M.131), *Japonica* (M.133) and *Hydrangea*. This same year they also built the steam fleeter *Tynemouth* (GY.163), which was lost on 13th April 1902 after running aground at Bempton Cliffs in Yorkshire, and the fish carrier *Swift* (FD.170 – **Photo. 32**) for Brixham Trawlers Ltd. She went to Hull in 1910 as H.99, owned by Kelsall Brothers & Beeching Ltd, Hull, until she was scrapped in 1936. *Minotaur* (GY. 840), built in 1898, was a small inshore steam trawler belonging to J.R. Mackrill, Grimsby. An interesting feature of the vessel is the absence of fore gallows, trawling sheaves being fitted to the bulwarks in their place. This ship went missing on 31st March 1915 in the North Sea with no survivors. Another handsome pair built by the company in 1898, for the Grimsby & North Sea Steam Trawling Co. Ltd, were the trawlers *Capricornus* (GY.750) and *Aquarius* (GY.714) both 114ft 2ins x 21ft 1in x 11ft 2ins, 80n. *Capricornus* was lost in 1914.

The Grimsby & North Sea Steam Trawling Company possibly used them as fleeters – although, and because they were fitted with fish wells, they may have gone single boating. Noticeable features on the plan are the stepped down keelson and the anti surge plates in the fish well. *Aquarius* went ashore south off Withernsea on Christmas Day 1904, becoming a total loss, and was replaced by another of the same name, GY.76. This **Aquarius** was hired for two months in 1915 by the Admiralty and her end came on 25th February 1945, when she struck a mine some 15 miles SE of the Outer Dowsing Light Vessel. *Capricornus* (GY. 750) was sunk by a German torpedo boat, 85 miles E by N of Spurn Point, on 22nd August 1914. These types of trawlers were often referred to as 'Camels' or 'Hansom Cabs' and were popular with English owners but the type never found favour in Scotland. *Minotaur* was an 'aft side job', fired from the engine room, with *Aquarius* and *Capricornus* being more conventional 'foresiders', fired from the fore end of the boiler.

In 1889, William Harkess of Middlesborough entered into an agreement with the Western Steam Trawling Co. Ltd of Bristol for the construction of two steam trawlers. These were yard No's 123 and 124, *Dartmouth* (BL.3) and *Avonmouth* (BL.4). The price for both ships was £7,796 and they were the first new steam trawlers to be registered in the south west. The driving force behind the Bristol company was Frederick Sellick, who saw that there were advantages to be gained by using the new fish dock at Milford Haven for steam powered trawlers. His first ship, *Bournemouth* (BL.2), was an ex-Hellyer's vessel from Hull, which had been built by Cook, Welton & Gemmell in 1887.

When Sellick entered into the contract for *Dartmouth* and her sister, he had somehow acquired a compound marine steam engine complete with boiler, which he supplied to the shipyard for the first vessel. In recognition, the builder awarded him £3,000. This comprised £1,000 in cash for the machinery and a further £2,000 in shares. This would prove a shrewd move as he was the only person in the company with the necessary skill to make it viable. Although all the vessels of the fleet were registered at Bristol, they worked principally out of Milford and fished mostly the Irish Sea grounds and later the west coast grounds off Scotland. When some of the vessels were transferred to Fleetwood after the First World War, they would fish as far afield as Iceland.

PLYMOUTH

Plymouth had a small trawling fleet which worked until the 1950s. In 1889, J.H. Luxton of Plymouth took delivery of the port's first steam trawler. She was *Reginald* (PH.75 – 110ft 7ins x 21ft x 11ft 2ins, 191g) and 55nhp, built of iron at Selby. She apparently led a charmed life, surviving a stranding on the 'break up coast of Scilly' in 1895, when she ran ashore SE of St. Marys in thick fog. At low water, her crew left the trawler and made a boiling of tea for themselves ashore. She was refloated at high tide with only minor damage.

As the industry entered the final decade of the 19th century, steam trawlers were growing in both size and number. These advances were brought about by the gradual decline of the sailing

Photo. 32: The fish carrier **Swift**. Note her open bridge with pole compass, quarterdeck flush with the rail, large winch abaft the foremast and lack of gallows. She has a black hull and funnel, with a small red bird on a white flag.

Plan 19a

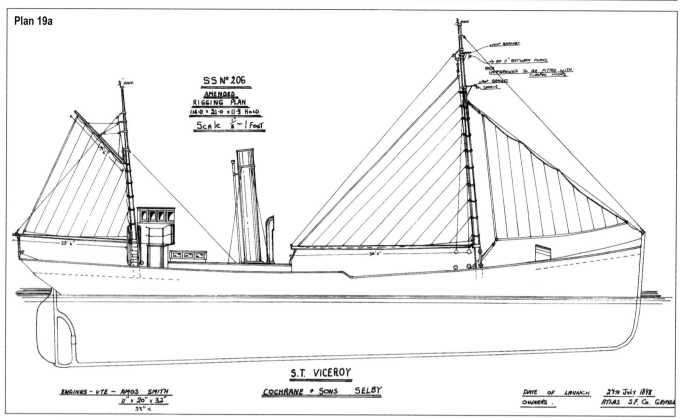

GENERAL ARRANGEMENT - VICEROY & CASSOWARY
Yard Nos. 206/7
Scale 1/8in - 1ft

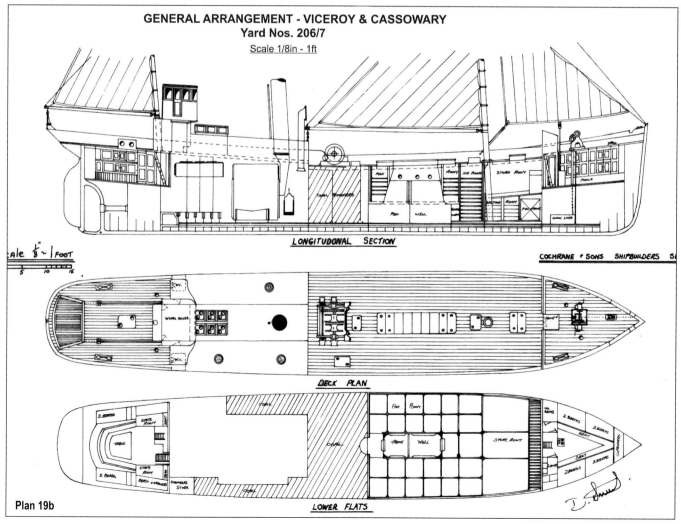

Plan 19b

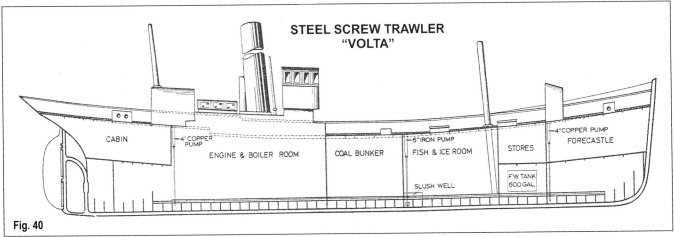

STEEL SCREW TRAWLER
"VOLTA"

CABIN — 4"COPPER PUMP — ENGINE & BOILER ROOM — COAL BUNKER — 6"IRON PUMP — FISH & ICE ROOM — SLUSH WELL — STORES — F.W. TANK 600 GAL — 4"COPPER PUMP — FORECASTLE

Fig. 40

smack and the demise of the older paddle tugs. Another factor was the opening up of more Distant Water fishing grounds and the introduction of the otter trawl. Until its introduction, the maximum length for a sailing trawler was 78ft overall, using a 50ft wide beam trawl. With the otter trawl, ships gradually grew in size until they reached over 200ft long. Specialist trawler builders were evolving along with engine builders. The compound engine was being replaced by the triple expansion type and dedicated engine builders such as Amos & Smith, Hall, Russell, Cooper & Co. and C.D. Holmes, etc, were to become familiar names to the trawler engineer.

Two of the larger steamers (other than fish carriers) built by Cochranes in 1899 were the fish well boats *King Harald* (GY.1097) and *King Erik* (GY.786), Yard No's 232 and 233 respectively (114ft x 21ft 6ins x 12ft, 227g). They were built for the Viking Steam Fishing Co. Ltd, Grimsby, and powered by engines of 12ins, 20ins, 32ins x 24ins stroke, *King Harald*'s being supplied by Amos & Smith, while those of her sister came from C.D. Holmes. These well boats were a development of the older well sailing smacks. The fish well was kept full of seawater, thereby allowing the fish to swim around so as to be 'sea fresh' when it arrived at market. The seawater was changed frequently by pumps on the steamers, whereas in the sailing smacks, the hull was pierced below the waterline allowing the seawater to wash in and out. By September 1889, *King Erik* had been converted to trawling and, in September 1903, she was sold to Frank Barrett of Grimsby. A year later she was sold to Norway as SD.33 and had a new boiler fitted in 1911. She was sold back to Frank Barrett in March 1915 as GY.474. She was requisitioned a month later as a minesweeper and returned in 1919. In April 1920, she was owned by Direct Fish Supplies Ltd, London, who went into liquidation in August 1922. She was bought by Thomas W. Bascomb of Grimsby in December 1922, who fitted her with another new boiler in 1929. In October 1935, Bascomb's were bought out by Fred Parkes, Blackpool, who in turn sold her to the Boston Deep Sea Fishing & Ice Co. Ltd, Fleetwood, in May 1940. In September 1941, she was sunk by a torpedo from *U141* with the loss of her fifteen man crew. Her sister *King Harald* was also sold to Frank Barrett in 1903 and he sold her to Denmark in 1912. Barrett bought her back again in April 1915 as GY.479. She was requisitioned in May 1915 and returned in 1919. She too was sold to Direct Fish Supplies Ltd, London and then to Thomas W. Bascomb, Grimsby in 1922. She went to the breakers in September 1935.

Other vessels of this type to be built by Cochranes in 1898 were No's 206 and 207, *Viceroy* (GY.786 – **Plan 19a & b**) for the Atlas Steam Fishing Co. Ltd, Grimsby, and her sister ship *Cassowary* (GY.634) for Thomas W. Bascomb, Grimsby. They were slightly finer than the previous two ships (114ft x 21ft x 11ft 6ins, 217g), with engines by Amos & Smith of 11ins, 20ins, 32ins x 23ins stroke. They were both fitted with sea water wells for the carriage of fresh fish but also had conventional fish rooms, where 'shelving' (best quality gutted) fish were kept on ice. A twin barrelled trawl winch is fitted but no gallows or fairlead rollers are shown. The enclosed wheelhouse abaft the funnel sits atop the galley and entrance to the engine room and after cabin. The open bridge wings are supported by the WCs port and starboard. No small boat is shown; this would have either been aft or on deck chocks near the foremast. This vessel was probably the last well boat built for UK owners. *Viceroy* went missing without trace on or about 7th December 1915 – one of eighty-seven Grimsby vessels lost that year. *Cassowary* was requisitioned as a minesweeper in November 1914, Admiralty No. 806, and fitted with a 6-pounder gun. She returned to Bascombs in 1919 as GY.634. In 1933, she was owned by the Almalgamated Steam Fishing Co. Ltd, Grimsby (ex-T.W. Bascomb).

Cochrane & Cooper's first steam trawler to be fitted with a triple expansion engine was No. 75 *Hugelia* (GY.472) for the North Eastern Steam Fishing Co. Ltd, Grimsby. Built in 1892, she was lost a long way from home on 19th February 1913, when she ran aground 5 miles west of Keis Kamma River on the Cape of Good Hope. She had been Capetown registered since 1912 and owned by the Cory Whaling & Deep Sea Fishing Co. Ltd. After Yard No. 93 *Imbrecaria* (GY.537) of 1893, none of Cochrane's trawlers had compound engines. This vessel, originally owned by the International Steam Trawling Co. Ltd, Grimsby, went to the North Eastern Steam Fishing Co. Ltd in 1902. They sold her to the Canadian Fishing Co. Ltd, Vancouver in 1919. These early steam trawlers were tough little ships; they had to be in order to withstand both the rigours of the trade and the rough treatment they received when coming alongside the landing and coaling berths. Proof of their strength was often their longevity, as with *Viola* (*see Epilogue, page 276*).

Another milestone in the history of the deep water side trawler was reached in 1896, when Iceland agreed to shelter British trawlers and allow them to use their ports, providing the vessel's gear was stowed. This paved the way for the exploitation of the Icelandic grounds, as the smaller trawlers from Aberdeen, in addition to

Photo. 33: *Frigate Bird*, an example of the smaller 'drifter/liner', with her capstan and pile of drift nets ahead of the wheelhouse. Her mast is lowered as it would be when laying to her fleet of drift nets. She has a brown hull, with black funnel and name scroll on wheelhouse.

the larger Humber ships, could now work in these hostile waters, secure in the knowledge they could run for shelter. Vessels such as the tiny *Thrush* (GY.491 – 93ft 6ins x 20ft x 11ft, 134g), built by Earles in 1893 and owned by the Pioneer Steam Fishing Co. Ltd at Grimsby might have fished these Distant Waters – and if not from Grimsby then possibly from Aberdeen, as the company had offices in both ports. She went north in November 1901 as A.508, owned by J. Harrow, Aberdeen. Three years later, they sold her to the Dee Steam Fishing Co. Ltd, Aberdeen, who ran her until 1916, when she was sold to A. Mitchell and A.M. Watson. By April the following year, she was back at Grimsby as GY.1055, owned by Sleights. She went for scrap in October 1924.

The year 1899 saw Cochrane & Cooper move from Beverley to new premises at Selby, where they were to remain until their demise in 1990. This move was dictated by a lack of capacity at the Beverley yard. In 1897, they turned away orders totalling £100,000 and Selby offered better rail and water transport facilities. The first steam trawler launched from this yard was No. 246 *Volta* (M.14 – 168g, **Fig. 40**) for Messrs Hancock & Galvin, Milford Haven, at an estimated cost of £6,000. She soon came under F.T. Ross of Hull's flag as H.111. Later, she was renamed *Venus* when sold to Serna & Co., Havana (Cuba) in 1906. In 1930, she was renamed again as *Raphael Doniphan* when owned by R. Doniphan of Havana, who kept her until 1945.

The sum total of new steam trawlers, steam liners and steam carriers constructed by the major building yards by the end of the 19th century was: Cochrane's, Beverley and Selby – 204 ships; Cook, Welton & Gemmell – 221; Earles of Hull – 120; Smith's

Dock, Middlesborough no listings until 1900; Hall, Russell – 53; and Alexander Hall – 37 ships. In addition, many more ships were built in twos and threes at other shipyards but these were the main trawler builders of the time. By the final decade, the trawling industry was firmly established, with the major centres at Hull, Grimsby and Aberdeen being supplemented by fleets from other important ports, such as Granton, Leith, Fleetwood, Liverpool, Milford Haven, Plymouth, and North and South Shields. The following list shows the deployment of the majority of Britain's steam trawlers for the year 1895. Aberdeen – 54, Hull – 160, Dundee – 3, Grimsby – 143, Granton – 26, Boston – 35, Leith – 9, Scarborough – 16, North Shields – 88, and Sunderland – 10. This is not perhaps as accurate as it might have been, as the Board of Trade were quite creative in their listings:

'It appears to be the peculiar function of the Fisheries Department of the Board of Trade to formulate statistics which shall be just sufficiently complete to bring into strong relief the importance of what is omitted from them.' E.W. Holt, *1895*

In 1892, the steam trawlermen of Sunderland and Tyneside were suffering the effects of over fishing on the Great Fisher and Dogger Banks. So much so in fact, that a good number of the vessels unshipped their trawling gear and refitted with long lines, and went after Halibut off the Faeroes. An observer of the time stated:

'It seems as if the Steam Liner will in time supersede the Steam

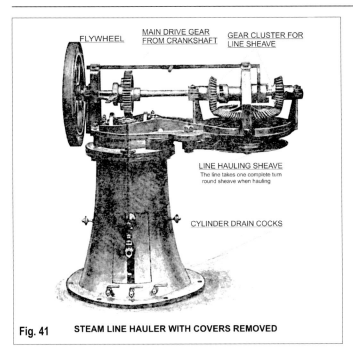

FLYWHEEL   MAIN DRIVE GEAR   GEAR CLUSTER FOR
          FROM CRANKSHAFT   LINE SHEAVE

LINE HAULING SHEAVE
The line takes one complete turn
round sheave when hauling

CYLINDER DRAIN COCKS

Fig. 41   STEAM LINE HAULER WITH COVERS REMOVED

Trawler, as they can be of less size and power, consequently less coal consumption; their fishing gear is less costly, the cost of a trawl and rope being from £100, to £150, while a set of lines can be had for about £40.'

Although this was not to be the case, liners worked in harmony with the trawlers, both on the Near and Distant Water grounds, often as far afield as Greenland and that loneliest of outcrops, Rockall. A small fleet of these steam, and later, motor liners worked out of Aberdeen until the late 1960s but, by this time, the few remaining boats were mostly owned by men from Kirkcaldy. It should also be noted that often steam liners were identical in size to their counterpart, the steam trawler, and many were converted from lining to trawling and vice versa.

LONG OR GREAT LINERS

To the inexperienced eye, these vessels, sometimes referred to as drifter liners, looked like trawlers, the immediate differences being size and the lack of gallows or winches. Where a trawler might have a couple of dhan buoys, the liner would have lots of them lashed along her casing. The long lines or great lines used

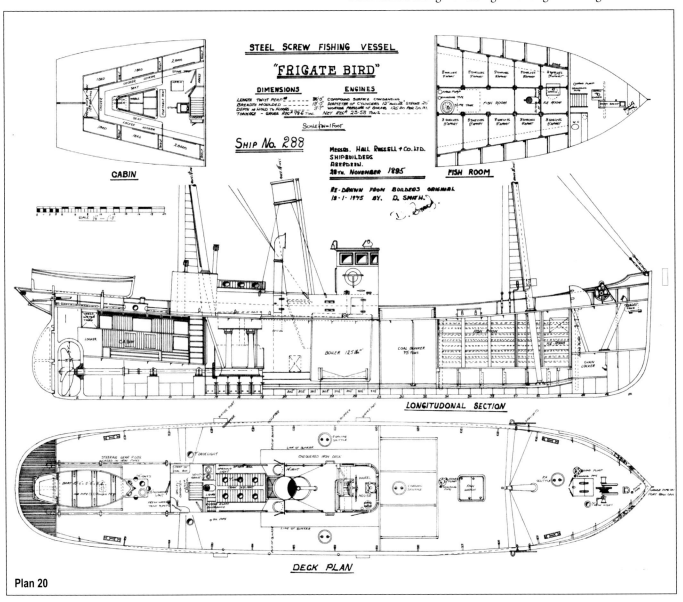

Plan 20

by these vessels were made up of between eighteen to twenty-four lines, each about 40 fathoms (240ft) long. Each of these separate lines had twenty-six cotton 'snoods' with hooks attached, spaced some 9ft apart. This spacing was necessary to prevent the hooks becoming entangled with each other. The great line, of 180 lines, all fastened together, made a total length of seven nautical miles, and the 4,680 or so hooks were all manually baited with herring. Great lines are shot around dawn and hauled again before dusk, the actual hauling in of the lines being done with the aid of a line hauler (**Fig. 41**). These were steam powered until the motor ships replaced the steamers, when they were hydraulically operated. The fish taken by these lines was predominantly the Halibut and the fishermen's greatest predator was the Dogfish, which would devour the hooked fish. Long liners could work in harmony with the steam trawlers as they fished on the rough grounds, which were of little use to their counterparts. Other traditional grounds were Faeroe, Orkney, Shetland, St. Kilda and Fair Isle. Even Greenland would on occasion be fished by these little vessels. These steam liners found life hard during the war years, owing to the fact that skilled crews were scarce, with most fishermen called up for active service. The method of fishing made them more vulnerable than trawlers, as they had to lay to their lines all through the hours of daylight. A 1956 list shows a marked decline in the number of ships. By then, most of the coal fired steamers were very old and were costly to run. Another factor in the decline of the great liner was the price of bait and yet again the scarcity of skilled crews. Line fishermen normally provided their own fishing gear and were paid solely on a share basis, so many men went on to the trawlers, which paid at least a minimum wage plus a 'poundage' share. The work of the great line fisherman consisted of long hours spent baiting the lines, removing the fish from the hooks and finally cleaning the catch before stowing it below.

A typical Aberdeen steam or great liner of the period was **Frigate Bird** (A.769 – 86ft bp x 19ft x 9ft 7ins, 98.6g – **Plan 20** and **Photo. 33**), completed on 22nd April 1895 by Hall, Russell of Aberdeen, as Yard No. 288, for George Main & Others, Aberdeen, at a cost of £2,770. She was launched by Miss Agnes Rennie Ritchie of 25 Ferry Road, Torry, with her two brothers, Alex and William, along with brothers-in-law George and Alex Main – the principal shareholders. The contract was paid off in three equal installments of £92 6s 8d, the first when the framing was up on 22nd February, the second when plating was completed on 21st March, with the final payment being made on completion. To the untrained eye, she very much resembled a steam trawler both in size and appearance. She had compound engines, supplied by the builders, of 12ins, 28ins x 20ins stroke. Steam was supplied from a return tube type boiler, working at 125psi. Her coal bunkers gave around twenty days steaming. As can be seen from the plan, she is a flush decked vessel with slightly more beam than a trawler of the same length but the main deck is a clear working space, uninhibited by any trawl gear. The favourite fishing grounds for the 'Birdie', as she was affectionately known by her crew, were the wild waters off Rockall. *En route* to the grounds, she would spend a couple of nights drift netting off the Shetlands for herring, which was cut up and used as bait. Out of season they used squid for bait. *Frigate Bird* was a family boat and, throughout her life, her sole agents were Meff Bros of Aberdeen. In 1921, she was sold to J. Bruce of Buckie, and A. Wood and J. Pirie of Portknockie, Banffshire. Later in 1926, she was sold to A.R.M. Bouquet & Cie, Lorient, France and renamed **Belon**. She apparently was seen and recognised when off the Dunkirk beaches in 1940 and went to the breakers in 1946. After the 'Birdie', the Ritchie family owned the steel steam liner *Redwing* (A.425 – 95ft x 19ft 9ins x 9ft 8ins, 119g and 40nhp), built at Govan in 1896, although she did not go to Aberdeen until 1901. She remained with the company until 1948.

Aberdeen had a long history with great liners as the following shows: 1901 – 47 steamers; 1935 – 35; 1950 – 34 steamers and 6 motor; 1951– 25 steamers and 6 motor; and in 1956 it had 3 steamers and 6 motor vessels.

Chapter 7: THE EDWARDIAN ERA AND THE YEARS UP TO THE FIRST WORLD WAR 1900-1914

Bigger and better trawlers was the cry that heralded the 20th century. Shipbuilders and owners alike were competing to produce the best designs. Labour was plentiful and cheap in the yards and there was no shortage of crews to man the new ships as they came on stream.

However, this century started very badly for the Humber ports. Hull lost seven ships in the February of 1900: *Ensign* (H.249), owned by the Great Northern Steamship Fishing Co. Ltd, which sank after a collision in the North Sea; *Deerhound* (H.81), owned by the Humber Steam Trawling Co. Ltd, and *Falcon* (H.321), owned by Pickering & Haldane's Steam Trawling Co. Ltd, were both sunk in the North Sea in the gale of 15th February. The Hull Steam Fishing & Ice Co. Ltd lost *Cyrus* (H.198) and *Bermuda* (H.296) in the same gale, whilst the Cargill Steam Trawling Co. Ltd, Hull, lost *Indian Empire* (H.369) and *British Empire* (H.313). The former sank on 15th, while the latter ran ashore at Bempton Cliffs and was declared a constructive total loss. Hull was to lose a further seven trawlers in 1900, whilst across the Humber, Grimsby was to lose four ships. Aberdeen lost three ships that year with a death toll of twenty-six. The first was *Tento* (A.90) only three months old and built by Alexander Hall for W. Slater & Sons, Aberdeen. She disappeared on or about 6th February. A bottle was found on the beach near Fraserburgh on 26th February, saying that she was disabled some 50 miles off Kinaird Head and required immediate assistance, and a lifebelt from the vessel was found three days later a few miles away. This amply illustrates the basic outfit of these early trawlers – no navigational aids, save a magnetic compass and hand lead line, no radar and no radio to summon help when needed. The only distress signals of the age were visual ones such as flares, burning nets, etc, to attract attention at night or frantically shouting and waving during the hours of daylight. It was desperate straits indeed when one's only hope for survival rested on a hastily scribbled message thrown overboard in a bottle.

As the century turned, Grimsby's trawling industry was to suffer another setback with the strike of 1901. The strike began on 1st July, when trawler engineers refused to sign on after the owners decided to introduce the 'share' system of remuneration for their crews. Violence flared, the offices of the Trawler Owners Federation were attacked and the building set alight, destroying equipment and records. The strikers were subjected to a police charge, during which many women and children were injured. Later, the Riot Act was read out to the crowd. This dispute eventually went to arbitration and the trawlermen received safeguards that the pay would not fall below that of their previous earnings, and with the added inducement of the new share system, could easily rise well above the old wage. In other words, the trawlermen had to work harder and longer, push themselves and their ships to the very limits in all weathers, to land a profitable catch of fish when no one else did, so as to receive their share. This share was not calculated on the gross profit but, on the net profit after all incidental expenses had been deducted. This strike was to set the pattern for all future disputes, in that the owners would make sure that any changes to pay and conditions would be made during the summer months. The owners had calculated the result of the strike, because the sale

of fish dropped off during the hotter months and it was in their interest to lay the fleet up until the demand rose again. Remember, trawlermen were employed on a casual basis and were paid only when they were working. Immediately the ship sank, pay stopped. If he was injured at sea and had to be taken ashore for treatment, his pay stopped and when he stepped ashore for his couple of days off between trips, pay stopped again. On the fishing grounds, he worked on average an eighteen hour day but often much longer and there was no strike pay for trawlermen, who were among the lowest hourly paid workers in Great Britain. By this time, vessels were working further and further afield; Iceland and Faeroe had been regularly fished since the steam trawlers first visited them in the 1890s. By 1904, trawlers were fishing off the coast of Morocco and 1905 saw them fishing the rich grounds of the Barents Sea and Russia, known to trawlermen as the White Sea Grounds. The North Sea was still the main workplace for the smaller vessels, as were the West Coast Grounds off St. Kilda, although by 1905, only 60% of the country's catch came from here, as opposed to fifteen years previously when they supplied almost the sum total; by 1914, this was to drop to around 40%. Nevertheless, though the ships could range farther and farther afield in search of fish, as stated previously, trawl caught fish would only remain fresh for a period of between sixteen and eighteen days when packed in ice. After this time, the catch deteriorated rapidly and even to miss a tide when returning from the grounds could mean the catch being condemned and sold for fish meal. This factor, for the most part, remained unchanged throughout the history of the side trawler. It governed the duration of the trip and restricted the actual fishing time on the far Distant Water grounds. One way to extend the fishing time was to design faster and more powerful ships, which could cut down the steaming time to and from the grounds.

By now, we see a pattern of 'traditional' fishing grounds manifesting itself at the main centres. Aberdeen skippers favoured the North Sea and Middle Water grounds of Faeroe, with occasional trips to Iceland. Hull, was becoming a dedicated Distant Water port, with its trawlers ranging far into Arctic waters. Her neighbour, Grimsby, had a powerful Distant Water fleet, backed up with a strong Near and Middle Water sector. Fleetwood men preferred to fish for Hake off the west coast of Scotland, with one or two ships going to Iceland. So as to take advantage of these more Distant Water fishing grounds, trawlers were gradually growing in both size and power. In 1900, Cochranes built Yard No. 280 *Golden Sunrise* (H.517 – 125ft x 21ft 6ins x 11ft 6ins, 226g) for Hall, Leyman & Co. Ltd, Hull, powered by engines (13ins, 22ins, 36ins x 24ins stroke) from C.D. Holmes. Her short life ended on 16th August 1908, when she sank off Flamborough Head. Around the same time, Cook, Welton & Gemmell launched *Oliver Cromwell* (H.490) for the Yorkshire Steam Fishing Co. Ltd, Hull, as Yard No. 250. At 125ft overall, she was almost identical to *Golden Sunrise*. She also suffered an untimely end, when she was wrecked off Iceland on 7th August 1905. It was to be 1906 before the Aberdeen builders Hall, Russell launched a similar size trawler, Yard No. 401 *W. Weatherly* (A.65), named after her local owners. She was sold to Holland in 1913 and renamed *Oceaan 1V*, with

Photo. 34: *Aboyne* on trials. Note position of ship's boat, wheelhouse with verandah and whaleback. She is in the Caledonian Company colours of light grey hull, brown superstructure and black funnel bearing a red cross on a white shield. She has a large number of people on board for these trials.

the registration IJM.202 and skippered by C. Zwart. A slightly larger trawler, *Princess Louise* (SN.18 – 130ft x 22ft x 12ft 8ins, 267g), was launched as Yard No. 416 by A. Hall for Dodds Steam Fishing Co. Ltd, Aberdeen. She was fitted with a steam refrigeration plant supplied by J.&E. Hall, London but was sold to Spain in 1909.

FOREIGN INTEREST IN STEAM TRAWLERS

After the turn of the 19th century, Holland and Iceland showed interest in our trawlers and purchased many ships from the UK fleet. This trend continued right up to the final years of the side trawler. Even when Holland was forging ahead with building her own motor sidewinders and beamers in the 1950s, many British vessels were sold to the enterprising Dutch. Aberdeen trawlers sold to Holland in 1912 were *Clydesdale* (A.182) and *Bannerdale* (A.126). Both were built by John Duthie in 1907 (115ft x 22ft x 12ft, 229g) for Bookless Brothers, Aberdeen. The builders offered to fit a whaleback for an extra £50 if required. They became *Odin* (IJM.168) and *Thor* (IJM.164), owned by NV Zeevisscherij, Maatschappi Ijsland. *Odin* was lengthened in 1917 to 135ft, her tonnage increased to 254 and her engines were rebuilt to give an output of 400nhp. The embryo Dutch fleet also comprised of English trawlers such as *Essex* (H.762), built for Pickering & Haldane's Steam Trawling Co. Ltd, Hull, in 1903 by Mackie & Thomson. This tough little ship had a few name changes during her long career. In 1929, she became *Amstelstroom* (IJM.91), then *Dirk* (KW.157), *Friesland* (HA.5) and finally *Hollandia* (IJM.78). In addition to these changes, she fished out of Fleetwood as FD.218 from 1940 to 1945.

Another smart ship that eventually went Dutch was *Aboyne* (A.183 – 16ft x 21ft 9ins x 13ft – **Photo. 34**), built in 1908 by J. Duthie for the Caledonian Steam Trawling Co. Ltd, Aberdeen and powered by a Lidgerwood engine (12ins, 20ins, 33ins x 23ins stroke). Her boiler was 12ft 6ins diameter by 10ft 3ins long, with three furnaces giving a working pressure of 180psi. One prominent feature was the stowage of the ship's boat. This was on top of the main engineroom skylight, just forward of the galley (a position common in Duthie built vessels). She became *Libra* (IJM.98), owned by N.V. Visscherij, Maats Neerlandia in 1933. In August 1914, she was requisitioned for minesweeping duties, given the Admiralty number 65 and fitted with a 6 pounder gun. She returned to commercial fishing in 1919. She was hired again in July 1940 as *Libra*, pennant No. FY867 and, with her Dutch crew, she went sweeping for mines until returned in 1945.

Iceland first ventured into steam trawling in 1899, when *Umbria* and *Utopia* (details under Mackie & Thomson's ships) arrived in Hafnarfjordur and although registered in Iceland, they were owned by Mr Pike Ward, a Devon fish merchant. This venture initially failed, as Iceland did not have any steam trained engineers. However, both ships returned in 1908 and *Umbria* was wrecked at Reykjavik in 1913. Iceland's first successful steam trawler was *Coot* (GK.310), built by Hamiltons of Port Glasgow in 1892. She was bought in Aberdeen in 1904 and arrived in Iceland in February 1905. She was followed in June by *Seagull* (M.112 – 104ft x 21ft 1in x 9ft 10ins, 146g, 50nhp), which had compound engines by Ross & Duncan, Glasgow. She was built at Castle Mill Steel Works (later T.R. Oswald) Milford as Yard No. 267 and accepted by Castle Steam Trawlers, Milford Haven, on 26th September 1894. She was purchased by a consortium in Reykjavik and registered as RE.100 but was not a success. This was blamed on her troublesome engines (apparently bought second hand by her builders) and again the lack of local engineering facilities.

FIFE BUILDERS

The small town of Kinghorn in Fife was home to Scott's Shipbuilding Yard, who constructed a number of steam trawlers. One such vessel was Yard No. 117 *May Queen* (LH.356 – 115ft x 23ft x 12ft – **Plan 21a & b**), built in 1903 for A. Kay, Edinburgh. The plan shows at first glance a simple vessel but on closer study she becomes quite interesting. Her deck layout shows

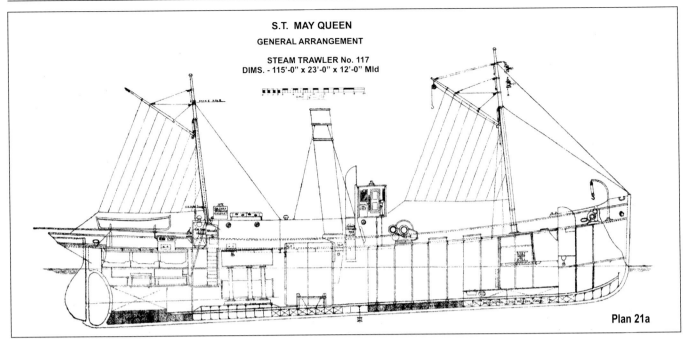

S.T. MAY QUEEN

GENERAL ARRANGEMENT

STEAM TRAWLER No. 117
DIMS. - 115'-0" x 23'-0" x 12'-0" Mld

Plan 21a

a steam anchor windlass forward and a radial davit for handling her fisherman's type anchor, which when stowed would be lashed inside the bulwarks. Aft of this is a companionway leading not as normal to the crew's fo'c'sle but to an under deck store, with a WC fitted to port. The ice room is immediately abaft the store, with three ice scuttles fitted on the deck above. Also stepped on the deck above this compartment is the foremast with its cast iron heel plate. The fore gaff would appear to be standing, as no jaws are shown but she is fitted with a throat halliard, so possibly (as with the mizzen) the jaws have been omitted. Two sets of peak halliards are shown, along with a metal gin block with a single whip. This may have been used both as a Gilson block and landing tackle for the catch. The fish room hatch leads to a rather smaller than normal compartment in a trawler of this size – at the forward end is a sliding door leading into the ice room. In comparison, the bunker space appears very large indeed, with short wings, four bunker lids and a square coaling hatch on deck. As no intermediate bulkheads are shown on the plan, it is doubtful if any of the catch could be stowed here, as would have been the case had the space been divided up and a tunnel fitted linking it up to the stokehold. A double barrelled steam trawl winch is fitted in front of the superstructure but no warp guides or gallows are shown on the

plan, although port and starboard fish pounds are fitted for sorting and gutting the catch.

At the fore end of the casing is the lamp room, with an inclined aft bulkhead. This bulkhead is fitted with a relief door for the stokehold. When this door and its partner at the forward end of the lamp room are opened, they provide additional ventilation for the trimmers and stokers working below. This arrangement, along with the single large stokehold cowl vent and twin fiddley gratings, was a most unusual one. Atop the casing is the steel wheelhouse fitted with an inverted compass on the roof and a standard binnacle in front of the helmsman. A door on the port side presumably leads on to a vertical ladder from the main deck. On the casing top, aft of the tall funnel, is a single 10ins mushroom vent and the opening skylight, giving light and air to the engine room, which housed the vessel's engines. At the aft end of the casing is a 280 gallon fresh water tank, feeding directly to the galley below. The galley funnel is absent, instead the fumes are led up the hollow steel mizzen mast to smoke holes fitted above the hounds. Two 'stable' type doors are fitted on the aft end of the casing, the port leading into the galley and the starboard to the engine room and the after accommodation. Between these doors is a towing hook. On *May Queen*, all the crew were housed down aft and not split

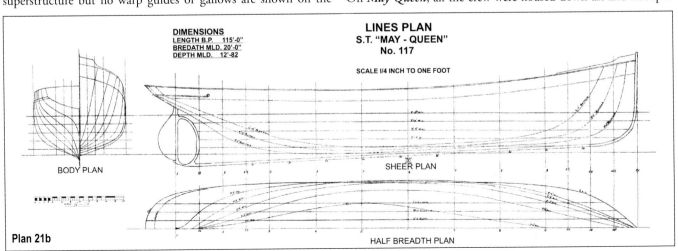

DIMENSIONS
LENGTH B.P.   115'-0"
BREDATH MLD.   20'-0"
DEPTH MLD.   12'-82

LINES PLAN
S.T. "MAY - QUEEN"
No. 117

SCALE 1/4 INCH TO ONE FOOT

BODY PLAN

SHEER PLAN

Plan 21b

HALF BREADTH PLAN

Photo: 35: *Lizzie Melling*, showing the ship's boat stowed aft and a full suit of sails. Note halliards for oil lamps. she has a grey hull, with black topped red funnel separated by a deep white band and fishing numbers on either side of the funnel.

up fore and aft as was the norm. This arrangement was not to be seen again until the Bremerhaven-built 'Northern' ships of the mid-1930s. Either side of the galley are pound boards, just about right for the aft gallows if fitted.

The port of Preston was not a registration found on many trawlers but one such vessel was *Lizzie Melling* (PN.45 – Photo. 35), built in 1904 by Smiths Dock for the Melling Steam Trawling Co. Ltd, Fleetwood, as Yard No. 754. Another trawler built by the same firm for the company in 1908, was *Lily Melling*, Yard No. 394, but she carried the registration FD.222 (there would appear to have been a revision of yard numbers in 1907; after 816, they revert to 337). Both trawlers were hired as minesweepers for the duration of the war in 1914. After the war, they were returned to their former owners and *Lizzie Melling* was to remain with them until she was scrapped at Dublin in June 1957. *Lily Melling* went to Aberdeen in 1933, as *Gareloch* (A.276) and owned by William Gove of Aberdeen. On 18th August 1935, she was returning home from a coaling trip to Methil in Fife (a favourite coaling station for Aberdeen boats) with a skeleton crew of five. She went ashore at Anstruther on the Billowness Rocks. The crew managed to walk ashore whilst carrying the engineer on a stretcher, who had suffered broken ribs during the stranding.

DOGGER BANK INCIDENT

Trawlermen were well accustomed to facing up to the natural perils of their calling, with scarcely a mention in the national press but this was to change suddenly on the night of 21st October 1904; the Dogger Bank Incident was more commonly known by the trawlermen of the Humber as the 'Russian Outrage'.

The incident was a direct result of the Russo-Japanese War. A fleet of Russian warships were en route from the Baltic to the Pacific, to reinforce the beleagured armada which had already been driven out of Port Arthur. Their intended route was via the North Sea, English Channel, Mediterranean Sea, Suez Canal and Indian Ocean and was under the control of Admiral Rozhestevensky. Amidst tales of Japanese trickery and intelligence reports suggesting

that they had disguised gunboats as trawlers and sent them round the globe to attack first, a very jittery Russian Navy opened fire on the British trawlers innocently going about their business.

The duration of the action lasted between ten and twenty minutes but in this short time, two men were killed, six others seriously injured and one trawler, *Crane*, sunk. Aboard this vessel, galley boy Joseph Smith, the skipper's son, had run up on deck only to find his father and third hand William Leggott both decapitated, the vessel's superstructure shot away and *Crane* herself sinking fast. Shells burst close to *Thrush* (H.703) and *Swift*, and a crew member of *Mino* was laid low in the pounds where he was gutting fish. The casualties were taken aboard *Gull*, where they were treated by the Mission Ship surgeon, Dr Anklesaria, who stated:

'I have never witnessed such a gory sight, two men lay on the deck with their heads blown to pieces. In the cabin, it was even more heartrending. Six men stretched any way they could, bleeding and groaning from the agony of their wounds.'

Nothing was known ashore until the evening of 23rd October, when *Moulmein* and *Mino* arrived back in Hull. The former vessel carried the bodies of *Crane*'s men, and both ships showed the scars of torn hulls and casings pierced by shrapnel. Both the national and world's press condemned the outrage and picture postcards were issued showing the shell damage to *Thrush* and other vessels of the trawling fleet. Such was the mayhem during the incident that the Russian ships also managed to fire on each other and at least two of their own men were killed as a result. The fact that the Russian ships failed to provide any assistance to the trawlermen after they abruptly ceased fire only served to compound the ill-feeling. A war between the Russian fleet and the Royal Navy was only narrowly averted, although they were shadowed all the way down to the Mediterranean and then barred by the British from sailing through the Suez Canal. An International Commission later awarded £66,000 to the fishermen involved.

FIRST WHALEBACK FO'C'SLE APPEARS

The name turtleback or whaleback is derived from the curved shape of a turtle's shell, or the back of a surfaced whale. In 1905, the first of Cochrane's trawlers fitted with a whaleback fo'c'sle head was launched, Yard No. 352 *Eske* (H.859 – 137ft x 22ft 3ins x 11ft 6ins, 289g), for J.H. Collinson, Hull. She was built specifically for the Distant Water grounds off Iceland, with 70nhp engines supplied by C.D. Holmes. She was the largest British trawler launched by Cochranes up to that date and received favourable press coverage over her design:

'The whaleback which is fitted forward, is one of the latest improvements, and greatly assists in keeping seas off the vessel, at the same time affording shelter for the crew when working at the fish.'

By 1910, she had been fitted with radio and allotted the call letters HFLB. In February 1915, she was requisitioned as a minesweeper (Admiralty No. 1225) and fitted with a 6 pounder AA gun and a 7.5ins bomb throwing mortar. Returned to her former owners in 1919, she was lost on 1st April 1930 off the Vestmannaeyjar Islands, Iceland, a location where she had worked for most of her days.

In 1906, Cochranes launched Yard No's 377 and 378, *Lord Nonburnholme* (H.900) and *Flamingo* (H.901 – both 130ft x 22ft 3ins x 12ft 9ins, 290g) for Pickering & Haldane's Steam Trawling Co. Ltd (**Photo. 36**). Their engines by Amos Smith were 13ins, 22.5ins, 37ins x 24ins stroke). By 1910, *Lord Nonburnholme* had transferred to the Yorkshire Steam Fishing Co. Ltd. They sold her to the Portugese in 1914, who renamed her *Lordello*. *Flamingo*

was lost off Iceland on 26th February 1911. The next large trawler launched by Cochrane's was Yard No. 379 *Ladysmith* (GY.183). She was 137ft long and owned by Henry Taylor & Bernstein, Grimsby, who named their ships after places in India. By 1919, she was owned by Taylor & Hopwood, Grimsby, who sold her to the Diamond Steam Fishing Co. Ltd, Grimsby in 1922. She crossed the Humber to Hull owners F. Crimlas in 1929 as *Golden Beam* (H.167), before going for scrap in 1939. Her plan shows a profile that was to become the standard for Distant Water ships until the late 1950s.

Ladysmith was requisitioned in August 1914 as Admiralty No. 4, fitted with a 12 pounder AA gun and used as a minesweeper, until released in 1920 and returned to Taylors. Her predecessor *Ladysmith* (H.726) was built as Yard No. 334 by Cook, Welton & Gemmell in 1903, for the Hull Steam Fishing & Ice Co. Ltd. She was a much smaller vessel (109ft x 21ft 5ins x 11ft, 181g, 65n), with 45nhp engines by Amos & Smith. She was the last of an order for five fleeters, all sister ships placed with the yard, the others being *Kimberley* (H.707), *Pretoria* (H.701), *Mafeking* (H.716) and *Johannesburg* (H.711). *Ladysmith* was lost after colliding with the steam trawler *Australia* in the North Sea on Christmas Day 1911. There were two trawlers named *Australia* fishing at that time. The first was GY.456, owned by the North Eastern Steam Fishing Co. Ltd, Grimsby, whilst the second and most probable assailant was H.1328, a fish carrier owned by the ill-fated ship's parent company. *Pretoria* was also lost by collision in the North Sea in 1924 and *Mafeking* was wrecked off Spurn Point at the mouth of the Humber on 18th October 1922; thus four of the quintet were lost within twenty years.

Another trawler similar to *Ladysmith* was *Carmania* (GY.268

Photo. 36: *Flamingo*. Note her whaleback, wheelhouse verandah and pole compass. Her jib and mizzen are furled and her trawl net is hoisted up the mizzen mast, either for drying or repair. The low position of her anchor shows that her windlass is on the foredeck below the whaleback, although she has a hand windlass aft of the breakwater. She is in Pickering & Haldane's colours.

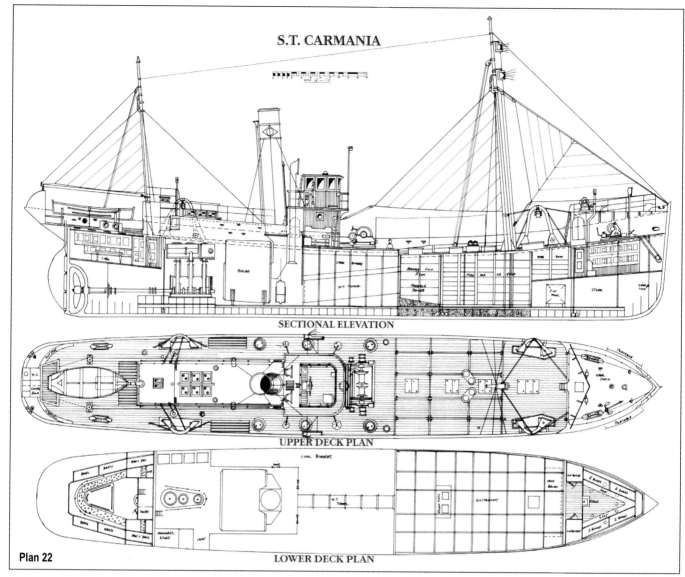

S.T. CARMANIA

SECTIONAL ELEVATION

UPPER DECK PLAN

Plan 22

LOWER DECK PLAN

– **Plan 22**). She was built on the south bank of the Humber at Grimsby by Charlton & Doughty, for the Grimsby Alliance Steam Fishing Co. Ltd. The chartroom below the wheelhouse is also the skipper's berth, an arrangement common aboard trawlers right up till the end. There is a void space behind this cabin, through which pass the cowl vent trunks – these continue up through the verandah behind the wheelhouse. Right aft is a WC with a lamp room to starboard. The plan view shows four large acetylene deck lamps swung out from the verandah, with another two above the aft gallows. The under deck layout is almost identical to that of *Ladysmith*, or indeed any of her type. In 1915, she appears as *Carmania 2*, when hired as a mine layer and mine sweeper with the Admiralty No. 3221. Her armament was a 6 pounder AA gun and she was returned to commercial fishing in 1919. She kept her original fishing number but under new owners, the Strand Fishing Co. Ltd, Grimsby. Her end came on 14th February 1929, when she ran ashore on the Kirk Rocks in Hoy Sound.

One trawler that led a long varied relationship with many owners was *Triton* (SA.61 – 120ft x 21ft 9ins x 12ft 6ins, 71n) (**Plan 23**), built by the Dundee Shipbuilding Co. in 1907 for T.J. Wales, Swansea. From the builders plan she looks no different to hundreds of similar steel vessels, except for the crew's fo'c'sle. This

was set half a deck lower than the foredeck, where normally it would be level or one whole deck below. In May 1915, she was requisitioned as a minesweeper with the Admiralty No. 1769. At the close of hostilities, she was released in 1919 to W. Sutherland, Aberdeen, as A.94. She then went to Thomas Hall, Edinburgh and, in 1925, she was owned in Grimsby by Jeffory & Walter Garrett of Grimsby, with a new number, GY.384. By 1930, her owners were T.W. Bascomb, Grimsby and, in 1931, she went to Charles Dobson of the same port. When war clouds again rolled over Britain, she was called up once more as Y.742, an armed patrol trawler in December 1939. In 1940, her role changed to that of a fuel carrier and, in 1944, her name was changed to *Wrangler*, until discharged in 1945. It was during her naval service that she again changed hands, this time to Hendersons Trawling Co. Ltd, a subsidiary of J. Marr & Sons Ltd of Grimsby. In 1946, she was finally sold for scrap to John Lee of Belfast.

WORLD WIDE APPEAL

The expertise of Britain's trawlers builders was by this time being much sought after by owners as far afield as South Africa, Buenos Aires and Pernambuco (now Recife). In 1907, Hall, Russells received an initial order for two small trawlers for The Societes

Pescadores, Buenos Aires. They were Yard No's 425 and 426, *Uno* and *Dos* (112ft x 21ft 6ins x 12ft 6ins) and cost £6,100 each. They were followed in 1908 by *Tres* and *Cuatro*, much larger trawlers (134ft x 23ft x 12ft 6ins) costing £9,375 for the pair. Another 112ft ship, *Cinco*, was built in 1909, followed in 1910 by the 134ft *Seis*, which cost, £8,700. The final two ships were launched in 1910 as *Siete* and *Ocho* (136ft x 23ft 6ins x 12ft 6ins), costing £8,877 each. Of this fleet, four of the ships later went to Russian owners; they were *Uno*, *Cuatro*, *Seis* and *Tres*, becoming T.31, T.34, T.36 and T.33 respectively. According to British Admiralty reports, they were seized along with another fourteen Russian trawlers on 3rd August 1918, while fishing the White Sea grounds, although it seems that eight of the ships might have been handed over by 'White' Russians. As RN ships, they carried the names *Sureaxe*, *Firmaxe*, *Coalaxe* and *Silveraxe*. They were sold in 1920, with *Sureaxe* becoming A.161, owned by the Harrow, Baxter Steam Fishing Co. She was requisitioned again from 1942 until 1945, serving as a target towing vessel. *Firmaxe* became *Cannamore* in 1921, *Coalaxe* was renamed *Calicut* also in 1921, and *Silveraxe* became *Finmark* (H.98). She was registered at Hull but operated by Lars Peter Brekke, of the Norwegian Consulate

and was wrecked at Kettleness near Whitby on 7th February 1926.

What a fine sight these new trawlers must have made, when resplendent in fresh paint they ran their trials in Aberdeen Bay. Photographs in the John Duthie Torry Shipbuilding Book show *Star of Liberty* (A.88) and *Star of Freedom* (A.151) leaving port on such a trip, packed with shipyard workers, owners representatives and crewmen, plus a harbour pilot, compass adjuster and possibly the yard manager – with their families all dressed up for the occasion. These pleasure trips stopped after the Board of Trade realised that the lifesaving equipment carried was totally inadequate to cope with an emergency. It later became a stipulation that all vessels running trials had to carry extra lifesaving gear for the trip but this only covered accredited representatives and necessary personnel. Another smart Duthie-built trawler was *Edinburgh* (A.897) of 1903 (115ft), for the Caledonian Steam Trawling Co. Ltd; she later went to Holland as *Zaanstroom III* (IJM.171). Accompanying her went another 1903 Aberdeen-built trawler from Hall, Russell's, *Strathcarron* (A.898), owned by the Aberdeen Steam Trawling & Fishing Co. Ltd; she became *Zaanstroom II* (IJM.171).

By now, foreign clients were ordering very much larger vessels and, in addition to trawlers, multi-functional ships for trawling,

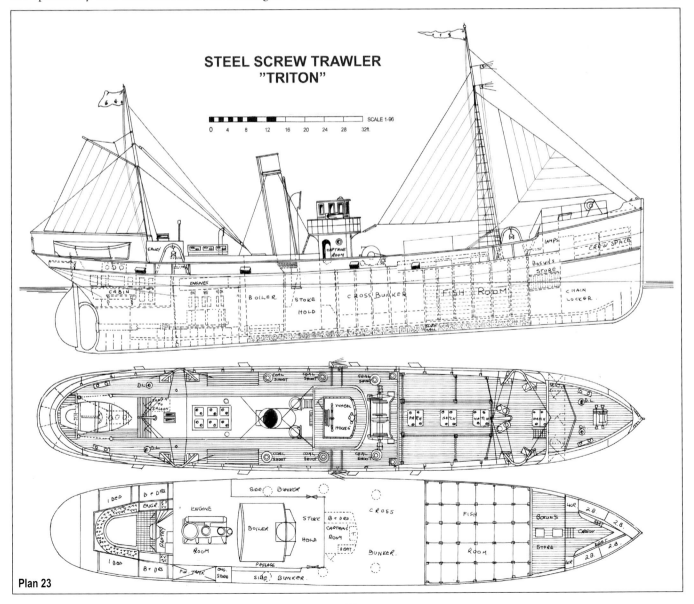

STEEL SCREW TRAWLER "TRITON"

SCALE 1-96

Plan 23

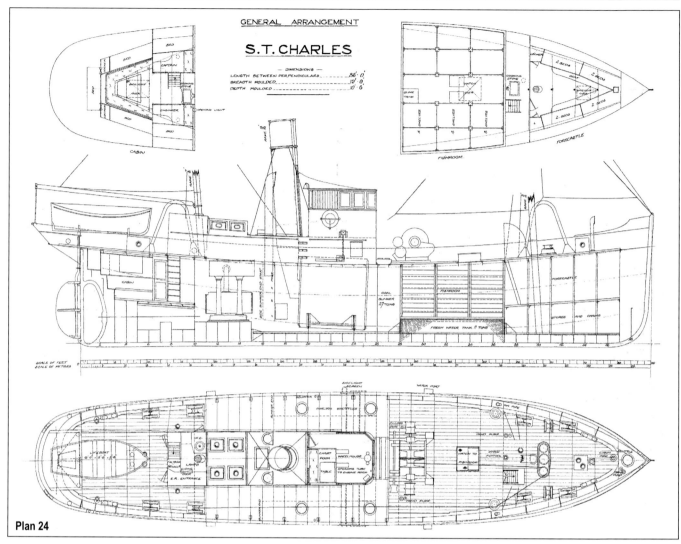

Plan 24

drifting and the salt cod trade were being built; these varied in length from 140ft to 160ft. When trawling, they were rigged with the otter trawl in the same fashion as British ships but they had very much larger fish room capacity. It was when pursuing the herring that they differed both in design and method to our drifters. Where we went out nightly to catch the 'silver darlings' and returned with the catch fresh for market and processing ashore, the French gutted, split, salted and packed the fish in barrels on board. To make space for this operation, the fish room fittings were stripped out and the space divided into five compartments by means of wooden bulkheads, and served by five deck hatches. When preparing for the trip, all the barrels full of salt are packed into these compartments ready

Photo. 37: The steam trawler and herring drifter *Aiglon* fitting out at J. Duthie's Torry shipyard. Note her bow rudder.

Plan 25

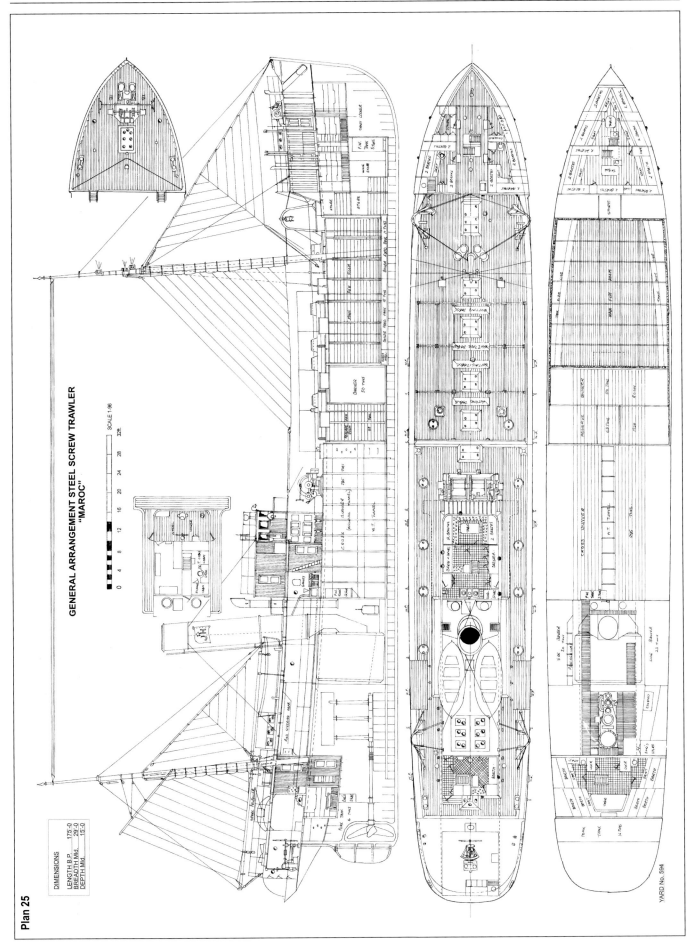

GENERAL ARRANGEMENT STEEL SCREW TRAWLER
"MAROC"

SCALE 1:96

0   4   8   12   16   20   24   28   32ft.

DIMENSIONS

LENGTH B.P.   175·0
BREADTH Mld.   29·0
DEPTH Mld.   15·0

YARD No. 594

for processing the fish at sea. A herring voyage would last anything from six to ten weeks, or until a full cargo was caught. One of the difficulties of using such a large vessel for drift net fishing in the traditional way would be that the ship could become windborne and if the wind was across the tide, then the vessel would foul the nets. These large ships were all fitted with bow rudders and this enabled the nets to be shot with the engines going astern, thus ensuring complete control of the operation. The bow rudder was manually controlled by way of a tiller and, when not in use, this was locked amidships by a specially designed pin. The third function of these vessels was the Newfoundland salt cod trade which, until this time, had been carried out by fleets of three masted schooners working from the French ports.

The French trawlers, when fitted out for this salt cod trade, removed the bulkheads in the fish room which left an empty hold. Some 200 tons of rock salt would then be packed into this space, ready for packing the cod after it has been gutted and split. By 1910, John Duthie and Smiths Dock had constructed some notable ships for foreign owners. From Aberdeen in 1904 came the steam trawler *Mars* (LR.1549), 130ft long, for E. Salmon of Lorient in France. She could be classed as a stretched North Sea trawler, without a whaleback but fitted with a verandah to the wheelhouse. The owners ordered a second ship from Duthie's in 1906. She was *Venus* and, with the exception of the stowage and type of boats, she was typical of the Distant Water ships seen on the Humber. A 24ft double ended ship's boat to port and a 16ft transom-sterned workboat to starboard, were carried on a deck over the casing abaft the funnel. No davits can be seen on the photograph but she has quite a long bobbin derrick fitted to the mizzen mast, which could double up as launching gear. Like her British sisters, she carries a full suit of fore and aft sails.

In 1910, an exception to these large French trawlers came in the form of Hall, Russell's Yard No. 478 *Charles* (85ft bp x 19ft x 10ft 6ins, 93n) for L. Veyrat, Dieppe, at a cost of £3,550. Her layout

is typical of UK ships except for her larger wheelhouse, which contained a chartroom, and her bare steel side decks over the wing bunkers. An 'aft sider', her compound engines were supplied by the builder. She was sold in 1918 to Abraham, Dieppe, and again in 1926 to Burolland (Dieppe). In 1947, she was converted to diesel and, by 1958, her owners were the Soc. Anon du Vapeur Charite, Dieppe (**Plan No. 24**)

Duthie's also built *Voador*, a small trawler for Pernambuco; *Elsie*, a 120ft trawler for Buenos Aires, with a single lifeboat stowed on the casing top; and a larger trawler, *Republica*, for Lisbon. She was 135ft long, fitted with a whaleback and twin ship's boats immediately aft of the funnel, on a boat deck extending out to the ship's side and launched by quadrantal type davits. In 1905, they launched the steam trawlers/herring drifters *Alexandra* (B.3000) and *Le Corsaire* (B.2980) for Boulogne. They were large ships (140ft x 22ft 6ins x 12ft 6ins), powered by engines of 12.5ins, 21ins, 34ins x 27ins stroke), with boilers of 13ft 6ins and 12ft 6ins diameter respectively, the larger working at 180 psi and the smaller at 200psi. *Alexandra* was owned by Pichon and *Le Corsaire* by Eugene Altazin, both of Boulogne. Pichon ordered an even larger ship from this yard in 1907; *Aiglon* (B.10) Yard No. 303, was 147ft in length and the builders fitting out photograph shows the bow rudder quite clearly. Being drifters, they were not built with whalebacks and this gave them a very sleek appearance (**Photo. 37**).

One of the larger type of French pre-war trawlers, built as Yard No. 594 by Cochrane's in 1914, must have been *Maroc* (175ft bp x 29ft x 15ft, 634g) for J.T. Huret, Boulogne (**Plan 25**). Her engines, supplied by Amos & Smith, were 15ins, 25ins, 42ins x 27ins stroke and were fed at 180psi, from a 15ft 6ins diameter boiler.

Outwardly, she was typical of any Distant Water ship of thirty years later, with the exception of her boat stowage and the central galley and messroom under the bridge. Her rod steering gear was linked by crown and bevel gearboxes, the gear being all internal which protected it from the elements. Another prominent feature

Photo. 38: *Patrie.* Her outline is more akin to an engines aft coaster, with her long foredeck. In addition to her two steel masts with fidded topmasts, she has a single sampson post midway between the wheelhouse and the foremast, with two cargo derricks, with the cargo winches just visible at the foot of the post. A large trawl winch can be seen in front of the superstructure and her twin lifeboats are carried in quadrantal davits.

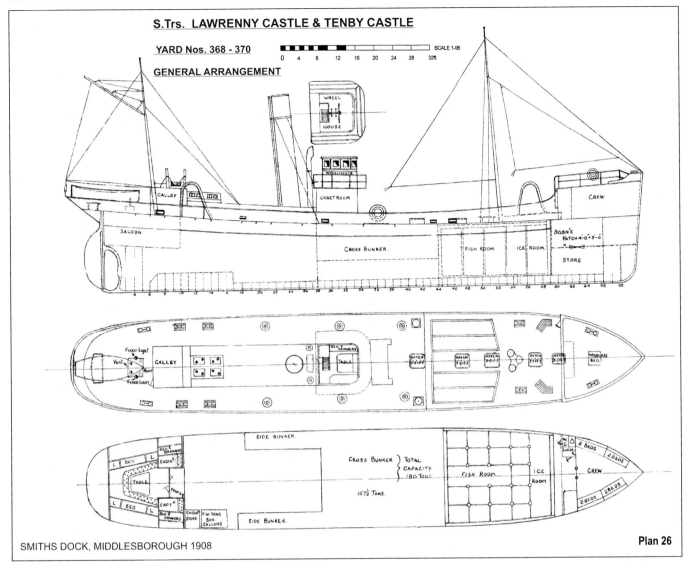

S.Trs. LAWRENNY CASTLE & TENBY CASTLE

YARD Nos. 368 - 370

SCALE 1·96

0 4 8 12 16 20 24 28 32ft.

GENERAL ARRANGEMENT

SMITHS DOCK, MIDDLESBOROUGH 1908

Plan 26

of *Maroc* was the height of her masts; this was necessary in the early days of wireless, enabling the aerials to receive and transmit at maximum efficiency. There is no doubt that this vessel was exceptional for the period, designed as an enhanced endurance trawler well able to spend many weeks working the distant Newfoundland cod grounds and, at the same time, offering the crew of forty-three at least some degree of comfort.

Smiths Dock, at South Bank on Tees, built the steam trawler *Star of Peace* for South Africa in 1903. Although only 115ft long, she was fully insulated and fitted with a refrigerating plant. They built the French steam trawler *Antioche* (LR.1563 – 125ft, 257g) for G. Conor, La Rochelle, in 1905, and of 490ihp. Her trials photograph shows a bridge forward of the funnel and what appears to be a light fo'c'sle deck level with the main rail. Larger and larger ships were being ordered by the French; E. Dufilhol, La Rochelle, took delivery of *Menhir* (L.568 – 145ft, 328g), of 562ihp, from Smith's Dock in 1905. A year later, they built the combination drifter/trawler *Augustin Le Borgne* (150ft, 300g) for the Society Anon Des Secher, Fecamp. The builder's photograph shows the ship carrying F.2 as her fishing number but the register shows this as F.1929. Both these vessels appeared to be flush decked but they had raised forecastles level with the main rail and their wheelhouses were fitted with open verandahs.

Another Cochranes ship similar to *Maroc* was *L'Atlantique*, Yard No. 738, built in 1917 for A. Coppin & Cie, Fecamp. However, by far the largest of the time must have been *Patrie*, Yard No. 739 (200ft bp x 32ft x 16ft, 787g – **Photo. 38**)

THE SPECIALIST BUILDERS

By the early years of the 20th century, specialist trawler builders were well established and, in addition to producing single vessels, they were offering prospective buyers ships from various standard designs or 'Classes'. Messrs Eltringham of South Shields built four 'Princes' in 1904: *Australian Prince*, *Canadian Prince*, *Celtic Prince* and *Highland Prince*. All of these ships went to Dutch owners in 1906, as *Amsterdam* (IJM.49), *Rotterdam* (IJM.50), *Dordrecht* (IJM.52) and *Gravenhage* (IJM.51). In 1908, Smith's Dock launched the first of their 'Castle' Class trawlers, *Lawrenny Castle* (SA.52 – 125ft x 22ft x 13ft), Yard No. 368 (**Plan 26**), and *Tenby Castle* (SA.53), Yard No. 370; both were owned by the Castle Steam Trawling Co. Ltd, Swansea (these two vessels were the lead ships for the Admiralty vessels of the same type.)

Both these trawlers were requisitioned for war service, *Lawrenny Castle* as a minesweeper armed with a 12 pounder AA gun, whilst *Tenby Castle* was used as a decoy ship, also armed with a 12 pounder. Both vessels were returned in 1919. One feature common to this class was the raised fo'c'sle head with no camber, whilst the long, level main deck had no raised section from the winch aft. *Lawrenny Castle*, along with another Smith's Dock built trawler, Yard No. 691 *King Edward* (SN.332) of 1902, was still fishing in 1990, although under Portugese owners.

In 1908, Smith's Dock built Yard No's 382 to 386, the sister ships *Bush* (M.227), *Angle* (M.225), *Apley* (M.226), *Caldy* (M.228) and *Slebech* (M229 – all 120ft x 21ft 6ins x 12ft 6ins, 222g, 86nhp), for the Neyland Steam Trawling & Fishing Co. Ltd, Neyland. They were slightly smaller than the 'Castles' and had no wheelhouse verandahs. The main deck was raised at the winch and they had the same flat raised fo'c'sle deck. All were hired for the duration of the First World War as minesweepers. The only casualty was *Apley* – destroyed after striking a mine off the Isle of Wight on 6th February 1917. By 1921, *Angle* was under the ownership of Croston Steam Trawling Ltd (Taylor & Tomlinson) of Fleetwood, as FD.57. In 1924, she was wrecked on the Bahama Bank off the Isle of Man. By 1930, *Bush* had become FD.60, operated by Scarisbrook Steam Trawlers Ltd, *Caldy* became M.198, owned by J.S. Pettit, and *Slebech* became M.199, in the ownership of J.B.B. Huddlestone, Milford. During the Second World War, *Bush* was again taken over by the Admiralty, as an armed patrol trawler and was returned in 1946 to Clifton Steam Trawlers Ltd, Fleetwood. Her last owners were Richard Fenton, Dundee, and it was as *Lynn Fenton* (DE.24) that she went to the breakers in 1954. *Caldy* was requisitioned again in December 1939 as a minesweeper and was returned in January 1940, to Westward Trawlers of Milford Haven, who owned her until 1962. Finally, *Slebech* was requisitioned as a

fuel carrier from December 1939 until January 1946, when she too went back to Westward Trawlers (her pre-war owners). She disappeared from the register around 1960. The early 19th century was a period of very rapid growth within the British trawling industry, with new ships being built at the rate of one every two days. Owners were clamouring for ships and the shipyards, with their plentiful supply of skilled labour, were sending them down the ways post haste. In the four years leading up to 1908, no less than 741 new steam trawlers were commissioned.

Scott of Bowling received an order in 1906 from the Double Steam Fishing Co. Ltd (Lune Steam Fishing Co. Ltd managers) of Fleetwood for four new ships (Yard No's 183/4/5/6). They were *Belmont* (FD.64), *Euston* (FD.67), *Elswick* (FD.78) and *Albany* (FD.82), all 115ft oa, 207g. The last was the shortest lived of the quartet, lost by stranding at Westport, Kintyre, on 28th December 1908. *Belmont* was requisitioned in June 1915 and returned in 1919. She went to Aberdeen as A.101 and was lost on 26th January 1928 when she grounded on the Horseback Rocks, adjacent to the lifeboat slip at Peterhead. All the crew were rescued by the rocket team but, badly holed and with her propeller gone, she rolled onto her beam ends and had to be broken up. *Euston* was called up for minesweeping duty in June 1915, only to be lost by a mine off Hartlepool on 12th February 1917. *Elswick*, the longest lived, was requisitioned a month later than her sisters, given a 6 pounder gun and fitted out for minesweeping. She was returned in December 1919 but twelve months earlier she had been sold to Grimsby owner W. Would, as GY.1264. He sold her in April 1920, to the Woodbury Steam Fishing Co. Ltd, Grimsby but, in September

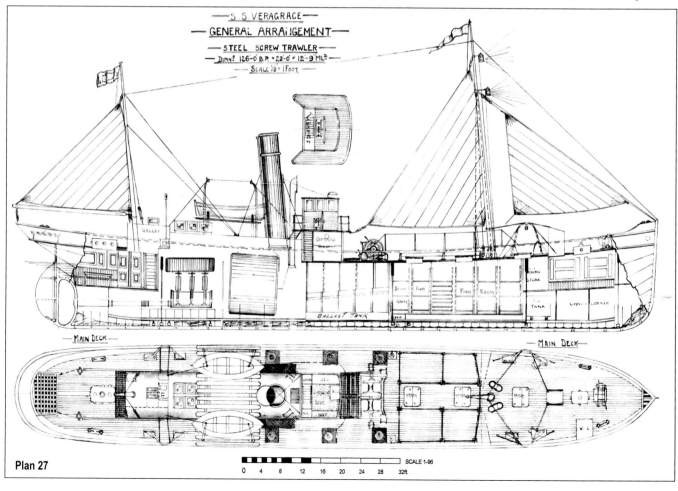

Plan 27

SCALE 1-96

0   4   8   12   16   20   24   28   32ft.

Photo. 39: *G.E. Foster*. An unusual design of trawler, with guardrails at the stern and quite a large wheelhouse. Although she is flying light, her freeboard still seems quite excessive.

1922, she returned to her former owners. In April 1925, she was bought by T.T. Irvin, Aberdeen and re-registered A.97. In 1931, she was transferred to Mrs Ethel Irvin, eventually coming to grief on 20th January 1942 after running aground near Peterhead.

Another smart new trawler which appeared at Fleetwood in 1908 was *Vera Grace* (FD. 211 – 126ft bp x 22ft x 12ft 9ins, 232g, 60nhp – **Plan 27**), built at the Panmure Yard of Dundee Shipbuilding Ltd. Her first owner was W.H. Sutcliffe, Fleetwood and later she went to H.B. Ingram and J. Marr of the same port. The blueprint shows a flush-decked ship, with the foremast stepped well back from the stem, although judging from her size and bunker layout, she would have been designed for Distant Water grounds. She has no fo'c'sle which must have made deck work rather uncomfortable. The accommodation layout is typical of the period, with the crew forward and the officers aft. One distinguishing feature of the ship is her two double-ended lifeboats stowed on a spar deck. She was requisitioned in August 1914 as a minesweeper and fitted with a 6 pounder AA gun. She was returned in 1919. Marr's sold her in 1941 to Thornton Trawlers of Fleetwood for £3,500 and she went for scrap in 1954. Prior to *Vera Grace*, in July 1905 the yard built *Gloria* (GY.78 – 130ft 280g) for Alec Black. Between 1908 and her return to Grimsby in 1920, she had three nationalities: *Gloria* of Holland, *Gloire* of France and *Skallagrimur* of Iceland. On her return in March 1920, she became *Pelham* (GY.1088)m undergoing another four changes of owner before she was scrapped in 1939. Another Fleetwood trawler from this yard in 1907 was *City of Edinburgh II* (FD.185 – 130ft bp, 300g, 80nhp) for Kelsall Bros. She featured four cowl vents on the casing top, above the boiler and machinery spaces. She was requisitioned as a minesweeper and armed with a 6 pounder gun in August 1914, being returned in 1919. She later became the Spanish vessel *Paco*, eventually going for scrap in 1954.

Two steam trawlers built by Cochranes in 1912 as Yard No's 534 and 535 were *G.E. Foster* (GY.739 – **Photo. 39**) and *Andrew Kelly* (GY.741 – 118ft x 22ft x 12ft 3ins, 228g), for the Canadian Fish & Cold Storage Co. Ltd, Prince Rupert, British Columbia but when

fishing from Grimsby they were managed by Thomas Robinson. Both became Canadian tugs in 1932 and in 1943 were renamed *Island Warrior* and *Island Commander* respectively. Their casings seemed shorter than normal and they had large wheelhouses with wing verandahs. As 'aft siders', they made work extra hard for the trimmers, when dragging the coal through the tunnel from the spare fish room to the stokehold. The stern was really where these trawlers differed, in that they had a form of vertical semi elliptical counter, with the bulwarks cut down to deck level just behind the after gallows. An open rail surrounds the counter, so they were probably wet ships in a following sea. The picture shows a very high freeboard and, even allowing for the fact that she is light ship, this seems greater than usual for a sidewinder

By around 1910, certain improvements were being incorporated in new ships and older vessels were gradually being updated. One such innovation was the See's Patent Ash Ejector (**Fig. 42**), which did away with the dangerous job of dumping the ashes over the bulwarks. As the sketch shows, a pipe ran from below, up through the main deck, terminating in an elbow that passed through the bulwarks. The ashes were shovelled into a hopper in the stokehold, the lid was locked and the ashes ejected from the hopper by a jet

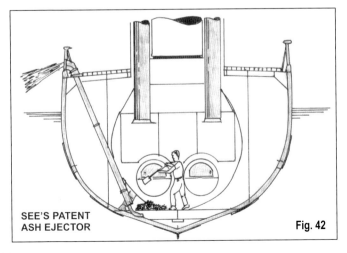

SEE'S PATENT ASH EJECTOR   Fig. 42

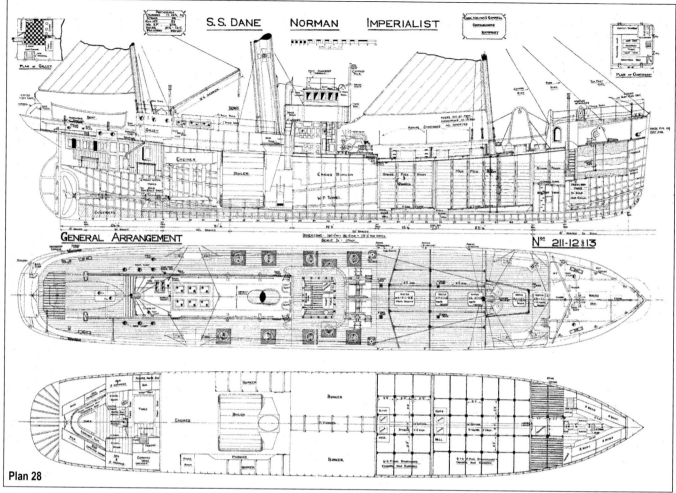

Plan 28

of steam. This was not an entirely new design, as the system was a development of the one fitted to merchant ships and it never really caught on with the trawler owners. This could have been due to either its initial cost or to the use of valuable steam for its operation. The innovators of this product were Messrs Trewent & Proctor of London.

A more common way of dumping ashes was the 'ash shoot'. The first Grimsby trawler to be fitted with ash shoots, in 1913, was *Passing* (GY.877 – 160ft x 26ft x 14ft 8ins, 459g). She was built by Cook, Welton & Gemmell, as Yard No. 261, for Alec Black's South Western Steam Fishing Co. Ltd and powered by engines from Charles D. Holmes of Hull, of 13ins, 22ins, 37ins x 26ins stroke, 68nhp. Until 1918, she was the largest vessel working out of Grimsby and was reckoned by many to be the ultimate pre-war British trawler. She went through a few changes of ownership (although only on paper as they all came under Alec Black's umbrella), until taken over by the Admiralty as a minesweeper in August 1914. She was returned in 1920 and sold to Belgium as *Boula Matari*, finally being sold to France under whose flag she was lost in 1928, as *Pacifique*.

The Imperial Steam Fishing Co. Ltd, Hull, took delivery of three Distant Water ships in 1911, from Cook, Welton & Gemmell, Yard No's 211, 212 and 213. They were *Dane* (H.227), *Norman* (H.249) and *Imperialist* (H.250 – all 140ft bp x 24ft x 13ft 4ins, 346g), with engines by Amos & Smith (13ins, 22ins, 37ins x 24ins stroke). These were supplied by steam at 200psi from a Scotch marine boiler 10ft 6ins long by 13ft diameter, which in

turn gave 520ihp and 87nhp. The yard drawing (**Plan 28**) shows a typical deep water trawler, with a raised whaleback fo'c'sle and a wood sheathed, fore/main deck stepping up to a quarterdeck. Her single port side anchor is handled by a centre line davit on the fo'c'sle head and a steam windlass on the deck below. The rod guardrails are replaced by drop chains to facilitate bringing the anchor inboard.

A breakwater is fitted across the after end of this raised deck, along with a central stove funnel for the crew's quarters and also a hand warping windlass. Below the fo'c'sle head to port is a WC and the entrance to the crew space below, whilst on the starboard side is the lamp room/bosun's store. A steep iron ladder runs down to the crew's quarters, which was heated by a bogie stove. The maindeck has five hatches. From fore to aft they lead to the net store, ice room and three fish room hatches, with the aftermost serving also as a coaling hatch for the after fish room/reserve bunker space. This deck is fully fitted for trawling and stanchions are fitted to the waist rails in order that a shelter may be rigged to shade the catch on hot summer days. A large twin barrelled trawl winch is fitted immediately in front of the casing, with a degree of shelter afforded to the winchmen by the verandah above. Strangely, no chequer plate is shown for boiler installation or renewal. The casing is typical for her class, with storm guardrails running the full length and also carried round the galley top. The wheelhouse has steam/hand steering gear, a folding chart table, inverted compass set in the roof and an engine room telegraph. A pole compass is fixed in front of the verandah, and the ship's brass bell and frame is hung above one of the opening carriage type windows. On the top of the wheelhouse is a storm rail of solid brass, which was to reduce the effect of any magnetic influence on the compass. Below the wheelhouse is the skipper's cabin, which doubles as a chartroom. It is fitted out with a wash hand basin, bunk and cushioned seats, with a wooden ladder leading to the deck above. At the aft end of the casing is the galley, with the entry on the starboard side. This door leads on to a short alleyway with stairs leading down to the engineroom, the aft cabins and a sliding door that leads into the galley, which had a tiled floor, range, etc. The engine room is typical of her class but free passage to the stokehold is restricted to the starboard side. Although seldom shown on plans, she must have been fitted with an electric generating plant, as the drawing shows an electric stern light. The after accommodation is divided into four compartments. At the foot of the access ladder is a small mess room with various cupboards and shelves. From here a door leads onto the after section, where there is a central coal fired heating stove complete with brass fender rail and mantle shelf, with a mirror over. At either side are two state rooms for the officers and the aft end carries four berths, a cushioned seat with a brass transom rail and a small triangular table. The poop house would have contained a WC and possibly a store. No port or starboard navigation lights are shown on the plan; presumably they would be on hinged light boxes either side of the verandah. *Imperialist* was destroyed after striking a mine in the North Sea on 6th September 1914, while some 40 miles ENE of Tynemouth.

Norman was requisitioned in May 1915 as a minesweeper and escort trawler, with the Admiralty No. 1575. In addition to her sweeping gear, she was armed with a 6 pounder AA gun and a bomb throwing mortar. Her name was changed to *Norman II* on 11th December 1915 and after the war, she went back to her former owners. By 1933, she was sailing under Hellyer's colours until called up again as *Dervish*, in June 1940, as a minesweeper. Unfortunately her days were numbered and she struck a mine in the North Sea off Spurn Point on 9th September of that year. The last of the trio, *Dane*, was also requisitioned in April 1915 and her name was changed to *Dane II* on 11th July of that year. After 1919, she returned to the Imperial Company and, in 1933, she was owned by the Dane Fishing Co. Ltd, Hull, until called up again as a minesweeper in January 1940 and given the number FY554. She was decommissioned in January 1946 and by 1947 was owned by H. Markham Cook Ltd of Hull.

In 1911, Smith's Dock received an order for twelve sister ships, Yard No's 483-494, for the Port of Blyth Steam Fishing & Ice Co. Ltd (117ft x 22ft x 11ft 7ins, 215g); their names were all pre-fixed *Lord* (See Appendix 4).

The second steam trawler to be laid down by Cook, Welton & Gemmell in 1912 was Yard No. 236 *Birch* (GY.677 – 118ft bp x 21.5ft x 11.5ft, 215g, 67nhp), engined by C.D. Holmes. She was built for William Grant, Grimsby and at first glance she looks just like any other vessel of the time (**Plan 29**). However, if one looks closely at her plan, one or two deviations from normal

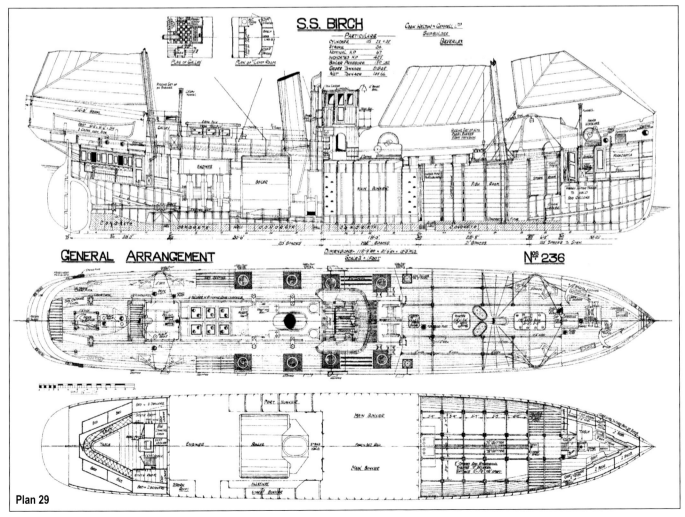

Plan 29

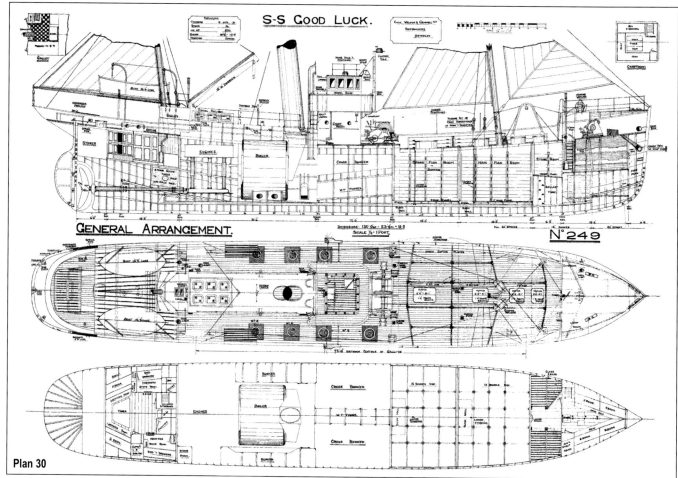

Plan 30

are apparent. Firstly her deck is on three levels; a raised foredeck runs aft, to the fore companionway, where it steps down some 12ins on to the maindeck and this deck steps up again to form a quarterdeck. This step up does not run square across the vessel, it angles back on either side of the trawl winch. The space below the wheelhouse, which would normally be occupied by the skipper, is actually a lamp room containing a WC (with a hinged top), a shelf for the lead line, and various other cupboards and storage shelves.

The skipper's berth is in the after accommodation, along with that of the two engineers and eight hands. This compartment has a coal stove for heating, with the stove pipe running up the inside of the steel tubular mizzen mast. The builder's drawing shows some very nice details, such as the two large anchors forward, with a smaller kedge anchor stowed beneath the boat aft. This was often the home of the spare propeller when carried. The combined anchor and mooring windlass is well drawn and even the compressor chock for the anchor cable is shown. The verandah is topped with a teak rail but as no pole compass is shown, it appears that she was a North Sea ship. The sidelights with their screens are drawn swung out on either side of this verandah. Her engine room skylight is teak, with an awning spar fitted over it. The plan view shows the four top sheaves on the casing and two strange 'sheet iron boxes' either side of the funnel, probably a type of fiddley grating, as they are in the wrong place for hauling up the waste ashes from the stokehold. This drawing is typical of the detail from this yard. She was requisitioned as a minesweeper in February 1915 and foundered in August the following year, after striking a mine off Great Yarmouth.

One of the earliest British trawlers to be fitted with twin lifeboats was *Good Luck* (H.497 – **Plan 30**), Yard No. 249 from Cook, Welton & Gemmell's Beverley yard, for the Humber Steam Trawling Co. Ltd, Hull. This upturn in crew safety came about after the tragic loss of the White Star Liner *Titanic* in April of that year, when the inadequacy of the life saving apparatus was highlighted and the Board of Trade introduced new rules for deep water vessels. She is a typical Icelandic trawler (130ft bp x 23ft 6ins x 12ft 6ins, 294g, 87nhp), with engines supplied by Amos & Smith. The drawing shows a hawse pipe on the starboard side, which means that she carried a stockless anchor, in addition to a fisherman's type on the port side, with its cable running through a hawse hole in the bulwarks under the whaleback. A pole compass is fixed to the front of the verandah, stayed back to the wheelhouse top by brass rods. The storm rail on the wheelhouse top is also brass in order to minimise magnetic influences on the main steering compass. The coast of Iceland was notorious for its interference on a magnetic compass, so every effort was made by trawler designers to reduce the ship's own magnetism by using non-ferrous metal fittings near the main compass. She was owned by the Humber Steam Trawling Co. Ltd, Hull, before being requisitioned as a minesweeper/escort trawler from April 1915 to 1919. By 1933, she was working out of Fleetwood as *Tranquil* (FD.425) and owned by Ashton & Welsh of Blackpool. Requisitioned again in February 1940 as a minesweeper, she was lost off Deal in June 1942.

Later on in 1912, Cook, Welton & Gemmel launched two pretty sister ships, *Rowsley* and *Suncloud*, Yard No's 251 and 252 (**Plan 31**). Similar in size to *Birch*, they were 'Hansom Cabs' but

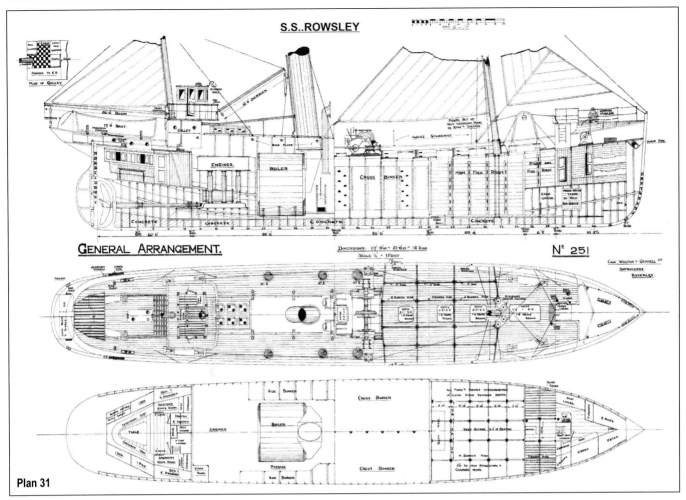

S.S. ROWSLEY

GENERAL ARRANGEMENT.

Nº 251

Plan 31

fitted with whaleback fo'c'sles (only a handful of this class were so fitted). *Rowsley* (GY.751) was built for W.H. Beeley (later Beeley & Sleight), who were to be her owners until 1947, when she went to Wyre Trawlers Ltd of Fleetwood. She finished with Ribble Trawlers Ltd, Fleetwood and went for scrap in 1953. Although working out of the Lancashire port, she kept her original GY registration. *Suncloud* GY.753, built for the Pelham Steam Fishing Co. Ltd of Grimsby, was sold to the North Western Steam Fishing Co. Ltd, Grimsby, in March 1914, and later to the Grimsby & North Sea Steam Trawling Co. Ltd. She went missing without trace on 24th June 1919, with no survivors, it being highly probable that she struck a mine and sank immediately. They were 117ft bp x 21ft 6ins x 12ft 3ins, 213g, with engines by Amos & Smith (12ins, 21ins, 34ins x 24ins stroke, 58nhp). As the drawing shows, they were very fine forward ('narrow-gutted' in trawlerman's terms) with a small whaleback. The standing rigging was set up with rods and sheaves from the sheer strake.

Thomas Devlin of Leith took delivery of three sister ships, *Commandant* (GN.36), *Coadjutor* (GN.41) and *Colleague* (GN.53), on 8th April 1915 from Hawthorns of Leith (Yard No's 139, 140 & 141 – 118ft bp x 22ft x 12ft 9ins). All three vessels were requisitioned during the First World War. *Commandant* was lost after striking a mine off the Sunk Light Vessel on 2nd April 1916 but her two sisters were returned to Devlin's in 1919. They spent the remainder of their careers working for the same owners, which proves that they must have been cost effective ships. With a bunker capacity of 120 tons and an endurance of around fifteen

days, they had capacity enough for working the North Sea, and the Faeroes. They both disappeared from the register in 1958, after no doubt being sold for scrap.

NEW STYLE OTTER BOARDS

Many new variations of trawl boards came on stream around this time, with each manufacturer claiming amazing results from their design. C.W. Brompton of Grimsby patented their 'Dreadnought' otter board, claiming that they were 100% stronger and considerably cheaper than other boards. They were fitted with two steel shoes that could be adjusted for fishing in deep or shallow water and the bottom shoe, which was made from a special rolled, hardened steel, could be renewed without taking the board to pieces. The timber used on these boards was pitch pine, with an oak base and with all bolt heads countersunk to minimise snagging on the net, or hooking up on obstacles littered around the seabed.

Other otter board manufacturers at this time included J.W. Loncaster of Hull, who patented their No. 17096, 'Reversible Loncaster Trawl Board' (**Fig. 21**, *page 41*) under the banner of the Fearnought Otter Board & Trawl Bobbin Company. This had a heavy bar and plate shoe, with spaces in the boards designed to reduce drag (a major load factor on both warps and engine power). Standard boards bearing the 'Dreadnought' stamp were also supplied by the firm (**Fig. 21**). The company patented metal, self connecting bobbins for the ground rope. They comprised of a four ribbed, split sleeve, which locked together around the wire; when damaged, it could be replaced much faster than the conventional solid type of bobbin.

Another reason for the streamlining of otter boards was the danger posed by the new submarine telephone cable, linking Thorshavn in Faeroe with Seydisfjord in Iceland. The operating concern, the Great Northern Telegraph Company, issued notices to owners and skippers, concerning the dangers of snagging, posed by using faulty shoes on beam trawl heads and otter boards. To this end, they suggested that:

'**A**. *All bolt heads on the inner side of an otter board should be round and smooth.*
B. *Nuts, if used at all, should be fixed on the outer side of the board, should project as little as possible, and should have their outer corners rounded off.*
C. *The bottom of the board should in no part be straight, but should be slightly curved from end to end.*
D. *The shoe should be smooth, and the bolts which secure it to the board should be countersunk.*
E. *The fore end of the shoe should be carried well up the front edge of the board where it should be made to fit closely to iron plates running up the front edge, and to terminate without projection, or indentation.*
F. *Generally, all attachments should be as simple and smooth as possible, and in every part of the board, the aim should be to afford no resting place for a cable if it should chance to be caught.'*

Our own Board of Trade issued several official notices to Owners and Skippers of trawlers, under the Submarine Telegraph Acts, 1885 and 1886, reminding them that:

'*The attention of the Board of Trade has been called to the injury which has been and may again be caused by trawlers to Submarine Telegraph Cables, and in view of the provisions of the above Act, they think it desirable to impress upon owners and skippers of both steam and sailing trawlers the necessity of examining from time to time the irons or heads of the trawls used on board their fishing vessels, and of keeping them in good condition. It has been pointed out that such injury to cables is exclusively due to the sharp edges, projecting points, bolt heads, &c., of old, worn, or carelessly repaired trawl irons. All trawls should therefore be frequently looked over, and particular care should be exercised in making all necessary repairs without delay. The Act imposes a penalty of imprisonment and fine upon any person who by culpable negligence breaks or injures a submarine cable.'*

This snagging of gear on the seabed was a major problem for fishermen. The strain thrown on the warps and associated deck fittings was tremendous, with often disastrous results. Warps would part, whipping across the deck, scything through anything in their path. Should nothing carry away, then, unless she could be worked free, the very ship herself might be dragged over on to her beam ends and possibly founder, as happened with the motor trawler *Hildena* (H.222) when she came fast off the west coast of Scotland in 1953. Speed is of the essence; to

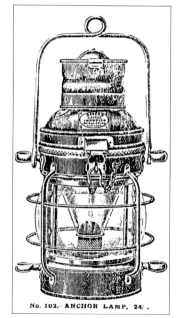

NO. 102.– ANCHOR LAMP. 24/.

Fig. 43

prevent this from happening, the winch brakes must be released immediately and the engines either stopped or put astern. Great skill is required by the skipper in order to free the gear and, even if successful, valuable fishing time would be lost while the crew repaired the damage to the net. The sea bed is covered with hidden fastenings not shown on any chart and their locations form an essential part of a skipper's knowledge, often handed down from father to son. The wreckage from two world wars, coupled to the everyday sinkings, added greatly to the danger of coming fast. These wrecks, however, often proved lucrative fishing spots for the skilful but the greatest care had to be taken in order to reap their rewards.

This problem almost vanished after 1930, when the fitting of echometers to trawlers became standard. Various new life-saving appliances were being offered to the industry – some were adopted but others never found favour. One of the latter and, again, a development from Merchant Navy practice, was the folding or collapsible lifeboat. The principal manufacturer was the Berthon Boat Co. Ltd and they supplied boats ranging from 8ft to 30ft overall, with capacities from three to sixty-three persons. Designed to stow flat either on deck or against the bulwarks, they could be ready for use within half a minute, when they would become '*The safest and most buoyant boats that can be desired*'. The price in 1910 for an 8ft boat was 10 guineas (£10 10s). More detailed charts were being published by Imray, Laurie, Norie & Wilson Ltd, specifically for fishermen's use, showing all territorial limits, currents, distances from point to point and all popular fishing grounds. The terminology used was common throughout the industry, making these charts more user friendly than the Admiralty versions. Although electric lights were slowly coming into use (the first such installation had been fitted to *Emu* (GY.1) in 1896), it would be many years before the BoT or the later Ministry of Transport agreed to remove oil lamps from ships inventories. One manufacturer was Davey & Co. of London, who supplied oil navigation lamps with both plain and dioptre lenses, in copper or galvanised housings. Prices ranged from 50s a pair for galvanised to 72s 6d for copper, both with plain lenses, to 95s a pair for copper, dioptric lamps (**Fig. 43**)

Improvements were slowly creeping into the sanitary and living conditions aboard trawlers but, on the home front, few houses had hot and cold running water, inside toilets, electricity or a bath. When ashore, the trawlerman could enjoy the hospitality of the Royal National Mission to Deep Sea Fishermen, with warm beds, good food, current newspapers, games rooms and hot baths. In Grimsby, the Fisher Lads Institute offered swimming baths and hot baths to fishermen. Charges were sixpence for a second class and one shilling for a first class bath, with a discount for buying twelve tickets and guaranteed 'no waiting'.

WIRELESS EQUIPMENT

If there was one item of equipment that did more to make the seaman's job safer, it was surely the introduction of wireless, so that seafarers could summon help, obtain weather forecasts

Photo. 40: Mark boat *Columbia* (H.42), showing the aerial array on the tall foremast.

gave a mean aerial height of 100ft above the waterline. The reader should pause for a moment and think of what this mast height really meant on a vessel the size of a trawler, the equivalent of an eight storey block of flats. So it was that, in June of 1913, these two ships sailed down the Humber towards the Danish coast, to test the new equipment. The performance exceeded all expectations with an average inter-ship range of 90 miles. *Othello*, with her smaller sets, worked Cullercoats Radio from a distance of 180 miles and with her sister at 100 miles. *Caesar* had no problem working Cullercoats from 270miles away, even when her aerial was lowered to a height of 65ft. Scheveningen Radio could still be raised at 195miles.

Delighted with these results, Hellyer's immediately placed an order with Marconi for three installations similar to that aboard *Othello* and one of the twin 3kw systems fitted to *Caesar*. These were duly fitted to the mark boat *Columbia* (H.42) and the trawlers *Bardolph* (H.296 – **Photo. 40**) and *Caliban* (H.76). These last two vessels were sister ships built in 1911 by Cook, Welton & Gemmell at Beverley as No's 217 and 218 (both 112ft x 22.5ft x 12.33ft, 215g, 87n), with engines by Amos & Smith (10ins, 16.75ins, 28ins x 24ins stroke, 46nhp, from a working pressure of 200psi). In early November 1913, *Caliban* left the Humber bound for the Dogger Bank under 'Vice Admiral' Windas. She was followed on 24th by Hellyer's flagship *Bardolph*, commanded by 'Admiral' Lynne and the mark-boat *Columbia*. This boat was, at the time, the last word in equipment, with a Marconi radio, wireless compass, directional aerials, searchlight and electric light. The sets fitted to *Columbia* were 3kw, each with a range of around 300 miles. Until then, ships returning to the fishing fleet had great difficulty actually finding it, as fishing grounds would frequently change. Searching for this elusive fleet was a costly business, losing valuable fishing time and burning up expensive coal. With *Columbia*, all this changed, for through the night she used rockets and her powerful searchlight to mark her position. Trawlers were then informed by loudhailer as to the exact whereabouts of the fishing fleet.

As soon as the flagship trawler *Bardolph* joined the fishing fleet, she made wireless contact with the shore and sent the following message to the President of the Board of Agriculture & Fisheries:

'Greetings from Lynn, Admiral, Hellyer's steam trawling fleet – the first British steam trawling fleet fitted with Marconi wireless telegraph apparatus and wireless compass. Fleet now 210 miles E.N.E. from Spurn'

In reply, Mr Runciman, congratulated the fleet by sending a radio telegram, praising the owners for their valuable pioneering joint venture with the Marconi company. Other inaugural messages were sent from the fleet. *Wireless World*, January 1914, stated:

'We can confidently predict that henceforth the fortunate trawlers possessing this equipment will wonder however it was they managed to exist without this aid to navigation and business enterprise.'

Of these wireless pioneers, *Othello* sank off Leathercoat Point, Kent after striking a mine. At the time she was an Admiralty controlled fishing vessel. *Bardolph* was sunk in the North Sea by gunfire from a U-boat, 115 miles S by W of Sumburgh Head on 5th June 1915. *Caliban* went the same way on 12th April 1917,

and market information. The latter enabled them to proceed to alternative discharge ports without first having to make a landfall, as by using radio direction beacons, a fairly accurate ship's position could be plotted. This market information was doubly important to the fishing skipper, as he had to catch his market when very few other ships were landing. This would ensure the highest price for his fish, thus ensuring a decent wage for the crew and profit for the owners. Even to miss one tide could put up to three weeks hard work in jeopardy, with the vessel ending up in debt. Possibly, it was these financial implications which concerned one owner enough that, in 1913, he set up an experiment using radio equipment for the first time aboard two of his vessels. The partners were Hellyer's Steam Fishing Co. Ltd, Hull and Marconi International Marine, one providing the ships, and the other the equipment and operators. They also asked the coastal radio stations of Germany, Holland and Norway to keep a listening watch for signals from the trawlers. The first problem to be overcome was that neither of the two vessels had any form of electricity on board, so portable generators were installed on the trawler *Othello* (H.956) and the carrier *Caesar* (H.874), which supplied enough power for the radio gear. *Othello* was fitted with two 0.5kw sets and *Caesar*, requiring greater range, with two 3kw sets, one a marine type and the other a portable military unit. After the installations were completed, it was discovered that the vessels' masts were not high enough for maximum efficiency, so wooden topmasts were fitted to *Othello* and two brand new wooden masts were fitted to *Caesar*, which

Photo. 41: *Bempton.* Note the height of her masts and port side gallows only, with spare trawl doors stowed alongside the casing. The wireless cabin is ahead of the funnel. Colour scheme of black hull, brown casing and black funnel, whilst the logo is a red cross on a white flag.

some 45 miles off Rattray Head on the Buchan coast. *Columbia* was torpedoed on 1st May 1915, while working under Admiralty instructions for fishing trawlers. The year 1915 was particularly bad for the fleeters: Hellyer's lost fifteen ships and the Hull Steam Fishing & Ice Co. Ltd lost eight. In all, Hull lost fifty-one ships in twelve months, whilst Grimsby lost eighty-seven vessels, Aberdeen lost thirty-seven. Fleetwood fared a little better, only losing three ships, one of which, *Lucerne* (FD.34), built at North Shields in 1906, was sunk by a submarine off Rattray Head. She was owned by J. Marr & Son and at the time she was working out of Aberdeen. As no provision had been made for radio sets when these early trawlers were built, they had to be shoe-horned into any available space. Until radio rooms were specified on the initial outfit, the wireless equipment was usually in the skipper's berth, with the aerial lead-in fitted on the wheelhouse roof. The 1938 statistics for Scotland showed a total of 334 steam trawlers and liners fitted with radios. Out of this number, 190 had transmitting and receiving sets, with the remaining 144 having receiving sets only.

The earliest trawler drawing that I have showing an 'as fitted', radio room is that of the sister ships *Filey* (H.8) and *Bempton* (H.19 – 115ft x 22ft 6ins x 12ft 4ins, 226g). Built for the Hull Steam Fishing & Ice Co. Ltd at the Beverley yard of Cook, Welton & Gemmell as Yard No's 284 and 285, *Filey* was launched in late 1913 and *Bempton* (**Photo. 41**) sailed in February 1914. Amos & Smith supplied their 49nhp engines. The drawing shows the Marconi Room as a steel tank some 8ft square by 7ft high, in which

lived the wireless operator and his equipment. It was entered by a companionway on the casing top and by descending a wooden ladder. Fitted to the roof were the forward two casing top sheaves which led the messenger wires to the winch and when they were in use, the conducted noise inside the cabin must have been most distracting for the operator. After the fitting of wireless equipment became standard, the radio room was usually placed at the rear of the bridge, with the steam steering gear separating it from the wheelhouse. Some of Crampins' ships, however, had the wireless cabin on the main deck at the forward end of the casing below the wheel house and in a similar position to that of *Filey* and *Bempton*.

From day one wireless operators were segregated from the rest of the crew. They were not employed by the owners but on contract to them from his parent company, Marconi, with the radio equipment. They were not part of the deck crew and neither were they engineer but although they ate their meals aft with the officers, they slept in the radio cabin. Ashore, the 'sparks' steered clear of the fishermen, they drank in their own pubs and often lived out of town in private houses. They worked closely with the skipper, acting as his technical assistant and although they drew the same 'poundage' as the crew, they were resented by them as they never handled the fish. When the later vessels were fitted with liver boilers, it became part of the 'sparks' job to tip the baskets of livers into the hopper and boil them down for the oil. This smelly distasteful job, however, only fell to the wireless operators on the Hull ships. The 'sparks' were the butt of all the jokes aboard a trawler and was considered to have a real cushy number. This of course was untrue; they had to study hard at college for a licence before ever setting foot on a trawler and, when at sea, his hours were long and demanding. More especially so when repairs had to be made to vital equipment. However, although the crew tormented them, the 'sparks' held their grudging respect, for the crew knew that, when danger threatened, these men were their only contact with the outside world.

To return to *Filey* and *Bempton*, the builder's plan (**Plan 32**) shows a flush-decked 'Hansom Cab' trawler. The small boat stowage was forward on the starboard side and they were designed as fleeters, with trawl gallows fitted only on the port side. They were remarkably well equipped, with a large searchlight on the open bridge and two compasses, a standard binnacle type and a pole compass in front of the verandah.

They have large water ballast tanks fore and aft. A store room is fitted right up in the eyes, with a timber ceiling, which is entered through the circular deck hatch in front of the windlass and down a vertical ladder. Below this hatch is a small cylindrical oil tank. The crew's fo'c'sle sleeps five and has a stove, small table, two wooden benches and a cupboard fitted with coat hooks. On the port side is a sealed cupboard for rockets, with a seat locker in front, and on the starboard side is the coal box for the stove. A door leads aft into another large store. This has a square hatch on deck and a lamp room on the starboard side. Below is a 1,200 gallon fresh water tank. A watertight bulkhead separates this from the main hold

which, were they dedicated trawlers, would be shown on the plan as 'main fish room' and fitted with shelves and partitions. This compartment is bare, with only a central floor open to the sides for the stowage of boxed fish and no ice room is shown, which would be necessary for the good condition of the catch. There is nothing out of the ordinary about the boiler and machinery spaces, and the only small point about the aft cabin is the rather large flour bin outside the captain's state room. On deck, there is a WC on the starboard side abreast the windlass, a set of Atkinsons centre bollards abaft the foremast and a limited arrangement of deck pounds. Her rig was standard for the time, with the exception of her masts which, if one projects the stays and the mast centrelines, give a height of around 90ft above the waterline.

From this, it seems that they were mark boats for the fleet, and used their searchlights and rockets to signal approaching trawlers before directing them to the fishing grounds. *Bempton*'s radio call sign was given as MFBR but no call sign was allotted to *Filey* until around 1946, when she received the letters GKVF, so it would appear that no wireless transmitter was actually fitted to her until then. *Bempton* was requisitioned in April 1915 as a minesweeper and fitted with a 12 pounder gun. She returned to civilian life in 1919, under the Hull Steam Fishing & Ice Co's flag. In 1937, they sold her to Heward Trawlers Ltd, London with the fishing number LO.192. In 1945, she was under the Loyal Steam Fishing Co. Ltd, Grimsby, as GY.29. They sold her in 1951 to the Aberdeen owners Alexander Hay and J. Mair, as A.673; she

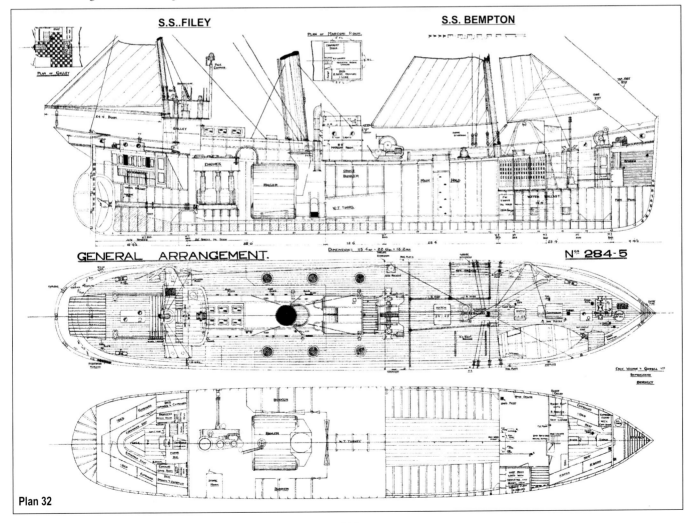

Plan 32

Photo. 42: *Filey* (A.232) in later years. The enclosed wheelhouse is now forward of the funnel and gallows are fitted both sides. No whalebacks were fitted to her or her sister.

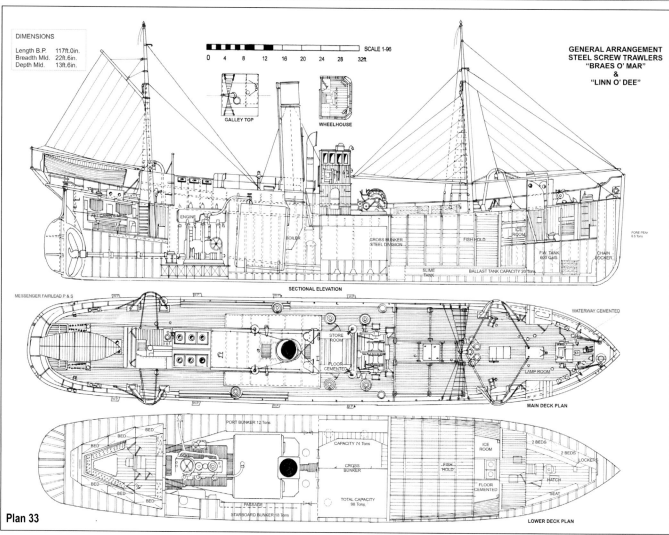

DIMENSIONS

Length B.P. 117ft.0in.
Breadth Mld. 22ft.6in.
Depth Mld. 13ft.6in.

SCALE 1-96

0 4 8 12 16 20 24 28 32ft.

GALLEY TOP

WHEELHOUSE

GENERAL ARRANGEMENT
STEEL SCREW TRAWLERS
"BRAES O' MAR"
&
"LINN O' DEE"

ENGINE

BOILER

CROSS BUNKER
STEEL DIVISION

FISH HOLD

ICE ROOM

FORE PEAK
9.5 Tons

SLIME TANK

BALLAST TANK CAPACITY 20 Tons

F.W. TANK
605 Galls

CHAIN LOCKER

SECTIONAL ELEVATION

MESSENGER FAIRLEAD P & S

STORE ROOM

FLOOR CEMENTED

WATERWAY CEMENTED

LAMP ROOM

MAIN DECK PLAN

PORT BUNKER 12 Tons

BED BED BED

BED

BED BED

CAPACITY 74 Tons

CROSS BUNKER

FISH HOLD

ICE ROOM

2 BEDS

2 BEDS

LOCKERS

HATCH

PASSAGE

STARBOARD BUNKER 18 Tons

TOTAL CAPACITY
98 Tons

FLOOR CEMENTED

SEAT

LOWER DECK PLAN

Plan 33

Photo. 43: HMT *Daisy*. Note the tall fidded topmast, the rail around the monkey island above the wheelhouse, her twin boat arrangement and trawl gallows. The space between the winch and mast would be a little short for commercial fishing operations. Note also the door into the vegetable locker and meat room, which replaced the hatch on the drawing.

was not in the 1959 register. Her sister *Filey* was called up for war service in March 1915, with the Admiralty, No. 1363. On 2nd October 1916, she went ashore on Tory Island, Donegal. She was salvaged and re-acquired in February 1918 as Admiralty No. 3826. On the cessation of hostilities, she returned to her former owners as H.19 and she too went to Heward's as LO.189. By 1948, she was working out of Aberdeen under A. Hay as A.232 and she went for scrapping at Antwerp on 15th June 1959.

I remember these two trawlers working from Aberdeen in the 1950s. By that time their wheelhouses were forward, as the photograph of *Filey* shows (**Photo. 42**). It was not until 1931 that the first Grimsby trawlers were fitted with experimental radios. The ships were *Suarian* (GY.901) owned by Harold Croft Baker & Sons, Grimsby and *Frascati* (GY.315), owned by the Strand Fishing Co. Ltd, Grimsby. The former vessel transferred to Sir Thomas Robinson & Son, Grimsby Ltd, fleet in February 1937, was requisitioned in June 1940 for minesweeping duties as FY1726 and was returned in November 1945. She eventually went to the Belgium breakers in October 1961. *Frascati* was sold to H. Markham Cook Ltd, Grimsby, in October 1933. A month later, she was owned by the Alfred Fishing Co., Grimsby and she worked commercially throughout the war, having been purchased by Bennett Trawlers in October 1941. In August 1945, she went to a London owner and, by 1947, she was owned by the British & American Salmon Curing Co. Ltd.

By 1915, Hawthorns were making a name for themselves as builders of fine steam trawlers, such as their *Braes o' Mar* and *Linn o' Dee*, Yard No's 143 and 144 (**Plan 33**). The windlass,

although hand operated, is fitted with a chain drive off a gypsy on the port side of the main steam trawl winch, which would have eased the anchor work considerably. *Braes o' Mar* (A.331) and her sister *Linn o' Dee* (A338) were built for the Standard Steam Fishing Co. Ltd, Aberdeen and followed the owners penchant for naming their ships after places on Royal Deeside. The former was requisitioned in September 1915 and returned to her owners in 1919. She was requisitioned again in 1939 as an armed patrol vessel and returned in 1940. *Linn o' Dee* was also requisitioned in 1915 as a minesweeper and returned in 1919. She was then acquired by J. Lockhart, Edinburgh, who remained her *Ocean Brine* (LH.78). Requisitioned again in 1939 as an armed patrol vessel, she returned to her owners in 1944.

DUTHIE'S SURVEY TRAWLERS AND OTHER ABERDEEN-BUILT SHIPS

The only drawing I have from the John Duthie Torry shipyard is a proposal for *Daisy* and *Esther* (125ft x 22ft 6ins, 475g), built as survey trawlers in 1911 and fitted for trawling, with double gallows, etc but minus any fishroom hatches (**Plan 34**). A trials photograph shows *Daisy* passing the old pontoon dock in Aberdeen harbour, with her very tall fidded fore-topmast and wireless aerials, with the lead in clearly shown on the wheelhouse roof (**Photo. 43**).

They are quite austere ships, with no whaleback but a double barrelled steam windlass for the two close stowing anchors. Being designed for naval use, their internal layout was quite different to that of a commercial trawler. The galley was on the main deck, under the fo'c'sle head, along with a forepeak paint store, petty

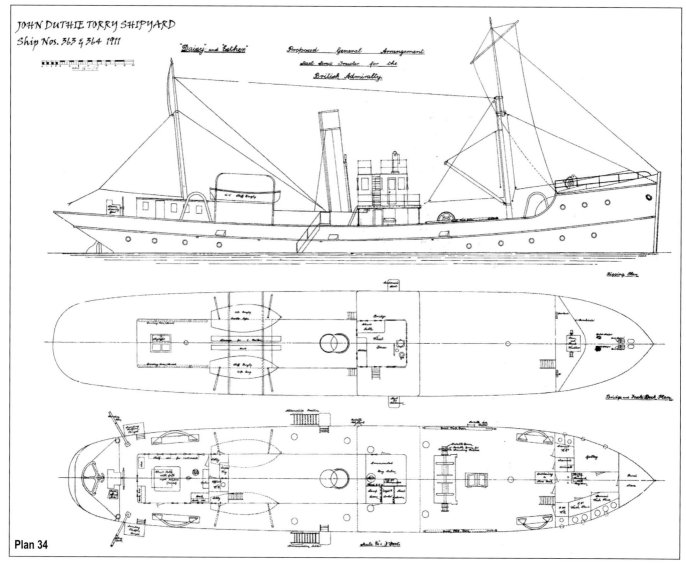

Plan 34

officer's and seaman's washrooms, and urinals. A small central hatch opening leads into the hammock and bag room (no bunks for the matelots aboard these trawlers). The seaman's mess deck occupied what would have been the fish room space on a conventional trawler, with natural daylight coming from portholes in the ship's side and a small skylight on the main deck in front of the trawl winch. The larger than normal wheelhouse contains a settee, in addition to the spartan outfit of ship's wheel, compass and engineroom telegraph. A standard binnacle sits on the wheelhouse roof but no aerial lead-ins are shown on the plan, although they appear in the trials photograph. Below the wheelhouse, in the space normally occupied by the skipper, is the Commander's cabin complete with coal heating stove and a box for no less than three chronometers. On the starboard side is the lamp room, a vegetable locker and a meat room. On the plan, a hinged flap is shown as the only access to the latter two compartments but, on completion, a door was fitted (*see* **Photo. 38**). No stokehold ventilators are shown on the drawing but again the photograph shows their positions. At the after end of the casing is a large cabin or survey room, fitted with a central chart table with a large skylight above. A door on the port side leads into the entrance lobby, with the officers' WC and ladder down to the after accommodation. A watertight door on the starboard side of the casing opens onto the ladder for the

engine room. The steam steering gear sits on the open deck aft under a protective casing, with the wheel exposed to the elements

The ship's boats comprise of a standard 16ft trawler lifeboat and a 16ft skiff dinghy, both stowed over the casing in front of the mizzen mast and fitted with radial davits. The bulwarks are fitted with various booms and platforms for the leadsman and sounding machine operator, plus the accommodation ladder. The tall topmast crosses a signalling yard not evident on the photographs. These two vessels were fitted out as minesweepers prior to the outbreak of the First World War and were among the handful of trawlers actually owned by the Admiralty at that time, forming the nucleus of the Auxiliary Patrol. After the hostilities, *Daisy* went to Fishery Protection duty and was based for a time at Yarmouth. Her sister was purchased from the Admiralty in 1919 for £6,500 by HM Customs, who spent a further £2,000 refitting the ship for her new role and changed her name to *Vigilant*. After some nine years service, she was sold to the Royal Swedish Customs Service for £2,200.

Another Duthie-built vessel that had a long working life was *Onetos* (A.592 – 115ft 3ins x 22ft 1in x 11ft 9ins, 217g). She was built for the National Steam Fishing Co. Ltd, Aberdeen, whose vessel names all ended in 'os' (*see* **Appendix 4**). She was hired as a minesweeper from August 1914 until 1919. By 1933, she was

Photo. 44: *Onetos*. The lack of winch and gallows denote that she is a steam liner. Note the short fidded topmasts for her wireless aerials. It appears that her whaleback was added later. She is outward bound passing the old Torry Dock, Aberdeen which disappeared in the 1970s to be replaced by an oil terminal.

owned by A.L. Banyard of Leith but, by 1937, she was owned by L. Carnie & Others, Glasgow. She was requisitioned in November 1939 as FY761, an auxiliary patrol vessel, until May 1940. By June, she was a minesweeper and, from April 1944, she served as a wreck dispersal vessel until her return in January 1946. This last conversion was for clearance work after the 'D' Day landings and she shared this duty with another two old trawlers, *Madden* (GN.101 – the ex-non standard 'Strath' Class *William Browning*, Hall, Russell's, 1917) and *Sunlight* (A.221 – ex-'Strath' Class *Thomas Graham*, Scott of Bowling, 1918). In addition, the War Department fleet comprised of a further twelve ships of the 'Isles' and 'Dance' classes. During her minesweeping duties, she was fitted with an LL sweep for magnetic mines, her official log entry for the 15th. August 1943, states: '*Damage repairs to LL sweep. Defects to LL sweep, 'O' will be completed 19/8. Expect to sail 20/8*'. Another entry in 1944 states: '*8th. Jan. Am informed by P.S.O. Aberdeen that 'O' has been taken by Admiralty for conversion to Demolition Store Carrier*'. The conversion work was taken in hand and the next entry reads, '*April 21st. Leith, 'O' now wreck dispersal vessel.*'

These three old trawlers were used to ferry stores and explosives to the wreck sites, which before the war would have been the responsibility of the three lighthouse boards but the proliferation of wartime wrecks forced the Admiralty to take a hand and so the Wreck Dispersal Department was formed. Its primary task was to clear the wrecks using explosives and obtain a 36ft clearance depth at low water. By the end of hostilities, there were still some 430 wrecks in home water channels and 150 in harbour approaches. After mine clearance, the dispersal work was estimated to take another two or three years to complete. As many of the harbour

wrecks lay in shallow water, they had to be either lifted or cut up where they lay. *Onetos* went to the Stephen Fishing Co. Ltd, Aberdeen and was re-registered as A.119. She worked as a great liner until going for scrap in 1960 (**Photo. 44**). At some point in their careers, presumably after the Second World War, both *Onetos* and *Sophos* were fitted with whalebacks but their sister *Lotos* remained 'as built' to the end and only *Onetos* was converted from trawling to lining.

Alexander Hall launched two sister ships in 1912, Yard No's 482 and 485, *Princess Beatrice* (SN.202) and *Princess Royal* (SN.209 – 117ft' x 22ft 6ins x 13ft, 213g), both for the Dodds Steam Fishing Co. Ltd, North Shields. They were nothing out of the ordinary for North Sea ships. Only very small differences are apparent from the builder's plan and these include the old fashioned side light houses with their screens placed on top of the port side WC and the starboard lamp room. In addition, she carries another set of side lights in hinged brackets either side of the galley casing. The entrance to the skipper's berth below the wheelhouse was by way of a square companionway on the aft side, rather than internally from the deck above. Their coal capacity would have given them about ten days duration but, as 'scratchers', they would seldom be away for more than a week at time. This was a local term; 'scratchers' went for short trips to the Near Water grounds and 'trippers' went usually to Faeroe but sometimes to Iceland. Both trawlers were requisitioned in 1914 for minesweeping duties. *Princess Beatrice* had a short naval career, being sunk by a mine off the Belgian coast on 5th October 1914. Her sister *Princess Royal* went back to her former owners and disappeared from the registers after 1939. Dodds had another two larger sisters built by A. Hall in 1914.

They were yard No's 496 and 497, *Princess Mary* (SN.27) and *Princess Alice* (SN.15 – 120ft 6ins x 22ft 6ins x 13ft, 225g). Their engines (12ins, 34ins x 24ins stroke) developed 57nhp/450ihp at 180psi. The crew's fo'c'sle slept eight hands, the entrance being shared with a WC compartment, the discharge pipe for which actually passed through the crew space. Their deck was typical of any Middle Distance trawler, although the wheelhouse was only about the size of that of a steam drifter, with a door on the port side, a verandah and a pole compass. Both were in action during the First World War. *Princess Mary* joined the navy in March 1915 and served as a hydrophone trawler until being returned in 1919. *Princess Alice* was called up in April 1915 as a minesweeper and sank a long way from home, after a collision on 6th March 1918, off Alexandria. In common with many trawlers, *Princess Mary* kept her Admiralty radio and D/F installation after the war, using the signal letters MFCK. She left Dodds sometime in the early 1930s and went to Granton as GN.11 for T.L. Devlin & Co. Ltd, Edinburgh. She was requisitioned again in 1940, as FY876, as a minesweeper and she was returned in 1945. She continued under Devlin's until being sold for £4,550 to the British Iron & Steel Corporation for scrapping at Charlestown on 19th November 1956.

ENGLISH YARDS

A 1913-built trawler that was to live to a ripe old age was *Ampulla* (GY.949). She was launched by Cook, Welton & Gemmell as Yard No. 273 for the Loyal Steam Fishing Co. Ltd, Grimsby. Her sisters were *Vindelicia* (GY.452), Yard No. 274, for the Great Grimsby & East Coast Steam Fishing Co. Ltd, and Yard No. 274A *Simerson* (GY 960 – 120ft x 22ft 6ins x 12ft, 248g) for the Standard Steam Fishing Co. Ltd, with 62nhp engines supplied by Amos & Smith.

Ampulla was requisitioned in September 1914 as a minesweeper and returned to Grimsby in 1919. She was called up again in 1940 as an armed patrol trawler, being sold out of service in 1946. During and post war, she was bought and sold on three occasions. The first time in May 1940 to Sir Alec Black, Grimsby and then from February to March 1943 she belonged to the Public Trustees, who passed her on to Grimsby Motor Trawlers Ltd. In April 1953, she went to Derwent Trawlers Ltd, Grimsby and finally to Ross Trawlers Ltd, Grimsby in 1959. She eventually went to the breakers at Ghent in February 1962. Her two sisters shared her longevity. *Vindelicia* was requisitioned in September 1914 as a minesweeper and returned to her owners in 1919. She was sold in February 1937 to H.G. Hopwood & C. Taylor Ltd, Grimsby and again in June that year to the Japan Fishing Co. Hired again in June 1940 as FY.1711, she served firstly as an armed patrol trawler, then as a refueller, until returned in December 1945. She sank on 4th December 1960, some 90 miles off Spurn Point. *Simerson* was hired in April 1915, also as a minesweeper and returned in 1919. She went along the same ownership path as *Vindelicia* and was also requisitioned again in July 1940 as an armed patrol trawler, until released in June 1946. She was to stay with the Japan Fishing Co. Ltd, Grimsby until July 1956, when they sold her to Belgium.

In 1913, the Standard Steam Fishing Co. Ltd took delivery of a new trawler from Cook, Welton & Gemmell who had moved to Beverley. She was Yard No. 259 *Strephon* (GY.810 – 120ft bp x 22ft 6ins x 12ft 10ins, 249g). She was requisitioned in March 1915 as a hydrophone trawler, with the Admiralty No.1233. Returned to the Standard Company in 1919, she worked for them until sold in March 1937 to H.G. Hopwood & C. Taylor Ltd of Grimsby. By June of that year, she was under the Japan Steam Fishing Co.

Photo. 45: *Margaret Duncan*, a rare photograph of a Liverpool trawler. Note the large complement aboard for her acceptance trials. She is shown in her original colours of light grey hull, brown superstructure and black funnel with broad yellow band. There is a red and yellow diagonal motif on a blue flag – the upper yellow segment shows a red 'D' and the lower red segment shows a yellow 'L'. Her fishing numbers are not strictly correct but are still very visible. Later her hull was painted black, as light colours did not wear well on trawlers.

Ltd's flag (a paper transaction, as the Japan Steam Fishing Co. Ltd belonged to Taylor). She was called up again in the Second World War as a minesweeper in August 1940, with the Admiralty number FY1829, and returned in February 1946 to Taylor, who kept her until she was sold to Holland in October 1961. A sister ship to this *Strephon* was Yard No. 258 *Silicia* (GY.809). Launched in 1912, she was handed over to her owners, the Great Grimsby & East Coast Steam Fishing Co. Ltd, in January 1913. She was also requisitioned for minesweeping duties from September 1914 and returned to her former owners in 1919. By 1937. she too was under the Japan Fishing Co. Ltd's flag and was called up for minesweeping again in August 1939. She was lost on 8th May 1941, after striking a mine off the Humber Estuary.

Also in 1913, Cochranes built Yard No. 557 *Margaret Duncan* (LL.123 – 120ft x 22ft x 12ft 4ins, 224g), with engines supplied by C.D. Holmes. She was built to the order of J. Duncan of Liverpool and looked every inch a classic deep water ship (**Photo. 45**). She was requisitioned in December 1914 as Admiralty No. 593, for minesweeping, and returned in 1919. In May 1934, she went to Grimsby as *Luda Lord* (GY.50), owned by the Dobson Ship Repairing Co. She was called up again in November 1939, as FY776, for minesweeping duties and later became a stores carrier, returning in November 1944. By March 1945, she belonged to the Wembley Steam Fishing Co., who sold her in February 1947 to the Vinur Steam Fishing Co. Ltd of Grimsby, who kept her until she went for scrap in November 1963, the very last vessel to be owned by the company.

Lowestoft in Suffolk received its first custom built steam trawler

in 1914 from Smith's Dock. She was Yard No .589 *Lolist* (LT.427 – 105ft x 21ft 2ins x 11ft 8ins,180g), built for W. Robbens & Co. Ltd, Lowestoft. A handsome ship, she was the owner's third steam trawler, his other two being ex-Hull ships built in 1894 by Cook, Welton & Gemmell as iron fleeters, Yard No's 117 and 118, *Adelaide* (H.239) and *Labrador* (H.246) respectively. *Lolist* served as a fishery trawler during the First World War and in 1938 she went to T. Bilton & Sons, North Shields but kept her LT registration. A year later she was owned in Dundee by the Den Fishing Co. Ltd, Dundee, who sold her in 1953 to John Murray of Buckie as *Lolist* (BCK. 29 – **Photo. 46**); note her smart appearance and the blue shading to her fishing numbers, so typical of Moray Firth vessels. Very few steam trawlers were registered at the Moray Firth ports, although a few were owned there. They worked out of Aberdeen and bore Aberdeen fishing numbers. Although the port had a large fleet of trawling smacks, these three ships were to form the nucleus of its steam trawling fleet. Smith's Dock Co. in Middlesborough were building their 'D' Class trawlers in the 1914 period and Yard No's 570 and 571 were *Delphine* (GY.958) and *Drusilla* (GY.951 – both 125ft x 23ft 6ins x 12ft 4ins, 250g) for Consolidated Fisheries Ltd, Grimsby (**Plan 35**). They were not unlike the builder's later 'Castle' Class trawlers, except they had a turtle-backed whaleback, as opposed to the flat-topped type common to the others. One feature that stands out is a pair of radial davits fitted on deck aft, for launching the boat; very few fishing trawlers actually had this arrangement, although another example was the 1912 Cochrane-built *Sapphire* (H.675 – 133ft 6ins, 289g) owned by the Kingston Steam Trawling Co. Ltd,

Photo. 46: *Lolist*. Her Engineer seems to be blowing out her boiler tubes. She has a black hull, separated from her red boot topping by a white line. Her wood grained casing had wooden wheelhouse windows and her funnel is buff, with a black top and a white 'M' in a red star. Her name and fishing numbers are in the traditional Scottish style for boats and drifters, being 'Rockwell Bold' with light blue shading, although the aft set have yet to be shaded.

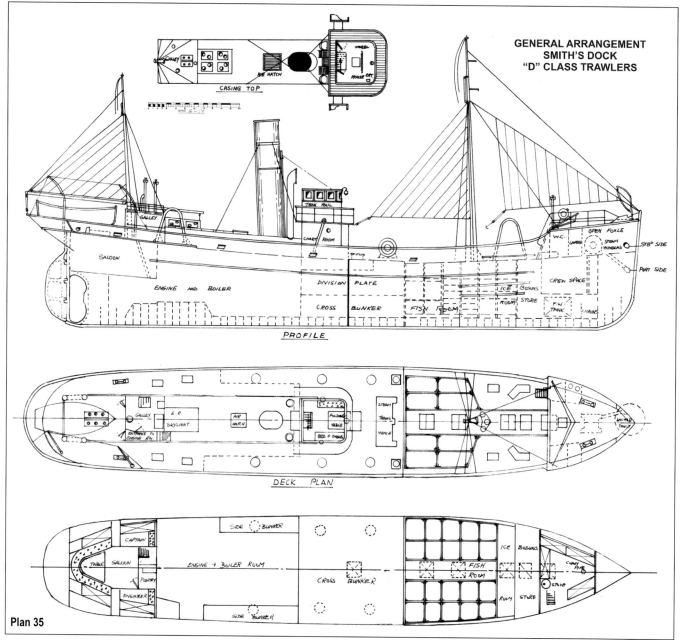

GENERAL ARRANGEMENT
SMITH'S DOCK
"D" CLASS TRAWLERS

Plan 35

Hull and lost off the Yorkshire coast on 1st March 1915, after striking a mine. Both *Delphine* and *Drusilla* were requisitioned as minesweepers for the duration of the First World War and were returned to 'Consols' in 1919. In 1934, they came to Aberdeen as *Delphine* (A.126) and *Drusilla* (A.133), owned by the North Star Steam Fishing Co. Ltd, Aberdeen. *Delphine* was sold to the Boston Deep Sea Fisheries Co. Ltd, Grimsby, in October 1939 and a month later, on 20th November, was sunk some 18 miles off Tory Island, Donegal, by gunfire from *U33*. Her sister *Drusilla* was sold for £4,750 to the City Steam Fishing Co. Ltd, Hull (Marr & Co.) on 31st October 1939. She was later sold to the Eton Steam Fishing Co. Ltd, Hull for £18,500 in January 1945. Her last owners in 1948, were Alfred Bannister (Trawlers) Ltd, Grimsby, and, as GY.223, she went to the breakers in 1959.

In 1916, Cochrane's built Yard No. 650 *St. Cuthbert* (GY.824 – 136ft 8ins x 23ft 6ins x 13ft, 311g) for the Victoria Steam Fishing Co. Ltd, Grimsby. She was a Distant Water vessel, with engines by C.D. Holmes (13ins x 23ins x 37ins x 24ins stroke).

She was requisitioned as a minesweeper in April 1916 and fitted with a 12 pounder, a 7ins gun and a bomb throwing mortar. During her naval service, she was bought by the New Docks Steam Fishing Co. Ltd, Fleetwood and received the new fishing number (FD.137). They later sold her to Canadian owners Ocean Trawlers Ltd, Halifax, Nova Scotia, in 1928. She was sold again in 1936 to Warren Transport Ltd, British Honduras, who converted her to a motor cargo vessel. By 1940, she was registered to St. Cuthbert Ltd, British Honduras. Owned by the Mc.Cormack Shipping Corporation, Panama since 1958, she was apparently still afloat in 1990.

Cochrane's also built Yard No. 722 *General Botha* (A.709 – 124ft 6ins x 22ft 6ins x 13ft, 244g) in 1916, for Dodds Steam Fishing Co. Ltd, Aberdeen. Her fishroom was fitted with acetylene gas lighting but there is very little else to set her apart from any other trawler of the time, although the deck plan shows a very fine fore-end, which would have made her quite fast but very wet to work. She served as a minesweeper from December 1916 until

1919. In February 1920, she went to Grimsby as GY.1025, owned by the Canute Steam Fishing Co. Ltd, Grimsby. In 1924, she returned to Aberdeen and, by 1932, she was owned by John Lewis Ltd, Aberdeen, as A.194. She was requisitioned again in July 1940 as a minesweeper and became a film star, playing the part of the German vessel *Konigin Louise* in the Air Sea Rescue documentary *For Those In Peril*. She returned to fishing in November 1945 with her former owners. By 1953, she was sailing under the flag of North Eastern Fisheries Ltd, Aberdeen and eventually went to Charlestown for scrapping on 15th November 1959. Even at the last, she remained little changed from the ship that slipped sideways into the River Ouse at Selby all those years ago.

In 1916, Alexander Hall launched Yard No. 522 *Lord Stanhope* (GY.931 – 115ft x 22ft x 12ft 9ins) for the Beacon Steam Fishing Co. Ltd, Grimsby. A typical North Sea trawler with no whaleback, she was immediately requisitioned for minesweeping work as Admiralty No. 2961. During her naval service she was sold to W. Smethurst of Grimsby and was returned in 1919. In 1920, she became GY.815 after being bought by D. Levinson, Grimsby who, in July 1922, sold her to Aberdeen owners A. Bruce & Others. She was renamed *Sansonnet* (A.862) in 1926. She was called up again as an armed patrol trawler in November 1939 and returned to W. Bruce in January 1940. On 3rd April 1940, she was bombed and sunk with all hands off Muckle Flugga in the Shetlands. This *Lord Stanhope* had been built to replace another of Beacon's trawlers of the same name, built at Hull by Cook, Welton & Gemmell in October 1898, as Yard No. 218 *Strephon* (GY.852) for the Standard Steam Fishing Co. Ltd, Grimsby. She worked out of Blyth from 1912 until 1914, when she was bought by Beacon's and renamed *Lord Stanhope* (GY.401). She was lost soon afterwards on 14th November 1914, after colliding with the Inner Dowsing Light Vessel.

DRIFTER/TRAWLERS

In addition to sailing smacks, by 1914 East Anglia had large fleets of steam drifters, which tended to be laid up when the herring season finished. In order to maximise their use, many drifters were temporarily converted to trawlers for fishing the North Sea and west coast grounds, reverting back to drifters when the herring season recommenced. This was not an entirely new venture, for the region had a number of 'converter smacks' which performed the same function, along with wooden steam drifter/trawlers.

Although not built for East Anglia, the vessel shown (**Plan No's 36a & b**) represents a typical example of the wooden type (93ft oa / 85ft bp x 19ft x 10ft 3ins, 95g, 173ihp). She was built for the owners account and first registered at Douglas, Isle of Man.

The last wooden drifter/trawler, *Wyedale* (YH.105 – 89ft x 20ft 1in x 10ft 4ins, 102g), left Great Yarmouth in 1960. She had been built in 1917 by Chambers Ltd, Lowestoft for C.J.H. Eastick Ltd, Lowestoft, with engines supplied by Elliott & Garrood. Most drifters were requisitioned in the First World War and after the cessation of hostilities, owners began to order dual purpose drifter/trawlers which could work all year round. The new steel ships were slightly larger than the normal steam drifter, around 94ft bp as opposed to the drifters 86ft. Their hulls were strengthened with cope irons for trawling, and the gallows and trawl winches could be removed when drift netting but, to reduce costs in later years, the after gallows were often left in place when herring fishing. By 1939, Great Yarmouth had only seventeen steam drifter/trawlers left, the 1930s depression having forced many owners to sell their ships for a fraction of their worth. The first post-Second World War steel drifter/trawler to land at Yarmouth was *Lord Anson* (LT.344 – 88ft 3ins x 19ft 1in x 9ft, 100g, 270ihp). She was built by Cochranes in 1927 as Yard No. 1008, for the Lowestoft Steam Herring Drifters Co. Ltd. She was later converted to motor and scrapped in 1956. The last steel drifter/trawler was *Merbreeze* (LT.253), built by Richards Ironworks as Yard No. 245 in 1931 for P.W. Watson, Lowestoft. She was requisitioned in November 1939 as FY953 for minesweeping duties and returned in 1945, when she was renumbered LT.365. In 1958, she transferred to Yarmouth owners C.H.J. Eastick but kept her LT number. They later sold her back to Lowestoft owners Merbreeze Ltd. In 1960, her steam engine was replaced with a Ruston & Hornsby NE59 type diesel and she went for scrap around 1976. *Ocean Lux* (YH.84 – 94ft 3ins x 20ft 1in x 9ft 7ins, 125g) was a typical steel drifter/trawler. She was built as Yard No. 628 by A. Hall, Aberdeen in 1930 for

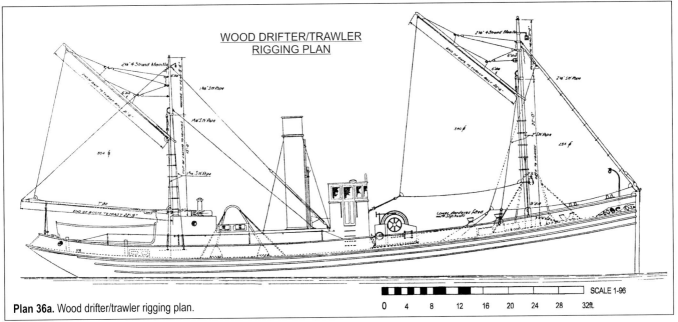

Plan 36a. Wood drifter/trawler rigging plan.

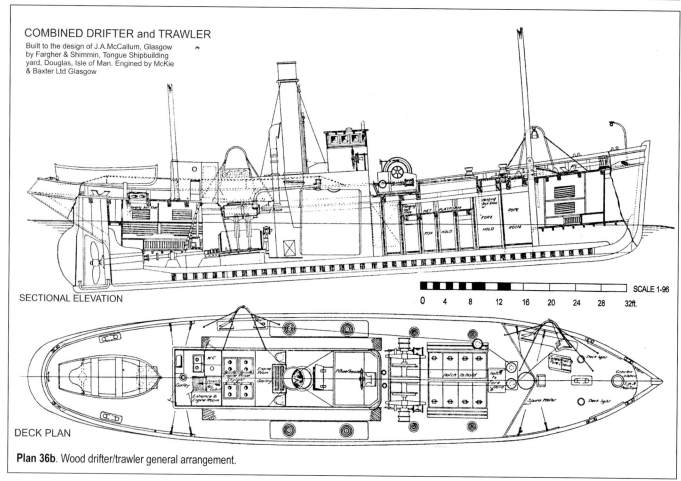

COMBINED DRIFTER and TRAWLER
Built to the design of J.A.McCallum, Glasgow
by Fargher & Shimmin, Tongue Shipbuilding
yard, Douglas, Isle of Man. Engined by McKie
& Baxter Ltd Glasgow

SECTIONAL ELEVATION

SCALE 1-96

0   4   8   12   16   20   24   28   32ft.

DECK PLAN

Plan 36b. Wood drifter/trawler general arrangement.

Bloomfields Ltd, Great Yarmouth. She was hired as a minesweeper in November 1939 and returned in 1945 but went for scrapping in 1956 when owned by W.H. Kerr, Milford. East Anglia's last ever landing from a steam drifter/trawler was at Lowestoft in January 1960. This was from *Silver Seas* (LT.235 – 94ft 1in x 20ft 2ins x 9ft 6ins, 117g, 350ihp, **Photo. 47**), built in 1931 as Yard No. 1103 by Cochranes for A. Catchpole, Kessingland, who sold her to the Silver Fishing Co. (Lowestoft) Ltd in 1946. She was converted to motor in 1960, before going to G.R. Wood, Aberdeen as A.56. She went for scrap in 1972.

Photo. 47: *Silver Seas* (LT.235) rigged for drifting. Her aft gallows remain in place, although her forward ones and winch have been removed.

BIG PRE-FIRST WORLD WAR SHIPS

Launched by Cook, Welton & Gemmell as Yard No. 286 in 1913, *St. Elmo* (H.3 – 136ft x 23ft 6ins x 13ft 6ins, 314g) was a large Distant Water ship built for the St. Andrew's Steam Fishing Co. Ltd, Hull. Her engines came from C.D. Holmes and developed 86nhp at 200psi. She carried 210 tons of coal, 45 tons of ice and 1,800 gallons of fresh water. This gave her a draught of 10ft forward and 15ft 9ins aft, with a service speed of 12 knots. She was requisitioned in May 1915 as a minesweeper, and armed with a 12 pounder and a 5ins bomb throwing mortar; she was returned in 1919. The drawing (**Plan 37 a & b**) is one of the earliest showing derricks fitted to both masts, essential when handling the heavy ground ropes used on the deep water trawls. These derricks and the Gilson tackles from the masthead, allowed the trawlerman to transmit the full power of the steam winch to whatever item of gear required moving, no mean feat on a small ship in a seaway. *St. Elmo* was lost after running ashore on the south coast of Iceland on 6th March 1921.

The last two large trawlers launched by Cook, Welton & Gemmell prior to the First World War were Yard No's 287 and 295, *Tervani* (GY.10) in March 1914 for Alec Black, Grimsby and *Ilustra* (GY.127) in June 1914 (160ft x 26ft x 14.75ft, 457g), both powered by a C.D. Holmes 89nhp engine. In October 1914, *Tervani* transferred to the South Western Steam Fishing Co. Ltd, Grimsby and was requisitioned in May 1915. By October of that year, she was under Bascombe's ownership but, unfortunately, her life with them was to be short, as she was sunk by a mine off Orford Ness on 5th December 1916. *Ilustra* was also taken into

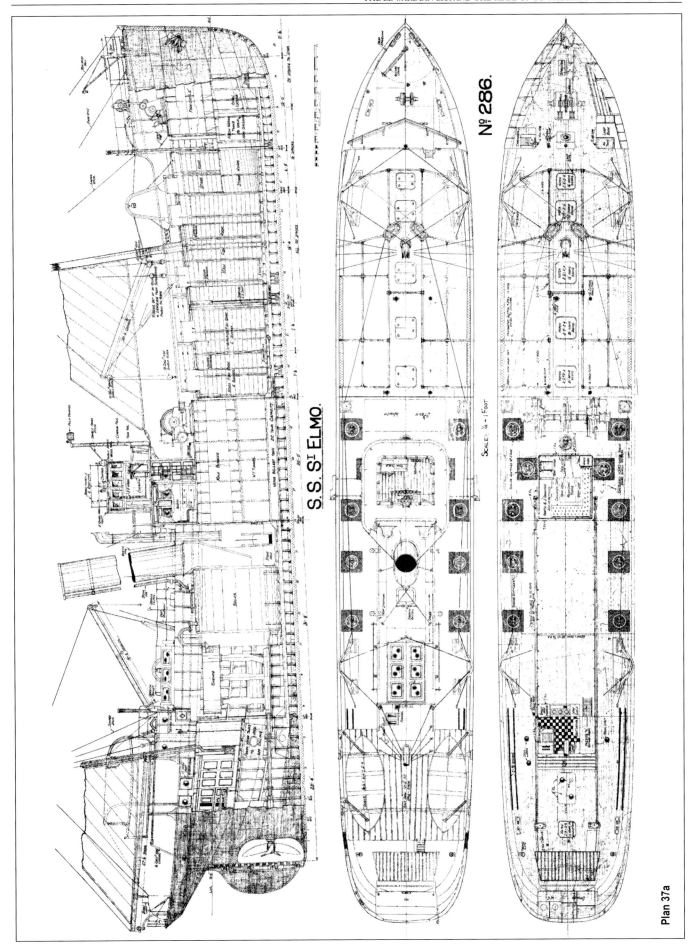

S.S. St ELMO.

Nº 286.

SCALE: ¼ = 1 FOOT

Plan 37a

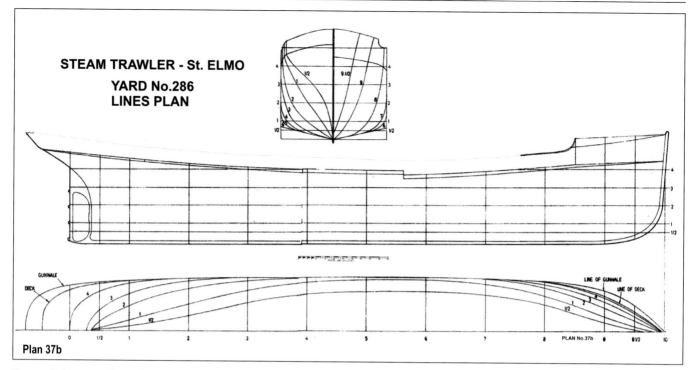

STEAM TRAWLER - St. ELMO
YARD No.286
LINES PLAN

Plan 37b

Bascombe's ownership. She was requisitioned as a minesweeper in August 1914, armed with a 4ins gun and a 6 pounder AA gun. She returned to Bascombes in 1919, only to be lost a year later at Paroe Bay, Iceland.

In June 1916, Cochranes launched Yard No. 656 *Marconi* (H.488 – 136ft x 24ft x 13ft 7ins, 322g, 86nhp) for F.T. Ross, Hull. She replaced her namesake, H.777, built by Cook, Welton & Gemmell as Yard No. 36 in 1903 (130ft, 261g), which had apparently been lost on 6th March 1909 by stranding but she appears in the 1910 register (this anomaly arises because the

registers are usually published the year following the collation of the records and often causes problems for researchers), whilst a trawler identical in both name and dimensions was hired from 1916 to 1919 as a minesweeper. The second *Marconi* was fitted with wireless and allotted the call sign MGDC. She was requisitioned from August 1916 as a minesweeper and returned in 1919. In August 1929, she was almost totally destroyed in the fire which swept through Hull's No. 2 Fish Market. She served in the Second World War as a minesweeper from March 1940 until her loss off Harwich on 20th September 1941. She had been lying to

Photo. 48: *Aspasia.* She is fitted with twin lifeboats in radial davits and has a WC and lamp room at the stern. She also has a railed verandah round the wheelhouse and a pole compass.

a buoy when she was rammed amidships by one of our patrol craft operating out of Ipswich and she sank within minutes. Her crew were picked up from their lifeboat by a local tug.

The last two really large trawlers built by Cochranes pre-war were for French owners. They were Yard No's 741 and 742, *Avant Garde* for Peche Francais and *Terra Neuve* for F.T. Huret, Boulogne (both 200ft bp x 32ft x 16ft, 790g). Their engines (15ins, 25ins, 42ins x 27ins stroke) were supplied by Amos & Smith. They were both designed for work off the Grand Banks of Newfoundland, where they spent many weeks on the grounds salting their catches before returning to port.

In late 1915, Smith's Dock built two sister ships for the Iceland Steam Fishing Co. Ltd, Grimsby. They were Yard No's 555 and 556, *Amplify* (GY.789) and *Aspasia* (GY.793 – both 140.6ft x 24ft x 13ft 2ins, 342g); note that the builders' photograph (**Photo. 48**) shows *Aspasia* as GY.794. They carried twin lifeboats on light spar decks either side of the engine room skylight, which were launched by radial davits. *Amplify* was requisitioned as a minesweeper in

February 1916, Admiralty No. 1982. She went ashore in January 1917 at Skeirascape, Castlebay, Barra and was a total loss. Her sister was called up in April 1916 also as a minesweeper, Admiralty No. 1996, and was returned in 1919. During her service, she was sold to W.G. Alnutt, Grimsby, in December 1917. She was sold again in January 1919 to a Gloucester owner, before a final sale to Portugal as *Lisboa*.

MORE ABERDEEN TRAWLERS

The building yards at Aberdeen were by this time concentrating on building the smaller type of 125ft trawler, mainly for the Near Water grounds but also for fishing off Faeroe. In June 1917, Alexander Hall launched Yard No. 532 *Cadorna* (GY.1072) for the Rushworth Steam Fishing Co. Ltd, Grimsby. She was immediately requisitioned and given the Admiralty No. 3055. In November 1917, she was bought by W. Richmond and was returned to them in 1919. By 1920, she had returned to Aberdeen as A.125 under the Aberdeen Pioneer Steam Fishing Co. Ltd colours (H.E. Stroud,

ABOVE: Photo. 49: *Ben Namur* ashore at Bay of Skaills, Orkney. A weaker vessel would have snapped in two with such an overhang. She is in standard Irvin colours of black hull, brown superstructure and black funnel, with two red bands.

RIGHT: Photo. 50: *Cadorna* (A.125) outward bound from Aberdeen in the early 1950s. She is in Stroud Steam Fishing's colours of black topsides over red boot topping, with a brown superstructure and black funnel.

manager). She was back in the navy in May 1940 as FY1651, converted for minesweeping duties and returned to the Aberdeen Pioneer Steam Fishing Co. Ltd in 1945. She later transferred on paper to the Stroud Steam Fishing Co Ltd, Aberdeen, who kept her until she went for scrap at Charlestown on 15th June 1961. In 1917, the neighbouring yard of Hall, Russells launched Yard No. 597 *Ben Glas* (SN.336) and Yard No. 598 *Ben Medie* (SN.340 – both 122ft x 22ft x 13ft 3ins, 98n, 78nhp) for Richard Irvin & Sons Ltd, South Shields. They were followed in 1919 by Yard No. 600 *Ben Heilem* (A.242) and Yard No. 601 *Ben Namur* (A.244), both identical to the former pair (**Photo. 49**). The first two ships cost £9,750 each, while the later pair cost £10,700 each. *Ben Medie* and *Ben Glas* were both requisitioned in 1917 as minesweepers and were returned in 1919. In 1927, *Ben Medie* became the first British steam trawler to freeze part of her catch at sea. She was fitted out as a floating test bed for a year and proved conclusively that white fish, quick frozen in brine at -20 degrees C and kept in refrigerated storage at -24 degrees C, would keep for some three months and, when defrosted, be as good as freshly caught fish. The industry was unfortunately not ready for the shore-side storage or distribution of frozen fish, so little more was done until the 1950s. Both vessels fished the North Sea and Middle Water grounds until being called up again in the Second World War; *Ben Medie* in January 1940 as

a minesweeper and *Ben Glas* in November 1939 firstly as an armed patrol vessel, later as a minesweeper and eventually finishing up as a refueller. *Ben Glas* was returned in October 1944 and her sister in March 1946. They worked for Irvins through the 1950s, keeping their SN registration but fishing out of Aberdeen. *Ben Medie* was wrecked on the Pentland Skerries on 7th October 1958. Her sister survived her by two years, going to Grangemouth for scrap in May 1960. *Ben Heilem* (A.242) was built to replace her namesake, in 1912 as A.470 for Irvins. The former ship cost £5,950 and her successor cost £10,700. She was the second of Irvin's Aberdeen trawlers to be requisitioned as a minesweeper in August 1914 and was given the Admiralty No. 97 (the first being *Ben Chourn* (A.40), Yard No. 545, requisitioned from new). She was wrecked on 8th October 1917 off Berwick on Tweed. *Ben Namur* (A.244) was scarcely a year old when she came to grief on rocks at the Bay of Skaills on the west side of Orkney. Nine of her crew were rescued but the mate, Alexander Lawrence, and a deckhand, Alexander Cordiner, both from Aberdeen, were swept overboard and drowned. The rescuers were alerted by the trawlers siren and distress flares. A line tied to a cask was floated ashore, and eight crewmen scrambled to safety. Before the skipper, William Coates could be rescued, the line snapped but he was saved shortly afterwards by the Stromness Rocket Brigade.

ABOVE: Photo. 52: *Ben Heilem* (A.242) entering Aberdeen harbour in the 1950s. She is in Richard Irvin's colours of black topsides over red boot topping, with brown casing and wheelhouse, and black funnel with two red bands.

LEFT: Photo. 53: *Ben Meidie* (SN.340) passing Hall, Russell's shipyard when outward bound from Aberdeen in the 1950s. Note the later addition of a whaleback forecastle. She is wearing the same Irvin colour scheme as *Ben Heilem* above.

Chapter 8: THE FIRST WORLD WAR

Trawlers have proved themselves of invaluable service to this country in times of aggression. They are sturdily constructed and possess excellent sea keeping qualities, such that the Admiralty possessed a few trawlers fitted out for minesweeping duties. They were soon augmented by the requisitioning of further ships for minesweeping, offensive and defensive anti-submarine work, patrol duties, convoy and escort work, and tenders to major warships. When war broke out in 1914, the fleets were at sea and knew nothing about the conflict until they returned. The Admiralty confined the ships to port, or to the inshore grounds, where their livelihoods would supposedly be unaffected. Alas, the plan misfired, as ports throughout the country were packed to capacity and fishermen were forced out of a living. About this time, the navy began wholesale requisitioning for the Royal Naval Patrol Service. Ships were hastily converted, their fishrooms became messdecks, trawling gear was swapped for minesweeping equipment and antiquated weaponry was fitted, before they were repainted in Admiralty colours. Open bridges with standard binnacles were fitted on top of the wheelhouses; unofficially termed 'Mount Misery', they allowed skippers to monitor the sweep wires.

Amongst the problems with these conversions was stability and seaworthiness, with the most important factor being metacentric height. It was standard Admiralty practice to incline and ballast each requisitioned vessel. In trawlers on wartime duties, account had to be taken, among other factors, of leaks caused by near miss gunfire and bomb shock. Also, as in peace time, trawlers operated in Arctic waters where the icing on deck and gun platforms could dangerously reduce stability. These factors influenced the minimum acceptable metacentric height of 12ins in the worst condition of the ship, namely in the arrival condition (or 'light ship') with all but 10% of fuel and stores consumed. In deep condition, the effect of the added weight of fuel, stores and water, etc, raised the metacentric height to nearly 24ins. Additions of top weight such as armament, mine-sweeping gear, anti-submarine gear, etc, made it necessary to add permanent ballast to obtain the minimum of 12ins metacentric height. The approximate amount of ballast fitted was as follows: Small trawlers of 115ft-125ft bp – 20-30 tons; medium trawlers of 124ft-150ft bp – 30-50 tons; large trawlers – 50-80

tons. Next to metacentric height, the freeboard is perhaps the most important single element affecting seaworthiness. The reserve of buoyancy, range of stability and dryness was primarily dependent on the freeboard given suitable metacentric height. The freeboard is a valuable guide to the reserve of buoyancy and corresponding stability of the vessel, and the following values were reached: Small trawlers – 27ins; medium trawlers – 30ins; large trawlers – 33ins (**Fig. 44**)

The Patrol Service is better remembered for its anti-submarine (A/S) and minesweeping duties (M/S). The Germans had mined all the channels leading in and out of our major ports, and huge stretches of the North Sea. The first losses were the Aberdeen trawlers *Crathie* (A.350) and *Thomas W. Irvin* (A.421), which were blown up on 27th August 1914 whilst attempting to clear a minefield off the mouth of the Tyne. The senior officer of the group was aboard *Thomas W. Irvin*, which went down in less than five minutes taking three of her crew with her. *Crathie* sank shortly afterwards with the loss of two men.

The silent enemy that these sweepers had to contend with was the moored contact mine, a buoyant, hollow steel spherical container, filled with around 600lbs of TNT. It was triggered by breaking off any one of the external horns. Each horn held a glass phial containing a chemical which activated the firing sequence. A heavy sinker weight lay on the bottom and the mine was tethered to this, at a pre-set depth, by a steel cable. It was this cable that had to be cut by the minesweeper, as once it was severed the mine would float to the surface, where it could be dealt with either by sinking or by blowing up. To prevent this they fitted small explosive charges, called 'obstructers', to the mooring wires. These would explode on contact with the sweep wire and cut it, thus effectively hindering the sweep until another wire could be rigged. Later, static wire cutters were fixed to a float. These severed the sweeper's cable, delaying her until new gear could be set up.

As a result, the death toll of men and ships began to rise. Armed enemy cruisers and U-boats wreaked havoc among our unprotected fishing fleets. The steam trawler *Tubal Cain* (GY.88) was sunk and her crew captured 50 miles off Iceland on 7th August 1914, by an armed merchant cruiser. This 227-ton trawler had

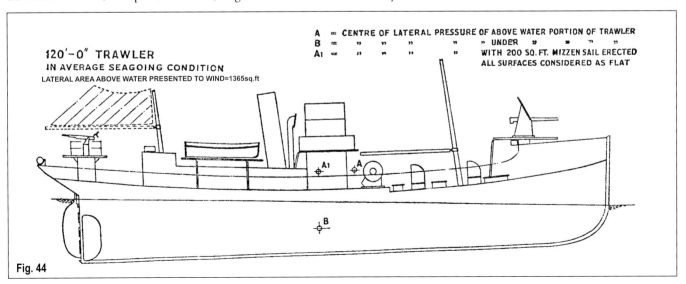

120'-0" TRAWLER
IN AVERAGE SEAGOING CONDITION
LATERAL AREA ABOVE WATER PRESENTED TO WIND=1365sq.ft

A = CENTRE OF LATERAL PRESSURE OF ABOVE WATER PORTION OF TRAWLER
B = „ „ „ „ „ UNDER „ „ „ „
A₁ = „ „ „ „ „ WITH 200 SQ. FT. MIZZEN SAIL ERECTED
ALL SURFACES CONSIDERED AS FLAT

Fig. 44

been built by Smith's Dock as Yard No. 784 in November 1905, for Rushworth & Atkinson of Grimsby and was fishing at the time of her loss. A few weeks later, the Boston fleet lost seven out of eight vessels in one day. During that fateful month, twenty-five steam trawlers were sunk and, by May 1915, the total had risen to ninety-one. This number does not include the sailing smacks which were still working the Dogger Bank and whose fleets were decimated by the enemy warships. Bounties were offered to trawler skippers for sinking U-boats. There were discussions on the arming of fishing vessels but it was not recommended, so the sinkings continued. In the opening days of May 1915, Aberdeen lost the trawlers *Martaban* (A.527), *Cruiser* (GN.54) and *Scottish Queen* (A.384). *Martaban* was originally a Hull-owned ship, built of iron in 1890 as Yard No. 57 by Cook, Welton & Gemmell of Hull, for Kelsall Brothers & Beeching Ltd. She was purchased in 1912 by R.&J. Moon, Aberdeen, who bought up old trawlers and had a butchery business supplying fresh meat to the local fleet. Her loss came on 2nd May, when she was sunk by gunfire from a U-boat, 22 miles E by N of her home port. Her crew took to the boat and, after some 17 hours of rowing, landed at Stonehaven. *Cruiser* (100ft x 20ft x 11ft 3ins, 38n, 50nhp) was built in 1898 as Yard No. 312 by Hall, Russells for Thomas Devlin, Edinburgh. She was sunk on the same day and in the same way as *Martaban*. Out of her crew of nine, four men, including her skipper, were killed and three were injured. They were rescued by the steamer *T.W. Stuart* and returned to Aberdeen. The next day, 3rd May, saw the loss of *Scottish Queen*, one of Aberdeen's oldest vessels, built along with *Scottish Belle* (A.512) by Scotts of Kinghorn in 1889 for Robert Brown of Aberdeen. She too was sunk by gunfire from a U-boat some 50 miles E.N.E. of the port. Her crew were rescued by another local trawler, *Jane Ross* (A.454). In June 1916, *Viceroy* (GY.786), built in 1898 for the Atlas Steam Fishing Co. Ltd, Grimsby, was lost with her crew of nine men on the North Sea grounds. The total British losses by the middle of 1916 amounted to some 237 trawlers and drifters. By the end of that bitter campaign, some 675 fishing vessels were sunk, both steam and sail, with the loss of 434 lives. Of these commercial fishing craft, thirty-four were sunk by enemy cruisers, 578 by U-boats, and sixty-three by mines.

By the end of 1916, the Navy had taken over so many fishing vessels that it was impossible to requisition any more if the supply of fish for the population was not to be imperilled. A newspaper report of the time stated:

'When war broke out there were 375 Hull owned trawlers and cutters. To-day, their number is 93, of which 32 are supplying the London market direct, leaving 61 for Hull, and 260 trawlers are, or were on Admiralty work. Over 3,000 fishermen and engineers have also gone into the Navy, so that the industry is but a shadow of its former self. The losses of life and property since the outbreak of the war have been heavy, 37 Hull trawlers have been lost through war risks.'

This was the picture the length and breadth of the country and, by February 1917, the Government was beginning to panic. They commissioned a special survey of commercial fishing trawlers, which proved that unless the few remaining vessels were safeguarded, the nation's supply of fresh fish would all but disappear. Since the outbreak of the war, only a handful of new

ships had joined the fishing fleet. The fleet was now working with the ships that the navy would not hire, owing to their age and size. Of the 1,900 steam trawlers fishing in 1914, 1,400 had been taken over by the Admiralty and used in the Auxiliary Patrol. The price of fish rocketed as landings fell, whilst the trawlers were finding it increasingly difficult to catch fish with any degree of safety. Under pressure from the Government, on 29th May 1917, the Admiralty issued their War Order N.67028, which effectively placed all remaining steam fishing craft under immediate requisition. This order was compulsory for all British registered trawlers but foreign vessels that were using our ports could also be hired with the consent of their owners. So it was that the Fishery Reserve of the Trawler Section was formed for these vessels, under the White Ensign. The objective was that the trawlers would fish in fleets of twenty ships, with limited protection provided by arming one or two of them as and when guns became available. They were to remain under the command of their civilian owners but came under the direct jurisdiction of the Navy. A token payment of one shilling per ship and one shilling per man per month when on hire was paid by the Government for the duration of their naval service, with all other running expenses being the responsibility of the owners. In addition to offering some degree of protection to the commercial trawlers, the measures were also designed to reduce the inflated price of fish. This would have the knock on effect of reducing the owners' profits, which had risen from £6,000-£7,000 in 1914, to around £30,000-£40,000 in 1917. The men on these fishing trawlers, because they were paid a percentage of the gross value of the catch, were benefiting from the high market prices.

In Grimsby, a Fisheries Committee was established. As this was formed on the instructions of the Admiralty, the members (all prominent local owners of course) were allowed full naval status to regulate the fish landings and rates of fishermen's pay. After many heated arguments and some threatening strike action, the matter was grudgingly resolved. The main stumbling block was that the committee wished to class all the remaining fishing trawlers as naval vessels. This meant that their crews were subject to the Naval Disciplinary Code and could not leave their trawlers at will, as was the norm. The agreement also meant that the men signed on articles for the duration of the war and not for the usual single trip. Eventually, the owners agreed to a settlement and the men's wages, although fixed, were increased marginally. This increased rate of pay for a trawler engineer at Grimsby, represented, £2 11s 6d a week, plus 10 shillings per trip risk allowance and 7s 6d per £100 on the ship's gross earnings. To encourage the men to stay in the same ship, the owners agreed a payment of £3 5s Quarter Money, paid for serving in the one ship for three months. The rates of pay for the men serving in the Trawler Section of the Royal Naval Reserve were as follows: Second hands/enginemen – 6 shillings a day; leading hand/leading trimmer – 4 shillings; deckhands, trimmers/cooks – 3s 6d; and boys – 1 shilling a day. All these, with the exception of the boys, received a war retainer of £1 per month. The men serving in the Auxiliary Patrol Fleet also received free kit on entry, plus 1s 5d a day messing allowance, whilst their families were given a separation allowance. After completing twelve months unbroken service, a rating was entitled to a gratuity of thirty days pay on discharge; again this was not given to the boys.

Owners who hired their vessels to the government in the early stages of the war were well rewarded. So much so that questions were raised in the House of Commons regarding the rates for the trawlers *Southern Prince* (SN.121) and *Ben Arthur* (SN.125) of the Port of Tyne Examination service. The original building costs for the vessels were £7,200 and £7,000 respectively. It was stated that the hire rate was £475 each per month and the total sum paid for each ship up to 31st March 1916 was around £8,200. This included all running and insurance costs, wages for a double crew and liability for replacement if any vessel was withdrawn for any reason whatever. Later, the hire rate for a 115ft trawler was about £132 per month and, after the war, they would be offered for sale as a '*really magnificent vessel, built to a special specification, and fitted with all improvements*' for around £11,750, which represented almost twice the cost of a similar pre-war ship but a vast reduction on the war-time price of a similar sized 'Strath' Class vessel.

PREPARATIONS FOR WAR – THE AUXILIARY PATROL

The use of contact mines had been instrumental in making the Admiralty seek a counter-measure, as enemy mines could strangle this country's coastal trade. Admiral Lord Charles Beresford saw the potential for using trawlers as minesweepers when he visited Grimsby early in 1907 and, by the end of that year, two vessels, *Algoma* (GY.6) and *Andes* (GY.5) had been hired and dispatched to Portland for trials. Both vessels were built by Edward Brothers of North Shields in 1899, for J.&G. Alward, Grimsby. They were small ships (106ft bp, 54n). Both vessels transferred to the Spurn Steam Fishing Co. Ltd, Grimsby in December 1911 and survived both wars. *Andes* changed her name to *Andros* (GY.5) in February 1937, remaining with the Bannister family until scrapped in March 1957. The results of the minesweeping trials, although not really conclusive, did show the potential for using trawlers. The first such vessels purchased by the Admiralty in 1909 were Goole Shipbuilding & Repairing Co's *Seaflower* (ex-*Osprey*, later *Sea Rover*), the Smith's Dock-built *Seamew* (ex-*Nunthorpe Hall*, Yard No. 388) and *Sparrow* (ex-*Josephine*), also from Goole Shipbuilding. These were given the Admiralty No's 1, 2 and 56 respectively, and they formed, along with a further fifteen trawlers, the nucleus of the Patrol Service in 1914. Included in this group were the Duthie-built *Daisy* and *Esther*, already described.

RNR TRAWLER SECTION

In the latter months of 1911, the RNR Trawler Section was formed. Initially, it included only ships from Grimsby and Aberdeen but later, trawlers from all the major fishing ports participated. However, by early 1914, it had become obvious that many more minesweeping trawlers would be required.

The Suffolk port of Lowestoft was the main depot for the Patrol Service and other large fishing centres also became fitting out bases so that, by the end of 1914, around 194 trawlers were either at the fitting out stage or converted and at sea. By this time, the sea lanes around our coasts had been the target for concentrated mining by both enemy surface ships and U-boats. Initially, minefields were only discovered after numerous casualties among coastal convoys and only then would the sweepers start clearing the channels. Results at first were poor, with a ratio of one mine swept for every ship sunk but once the main mine laying areas had been identified and the number of trawlers increased, this went up to 85 to 1. One of the main reasons for the loss of minesweepers during the early stages was the trawler men's desire to help fellow seafarers

when in trouble. Hence, they would steam at full speed to the assistance of their stricken comrades, only to find themselves in the same predicament after striking another mine from the same field. With the pressure of keeping the main lanes open, many secondary minefields remained untouched until after hostilities ceased, when the ships could be assigned to sweep them. Other trawlers were used as armed patrol (AP) and anti-submarine vessels (AS). Their task was to protect the coastal convoys, and attempt to destroy the minelayers. AS ships worked in groups or units of four trawlers and one armed yacht, which was designated as the unit leader and carried wireless equipment.

TRAWLER ARMAMENT

Trawlers were first issued with either 3 pounder or 6 pounder guns but, as the enemy's efficiency increased, it became necessary to fit 12 pounders, along with pom-poms, howitzers, bomb throwing mortars and hydrophones for seeking out the U-boats. In addition, five rifles and three pistols were stowed in the wheelhouse. Initially, guns were mounted on a 13ins diameter platform above the casing but later bow mountings became standard. However, in July 1918, the Admiralty instructed the builders to fit both mountings. In April 1918, 4ins guns were successfully trialled on the 'Mersey' Class trawler *Thomas Jago*, fitting out at Cochranes, and the 'Castle' Class *Giovanni Guilti*, building at Ailsa. A rough guide to the calibre of these guns would be: (I) A 3 pounder gun, 45.4 calibre on a 4 cwt mounting (Nordenfelt type), or a 5cwt 40 calibre mounting (Hotchkiss type) similar to 47mm with a 1.85ins bore; (II) A 6 pounder gun with 6cwt 42.3 calibre mounting (Nordenfelt type) or an 8cwt 40 calibre (Hotchkiss) similar to 57mm, with a 2.24ins bore; (III) A 12 pounder gun with 8 or 12cwt mountings of 28 or 40 calibre, similar to the 3ins and 76mm. The bore of the 12 and 15 pounders was about 3ins but there were some differences in the ammunition weight used. The 3 pounder Hotchkiss was introduced into the Royal Navy in 1886, as a quick firing gun designed to ward off attacks from torpedo boats. The weapon had the advantages of being easy to maintain and simple to use, making it ideal for trawler use. The total weight of the gun and mounting was around 11cwt, making it suitable for fitting either on the trawler whalebacks or on the casing top. When the larger calibre weapons arrived, the 3 pounders were removed and fitted to the smaller steel and wooden steam drifters.

NAVAL TRAWLER BUILDING PROGRAMME

By 1916, there were no civilian trawlers left for the navy to hire. Since the outbreak of the war, the Admiralty had requisitioned every fishing trawler of suitable size and power for Patrol Service duties. It became abundantly clear that, with the rate of war losses, the commercial fishing fleet would be seriously depleted if and when the war ended. The trawler builders, too, were struggling to keep going, as very little new tonnage had been ordered since the outbreak of hostilities. Spurred on by the desperate need for new ships, the Admiralty decided to implement its own building programme. Until this time, naval trawler construction was a relatively slow, easy affair but things were about to happen and very soon three prototypes had been selected from builders' standard designs. These were Hall, Russell's 'Strath' Class; Smith's Docks 'Castle' Class; and Cochranes 'Mersey' Class. The choice had been based on the availability of specifications and drawings, coupled to the future requirements of a peacetime trawling fleet and 540 were built in total, with a breakdown as follows:

	Strath	Castle	Mersey	Total
Delivered by 11.11.18	89	127	69	285
Unarmed M/S	14	18	8	40
Completed as Fishing Tr.	46	52	35	133
Cancelled	18	20	44	82
Totals	**167**	**217**	**156**	**540**

Table from *British Warships 1914-1918* by Ditmar & Colledge

Some trawlers were already on the stocks by November 1916 and these 'non-standard' ships were taken as part of the initial order and listed under the class that was nearest to their dimensions. War shortages meant changes to materials – brass and copper fittings were changed for galvanised iron, whilst pitch pine used on decks below the upper deck was replaced by red or yellow deal and upper decks were steel fitted with tread strips. With the exception of the Commanding Officer's cabin, linoleum was deleted from all floors and due to the shortage of flax, mizzen sails only were fitted. To economise on labour and materials, certain fittings were deleted, including deck sockets for fish pounds, fish discharging derricks and gear, Gilson tackles and slings, awning stanchions and eyeplates, ring bolts, wood chocks and fairleads required only for fishing.

The system of naming these new vessels used the names of Petty Officers and seamen from the muster rolls of HMS *Victory* and HMS *Royal Sovereign* at the time of the Battle of Trafalgar. There seems a subtle irony here, as the majority of the men honoured had been assigned to the fleet by magistrates as an alternative to prison, after being convicted of smuggling. These seamen were far too valuable to Nelson's navy to be wasted languishing in a shore gaol, so they and their press-ganged shipmates formed the backbone of the British Battle Fleet.

COST OF ADMIRALTY TRAWLERS

Bearing in mind that these trawlers were ordered in large numbers and required the full output of all the country's trawler builders, it was necessary to lay down rules to prevent firms quoting unreasonable prices which would delay the tendering process. The result was that ships were ordered according to each shipyard's capacity and builders were instructed to proceed under the *Defence of the Realm Regulations 8A*, which required a firm price for the work. If any of the prices were unacceptable, the Admiralty had the final say as to the amount to be paid. To keep costs to a minimum, builders were told not to insure the vessels and to remove guarantee clauses from their tenders. In the main, builders' prices were accepted but sometimes they had to be renegotiated until an agreeable price was reached. Costs increased as the programme evolved, owing to the recurring advances in wages and materials:

Type	Earliest £ Main Firm (hull only)	Latest £ Main Firm (hull only)	Highest £ Any Firm (hull only)	Approx. Average £ Total Cost (hull & machinery)
Mersey	£10,716	£12,400	£16,700	£22,000
Castle	£ 9,316	£10,100	£14,200	£21,000
Strath	£ 7,156	£ 9,800	£12,100	£18,200

Table from Admiralty records showing cost increases.

SMITH'S DOCK 'MILITARY' GROUP

In 1915, the company received an order from the Admiralty for ten 'Military' type trawlers, valued at £93,800. They were as follows: Yard No. 596 *Lancer*, Admiralty No. 1151 (B); 597 *Bombardier* 1517 (A); 598 *Brigadier* 1530 (B); 599 *Dragoon* 1152 (B); 600 *Gunner* 1153 (B); 601 *Sapper* 1162 (B); 602 *Fusilier* 1163 (B); 603 *Carbineer* 1164 (B); 624 *Highlander* 1526 (C); and 625 *Trooper* 1541 (C). Although classed the same, there were three different sizes of trawler, as indicated by the letters: A – 130ft x 24ft x 13ft 3ins, 303g; B – 130ft x 23ft 6ins x 12ft 9ins, 276g; and C – 118ft x 22ft 6ins x 12ft 6ins, 239g.

It would appear that these vessels, although given a naval classification, were civilian designs already on the stocks. Out of the ten ships, three were lost on active service. *Carbineer* was wrecked on 18th May 1915 off Crebawethan Point. Her name passed to *Fusilier*, after she was sold out of service on 11th March 1920. She became *Carbineer II* (GY.1048), owned by the Consolidated Steam Fishing & Ice Co. Ltd, Grimsby. In September 1927, she was transferred on paper to Consolidated Fisheries Ltd (Consolidated Steam Fishing & Ice Co. Ltd until earlier that year). In 1930, she was lengthened to 138.7ft and, in April 1942, she was bought by Bennett & Co. Ltd, Grimsby. This was after being hired as an armed patrol trawler in May 1940. At the end of that year, she changed to a boom defence vessel, until returned in July 1946. There are discrepancies between Colledge's book, Cox's book on Grimsby trawlers and the Smith's Dock builder's list; the latter states that, along with another six ships, Yard No's 597 to 602, all were cancelled while on the stocks, while Cox states that *Carbineer* was sold to the Ministry of War Transport in May 1944. The other two casualties were *Sapper*, which foundered off the Owers Light Vessel on 29th December 1917, and *Lancer*, which sank after a collision near the Brighton Light Vessel on 18th July 1918. The most unusual ship of the group was *Gunner*. Commissioned as a 'Q' Ship, she was armed with one 4ins gun, two 12 pounders, two 6 pounders and two 14ins torpedo tubes. During her wartime service she went under the names *Borgia*, *Planudes*, and *Q.31*. She was sold in 1920 as *Temehani* and, in 1926, became *Millimumul*.

HALL, RUSSELL'S 'STRATH' CLASS

Hall, Russell's 'Strath' Class was based on their Yard No. 576 *Strathlochy* (123ft x 22ft x 10ft, 311g), ordered by the Aberdeen Steam Trawling & Fishing Co. Ltd in 1916 (**Plans 38 a & b**) at a cost of £6,550. Engines were 525ihp, which gave 10.5 knots. Armament varied, usually one 3ins gun and twenty-four mines. Their complement was normally fifteen but up to eighteen if a wireless transmitter (WT) was fitted. The first 'Strath' was *George Borthwick*, Admiralty No. 3621, launched on 21st June 1917 and handed over to the Admiralty on 3rd August from Hall, Russell's as Yard No. 611 at a cost of £12,316. Armed with a 12 pounder gun and a 3.5ins bomb throwing mortar, she served as a minesweeper and hydrophone trawler until sold in 1921 to the Consolidated Steam Fishing & Ice Co. Ltd, Grimsby as *Annabelle* (GY.1314). She was sold to Aberdeen owner David Wood in 1934, as *Annabelle* (A.101). Requisitioned again in November 1939 as an armed patrol trawler, she was released in December 1944. She worked for fifteen years under Wood's ownership, until going for scrap in 1959. By this time she had been fitted with a whaleback and wheelhouse verandah. Another standard 'Strath' from Hall, Russell's was *James Bentole*, Yard No. 612, launched on 21st June 1917 as Admiralty No. 3622, a hydrophone trawler. She was sold out of service in 1922 and her name changed to *Fort Robert* (A.878), owned by William Masson of Aberdeen. She was requisitioned again in November 1939 as a minesweeper (FY762) and was decommissioned in August 1945, going to the Looker Steam Fishing Co. Ltd, Aberdeen. She went for scrap on 6th September 1960 at St. Davids on the Forth. The twenty 'non-standards' (**Photo. 44**) taken over from various builders measured from 115ft to 122ft bp x 22ft to 22ft 6ins and among them was *Matthew Crooke*, Admiralty No. 3655, launched by Alexander Hall on 2nd October 1917 as Yard No. 534. She was sold out of service in 1921 and renamed *Fortrose* (A.801), owned by John Lewis Ltd. In May 1940, she was requisitioned as an armed patrol trawler until returned in 1945 to the Stephen Fishing Co. Ltd, Aberdeen. Like *Annabelle*, she had a whaleback but no wheelhouse verandah. She went for scrapping in Holland in June 1961. Another of these ships was *George Coulston*, Admiralty No. 3660, also built by Halls and launched on 27th April 1918. She served as a hydrophone trawler, armed with a 12 pounder and a

3.5ins bomb throwing mortar, until sold in 1922. She first went to Glasgow owners as GW.38 but, in July of that year, she was bought by Miss A. Lewis, Aberdeen as *Doonie Braes* (A.881). It seems that she never actually worked as a trawler, for records show that for the majority of her life she fished as a steam liner. In the Second World War, she served from May 1940 until January 1945, both as a dhan layer and an armed patrol trawler. After release, she went to George Walker, Aberdeen and, by 1947, she was owned by Alexander King & Others, Aberdeen. Her end came on 20th April 1955, after she ran aground on the Old Man of Hoy when homeward bound with a full catch, including some six and a half tons of line caught halibut. Her distress flares were seen by a naval MFV from Scapa Flow, which closed in to the wreck, enabling the liner's crew to row to the naval craft.

'STRATH' CLASS BUILDERS

In addition to the parent yard of Hall, Russell, who built forty-seven 'Strath' Class vessels, the remainder of them came from the following builders: Alexander Hall – five; John Duthie – eight; Fullerton – eight; Fleming & Ferguson – seven; Montrose SB –

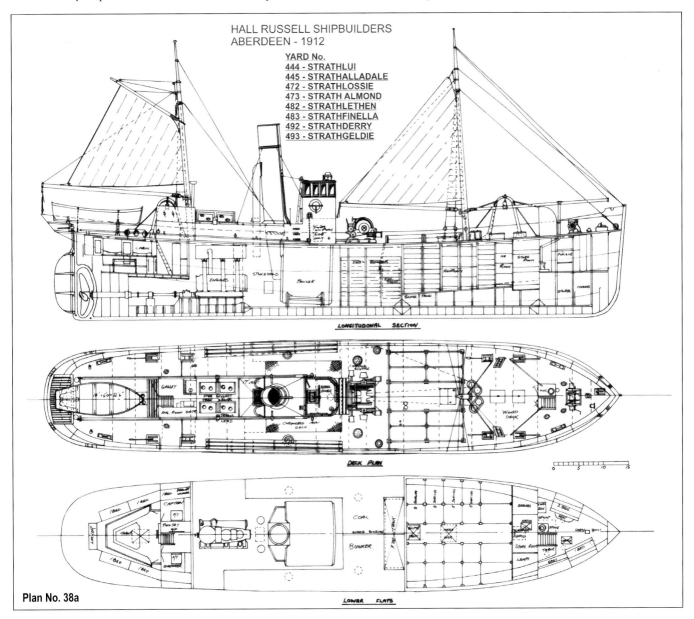

HALL RUSSELL SHIPBUILDERS
ABERDEEN - 1912

YARD No.
444 - STRATHLUI
445 - STRATHALLADALE
472 - STRATHLOSSIE
473 - STRATH ALMOND
482 - STRATHLETHEN
483 - STRATHFINELLA
492 - STRATHDERRY
493 - STRATHGELDIE

LONGITUDINAL SECTION

DECK PLAN

Plan No. 38a

LOWER FLATS

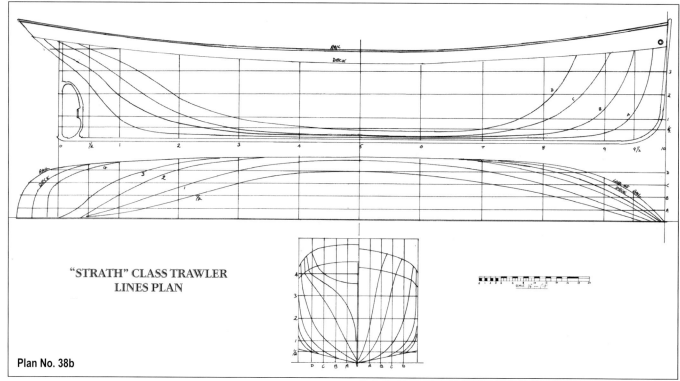

"STRATH" CLASS TRAWLER
LINES PLAN

Plan No. 38b

eight; Rennie & Forrestt – fifteen; Hawthorns – sixteen; G & M. Ritchie, Whiteinch – six; Williamson, Workington – six; Murdoch & Murray – five; Scott & Co – six; Abdela & Mitchell – five; and Ouse Shipbuilding – four; making a total of 146 ships. This excludes the twenty-one ships cancelled after November 1918. Two of Rennie & Forrestt's trawlers, *George Ireland* and *Henry Jennings*, were used by the Admiralty as test ships for water-jet propulsion units. Because of their unsuitability, they were not handed over until 25th October 1919 and 22nd July 1919 respectively, after reverting back to single screw ships.

Representative ships of the 'Strath' Class were vessels built at Fleming & Ferguson of Paisley. Their earliest three ships were Yard No's 443, 444 and 445: *Thomas Collard*, launched 11th July 1917; *John Corwarder* on 20th September; and *Benjamin Coleman*, launched on 2nd November of that year. *Thomas Collard*,

Admiralty No. 3686, was also armed with a 7.5ins bomb-throwing mortar; she was sunk by a U-boat on 1st March 1918, north of Rathlin Island. *John Corwarder*, Admiralty No. 3685, served as a minesweeper until sold in 1919. By 1923, her name had changed to *River Nith* (GY.289), owned by the Consolidated Steam Fishing & Ice Co. Ltd, Grimsby. They moved her to Lowestoft in December 1938, changing her name to *Gunton* (LT.319). By 1956, she was working out of Aberdeen as *Gunton* (A.12), owned by Craigwood Ltd, Aberdeen. She eventually went for scrapping at Charleston on 2nd November 1959. The last of the trio, *Benjamin Coleman*, Admiralty No. 3687, also served as a minesweeper throughout the First World War, until sold on 16th November 1921. She became *Benjamin Coleman* (GW.37), owned by John S. Boyle, Glasgow, until requisitioned in November 1939 as an armed patrol trawler, being returned in September 1945.

Another trio of ships built at Fleming & Ferguson's were Yard No's 454, 456 and 457, *John Dunkin*, *William Harvey* and *Arthur Herwin* (**Plan 39**). The minesweeping gear shown on the plan consists of a pair of 9ft kite otters stowed behind the after trawl gallows. The towing pendants run from strain indicators mounted on deck aft, then forward through the blocks at the end of the winch wires and out over the stern. Electric wires lead from the strain indicators, along the casing side, to the repeater display in the wheelhouse. If the charge made contact with an underwater object such as a U-boat, it could be detonated electrically from the wheelhouse, or by an internal contact detonator on the charge itself. Like the earlier ships, the strain indicators were wired to panels in the wheelhouse and the engine room telegraph repeater was fitted outside on the verandah. Round the wheelhouse top is a canvas covered wooden guardrail. The companionway for the mid-ship accommodation is forward of the foremast and that for the forward crew space is ahead of this. The main steam trawl winch is used for minesweeping, with trawl gallows fitted fore and aft. All the standing rigging is set up using deadeyes and layards.

Photo. 50: Requisitioned trawler ***Ben Earn*** with her crew at 'harbour stations'. At 122ft, she is similar to a non standard 'Strath'. The photograph shows the amount of top hamper fitted to these minesweepers. Armed with two 12 pounders and a machine gun on the bridge wings, her boat is stowed aft of the funnel on the starboard side. She still carries her trawl winch and forward gallows.

The *John Dunkin*, Admiralty No. 3727, was launched on 6th August 1918. She became *Pekin* in March 1919 and, in May of that year, she was loaned to the US Navy for three months, under her original name. She was sold in 1921 as *John Dunkin* (GW.35) owned by John S. Boyle, Glasgow. She does not appear in the registers after 1939. *William Harvey*, Admiralty No. 3816, was launched on 10th November 1919, too late for war service and was finished off as a fishing trawler. Sold later that year, her name was changed to *River Orchy* (GY.291) owned by the Consolidated Steam Fishing & Ice Co. Ltd. She was transferred (on paper) to the Consolidated Fishing Co. in September 1927 and they in turn sold her to Lowestoft as *Flixton* in December 1938. She was requisitioned in August 1939 as a port examination vessel and was returned in July 1946. She was reregistered as *Flixton* (SN.120) under the ownership of R. Hastie & Sons, North Shields. The last of the trio, *Arthur Herwin*, Yard No. 457, launched on 19th December 1919, carried the Admiralty No. 3817. She was sold while on the stocks and was delivered as *River Lossie* (ME.121) to the Montrose Fishing Co. Ltd on or around 23rd January 1920 (they also purchased around twenty other ex-naval trawlers). By

1923, she had been sold to the Consolidated Steam Fishing & Ice Co. Ltd as *River Lossie* (GY.279). In 1935, she was sold to George Cormack of Nigg, Aberdeen as A.332. By 1939, she was owned by George Craig, Aberdeen and was fitted with wireless. She twice hit the local headlines in 1939. The first occasion was on 30th October, when she rescued the crew of the *Cairnmona* of Newcastle, which had been torpedoed by *U13* off Rattray Head, and the second on 7th December, when she became one of the first Aberdeen trawlers to be attacked by German aircraft, while fishing off Buchan Ness on the Aberdeenshire coast. She was requisitioned in June 1940 as an armed patrol trawler and was returned in February 1945. By 1947, she was owned by J.W. Johnstone, Aberdeen. Her end came on 27th March 1953, when she ran aground on Robbie Ramsay's Baa, while running into Lerwick harbour for shelter. She soon became a constructive total loss but fortunately no lives were lost

The final 'Strath' Class trawler to be built by Fleming & Ferguson was Yard No. 449 *Thomas Dennison*, Admiralty No. 3723. She was a typical North Sea trawler but fitted with a wooden rail and standard binnacle. Below deck, the crew's fo'c'sle had bunks for four hands and was heated by a small coal fired bogey

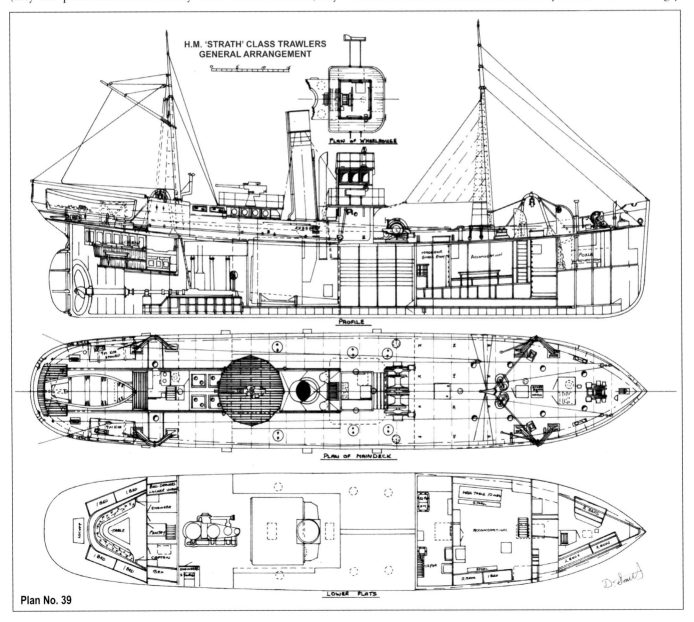

Plan No. 39

stove. Between this compartment and the main bunker space were storerooms, an ice room and fish room, with their attendant deck hatches. There was nothing untoward about her profile, except for her triatic fish landing span set up at the stem head. She was sold in December 1919 to H. Mitchell, Grimsby as *The Tower* (GY.608). In March 1920, she went to the Tower Fishing Co. Ltd, Grimsby, who later sold her to the Arctic Steam Fishing Co. Ltd, Grimsby, in June 1937. She was requisitioned in November 1939 as FY889 and returned in February 1945. When under Royal Navy control, she was sold in April 1941 to George Craig, Aberdeen, as A.585. In March 1945, she went to George Robb & Sons Ltd, Aberdeen as *Viking Freedom* and was finally broken up at Charlestown on 9th August 1960; her scrap value was £2,311.

SMITH'S DOCK 'CASTLE' CLASS

This class were based on the builder's mercantile *Raglan Castle* (SA.30 – 134ft oa x 125ft bp x 23ft 6ins x 12ft, 360g, 480ihp), with a speed of 10.5 knots. She was taken over in November 1915 and used as a trials ship for minesweeping and mine laying duties, until sold in 1919. Armament on the ships in the class varied but was normally one 3ins gun. They had a complement of eighteen, including three wireless operators when carried and cost £21,000 in total for hull and machinery. In addition, the class carried some 160 tons of coal which gave an endurance of thirty days at sea. The first standard 'Castle', *Nathaniel Cole*, was delivered on 4th May 1917 from Smith's Dock, with the Admiralty No. 3507. She sank shortly afterwards at Buncrana off Lough Swilly, Ireland on 6th February 1918.

Some eighteen 'non-standards' were taken over from various builders prior to the standard building programme. These ranged from 117ft 6ins to 125ft bp and from 22ft to 23ft 6ins beam. They included such ships as *John Burlingham*, Admiralty No. 3600, launched by Cook, Welton & Gemmell on 21st April 1917, as Yard No. 363 for G.F. Sleight & Co. Ltd, Grimsby; the vessel measured 125ft bp x 22ft x 13ft, 266g, 80nhp and was engined by Amos & Smith. She was fitted out as a minesweeper with one 12 pounder and a 7.5ins bomb throwing mortar. In April 1920, she was sold to her intended owners as *Rehearo* GY.829. She remained with Sleight's until requisitioned again in September 1940 as a minesweeper, returning to civilian life again in December 1945. Her owners were recorded as G.F. Sleight & Sons Ltd and she stayed with them until going for scrap at Krimpen in April 1961. Another 'non-standard' pair launched from Smith's Dock on 9th January 1917 were *Festing Grindall*, Yard No. 662, Admiralty No. 3501, and No. 663 *John Gillman*, Admiralty No. 3502. They measured 117ft 4ins x 22ft 6ins x 13ft 1in. As minesweepers, their armament consisted of the ubiquitous 12 pounder and a bomb throwing mortar. *John Gillman* was sold in 1920 to North Eastern Fisheries Ltd, Aberdeen as A.230. In the mid 1930s, she starred in the GPO film *North Sea*, about radio at sea, which portrayed an excellent overview of life aboard a North Sea trawler. In May 1946, she became GY.273 owned by J. Clayburn and, in July 1947, she was sold to the Consolidated Steam Fishing (had & Ice been dropped?) Co. Ltd, Grimsby; she was eventually scrapped at Gateshead on 8th December 1954. Her sister, *Festing Grindall* (A.630) was also owned by North Eastern Fisheries Ltd, Aberdeen (R.W. Lewis) after the war and came to grief on 4th October 1928, whilst on a coaling trip to Granton. She ran ashore in thick fog

at Fife Ness and her crew took to the boat, reaching the nearby Balcomie Sands without further mishap.

Another sixty 'Castle' Class trawlers were built in Canada by various shipyards, of which the Admiralty took over thirty-six. Out of the remaining twenty-four, nine were manned by the US Navy, with the rest having Royal Canadian Navy crews.

The first *Raglan Castle* – not be confused with a second *Raglan Castle* (SA.6) – was launched on 12th May 1919 from George Browns as the 'Castle' Class trawler *George Greaves*, Admiralty No. 3790. She was sold later that year and although registered at Swansea, was owned by the Consolidated Steam Fishing & Ice Co. Ltd, Grimsby. She was requisitioned again in August 1939 as FY631, an armed patrol vessel. After the end of the war, she was purchased by the Admiralty, who later sold her in September 1947 to the Ceylon Government

'CASTLE' CLASS BUILDERS

In addition to the forty vessels launched from the parent yard, a further eighteen ships were cancelled in 1917, to allow Smith's Dock to complete their gunboat building programme. The remainder came from the following builders: Cook, Welton & Gemmell – fifty-six; C. Rennoldson – thirteen; J.P. Rennoldson – fourteen; Goole SB – fourteen; Lobnitz – eight; Ferguson – five; Bow McLachlan – twenty-four; George Brown – thirteen; John Duthie – five; Ailsa, Ayr – none; Ailsa, Troon – seven; Chambers – two; Hepple – six; Fletcher & Fearnall – two; Cox, Falmouth – two; and Harkess, Middlesborough – two; a total of 222 ships. This has been compiled from the builder's lists. In addition to the tally above, another twenty vessels were cancelled, with some of them being completed as commercial fishing trawlers (Note: this does not tally with the table found in Colledge's book, which lists 217 ships).

The standard military 'Castle' Class anti-submarine trawlers were heavy looking Middle Water ships, with flat topped forecastles. They had the normal trawler casing, with a verandah round the wheelhouse and a storm rail on the wheelhouse top. Abaft the funnel was a steel circular bandstand for the 12 pounder gun. The casing was strengthened in way of this bandstand by plate gussets. The wooden bandstand decking was laid either radially or fore and aft. The ship's boat, stowed behind the galley, restricted the working space aft, where she carried two rails for her type 'D' depth charges, and twin chutes for the type 'G' towed charges. A companionway lead down to the midships crew space and mess deck, which were in the fish room space. Apart from this and the gun, there was nothing to distinguish her from a fishing trawler. As with the 'Straths', quite a number of these vessels were fitted out as fishing trawlers after being completed too late for war service. The Cook, Welton & Gemmell plan covers a number of these vessels, their Admiralty names and numbers being as follows:

Yard No. 403 *John Gulipster*, No. 3782
Yard No. 404 *Philip Godby*, No. 3783
Yard No. 407 *George Aiken*, No. 4291
Yard No. 408 *John Aitkenhead*, No. 4292
Yard No. 409 *John Ashley*, No. 4293
Yard No. 410 *Egilias Akerman*, No. 4294
Yard No. 411 *Thomas Adney*, No. 4295
Yard No. 412 *Dominic Addison*, No. 4296
Yard No. 413 *Isaac Arthan*, No. 4297
Yard No. 414 *Andrew Apsley*, No. 4298

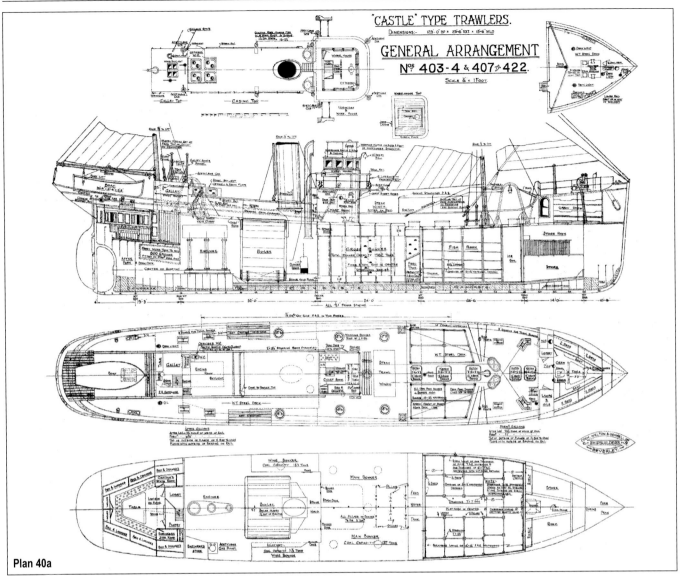

Plan 40a

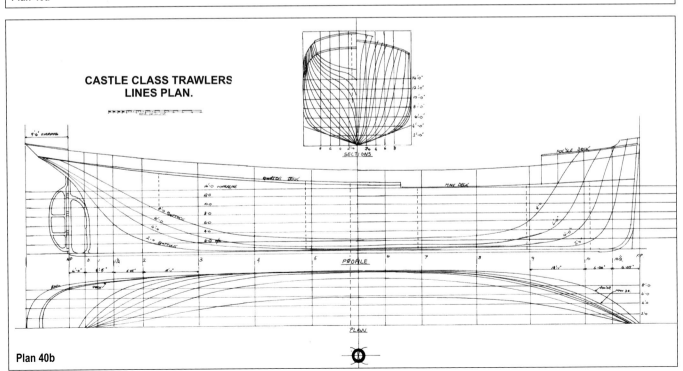

CASTLE CLASS TRAWLERS
LINES PLAN.

Plan 40b

Painting 3: 'Castle' Class trawler **William Brady**. Built at Beverley as Yard No. 380, LO.347. The painting shows her in 1940 as FY4112. She was returned in 1946 and renamed **Tokio** (GY.167 in 1951). COURTESY S. FARROW

Yard No. 415 *Joshua Arabin*, No. 4299
Yard No. 416 *Thomas Altoft*, No. 4300
Yard No. 417 *Charles Antram*, No. 4401
Yard No. 418 *George Adgell*, No. 4402
Yard No. 419 *Thomas Allen*, No. 4403
Yard No. 420 *Thomas Alexandra*, No. 4404
Yard No. 421 *Andrew Anderson*, No. 4405
Yard No. 422 *Thomas Boudige*, No. 4406 (**Plan No. 40 a & b**)
The eight crewmen were housed in a fo'c'sle on main deck level, with daylight provided by two fixed ports on the after bulkhead and two deck lights. A short lobby led out onto the deck, where to port is a WC and to starboard the lamp room. One major point regarding these ships was their all steel decks, though later wood-sheathed. The skipper's working cabin/chartroom below the wheelhouse is quite roomy for a trawler of this size and no doubt the radio gear was housed here before proper wireless cabins were introduced.

Up to Yard No. 411 *Thomas Adney*, the entrance from the deck was by a teak door on the port side. On later ships, a steel door was fitted. The drawing shows a standard binnacle, which would have been replaced by a pole compass fitted to the front of the verandah for commercial fishing (**Photo. 45**). The fish rooms, at 18ft long, were also quite small. The bunker space ran well forward and was separated from the fish room by a void space, which held a boiler feed tank. After Yard No. 414, this tank was removed and the fish room extended aft, which added another 24ft. All the deck lighting was the acetylene type, with the gas plant fitted in the engine room. Their bunker capacity was 162 tons, which gave them sixteen to eighteen days steaming. Three sails are shown but no fish or bobbin derricks.

Looking at the brief histories of just a couple of the above trawlers, we see that, in May 1919, *Philip Godby* came under the ownership of H. Smethurst, Grimsby as GY.309. In February 1920, she fished for the Derby Steam Trawling Co. Ltd, who sold her in November

1921 to Bootle owners. She transferred to Fleetwood in March 1922, as *Cisnell* (FD.405), owned by the Neva Steam Trawling Co. Ltd, Fleetwood. They in turn sold her in 1924 to Milford owners Thomas Jenkerson, as *Togimo* (LO.122). She was sunk on 11th February 1940 by gunfire from *U37*. Yard No. 408 *John Aitkenhead* was launched on 19th December 1918 and was sold as *Polly Johnson* (H.322) to W.A. Massey & Sons Ltd, Hull in 1919. She stayed with one owner and sank twice during her lifetime. The first occasion was on 23rd November 1927, in Fraserburgh harbour. Raised soon afterwards, she went back to sea. She was requisitioned in August 1939 as a minesweeper but was sunk for the second and final time on 29th May 1940, following a direct hit from German bombs whilst taking part in the evacuation from Dunkirk.

Another of the class, *George Cousins*, was completed by Ailsa at Ayr as a fishing trawler. She went to the Blackburn Trawling Co. Ltd, Fleetwood (as FD.343) in 1919. By 1933, she was owned by Blackburn & Robertson, Fleetwood. They sold her to the Iago Steam Trawling Co. Ltd, Fleetwood in 1935. Requisitioned as a minesweeper in August 1939, she was returned in July 1945. By 1947, she was owned by Haven Trawlers Ltd, Milford (Robert Lewis, manager). They in turn sold her to Aberdeen as A.681 under the flag of the Harrow, Baxter Steam Fishing Co. Ltd and she went for scrap in 1956. While working out of Aberdeen, it was said she had a full colour painting of 'Superman' emblazoned on her boiler face. Ailsa also launched Yard No. 333 *Emmanuel Camelaire*, Admiralty No. 3717, on 25th April 1918. She served as a minesweeping trawler, armed with the standard issue 12 pounder. She was sold out of service in 1921 and went to Belgian owners as *General Franqui*, for use as a tug and salvage vessel. In November 1938, she went to Grimsby as *Brabant* (GY.544), owned by the Rhondda Steam Fishing Co. Ltd, Grimsby (Consolidated Fisheries). She was requisitioned as a minesweeper in August 1939 and returned in December 1949. Although under Admiralty control, she was sold in January 1944 to Clifton Steam Trawlers Ltd, Fleetwood as *Brabant* (FD.239), who kept her until she went for scrap in 1959. The post war market price for an ex 'Castle' Class trawler was from £8,000 to £9,500 (see **Photo. 51** *Concertator* for an example of post war fishing conversion).

When listing these later trawlers, and in addition the cancelled vessels, a certain amount of confusion arises with the Cook, Welton & Gemmell ships in Colledge's book. He lists the cancelled 'Castles' as (Admiralty names and numbers):

Ephraim Bright, No. 4407 – later *Mai*
James Baird, No. 4411 – later *Ijuin*
John Benson, No. 4409 – later *Kari Solmundarson*
James Boyle, No. 4144
Matthew Berryman, No. 4412 – later *Righto* (GY.1267)
Richard Bane No. 4410 – later *Kyoto*)
William Bennett, No. 408 – later *Njordur*)
William Burte, No. 4413 – later *Reboundo* (GY.1268)

However, the builders list shows the above seven vessels with their later names as Yard No's 423 to 429 and only *Righto* and *Reboundo* are of similar size to the war time 'Castles'. *Mai*, *Njordur* and *Kari Solmundarson* all measured 140ft bp, whilst *Kyoto* and *Ijuin* measured 128ft bp, which was still larger than the standard 'Castle'. The eighth ship, *James Boyle*, appears to have been cancelled completely but a trawler of similar size, Yard No. 435 *Windward Ho*, was launched in 1920 for Hull owners. She went to Grimsby in 1929 as GY.158, owned by H. Croft Baker & Sons, Grimsby. When war broke out again, the Admiralty took her over in October 1939 as FY574, for minesweeping duty,

returning her in 1945. She was sold again in 1951 to the Diamond Steam Fishing Co. Ltd, Grimsby and renamed *Okio*. She stayed with them until being scrapped in February 1962 at Sunderland. One of Hepples' four ships was *William Carberry*, Admiralty No. 4479, delivered on 13th December 1919 as fishing trawler PH.69. She was later sold to Spanish owners as *Micaela De C.*

COCHRANE'S 'MERSEY' CLASS

This class of steam trawlers were based on Cochranes Yard No. 647 *Lord Mersey* (H.247 – 148ft x 23ft 6ins x 13ft, 324g, 60ihp), which had a speed of 11 knots. She was launched in 1915 for Pickering & Haldane of Hull, with the Admiralty No. 1991. *Lord Mersey* served as a minesweeper armed with a 12 pounder and a 7.5ins bomb throwing mortar. She was released in 1919 and went back to her former owners. Armament varied, with either one or two 12 pounders plus two 20mm guns and she had a complement of twenty. The first of the standard 'Mersey' Class was *John Quilliam*, Admiralty No. 3541, launched on 12th March 1917 from Cochranes as Yard No. 801. Her engines by C.D. Holmes were numbered A (for Admiralty) 1. She served as a hydrophone trawler until being sold in 1921, as *Dana*.

There were seven 'non-standard Merseys' built, five by Cochrane's and the remaining two by Cook, Welton & Gemmell. They ranged from 120ft 6ins to 138ft 6ins and from 248g to 400g. The largest of these vessels was *William Westenburgh*. She was laid down by Cochrane's as Yard No. 756 *Lord Talbot*, for Pickering & Haldane's Steam Trawling Co. Ltd, Hull. She was the third trawler of a four ship order by the company, the

Photo. 51: *Concertator* (A680), was the ex-Admiralty 'Castle' Class *John Thorling*, built by Smith's Dock in 1917. Sold out of service in 1920 and renamed *River Kent*, she became FD.75 after being purchased by the River Steam Fishing Co. Ltd. Fleetwood. Sold in 1939 to T.L. Devlin of Leith as *Concertator* (GN.8), she was requisitioned that year as a minesweeper and sold in 1945 to J. Marr & Son, Fleetwood as FD.276. She is seen passing Hall, Russell's yard in the 1950s, with her new Aberdeen fishing number but prior to being renamed *Thomas Stephen* by her owners the Stephen Fishing Co. Ltd, Aberdeen.

others being *Lord Byng, Lord Birkenhead* and *Lord Carson*. They were all the same size as the standard 'Mersey'. In the First World War, *William Westenburgh*, Admiralty No. 3577, served as a minesweeper armed with two 12 pounders. She was sold to her original Hull owners in 1921 reverting back as *Lord Talbot*. In May 1928, she went to Grimsby as *Lord Talbot* (GY.463), owned by the Perihelion Steam Fishing Co. Ltd. In January 1931, she moved to Aberdeen and her name was changed in late 1932 to *Star of the Realm* (A.147); she was owned by the Walker Steam Trawl Fishing Co. Ltd, Aberdeen. She frequented Greenland under skipper Thomas Watson of Torry, who was the local expert on these grounds. Just before her name change in October 1932, she hit the headlines after saving the 'Flying Hutchinsons'. Their amphibian plane had crash landed in the sea near Angmagsalik, after taking off from Julianehaat, Greenland whilst on a flight from New York to Edinburgh. Their SOS was picked up by *Lord Talbot* and she began a search for the survivors, assisted by the Aberdeen trawlers *Mount Ard* (A.156) and *Star of Victory* (A.4). By nightfall, skipper Watson's trawler had located the family after sighting their flares. There was heavy pack ice in the vicinity but the trawler eventually reached the position and launched a boat. The mate, who was in charge of the boat, decided that the swell was too bad to attempt a rescue in darkness, so he sent the boat back to *Lord Talbot*, while he remained with the survivors. By noon the following day, the parents and their two daughters Kathryn and Janet, along with their four man crew, had been landed at the settlement of Finsbu and the trawler returned to the fishing grounds. Could this have been the first instance of an Air-Sea Rescue in peacetime?

Lord Talbot went back to Grimsby in February 1933 as *Star of the Realm* (GY.475), under the Crampin Steam Fishing Co. Ltd's banner. By June 1934, she was owned by the Malmata Steam Fishing Co. Ltd, Grimsby, who sold her to Denmark in February 1938. By the beginning of the Second World War, she was Norwegian owned as *Nordstjornan* (TN.131). Requisitioned in January 1940 as *Star of the Realm* again, Admiralty No. Z.105, she served as a boom defence vessel until sold in May 1946. The *British Fisheries Directory* for 1947 shows her under the ownership of W.R. Metcalf, Falmouth, who were still her registered owners in 1948-9. She went to the breakers at Spezia in February 1962.

'MERSEY' CLASS BUILDERS

In addition to the eighty-two ships completed by Cochrane's, the remainder of the class were constructed by the following builders: Cook, Welton & Gemmell – two; Goole SB – fourteen; Lobnitz – eight; Ferguson – six; making a total of 112 ships, which excludes the forty-four ships cancelled after November 1918. Many of these vessels were completed as fishing trawlers. Six of these cancelled ships were to have been built at the new John Lewis yard at Aberdeen but the company were busy constructing wartime coasters.

It is obvious that Cochranes were prolific builders of trawlers, having launched eighty-two 'Merseys' in a space of a little under two years. Their work record shows that, for 1917, they built forty-four Admiralty trawlers, a total of 14,013.06 gross tons, with a total power output of some 25,37ihp. In 1918, they launched twenty-eight steam trawlers and eight 'KIL' Class patrol gunboats. That year's totals were 13,288.36 gross tons and 27,720ihp. In order to pursue such an aggressive building programme, considerable improvements and extensions to the yard had to be made. These,

coupled with standardisation in building methods, enabled the company to achieve maximum efficiency. The shipyard, situated at Selby, some fifty miles from the open sea, was capable of building ships up to 1,000 tons. Sited on the banks of the River Ouse, it was only possible to sideways launch completed hulls on a spring tide and during this wartime building bonanza, they were launching two ships simultaneously every fortnight. The trawlers were more or less completed at Selby, except for the installation of the machinery, which was carried out in Queen's Dock, Hull. The fifty mile trip from Selby to Hull usually took four to five hours, depending on the rate of the ebb tide.

There were five slipways in all, each capable of handling two 325g trawlers at a time. When the larger 525g patrol gunboats were being built, only four of the slips could be used. From the time of laying the keel to preparing the ship for towing down the river took some three months. The programme was worked out thus: 1st pair – framing; 2nd pair – inside steel work; 3rd pair – plating; 4th pair – rivetting; and 5th pair – caulking and launching. The sequence of operations was finely tuned, so that the respective main trades worked for two weeks on each pair, before passing on to the next pair, making for a strict rotation of work, thus minimising production delays. In common with most yards of the time, Cochranes relied on steam as the main source of motive power. This was changed to electricity in October 1918 with minimum disruption to the work schedule. The majority of the changeover was done at weekends and whenever time allowed. A short strike during January 1919 permitted the work to be completed ahead of time. After the changeover, the slipways were served by Clarke Chapman electric winches, which proved a great improvement on the cumbersome crane work. An overhead runway was installed, to ease congestion when using ground trolleys for moving materials around the yard. From the layout of the yard, it is evident that all the workshops were arranged so as to facilitate the various stages of construction. The shipyard was more or less self-contained, with fittings such as bollards, stanchions and davits all being made in-house. The joiner's shop fabricated all the internal cabin fitments from standardised patterns. This allowed the work to go on independently of other yard departments. The yard had a timber buying policy in place well before the war, purchasing large stocks of timber at least three years ahead of requirements. This allowed ample time for seasoning prior to it being used. In addition to the naval construction, the yard built a further eighty-eight trawlers for private owners during the war years (**Photos 52 a, b & c**)

Cochrane's 'Mersey' Class ships, Yard No's 801 to 836, were all Admiralty trawlers (Yard No., Admiralty name & No.):

Yard No. 801 *John Quilliam*, No. 3541
Yard No. 802 *George Bligh*, No. 3542
Yard No. 803 *John Yule*, No. 3543
Yard No. 804 *John Pascoe*, No. 3544
Yard No. 805 *Andrew King*, No. 3545
Yard No. 806 *Thomas Atkinson*, No. 3546
Yard No. 807 *Edward Williams*, No. 3547
Yard No. 808 *George Brown*, No. 3548
Yard No. 809 *Alexander Hills*, No. 3549
Yard No. 810 *William Ram*, No. 3550
Yard No. 811 *Charles Adair*, No. 3551
Yard No. 812 *William Rivers*, No. 3552
Yard No. 813 *Lewis Reeves*, No. 3553

Photo. 52a: A 'Mersey' Class trawler in frame.

Photo. 52b: 'Mersey' Class trawlers on the stocks.

Photo. 52c: 'Mersey' Class trawlers under construction at Cochranes Yard, Selby.

Yard No. 814 *Lewis Roatley*, No. 3554
Yard No. 815 *James Adams*, No. 3555
Yard No. 816 *George Andrews*, No. 3556
Yard No. 817 *Robert Bookless*, No. 3557
Yard No. 818 *Thomas Bailey*, No. 3558
Yard No. 819 *Robert Barton*, No. 3559
Yard No. 820 *Richard Bulkeley*, No. 3560
Yard No. 821 *Michael Clements*, No. 3561
Yard No. 822 *John Cormack*, No. 3562
Yard No. 823 *Christopher Dixon*, No. 3563
Yard No. 824 *Samuel Dowden*, No. 3564
Yard No. 825 *James Buchanan*, No. 3565
Yard No. 826 *John Ebbs*, No. 3566
Yard No. 827 *Fraser Eaves*, No. 3567
Yard No. 828 *George Fenwick*, No. 3568
Yard No. 829 *Henry Ford*, No. 3569
Yard No. 830 *John Felton*, No. 3570
Yard No. 831 *Daniel Fearall*, No. 3571
Yard No. 832 *Thomas Thresher*, No. 3572
Yard No. 833 *John Welstead*, No. 3573
Yard No. 834 *Thomas Whipple*, No. 3574
Yard No. 835 *George Westphall*, No. 3575
Yard No. 836 *James Wright*, No. 3576

The original builders design concept, shows all these vessels as fishing trawlers. In order to give some idea of the life span of two of these ships, I have chosen the first and last.

John Quilliam was launched on 12th March 1917, fitted out as a hydrophone trawler and armed with a single 12 pounder gun. She was sold out of service in 1920 and renamed *Dana*. Under her new Danish owners, she was to scour the oceans of the world as an ocean research ship. *James Wright* was delivered on 15th March 1918 as a minesweeper and was sold in 1921 as *Lord Ancaster* (H.662). In 1935, her name was changed to *Westcoates* (H.662), owned by J. Marr & Sons Ltd, Hull and sold in 1939 to the Loch Line as *Loch Moidart*. Under this name she was requisitioned in June 1940 as an armed patrol and minesweeping trawler, a role she played until returned in January 1946. She was owned finally by J.&U. Smith & H. Richards, Hull, going to the breakers in 1947.

DEPTH CHARGE TRAWLERS

Cochrane's drawing for ship No's 843-851 covers the following trawlers (Admiralty name & No.):

Yard No. 843 *Richard Jewell*, No. 3836
Yard No. 844 *Thomas Johns*, No. 3837
Yard No. 845 *William Jones*, No. 3838
Yard No. 846 *Samuel Jameson*, No. 3839
Yard No. 847 *Thomas Jarvis*, No. 3840
Yard No. 848 *William Inwood*, No. 3841
Yard No. 849 *James Jones*, No. 3842
Yard No. 850 *William Johnson*, No. 3843
Yard No. 851 *Andrew Jewer*, No. 3844

The builder's general arrangement drawing for these trawlers depicts a very different vessel from the 'Fishing type' (**Plan 41 a & b**). They are very much minor war vessels, with their two gun mountings, the disposition of the small boat and the depth charge rails aft. The raised fo'c'sle head has collapsible wire rails and stanchions replacing the usual fixed type. The hand warping windlass and breakwater have been removed and the 13ft diameter bandstand for the forward 12 pounder gun sits in their place. Below the fo'c'sle head, the layout is identical to the earlier ships, as is the crew's space on the lower deck. Aft of the crew's fo'c'sle is a large store room, with the 1,000 gallon fresh water tank for the galley fitted below the floor. A watertight bulkhead separates this from the wireless cabin, officers' berth, crew and petty officers' messroom. These have been shoe-horned into what would have been the ice room and forward fish room. Below the messroom floor are the boiler feed water tanks, with a total capacity of 2,500 gallons. The magazine lies between the messroom and the reserve bunker space, separated by WT bulkheads. From here on aft, the below deck arrangement is similar to the earlier type. The weather decks are bare steel, with diagonal tread strips rivetted on the foredeck. The five fish, ice and store room hatches are still fitted.

The middle hatch has been converted to a companionway for the messdeck and the hatch over the magazine is fitted with an ammunition davit. Four 8ins diameter deck lights, with sliding wooden covers, are fitted to supply daylight to the accommodation below. An aerial trunk is shown inboard of the after leg of the

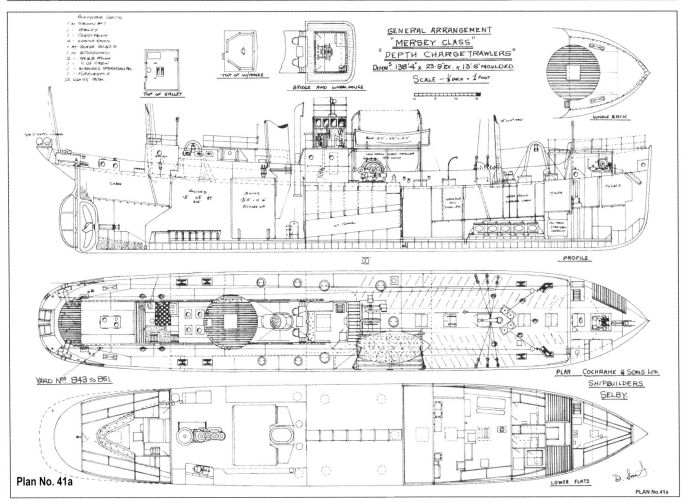

Plan No. 41a

starboard gallows. The transom-sterned trawler-type boat sits on a light spar deck, level with the verandah. The main steam trawl winch has a capacity for 1,000 fathoms of trawl warp. At the forward end of the casing is the chart room. This has a door to starboard, leading from the deck, and a wooden ladder leading up to the wheelhouse. The wheelhouse contains the main Donkin patent steam and hand steering gear, engine room telegraph, folding chart table and inverted steering compass, plus railway carriage type windows all round. On the roof sits a binnacle, surrounded by a canvas covered guard rail, topped with a canvas dodger; such were the comforts on 'Mount Misery'. Between the funnel and the galley is the after gun bandstand, with a fixed guard rail, sparred deck and ready use racks for ten shells. Immediately in front of this, on the casing top, is a small hatch over the boiler safety valves. At the after end of the casing is the galley, with an officers' WC to port, complete with a *Porcelain closet with wooden seat*. The soil pipe and storm valve are shown passing through the port side shell plating. At the stern are twin depth charge rails, with their four 'D' type charges, and either side of the quarter are the towed

charge launching trays (or chutes). Although not shown on the drawing they were fitted with tall, fidded, wooden topmasts above the steel mizzen. Full electric and acetylene lighting was fitted, with the latter positioned as follows: one in after saloon; one in stokehold; one in galley; two in messroom; one in chart room; one in CO's cabin; two in engineroom; one in radio cabin; one at gauge glass; and one in fo'c'sle. She has another gun platform over the

Plan No. 41b

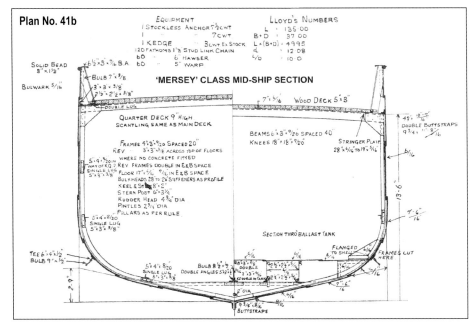

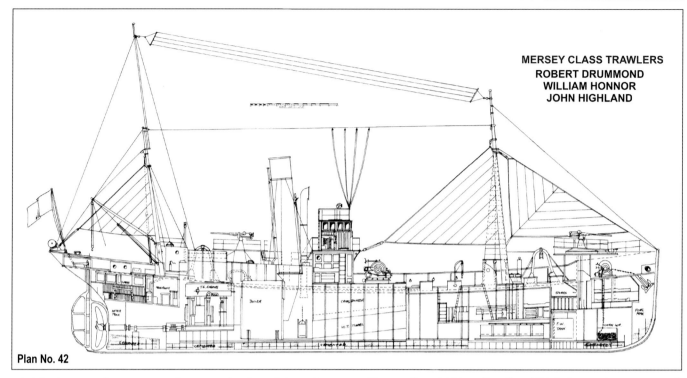

MERSEY CLASS TRAWLERS
ROBERT DRUMMOND
WILLIAM HONNOR
JOHN HIGHLAND

Plan No. 42

whaleback as per the 1918 specifications. The first of these ships, *Richard Jewell*, launched on 6th August 1918, does not (according to Colledge's book) conform to the drawing, as he lists her as having only one 6 pounder AA gun. This is not a criticism of Colledge, as builders' drawings are notoriously deceiving. She was sold to the Pickering & Haldane Steam Trawling Co. Ltd, Hull as H.646 in 1922. In December 1928, she was sold to J. Little, Grimsby who renamed her *Fairway* (GY. 488). In May 1929, she changed hands again to the Rinovia Steam Fishing Co Ltd. Requisitioned in May 1940 as FY1551, an armed patrol/minesweeping trawler, she was returned in March 1946. In 1942, whilst on war service, she was sold to J. Marr & Sons Ltd as *Fairway* (FD.140) for £9,250. She eventually went for scrap in 1955.

Yard No. 851 *Andrew Jewer* was delivered on 4th December 1918. She appears to have been fitted with only one 12 pounder. By September 1920, she was serving as the gunnery tender *Nith*

and later, in June 1922, as *Excellent* (T.47). During her service with the gunnery school at Whale Island, she sported a black hull and yellow funnel. She went through the Second World War unscathed and was sold out of service in 1946. Her name was changed to *Malvern* (A.234) owned by the Malvern Steam Fishing Co. Ltd, Aberdeen (George Craig, manager). In 1949, she went to Milford as *Lady Jill* (M.295), owned by Yolland Brothers, Milford and eventually went for scrap in 1954. Although most of Cochranes standard 'Merseys' were built to the same original design, there were deviations. The nett tonnage increased by around 17.5 after Yard No. 838 *John Welstead*. Her successors from Thomas Whipple onwards all measured 149.5 nett, although their other tonnage measurements remained the same. This points to a reduction of either crew or machinery spaces. If one takes the standard measure of 100 cubic feet equalling one to,n then a reduction of around 1,750 cubic feet of space was achieved.

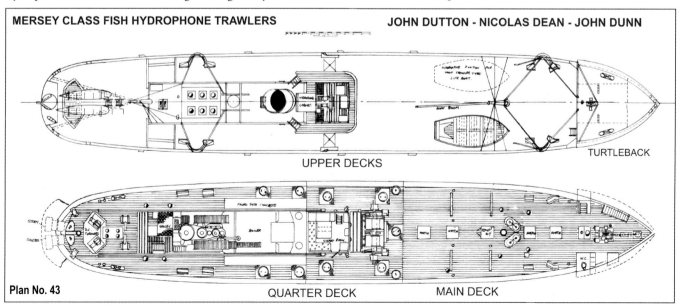

MERSEY CLASS FISH HYDROPHONE TRAWLERS

JOHN DUTTON - NICOLAS DEAN - JOHN DUNN

UPPER DECKS

TURTLEBACK

Plan No. 43

QUARTER DECK

MAIN DECK

The general arrangement drawings from Ferguson Brothers, Port Glasgow, show the depth charge trawlers *Robert Drummond*, *William Honnor* and *John Highland*, Yard No's 233, 240 and 241 (**Plan 42**). In contrast to the Beverley-built ships, these have fully planked decks but otherwise they are almost identical. The elevation shows the full rigging detail which emphasises the height of the masts and aerial arrangement. The triatic stay carries four signal halliards which terminate on the guard rail, near the two flag lockers on the wheelhouse top, and the rigging for the mizzen boom shows it set up as a depth charge loading derrick. Aft they have a pair of towed charges chutes and twin depth charge rails with their release mechanism. On some ships, these depth charges could be released from the wheelhouse. *Robert Drummond*, Admiralty No. 3742, was launched on 4th of May 1918. The plan shows a pair of 12 pounders but Colledge only credits her with one. She was sold in 1922 as *Robert Drummond* but she was renamed *Salmonby* in 1924 and was lost on 23rd March 1926. *William Honnor*, Admiralty No. 3796, was launched on 26th August 1918 and served as an armed escort, armed with a single 12 pounder. She was sold in 1922 and renamed *Grimurkamban*. She was sold again in 1927 as *William Honnor* and later that year as *Sprayflower*. In 1928, she became *Bragi* and sank off the Wyre Light in October 1940. The third ship of the order, *John Highland*, Admiralty No. 3797, was launched on 23rd September 1918. She served as a minesweeper and, according to Colledge, had only one 12 pounder. She was sold in 1920 as *Ocean Ensign*; In 1927, she became *Almirante Jose De Carranza* and was lost off Cape Vilano in September 1940.

Another trio of 'Merseys' from Fergusons were *John Dutton*, *Nicolas Dean* and *John Dunn*, Yard No's 230, 231 and 232. They are listed on the GA drawing as '*Fish, Hydrophone Trawlers*' and have a few differences from the normal 'Mersey' (**Plan 43**). Again the decks are wood sheathed but the trawler-type transom sterned boat

can be stowed on deck chocks, either on the port or starboard side of the foredeck and is launched using the foremast derrick. They are armed with only one 12 pounder mounted on its bandstand, abaft the funnel base only shown on plan. The wheelhouse has a steel hydrophone cabinet built onto its after side. This necessitates the verandah wings being lengthened, with the casing ladders set diagonally, as opposed to the usual fore and aft arrangement. The real differences come at the stern. One deck plan shows an anti-submarine arrangement, with twin double depth charge rails on the counter and hinged discharge doors set in the bulwarks. Two depth charge throwers are positioned on deck between the rudder head and the cabin skylight. This is the only First World War drawing that I have seen which shows these throwers.

The other section of the drawing shows the after arrangement when rigged as a hydrophone trawler, with twin wire reels on the centreline, an 'A' frame mounted over the counter with its guide sheave, torpedo shaped floats and weights for the sensitive equipment. It is possible that this drawing, although for three ships, shows the arrangement for the two types that normally worked together in harmony. This was of necessity, as the hydrophone trawler had to remain stationary, with her propeller stopped, as the cavitations from a turning screw set up spurious echoes which confused these early sets. Once a target had been located, her partner the anti-submarine trawler moved in for the kill, directed by the listening vessel. It was not only these vessels that worked in pairs; the minesweeping trawlers would tow a sweep wire between them when working the 'A' type sweeps used at the outset of the war. These were replaced by single ship sweeps, where the towing vessel streamed a kite otter board, which held the wire well away from the stern of the ship. A further development was the Oropesa sweep, named after the trawler in which it was first tested. This showed the way forward for moored minesweeping and enabled the

Photo. 53: *Cherwell* showing her naval configuration but still unmistakably a steam trawler.

Photo. 54: *Explorer*. A larger superstructure has been fitted for extra laboratory and crew accommodation, and no port side gallows are fitted. The hull is painted black with a white band. She has wood grained superstructure and a cream funnel with a black top. No fishing numbers are carried. The tall stove chimney ahead of her foremast is for the accommodation in the hold space.

navy to be twenty years ahead of any of its counterparts by 1939.

John Dutton, Admiralty No. 3739, appears to have been the anti-submarine ship of the trio, with *John Dunn*, Admiralty No. 3741, the hydrophone trawler. The former vessel was sold in 1921 and later became *Karlsefni*. Her sister, was sold in 1923 and later had her name changed to *Florence Brierley* (FD.105), owned by Clifton Steam Trawlers Ltd, Fleetwood. She was requisitioned again in January 1940, as a boom defence vessel, and was returned in August 1946. She then went out to Capetown under the same name but to new owners, the East Fisheries, Capetown. She went for scrap in 1959. *Nicolas Dean*, Admiralty No. 3740, was launched on 11th March 1918. She was armed with a single 12 pounder plus a 3.5ins bomb throwing mortar and was listed as a hydrophone trawler. She was sold in 1921 and renamed *Notre Dame De France*. In 1925, she was *Willoughby* and, by 1928, *Svidi*, last reported at Breidafjord in December 1941.

Not all 'Merseys' ended up as fishing vessels; for example, Cochranes Yard No. 874, *Henry Lancaster*, Admiralty No. 4231, served as an unarmed mark buoy vessel during hostilities She was sold in August 1921 to the Aberdeen Mutual & General Marine Insurance Co. Ltd and extensively altered, with the addition of increased accommodation, extra electric light, special windlass and lifting gear, gangway doors, extra boats, etc, and was employed in marking the navigable channels through minefields. By 1937, her name had changed to *Longtow*, owned by James Dredging, Towing & Transport Ltd, London. She was requisitioned in September 1939, as the tug/salvage vessel *Long Tow* (O/N W.93) at a hire rate of £105 5s per month. In 1943, she was bought by R.A. Beazley of London and was returned in November 1945. By 1948 she had changed hands yet again, this time to the Overseas Towage & Salvage Co. Ltd of London. After a varied career, she was sold to the British Iron & Steel Corporation, who transferred her to T.W.

Ward Ltd, Sheffield and she was broken up in 1951 at Grays, Essex.

Some of the other 'Merseys' were kept by the Navy after the war for fishery protection duties. These included:

T.29 *Boyne*, ex-*William Jones*; *Boyne* in WW2, sold in 1946 and renamed *Nypuberg*, she went for scrap in April 1957

T.03 *Cherwell*, ex-*James Jones*; *Cherwell* in WW2, boom defence vessel, sold 1946 (**Photo. 53**)

T.17 *Colne*, ex-*Isaac Chant*; *Colne* in WW2, sold in 1946

T.35 *Doon*, ex-*Fraser Eaves*; *Doon* in WW2, sold 1946

T.48 *Foyle* ex-*John Edmund* (later *S.A.N. Sonneblom*); *Foyle* in WW2. She remained with the War Department after 1946.

Another of the class, *John Felton*, launched by Cochrane's as Yard No. 830 on 1st November 1917, was armed with the usual 12 pounder plus a 6ins bomb throwing mortar. She was sold out of service in 1921 but she kept the same name. Her new owners were the Department of Agriculture & Fisheries (Scotland) and, after a major conversion, she was commissioned in July 1922 as *Explorer* (**Photo. 54**). In her new role she carried scientists and technicians who monitored water temperatures, salinity relating to fish stocks and tested new fishing gear. Requisitioned in 1939, she served as an examination vessel based at Rosyth, until released in April 1946 and returned to the Department of Agriculture & Fisheries (Scotland). She was taken out of service in 1955, when her successor was launched by Alexander Hall, after which time she sailed to Charlestown for breaking up. Her scrap value was £5,600.

EX-'PORTUGUESE' CLASS

If one is to classify First World War Naval trawlers by types, then there are two other groups to be considered. The first was the 'Portuguese' Class, an odd assortment of British-built ships purchased by the Admiralty for £80,788 in September 1915. They came from builders such as Cook, Welton & Gemmell, John Duthie, Mackie

& Thomson, Goole Shipbuilding & Repairing Co. and Alexander Hall. They were originally constructed as the British trawlers:

Lucida by Goole Shipbuilding in 1911 (later *Bicalho*, later *Crucis*) Admiralty No. 172 and sold in 1919 as *Rio Minho*

Baron Ruzette by Mackie & Thomson in 1909 (later *Mindello 2*, later *Corvi*) Admiralty No. 173 and sold in 1919 as *Rio Zezere*

Loch Laggan by Alexander Hall in 1903, as A.910 for the White Star Steam Fishing Co. Ltd, Aberdeen (later *Monchique*, later *Cygni*) Admiralty No. 174 and sold in 1919 as *Rio Vouga*

Alberia by Cook, Welton & Gemmell in 1910 (later *Rio Tedjo*, later *Arcturus*, then *Arcturus 2*), Admiralty No. 175 and sold in 1919 to Cruz Brothers

Vinca by Goole SB in 1907 (later *Neptuno* later *Algenib*), Admiralty No. 176 and sold in 1919 as *Rio Douro*

Ben Alligin by Duthies in 1906 (later *Cabo Verde*, later *Antares*, then *Antares 2*) as A.74 for Richard Irvin & Sons Ltd, South Shields. Admiralty No. 177, she was sunk by gunfire on 2nd May 1918 after a collision off Gibraltar (the only war casualty of this class)

Star of Freedom by Duthies in 1907 (125ft x 22ft 9ins x 13ft 9ins) as A.151 for the Walker Steam Trawling & Fishing Co. Ltd, Aberdeen (later *Victoria Laura*, later *Altair*, then *Altair 2* in 1917), Admiralty No.178 and sold in 1919 to Cruz Brothers

Caithness-Shire by Mackie & Thomson in 1901, as A.375 for the Shire Steam Fishing Co. Ltd, Aberdeen (later *Maria Amalla*, later *Algol*), Admiralty No. 179 and sold in 1919 as *Rio Lima*

Hebden by Duthies in 1908 as FD.223 (126ft x 22ft 6ins x 12ft 9ins) for J. Potter, Blackpool and fitted with WT (later *Georgina*, later *Chire*, later *Achernar*), Admiralty No. 180 and renamed *Rio Guadiana* in 1919.

'ARMENTIERS' CLASS

This second group of twelve trawlers (139ft x 23ft 6ins x 13ft 6ins, 320g, 480ihp) with a service speed of 10.5 knots and a complement of eighteen, came from Canadian yards in 1917 and 1918. Although initially designed to carry two 12 pounders, it appears only one was ever fitted. They were the product of three yards: Polson Iron Works – six ships; Canadian Vickers – four; and Kingston SB – two. Polson's vessels, strangely enough, were built of iron, with their construction overseen by the manager of the Canadian Steamship Line and the Navy Department. Steel was used for the other ships. Designed as patrol vessels for the Atlantic seaboard, all survived the war and went into commercial fishing, working for the Canadian Department of Marine & Fisheries. Three of the survivors were requisitioned for service in the Second World War.

EX-GERMAN PRIZE TRAWLERS

These were a group of twenty-eight German fishing trawlers, all bar one captured by Royal Naval units. The odd man out was *Clonsin*, which was detained whilst in Aberdeen in 1914. After capture they went to Grimsby until converted. Most went out to the Mediterranean. At first their names were suffixed 'sit' but after November 1915 this was changed to 'sin'. Two ships were lost, *Charlsin* sunk on 30th September 1917 off Marseh Matruh by *U74* and *Crownsin* by a mine off Malta on 4th May 1916. The remainder were sold after the war, with some finding their way into the British trawler fleet.

These then were the naval trawlers that formed the greater part of this nation's mine counter offensive during the First World War. Along with their requisitioned sisters, they carried out their duties as escorts, anti-submarine and hydrophone trawlers, decoy ships, boom defence vessels and, most of all, as minesweepers.

EX-RUSSIAN 'AXE' CLASS

Also on the navy's books were the seventeen ex-Russian 'Axe' Class trawlers built for the Russian Navy. They came from an assortment of builders: Smith's Dock; Cochranes; Hall, Russells; Goole Shipbuilding; Edward Bros; and Aitken & Scott of Glasgow. Nine of these Russian ships were seized in the White Sea in 1918 during the Royal Navy's campaign against the Bolsheviks, with a further

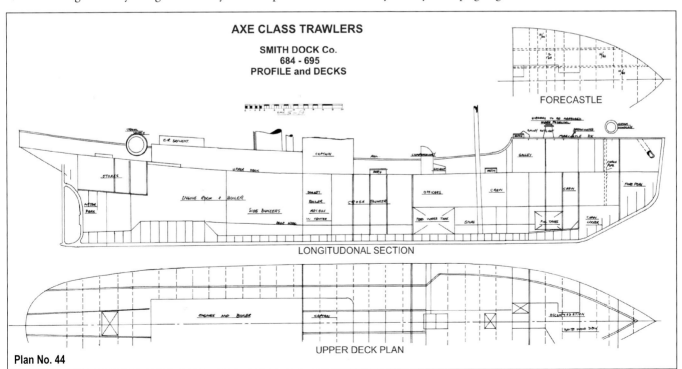

AXE CLASS TRAWLERS

SMITH DOCK Co.
684 - 695
PROFILE and DECKS

FORECASTLE

LONGITUDONAL SECTION

UPPER DECK PLAN

Plan No. 44

eight ships accepted from the White Russian authorities. Their dimensions were 130ft x 23ft 6ins x 12ft, 296g or 135ft 6ins x 23ft 6ins x 12ft 6ins, 304g, with engines of 490ihp giving 10.5 knots, or 500ihp giving 11 knots. Propellers were four blade, cast steel (later cast iron), 9ft 3ins dia. x 11ft 3ins pitch and a surface area of 33 sq. ft. Armed with one 3ins gun, they carried a crew of eighteen.

Six of the above class came from Smith's Dock. They were built in 1916 as part of a Russian order, Yard No's 684-695, numbered T.13 to T.24. The builder's annotations on the back of their file copy of the GA gives the following details (Admiralty name & No.:

Goldaxe, No. 4331 ex-T.13
Stoneaxe, No. 4332 ex-T.14
Battleaxe, No. 4333 ex-T.16
Iceaxe, No. 4334 ex-T.17
Poleaxe, No. 4335 ex-T.19
Woodaxe, No. 4336 ex-T.20
Ironaxe, No. 4337 ex-T.22

The builder's blueprint (**Plan 44**) dated 24th February 1916 and approved by the British Corporation, shows a hybrid type of trawler specially strengthened for ice. They have a long flat fo'c'sle and the stem is cut back icebreaker fashion below the waterline (hence the suffix '*axe*'). The rudder was a standard trawler fitment but their semi-elliptical counter sterns were quite ugly. Their long flush maindecks were mostly bare steel, with wood sheathing extending only from the main fish room hatch forward. The fo'c'sle deck carries a steam windlass and a pedestal mount for the forward gun. The lower deck is fitted out for both officers and crew, with the former using the refurbished fish hold. This was entered by a companionway fitted over the main fish room hatch. The steam trawl winch was fitted aft of the main casing, a position better suited for minesweeping. At the forward end of the casing is the captain's berth and above this is the wheelhouse, unfortunately not shown on the drawing. They were fitted with large storerooms aft, in the space normally occupied by the trawler's officers, now used for storing minesweeping gear. No lifeboats are shown on the plan but, presumably, they would have been carried either on the foredeck or on the casing top well clear of the working deck. Post war, the stern bulwarks were replaced by semi-elliptical counter sterns.

Goldaxe was taken over on 1st June 1916 as a minesweeper and in September 1920 was renamed *Garry* (T.63). She remained in the navy and served again in the Second World War, until sold in 1946 and broken up. *Stoneaxe* was also taken over on 1st June 1916 for minesweeping. In 1920, she became *Liffey* (T.81), part of the Fishery Protection Squadron and was often to be seen in Grimsby. She served again in the Second World War until sold in 1947. *Battleaxe* was taken over in September 1920 by the Admiralty and renamed *Dee* (T.20), serving in the navy through the Second World War until sold out of service as *Safir* in 1946. She was named after another requisitioned trawler of the same name, built in 1893 by Earles as GY.513 for H. Morris, Grimsby. She was sold in February 1897 to the 'D' Line Fishing Co. Ltd, Grimsby and she came under naval control as a fishery trawler from 1918 to 1919, when she was owned by J.A. Smith Trawling Co. Ltd, Hull. He sold her in 1922 to W. Would of Grimsby and she went for scrap in March 1924. *Iceaxe* became *Kennet* (T.78) in September 1920 and served again as a minesweeper in the Second World War, until she was sold out of service in 1946 and broken up. *Woodaxe* was purchased from the builders and served as a

minesweeper until sold to the French navy in December 1918. *Ironaxe* was also sold to the French navy in December 1918 as *Commandant Vergoignan*. She returned to the UK in 1922 and reverted to her former name, which she carried in the Second World War when she served as a salvage vessel, until returned in 1945 to the Fishing Vessels Salvage Association, Aberdeen. Of the other 'Axe' Class ships, three were built by Hall, Russell and have already been described. They were *Coalaxe*, *Firmaxe* and *Sureaxe*. Goole SB built *Steamaxe*, Edwards built *Frostaxe* and Cochrane's built *Poleaxe* and *Greataxe*, This latter ship was laid down at Govan in 1889 by D. Macgill but completed by Cochrane & Cooper Ltd, Govan as *Windsor Castle* (H.49) for J.A. Smith Trawling Co. Ltd, Hull. She was sold to France in 1903 and renamed *Alcyon* (D.1433). In 1913, she was sold to Russia and renamed *Wostock*, later commissioned as T.6. After her transfer to Great Britain, she became the Royal Navy's *Greataxe*. In May 1920, she was sold to John Lewis Ltd, Aberdeen as *Greataxe* (A.371). They sold her to William Masson & Others, Aberdeen in 1923 as *Roslin* (A.371). She ran aground in atrocious weather off the mouth of the River Ythan on 4th August 1937, when two crewmen were saved but six men perished during a gallant rescue attempt by the Aberdeen lifeboat. She was later written off as a 'Total Loss'.

During the war, there was some resentment against the seemingly higher wages earned by fishermen. The Admiralty tried to offset this discrepancy by the payment of salvage money to the naval trawler crews. This was very difficult to regulate and, in most cases, there was a protracted time lag between men claiming salvage money and actually receiving it. The case of HM trawlers *Esher*, *Evangel*, *King Erik*, *Nodzu*, *Spider* and *Thunderstone* was typical of many. They had been instrumental in saving the steamer *Formosa* on 14th November 1915 but it was to be another two full years before the awards were made. The announcement was made public on 24th November 1917. By this time, some of the recipients were unfortunately dead, such as the crew of *Evangel*, sunk by a mine off Milford Haven on 25th March 1917.

Not all salvage claims were plain sailing either, as the case between the crews of the armed trawlers *Fusilier* and *Kinaldie*, and the Swedish steamer *Carrie* proved. The latter was on passage from Glasgow to Nantes, with a munitions cargo for the French government, when she was attacked and set on fire by a U-boat some 20 miles south of the Wolf Rock Lighthouse. The German commander ordered *Carrie*'s crew to abandon their vessel and take to the boats. Shortly afterwards, the two trawlers came on the scene but, by this time, the U-boat had disappeared. The steamer's crew refused to reboard their vessel, so a trawler boarding party was put aboard and *Carrie* was towed into Falmouth. *Kinaldie*'s crew lodged a salvage claim against the Swedish owners of the steamer. The owners refuted the claim, on the grounds that *Carrie* was merely saved from war risks, that it was the duty of HM ships to save the cargo as it belonged to an Allied Government and that the actual saving of the vessel was a mere incident in the saving of this cargo. *Carrie*'s crew, when under oath, denied refusing to reboard their ship, stating that they were ordered not to by the trawler captains. This naturally was refuted by the trawler officers and their official log books were given in evidence. After much legal wrangling, with claim and counter claim being made, a settlement was reached with the trawler crews receiving £750, which worked out at £375 per ship, to be divided between the crews.

Chapter 9: THE FLEETS RECOVER

Wartime losses had been staggering and the peacetime fleet was a shadow of its former self. Hull lost over 130 trawlers, Grimsby 304, Fleetwood over thirty, Aberdeen over eighty vessels and all the other trawling ports suffered considerable losses in ships and men. The ships could be replaced relatively quickly but trained fishermen were a different matter, as it takes around four years for a deckhand to become proficient. By August 1919, almost all of the requisitioned trawlers had been decommissioned and, by 30th April 1920, the RN Trawler Section had been completely disbanded. The ships returned to their former trade, some to their original owners and others to new ones but many craft were showing their age and were in need of replacement. These came in the form of the Admiralty built 'Strath', 'Castle' and 'Mersey' classes. By the early 1920s, the country was in a depression but the stocks of fish had been revitalised during the war through under-fishing. New trawlers were needed to take advantage of these stocks and it was found to be cheaper to purchase the ex-naval ships and convert them for fishing, rather than commission new vessels. A 'Castle' Class trawler would fetch from £8,000 to £9,500 at auction, which was a fraction of the cost of a new ship. The dispersal of these standard trawlers was relatively localised, with the 'Straths' going to Aberdeen, the 'Merseys' to the Humber ports and the 'Castles', primarily to Fleetwood, the West Coast ports and the Humber, with a few ending up with London registrations.

One significant change at Hull was that the 'Boxing Fleets' of Hellyer and the Great Northern Steamship Fishing Co. Ltd

were wound up and their vessels went 'single boating'. The other two prominent 'Fleeting' firms of Gamecock and Red Cross amalgamated in 1921, with a total of eighty-eight trawlers, under the Kelsall Brothers & Beeching Ltd banner. This rationalisation was no doubt brought about by the loss of so many 'Fleeters' during the war years. The company finally went into voluntary liquidation in 1936.

Grimsby ordered ninety-seven new trawlers throughout the 1920s. They were all Middle Water ships, with only a couple built for the Distant Water grounds. These smaller ships would still make trips to the Icelandic grounds, but not on a regular basis.

Aberdeen purchased some seventy smaller ships from south of the border, as a stop gap until the ex-naval craft were released for sale. Among these were six ex-German prize trawlers which had served in the Mediterranean. *Cairnrigh* (A.377 – ex-*Cachosin*, ex-*Doktor Kuugler*) was built by Seebeck at Geestemunde in 1912. She came under the ownership of Thomas Davidson, Aberdeen, in March 1920. She disappeared from the register in 1938. *Caersin* (A.427 – ex-*Dora*) was built by Wenke at Bremerhaven in 1892. After the war, she was sold to Nicholas Cook, Aberdeen. It was by an irony of fate that she met her end off Aberdeen on 28th November 1926, after a collision in the Moray Firth with her sister ship, *Cambrisin*. The latter vessel took her in tow but she foundered in sight of home. Fortunately, her crew were rescued by *Cambrisin* (A.426 – ex-*Orion*), built by Wenke of Bremmerhaven in 1891. Like her sister above, she came to Aberdeen owner

Photo. 55: *Keith Hall* ashore at Birsay, Orkney showing the clean deck layout of a steam liner. Note the slender funnel, a common feature of German-built trawlers of the period.

Photo. 56 *Robert Murray*, note her flat topped forecastle, pole compass and the liver oil boiler alongside the funnel. Shown in Cygnet's colours of black hull with black topped yellow funnel separated by a red band.

Nicholas Cook in March 1920. Both vessels had been captured on 30th September 1915, *Caersin* by HMS *Penelope* and *Cambrisin* by HMS *Cleopatra*.

Another of these ships was *Keith Hall* (A.636, ex-*Carbosin*, ex-*Darmstadt*) built by Bremer Vulcan, at Vegesack in 1896. She too had been captured by HMS *Cleopatra* along with the two previous ships. In October 1920, she was sold to Ellis & Meff Ltd, Aberdeen, who worked her as a liner. Her fishing career was short lived, ending on the rocks of Birsay in the Orkneys at 17.50 hours on Sunday 27th November 1921 (**Photo. 55**). One man, George Neilson of Torry, Aberdeen was swept overboard and lost while helping launch the ship's boat. The remainder got away in the boat and were rescued by the Stromness lifeboat. *Birkhall* (A.378, ex-*Clonsin*, ex-*Dr Robitzsch*) was built by Seebeck, at Geestemunde in 1911. She too came under Meffs' ownership until she left the register in 1940. Another of Meffs' ships that came north to work after the war was *Leith Hall* (A.632, ex-*Culbasin*, ex-*Nereus*) built by Tecklenborg, at Geestemunde in 1893. These formed some of the thirteen ex-German trawlers that came to Aberdeen in 1920. There were another five German trawlers bought in 1922 by the Walker Steam Trawl Fishing Co. Ltd, Aberdeen and given 'Star' pre-fixes but they were unsuitable for the work and were sold back to Germany a year later.

Grimsby bought at least one of these ex-German trawlers in July 1920. She was *Keelby* (GY.1161), first owned by A. Phelps but, in September of that year, she in the ownership of the Keelby Steam Fishing Company. Apparently, this was commonplace in Grimsby, when the owner had only one ship. Soon afterwards, she foundered some 10 miles SW of Heligoland on 10th July 1921. The circumstances leading up to her loss were quite bizarre. Running short of coal, she entered Geestemuende and was stoned by an angry crowd. The German pilot fearing for his life, fled

the vessel, which drove ashore in shallow water and foundered. The exhausted crew rowed for over eight hours before reaching Heligoland. She had been recognised as the ex-German trawler *Burgomaster Schmidt* and, when alongside, had been boarded by an angry mob shouting, "*We sink you tonight, English Swinehund.*"

THE HUMBER'S FIRST POST WAR SHIPS

Cochrane's last official Admiralty trawler was *Jeremiah Lewis*, Yard No. 877, and the remaining 'Merseys', Yard No's 878-899, were all finished off as fishing trawlers. Fifteen were launched with Admiralty names and were later renamed, while the remaining eight had names chosen by their civilian owners. The first of this group of ships was Yard No. 892, launched as *Lord Ernle* (H.113) after being laid down as *Peter Magee*. She was sold to Grimsby in July 1929, as *Lord Ernle* (GY.109), owned by the Perihelion Steam Fishing Co. Ltd, Grimsby, She was lost by stranding on Bempton Cliffs, Yorkshire on 2nd March 1937 – one of four Grimsby trawlers lost that year. Her call sign GBDF transmitted by her radio operator Stephen Codling was picked up by Lt E. Taylor, the harbourmaster at Bridlington and a well known local radio ham. He alerted the rescue services and the Bridlington and Flamborough lifeboats were launched. This was indeed luck, as a couple of years earlier, on 24th September 1935, the Hull trawler *Skegness* (H.14) ran ashore at the same spot with the loss of all hands. The night of *Lord Ernle*'s ordeal was very foggy, with a heavy swell running. Fifteen minutes after striking, around 23.30 hours, she lost all her power and was bumping heavily on the rocks. At the time of her stranding the trawler carried a brand new ship's boat. This was put aboard at Stromness, to replace her original one that had been lost on the way to the grounds. This new boat began to fill with water immediately it was launched, owing to the bung not being fitted. A brush handle was cut down for a plug but the boat was washed away before any of the crew could use it. When the Flamborough pulling lifeboat arrived, she quickly got a line aboard the stricken vessel, aided by the headlights from a couple of cars on the cliff top. After the first man was rescued by breeches buoy, the line parted. All the remaining crewmen had to jump overboard with a line and be pulled aboard the lifeboat. The trawler skipper at the time was Arthur Phillipson, who along with his fourteen man crew, was returning from the White Sea with some 1,200 kits of fish. This catch posed a problem for the rescuers, as due to the pounding, the hull split open and the sea was awash with dead fish. The lifeboat sustained some considerable damage in her attempts to get alongside but the skill of Coxswain Leng and his crew saw her safely through with all the trawlermen aboard. After this latest stranding at Bempton, theories abounded as to why these ships had come to grief and the most popular one was that the location had become 'Ironbound' with all the broken iron and steel hulls that littered the cliffs. This caused vessel's compasses to give false readings, thus leading them to their doom.

Other ships from this last batch of 'Merseys' were *Springbok* (H.137 – Admiralty *Henry Marsh*) and *Robert Murray* (FD.90 – **Photo. 56**). The former was owned by the East Riding Fishing Co. Ltd, Hull. She was sold to the Strand Fishing Co. Ltd, Grimsby in January 1929. In February the following year, her name was changed to *North Cape* (GY.494) and she disappeared off Iceland around 16th March 1931 with all hands. *Robert Murray* was owned by the Admiralty until sold in March 1923 to the Commissioners of Public Works, Eire. In January 1926, she passed briefly through the hands of George Young & Richard Fleming, Donegal, who sold her on 2nd February to the Cygnet Steam Fishing Co. of Fleetwood who kept her until 1938. She then went to Thomas Cardwell & Robert H. Bagshaw, Fleetwood, who renamed her

Northlyn (FD.90). She was requisitioned in October 1939 as a boom defence vessel, Z.103, at £106 6s a month and returned in January 1946. By 1953, she was owned by the Cevic Steam Fishing Co. Ltd, Fleetwood, who sold her to the St. Andrews Steam Fishing Co. Ltd, Hull. She went to the breakers torch at Brughes in April 1955. This last batch of seven 'Mersey's all had flat topped fo'c'sles, in contrast to the nicely rounded whalebacks of their predecessors.

Cochranes' Selby yard's first true post-war commercial fishing trawler was *Lord Lonsdale* (H.32). She was the lead ship of a twelve vessel order for Pickering & Haldane's Steam Trawling Co. Ltd, Hull, built between 1924 and 1926. This order comprised:

1924 deliveries:
No. 934 *Lord Lonsdale*, H.32
No. 935 *Lord Balfour of Burleigh*, H.36
No. 936 *Lord Derby*, H.71
No. 944 *Lord Chelmsford*, H.96
No. 945 *Lord Inchcape*, H.102.

1925 deliveries:
No. 946 *Lord Winterton*, H.130
No. 947 *Lord Islington*, H.151
No. 977 *Lord Mountbatten*, H.225
No. 978 *Lord Bradbury*, H.251

1926 delivery:
No. 990 *Lord Devonport*, H.284

Two of the ships were later lost, **Lord Devonport** on 18th March 1928 after running aground on the Island of Hoy in the Orkneys and **Lord Inchcape** after striking a mine off Plymouth on 20th October 1940. She had been requisitioned in August 1939 as a minesweeper, FY1611, but was under Hellyer ownership at the time. She was salvaged and returned to duty until released in 1945.

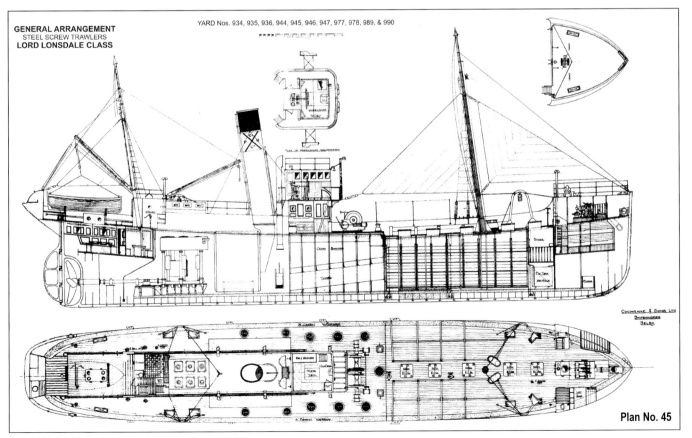

GENERAL ARRANGEMENT
STEEL SCREW TRAWLERS
LORD LONSDALE CLASS

YARD Nos. 934, 935, 936, 944, 945, 946, 947, 977, 978, 989, & 990

Plan No. 45

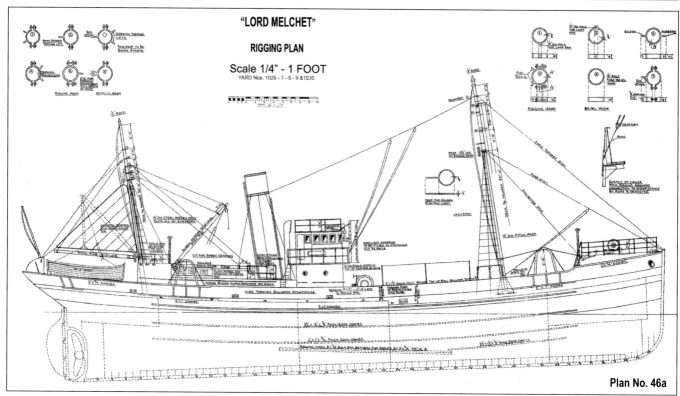

"LORD MELCHET"

RIGGING PLAN

Scale 1/4" - 1 FOOT

YARD Nos. 1026 - 7 - 8 - 9 &1030

Plan No. 46a

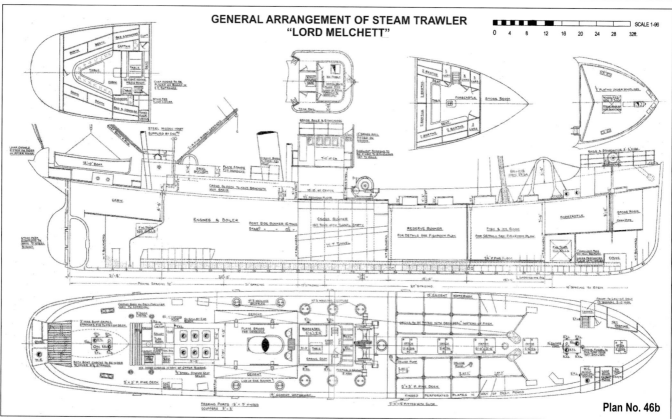

GENERAL ARRANGEMENT OF STEAM TRAWLER "LORD MELCHETT"

SCALE 1-96

Plan No. 46b

Hellyer's sold her to Holland on 24th May 1947, becoming *Petten* (IJM.49). Another ship of the class to be sold to Dutch owners was *Lord Chelmsford* and she changed hands on 18th January 1937, to become *Norma Maria*. The builders drawing (**Plan 45**) shows a second generation 'Mersey'-type trawler with the traditional whaleback fo'c'sle, and with a greater rake to the masts and funnel, which gave them a sleeker, more purposeful profile.

The only other outward change was the steering gear housed in a separate compartment abutting the wheelhouse. The doors into the wheelhouse are on either side of the after bulkhead, which made for a more sheltered entrance. The binnacle has been removed from the wheelhouse roof and replaced with the more usual inverted compass. Bunker capacity was increased by three tons to 187.

They built another batch of stretched 'Merseys' (140ft x 24ft x

14ft, 345g, 134n) for Pickering & Haldane's Steam Trawling Co. Ltd in 1928, with engines by Amos & Smith:

No. 1026 *Lord Deramore* (H.461)
No. 1027 *Lord Hewart* (H.475)
No. 1028 *Lord Grey* (H.500)
No. 1029 *Lord Irwin* (H.501)
No. 1030 *Lord Melchett* (H.1)

Lord Melchett was requisitioned in August 1939 for minesweeping duties and returned in April 1946. She went to the Lord Line in 1947 and, in May 1948, she went to Grimsby as GY.577, owned by the Premier Steam Fishing Co. Ltd. In July of that year she was renamed *Nelis*. She worked out of Aberdeen for a short spell in 1955, before going to Fleetwood as FD.119, owned by the Fern Leaf Fishing Co. Ltd, who sent her to the breakers in 1957 (**Plan 46 a & b**).

A slightly smaller trawler built by Cochranes in 1929 was Yard No. 1039 *Tehana* (LO.132 – 135ft bp x 24ft 9ins x 14ft 3ins, 333g) and 99nhp, for Brand & Curzon Ltd, Milford. Her appearance was very similar to the previous vessels but, being smaller, her fo'c'sle was fitted for only eight men. Her trawl winch came from Robertson's of Fleetwood. An uncommon feature are mooring bollards either side of the chartroom, whilst the wireless cabin was fitted behind the wheelhouse, a position which became the standard for all later ships. By 1937, she was owned by the Boston Deep Sea Fishing & Ice Co. Ltd, Fleetwood as FD.132. She was requisitioned in August 1939 as FY525, firstly as a minesweeper and latterly as a wreck dispersal vessel, being returned in March 1946. In 1948, the register shows her still under Boston Deep Sea Fishing & Ice Co. Ltd ownership and working from Fleetwood as LO.9. Apparently she went to Grimsby later that year as either *Satern* or *Saturn* but I can find no record of her under these names, although a *Saturn* (ex-*Tehana*) was sold to Poland in late 1948 and scrapped in 1964. The confusion arises from differences in the lists given in Mark Stopper and Ray Maltby's book of the Boston Company, and Peter Horsley and Alan Hirst's book on Fleetwood trawlers. The former states that a *Tehana* (FD.132) measuring 135ft and of 333 tons was built at Middlesborough in 1924. The latter gives a similar vessel, *Tehana* (FD.132) but built at Middlesborough in 1929. Neither of these dates figure in the Smith's Dock records with respect to a *Tehana*. Another anomaly appears in an annotation to the builders lists, which shows her as *Saturn* and scrapped in 1974.

The first true post-war commercial trawler built by Cook, Welton & Gemmell in December 1920 was Yard No. 434 *Sturton* (GY.1241 – 120ft bp x 22ft 6ins x 12ft 10ins, 250g), for the Victoria Steam Fishing Co. Ltd, Grimsby, with engines supplied by Amos & Smith, of 74nhp at 180psi. In December 1929, she transferred to the Lindsey Steam Fishing Co. Ltd. She was requisitioned in August 1939 as FY1595, firstly as a minesweeper and finally as a refueller, until returned in October 1944. She remained with Lindsey's until she was sold to Holland in 1961.

The Hellyer Steam Fishing Co. Ltd, Hull placed an order with Cook, Welton & Gemmell in 1925 for five new ships:

Goth (H.211), Yard No. 468
Angle (H.212), Yard No. 469
Norse (H.21), Yard No. 470
Kelt (H.236), Yard No. 471
Pict (H.250), Yard No. 472

A sixth ship built to the same drawings was *Tervani* (H.260), Yard

No. 473 (147ft bp x 25ft x 14ft 6ins, 394g, 99hp), for Henriksen's of Hull. They were large vessels built for the Distant Water grounds. They had a reputation as 'coal gobblers', being very hard ships to fire, and Hellyer's *Goth* and *Kelt* were often referred to as 'punishment ships' by the crews. These were the trawlers that recalcitrant firemen had to ship in until they had made up for any indiscretions and then were allowed back onto the easier ships. Almost 100 tons of coal was carried in the reserve fish room or reserve bunker space, all of which had to be shovelled into baskets and dragged through the 3ft square tunnel into the stokehold. Once all the spare coal had been used up, the hold had to be washed out ready for stowing the fish. The shortest-lived vessel of the group, *Norse* (H.219), was wrecked at Keflavik on the south west coast of Iceland on 5th March 1929. She was replaced in 1930 by another Cook, Welton & Gemmell ship, *Norse* (H.348), albeit a slightly smaller vessel (140ft 3ins x 24ft 6ins x 13ft 3ins, 351g, 96nhp). She was sold to Grimsby and requisitioned in August 1939 as a minesweeper, Admiralty No. FY1628. Her owners were Shire Trawlers Ltd, Grimsby and her fishing number changed to GY.129. She was returned in November 1944 and spent a short time at Hull again, before being sold to Faeroe as *Krossteinur*.

Another three of the Hellyer ships, *Angle*, *Kelt* and *Pict*, were sold in 1937. *Angle* went to Norway and was owned by Astrup AS, Kristiansund. *Kelt* also went to Norwegian owners AS Bergens Fiskeriselkap of Bergen but she appears to have been registered at Oslo. The fifth Hellyer trawler, *Goth*, was requisitioned as a minesweeper in August 1939, given the Admiralty No. FY649 and was sold out of service in November 1945, returning to Hellyer's. They sold her to the Ocean Steam Trawling Co. Ltd, Grimsby in 1947, who sold her to the Wyre Steam Trawling Co Ltd, Fleetwood, as FD.52 in 1948. Her new owners were not to have her for long, as she foundered off Iceland that same year with the tragic loss of all hands. The first and the only wartime loss was *Lord Deramore*, which ran aground at Horno Island, on the north coast of Norway near Vardo, on 5th March 1953 and was a total wreck. The last ship of the batch, *Tervani* (H.260), was ordered by Henriksen & Co. Ltd, Hull, who owned her until her loss on 7th February 1943. At the time she was a requisitioned trawler, called up in October 1939 for armed patrol duties. In 1941, she was converted for minesweeping and was torpedoed by the Italian submarine *Acciaio* off Cape Bougaroun, North Africa. The builders general arrangement diagram (**Plan 47**) shows powerful looking ships, with a roomy whaleback, quarterdeck, solid steel plated verandahs and double lifeboats carried in radial davits.

In 1929, the yard launched three sister ships for the Hull Northern Fishing Co. Ltd, as Yard No's 528, 529 and 530. They were *Dromio* (H.94), *Cassio* (H.138) and *Orsino* (H.115), all with the same dimensions (147ft 7ins bp x 25ft 4ins x 15ft 6ins) and engines (13.5ins, 23.5ins, 38.5ins x 26ins stroke, producing 99nhp at 210psi). Designed for the Faeroe and Iceland grounds, full electric lighting was provided by a Robey 6kw generator. The trawl winch, strangely enough, was manufactured by the Strath Engineering Co. of Aberdeen, who were better known for the smaller winches that they fitted to the North Sea ships (**Photo. 57**). Both the *Orsino* and *Cassio* went to Dutch owners in 1938. The former was renamed *Walrus* (IJM.24) and the latter *Flamingo* (IJM.25). This sale along with many others around this period was no doubt influenced by the poor fishing experienced by British

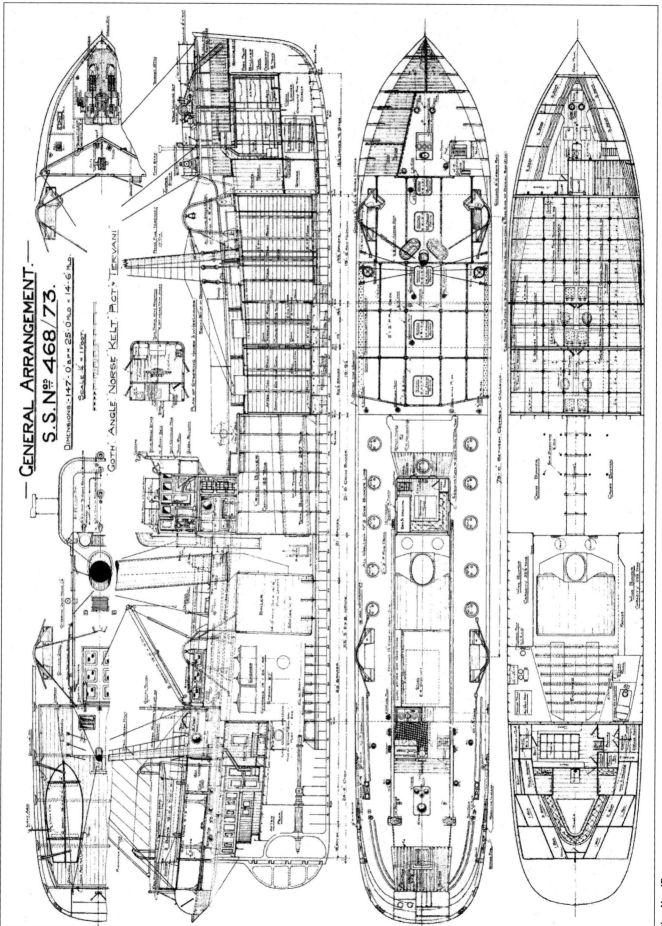

— GENERAL ARRANGEMENT. —
S.S. Nᵒˢ 468/73.

Dimensions :- 147′·0 b.p × 25′·0 mld × 14′·6″ mld.

Scale ¼″ = 1 Foot.

Goth. Angle Norse Kelt Pict Tervani

Photo. 57: 'Strath'-type trawl winch. The 'spooling on' rollers are at the front of the winch and the pound board stanchions are in the foreground. The wing bollard appears very far inboard, which would make the after warp cross the deck and form a hazard.

vessels. After 1919, things had been good but the fleets were soon built up to surpass their pre-war numbers and the results of over-fishing were evident by the second half of the thirties. *Dromio* was requisitioned as a minesweeper in August 1939 but was lost by collision off Whitby on 22nd December 1939.

LOYALTY TO SMITH'S DOCK
In 1906, Smith's Dock began a relationship with the Cardiff trawler owners Neale & West Ltd. It commenced with Yard No. 805 *Hirose* (C.F.20) and ended twenty-four years later in 1931, with Yard No. 927 *Sata* (C.F.30). In 1927, they launched *Hatsuse* (C.F.21 – 38ft 6ins x 13ft 6ins, 108n, 99nhp). She was one of the earliest steam trawlers to have a cruiser stern and balanced spade type rudder, an adaptation of the builder's whale catchers of the period. This configuration on the whale catchers, with their cut away forefoot, gave them great manoeuvrability, so necessary when chasing the whale but the trawler kept the deep forefoot. The balanced rudder's advantage over the standard door type was evident in higher speed work but, when underway at reduced speed, it tended to default to a neutral off-centre position. The helmsman required a greater degree of concentration in order to hold a course as, if neglected, the ship would sheer off. This was more noticeable when running before a following sea.

Hatsuse's stern was not strictly a true cruiser type, having a rounded spoon-like shape in elevation, which was often referred to as a semi-cruiser stern. Requisitioned in August 1939 as minesweeper FY1749, she was returned in May 1946 to her former owners and went for scrap at Newport on 16th January 1956. She was followed in 1928 by *Honjo* (C.F.26) and *Sasebo* (C.F.27), Yard No's 853 and 854. The marked up builders profile shows that they were based on the design of *Hatsuse*, as the same drawing had been used with heavy alterations. An extra frame was added forward of number 60 and the aft end was also revised. They kept the cruiser stern but a cast frame was fitted to house the Oertz type semi-balanced rudder. This was operated by steam steering gear located in the wheelhouse (not shown for the earlier ship). The rudder post was tilted forward, so as to bring it perpendicular when the trawler was trimmed down by the stern, as was normal. These alterations changed their length somewhat. By adding the extra

frame, the length bp increased by 21ins. By changing the rudder type, the post was moved forward, which decreased the length bp by 17ins when measured from the centre-line of the post, so the actual registered length increased by only 4ins. The foremast was stepped on the main deck, which had been strengthened with girders and tie bars. A hand operated windlass had been fitted on the whaleback to handle the fisherman type anchor. This was also chain driven from the main trawl winch. The crew's fo'c'sle was below the whaleback on main deck level, with a WC to port and a lamp room to starboard. Below the wheelhouse is the chartroom/skipper's day cabin. The mizzen mast passes through the forward end of the galley, not as normal at the aft end, whilst the after accommodation appeared quite small for a vessel of this size. *Honjo* was requisitioned in October 1939 as a minesweeper, armed with a 12 pounder and given the Admiralty No. FY 661. She was blown up at Gibraltar by Italian frogmen on 18th January 1942. Her sister was also called up in 1939, as FY828 for minesweeping duties and was released in February 1946, returning to Neale & West of Cardiff. She went for scrapping at Boon on 7th July 1956. These two ships were followed in 1929 by *Asama* (C.F.18) and *Nodzu* (C.F.22), Yard No's 894 and 895, both built to the same design as *Honjo* and *Sasebo*. *Asama* was requisitioned in August 1939 as a minesweeper. She was attacked and sunk by enemy aircraft whilst on a sweep off Plymouth on 23rd January 1941. *Nodzu* also served as a minesweeper until being returned in November 1945. Neale & West ran her until 1957, when they sold her to the Dalby Steam Fishing Co. of Fleetwood as FD.49. She went to the breakers at Preston in 1959.

LARGEST GRIMSBY TRAWLER OF THE PERIOD
This honour fell to *William Grant* (GY.25 – 189ft 3ins bp x 29ft 6ins x 13ft 2ins, 727g), purchased by Grant & Baker Steam Fishing Co. Ltd, Grimsby in 1929. Originally a French trawler, built at Nantes in 1921 as *Sagittaire*, she was a Grand Banks fleeter that fished with dories and was to be the ultimate trawler, size-wise, until after 1945. She was not a very pretty ship, with her long flat topped whaleback and large wheelhouse with solid steel plated verandah. Both her masts carried fidded topmasts for the aerials, the mizzen was quite lofty and the fore topmast was stayed well forward. She carried two lifeboats on light spar decks either side of the galley and immediately aft of the after gallows in radial davits. She was sold in June 1932 to the Howe Steam Fishing Co. Ltd, Grimsby, who renamed her *Gatooma* (GY.25) in March 1933. In 1934, she was again sold to Samuel Franklin, who in turn sold her to Italy in 1938 as *Enrico Gismond*. She ran ashore at Pantelleria on 18th May 1943. When the new No. 3 Fish Dock at Grimsby was opened on 4th October 1934, it was *Gatooma* that the engineers used to physically check their calculations with regards to the size of the lock pits.

THE SCOTTISH YARDS
The first new post war trawler to be built for the port of Fleetwood, *Gava* (FD.380 – 125ft, 257.5g) came from A. Hall, as Yard No. 579 in 1920, for the New Docks Steam Fishing Co. Ltd. Requisitioned in November 1939 as an armed patrol trawler, she assisted with the evacuation of Dunkirk. During her service, when under the command of an RN Lieutenant and acting as guard ship for a fleet of fishing trawlers, her fishing skipper decided to try a

Photo. 58: *Gava* clearly showing her ash shoots and pole compass. Her bag ropes are triced up to the shrouds and she has bridge wings either side of her wheelhouse, rather than a full verandah. She is seen here passing the No.1 Pontoon Dock in Aberdeen harbour.

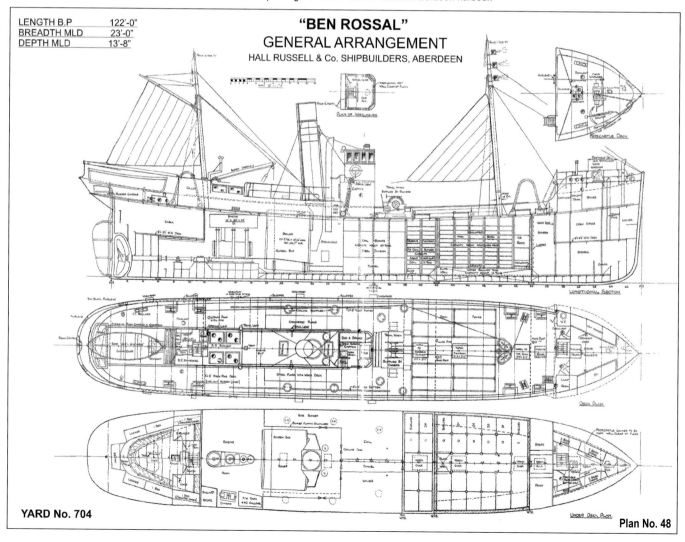

LENGTH B.P	122'-0"
BREADTH MLD	23'-0"
DEPTH MLD	13'-8"

"BEN ROSSAL"
GENERAL ARRANGEMENT
HALL RUSSELL & Co. SHIPBUILDERS, ABERDEEN

YARD No. 704

Plan No. 48

haul for himself. No sooner had he shot away his trawl and begun towing, than he was contacted by an Aberdeen trawler warning of a U-boat in the vicinity. The RN officer ordered him to cut away his gear. He 'politely' refused and calmly hauled his gear; fortunately, the enemy vessel never appeared. After the war, in June 1946, she went to Clifton Steam Trawlers Ltd, Fleetwood and, by 1950, she was *Gava* (A.676 – **Photo. 58**), owned by the Stroud Steam Fishing Co. Ltd, Aberdeen. She remained a coal burner to the end, with a small liver oil boiler fitted immediately behind the funnel. The rendered down oil was stored in 40 gallon drums, which were lashed to the storm rail. She left Aberdeen on her last trip to the breakers at Boom on Hogmanay 1959.

In 1929, Hall, Russell's of Aberdeen launched two sister ships, No. 703 *Ben Rossal* (A.65) and No. 704 *Ben Roy* (SN.61 – 122ft bp x 23ft x 13ft 3ins, 114n, 260g), both for Richard Irvin & Sons Ltd, North Shields and costing £10,788 each. They were North Sea ships but could also work the Faeroese grounds. The drawing (**Plan 48**) shows a stretched 'Strath' trawler fitted with a quite high whaleback. This was fitted with the usual breakwater, which incorporated a skylight trunked to the crew's fo'c'sle below. She carried a fisherman's anchor and hand windlass, which could be belt driven from the trawl winch if necessary. Six berths were provided forward, with another four in the after cabin. For extended trips to Faeroe, the reserve fish room could carry an extra 31 tons of coal. Electric lighting was provided by a dynamo in the engine room. *Ben Rossal* was requisitioned in September 1939 as a boom defence vessel, Admiralty No. Z120. In 1942, she was sold to Carnie &

Gibb Ltd, Granton and returned to them in March 1946 as *Mary Paton* (GW.15). She was scrapped by Walter Brechin at Granton in 1960. *Ben Roy* was requisitioned in February 1940 as a minesweeper and returned in 1945, transferring to Aberdeen as A.604 owned by Alexander Bruce & Others Ltd. In 1958, she transferred to D. Wood and E.C. Mathieson, Aberdeen, going for scrap in 1959.

The Dalmuir yard of Beardmores was not well known in trawler building circles, tending as they did to concentrate on larger ships but, in 1928, they launched *Hannah E Reynolds* (A.322 – 120ft 7ins bp x 23ft 1ins x 12ft 5ins, 98n, 253g, 84nhp) for William Leith and John F. Reynolds Ltd, Aberdeen. I include her as an example of a Beardmore-built vessel and the only British-built steam trawler I have come across with a flat counter stern, as opposed to the traditional semi-elliptical type. The builder's general arrangement drawing (**Plan 49**) shows a flush decked vessel with no whaleback. Her bunker space runs well forward, giving her a rather restricted fish room. The companionway entrance to the crew's fo'c'sle is a peculiar wedge shape, owing little to aesthetics but cheap to construct. She does not appear to have the usual inverted steering compass outside, instead a standard type binnacle is fitted inside. Another addition is the two cowl vents in front of the main engine room skylight for additional air to the machinery space. Aft on the stern are a WC to port and a lamp room to starboard. The triatic stay has a chain insert where it passes above the funnel. By 1939, she had gone to the Boston Deep Sea Fishing & Ice Co. Ltd, Fleetwood but retained her Aberdeen number. She was destroyed by enemy aircraft in St. Margarets Bay, Dover on 18th August 1940.

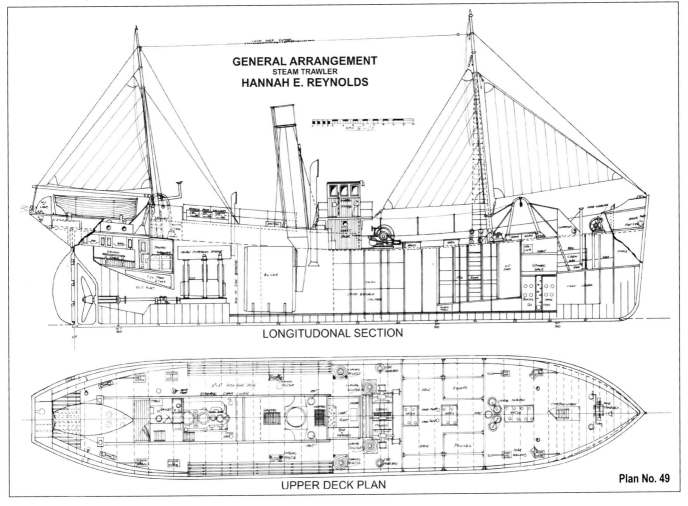

153

THE LEWIS FAMILY OF ABERDEEN

This company began in the village of Cove, south of Aberdeen, when John Lewis set up in business as a wooden boat builder in 1870. He moved to Aberdeen shortly afterwards and had a small yard at Pointlaw, and then to Torry in 1886. In 1890, he acquired the agricultural engineering firm Joss & Sinclair and became marine boiler and engine makers, building their first ship, the coaster *Wyndhurst*, in 1917. She was No. 52, which was to be first of the company's Yard numbers. They did not build any trawlers until Yard No. 100 *Braemar* (A.252 – 115ft x 22ft x 12ft 9ins, 93n, 56nhp), launched on 27th August 1927 for James Christie, Aberdeen but managed by Lewis; by 1933, she was owned outright by him. She was purchased by the navy in April 1940 as a dhanlayer and renamed *Jennifer* and laid up in 1942. She was sold to Neale & West Ltd, Cardiff as *Braemar* (CF.38). By 1953, she was back home in Aberdeen as A.656, owned by North Eastern Fisheries Ltd and she went for scrap in 1958. They ordered *John E Lewis* (A.294) from Hall, Russell's as Yard No. 464 on 13th January 1909, at a cost of £3,350. This appears rather cheap for a 125ft trawler, when one considers the going rate for a 115ft vessel was around £5,500. One possibility is that Lewis supplied the machinery outfit, thus reducing the cost. This trawler was sold to Portugal in 1910 and renamed *Norte*. She returned to Aberdeen as *Norseman* in 1916 and was attacked and subsequently scuttled by a U-Boat on 31st August 1918 off Safi, Morrocco. She was replaced by her namesake, A.354, from Hall, Russell in 1911, Yard No. 484, again at a special price of £3,400. Requisitioned as a minesweeper in August 1914, she was lost on 16th January 1918, near the Cork Light Vessel off Harwich.

John and Andrew Lewis, in addition to being shipbuilders, were also trawler owners in their own right. In 1896, they took delivery of their first steam trawler, *Linnet* (A.816) from Alexander Hall, Yard No. 364, a relatively small vessel (96ft 9ins, 124g) and powered by a compound engine. In 1900, they sold her to Peverell & Mason, Aberdeen but bought her back again in 1907. They had another *Linnet*, with a 30nhp compound engine, built in 1887 as *Her Majesty* (H.24 – 90ft, 102g) by Head & Riley of Hull, Yard No. 22, for William Wolfe of St. Andrew's Dock, Hull, who named her after the reigning monarch. She was bought by John Lewis Ltd, Aberdeen in 1899. In 1901, after the death of Queen Victoria, her name was changed to *Linnet* (A.43). She was requisitioned in June 1915 as a boom defence vessel (later a fishery trawler) and was returned in July 1918. She worked for the Lewis family until 1929, when she was sold to Edward J. Hellings of Milford Haven, becoming *Linnet* (M.61) in 1930. Her Milford registry was closed in August 1938 when she was scrapped at Llanelly.

Their next new ship, also from A. Hall's as Yard No. 412, was *Nightingale* (A.20), launched in 1904 as a steam liner but she left the local register in 1913. She was followed in 1906 by *Swallow* (A.76), built by Hall, Russell as Yard No. 400 – 115ft, 204g). Requisitioned in August 1914, as a minesweeper, with the Admiralty No. 261, she was returned to Lewis's in 1919. By 1933, her owners were A.F.&J. Wood Ltd, Aberdeen but she does not appear in the register after 1939.

One of the fascinating aspects of fishing vessel research is the number of ships that have the same name, often from the same port, at the same time. Such was another *Swallow* (A.112), a small vessel (94ft, 134g) built by Earles of Hull in 1893, as GY.489, for the Pioneer Steam Fishing Co. Ltd, Grimsby. In August 1898, she came to Aberdeen as A.112, owned by J. Caie (Torry) Ltd and she met her end in September 1905, when she was wrecked at Sealskerry, Orkney. In 1915, Lewis's took delivery of the strangest named trawler ever to be registered at Aberdeen, *Morococala* (A.238 – 125ft, 264g). Her bare hull was supplied by A. Hall, as Yard No. 503, with the engines and boiler, etc, coming from Lewis's yard; she was the largest of their small pre-war fleet. Requisitioned in April 1915 as a minesweeper and armed with a 6 pounder, she sank after striking a mine off the Daunt Rock Light Vessel on 19th November 1917.

A year later, the company took delivery of the first of a trio of trawlers from Cochrane's of Selby. This was Yard No. 710 *Kate Lewis* (A.620 – 117ft 6ins, 207g). Her engine was supplied by the Abernethy Company of Aberdeen as No. 893. Purchased in August 1917, she was to remain in naval service until 1939 as both a minelayer and sweeper. She was sold to Carnie & Gibb of Granton, renamed *Noreen Mary* and later sunk by a U-boat on 5th July 1944 whilst fishing off Cape Wrath. The next two trawlers from Cochranes were Yard No's 711 and 725, the sister ships *Ann Lewis* (A.621) and *Feugh* (A.706); both were 121ft and 216g, and both were engined again by Abernethy (I presume these engines were shipped by sea from Aberdeen to Hull, rather than towing the hulls north to have them fitted). *Ann Lewis* was taken over by the Navy in December 1916 as a minesweeper. In 1920, she was bought by J. Stookes of Grimsby, who renamed her *Fifth Lancer* (GY.802). In April the following year, she reverted to her former name but kept her GY registration. She returned to Aberdeen owners the Stephen Fishing Co. Ltd in 1931, who changed her name to *Jean Edmonds* (A.174). In 1944, she was again owned by the Lewis family, who sold her in 1946 to Richard Irvin & Sons Ltd, Aberdeen. She went to the breakers in Brussels on 16th May 1962.

Her sister, *Feugh*, named after a place in Aberdeenshire, had a more varied career after she was sold by Lewis in 1919 to the British Trawling Co. Ltd, Bootle. They sold her a year later to the Derby Steam Trawling Co. Ltd, Fleetwood. In February 1922, she was sold to the Godby Steam Fishing Co. Ltd, Fleetwood and she was re-registered as FD.403. On 8th March 1923, she went ashore near Blackpool but her crew and catch were saved and she was later refloated. In September 1924, she was bought by Thomas D. Lees, Bonnington, Edinburgh and re-registered at Granton as GN.24. In November that year, Lees sold her to the Crampin Steam Fishing Co. Ltd, Grimsby and the following year her registry changed to GY.366. In November 1927, she was sold to Trawlers (White Sea & Grimsby) Ltd, Grimsby, who renamed her *Berenga*. A year later she was hired as a minesweeper at £64 6s 4d a month. She was returned to her owners in February 1940 but was requisitioned two months later as a barrage balloon vessel. She was still under Naval control in 1942 when she was sold to Trawlers Grimsby Ltd (a different company from that above) and she was returned to them in September 1945. Three months later, she was sold to United Trawlers Ltd, Milford Haven who ran her until 1951. They then sold her to Atlantic Trawlers Ltd, Edinburgh but she was registered as *Springleigh* (M.192) and continued to work from Milford. Her last owner, South Western Trawlers Ltd of Milford Haven, bought her in 1953 and renamed her *Lydstep*. She went for scrapping at Castle Pill, Milford in May 1955.

Lewis's five later Aberdeen registered vessels were almost all prefixed 'Fort ' (see **Appendix V**).

Chapter 10: 1930s – DECADE OF DEVELOPMENT

This was a period of far reaching technical improvements in trawler design, outfitting, construction and cod liver oil processing. New stern shapes were being incorporated, which gave greater buoyancy and speed. Spade and semi-balanced rudders, with steam and, later, hydraulic steering gears were introduced so that, by the middle of the decade, most of the new Distant Water ships had cruiser sterns with either semi or full balanced rudders. Later, in the second half of the decade, cut away spoon and Maierform stems appeared. The former, found on the large Bremerhaven-built Northern boats, was a derivation of the whale catcher bows being constructed by the yard at that time. The latter shape was first seen on *Kingston Agate* (H.489), built by Cook, Welton & Gemmell in 1937 as Yard No. 640. Electric lighting became standard, whilst in the electronics field, trawlers were catching up with the larger merchant vessels. Wireless telephony was replacing wireless telegraphy but Morse code, along with the Morse key, was to remain in use until almost the end of the trawler era. Early telephony worked on the 'simplex' system, where only one person could talk at a time, hence the necessity of using "*over to you*" or simply "*over*". Later, the 'duplex' systems came into use and the air was alive with the crackle of ships all talking to each other simultaneously. Direction finding equipment and echo sounders for depth finding came into more regular use, and radio officers were making up the working complement of Distant Water trawler crews. In the engine room, exhaust turbines were giving more power and greater economy. Steam heated liver oil boilers with storage tanks were becoming standard fitments on the deep water ships.

ECHO SOUNDERS

The forerunner of the 'echo sounder' or 'echometer' as we know it was unrelated to either navigation or fish-finding. The first experiments took place in Lake Geneva in 1827, by Colladin and Sturm, who developed a means of accurately measuring the speed of sound through water. Later, in 1842, Dr Joule discovered the principle of magneto-striction. His experiments proved that if a metal such as nickel was surrounded by the fluctuations of a magnetic field, it would expand and contract. This movement converted the electrical pulses into acoustic pulses, a phenomenon which worked equally well when reversed. In the early 1900s, Pierre and Jacques had discovered a similar behaviour in the piezo-electric excitement of quartz, which led to a Dr Langevin's discovery that acoustic beams could be formed in water. However, it was not until the mid 1920s that all these results came together and Henry Hughes & Son of London produced the world's first ultrasonic echo sounder, using the properties of magneto-striction. They developed a series of 'sonic' echo sounders (where the transmitted pulses were within the audible frequency range) for the Admiralty in 1926. These sets utilised a spring-loaded electro-magnetic hammer, which acted on a diaphragm under the ship's hull. The transmitted sound pulse would reverberate back from the seabed, through a carbon microphone, to the operator's headset. He would then read off the moment of reception on a rotating dial, thus giving the depth of water. However, these low frequency sets suffered a great deal of interference from air bubbles passing under the bottom of the

ship, so in order to arrive at an accurate figure, the vessel had to be stopped. By 1930, Hughes had overcome this problem with the development of the ultrasonic mirror signal oscillator. This gave the company's products the well known MS prefix still in use today. Used in conjunction with mechanical timing, accurate soundings could be taken at full speed. The next step was the introduction of the Hughes Type MS.3 starch iodide or 'wet' paper recorder in 1933. This gave a paper print-out of the soundings.

During this period, Marconi founded the Sounding Device Company to manufacture its 'Atlantic' and 'Pacific' sounders. These units used the principle of the piezo-electric quartz oscillator, rather than the magneto-striction method favoured by their competitors. However, Marconi did utilise the MS system after 1940. These two sounders displayed their results in two different ways. The former used a meter, while the latter reproduced the soundings by means of a pen working on dry paper.

The echo sounder first attracted the attention of fishermen in the early 1930s. Initially installed as a navigational aid, it soon became apparent that it had another important use as a fish finding tool. The first British skipper to use the sounder to locate

Photo. 59: A rare aerial view of a steam trawler, showing RAFA *Adastral* on torpedo recovery exercises in February 1930 and still carrying the bandstand for her 3 inch gun. Recovered torpedoes can be seen on her side deck. She was built by Ritchie Graham at Glasgow in 1919 as the 'Strath Class' trawler *William Gillett*. She was sold to the Air Ministry on 9th March 1921 and converted into a weapons recovery vessel for the Marine Craft Section. Disposed of 5th July 1946.

fish shoals was Ronnie Balls of Yarmouth, in his steam drifter *Violet and Rose* (YH.757) in 1933. Ronnie used a Marconi echo sounder and he kept detailed records of his findings over a seven year period. The problem with these early sets was that the echo, a tiny spot of light flashing over the fathom scale, was momentary and could not be held or repeated; once the echo had gone, it was lost forever. Nevertheless, it was found that by interpretation, these fleeting echoes could identify shoals of fish, wrecks, etc. The Norwegian scientist Oscar Sund used a Hughes Type MS.3 Echometer to locate shoals of cod from the research vessel *Johan Hjort* off the Lofoten Islands in 1935, thus establishing the instrument as a definitive fish finding aid. During the Second World War, the Navy further developed the principles of the echo sounder into the 'Asdic' set, named after the Allied Submarine Detection Investigation Committee which had been set up after the First World War to detect submerged U-boats.

ELECTRIC WELDING

This was slowly making its presence felt in the trawler building industry, with many internal bulkheads fabricated in this manner. External cope irons and chafing bars were welded to the hulls, giving a stronger, smoother finish. Two examples of this 'part welded' construction were *Imperialist* (H.2), built as Yard No. 1058 by Smith's Dock in 1939 (with the butts of her shell plating electrically welded) for the Hull Northern Fishing Co. Ltd, Hull, and *Lord Nuffield* (H.373), built as Yard No. 1183 by Cochrane & Sons in 1937 for Pickering & Haldane's Steam Trawling Co. Ltd, Hull ('E' strake part electrically welded). The former was requisitioned in August 1939 as FY126, an anti-submarine trawler. In 1943, whilst attached to the Gibraltar trawler force, she attacked and damaged *U732*. The U-boat was forced to surface where she was later sunk by the destroyer HMS *Douglas*. *Imperialist* was

returned to her former owners in October 1945. On 9th October 1959, she had to be beached at Scarborough after a collision. In 1965 she transferred to Fleetwood as FD.83, owned by the Wyre Steam Trawling Co. Ltd, Fleetwood and went to the breakers in 1966. *Lord Nuffield* was requisitioned in September 1939 as FY221 and converted for anti-submarine work. While stationed at Gibraltar, with skipper Lieutenant David Mair in command, she successfully attacked and sank the Italian submarine *Elmo* (1,260 tons). She was returned to her former owners in December 1945 and was transferred to Fleetwood as FD.88, owned by Wyre Trawlers Ltd. Scrapped in 1967, she was the last of Lord Line's pre-war trawlers.

LIVER BOILERS

The first sign of liver boilers on builder's drawings appears in 1931. These were fitted to three Lewis-built trawlers, Yard No's 116 and 117, *The Way* (SN.134) and *Rightway* (SN.121), and Yard No. 125 *Fort Royal* (A.171). This was to prove a great forward step in the treatment of the livers. Up to this time, they had been packed in barrels or casks which were then lashed down on deck aft until the trawler reached port, by which time the contents could have a rather unpleasant odour. Here they would be off-loaded and taken to a shore factory for processing into the valuable oil. The fishermen received a payment, 'liver money', which was an added bonus to their normal earnings. By boiling down the livers at sea, the resulting oil fetched a higher price, which was reflected in the payment. The oil was stored in special tanks. At Aberdeen, the oil was taken by small tank barges, the *Isco*'s (named after Isaac Spencer & Co., the local refiners). At Hull, it was *Seven Seas*, an oil barge, that shipped the oil from the trawler and after stringent purity tests had been done, the oil was pumped into road tankers to be taken to the Marfleet Refinery. On the later Hull ships, the job of rendering

Photo. 59a: *Reformo* showing cod liver boiler aft of her funnel, atop the casing. Her forecastle deck is flush with the rail and her trawl net is strung out to dry along the casing. Note how the mainrail rises up forward.

down livers fell to the radio operator but on other ships the crew did this work. Owing to the rather obnoxious gasses given off, the liver boilers were relegated to the very stern of the ship to prevent these gasses entering the accommodation. This, however, presented another problem, that of manually transporting the heavy baskets of livers from the gutting pounds to the aft end of the ship. This was a hazardous occupation, as on a large ship upwards of 60 tons of livers had to be carried along the exposed side decks, often totally submerged in freezing water, hanging onto the ship with one hand, and the precious basket with the other. Many men have been swept to their deaths in the execution of this task, which at the end of the trip gave them a small extra allowance for their trouble. As far as I can ascertain, the first Hull trawler to be fitted with a liver boiler was *Loch Torridon* (H.198), built in 1930 by John Lewis, as Yard No. 112, for the Loch Line Trawling & Fishing Co. Ltd, Aberdeen. The working of this new device fell to Arthur Chapple, who was given only very brief instructions as how to operate it and produce the oil at sea. He managed to render the livers down but in doing so scalded his left arm and still had the scars in 1989 (for details of *Loch Torridon*, see page 159).

A report on these new boilers, written with regards to a later Cochrane built trawler states:

'The location of the cod liver boilers in a house on deck can be seen from the GA drawing. Two of these boilers, made by the St. Andrew's Engineering and Shipwright Company of Hull, are installed, and work in connection with the liver oil tanks placed immediately below deck at the after end of the engine-room. It may be mentioned that the bulkhead separating the liver boiling room from the pantry, is of insulating material. The livers are fed by hand into the boiling tanks, which are constructed of mild steel plates welded together. Steam is led into the bottom of the tanks and discharged among the livers, causing the oil to separate. Water connections fitted on the tanks are used for raising the oil levels and for swilling out purposes. From the top of the tanks, vapour

pipes are led to the atmosphere, and large gunmetal sluice valves are fitted on the bottom for discharging the foots or residue. The oil is drawn off from the front of the tanks by suitably placed draw-off cocks, and is run through a strainer into the storage tanks below, which are four in number and have a combined capacity of 7 tons. Boiling the livers on board ship, while the vessel is still at the fishing grounds is now becoming general practice on modern trawlers, and of course, makes for greatly improved quality in the resulting oil, by reason of the perfect freshness of the livers when treated.' Shipbuilding and Shipping Record, *July 1933*

Another location and smaller type of boiler (as fitted to *Gava*) was also fitted to *Reformo* (A.224) in the 1950s (**Photo. 59**); it can be seen on the casing top immediately behind the funnel. Most of the Aberdeen trawlers had small boilers fitted under the wheelhouse. *Reformo* was built by Dundee Shipbuilders in March 1899 as *Windsor Castle* (GY.1101 – 119ft, 241g, 80nhp) for the Castle Line Steam Fishing Co. Ltd, Grimsby, with engines by Cooper & Greig Ltd. Five years later, she was sold to Denmark and renamed *Dannebrog*. She returned to Grimsby in October 1911 as *Mollyhawk* (GY.654), owned by Thomas W. Bascomb, Grimsby. She spent the war years as a fishery trawler at a shilling a month hire rate for crew and owner. They in turn sold her in May 1914 to the Bianco Trading Co. Ltd, Grimsby. She changed hands again in September 1916, going to the Record Steam Trawling Co. Ltd, Grimsby. They kept her two months and sold her to R.D. Clarke, who sold her to G.F. Sleight in June 1917 and renamed her *Reformo* in 1919. She came to Aberdeen owners J.E. Lawrie, & T.R. King in 1934, was requisitioned for harbour service in 1941 and returned in 1946. Apparently, when she had her new wheelhouse fitted, the skipper's berth was relocated from the after accommodation to the forward end of the casing and the liver boiler repositioned on the casing top. Originally built with an open deck, sometime during her life she was fitted with a fo'c'sle deck flush with the rail.

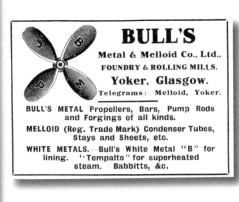
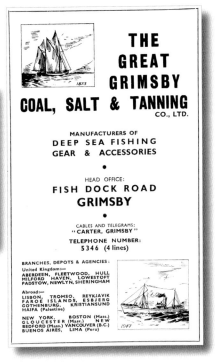

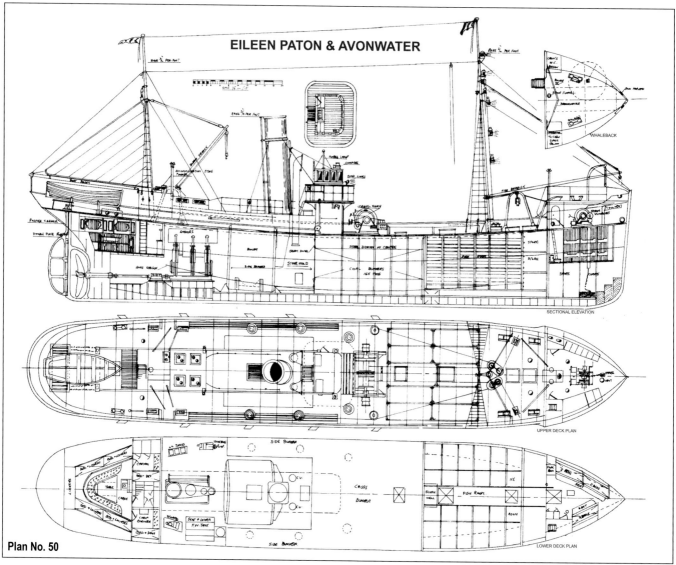

EILEEN PATON & AVONWATER

Plan No. 50

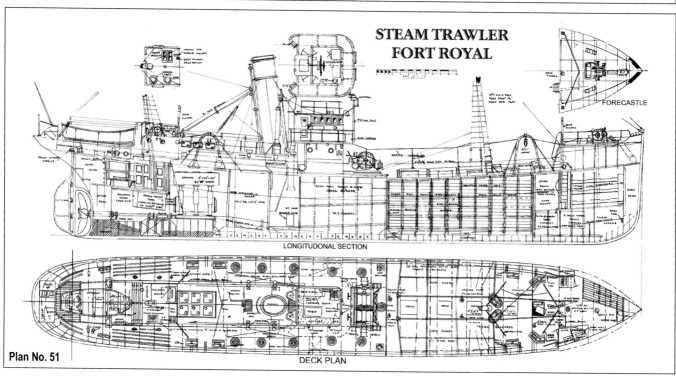

STEAM TRAWLER
FORT ROYAL

Plan No. 51

Chapter 11: NOTABLE ABERDEEN SHIPS OF THE 1930s

In 1930, John Lewis launched Yard No. 123 *Avonwater* (A.142 – 123ft 6ins bp x 23ft x 13ft 6ins, 260g) for the North Star Steam Fishing Co. Ltd, Aberdeen (**Plan 50**). She was almost identical to *Ben Rossal*, with the exception of her wheelhouse verandah. One feature of these smaller Scottish vessels was the net gratings either side of the casing against the bulwarks. Their use was two-fold; firstly they provided a slightly raised platform when hauling the net and, secondly, they were used to stow the net when on passage (the Humber ships had a wire span running through the bulwark stanchions, possibly for this purpose). Another feature was the steam anchor windlass positioned on the main deck below the whaleback. In common with many vessels being launched by this date, she was fitted with radio. *Avonwater* was requisitioned in September 1939 as a boom defence vessel, with the Admiralty No. Z119, and was returned in May 1946. By 1947, she had changed hands and was under Shire Trawlers colours but still Aberdeen registered. In 1948, she was sold to the Ardrossan Trawling Co. Ltd, Granton and renamed *Eileen Paton* (GW.22); she was scrapped on 15th January 1960 at Granton.

In 1931, the yard launched two entirely different designs of trawler. The first, a pair of sister ships, Yard No's 116 and 117, *The Way* (SN.134) and *Rightway* (SN.121 – 122ft 6ins bp x 23ft 13' 6ins, 116n, 69nhp) were for the Crater Steam Fishing Co. Ltd, North Shields. The builder's general arrangement drawing depicts a North Sea trawler, also capable of making Iceland trips. She had a straight stem, semi-elliptical counter stern and a short, raised whaleback. Her main deck was flush throughout and she was devoid of a wheelhouse verandah. She was divided up into four watertight compartments, with little hope of remaining afloat if badly damaged anywhere between the fish room and the inner propeller shaft coupling. Below the whaleback, to starboard was the liver boiler house. After being rendered down, the oil passes into two 150 gallon storage tanks below. On return to port it was pumped out of the tanks, using a semi-rotary pump fitted to the outside of the boiler house. There was no spare fish room for reserve bunkers. With a normal trip of around five to seven days, her main bunkers were adequate for longer trips, the builders stating:

'The vessels whilst fulfilling all the ordinary functions of North Sea trawling, have been so designed that bunkering arrangements below deck are sufficient for Iceland trips to be made.'

In 1935, *The Way* was purchased by John Craig of Aberdeen. She was requisitioned in September 1939 as a boom defence vessel, with the Admiralty No. Z127, and was returned in July 1945. Her sister ran ashore at Collieston near Aberdeen in 1932.

Lewis's other trawler of note in 1931 was Yard No. 125 *Fort Royal* (A.171 – 140ft bp x 24ft x 14ft, 351g, 79nhp – (**Plan 51**), built for their own account. A far larger ship, she was fitted with wireless from the outset. The builder's drawing shows a nicely proportioned, sturdy Distant Water ship, with a quarterdeck. Were it not for her counter stern, she could quite easily have been mistaken for an early oil burner built in the mid-1940s. Below the whaleback to starboard is the liver boiling house, with twin

boilers. These boilers are heated by steam piped from the main boiler. After the oil has been removed and piped to the two 450 gallon storage tanks, the offal is shot overboard using waste steam. The poop house has a double WC to port and a store to starboard. The foremast is of pitch pine 15ins diameter and is raked 1.5ins per foot. Both electric and oil navigation lamps are carried, and full internal electric lighting is supplied by the two dynamos fitted on the starboard side of the engineroom.

Fort Royal was among the first Distant Water ships to be specifically built for Aberdeen owners. These local businessmen were quite content to allow their skippers to work the North Sea grounds, making shorter trips and landing their catches in prime condition, thus obtaining good prices. The traditional grounds for the Aberdeen vessels were the Viking Bank, the West of Shetland grounds, St. Kilda, Rockall and the Flannan Isles, with occasional trips to Faeroe. She was bombed by two Heinkel III aircraft off Aberdeen on 9th February 1940, going down in less than three minutes. One other local firm of trawler owners, Loch Line, were keen on working the Distant Water grounds, the round trip for which was far shorter than that of a Humber-based vessel. The main customers for Icelandic cod were the fish and chip shops of industrial middle England, which meant a protracted rail journey. In addition, there were no coal mines close to the port (as with the Humber ports), so fuel had to be brought in either by rail or by sending the trawlers with scratch crews south to the Forth for bunkers. The company had three such vessels built by the Lewis yard: *Loch Carron* (A.23), launched by Mrs Malcolm Smith Jnr on 9th May 1929; *Loch Torridon* (A.96), launched 12th February 1930 by Miss Agnes Thomson; and *Loch Ard* (A.151), launched 5th March 1941 by the manager of Loch Line, H.A. Holmes. They were Yard No's 103, 112 and 118 respectively (and all 150ft x 24ft x 14ft, 351g, 79nhp). Although they were all Aberdeen registered and identical to *Fort Royal*, it appears that they spent most of their time fishing out of Hull:

'The vessels have been built to class Lloyd's 100 A.1., but scantlings are considerably in excess of regulations. The deck fittings and gear are also of a specially heavy type to meet the severe conditions of service. Specially designed trawl winches of the latest pattern, all gears being machine cut, have been built and will be fitted on board by the builders. Special attention has been paid to fishroom arrangements etc., to ensure the landing of fish in the best possible condition. Part of the fishroom can also be adapted as a temporary bunker, for the carrying of additional coal for longer voyages. A complete electrical installation will be arranged with a generating set having a 5.K.W. capacity, this is to ensure ample power for the deck floodlights etc., when the vessel is working during the winter season. An emergency lighting set of 1.5.K.W. capacity will also be fitted as a stand-by.' J. Lewis launch report

The last of the trio, *Loch Ard*, was unfortunately the first to be lost, on 16th January 1934. After calling in at Aberdeen whilst on passage to the Icelandic grounds, she disappeared without trace. By 1935, the other two ships were Hull registered, as *Loch Carron*

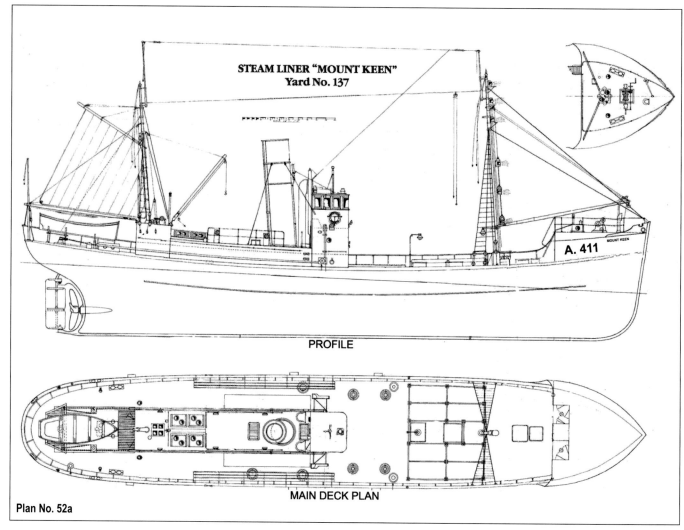

STEAM LINER "MOUNT KEEN"
Yard No. 137

A. 411

MOUNT KEEN

PROFILE

MAIN DECK PLAN

Plan No. 52a

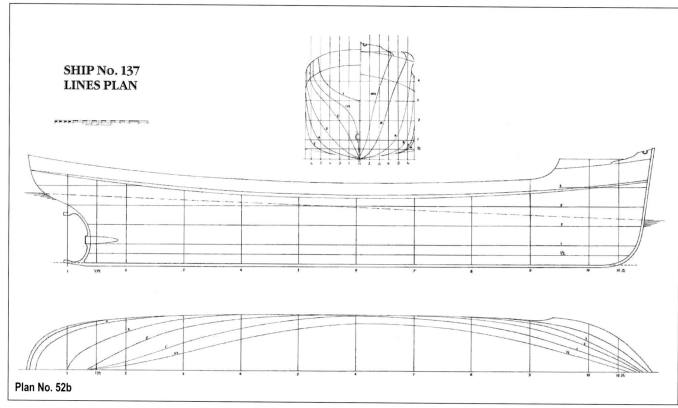

SHIP No. 137
LINES PLAN

Plan No. 52b

Photo. 60: *Mary White* showing her clean lines and rivetted construction. Also of note are her numbers and name, white on black as per the rules.

(H.190) and *Loch Torridon* (H.198), owned by the Caledonian Fishing Co. Ltd, Aberdeen. They disappeared from the register in 1940.

In 1935-6, John Lewis built three sister ships (all 134ft x 23ft 4ins x 13ft 6ins, 271g, 470ihp): *White Pioneer* (NE.3) for White Trawlers of Hebburn on Tyne; *Fort Rannoch* (A.398) for J. Lewis of Aberdeen; and the steam liner *Mount Keen* (A.411), for Dodds Steam Fishing Co. Ltd, Aberdeen. The builder's drawings (**Plans 52a & b**) for *Mount Keen* show a flush-decked North Sea ship, with a whaleback fo'c'sle, semi-cruiser stern and balanced rudder. Her main fish room is quite small and there is a cold cabinet shown on the port side aft, for storing her frozen bait when she went long lining (the other two ships did not have this cabinet). Aft of the relatively small fish room are the main bunkers. These run well forward and take up what could have been useful fish room space. A fish derrick is shown on the foremast and a single bobbin derrick is fitted on the front of the galley casing.

White Pioneer, Yard No. 134, was launched on 1st August 1935 and sailed for her home port on 7th September. Her engines were supplied by White's Marine Engineering of Hebburn, part of the owners other interests. The builder's press release states:

'The vessel is interesting in respect that she will be fitted with the White Patent Combination Marine Engine, built by Messrs. White's Marine Engine Engineering Co Ltd., Hebburn-on-Tyne, and installed by John Lewis & Sons., Ltd. The Combination Engine consists of a fairly high speed compound marine engine using superheated steam, exhausting into a low pressure turbine both geared onto the propeller shaft. With this arrangement the racing of the propeller is practically eliminated, hence it should make an ideal arrangement for trawlers when towing gear. In heavy weather this should be of great assistance to the vessel in working conditions, and it is claimed by the Engine Builders that the actual time of trawling may be improved by about 50%.'

At some period during 1936, she was renamed *Mary White* and was photographed in dry-dock after a repaint (**Photo. 60**). She was requisitioned in January as a boom defence vessel, Admiralty No Z.147, and was returned in February 1946. In 1948, she was sold to the Newhaven Trawling Co. Ltd, Granton and renamed *Luffness* (GN.57). Her end came on 27th January 1958, after running aground on the ledge of the North Pier, Aberdeen (**Photo. 61**). Her crew were rescued by the Aberdeen pilot cutter but the ship, stuck hard and fast and battered by the winter gales, was a hazard to navigation in the channel. She was cut down to a hulk and towed to a spot three miles off Cove, where the hull was scuttled.

Fort Rannoch (A.398), Yard No. 136, was launched on 30th December 1935 and was engined by the builders, sailing on her maiden trip on 24th January 1936. By 1937, she was registered at Dublin but still owned by Lewis in Aberdeen. She was later taken over by the Dublin Trawling, Ice & Cold Storage Co. Ltd. By 1953,

Photo. 61: *Luffness* aground on the ledge of the North Pier, Aberdeen in late January 1958.

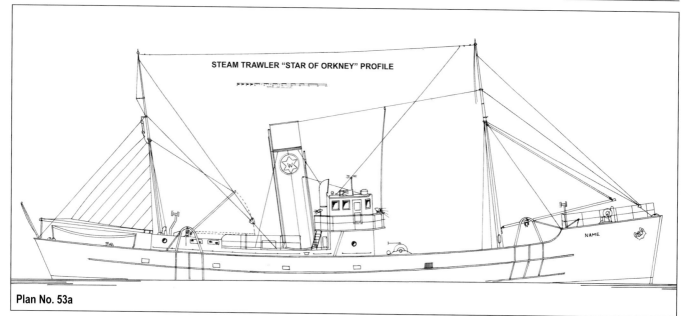

Plan No. 53a

she was owned by T.L. Devlin & Sons Ltd, Granton and registered as GN.14; she went to the breakers at Grangemouth in September 1963. *Mount Keen*, Yard No. 137, was launched on 17th June 1936, engined by her builders and sailed on 7th August; she was the firm's last pre-war trawler. She was hired in August 1939 as a minesweeper, FY684, and returned in April 1945 to Dodd's. They sold her to North Eastern Fisheries Ltd, Aberdeen in 1954, who ran her until she went to the breakers in 1965. In addition to trawling, she also went long lining for a spell under skipper John Leiper and after the war she was fitted with a wheelhouse verandah and pole compass.

Over the water at Footdee in 1936, Hall, Russells constructed Yard No. 741, *Star of Orkney* (A.421 – 125ft bp, 137ft 9ins oa x 23ft 6ins x 13ft 9ins, 440g – **Photo. 62**) for the Walker Steam Trawl Fishing Co. Ltd, Aberdeen, for the sum of £13,000. She was launched on 5th August at 3.30pm and ran trials on 31st. Payment terms were four equal instalments; the first when she was in frame, next when plated, third when launched and the last payment after acceptance trials. Her delivery was given as six months from date of order. She was to be the yard's last steam trawler for British owners before the onset of the Second World War and the first

Photo. 62: *Star of Orkney* heading up channel on a summer's day; note the awnings helping to shade the fish room and as yet no radar is fitted. She is in Walker Steam Trawl Fishing Co. Ltd colours of black hull with red boot topping and wood grained superstructure. The funnel is grey, with a black top and white 'W' on a red star, on a blue edged white disc.

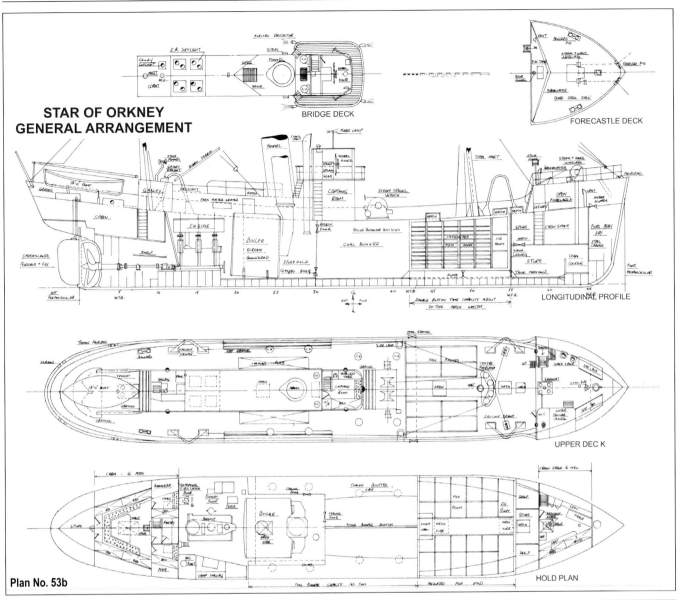

STAR OF ORKNEY
GENERAL ARRANGEMENT

BRIDGE DECK

FORECASTLE DECK

LONGITUDINAL PROFILE

UPPER DECK

HOLD PLAN

Plan No. 53b

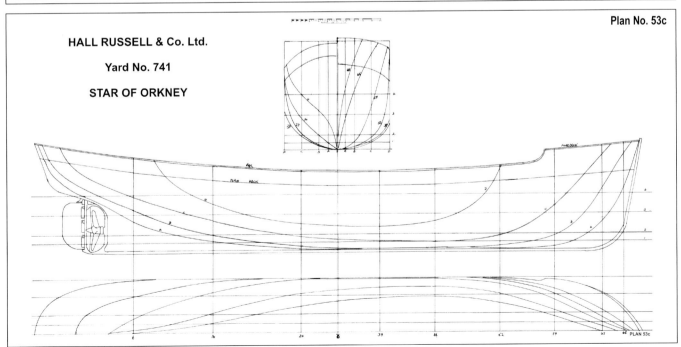

Plan No. 53c

HALL RUSSELL & Co. Ltd.

Yard No. 741

STAR OF ORKNEY

of her class. The remainder were all built as 'Round Table' Class minesweepers and they were among the best looking coal burners registered at Aberdeen (**Plan 53 a, b & c**). They were similar in size to Smith's Dock's 'Castle' class but there the similarity ends. The 'Castles' were most austere looking ships, whilst *Star of Orkney* was a handsome example of the Middle Water trawler, capable of working off Iceland and Faeroe, in addition to the North Sea and West Coast grounds. The drawing shows a flush-decked ship, with a streamlined double plate rudder and fin fitted in the propeller race to assist flow. Her slightly squatter, well-raked funnel, gives her the air of a mid-1940s oil burner. The starboard stokehold vent on the plan clearly shows the ash door, no shoots being fitted to this class. Her foremast is steel and the mizzen wood. *Star of Orkney* was hired as a minesweeper, FY683, in August 1939, at a rate of £177 9s. per month and released from duty in September 1946.

Before returning to fishing, she underwent a full survey at Alexander Hall's Aberdeen, prior to undergoing conversion. In common with most trawlers that had been requisitioned for war

service, she had been quite badly knocked about and a fair amount of repairs were needed before she could be accepted by her owners. The surveyor's ledger gives four full pages of items requiring repair or replacement, with the first meeting held on board at 2.30pm on 13th December 1945, with the vessel afloat, those attending being Mr Bissett, Mr Webster and the surveyor. At this meeting, they arranged for Admiralty removal of all war-time equipment. Further surveys were carried out on 22nd December, when a list of all of the damage to the hull upwards from the sheerstrake was made. An engine survey was undertaken by Lloyd's surveyor, Mr Stevenson, whilst their Mr Robinson carried out a boiler survey on 14th February 1946. On 4th March, she was put onto pontoon No. 3, where a full hull survey was held, the first occasion that the owner Mr. Walker was present. The claim for all the repairs was sent to the Government on 31st October 1946 and amounted to £1,040. Added to this was an extra month's hire rate and £75 for surveyor's fees, which brought the total to £1,292 9s. *Star of Orkney* continued to fish out of Aberdeen until going to the breakers in 1964.

Chapter 12: 1930s HUMBER FLEETS AND DESIGN IMPROVEMENTS

SMITH'S DOCK'S CRUISER STERNS

In 1936-7, Smith's Dock built replacements for *Angle*, *Pict* and *Kelt* (164ft bp x 27ft 1in x 14ft 3ins, 462g, 99nhp) as Yard No's 1005, 1009 and 1020. These larger cruiser sterned ships were owned by the Hull Northern Fishing Co. Ltd and carried the port letters H.307, H.298 and H.398 respectively. *Angle* was requisitioned as FY201 in September 1939 and served as an anti-submarine trawler until her release in October 1945, when she came under Hellyer's ownership. *Kelt* was also requisitioned in September 1939 as an anti-submarine trawler and given the Admiralty No. FY112; she was sold in 1945. The last of the trio, *Pict*, served from August 1939 as the anti-submarine trawler FY132, until sold out of service in 1946. These two ships were bought back by their former owners after the war, as *Kelt* (H.193) and *Pict* (H.162). *Kelt* was later sold to the Devon Fishing Co. Ltd of Hull in 1953 and her sister had her name changed to *Carthusian* (H.162) in 1948, after being purchased by the Eton Steam Fishing Co. Ltd of Hull. Both went for scrapping in 1957.

At Fleetwood, the Iago Steam Trawling Co. Ltd ordered two new ships from Smith's Dock in 1930; Ship No's 928 and 929, *Red Gauntlet* (LO.33) and *Admiral Sir John Lawford* (LO.42 – both 134ft 3ins bp x 24ft x 14ft 3ins, 338g, 99nhp). These ships were the first new trawlers for the firm's Fleetwood operation. The company was formed after the First World War by Commander E.D.W. Lawford, after being invalided out of the Royal Navy. His first vessel, purchased second hand from Hellyer's of Hull, *Iago* (H.963), was actually registered in his wife's name and gave the company its title. Initially, he worked his fleet out of Milford Haven, before moving to Fleetwood in 1930. Lawford, unlike many owners, placed great store on the welfare of his employees

and was saddened when someone left to work for another firm. He endeavoured to improve the crew's accommodation, by moving them out of the fo'c'sle and into better quarters aft. He fitted his vessels with wireless telegraphy equipment and later, after 1933, with radio telephone sets. He was regarded as a dynamic reformer, determined to give his crews the best ships and equipment with which to do their job, which included the fitting of echo meters for fish finding when they became available after 1931.

These two trawlers were sturdy, powerful looking ships, well able to fish the Distant Water grounds and their white painted hulls gave them the air of private yachts. The builder's steelwork drawing shows them as having the straight trawler stem, coupled to the new cruiser stern, which Smith's Dock were instrumental in promoting, and spade rudders. They were rivetted throughout, with flat topped fo'c'sle heads and quarterdecks. They carried stocked fisherman-type anchors, which were handled by a windlass on the whaleback. These ships also had a pair of cowl vents on the casing top in front of the main engine room skylight, which gave additional fresh air to the machinery space. Wooden fidded topmasts were fitted to carry the wireless aerials. *Red Gauntlet* was requisitioned in August 1939 as a minesweeper, fitted with a 12 pounder gun and given the Admiralty No. FY900. She was sunk in the North Sea on 5th August 1943, after being hit by a torpedo fired from a German E-boat. *Admiral Sir John Lawford* was also requisitioned at the same time and for the same duties. In May 1944, she switched to wreck dispersal work, until being released in 1946. Converted to oil firing in 1950, she was sold in 1961 to the Milford Steam Trawling Co. Ltd and renamed *Milford Admiral* (M.224), going for scrapping on 8th January 1962 at Briton Ferry.

As previously mentioned, the Cardiff firm of Neale & West Ltd

Photo. 63: *Huddersfield Town* (H.261) entering Aberdeen, showing light grey topsides over red boot topping. She has a wood grained superstructure and a black topped light blue funnel, separated by a broad white band surmounted by the company's crown logo.

had four sister ships built to the same design as the Iago vessels. They were Yard No's 913 and 914 *Naniwa* and *Muroto*, built at Stockton, with *Oyama* and *Sata*, Yard No's 926 and 927 built at Middlesborough. The builder's blueprints show a conflict of sterns, with the Middlesborough ships having a spoon type cruiser stern with an Oertz style rudder, and the Stockton ships with a typical cruiser stern and spade rudder.

CONSOL'S 'FOOTBALLERS'

The Consolidated Steam Fishing & Ice Co. Ltd's new naming scheme appeared in the early 1930s, when their ships were named after football clubs. Smith's Dock built the first of the class as Yard No. 952 *Arsenal* (GY.505). The yard's order book shows her purchase price as £19,871, with her sisters costing around the same. She was the first of ten ships to be built by the yard that year, with five more of them 'footballers'. Of these, the first was Yard No. 953 *Aston Villa* (GY.508). She was purchased by the Admiralty on 11th July 1936, renamed *Mascot* and was later converted to a depot ship for the coastal forces, as *Vulcan*. She was sold out of service on 5th February 1947, going to Fleetwood as *Fotherby* (FD.262) owned by the Boston Deep Sea Fishing & Ice Co. Ltd and was converted to oil burning. They sold her to Israel in 1951 as *Miriam* and she finished up under Polish colours as *Pollux*.

Next came Yard No. 954 *Derby County* (GY.514), which was requisitioned in August 1939, as an anti-submarine trawler, FY171, and sold to the Hull (Steam Fishing & Ice Co. Ltd in March 1946. They sold her back to Consols in November that year as GY.194 for £20,000. She was sold again in February 1964 to Belgium. Yard No. 955 *Spurs* (GY.515) was requisitioned as anti-submarine trawler FY168 in September 1939 and sold to the Hull (Steam Fishing & Ice Co. Ltd in January 1946. Consol's bought her in November as GY.148, and she went for scrap on 7th February 1962 at Dunston on Tyne. Yard No. 956 *Sheffield Wednesday* (GY.519) was sold to Dutch owners as IJM.12 on 17th June 1937 and taken over by the Admiralty in 1940. She was destroyed by an explosion at Gibraltar on 18th January 1942. Yard No. 957 *Huddersfield Town* (GY.521) was requisitioned in 1939 as the anti-submarine trawler FY197 and sold to the Hull (Steam Fishing & Ice Co. Ltd in April 1946. She was purchased again by Consols in that November as GY.261, for around £22,000. By June 1962, she was *Leeds United* (GY.261) and was sold a year later to the Boston Deep Sea Fishing & Ice Co. Ltd, Grimsby, who only kept her until the September, when she was sold to Holland (**Photo. 63**).

All these five ships were sisters (155ft x 26ft 5ins x 12ft 2ins, 700ihp), with the cruiser stern and spade rudder favoured by Smith's Dock and a flat topped fo'c'sle instead of the more usual curved whalebacks. The crew were in the forward cabin with the officers aft. The skipper had his own cabin below the wheelhouse. All the crew ate in a dedicated mess room aft. A steam windlass was fitted on the fo'c'sle head and the main trawl winch had a capacity of 1,200 fathoms. Steering gear was the Donkin vertical type, allowing both hand and power operation. All internal bulkheads were electrically welded, along with the tunnel through the bunkers,

Photo. 64: *St. Nectan* having problems with her gear. The trawl doors are hanging on dog chains and her trawl warp appears to be strung out below the boat deck for repair. Note her polished brass portholes behind the wheelhouse and the escape port below the verandah. She is in Hamling colours of black hull with white band and wood grained superstructure, with a black topped yellow ochre funnel and a broad white band over a narrow black band.

the double bottom and fresh water tanks. Externally, some of the deck fittings were welded, as were the chafing bars on the hull. A liver boiling plant and oil storage tanks were in the specification, along with direction finding (DF) equipment and echo-sounding apparatus. They proved to be very economic ships to run, with an average consumption of between 7.5 to 8 tons of coal per day and a mean speed of 11 to 12 knots. This with a bunker capacity of 300 tons, gave them some thirty-five days steaming.

The other five ships built by the yard for Consols were for their Cardiff station. They began with Yard No. 958 *Barry Castle* (GY.53), which went to Grimsby in June 1934 as *Manchester City* (GY.53). She was requisitioned in August 1939 as FY198, an anti-submarine trawler and renamed *Peridot*. She sank after striking a mine off Dover on 15th March 1940. Yard No. 959 *Camarthen Castle* (GY.62) went to Grimsby in May 1934. In June, her name was changed to *Leeds United*. She was requisitioned in September as an anti-submarine trawler, FY196, and sold to Hull owners Hamlings in November 1946 as H.172. In 1947, she came back to Consol's renumbered GY.386. In March 1958, they sold her to the Rhondda Steam Fishing Co. Ltd, Grimsby and she went to the breakers at Sunderland on 30th January 1962. Yard No. 960 *Dynevor Castle* (SA.17) came to Grimsby in December 1937 as *York City* (GY.530). She was requisitioned in August 1939 as an anti-submarine trawler FY110 and sold to the Hull (Steam Fishing & Ice Co. Ltd in November 1945. Consols re-acquired her in February 1946 as *York City* (GY.193) and she worked for them until going to the breakers in Bruges on 22nd December 1964. Yard No. 961 *Pembroke Castle* (SA.25) went to Grimsby as *Lincoln City* (GY.529) in December 1937 and served as an anti-submarine trawler from September 1939, until her sinking off the Faeroes by hostile aircraft on 21st February 1941. These five sisters were almost identical to the first batch – 155ft bp x 26ft 4in x 12ft 2in, 386g, 99nhp.

In 1934, Smith's Dock launched another batch for Consol's, mostly 'footballers'. Often referred to as the 'second Batch' (157ft bp x 26ft 7ins x 12ft 7ins, 419g), they cost around £21,000 each. They were the first of Consol's ships to have all electric welded quarterdecks. Yard No. 968 *Grimsby Town* (GY.81) was hired as the anti-submarine trawler FY125 in August 1939 and sold in November 1945 to the Hull Steam Fishing & Ice Co. Ltd. She returned to Consols in January 1946 as GY.136 but was lost on 23rd April after running aground in Iceland. Yard No. 969 *Preston North End* (GY.82) was requisitioned in September 1939 as the anti-submarine trawler FY230, being returned in 1945. She was ultimately lost by stranding on 14th April 1950, on the rocks of Geirfuglagladrangar Reef, Iceland. Yard No. 976 *Blackburn Rovers* (GY.102) was requisitioned in August 1939 for anti-submarine duties as FY116. She sank a year later in the North Sea from '*unknown causes*'. Yard No. 977 *Jean Eva* (GY.104) changed her name in April 1938 to *Wolves*. She was requisitioned in August 1939 as an anti-submarine trawler, FY158, and returned in October 1945. During her naval service she was sold to the Bunch Steam Fishing Co. Ltd, Grimsby and, in June 1947, was renamed *Patuadi* (GY.104), going for scrap in 1961. Yard No. 978 *Leicester City* (GY.106) was requisitioned in September 1939 for anti-submarine duties as FY223 and was returned in March 1946. On 22nd March 1953, when homeward bound from Iceland under skipper G. Johanason with a crew of twenty, hands she went ashore

in thick fog at Breibuster Head, Hoy and immediately heeled over 45 degrees. Not knowing how close to shore they were, the skipper ordered 'abandon ship' and the crew launched the lifeboat and two rafts, which were quickly overwhelmed by the seas. Fourteen of her crew were picked up by the Stromness lifeboat under the command of Coxswain William Sinclair but, unfortunately, three of them died before reaching port. At her home port of Grimsby, there was some confusion when the lost trawler's name was given as *Leicestershire* (this was the name of another Grimsby ship lost with all hands on Hoy on 28th January 1938). The owners thought that *Leicester City* might be refloated, so they sent the salvage vessel *Salveda* north but she was deemed a constructive total loss. The final ship of the order was Yard No. 979 *Stoke City* (GY.114). She was requisitioned in September 1939 for anti-submarine duties as FY232 and returned in 1945, eventually going for scrap on 16th April 1964.

In 1937, they ordered two further ships from Smith's Dock, costing around £29,500 each. They were Yard No. 1028 *Mareham* (GY.42), which was renamed *Coventry City* in December 1938 and requisitioned as the anti-submarine trawler FY267 in September 1939. She became one of the group of twenty-four asdic trawlers loaned to the US for convoy and anti-submarine work in 1942 and was returned in August 1945. She continued to work for Consol's until she went for scrap on 17th April 1964 at Inverkeithing. Yard No. 1029 *Aston Villa* (GY.428) was requisitioned as an anti-submarine trawler in September 1939, as FY261. She was lost at Namsos on 3rd May 1940 while serving with the 16th Anti-Submarine Striking Force, which was engaged in the evacuation of Norway. At the time of her loss, she was commanded by the group's senior officer, Lieut. Commander Sir Geoffrey Congreve. Two further trawlers were ordered in 1938, at a similar price to the two earlier ships, Yard No. 1030 *Norwich City* (GY503) and Yard No. 1031 *Notts County* (GY.487 – 190ft oa x 178ft 8ins bp x 28ft 6ins x 15ft, 541g). *Norwich City* was requisitioned in September 1939 as the anti-submarine trawler FY229. She went to the US in 1942, and was returned in April 1946. She worked for Consols till she went for scrap at Inverkeithing on 12th April 1964. *Notts County* was requisitioned in September 1939 for anti-submarine duties, as FY250. She was sunk off south-east Iceland by a torpedo fired from *U701* on 8th March 1942. This was the last vessel built by Smith's Dock for Consol's before the Second World War; all were powerful, heavy weather ships and were snapped up by the Admiralty as anti-submarine trawlers.

THE 'NORTHERN SAINTS'

The 'Northern Saints' was the nickname given to the Saint-named Hull trawlers owned by Thomas Hamling & Co. Ltd, Hull. They ordered a series of eight sister ships from Cook, Welton & Gemmel in 1936 and 1937, Yard No's 612 and 613, 617-620, and 634 and 635: *St. Cathan* (H.353), launched on 19th August 1936, by Miss Nasha Muirhead Murray, ran trials on 30th September (light) and 2nd October (loaded); *St. Goran* (H.356), launched 5th September by Miss Molly Johanesen, ran trials on 20th October (light) and 22nd (loaded); *St. Kenan* (H.360), launched on 1st October by Miss Eilean Ellis, ran trials on 12th November (light) and16th (loaded); *St. Loman* (H.381), launched 15th October by Mrs Precious, ran trials on 7th December (light) and 10th (loaded); *St. Nectan* (H.411) launched on 2nd November

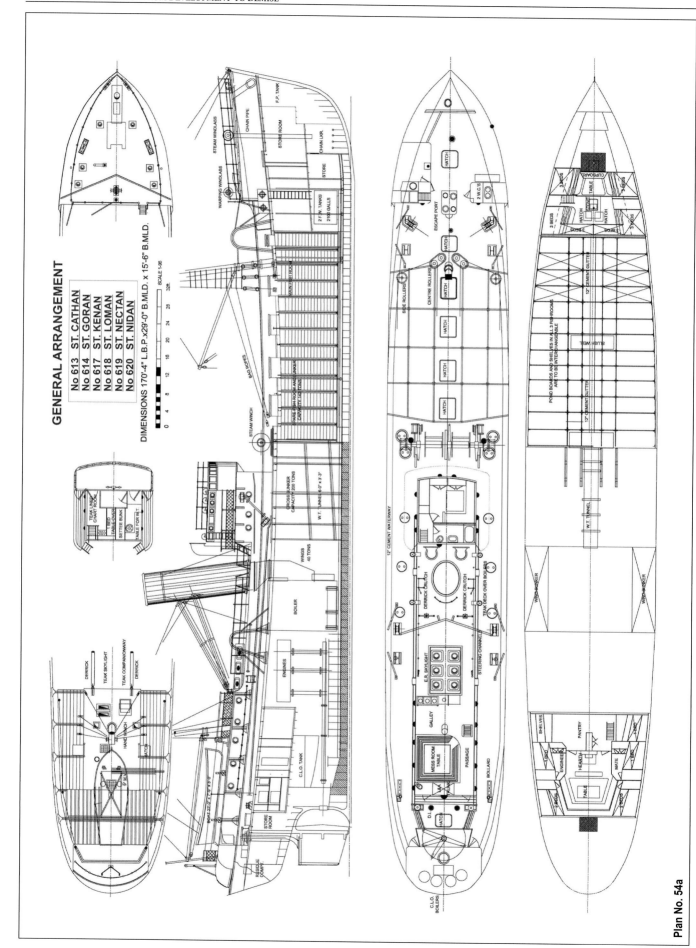

GENERAL ARRANGEMENT

No 613	ST. CATHAN
No 614	ST. GORAN
No 617	ST. KENAN
No 618	ST. LOMAN
No 619	ST. NECTAN
No 620	ST. NIDAN

DIMENSIONS 170'-4" L.B.P. x 29'-0" B.MLD. x 15'-6" B.MLD.

SCALE 1÷56

Plan No. 54a

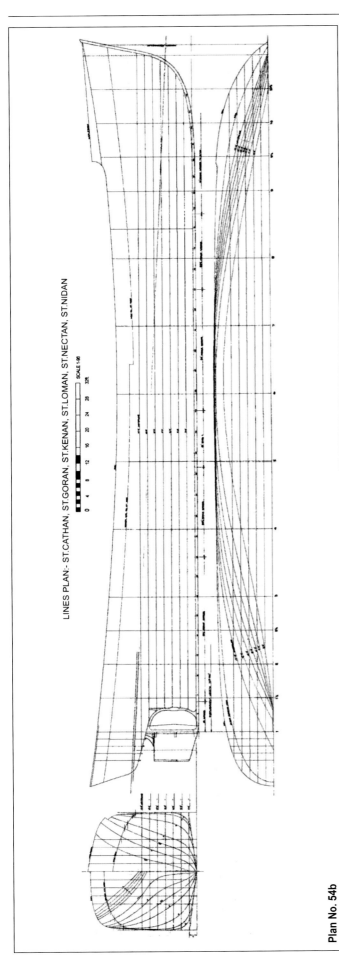

LINES PLAN:- ST.CATHAN, ST.GORAN, ST.KENAN, ST.LOMAN, ST.NECTAN, ST.NIDAN

SCALE 1-96

Plan No. 54b

by Miss Greaves and ran trials on 7th January 1937 (light) and on 11th (loaded); *St. Nidan* (H.412), launched on 30th November by the Hon. Katherine M. Hotham, ran trials on 18th January 1937 (light) and 21st (loaded); *St. Elstan* (H.484), launched on 23rd September 1937 by Miss J. Hall, ran trials on 16th November; *St. Wistan* (H.486) launched 21st October 1937 by Miss V. Hosdell and ran trials on 10th December. The last two ships' trials are only given as a single date; presumably this was their fully loaded test runs. These would have been the final acceptance trials before being handed over to their owners.

They were designed as Distant Water ships (170ft 4ins bp x 29ft x 15ft 6ins, 565g) and were engined by C.D. Holmes (15ins, 25ins, 42ins x 27ins stroke), supplied with dry superheated steam at 220psi from a single 15ft 6ins diameter Scotch boiler. The builder's drawings (**Plan 54 a & b**) must be the most well worn of any that I have and have been redrawn by Donald Leiper. This was the first builder's general arrangement drawing that I acquired back in 1963, from the superintendent at St. Andrews Steam Fishing Co. Ltd, Hull, after I had spent many hours crawling over *St. Nectan*. Outwardly, she had changed little from new but by then she had two lifeboats, was oil-fired and had been fitted with radar, and the illustration of her (**Photo. 64**) shows her working on a rare calm day in the Arctic. They were extremely well proportioned ships, with raked bar stems, flared bows, whaleback fo'c'sle, quarterdecks, full cruiser sterns with Oertz rudders, and fairing plates fitted to the sternpost.

St. Nidan was a very short lived ship, being sunk off the Shetlands by an enemy U-boat on 2nd October 1939 whilst returning from Iceland. Unfortunately, this made her the first Hull trawler to be lost to the enemy in the Second World War. The U-boat's Captain allowed all *St. Nidan*'s crew to leave their vessel before he sank her. She came to light again early in 1996, when underwater contractors Sub-Sea Ltd were surveying the seabed for the new Foinaven Oilfield off the west coast of Shetland.

The remaining ships were requisitioned in early 1940, for anti-submarine duties and nicknamed 'Fighting Saints' by their crews. Two of these never returned. The first loss was *St. Goran*, on 3rd May 1940, when she was attacked and badly damaged by German aircraft during the Namsos raid and had to be scuttled. Her sister *St. Cathan* formed part of the group loaned to the US Navy in 1942. She sank after colliding with the merchant ship *Hebe* off South Carolina on 11th April that year. These ships were constantly in the thick of the action, both on the Atlantic and Russian convoys; *St. Elstan* with convoy PQ16 was loaded with injured survivors from seven merchantmen and was under persistent air attack. *St. Kenan* almost foundered on the approach to Murmansk, when she was blown onto her beam ends during a gale. *St. Loman*, veteran of Namsos, attacked and sank a U-boat while she was on convoy protection duty in the Atlantic in July 1940. A few trips later, in December, she became a casualty after being rammed by a large freighter. She managed to limp into Aberdeen with the water almost up to her boiler fires. *St. Loman* also went to the US but came safely home in July 1946.

After the war, the remaining six trawlers rejoined the fishing fleet. All were converted to oil burners in the late 1940s and gave good service until going for scrap in the 1960s. *St. Kenan* was sold to Boyd Line Ltd, Hull in 1951, renamed *Arctic Invader* and went to the breakers in Antwerp, on 23rd August 1966. *St. Loman* was

Photo. 65: *Fighter* showing the standing gaff on her foremast. No ash shoots are fitted but there appears to be a support rail for them on the casing. She is wearing Alex Black's colours of white hull with black line at deck level and dark wood grained superstructures. Funnel colours are white with the logo of a white star on a blue flag.

also sold to Boyd's in 1951, becoming *Arctic Adventurer*. On 8th December 1964, three men were killed from a boiler explosion which severely damaged the vessel, so much so that she was towed to Ghent breakers on 25th January 1965. *St. Nectan* remained with Hamlings until she went for scrapping in 1967. *St. Elstan* also remained with Hamlings until broken up in Belgium, along with her sister *St. Wistan*, in January 1966.

BLACK'S 'WHITE ELEPHANT' FLEET

The Earl Steam Fishing Co. Ltd, Grimsby, owned by Sir Alec Black, had six handsome trawlers delivered in 1937. They were truly splendid ships and because of their hull colour, were affectionately dubbed 'The White Elephant Fleet'. Earl's did not run them for long and by the outbreak of the Second World War, most had been sold. The first four vessels came from Cochrane's yard: *Man O' War* (GY.396), Yard No. 1179; *Le Tiger* (GY.398), Yard No. 1180; *Fighter* (GY.42), Yard No. 1181; and *Daneman* (GY.426), Yard No. 1182 – all 17ft bp x 28ft 6ins x 15ft 6ins, 516g, 156nhp, with engines supplied by Amos & Smith. The picture of *Fighter*

Painting 6: *Italia Caesar*. S. FARROW

(**Photo. 65**) shows here with a bone in her teeth in the North Sea. She looks every inch the thoroughbred, with her well raked stem and cruiser stern. Note the two dhan buoys lashed to the forward shrouds and the Carley floats on the boat deck aft. A peculiarity, only found in these ships, was the standing gaff at the foremast head. This was used with a 'whip' to land baskets of fish at the fish market (a throwback to the method used by early steam colliers when discharging baskets of coal). The other two vessels came from Cook, Welton & Gemmell: *Italia Ceasar* (GY.442), Yard. No. 625, was launched on 27th April by Miss M. Cook. She ran her trials on 14th and 21st July (**Plan 55**); *El. Capitan* (GY.450) Yard No. 626, was launched by Miss Nancy Boyes on 24th May and ran her trials on 28th and 31st July. Both vessels were the same size as Cochrane's trawlers, their engines being supplied by C.D. Holmes with identical horsepower

By October 1938, *Fighter* and *El. Capitan* had been sold to Crampins and renamed as the cricketers *Wellard* and *Compton* respectively, although the latter ship's registered owners were the Perihelion Steam Fishing Co. Ltd, Grimsby (a Crampins subsidiary). In June 1939, Hudson Brothers (Trawlers) Ltd, Hull purchased *Compton* and renamed her *Cape Warwick* (H.272). After conversion to oil fuel in August 1949, photographs show she was equipped with two boats in Welin davits and a wheelhouse verandah and the foremast had a cross tree in place of the gaff. In 1955, she was sold to Henriksen & Co. Ltd, Hull and renamed *Evander*, going to Belgian breakers in February 1966. *Wellard* was purchased as an anti-submarine trawler (FY137) in August 1939. She was loaned to the US Navy in 1942 and was sold out of service in 1945. Her sale was handled by the Hull (Steam Fishing & Ice Co. Ltd, who passed her back to Crampins with the new fishing number GY.300. She went to Ghent breakers in August 1961. December 1938 saw *Daneman* sold to Hellyer's of Hull. She was requisitioned in August 1939 as FY123, an anti-submarine trawler. Along with her sister *Man O' War*, she formed part of the 21st Striking Force at Namsos. Later, she was one of four trawler escorts on convoy PQ18, the last of the PQ convoys that fought their way to Murmansk through ice, gales and numerous aircraft attacks, often acting as rescue ships picking up crews of

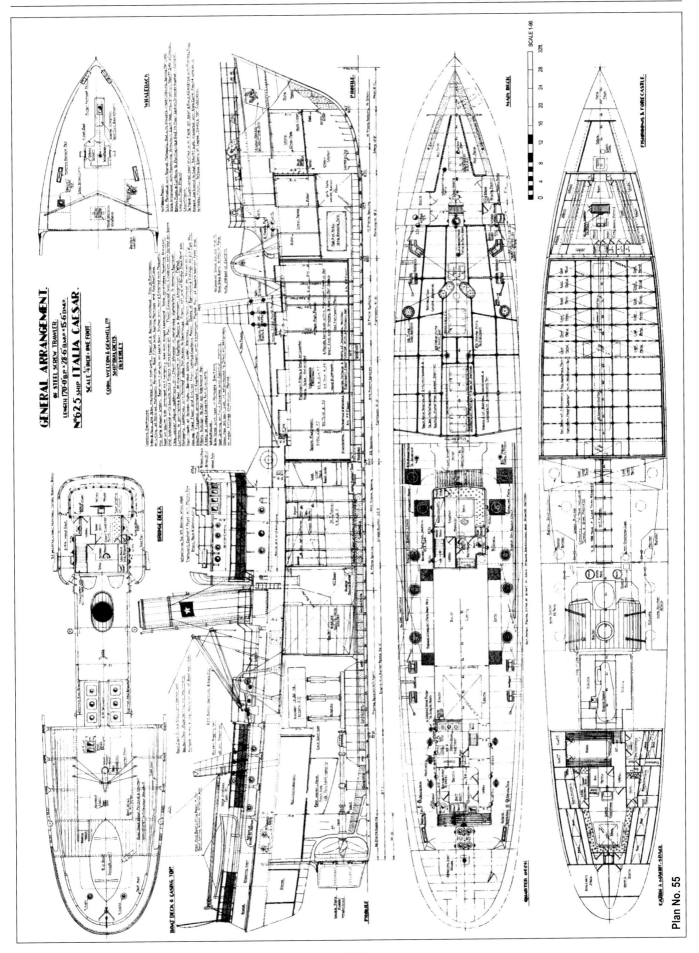

GENERAL ARRANGEMENT.
OF STEEL SCREW TRAWLER.
LENGTH 170-0 B.P. × 28-6 B.MLD × 15-6 D.MLD
No 625 SHIP ITALIA CAESAR.
SCALE ¼ INCH = ONE FOOT
COOK, WELTON & GEMMELL LTD
SHIPBUILDERS
BEVERLEY.

WHALEBACK.

PROFILE

BRIDGE DECK.

BOAT DECK & CASING TOP.

PROFILE.

MAIN DECK.

SCALE 1:96
0 4 8 12 16 20 24 28 32ft.

FISHROOMS & FORE CASTLE.

QUARTER DECK.

CABIN & SHELTER DECK.

Plan No. 55

stricken merchantmen. She struggled into Dvina Inlet in the teeth of a howling gale but, by this time, all her fuel had been used up and the crew broke up the woodwork in order to keep steam on. This was to no avail, as she foundered on a sandbank and had to be abandoned. It was two weeks later before the Russians condescended to tow her off, enabling her to hobble back to Belfast with a homeward bound convoy, for repairs. She met her end in May 1943, when she foundered whilst under tow in the North Atlantic, after striking pack ice. On the Russian run, these trawlers worked to the limits of their endurance, as not only did they steam many hundreds of extra miles picking up survivors, following Asdic contacts and rounding up stragglers, they had to waste valuable steam constantly thawing out the guns and other deck equipment. *Man O' War* was requisitioned in August 1939, as FY104, an anti-submarine trawler, and was returned in 1945. She was purchased by Hellyer's of Hull as *Man O' War* (H.181).

She kept her original name throughout her working life, taking it with her to the breakers at Inverkeithing on 9th December 1963. *Le Tiger* (apparently named after a comic character) was sold in August 1938 to Hellyer Brothers Ltd, Hull, who sold her back to Earl's some four months later. Purchased in December 1939 as FY243, an anti-submarine trawler, she went on loan to the US in 1942 and, on 3rd July, whilst escorting convoy BA.2 to Archangel, she sank *U215* after it had sunk the liberty ship that the trawler had been standing by. She was sold by the Admiralty in October 1945. Passing by way of the Hull Steam Fishing & Ice Co. Ltd. to the Loyal Steam Fishing Co. Ltd, Grimsby as *Regal* (GY.312). They in turn sold her to the Hull owners Hellyer's, as *Othello* (H.58), in late 1948. She was the only one of the six ships to remain a coal burner to the end and it was as Hull's only surviving coal steamer she went to the breakers at Ghent on 19th April 1963. *Italia Ceasar* was sold to Jutland Amalgamated Trawlers Ltd, Hull in 1938 as *Lady Elsa* (H.286_. Purchased as FY.124, an anti-submarine trawler in 1939, she went to the US in 1942, being returned in 1945. Jutland's sold her in 1950 to Lord Line and she worked for them as *Lord Tay* until going for scrap on 20th November 1964, at Grays in Essex.

COOK, WELTON & GEMMELL AND JUTLAND'S 'LADIES'

Jutland Amalgamated were a respected Hull company, who prefixed all their ships with '*Lady*', hence the nickname of 'Lady Boats'. The owners had an excellent working relationship with Cook, Welton & Gemmell, who were to build all their new ships. All their vessels were of the Distant Water type, with cruiser sterns and Oertz rudders. They were fitted with the latest wireless and navigational equipment, including, fathometers. In 1938, the fleet comprised:

Lady Adelaide (H.4.), Yard No. 586
Lady Beryl (H.222), Yard No. 605, 1935
Lady Hogarth (H.479), Yard No. 623, 1937
Lady Jeanette (H.466), Yard No. 616, 1937
Lady Lillian (H.467), Yard No. 575, 1933
Lady Madelaine (H.85), Yard No. 592, 1934
Lady Philomena (H.230), Yard No. 606, 1936
Lady Rosemary (H.477), Yard No. 622, 1937
Lady Shirley (H.464), Yard No. 615, 1937

Lady Adelaide was purchased by the Admiralty in 1939 as an anti-submarine trawler and renamed *Beryl* (T.34). She was sold in 1946 to the Iago Steam Trawling Co. Ltd, Fleetwood as *Red Knight* (LO.445) and went for scrap on 27th November 1962 at Barrow. *Lady Beryl* was requisitioned in August 1939 as an anti-submarine trawler and returned to Jutland's in 1945. *Lady Hogarth* was requisitioned in October 1939 for armed patrol duties, then used as an anti-submarine trawler from December 1940 and returned in 1945. *Lady Jeanette* was tragically lost on 8th March 1939, in sight of the Hull fish dock, having anchored to await the tide before entering. There was a gale blowing and the spring tide was ripping up the river. Her anchor started dragging and she went ashore on a mud bank, in the dark, within hailing distance of safety. Within minutes of grounding, the tide swung her broadside and she capsized. Out of her complement of eighteen, nine were rescued from the swirling waters by the tug *Triume* and *Cite de Paris*, a powered barge from Grimsby, but the other nine perished. *Lady Lillian* was purchased in 1939 as an anti-submarine trawler and renamed *Jade* (T.56). She was attacked and sunk by enemy

Photo. 66: *Alsey* as built, with semi-elliptical counter, single boat and no radars.

Photo. 67: *Alsey* post-war, showing her after conversion with cruiser stern, twin boats and radar masts. Her hull is grey with a white line, whilst the funnel is grey with a black top, with the company logo of a red bordered white cross on a blue flag..

aircraft in Grand Harbour, Malta on 22nd April 1942 and was subsequently broken up where she lay in 1943. *Beryl*, *Jade* and *Moonstone*, at 615 tons apiece, were the largest of Jutland's fleet to enter Admiralty service.

Lady Madelaine was purchased by the navy as an anti-submarine trawler in 1939, renamed *Moonstone* (T.90) and sold in 1947 to Iago as *Red Lancer* (LO.442). She went to the breakers in Glasson Dock in January 1964. *Lady Philomena* was requisitioned as an anti-submarine trawler, FY148, in August 1939 and returned to Jutland's in October 1945. *Lady Rosemary* was purchased as the anti-submarine trawler FY253 on 28th April 1940 but was loaned to the US from March 1942 until the October. She was laid up from September 1945, until sold to the Kingston Steam Trawling Co. Ltd, Hull as *Kingston Ruby* (H.477); she went for scrap on 20th March 1963, at Ghent. *Lady Shirley* was requisitioned on 27th May 1940, as an armed patrol trawler. In January 1941, she changed to an antri-submarine vessel and was posted to Gibraltar, where she worked with the trawlers *Lady Hogarth* and *Erin*. Their task when not hunting submarines was escorting tankers to port after they had been detailed off from their convoy. She was on a lone patrol south of the Canaries when, at around 10.00 hours on 4th October 1941, she surprised *U111* running on the surface. A surface action followed, with the enemy submarine being destroyed. After this, *Lady Shirley* was a marked ship and she was torpedoed and sunk by *U374*, off Gibraltar, on 11th December of that year; there were no survivors.

CRUISER STERNS

By 1929, Cook, Welton & Gemmell were experimenting with

cruiser sterns. Jutland Amalgamated Trawlers Ltd of Hull ordered *Lady Eleanor* (H.50), which was delivered in June as Yard No. 520 (140ft 2ins bp x 24ft 6ins x 13ft 2ins, 360g). She had a straight stem and cruiser stern. In March 1937, she was sold to the Loyal Steam Fishing Co. Ltd, Grimsby as *Equerry* (GY.375). She was requisitioned as the minesweeper FY668 in August 1939 and returned in April 1946. She later had a complete new raked bow section added, which increased her length to 169ft 8ins and put her weight up by around 10 tons. She worked for Loyal's until going for scrap in August 1958.

In 1933, Cochrane's broke new ground with their first cruiser-sterned trawler, Yard No. 1108 *Cayton Wyke* (H.440 – 150ft bp x 25ft 6ins x 14ft, 372g) for the West Dock Steam Fishing Co. Ltd, Hull and engined by C.D. Holmes. She was requisitioned in August 1939 as an anti-submarine trawler, Admiralty No. FY191, but was sunk by a torpedo from an E-boat off Dover on 8th July 1940.

The next ship (and their first cruiser stern conversion) was Yard No. 1109 *Alsey* (GY.460 – 150ft bp x 25ft 6ins x 15ft, 400g), built for the Rinovia Steam Fishing Co. Ltd, Grimsby and engined by Amos & Smith. She was sold by Rinovia in April 1935 to the Alsey Fishing Co, Ltd (a subsidiary) and was lengthened in 1939 (166ft 6ins bp/180ft oa) at a cost of £5,000. This refit gave her a new flared bow with a raked stem, a new wheelhouse and a boat deck aft with twin boats (**Photos 66 & 67**). She was hired as a mine layer from February 1940, until being released in 1946. In December 1960, she was renamed *Ross Archer* following the takeover of her owners by the Ross Group. She went to the breakers in Belgium in May 1963.

Photo. 68: *Bayflower.* Note the dhan buoys lashed to her rigging, close stowing anchors and netting fitted to the wheelhouse verandah rails, with ash shoots on the funnel. She has a black hull with a white line and whaleback, and wood grained superstructure. The funnel is buff with a black top and the house flag is white with a blue border and red St. Andrew's cross.

The first batch of Cochrane's cruiser sterned trawlers of note were:

Yard No. 1111 *Bayflower* (H.487)
Yard No. 1115 *Lord Lloyd* (H.508)
Yard No. 1116 *Rockflower* (H.511)
Yard No. 1117 *Lord Plender* (H.517)

They were all the same size (163ft x 25ft 6ins x 14ft 6ins, 396g), with the 'Flowers' built for the Yorkshire Steam Fishing Co. Ltd, Grimsby and the 'Lords' for the parent company, Pickering & Haldanes. The engines for the first pair came from Amos & Smith, while C.D. Holmes supplied the others. *Bayflower* (**Photo. 68 and Plan 56 a & b**) was typical of the quartet, with the photograph showing a handsome Arctic trawler running trials at full load trim, well designed to work the Distant Water grounds of Iceland, Bear Island and the White Sea. The hull was divided into five watertight compartments, with a watertight door fitted at the after end of the tunnel between the stokehold and spare fish room. She was a rivetted ship but her external cope irons were welded to the hull. Her deck sheathing was of British Borneo white wood, chosen for its light weight, straight grain and hard-wearing properties. The crew's fo'c'sle is further aft than normal and entered by a companionway to port under the whaleback. The main fish room had received much thought by the builders. It was fully insulated under the main deck and floor, as well as the fore and aft bulkheads. This insulation comprised of 6ins of Noel plastic cork, faced with hard setting white cement. Both these materials came from the Cold Storage & Heating Co. of Hull. Another innovation by this company was the fabrication of the wing bulkheads, which were much lighter than usual but with no compromise to their strength. All corners had a large radius which allowed for ease of cleaning, and ensured that there was no corner in which fish offal could be trapped. The 'Triton' model trawl winch supplied by C.D. Holmes

had barrels of 36ins diameter, and cylinders of 9ins diamter by 14ins stroke. The single barrel steam anchor windlass came from Gemmell & Frow, and the side and centre trawl bollards were by Amos & Smith.

Bayflower and *Rockflower* were fitted with the latest design of Gemmel & Frow steam-hydraulic steering gear, whereas *Lord Plender* and *Lord Lloyd* were equipped with the more common steam/hand operated steering gear, utilising rods and chains. The raised part of the casing aft is longer than normal and houses the galley/pantry between and the liver boiling house. These were the first vessels built by Cochrane's to have the liver boiling house fitted as part of the main casing. A door to starboard leads into a lobby which serves the engine room, the galley and the after cabin below. Her engines (13ins, 22.75ins, 37ins x 26ins stroke) developed 650ihp at 115rpm, giving 12 knots. Full electric lighting and power for the radio and navigation equipment is supplied from an 8.kw, 100 volt generator, driven by its own vertical enclosed steam engine. *Bayflower* ran ashore on 21st June 1937, at Noss Head, Wick. She was refloated and sold to Grimsby. In February 1939, she became GY.19, owned by the Standard Steam Fishing Co. Ltd, Grimsby (known locally as 'Butts') and, in May of that year, her name was changed to *Saon*. She was purchased by the Admiralty in September 1939 as the anti-submarine trawler FY159. In October 1939, she was patrolling the Dover Straits in company with *Cayton Wyke* and HMS *Puffin* when they attacked *U16* off the Goodwin Sands. They drove the U-boat onto the sands, where it was destroyed. A year later, *Saon* rescued the thirty survivors from the trawlers *Blackburn Rovers* and *Westella* after they had come to grief in a British minefield (official records differ with regard to the actual position of these two trawlers at the time of their loss, the former's position was given as 'North Sea' and the latter as 'Dunkirk'). She was sold in 1946 to the Hull Steam Fishing & Ice

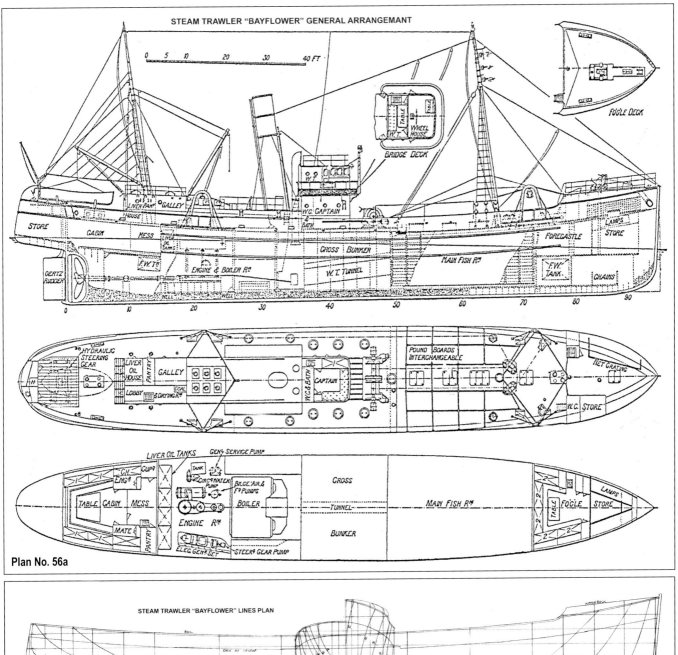

STEAM TRAWLER "BAYFLOWER" GENERAL ARRANGEMANT

Plan No. 56a

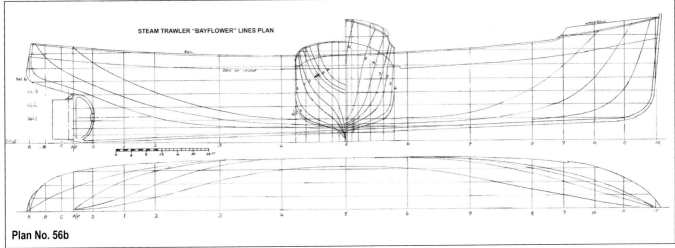

STEAM TRAWLER "BAYFLOWER" LINES PLAN

Plan No. 56b

Co. Ltd, who acted as brokers for many ex-admiralty trawlers. She returned to Grimsby and her former owners in November 1946, renumbered GY.139, and went to the breakers in August 1958. Her sister, *Rockflower* (H.115), was sold to the Great Grimsby & East Coast Steam Fishing Co. Ltd in February 1939, as GY.27. Two months later, she was renamed *Thuringa*, with the same

fishing number, but was requisitioned for anti-submarine duties in March 1940 as FY106. She was lost to an enemy mine in the North Sea on 28th April that same year.

The other two sisters, *Lord Lloyd* and *Lord Plender*, were both purchased for anti-submarine duties in August 1939 and given the Admiralty No's FY157 and FY181 respectively. Both were sold out

Photo .69: *Reptonian* in 1950, having changed little since her launch. Note her starboard ash shoot in the process of being lowered, the dhan buoys on her rigging and the two carley floats lashed to the mizzen shrouds; also visible are her pole compass, DF Loop and morse lamp. Eton's ships were all named after English public schools. ***Reptonian has a*** black hull with white band, wood grained superstructure and a black topped white funnel, with diamond and 'E' picked out in blue. Note also the additional fishing signal basket on the foretopmast stay.

Photo. 70: *Alexandrite*, seen leaving Aberdeen for the fishing grounds, was one of the larger steamers to operate out of the port. She is in North Star colours but still carries her 'H' registration and note the radar repeater on her mizzen mast.

of service in 1946, being bought by Lord Line of Hull (formerly Pickering & Haldane's, their original owners) and renumbered H.263, and H.191. In 1958, they were sold to Wyre Trawlers Ltd of Fleetwood, *Lord Lloyd* as FD.52 and *Lord Plender* as FD.59. They worked from the Lancashire port until going to the breakers in the 1960s; *Lord Plender* in December 1962 to Passage West and her sister to Troon the following September, making her the very last coal burner to work out of Fleetwood.

In 1933, Hellyer Brothers ordered *Basque* (H.521), Yard No. 581 – 154ft 6ins bp x 25ft 6ins x 13ft 9ins, 409g) from Cook, Welton & Gemmell. In 1939, she was renamed *Istria* and was subsequently purchased as an anti-submarine trawler, FY150, and sold out of service in 1946. She was renamed *St. Arcadius* and, in 1947, was sold to the Eton Fishing Co. Ltd as *Reptonian* (H.363 – **Photo. 69**). The photograph shows her single wooden lifeboat, with the mizzen boom rigged for handling. Carley floats are lashed to the mizzen shrouds, an additional life saving feature, which was an interim measure until the inflatable raft became universally available. Costing around £40,000 when new, she still looked the typical 1930s Distant Water trawler, with cruiser stern and Oertz rudder. Eton's sold her on 26th October 1950 to Marr's for £30,000 as FD.171. They in turn sold her to the Dinas Steam Trawling Co. Ltd, Fleetwood, for £39,625 on 24th May 1951 (a pretty shrewd investment for Marr's). She went for scrapping on 16th January 1959 at Preston, coal-fired to the end

A Hull trawler that came to Aberdeen in 1951 was *Alexandrite* (H.7 – 131ft bp x 24ft 6ins x 13ft, 313g,113n), built in 1934 by Cook, Welton & Gemmell for the Kingston Steam Trawling Co. Ltd, Hull; she was cruiser sterned and smaller than *Reptonian*. She was requisitioned in September 1939 as minesweeper FY560 and returned in November 1945. In 1949, she was sold to Marr's for their Fleetwood operations, for £30,250 but they sold her to the North Star Steam Fishing Co. Ltd, Aberdeen, for £29,000 in December 1951. Her funnel was replaced in November 1955 after her conversion to oil fuel but she always retained her Hull number. and she was scrapped at Grangemouth on 2nd of November 1963 (**Photo. 70**).

FIRST EXHAUST TURBINE

In 1934, the Kingston Steam Trawling Co. Ltd ordered *Kingston Cornelian* (H.75 – 169ft bp x 16ft 6ins x 15ft 3ins, 450g, 174n, 112nhp) from Cook, Welton & Gemmell, Yard No. 593. She was a break with tradition for, instead of the usual engines, she was fitted with a set of compound engines and a Bauer-Wach exhaust turbine supplied by C.D. Holmes, and was among the largest trawlers out of Hull at the time of building. She was constructed with a by now familiar cruiser stern, Oertz streamlined rudder and steam/hand steering gear. Her Triton-type 1,200 fathom trawl winch and her 1,500 gallon liver oil storage tanks were supplied by C. D. Holmes, whereas her steering gear and windlass came from Gemmell & Frow.

The propelling machinery comprised a high-pressure compound engine exhausting into a low-pressure turbine, transmitting its power to the main shaft through a hydraulic coupling and gearing. The oil-operated, servo-motor for change over purposes was worked by a small lever at the engine control platform. The compound engine and also the boiler, were made and installed by Charles D. Holmes, whilst the low-pressure turbine was constructed by Swan

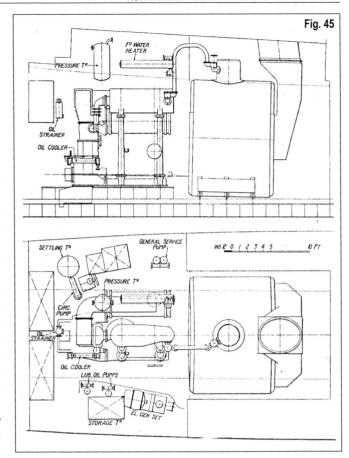

Fig. 45

Hunter & Wigham Richardson Ltd, at their Neptune Works, Walker-on-Tyne. The diameters of the cylinders were 13.5ins, and 27ins, and the stroke 27ins. An Edwards type air pump and feed and bilge pumps were driven by levers off the high-pressure engine, while the separate centrifugal circulating water pump of Holmes make was installed for the condenser, which was of the Wier regenerative type and of ample size, giving a vacuum of 29ins under full power. The boiler was of the three furnace, cylindrical type, 14ft 6ins inside diameter by 10ft 8ins long, with a working pressure of 215psi. On trial, it was found that the compound engine, which was of the balanced type, was manoeuvred with the greatest of ease, the compound engine being used alone when going astern. The total ihp was 750 but the designed speed of 11.75 knots was obtained during trials with an ihp of 630, the turbine developing about 27% of the total power employed. These trials were carried out on a fully loaded displacement. Included in the auxiliaries were two Weir vertical simplex steam pumps, located on the Starboard side of the engine room, each being capable of dealing with the lubrication requirements at full power, so that one served as a stand-by. An 8kw dynamo for lighting was supplied and fitted by Wm Broady & Son, Hull. A Vickers Diamond-type feed water heater, with automatic change-over valves and a Michell-type thrust block was also embodied in the turbine unit (**Fig. 45**).

She had a crew of twenty, with fo'c'sle berths for fourteen. The crew all took their meals in a mess room aft, which was far more convenient than taking food to the forward crew space. Her wireless equipment was supplied by the Marconi Company, who also furnished the echo-meter. She was purchased in August 1939, as an anti-submarine trawler, FY121, but sank on 5th January 1940 off Gibraltar, after a collision.

Kingston Cornelian was the lead ship for a class of five, the others being: *Kingston Cairngorm* (H.175); *Kingston Ceylonite* (H.173); *Kingston Chrysoberyl* (H.177); and *Kingston Crysolite* (H.169). In 1936, Cook, Welton & Gemmell built a further four Arctic trawlers for Kingston's, all fitted with coupled Bauer Wach exhaust turbines. They were: *Kingston Cyanite* (H.237); *Kingston Coral* (H.241); *Kingston Cameo* (H.272); and *Kingston Crystal* (H.281 – all 160ft 5ins x 26ins 6ins x 15ft 3ins, 432g – for details see **Appendix 4**).

FITTING OF SUPERHEATERS

Superheated steam was tried prior to the First World War but did not live up to expectations, probably because no modifications were made to accept the 'Schmitt' type superheaters in the Admiralty's experiments, whilst it was some years before suitable lubricants were developed. By the early 1930s, the superheater was again being looked at as a means of reducing running costs for larger Distant Water vessels. The exhaust turbine had been a great success but even the first British vessels so fitted were running on wet or saturated steam, while their German counterparts were using dry superheated steam for greater efficiency. These new trials with superheaters did not show a great improvement on earlier pre-First World War ships. This was due to poor specifications given to the engine builders, with resultant power deficiencies causing an unacceptable loss of three to four rpm. One of the problems originated from the positioning of the pressure type feed water filter, underneath the platform between the engine and boiler. This made routine maintenance very difficult especially in bad weather, so it would choke up and allow oil to pass into the boiler. Another factor in the power loss was traced to salt choked 'U' bends in the superheaters themselves, caused by using sea water without fitting an evaporator. The nature of a steam trawler's work demands that the boilers are worked to their maximum capacity and with a seawater feed, and the vessel pitching and rolling heavily, priming could occur, even with large steam domes fitted to the boilers.

The steam leaving the surface of the water in a boiler carries with it a certain amount of water in droplets. If this becomes excessive, the boiler is then said to be priming. The cause of priming may be either too high a level of water in the boiler or that it contains an undue amount of impurities. If these cause foaming, large quantities of water will pass over in the steam. Under these conditions, it is very difficult to maintain the correct level of water in the boiler and if a superheater is fitted, the temperature of the superheated steam will drop. Priming may cause damage to the machinery, reciprocating engines being particularly liable to suffer if the steam entering the cylinders contains an undue quantity of water. Even if no damage is done, priming may cause a reciprocating pump to stop. The greater the quantity of steam being generated in a boiler, the more likely it is to prime. Therefore, in the event of priming, the rate at which fuel is being burned should be reduced, particular attention paid to the water level in the boiler and every available means employed to drain water from the steam before it reaches the engines. (Based on *B.R.77 Machinery Handbook*, Admiralty, 1941).

Three main advantages in using superheaters immediately became apparent after the machinery installations had been improved:

1. An increase in the volume of steam to each pound of water evaporated, according to the degree of superheat applied. With 200 degrees, the superheated steam volume increases by some 35%.

2. Less loss due to condensation.

3. A rise in the operating temperature of the engine. This results in an increase of thermal efficiency. Also, steam superheated to 200 degrees Fahrenheit has less weight to do the work, with the result that the boiler has to evaporate less water.

The temperature at the base of a steam trawler's funne was around 700 degrees Fahrenheit. This accounts for the high degree of superheat obtained with a simple straightforward design of superheater, such as the smoke tube type. This design offered an efficient, relatively maintenance free method of improving the performance of the Scotch Marine Boiler. The main four types of superheater available were:

1. The uptake type
2. The combustion chamber type
3. The smoke tube type (mentioned above)
4. The smoke tube type with the ends of the elements projecting into the combustion chamber

There was another advantage to using superheated steam, which was when 'blowing down' or clearing the smokebox tubes of soot. The amount of soot deposited in the tubes depended on the quality of coal supplied and with the poorer grades naturally came the higher build up of soot. This could be blown out of the tubes any time during the trip, either by dry steam pressure or, on the earlier superheater installations, by using a steam lance. On a non-superheated vessel running only on wet steam, this filthy task had to be done manually by the firemen. First the trawler would lay to and the fires damped down. The firemen would then attack each of the three smokeboxes in turn, with what was basically a flue brush and scraper, while balancing on a joiners trestle. The soot would then be hauled up on deck in ash buckets and dumped overboard. When he was satisfied with the result, the fires would be built up again and steam raised as soon as possible. Time was of the essence when a trawler was at sea. Near Water ships often had their boiler tubes cleaned out between trips by a shore gang. In order to take full advantage of dry steam, the complete machinery installation often required some degree of modification. Feedwater heaters had to supply water at a constant high temperature to the boiler. The condensers had to carefully managed to give as high a vacuum as practical and all ancillary pipe work required lagging, almost up to the standard of that found aboard a high class liner. Compared to the earlier 'Mersey' Class of trawler that burned 9 to 10 tons of coal per day to give an average speed of 10 knots, these much larger superheated ships consumed about 8.75 tons per day, for a speed of 12 knots.

FORCED DRAUGHT FIRING

Although this method of assisted firing was only necessary in the later oil-fired ships, it was used to advantage on some of the larger coal burners. The most common was the Wallsend Howden System, more usually referred to as simply the Howden System. As the name implies, this was a method of inducing air into the combustion chamber, thereby increasing the thermal efficiency of the fuel, very important when poor quality coal was burned. The engineers and firemen had naturally to receive training on the operation of the plant. These men were not certificated by the BoT,

Photo. 71: _Cape Barfleur_. She carries a single boat on a full width boat deck, ash shoots on the funnel and a pole compass. She is in Hudson's colours of black hull with a white band and the funnel is black with a broad white band. Note the angled tube for the steering chain below her verandah.

nor in the early days were the majority of them skilled mechanics, so usually, apart from running repairs, most adjustments and servicing was hurriedly done by the shore staff during the vessel's short turn-round period. Great skill and dedication were required to maintain and operate steam trawler machinery when at sea in all weathers. Typical examination questions for trawler engineers would be:

QUESTION: What is the use of a Feed Pipe Escape Valve and where is it fitted?

ANSWER: The Feed Escape Valve is generally fixed between the suction and discharge valve. It acts as a Safety Valve in the case of the Discharge Valve Seat lifting and in the event of the Feed Check Valve being shut when starting the engines. If no Escape Valve fitted, the Check Valve is unadjustable and of course there is only one boiler.

QUESTION: If the HP Connecting Rod broke or the Crank Pin or Web broke, what would you do?

ANSWER: Take away broken parts of Connecting Rod, draw Slide Valve and work with reduced pressure, as the steam will go direct into IP. casing. If Crank Pin or Web, clear away broken parts, also Connecting Rod, take out Slide Valve, and work with IP and LP Engines with reduced pressure.

REFRIGERATED FISH ROOM AND SPEED RECORD

In August 1934, Cochrane's completed Yard No. 1123 **Lord**

Hailsham (H.82 – 155ft x 26ft x 15ft, 445g, 179.3n, 99nhp) for Pickering & Haldane's Steam Trawling Co. Ltd. She was a Distant Water ship, engined by Amos & Smith. She had a cruiser stern with semi-balanced rudder and Gemmell & Frow hydraulic steering gear. Her hull was both rivetted and welded, with the strake of plating above the waterline and the hull beadings electrically welded. Welding was specified on the shell plating to help eliminate shock damage to the plates and seams caused by gear slamming into the side, when working in heavy weather. Slight improvements in crew accommodation were incorporated, with single cabins aft for the officers and a bathroom for all the crew to use. The wireless equipment comprised a dual purpose Marconi 60 Watt telephony/telegraphy set and a DF set. Henry Hughes supplied the echometer (which appears to have been the first installation of its kind on a steam trawler) and a Walkers log was also fitted. However, the main advance was in the fish room, which was fitted with a refrigeration plant. Its function was to keep the temperature of the main hold just above freezing point, which would relieve the ice of this duty, allowing it to solely preserve the catch. The after fish room being in close proximity to the bunkers could be kept at 34 degrees Fahrenheit, instead of the 42 to 44 degrees possible with ice alone. The plant was a 3hp Hallmark type. The methyl chloride coolant passed through grids of 1,500ft of 1.5ins bore steel tubing placed in the sides,

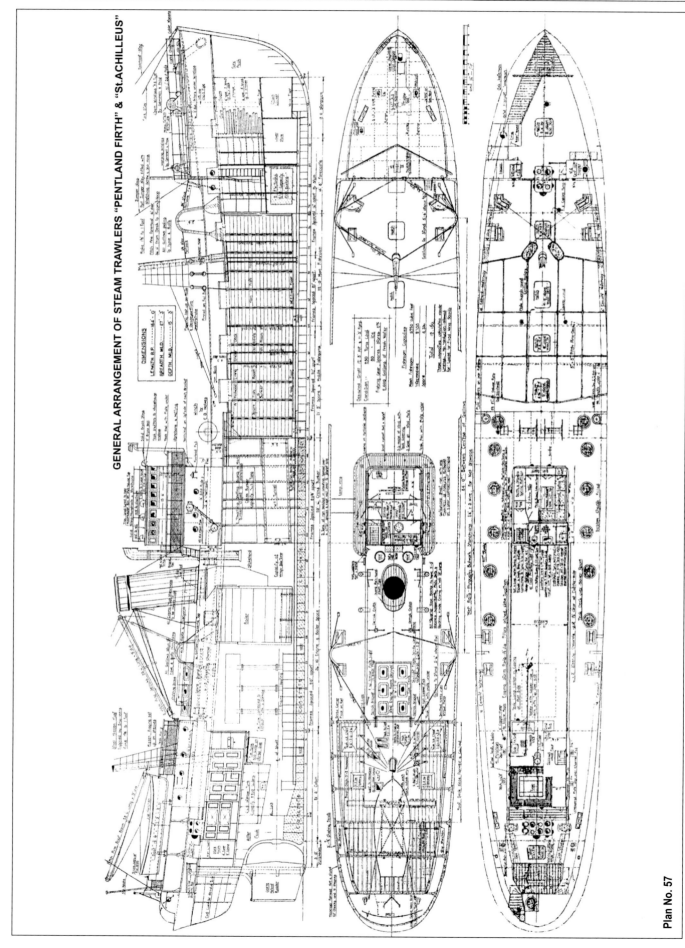

GENERAL ARRANGEMENT OF STEAM TRAWLERS "PENTLAND FIRTH" & "St.ACHILLEUS"

Plan No. 57

forward and aft bulkheads, and below the deck. The temperature was thermostatically controlled and an extraction fan was fitted to remove the toxic gas in the event of a coolant pipe leaking. This set up was powered by a dedicated generator fitted in the engine room. *Lord Hailsham* was requisitioned as an anti-submarine trawler in August 1939, FY109, and was lost in the English Channel on 27th February 1943, to an E-boat torpedo.

Until 1934, the normal speed for a trawler was around 10.5 knots, with an occasional top speed of 11.5 knots. For quite some time, owners had been demanding a 12-knot trawler, with speed the main requisite for success, allowing the vessel to spend longer on the grounds. In November of that year, Cochrane's gave the industry what they wanted. *Cape Barfleur* (H.105 – 160ft x 25ft 6ins x 15ft, 457g, 800ihp), Yard No. 1127, was engined by C.D. Holmes. She was built for Hudson Brothers (Trawlers) Ltd, Hull and broke the 12 knot barrier. On light trials, she clocked up 12.97 knots, with 12.154 knots loaded and was hailed as another milestone in trawler design (**Photo. 71**). Her hull model had been extensively tested at the National Physical Laboratory ship tank at Teddington.

Cape Barfleur had a cruiser stern and the flared bows were designed to prevent her digging her nose in and shipping water. This in turn would add weight, which would slow her down even further. Her liver boiling plant, supplied by the engine builders, was housed in the poop house, with storage tanks below for 8 tons of oil. The waste (or 'foots') was stored separately and could be discharged ashore for further extraction (**Plan 57**). The deck crew were housed in the fo'c'sle but they took their meals in a mess room fitted in the casing ahead of the galley. Two hip baths were also provided in an adjacent compartment. The skipper's accommodation below the wheelhouse was exceptionally well fitted out with mahogany panelling and chrome plated fittings. He had a personal wireless set and the cabin was heated by an electric fire. His bathroom had a marble bath with full hot and cold water. The after crew space had berths for six men, with separate cabins for the mate and Chief Engineer. Another improvement was that the two trimmers shared their own cabin, which allowed them better access to their workplace. Navigational equipment included a 300 watt Marconi radio telephony /telegraphy set and direction finding (DF) equipment. In addition, she had echo sounding gear and a Trident electric log, complete with a repeater in the wheelhouse. Full electric lighting was fitted throughout.

By this time, most Distant Water ships were fitted with two lifeboats but the photograph shows only a single boat carried on the boat deck aft. It is, however, supplemented by Carley floats lashed either side to the mizzen shrouds. She was commanded on her maiden trip by crack skipper J. Myers who, in *Cape Trafalgar*, made a record number of twenty Icelandic trips in twelve months. *Cape Barfleur* was purchased by the Admiralty in 1939 and renamed *Amber* (T28), becoming an anti-submarine trawler of the 'Gem' Class. She was sold out of service in 1946 and renamed *Etonian* (H.333), owned by the Eton Fishing Co. Ltd, Hull. In 1950, she became Boyd's *Arctic Crusader* (H.333) but reverted to *Etonian* in 1952. In 1955, she was renamed *Glenella* (H.333) when purchased by Marr & Sons, Fleetwood for the sum of £27,250 (cost £20,000 when new). She went for scrap on 13th May 1957, after being bought by the British Iron & Steel Corporation (Salvage) Ltd.

Cook, Welton & Gemmell were running neck and neck with Cochrane's in the development of the 12-knot trawler. In late 1934, they built *Pentland Firth* (H.123 – 164ft x 27ft 3ins x 15ft 3ins, 485g, 154nhp) for the Firth Steam Trawling Co. and *St. Achilleus* (H.127) for Thomas Hamling & Co., Yard No's 577 and 595 (**Plan 56**). They were powerful Distant Water sister ships, both engined by C.D. Holmes. Designed with cruiser sterns, Oertz rudders, and flared bows, they bunkered 330 tons of coal and 90 tons of ice. On fully loaded trials, *Pentland Firth* attained 12.25 knots over the measured mile, achieved on a design draft of 17ft 3ins aft and 11ft 3ins forward, with 250 tons of coal, 80 tons of ice, 2,000 gallons of fresh water, and a full inventory of fishing gear and stores on board. Their Triton trawl winches were supplied by the engine builders, each having a capacity of 1,200 fathoms per barrel, and were fitted with automatic spooling gear for guiding the warps onto the drums. Their steering gear was both hand and steam powered, and was furnished by Donkin's of Newcastle, with the steering engines fitted in a sealed compartment abaft the wheelhouse. The steering chains ran in a trough under the alleyway floor on either side, thence over an external roller fairlead, before passing through a set of down pipes to the deck. At the after end of the bridge is the radio room, with an athwartship berth for the operator and a small table for his equipment. Cod liver oil boilers were fitted as standard and full electric lighting was provided by twin generating sets, each capable of supplying all the vessel's needs. The crew ate in a mess room on the main deck, aft of the galley and the crew's bathroom in the steering flat had both a hot and cold water supply. An interesting feature of these ships was the single lifeboat, mounted on chocks fitted with wheels that ran in athwartship tracks, which allegedly permitted fast launching of the boat over either quarter.

Pentland Firth was requisitioned in August 1939 as an anti-submarine trawler, Admiralty No. FY108. She was loaned to the US and was lost by collision on 19th September 1942. Sadly, her sister had an even shorter life. Requisitioned as an anti-submarine trawler, Admiralty No. FY152, in August 1939, she was lost by a mine on 31st May 1940, while taking part in the evacuation from Dunkirk.

In addition to new building, older trawlers were modernised so as to remain competitive. One such vessel was the Hull trawler *Leonidas* (H.267 – 140ft x 24ft 6ins x 13ft 5ins), built by Cook, Welton & Gemmell in July 1930 as Yard No. 548, for Christensen & Co. Ltd, Hull. She was a standard Middle/Distant Water ship, with straight stem, short whaleback fo'c'sle and counter stern. In 1935, she was slipped for six weeks at Smith's Dock. They cut away her stem and stern, replacing them with a raked flared bow, complete with long flat topped fo'c'sle head, and cruiser stern with a double plate semi-balanced rudder. Her length increased to 151ft 6ins and her speed went up by 1.5knots. She was sold to Hudsons in 1938 and renamed *Cape Barracouta*. Requisitioned in August 1939, originally as an armed patrol vessel but later as a minesweeper, she was returned in January 1946. In May 1947, she went to Trawlers Grimsby Ltd as *Cape Barracloutha* (GY.479) but, a year later, she went to Heward Trawlers Ltd, Fleetwood, becoming their *New Prince* (LO.471); she fished out of this port until going for scrap in 1955.

Gradually, the humble steam trawler was coming of age, with larger, more powerful and comfortable vessels joining the fleets.

Photo. 72: *Hendren*. Note the pole compass, DF loop, ash shoots and single lifeboat, whilst the angled pipes carrying the steering chains from the wheelhouse can be seen below the verandah. She is in Crampin's colours of black hull with white band and red boot topping, and has a black-topped yellow funnel, separated by a blue band bearing a yellow 'C'. The ball on the forestay denotes that she is at anchor.

Photo. 73: *King Sol*, seen lying on a buoy on 'short slip' waiting to enter Grimsby. She is in in Rinovia's light grey colour scheme, with wood grained superstructure and houseflag on the funnel. Note the binnacle on the wheelhouse top (rather than the normal pole compass). Her Red Ensign denotes that she has returned from the fishing grounds. The port registration letters contradict the rules, as they are not white on black.

Hull alone, from February 1933 until November 1934, took delivery of no less than forty new ships, with the total value of approximately £1,000,000. They comprised the following: Kingston's – eight ships; Hellyer's – six; Pickering & Haldane – five; Yorkshire Steam Fishing Co. Ltd – four; Hudson's – four; Jutland Amalgamated – three; Hamlings – three; Odssens – three; Smith's – one; Red Cross Fleet – one; and Henriksen's – one.

During the same period, Grimsby took delivery of twenty-three large, 160ft, Distant Water ships: Atlas – two; Consols – two; Crampins – two; Bunch – one; Perihelion – four; Gresham – one; Shire's – eight; and Rinovia – three. These large ships were built to take advantage of the new larger No. 3 Fish Dock extension opened in 1934. The smallest of this group was *Hampshire* (GY.85 – 160ft x 26ft 7ins x 12ft 3ins, 425g, 160n). She was built by Smith's Dock in 1934 (although possibly ordered under another name, as the builder's list shows no ship of this name that year) and owned by the Hampshire Fishing Co. Ltd, Grimsby (Shire's). She was purchased as an anti-submarine trawler in September 1939, as FY173. She was sold to the French navy in November 1939, as *La Toulonnaise*, and broken up January 1960.

Slightly larger was *Hendren* (GY.128 – 161ft x 26ft 6ins x 14ft 2ins, 441.25g, 133nhp), built by Cochranes in 1935 for

the Perihelion Steam Fishing Co. Ltd (Crampin's), as Yard No. 1131, and engined by Amos & Smith. She was a rivetted ship, with the 'E' strake immediately above the waterline electrically welded. Her hull was quite deep for her length which would have made her quite tender when light-ship. She looked a business-like Distant Water vessel, with her straight stem and cruiser stern. Two close-stowing anchors were carried but again only one boat. Her masts and funnel are well raked, with ash shoots fitted alongside the funnel. She was fitted with the full navigational suite for the time, with DF loop and Morse signalling lamp on the wheelhouse top (**Photo. 72**). She ran under Crampin's colours for four years, until going to Hull in May 1939 as *Stella Pegasi* (H.90), owned by Charleston-Smith Trawlers Ltd, Hull. She was requisitioned in September 1939 as an anti-submarine trawler, FY155, and was returned in April 1945. In April 1947, she became *Arctic Crusader* (H.90), of Boyd Line. In September that year, she was sold to Trawlers Grimsby Ltd and renamed *Mountbatten* (GY.477). In August 1949, after running aground at Rodoysfjord, she was sold to Norwegian owners who kept her British name. They in turn sold her in 1951 to Germany but she sank in the Elbe estuary whilst under tow to Hamburg.

In 1936, the Rinovia Steam Fishing Co. Ltd (an Icelandic owned firm formed in the late 1920s, whose ships all had grey hulls with the Icelandic flag on their funnels) took delivery of two new ships from Cochranes. They were *Stafnes* (GY.297 – 160ft x 26ft 6ins x 15ft, 454g), Yard No. 1152, and the slightly larger *King Sol* (GY.338 – 163ft 5ins x 27ft 6ins x 15ft, 486g, 129nhp), Yard No. 1168, with engines supplied by Amos Smith. *Stafnes* was requisitioned in September 1939, as FY192, an anti-submarine trawler, returning to Rinovia in 1945 as GY.172. In March 1947, she was sold to the Kopanes Steam Fishing Co. Ltd, Grimsby (a subsidiary). In December 1960, she was renamed *Ross Searcher* after the company were taken over by the Ross Group and went to the Belgian breakers in May 1963. *King Sol* cost Rinovia £23,600 (**Photo. 73**). She was requisitioned as FY235, an anti-submarine trawler, and returned to Rinovia in December 1945. One of her wartime duties was to escort the UK section of the ill-fated Russian convoy PQ17 from Scotland to a rendezvous with the main convoy off Iceland. After her return to commercial fishing, she worked for the same owners until going for scrap on 4th February 1961 at Bruges.

Chapter 13: GERMAN-BUILT 'NORTHERNS' AND BRITISH EXPORTS

In 1936, MacFisheries Ltd of Fleetwood, part of the massive Unilever conglomerate, placed an order for fifteen steam trawlers with Germany. The builders were Deutsche Schiff und Maschinenbau, A.G. Werk, Seebeck, Wesermunde, Bremenhaven. Macfisheries were shrewd businessmen and with the German economy almost on its knees from rampant inflation, a deal was struck for the construction of the new ships. Part of the agreement was that these ships would form a segment of Germany's First World War reparation payments, thus utilising some of these frozen credits. The agreement was that they would deliver two ships per month. In October 1937, the firm of Northern Trawlers Ltd was formed, as a subsidiary of Associated Fisheries Ltd, Grimsby, to take over these trawlers that had been operating out of Fleetwood and Hull. They were as follows (for more details see **Appendix 4**): *Northern Chief* (LO.165), *Northern Dawn* (LO.136), *Northern Duke* (LO.169), *Northern Foam* (LO.153), *Northern Gem* (LO.109), *Northern Gift* (LO.166), *Northern Isles* (LO.172), *Northern Pride* (LO.104 – **Photo. 74**), *Northern Princess* (LO.170), *Northern Reward* (LO.168), *Northern Rover* (LO.164), *Northern Sky* (LO.162), *Northern Spray* (LO.140), *Northern Sun* (LO.161) and *Northern Wave* (LO.120).

These were very rakish, powerful, triple-deck ships, well in advance of their time. A key consultant during their design was Commander Lawford, the forward-thinking owner of Iago Steam Trawling Co. Ltd. They were very Teutonic looking vessels, with spoon bows, flush main decks and heavy cruiser sterns (**Plan 58 a & b**). They were a radical change from the traditional British trawler but they proved to be most efficient and were excellent sea-ships (187ft x 28ft x 16ft), drawing 13ft forward and 16ft 6ins aft on a displacement of 1,147tons. This included 300 tons of coal, 90 tons

of fresh water and 90 tons of ice. The main engine had a double reduction geared Bauer-Wach exhaust turbine, with superheated steam supplied at 220psi, developing 484ihp without the turbine and up to 1,000ihp with it coupled up. A propeller of 11ft 5ins diameter, with a pitch of 10ft 1ins and running at 124rpm, gave a fully loaded trials speed of 13 knots, on a coal consumption of around 7 tons per 24 hours. When on passage to and from the Distant Water grounds, most of the ships achieved between 13 and 14 knots but when on war service, *Northern Spray* made 17 knots pursuing a U-boat. After the war, whilst fishing, she raced *Thomas Tompion*, which had a twenty minute start placing her fully four miles ahead. *Northern Spray* beat the newer ship, however, whose skipper Tess Johnson remarked that "*a rusty tin can had wiped out his 20 minute advantage*" and he ordered a main engine overhaul before putting back to sea. On another occasion, *Northern Gem* clocked up 16 knots when running into Honingsvaag from Bear Island with an injured seaman (**Photo. 75**).

Electricity was provided by a steam generator for everyday use and a stand-by diesel generator for use in port or in an emergency. Ancillary equipment included a calorifier for de-icing the fishing gear and an evaporator with a brine pre-heater for economical feed water replacement. Four liver oil boilers were fitted in a dedicated house right aft, with storage tanks below. No ash shoots appear on the plans or photographs, so presumably they were fitted with ash ejectors. One major improvement in these vessels was in the tunnel used to move the coal from the after fish room to the stokehold. In British trawlers this was a very cramped space but aboard the German ships this tunnel was almost seven feet high and had a set of rails on which ran a wheeled coal truck. The trimmers must have found this a lot easier than hauling the coal through in baskets.

Photo. 74: *Northern Pride* on builders trials in Iago Steam Trawling Co. Ltd's colour scheme of white hull and black funnel with red band. Note the swastika flag at the gaff, her spoon bow, recessed anchor pockets and triple decked superstructure, topped off with a wooden dodger round her binnacle on the wheelhouse top. No boat decks were fitted to this class, boats being suspended in patent davits. Note the port registration as per the rules of white on black.

Photo. 75: *Northern Gem* in later 'Northern' colours of black hull with white band, brown casing with white wheelhouse and a black-topped grey funnel separated by a white band. Their port registration was changed to Grimsby post war. The mizzen mast has been replaced with a steel pole mast on the funnel.

Crew accommodation was provided for some twenty-eight hands, including eighteen deckhands. These were housed in both the fo'c'sle and in a large cabin on the upper deck, at the forward end of the casing (the skipper's cabin/chartroom on UK ships). This was fitted out for twelve hands and contained a WC, and ample locker and wardrobe space. It was well lit by both electricity and natural daylight, with ventilation by way of passenger ship-type, vent trunks.

On the bridge deck above was the captain's cabin and dayroom, with a large toilet compartment and a fully fitted wireless cabin. The latter had the latest radio equipment installed, at an estimated cost of some £2,000. At the rear of this deck was the steam steering gear house. From here, rods and chains led along the casing top on a level with the raised galley casing and terminated at the tiller head on the deckhouse top, in front of the liver boiling house. This was another first for a British owned trawler, as usually these rods and chains ran along the casing side at deck level. The liver boilers were of a different design to the British egg timer shape, being large copper boilers with drain taps at fixed intervals on their faces to drain off the oil. In practice, these proved less efficient than the UK boilers, as it was impossible to separate all the oil from the foots (or offal), resulting in a reduction of the 'liver money' paid to the crew. The wheelhouse had a proper chart room attached. No pole compass was carried, a standard compass in a binnacle being fitted on the wheelhouse roof ahead of the DF loop aerial. Around the front was a solid bulwark with a wind deflector all round. A messroom was built in at the after end of the casing,

which could be reached by all the crew in heavy weather via the engine room. This did away with the dangers of negotiating the often flooded open deck during the long hours of darkness common to the northern latitudes. Another improvement was in the size of the net store. It was large enough to lay out a full trawl net and could be accessed during heavy weather by way of a scuttle in the fo'c'sle, thus keeping the foredeck hatches watertight. At the after end of the casing could also be found the large galley, washroom and provision store. The after accommodation below had separate cabins for the mate, first and second engineers, and the cook. The after cabin was further fitted out for four men. The two lifeboats were carried whale catcher fashion in Schatt davits. When new, all these ships sported white hulls but some were soon repainted black. *Northern Foam* (LO.153) had an all black hull and *Northern Gift* (LO.166) had a white spirketting plate forward, whilst her liver house aft was also white; her foremast had very little rake as compared with her sisters.

These very large Distant Water trawlers proved impracticable for Fleetwood operations and, by 1937, they had transferred to Grimsby, under the Northern Trawlers banner. Snapped up by the Navy at the outbreak of war, as armed trawlers, they excelled themselves as part of the Northern Patrol, working in the very waters for which they had been so ably designed and constructed. This work was one of the toughest, most wearisome and boring duties to befall 'Harry Tate's Navy' (nicknamed after that music hall star's act as a well-meaning amateur). They patrolled the Denmark Strait, one of the grimmest stretches of water in the northern hemisphere. The men were ill-

Plan No. 58a: Original coal fired ships.

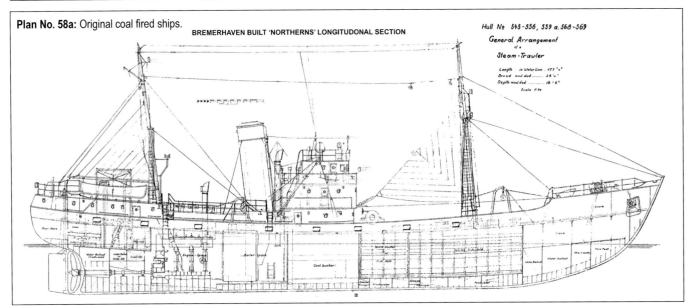

BREMERHAVEN BUILT 'NORTHERNS' LONGITUDONAL SECTION

Hull No 545-556, 559 a. 568-569

General Arrangement
of a
Steam-Trawler

Length in Water Line ... 177'0"
Bread mot ded .... 28 ½"
Depth moulded .... 16'6"
Scale 1:96

equipped for operating in these waters, as the Navy had no cold weather clothing available for crews of minor war vessels. Until such times as the ships were adopted by groups of townswomen, who knitted jerseys, balaclavas and stockings for them, the crews spent weeks on end enduring the misery of the weather. This was unlike fishing, where they knew that after two weeks 'down North' on the grounds, they would be steaming homewards for two days respite. On the Northern Patrol, they were lucky to see one night ashore per month at their Orkney base.

They were not restricted to this duty and they served with distinction all over the globe from 1939 until 1945. *Northern Pride* (FY105 – **Photo. 76**) took part in the Namsos evacuation as part of the 11th Anti-Submarine Striking Force, whilst the crew of her sister, *Northern Gem* (FY194), had their own adventure at Narvik. The trawler observed an enemy plane crash landing in the snow on the edge of the fjord. An armed party went ashore, only to be captured by the enemy. The plane, unknown to the trawler's crew, was a troop carrier. Not only were they taken prisoner but they were forced to strip down to their underclothes in the freezing conditions, before being marched away. Luckily, their plight was spotted by another trawler, which scattered the Germans with a couple of well placed salvos, and allowed the shivering sailors to escape and shelter in a small hut. Shortly afterwards, they were rescued and returned to their vessel. The first of the class to be lost was *Northern Rover*, sunk off Northern Scotland in October 1939.

Five of the ships were loaned to the United States for anti-submarine duties on America's east coast, in 1942: *Northern Chief, Northern Dawn, Northern Duke, Northern Princess* and *Northern Reward*. Of the quintet, *Northern Princess* failed to return home after the war, as she was torpedoed by *U94* on 7th March 1942 in the western Atlantic (although the official report states '*by unknown causes*'). Prior to her departure for the US, *Northern Dawn* worked out of Londonderry as part of the 45th Escort Group. In the autumn of 1941, she was fitted with RDF (Radar) at Harland & Wolff's yard in Belfast and I believe that she was the first armed trawler to be fitted with this type of radar set up. The scanner was fitted atop a tall lattice structure built over the engine room skylight, which brought the lantern containing the Type-271 scanner above the top of the funnel. Another

distinguishing feature was her crow's nest on the foremast above her signal yard, whereas all her sisters carried the yard above the crow's nest. The only other two ships of the class lost in World War Two were *Northern Rover*, sunk by *U-59* somewhere between Iceland and Faeroe in November 1939, and *Northern Isles*, which went ashore near Durban on 19th January 1945

The 'Northerns' were heavily armed vessels, carrying a variety of weapons, and depth charge arrangements. Defensive armament was usually a 4ins quick firing Mk IV gun on a Mk IX mounting, on a bandstand forward, Oerlikons or Lewis guns on the bridge wings and twin Vickers 0.5in guns on a Mark IV mounting aft on the casing top. Were it not for their spoon bows, they could have easily been mistaken for the naval-built trawlers. Their mizzen masts were removed and replaced with an aerial mast on the front of the funnel, with an ensign gaff on the aft side. All were fitted with Asdic, lifeboats were replaced with an Admiralty 27ft whaler to port and a 16ft transom sterned, trawler-type boat to starboard. Carley floats with their skids were attached to each side of the messroom casing aft. It appears that in all cases their trawl winches were removed. After the war, the remaining twelve ships returned to Grimsby and, in 1947, three of the class were sold to Iceland: *Northern Chief* (GY.445), renamed *Gylfi*, owned by Gylfi H/f, Vatneyri, Iceland. She was sold in 1950 to German owners Ludwig Janssen and renamed *Island* and went to the Hamburg breakers W. Ritscher on 15th July 1957; *Northern Gift* (LO.166), renamed *Kari*, owned by Alliace, H/f, Iceland, sold to Ludwig Janssen in 1950, new name *Gronland*, finally going to the Hamburg breakers on 7th March 1957; and *Northern Reward* (GY.431), renamed *Vordur* and owned by Vordur H/f, Patreksfirdi, Iceland. She was lost off the south coast of Iceland on 29th January 1950.

Before rejoining the fishing fleet, these naval trawlers had to be completely refitted and repaired after their gruelling six years spent as warships. Some of the trawlers were overhauled and refitted at Hebburn on Tyne. The drawing shows *Northern Duke* fitted for burning oil fuel in November 1946 and quite a few changes have been made to the vessel. The main one, of course, is that the coal bunker has been replaced by fuel oil bunkers (she was the first Grimsby trawler to be converted after the war). The fish room is now totally dedicated to storing the catch. The rest of the class

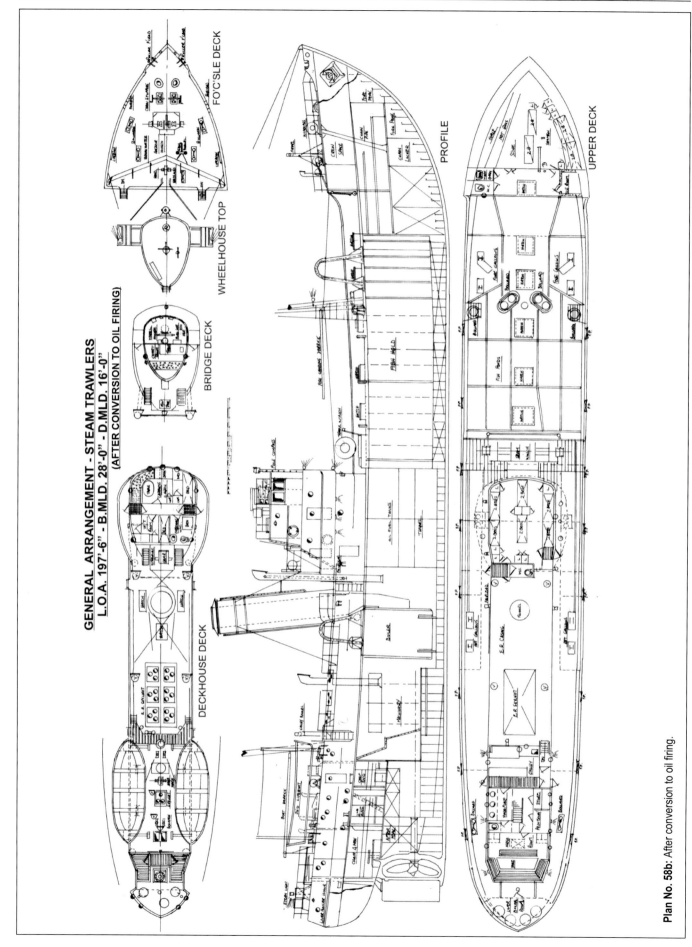

GENERAL ARRANGEMENT - STEAM TRAWLERS
L.O.A. 197'-6" - B.MLD. 28'-0" - D.MLD. 16'-0"
(AFTER CONVERSION TO OIL FIRING)

FO'SLE DECK

WHEELHOUSE TOP

BRIDGE DECK

DECKHOUSE DECK

PROFILE

UPPER DECK

Plan No. 58b: After conversion to oil firing.

were all later converted to oil (**Plan No. 58b**), with the exception of *Northern Dawn* and *Northern Pride*. Forward, the large storeroom space under the fo'c'sle head was divided centrally and accommodation for eight deckhands built into the starboard side. It seems that all the ships were so modified as photographs show the 'H' type stove pipe on the whaleback.

The domestic ice room is still on the starboard side but the lamp room to port has been replaced with a WC and wash/drying room. The twelve man cabin is still on the upper deck level below the skipper's and wireless operator's cabins but above this upper level are the most pronounced outward changes. The wheelhouse has been given enclosed wings on either side that reach out to the full width of the verandah. The latter has been faired into these wings and no longer goes around the front of the wheelhouse. The outboard facing entrance doors to the wheelhouse have been moved to the aft side of the wing extensions, giving more shelter. A pole compass has been fitted to the wheelhouse front and the standard binnacle removed from the top. The navigation lights have been moved from the verandah onto the wheelhouse roof and the enclosed windbreak around the forward side has been changed for open guard rails. Her lifeboats are now carried in Welin-type davits and the plan shows the mizzen boom rated for boat handling. *Northern Duke* still carried her mizzen mast, along with her davit arrangement. No radar is shown on the plan and when this was fitted, her mizzen mast was removed. An aerial mast was fitted to her funnel and a single ensign staff/aerial mast was fitted on her boiler casing. This again differed from her sisters as, with the exception of *Northern Foam* and *Northern Wave*, they carried twin aerial masts aft.

In 1955, *Northern Wave* was selected by the White Fish Authority for use as an experimental freezer trawler, with the capital for the project coming directly from the Treasury. Her freezers, designed by the Torry Research Station, Aberdeen, were of the six-station type. These were an improvement on the earlier four-station type used on the research vessel *Keelby* in 1950. The refrigerant was fed directly onto the freezer plates through flexible hoses. For defrosting, hot gas was used and to release the blocks of frozen fish, the plates were separated by means of spring jacks. By the end of August 1956, *Northern Wave* had completed eight experimental trips, in each case freezing the first thirty tons of white fish caught and storing the blocks at -30 degrees centigrade. When she landed her catch at Grimsby, these test blocks were thawed out and distributed to the trade for assessment. The modifications provided a cold store at the forward end of the existing fish room, with the freezing plant in the adjoining forward compartment. Even in the roughest weather, the installation was virtually trouble-free and paved the way for the commercial freezing of fish at sea. Although they were all classed as sister ships, and to the outsider they looked identical, there were subtle differences that could be spotted by the experienced trawlerman immediately they appeared over the horizon.

Photo. 76: *Northern Pride* in her wartime role; the bow shape can be clearly seen

BRITISH TRAWLERS FOR SOUTH AFRICA

In 1924, Hall, Russell's began building steam trawlers for Irvin & Johnson (South Africa) Ltd, an association that was to continue through to the stern trawlers of 1965. The first three ships ordered, Yard No's 684, 688 and 689, were *Disa*, *Nerine* and *Arum*, 'Strath' Class trawlers (115ft x 22ft x 12ft 9ins) costing £10,780 each. If one considers them rather small for working off the Cape, their successors, *Freesia*, *Gertrude W* and *Rochea*, Yard Nos. 706, 707 and 708, were even smaller (86ft x 18ft 6ins x 10ft) and cost £10,580 for each ship.

In 1934, they launched another four 125ft trawlers for the company and from then on the vessels gradually grew in size. This quartet comprised Yard No's 729, 731, 733 and 734, *Bluff*, *Babiana*, *Aristea* and *Grassula*. They were cruiser sterned ships, with double plate streamlined rudders, flush-decked except for a whaleback fo'c'sle. They were of all rivetted construction, with the exception of the shell beadings which were electrically welded. Their total complement was twenty-one hands (fourteen in the fo'c'sle). The skipper's berth was below the wheelhouse, with the engineer and the mate in separate small cabins aft. The remainder of the four 'officers' slept in the after cabin. Their fish rooms were well insulated by necessity, as they had been specifically designed to work in warm climates. Wheelhouse verandahs were solid steel plated and as they worked well away from the magnetic North Pole, they did not require pole compasses. Ventilation for the machinery spaces was by way of four cowl vents, engineroom skylights and fiddley gratings. The main engines were 550ihp and constructed by the builders, and the trawl winches had a capacity of 850 fathoms per barrel of 2.75ins warp. Full electric lighting was provided by a Robey compound steam engine, driving a 5kw Laurence Scott dynamo. Wireless telephony, and depth-sounding equipment were fitted, along with Donkin's hand and steam steering gear. They carried two double ended ship's boats on a raised platform over the main engine room skylight, with twin bobbin derricks double rigged for launching.

Irvin's next four ships and their last before 1939, were: Yard

No. 737 *Anenome*, No. 738 *Morea*, No. 745 *Protea* and No. 747 *Petunia* (all 130ft x 24ft x 14ft), costing £14,650 each. They were similar to the last batch, with the exception of their lifeboats, which were stowed on a boat deck aft between the galley and the poop house, and launched by radial davits. These larger vessels were all fitted with close stowing anchors and direction finding gear, in addition to their standard Marconi wireless installations.

HALL, RUSSELL'S FRENCH SHIPS

Another client of Hall, Russell's at this time was Joseph Duhamel, Les Pecheries de Fecamp. His ships were immense compared with Irvins and were dual purpose vessels designed for the Grand Banks trade. His first pair, ordered in 1920 as Yard No's 674 and 675, were *Simon Duhamel* and *Cap Fagnet* (170ft x 27ft x 15ft 6ins). Classed as raised quarterdeck ships, they cost £17,500 each. In 1923, he ordered a similar ship, *Bois-Rose*, Yard No. 682, the price for which had risen to £23,000 and in 1927, Yard No's 691 and 700, *Senateur Duhamel* and *Joseph Duhamel*, were delivered, costing £24,750 each. They were large counter sterned vessels (190ft x 31ft x 17ft 4ins), with the first triple deck superstructures to be fitted to British-built trawlers. They carried three boats on a boat deck aft, two large double ended lifeboats and a 12ft dinghy. After the fall of France, *Senateur Duhamel* served in the Royal Navy from January 1941 as an anti-submarine trawler. She was loaned to the US Navy but, on 6th May 1942, was lost after a collision off Wilmington. Her sister *Joseph Duhamel* also served the British war effort, by bringing fresh fish from Iceland to Hull, as part of the Icelandic Carrier Service.

A year later, another 190ft trawler, *Simon Duhamel II*, Yard No. 717 was ordered. All Duhamel's ships were fitted with comprehensive powerful radio outfits, including DF sets. Duhamel's penultimate pre-war ship from the Aberdeen yard was an oil burner, possibly the first such steam trawler built in the UK. Yard No. 732 *Vikings*, built in November 1935, was massive (206.7ft x 34.45ft x 19.19ft, 1,150g – **Photo. 77**). Her main engine was a four-cylinder compound, of two 15ins and

two 32ins cylinders by 32ins stroke, which developed 207nhp. A cruiser sterned ship, she had an Oertz rudder and steam steering gear. Her radio equipment included a DF set and an echo sounder. After the fall of France, she was taken over by the Admiralty in August 1940 as the anti-submarine trawler *U78* and crewed by the Free French. She was sunk by *U542* off Syria in April 1942 (the French give the date as 30th April but Admiralty report states 17th). She was replaced by another Hall, Russell ship in 1947, Yard No. 796, also *Vikings* and identical in both size and power to her predecessor. Hall, Russell's last trawler launch prior to the Second World War was also an oil burner for Mr Duhamel, named *Bois-Rose*, Yard No. 751 (216.5ft x 55.4ft x 20.5ft, 1,374g), built in 1940. She apparently escaped any war service but disappeared from the register in 1948. These large trawlers would be away from home between four and six months, and whereas British trawlers packed their fish in ice, the French preserved the catch by splitting open the fish, removing the back bone and packing them in salt.

Photo. 77: *Vikings* as an armed trawler. Her superstructure is larger than that of British trawlers, and her gallows have been removed for war service. Note the unprotected 12 pounder gun, searchlight platform and crow's nest lookout positions on the masts.

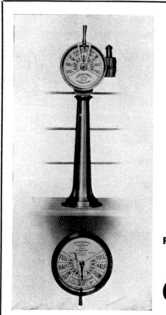

Chapter 14: THE END OF THE 1930s

By the middle of the decade, Britain's trawling fleet stood at 1,648 vessels, divided up as follows: Hull – 330 ships, Grimsby – 493, Aberdeen – 285, Fleetwood – 147, Milford Haven – 83, Granton – 65, North Shields – 67 and Lowestoft – 67, with the other ports totalling 111 ships between them. The age of the ships could be broken down thus (Port letters have been used):

Age Years	H	GY	A	FD	M	GN	SN	LT	Others
Under 10	156	60	29	9	3	3	2	10	22
10-15	30	3	3	4	4	0	0	3	3
15-20	53	131	82	52	37	24	36	9	21
20-25	37	121	63	44	3	27	19	6	20
Over 25	54	178	108	38	36	11	10	39	45

Thus it can be seen that by far the greatest investment in new ships was at Hull, with over 47% of the fleet less than ten years old. Grimsby's amounted to 12%, Aberdeen's 10% and so on.

With the peaceful years of the thirties drawing to a close, the steam trawler had reached maturity. The fleets, decimated by the First World War, had been rebuilt with larger more powerful ships, equipped with all the latest electronic gear for navigation, fish-finding and communications. Although fishing was still a gamble, the latest vessels had evened up the odds but the catching power of these ships were proving to be their Achilles heel. The Near and Middle Water grounds were showing signs of over fishing. These were still the main fishing grounds for the UK fleet, supplying the home market with fresh, high quality fish. In 1913, the total catch from the Near and Middle Water grounds amounted to 274,500 tons but the post war years from 1920 to 1922 saw record landings of up to 320,750 tons, brought about by the lack of fishing during the years of hostility. During the next two years, the catches dropped to 240,600 tons and, by 1935, the total catch from these grounds dropped to around 189,450 tons. It was further computed that the actual fishing time on the North Sea grounds had dropped by 13%, since 1925, with a further drop of some 30% in the hourly quantity of fish caught.

On the other hand, landings from the Distant Water grounds of Iceland, Bear Island, the Barents (White) Sea and the North Cape of Norway had risen from 105,000 tons in 1913 (20% of the total quantity of white fish landings) to 315,000 tons in 1935 (45% of the total). From this catch, Iceland accounted for three fifths, with the other grounds making up the balance. These Distant Water ships also encountered problems of an inverse nature during the hot summer months, when their catches would arrive in a condition of doubtful freshness. The owners found themselves faced with an often glutted market, with prices dropping to next to nothing. Hull owners, in 1932, agreed to a voluntary restriction of fishing on certain Distant Water grounds during the months of June, July, August and September. The Government addressed this problem in 1933, when they issued the Restriction of Fishing in Northern Waters Order, which prohibited the landing in Britain of any fish caught off Bear Island and the White Sea during the above months. Another round of trade agreements in 1933 restricted the landings of fish by foreign vessels, which had grown from 500,000 tons in 1913, to over 100,000 tons in 1930. This in turn allowed our own vessels a greater share of the home market.

This market as a whole was, by the mid-thirties, suffering the effects of the world depression. Prices were falling, especially for the higher quality Near Water fish, which bore the brunt of the market forces. The average gross earnings for Near and Middle Water trawlers in the years 1924 and 1934 at the five major ports were:

GROSS EARNINGS IN £S

Year	Hull	Grimsby	Aberdeen	Fleetwood	Milford
1929	8,657	7,171	6,628	11,042	8,644
1930	7,690	6,147	5,876	9,445	8,254
1931	6,741	5,677	5,579	8,112	7,750
1932	6,115	5,565	5,360	7,901	6,876
1933	6,011	5,972	5,608	8,552	7,170
1934	6,342	5,911	5,932	8,398	8,510

NETT PROFITS (+) or LOSSES (-)

Year	Hull	Grimsby	Aberdeen	Fleetwood	Milford
1929	+1,137	+344	+277	+1,284	+472
1930	+ 274	-279	-260	+ 164	- 21
1931	+ 89	-333	-459	- 335	- 452
1932	+ 17	-170	-345	- 39	- 294
1933	+ 376	+ 81	-176	+ 233	- 311
1934	+ 345	+ 9	+ 70	+ 71	+331

Taken from the *White Fish Industry Report*, HMSO 1935

Although there was a gradual upward swing in 1933 in the profits for the Near and Middle Water ships, this fell way short of the 1929 figures.

The Distant Water fish too was fetching lower prices, although even with the fishing restrictions, the vessels continued to show a good return. This accounts for the number of new ships coming on stream in the thirties. On the whole, Distant Water fishing was more remunerative than trawling on the other more local grounds but with regard to the higher capital and running costs, Distant Water ships had to show far higher gross earnings in order to remain viable:

GROSS EARNINGS IN £S: Distant Water Ships

Year	Hull	Grimsby
1929	15,569	13,132
1930	13,327	12,093
1931	11,894	10,547
1932	11.429	10,292
1933	12,081	10,962
1934	13,070	12,427

NETT PROFITS (+) or LOSSES (-)

Year	Hull	Grimsby
1929	+2,601	+1,157
1930	+1,373	+ 396
1931	+ 957	- 300
1932	+ 816	- 434
1933	+1.202	+ 192
1934	+1,834	+ 744

Taken from the *White Fish Industry Report*, HMSO 1935

Again there was a marked fall in profit related earnings after 1930; this starts to show a small rise in the last two years but was still way below the 1929 figures. Possibly owners of Distant Water ships suffered in the early 1930s, by investing in new tonnage immediately after the remarkable success of Bear Island in 1928. No one envisaged the crash of 1929-30 and, during this period, 158 new vessels were ordered at a total of £2.5 million. The market was falling by 1931, possibly from over-catching and under-marketing, and many older smaller vessels were laid up, with owners setting minimum prices below which they refused to sell their fish.

RUNNING COSTS

The biggest outlay for trawler owners was undoubtedly fuel. In the mid-thirties, the fleet consumed 3.5 million tons annually, accounting for around 25% of running costs at Hull and Grimsby, and around 28% at Aberdeen, Fleetwood and Milford Haven. The variation in price was blamed on the cost of shipping the coal from the coalfields and at Aberdeen, it was often more cost effective to send a trawler with a scratch crew to Methil for bunkering, returning home in time for her own crew to take her back to sea. This cost for coal was set against the trawler's gross earnings, with a few owners charging it out at cost but most marking it up, at between 6d to 4 shillings a ton. Some owners had shares in the nearby coalfields and could operate their own pricing policy when supplying the trawlers.

The second major item of expenditure was the crew's wages, which averaged around 27%. Although this appeared to be higher than the fuel bills, one should bear in mind the fact that trawler crews were paid by results out of the nett profits for the trip, after all the other running costs had been deducted. Skippers and mates were paid on a share of the nett catch only but some owners had agreements whereby skippers were paid bonuses when the value of the catch exceeded a certain figure. The rest of the crew were paid a small weekly wage, supplemented by their share, or 'poundage' plus their liver money.

Next in line was depreciation, plus the upkeep of the vessel, which included repairs and the replenishment of gear and stores, which amounted to around 25%. Again, older ships required more running repairs and more frequent surveys, which would cause them to miss trips, further reducing their cost effectiveness. Other expenses included, ice, insurance, commission to fish salesmen, harbour dues, etc, which amounted to a further 22%. If one adds the above figures together they show an average outlay of between 99 and 102 per cent, which gave from a net loss up to a profit of 1%. The latter figure was for Hull, where the trade was well organised and more efficiently managed than at other ports. The following costs are based on Hull and Grimsby, the main Distant Water trawling ports. When comparing these figures, the reader should bear in mind that, for the same period (the mid-thirties), the majority of the ships were newer and more fuel efficient than their counterparts in the Near and Middle Water trade.

AVERAGE EXPENSES (%):	Hull	Grimsby
Coal	19	21
Upkeep of vessel	19	19
Other expenses	22	26
Wages for skipper and crew	26	28
TOTAL EXPENSES	**86**	**94**
NETT PROFIT	**14**	**6**

Here again, the effects of efficient management working practices are evident between the two ports. This, however, does not paint the true picture on the profit side, as it was common knowledge, in Hull at least, that on average 50-100 or so 10 stone kits of the best fish, from every Distant Water ship, would leave the dock by way of the 'Ghost Train'. No records were kept for these consignments, as payment was strictly cash. If one takes an average price of say £5-6 a kit, this amounted to a nice earner for the owners. Another factor prevalent throughout the industry was the high loss rate of trawlers. In the years from January 1930 until August 1939, 159 trawlers were irrevocably lost, along with hundreds of men, from four of the major ports. Hull lost forty-two ships, Grimsby lost forty-eight, Aberdeen lost forty-four and Fleetwood lost twenty-five. Truly, trawling was ever a very risky commercial enterprise both for the owners and crews.

The last pre-war trawlers on the building stocks in 1939 were almost all taken over by the Admiralty and finished off as warships, forming the 'Tree' Class.

LAST PRE-WAR SHIPS

Cochrane's last big pre-war trawler was Yard No. 1205 *Cape Finisterre* (H.178 – 175ft bp x 30ft 6ins x 16ft, 590g), built for Hudson Brothers (Trawlers) Ltd. She was a powerful deep water ship and the last of a three-ship order, the other two being *Cape Siretoko* (H.106), Yard No. 1200, and *Cape Passaro* (H.135), Yard No. 1199. She was requisitioned in February 1940, as an anti-submarine trawler and armed with a 12 pounder, plus a depth charge array aft. Her naval career was cut short in August that year when she was sunk by enemy aircraft off Harwich. Her sisters were also short-lived. *Cape Siretoko* was requisitioned as FY263, an anti-submarine trawler, in September 1939. She was sunk by enemy aircraft at Namsos in April 1940. The Germans raised her and renamed her *Gote* but she was finally sent to the bottom by our aircraft on 11th May 1944 off Makkaur. *Cape Passaro*, also hired in September 1939, sank after an attack by enemy planes off Narvik in May 1940.

This *Cape Finisterre* should not be confused with her forerunner H.310, also built by Cochrane's but as Yard No. 1085 in 1930 and a much smaller vessel (140ft bp x 24ft 6ins x14ft, 347g,145n). She was the last of an order for four sister ships: *Cape Guardafui* (H.255), Yard No. 1082; *Cape Kanin* (H.258), Yard No. 1083; and *Cape Spartivento* (H.286), Yard No. 1084. These earlier ships were part of a group of twenty trawlers purchased in 1935 by the Admiralty to combat the Abyssinian Crisis. Classified as the 'Tree Group', they were named after trees and converted for mine sweeping. Their naming policy was passed on to the later 'Tree' Class of Admiralty-designed trawlers.

Cape Finisterre became *Cypress* (T09) and survived the war, being sold to Faeroe in 1946 as *Vardberg* and broken up at Fredrikssund in May 1959. *Cape Guardafui* became *Hawthorn* (T32) and she too was sold to the Faeroese in 1947 as *Havborgin*, and broken up at Thisted in 1982. *Cape Kanin* became *Syringa* (T55– **Photo. 78**). In 1946, she was sold to Granton owners Thomas H. Scales & Sons Ltd as *Davarr Island* (GN.23). She returned to her original owners in 1948 as *Cape Kanin* (H.586), eventually going for scrap in 1954. *Cape Spartivento* became *Willow* (T66), later being sold to Faeroe as *Trondur-I-Gotu* in 1946 and scrapped at Hamburg in 1957.

Photo. 78: *Syringa* ex-*Cape Kanin*. 'Mount Misery' has been enclosed, forming an upper conning position. She still carries gallows and the 'Kite' can be seen on the aft gallows. She is fitted with a 4ins quick firing Mark IV gun on a Mark IX mounting and her boats are mounted on deck extensions either side of the funnel, whilst her trawl winch remains in its original position.

Cochrane's also launched their first oil burning steam trawler in 1939, as Yard No. 1201 *Akita* (CF.4 – 130.7ft x 24.5ft x 11.9ft, 314g, 124nhp, O/N.162133), for Neale & West Ltd, Cardiff. The Admiralty immediately requisitioned her for minesweeping duty as FY.610 at £235 per month and she was returned to her original owners in October 1945. After her owners closed their Cardiff operations in 1956, she was sold to the Boston Deep Sea Fishing & Ice Co. Ltd, Fleetwood as *Boston Heron* (FD.48). A year later she went to Milford Fisheries Ltd, who chartered her to the Ministry of Agriculture & Fisheries and the White Fish Authority for investigative work off the west coast of Ireland. She was sold again in December 1961 to Merchants (Milford Haven) Ltd but the following year she drove ashore on a reef off the Island of Scalpay, with the loss of seven of her twelve man crew and was written off as a total loss.

Cook, Welton & Gemmell launched one of their last big pre-war trawlers in November 1937, as Yard No. 640 *Kingston Agate* (H.489 – 161ft 9ins bp x 27ft x 15ft 3ins) for the Kingston Steam Trawling Co. Ltd, Hull. Her naming ceremony was carried out by Mrs A. D. Campey on 18th November and she completed her trials on 23rd December. In September 1939, she was requisitioned as an armed boarding vessel and anti-submarine trawler, with the Admiralty No. FY212. Her call to fame came in August 1941 when, in company with *Northern Chief*, she picked up the crew of *U570* after it had surrendered to a Lockheed Hudson of Coastal Command in the Atlantic. The rescue was undertaken during a lull in foul weather by *Kingston Agate*'s First Lieutenant Jock Campbell, who crossed over to the enemy vessel in a Carley

float and passed a towline so she could be salvaged by *Northern Chief*, even though thirty foot seas were still running and twice he was almost washed off the casing whilst attempting to make the tow fast. The U-boat's crew were ferried to *Kingston Agate*, with the last German dragged on board some thirty hours after the surrender. The U-boat later sank. In January 1946, she returned to her Hull owners who converted her to an oil burner in March 1950 and she went to the breakers in 1964.

Cook, Welton & Gemmell's last trawler ordered commercially in 1939 was *Vizalma*, Yard No. 656, for the Atlas Steam Fishing Co. Ltd, Grimsby, launched on 11th April 1940 and requisitioned by the Admiralty while still on the stocks on 15th June. After

Photo. 79: *Vizalma* (GY101) on Doig's slip. Note the classic Distant Water hull shape, bilge keels and Oertz rudder. Her lifeboats are hung in radial davits and the twin radars can be clearly seen. She wears a black hull with a white band and wood grained superstructure. The funnel has a white 'A' on yellow over blue bands, bordered by white rings on black.

Painting 6: *Macbeth* in Hellyer's colours. Note her tall radar mast and radial davits, whilst her mizzen mast has been replaced by a pole mast ahead of the funnel. COURTESY S. FARROW

her completion on 12th August, she was allotted the Admiralty No. FY286. After a distinguished war service, much of it spent on the Russian convoy run, she was returned to Letten Bros in late 1945, when she underwent a four month major refit. Her forward crew accommodation was fitted with a modern combustion stove supplying the radiators, with a hot water system for crew's washrooms. Allotted her GY.101 fishing number, she sailed for the White Sea grounds on 3rd January 1946 under Skipper Jack Evans. In 1964, she was sold to Clayton & Davie and went to Dunston on Tyne on 4th November for scrapping. (**Photo. 79**)

Further north at Middlesborough in 1938, Smith's Dock launched three sister ships for the Hampshire Fishing Co. Ltd (Shires). They were Yard No's 1033, 1034 and 1035: *Ayrshire* (GY.520), *Fifeshire* (GY.524) and *Argyllshire* (GY.528 – all 175ft 8ins x 28ft 6ins x 15ft, 540g). Although all managed under the Shire Company umbrella, they were owned by Ayrshire, Fifeshire, and Banffshire fishing companies respectively. *Ayrshire* and *Fifeshire* were requisitioned in September 1939 as anti-submarine trawlers with the Admiralty No's FY225. and FY551. On a cold blustery February day in 1940, both ships were some seventy miles east of the Orkney's on passage for their base at Rosyth, when they were surprised by a pair of Heinkels. Although painted grey and classed as warships of the 11th Anti-Submarine Striking Force, their only defensive armament consisted of a pair of Lewis guns apiece. *Fifeshire* received two direct hits from enemy bombs and disintegrated. *Ayrshire* now bore the full brunt of the attack. Four times the aircraft bombed and strafed the trawler but her Skipper, Sub-Lieutenant Dixon, skilfully conned his vessel thus saving her. She was very badly mauled but remained afloat. After the aircraft left she picked up the only survivor from her sister.

Ayrshire again came to the fore during the disastrous PQ17 convoy, when she shepherded the last four merchantmen into Archangel, the remains of the thirty-seven ship convoy to Russia. In October 1945, she went back to civilian life as *Macbeth* (H.113), owned by Hellyer Brothers Ltd, Hull. Converted to oil fuel in 1950, they ran her until 1964, when they sold her to Wyre Trawlers Ltd, Fleetwood, as FD.74. She went to the breakers in 1966. *Argyllshire* was also purchased in September 1939 as an anti-submarine trawler. She was sunk by an E-boat off Dunkirk on 1st June 1940. These were followed in 1939 by the Smith's last pre-war steam trawlers,

Yard No's 1058-60, *Imperialist*, *Norman* and *Esquimaux* (190ft 7ins oa, 520g), all sisters for the Hull Northern Fishing Co. Ltd. They were sturdy ships, and among the first trawlers to have all the butts of their shell plating electrically welded. They almost immediately transferred to the parent company Hellyer's but *Norman* does not appear in the registers after 1942 and *Esquimaux* (H.29) was requisitioned in 1939 as *Alouette* FY.101 and was torpedoed by *U552* off Portugal on 14th September 1942. The last of the three, *Imperialist* (H.2), was beached at Scarborough in October 1959 after a collision in the North Sea. She was patched up on the beach and later towed to Hull for repair. In 1965, she was sold to Wyre Trawlers Ltd and renumbered FD.83, working out of that port until she went for scrapping at Troon on 20th November 1966.

As for the two Aberdeen builders, Hall, Russell's last pre-war trawler was *Star of Orkney*, whilst *Mount Keen* of 1936 was the last Lewis ship. After this period, the trawler building yards switched to war construction. They concentrated on the new naval trawler types rapidly being put into production, along with other classes of escorts and minesweepers.

THE MISSION SHIPS – END OF AN ERA

The work of the Royal National Mission to Deep Sea Fishermen (RNMDSF) is well known. It was founded by Ebenezer J. Mather in 1881, after he was appalled by the miserable, cruel and often deadly trade of the smacksmen. These men were separated from the normalities of shore life and their very existence was dominated by work, weather and market forces. Cooped up on small sailing trawlers, they worked the wild waters of the Dogger Bank. Comforts were non-existent and the only respite from work was by getting horribly drunk on the obnoxious liquor sold by the Dutch Copers. Death and maiming were commonplace, and sickness had no other remedy than work. The Mission equipped their own sailing smacks as seagoing refuges, offering a little spiritual and a lot of simple comforts, as well as medical support, to the men of the fishing fleet. Not confined to Near Waters, the Mission sent the hospital smack *Albert* to the Newfoundland cod grounds in June 1892. She was to inaugurate the Greenfell Mission in Labrador and lived to a ripe old age, being lost in 1968, after losing her propeller somewhere south of Cape Desolation. Fortunately, all her crew were rescued by a Norwegian vessel but soon afterwards *Albert* foundered in the ice.

On 19th December 1899, Hawthorn's of Leith launched the first steam trawler/hospital ship for the Mission to Deep Sea Fishermen (later to carry the 'Royal' pre-fix), *Alpha* (LO.24 – 145ft oa, 85n, 274 g, 65nhp – **Photo. 80**) She was the Mission's thirteenth ship, with the others all being sailing smacks, and was dedicated off Billingsgate, on 18th May 1900, by the Bishop of London. Most of her life was spent working with the boxing fleets of Hellyer's and Kelsall & Beeching's Gamecock fleet. In 1904, she was caught up in the 'Dogger Bank Outrage' and was badly damaged by a Russian shell. The damage claim amounted to £3,906, which was eventually settled by the perpetrator's government. Requisitioned

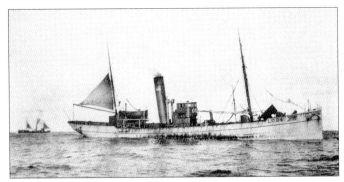

in 1915 as a minesweeper, she returned to her work with the fleets in 1919. She was taken off station in 1922, laid up and sold to Carver's of Great Yarmouth in 1925.

The 14th mission steamer sailed from her builders in Leith in 1902, for dedication in the Thames. *Queen Alexandra* (LO.51 – 231g, 85n, 65nhp) was similar to her predecessor and spent her early days working with the Red Cross Fleet (**Photo. 81**). She worked with the fleet through the war and when the Red Cross and Gamecock fleets were joined in 1931, she continued as a hospital ship until being laid up in 1932, going for scrap in 1934. The next steam hospital ship was *Joseph and Sarah Miles* (LO.175), an identical ship, also built by Hawthorn's and dedicated at Leith on 11th November 1902. She, too, was with the boxing fleet when the Russian navy attacked without warning on 21st October 1904 and she brought three wounded men back to Hull from the trawler *Crane*. She ran aground in 1911 but was successfully refloated without damage. She was requisitioned in April 1915 as a minesweeper and armed with a 12 pounder. On returning to her mission duties, she was chartered by Ministry of Agriculture & Fisheries for research work on the North Sea grounds. Afterwards, she continued her work with the fishing fleets until October 1936, when it was decided that she was no longer commercially viable and that her facilities were under-utilised. She went to T. Ward's for breaking on 19th March 1937.

By this time, it was becoming obvious that the spiritual and medical costs of running steam trawlers, even when fishing commercially, were prohibitive, so it seems strange that the mission ordered yet another new ship in 1936. Maybe their reason was clouded by the goodwill of the donor, Miss. Violet Wills, who

gifted the ship, named after her late father *Sir Edward P Wills* (LO.197 – 100ft bp x 21ft x 11ft). She was launched from the Goole Shipbuilding & Repairing Co's yard on 13th February 1937. The builder's drawing (**Plan 59**) shows a very 'sit up and beg' vessel, with a very short whaleback, tall wheelhouse, cruiser stern with a barn door rudder and four bladed cast iron propeller. She was fully fitted for trawling but her deck pounds are only on the port side, with a motor launch carried on deck to starboard. In addition, she had a single ship's boat aft, launched with the mizzen boom. The skipper's berth is below the wheelhouse, which he shares with the Marconi radio set. Forward accommodation was for two missionaries, with a dispensary and bathroom.

Owing to her small size, she was not equipped with steam steering gear and the 4ft diameter wheel needed twenty-six turns from hard over to hard over. A dynamo in the engine room supplied electric light for the whole ship and the boiler superheater delivered dry steam at 210psi. Her dedication took place on 23rd April 1937, by the Bishop of Plymouth, in Brixham harbour. Up to the outbreak of the Second World War, she cruised the east coast. It appears she was under utilised as the boxing fleets had all been disbanded by this time and the North Sea was now the domain of the single boater, which were more difficult to keep track of. Requisitioned in September 1939, she served throughout the war, with her original complement, as an examination vessel at Yarmouth. She was returned in August 1945 and with little real mission work left for her afloat, was sold in 1947 to the Vigilant Fishing Co. of Lowestoft, renamed *Mary Heeley* (LT.308) and was lost off the Isle of Man in 1950. *Sir Edward P Wills* was the last new vessel built for the Royal National Mission to Deep Sea Fishermen and the end of a seagoing lifeline to fishermen stretching back to 1881. It continued to do sterling work ashore, offering home comforts to seamen in strange ports, supplying fresh clothes after shipwreck and always being the first to break the dreadful news that loved ones had been lost at sea. Many wives have fainted at the sight of the Mission man coming to their door, knowing only too well the tidings he bore.

The families of fishermen are well accustomed to losing their husbands and sons, either separately or together. Often these men sailed on the same ships, along with uncles, nephews and cousins, so that when a trawler foundered there was great personal tragedy for those left behind. In some cases, the men had been prudent

ABOVE: Photo. 80: *Alpha* (LO.24) on the fishing grounds. The RNMDSF flag is on her funnel and also ahead of her fishing number, where the bow scroll can just be picked out. The port side forward otter board note is hanging in its chains and her mizzen is set but her staysails are furled. Note her boat stowage. The hull appears to be white.

RIGHT: Painting 7: *Queen Alexandra* (LO.51). Her bow scroll carries the message 'PREACH THE WORD' and the flag at her foremast signals that a prayer meeting is to be held on board.

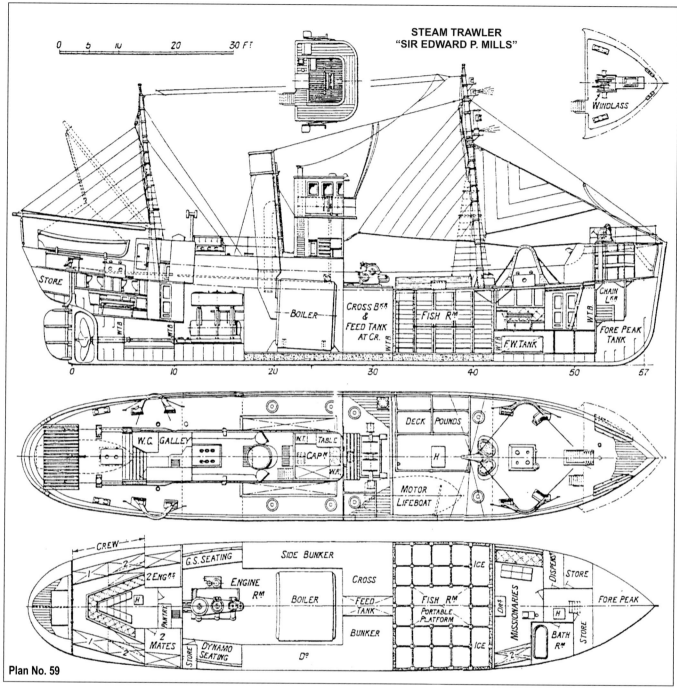

STEAM TRAWLER
"SIR EDWARD P. MILLS"

Plan No. 59

enough to take out insurance cover but many were uninsured and the dependents had to rely on charity for survival. Even an insurance policy was sometimes no guarantee of financial assistance, as some of the less reputable companies tried their best to wriggle out of settling a claim. One instance of this occurred in early 1915, when a fisherman (a member of the RNR) was washed overboard from his trawler. He had previously taken out life cover and the policy carried the start date of 14th November 1914. After his demise, when his wife attempted to claim on the policy, she met with a downright refusal to pay out. The company maintained that the policy was for a fisherman, when in fact he was a member of the RNR and awaiting call up. The desperate widow took the insurance company to court but, unfortunately, the county judge ruled for the insurers, stating that the policy twas in fact null and void. After much effort, the widow brought the case before Mr Justice Lawrence and Mr Justice

Allen. These learned gentlemen overturned the original decision and the family eventually received their father's insurance money.

Yet another example of hardship was when fishermen were taken prisoner after their trawlers had been sunk. The majority were incarcerated in Germany but some went to Austria. These fishermen were treated no differently to uniformed combatants. Normally, fishermen are well enough fed but in the camps, they were malnourished and ill-treated beyond the bounds of civilised humanity and not until the RNMDSF stepped in were some of the hardships alleviated. In 1917, the Board of Trade issued a list of 342 fishermen detained as prisoners of war. Three fishermen had died in captivity and twenty-one had been released. The prisoners came from fifty-seven vessels. When the war eventually ended, these men came home to rejoin their comrades and once more go out with the tide in search of a livelihood from deep sea trawling.

Chapter 15: THE SECOND WORLD WAR

Following the declaration of war, it immediately became obvious that the enemy were determined to bring the United Kingdom to its knees, by instigating a sub-sea offensive using U-boats and mine laying. This new menace was to prove much more effective than that of the previous war and, if proof were needed, it came on the evening of 3rd September 1939, when the liner *Athenia* was torpedoed and sunk some 250 miles off the Irish coast. The very next day, it was found that the approaches to the Thames, Humber and Tyne had all been mined, effectively bringing all traffic to a standstill. Once again, the fishermen of Britain with their ships were called up, as 'Operation Sweep' began. The trawlers, drifters and motor fishing vessels were requisitioned and sailed for their commissioning ports. Here they were refitted and issued with the same antiquated weaponry as they had discarded in 1919. All the RNR men were called up and assembled at Sparrows Nest Park at Lowestoft, a transit camp and the headquarters of the Royal Navy Patrol Service. It was soon renamed as HMS *Pembroke X* but later became HMS *Europa*. It was from this hastily converted seaside music hall that crews were moulded into the Navy's ways before being drafted to their ships. A few of these recruits had the misguided notion that the Royal Naval Patrol Service was a dashing and elite branch of the senior service (it never quite enjoyed the first part but as to the 'elite', 'Harry Tate's Navy' was a company many aspired to be a member of as the war progressed). When, however, they saw the vessels in which they were going to war, many of their number were not overly inspired. If the ships disillusioned them, the crew members, as in the first war, impressed them even less; hard bitten Arctic and North Sea trawlermen, soft spoken men from the Western Isles, rough driftermen and longshoremen from Norfolk and Suffolk, with scarcely a regular naval officer among them. Their use of nautical terminology, interspersed with colourful slang phrases, must have reflected very strongly on the wisdom of the recruits' decision to go to war in trawlers. Fish rooms were converted into messdecks and wardrooms. Whalebacks sported a 12 pounder Q/F gun, and wheelhouses were built up to accommodate asdic houses and more sophisticated communications equipment. Bandstands and zareebas were added to carry close support anti-aircraft weapons and depth charge arrays were fitted aft. Space was always at a premium aboard trawlers and shared messing arrangements for seamen and stokers came as something of a short, sharp, culture shock. After initial reservations had been overcome, trawler crews became close knit teams of first class fighting men, well able to take on the enemy in any theatre of the war, from the frozen waters of the Northern Patrol and Russian runs, to the baking heat of the Indian Ocean and the Mediterranean convoys to Malta and Crete.

The Distant Water, ex-fishery trawlers generally fell into two main groups: anti-submarine striking forces or mine sweeping groups. These could be further sub-divided into armed patrol, armed boarding and rescue ships. Their exceptional sea keeping qualities enabled these vessels to remain at sea when the larger, more charismatic destroyers had to run for shelter. Smaller Middle and Near Water trawlers were used as sweepers for both moored and magnetic mines, dhan layers, harbour patrol vessels, store carriers and any other task that their naval masters could dream up for them. This war was to exact a high price in both ships and men from the fishing fleet, and the Patrol Service. By the end of October 1940, Hull had lost thirty-five ships, Grimsby forty, Aberdeen twenty-one and Fleetwood twenty-nine. It is difficult to obtain firm figures for human losses during this period but it appears that around 40% of the trawlers were lost with all hands. By the end of the war, the English trawler fleet had lost a total of 124 vessels whilst fishing, twenty-four from unknown causes, twenty-five from mines, twenty-three from air attack, thirteen from U-boat gunfire and thirty-nine from collision, stranding or other marine causes. In addition, 146 trawlers were lost on war service. Aberdeen alone lost thirty-five ships by enemy attacks and mines, and fourteen trawlers were lost to other marine perils.

Throughout the war, fishing still continued but on a much smaller scale, using the few trawlers not called up for war service. Fishing grounds were closed, including almost the whole of the North Sea, Bear Island and the Norwegian coast. This had the effect of funnelling all the fishing into the west coast grounds of Scotland, the Hebrides, the north west of Ireland and the prolific hake grounds off the south west of Ireland, plus the Distant Water grounds off Iceland. This change in location made Fleetwood England's number one port, with Milford Haven ranking a close second. In Scotland, Aberdeen's depleted fleet worked these grounds in addition to those off Iceland. By the latter years of hostilities, the Irish grounds had to be given up, as enemy U-boat activity made them too hazardous to work. Not only were those trawlers still fishing unfit for war service but their skippers and crews were either medically unsuitable for the Navy or had been brought out of retirement to man them. Grimsby lost her first trawler on 28th October 1939. This was *Lynx II* (GY.401), under skipper A. Cressey, who took his vessel to the aid of the Hull trawler *St. Nidan* after it had fired flares to say that she was being attacked by a U-boat. The German Captain sank his second trawler that day by gunfire and scuttling charges, after forcing the crews to take to their boats. Fortunately, both crews were rescued and taken to Stornoway. Thus our two main Distant Water ports both lost their first ships to the Germans on the same day. The first Aberdeen registered trawler to be lost to the enemy was *Delphine* (A.126), sunk by *U33* off Tory Island on 20th November. Built in 1914 by Smith's Dock as one of their 'D' Class for Consolidated Fisheries Ltd, Grimsby, she originally had the number GY.958. In September 1934, they sold her to the North Star Steam Fishing Co. Ltd, Aberdeen as A.126. She was sold again in October 1939 to the Boston Deep Sea Fishing & Ice Co. Ltd and transferred to Fleetwood. So it was that officially Aberdeen and Fleetwood both suffered the same loss, although Fleetwood had lost her first trawler, *Arlita* (FD.188), in early September while working off the Flannan Isles

TRAWLER REQUISITIONING

The navy boasted only a handful of 'Minor War Vessels', the official terminology for fishing vessels. Mostly they were the left-overs from the previous war as follows: 'Strath' Class – one; 'Castle'

Class – three; 'Mersey' Class – fourteen; 'Axe Class' – four; and 'Armentires' Class – three. Requisitioning swelled the fleet by some seventy-five 'Straths', 125 'Castles' and thirty 'Merseys', plus two 'Axe' and two 'Military' Class ships, along with fifteen ships named after 'Gems' (**Photo. 72**) and outfitted as anti-submarine vessels. A further twenty-ship purchase was made between 1936 and 1939, the ships being designated as minesweepers, and anti-submarine and boom defence vessels.

In 1939, six whale catchers were bought off the stocks and finished off as anti-submarine ships. This was a woefully inadequate fleet with which to counter the German mining offensive in the first eighteen months of the war. It should be noted that all the above were groups rather than classes. After this period, new naval classes of trawler began to leave the yards to swell the ranks of the mine hunters, and asdic trawlers:

Out of a total of some 1,030 steam trawlers available at the outbreak of the war, about 816 were requisitioned at one time or another, the maximum number on naval service at any one time being around 690. The number requisitioned during the first three months of the war was about 330. Towards the end of 1939, when the magnetic mine first made its appearance, there was another heavy demand for minesweeping and about 190 more vessels were requisitioned. As countermeasures to the magnetic mine were devised and fitted, some of these vessels were returned to the fishing industry but others were taken up for various purposes following the collapse of France, to the extent that by January 1941, the total number on service reached the figure of 690 referred to. The number available for fishing was only about one-quarter of the pre-war fleet and the catching power was even less, as practically all the larger and more efficient ships had been taken. Another

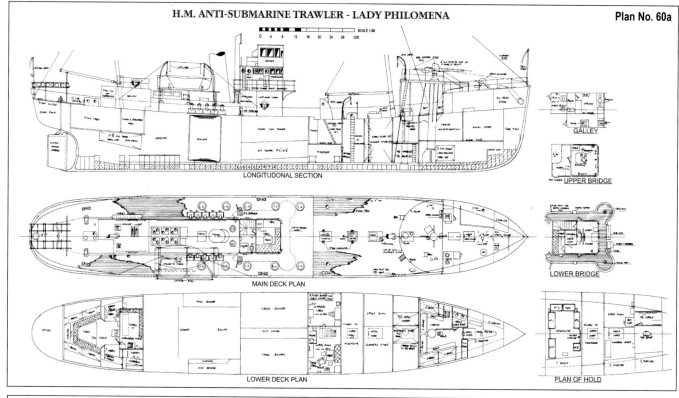

H.M. ANTI-SUBMARINE TRAWLER - LADY PHILOMENA

Plan No. 60a

LONGITUDONAL SECTION

MAIN DECK PLAN

LOWER DECK PLAN

GALLEY

UPPER BRIDGE

LOWER BRIDGE

PLAN OF HOLD

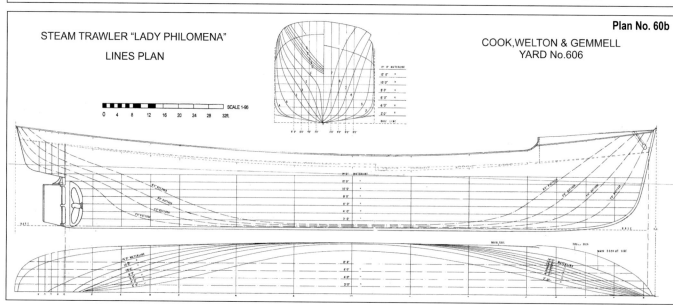

STEAM TRAWLER "LADY PHILOMENA"

LINES PLAN

COOK, WELTON & GEMMELL
YARD No.606

Plan No. 60b

factor which must be taken into consideration is that the age of the vessels still left to fish necessitated constant repairs often of a major character. The time spent in port was thereby considerably increased over the average of the pre-war years. Catches fell to below one-quarter of the pre-war figure. The position remained substantially the same until the end of August 1944, when the improvement in the war situation made possible a steady flow of releases which continued up to VE day, after which the number of releases was only controlled by the capacity of the reconditioning yards to take the vessels in hand. Taken from the *Report of the Sea Fisheries of England and Wales, 1939 to 1944*, HMSO

Typical of the requisitioned Distant Water ships was Cook, Welton & Gemmell's Yard No. 606 *Lady Philomena* (H.230 – 155.7ft bp x 26ft x 15ft, 157n, 417g, 105nhp – **Plan 60 a & b**), launched on 9th January 1936 for Jutland Amalgamated Trawlers Ltd, Fleetwood. Her engines, supplied by C.D. Holmes, were fitted with a coupled Bauer Wach exhaust turbine. She was requisitioned in August 1939 as an anti-submarine trawler, FY148, and her defensive armament comprised a single 4ins Q/F Mark IV gun on a Mark IX mounting, with a couple of Lewis guns on the wheelhouse verandah. For anti-submarine work she was equipped with Asdic, two depth charge throwers and twin D/C rails. The conversion drawing shows the Asdic room and retractable Asdic dome fitted in the bowels of the vessel below the foremast. This compartment is linked to the bridge by means of an Asdic repeater fitted on the upper bridge. Being an ex-fishery trawler, all the crew had proper bunks rather than naval style hammocks and an interesting feature is the dedicated wash place fitted in the crew's fo'c'sle, rather than on deck under the whaleback. A single ship's boat was carried, supplemented by a large Carley float. The usual small enclosed upper bridge houses the main binnacle and no less than eight speaking tubes for internal communication. *Lady Philomena* was returned to fishing in October 1945 as H.167, managed by Thomas Hamling & Co. Ltd. In 1947, she was renamed *St. Attalus* and, in 1948, she became *Onslow*, owned by the Hessle Fishing Co. In 1956, she transferred to Fleetwood's Mason Trawlers Ltd as *Onslow* (FD.50) and she went to the breakers at Preston on 11th May 1960.

TYPES OF ENEMY MINES
The new enemy mines were far more advanced than just the contact type used in the First World War and the minesweepers had to learn how to deal with the various types: acoustic, magnetic, magnetic-acoustic, submarine acoustic-magnetic (SAMMY) and the enemy-moored magnetic-acoustic (EMMA). In addition, there were varying permutations of influence mines to be destroyed before a channel was declared open. Mines destroyed their targets in two distinctly different ways; the contact mine (as the name implied) exploded on contact with a vessel's hull, inflicting visible structural damage and usually blowing her bows off. The influence mine exploded on the seabed underneath the ship, generating massive pressure or shock waves which broke the ship's back. The first sign that the latter type of mines had been laid was when a dull 'crump' sound was heard. The disabled vessel would veer from the formation out of the swept channel, into the moored minefield, where the contact mines would finish her off. The enemy were very cunning with these influence mines, fitting delayed action timers which would be armed by the first vessel passing overhead but not

exploding until the pre-determined number of ships had passed. This of course made them exceptionally hard to sweep, as pass after pass had to be made over the field before they could be detonated. The mainstay of the moored minesweeping gear was the Oropesa Sweep, developed after the First World War. It consisted of a steam trawl-type double-barrelled towing winch, and port and starboard sweep wires, with a normal length of 160 fathoms. An otter was attached at the outer end of the sweep wire, by a wire pendant leading to the torpedo-shaped float on the surface. The length of the pendant depended on the sweeping depth and the otter kept the wire at the correct depth, just like otter boards kept a trawl net's mouth open.

At the inboard end of the sweep wire was the 'kite' – similar in shape and function to the otter. It kept the entire length of the sweep wire at a constant pre-determined depth. Both the kite and the otter were steel rectangular frames, fitted with transverse angled blades which forced the board down in the water. Also fitted at the outer end of the sweep wire were explosive cutters, which severed the mine's mooring cable. It then floated to the surface where it was sunk or blown up by gunfire. The enemy tried many ways to combat this sweep, even to replacing the mooring wires with chain, which proved very difficult to cut. Various sweeping formations were laid down, such as the 'H' formation, with vessels in line abreast streaming either single or double sweeps. With the former, around 50% of the channel was swept and with the latter around 62%. Another pattern was the 'G' formation. Here the sweepers would follow the float of the ship in front, thus cutting an angled swathe through the minefield. Finally there was the 'K' sweep, where the ships steamed in two lines one behind the other at an angle of 27 degrees from the ship in front. Each sweeper was four cables abreast and four cables astern of each other, with all ships streaming double sweeps thus effectively covering a wide channel in one run.

The next problem for the sweepers manifested itself in the form of the magnetic mine. This lay on the bottom in shallow water (around 180ft) and was triggered by the magnetic influences from a passing ship. The main problem in combating this mine was that every steel ship had an inbuilt magnetic field wrought into the vessel by the builders rivetting hammers, etc. This magnetic field stayed with the vessel all her days and varied in strength depending on the aspect of her building berth, whether laid down north-south or east-west. Most ships built in the northern hemisphere have a magnetic force that projects a downward field of north polarity.

The first anti-magnetic sweep was 'one mine, one sweep', known as the 'skid sweep'. A small barge-like, flat bottomed raft was encased in a long electrically charged cable and the first skids carried their own on-board generator, although this type was almost impossible to hear from the towing ship and it was discontinued. After detonating a mine the skid usually disintegrated, tangling the towing wire and electric cables together. The system worked after a fashion and the idea of using an electrical current to set off mines led the scientists to their next counter-measure.

This next sweep was devised with a combination of thirty-four steel bars, approximately 3ins in diameter and 6ft long, which were spaced some 15ft apart along the 700ft sweep wire. These bars were heavily magnetised, with the poles reversed on alternate bars, the combined magnetism equalling that of a large merchant ship. These bars were suspended from the sweep wire

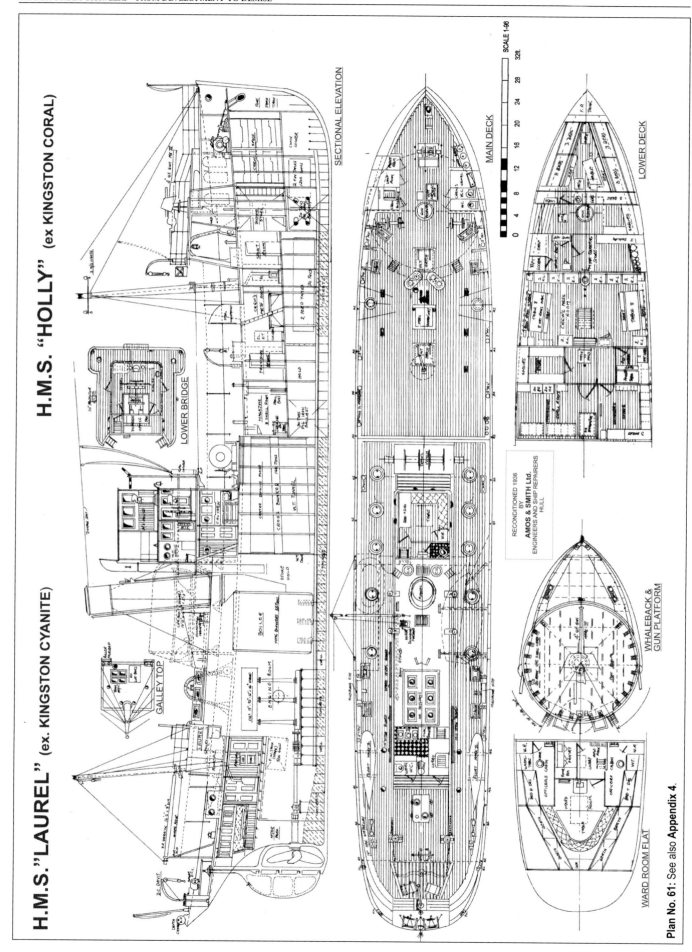

H.M.S. "HOLLY" (ex KINGSTON CORAL)

H.M.S. "LAUREL" (ex. KINGSTON CYANITE)

SECTIONAL ELEVATION

LOWER BRIDGE

GALLEY TOP

MAIN DECK

LOWER DECK

SCALE 1:96

RECONDITIONED 1936
BY
AMOS & SMITH Ltd.
ENGINEERS AND SHIP REPAIRERS
HULL

WHALEBACK &
GUN PLATFORM

WARD ROOM FLAT

Plan No. 61: See also **Appendix 4.**

by 40ft long wire pendants and the sweep wire itself was buoyed along its length with a series of floats. Although the sweep worked quite well, handling it was fraught with danger. They had to be stowed correctly, otherwise the bars would flail about madly, smashing anything in their path. At night or in anything of a sea, the 'bosun's nightmare', as it was termed, needed careful handling. As the wires and colour coded bars washed around the deck, they got into a snarl up of men and gear. The sweep was later modified, with the length of the weights reduced from 6ft to just 20ins and their number increased to seventy, with no effect on efficiency. The story goes that one seaman remarked woefully to his mate, "*When one of them new weights hits us, we'll only need two stitches instead of twenty*", and he chirped, as an afterthought, "*We can use the cut off bits as sinkers for fishing lines*". Even with this new sweep, steel trawlers were still blown up, so the boffins had to devise a cloaking device in order that they could safely go about their business of mine clearance. This evolved as the de-gaussing method, in which heavy electrical cables were fixed round a ship's hull at main deck level and energised by an electric generator. This effectively neutralised the magnetic influences in the vessel, giving her an immunity from the magnetic mine.

Early trials showed the cables strung round the outside of the hull. Later, they were encased in trays or ducting but still on the outside. However, damage to the cables still occurred in heavy weather or by coming alongside too enthusiastically and the solution was to fit them internally, when the ships were being built or refitted. The real solution to the magnetic mine came in 1940, with the 'Double-L sweep' or 'LL' for short. It was formed by passing an electrical charge through two differing lengths of buoyant cable, lashed together and towed astern. The first sweeps were only single cables and were only half as potent as the 'doubles'. The Mark 1 LL sweep consisted of a 525 yard length and a 125 yard length seized together and each fitted with a 50ft electrode. The power at first came from banks of car batteries but these were soon replaced by generators, which developed from 35kw on the early sweeps, up to 220kw on the later types. The sweep was pulsed every minute with 3,000 amps, which effectively swept a path some 270 yards long when steaming at 8 knots. The

trawlers used the Mark 2 sweep, powered by a 70kw generator, pulsing for 5 seconds every 60, and towed at 6 to 8 knots.

Next came the acoustic mine. This was another influence type device, triggered by the sound waves generated by a passing ship. An early attempt at dealing with this type was by firing bursts of machine gun bullets into the water ahead of the ship. This did have a modicum of success but as ammunition was at a premium, this method soon fell from favour. The real counter-measure came from, of all places, the construction industry, in the form of the pneumatic hammer. The most common type was manufactured by the Kango Company and so was born the 'Kango' or 'Hammer' sweep. Initially, they were fitted internally against a steel plate set in the flooded forepeak but, after a couple of unexplainable explosions destroyed two sweepers, this method was discontinued. It was replaced by the external bow fitting, whereby a steel 'A' frame was fitted to the bows. This could be raised when not in use but when sweeping, it projected below the keel of the sweeper. To this was fixed a conical steel bucket, inside which was mounted the Kango hammer. This produced 'white noise', which proved exceptionally effective against the acoustic mine. As the war progressed and the mining offensive became more intensive, not to mention more cunning, sweepers had to be fitted with a variety of counter measures. No longer were trawlers only equipped for sweeping a single type of mine, they carried at the very least two sets of sweep, one for moored contact mines and the other for either magnetic or acoustics

NAVAL TRAWLERS 'BASSET' CLASS

The Navy had not forgotten the usefulness of trawlers from 1914 and had studied their design in order to draw up a similar type, suitable for naval duties (**Photo. 82**). This design evolved as the 'Basset' Class of naval trawlers, with the lead ship being launched from Robb of Leith on 28th September 1935 and given the Admiralty No. T68 (160ft 6ins x 27ft 6ins x 14ft 6ins, 460g, 850ihp). Her service speed was 12 knots and her complement thirty-three in total. She was the forerunner of twenty-five of her class, with another four ships destroyed on the stocks when the Japanese invaded Rangoon. The builder's revised general arrangement drawing (**Plan 62**) bears

Photo. 82: *Bassett*, with her straight stem, was the forerunner of the Second World War naval trawlers.

H.M.TRAWLER - BASSET TYPE

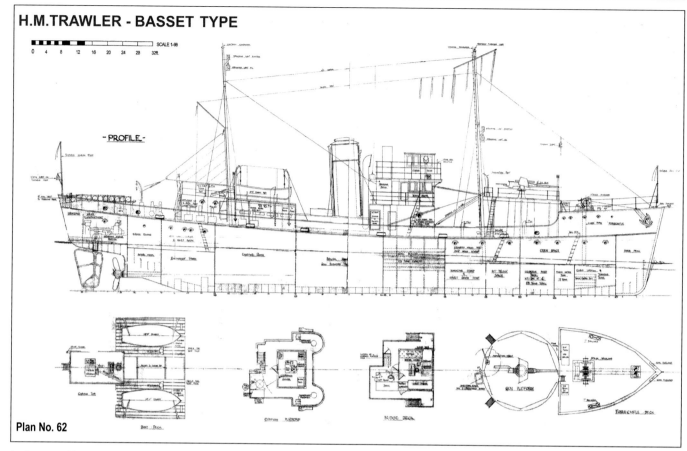

Plan No. 62

little resemblance to a civilian trawler of the period, being more like a pre-war naval sloop but with a raked stem, masts and funnel. Coal fired, they had full cruiser sterns with balanced rudders fitted to a skeg. One thing these ships did have in their favour, as opposed to their civilian counterparts, was the ability to remain afloat longer after sustaining a fair degree of damage. This was due to having seven watertight bulkheads, which divided the vessels into nine compartments. They were designed as anti-submarine trawlers, so their surface weaponry was limited and consisted of the single 4ins gun with a couple of light machine guns for anti-aircraft protection. *Basset* herself survived the war and was sold on 15th September 1947 and renamed *Radford*. She was followed by *Mastiff* (T10), a slightly larger vessel at 163ft 6ins oa and 520 tons. The extra length came from the fitting of a raked stem, which became standard on all following ships. Launched by Robb's on 17th February 1938, she was lost on 20th November 1939 after striking a mine in the Thames estuary. A further four ships were built in Canada, one each from Collingwoods, Burrards, Mortons and Canadian Yarrow shipyards. All served in the RCN and were sold to China after the war. The remaining nineteen vessels were part of an order placed with Indian yards for service with the Royal Indian Navy. These trawlers were 25 tons heavier than their British counterparts and carried fifteen more crew.

'TREE' CLASS

This class was a direct descendant of the earlier 'Basset' Class. Twenty ships were built in UK, with the first pair, *Rowan* (T119) and *Walnut* (T103) coming from Smith's Dock on 12th August 1939, as Yard No's 1070 and 1071 – 164ft oa / 150ft bp x 27ft 6ins x 10ft 6ins, 530g, 850ihp). Their uprated sweeping gear,

depth charge outfits and defensive armament gave them a 70 ton higher outfit weight than earlier ships. They were designed from the outset as dual purpose minesweeping and anti-submarine ships, carrying a crew of thirty-five officers and men. Some saw service as dhan layers, with reduced anti-submarine and surface to surface capabilities. The usual 12 pounder high angle gun was replaced by a pair of single 20mm Oerlikons. The dhan layers task was to accompany the sweepers and buoy the swept channel. Each would carry fifty-two dhans, with usually half this number in ready use racks on the upper deck. This class of trawler was all-rivetted, with a bar stem and all steel weather decks. They were sub-divided into eleven compartments by no fewer than nine watertight bulkheads. As minor war vessels, they were designed to take a fair bit of punishment, although six of the class were lost whilst on war service. Costing around £53,100 each, they were built by nine shipyards as part of the War Emergency Programme and their build time averaged about seven months a ship. Spare propellers were supplied at a further cost of £50 each. Unfortunately, *Juniper* had a relatively short life. She was launched from Ferguson's Yard on 15th December 1939 and given the Admiralty No. T123 but was sunk off Norway on 6th June 1940, by gunfire from the German cruiser *Admiral Hipper*. Another five of the class were lost during the war; *Almond*, *Ash*, *Chestnut* and *Hickory* by mines, and *Pine* by an E-boat torpedo. One of the remaining ships, *Acacia* (T.02), launched by the Ardrossan Dockyard on 7th March 1940, was purchased by the Scottish Home Department in November 1947 as a Fishery Patrol trawler and commissioned in September 1948 as *Vaila*. She carried out her protection duties until caught in whiteout conditions off the Isle of Lewis on 6th January 1957. She was driven ashore, and became a total loss.

'DANCE' CLASS

These were yet another development of the 'Basset' Class but whereas the 'Tree' Class were mainly minesweepers, the 'Dance' Class were primarily anti-submarine and escort trawlers (160ft 6ins oa x 150ft bp x 27ft 6ins x 10ft 6ins, 300g, 850ihp). They carried a forward 4ins gun, with a pair of Lewis guns on the bridge wings and an Oerlikon platform over the aft end of the casing. Twin depth charge rails were fitted aft, each holding twelve charges, and a D/C thrower was positioned on either side of the galley. The funnel and stokehold ventilators were slightly taller than on earlier vessels. Apparently, with the funnel being so close to the bridge, smoke was a problem. On earlier ships, its top was almost at the same level as the watchkeepers, making their life very unpleasant at times. Some ships had two masts but many of the class had the mizzen removed and the foremast replaced by a tripod mast on the foreside of the funnel. The funnels on these single-masted ships had an extension cowl piece fitted, similar to American-built escorts.

Mazurka was sold out of service in March 1946 and her sister, *Minuet*, transferred to the Italians in the same year as RD.307. Another three ships also went to Italy that year, namely *Gavotte* (T115), *Hornpipe* (T120) and *Two Step* (T.142 – ex-*Tarantella*), becoming RD312, RD316, and RD308 respectively. In all, twenty 'Dance' Class trawlers were built by the same yards as previously, with build times varying from seven to fifteen months. Only one of the class, *Sword Dance*, was lost in action, after a collision in the Moray Firth on 5th July 1942. As the war progressed and the need for greater endurance escorts arose, some of the class, like *Cotillion* (T.104), from the Ardrossan yard, had their fo'c'sles lengthened in a similar fashion to the 'Flower' Class corvettes.

'SHAKESPERIAN' CLASS

Yet another development of the Admiralty trawler classes, this twelve ship group took their names from the Bard's characters (164ft oa / 153ft 8ins bp x 27ft 9ins x 14ft 1in, 545g, 950ihp). They were slightly larger than the 'Dance' Class and were the most powerful of all the 'Basset' descendants, with a service speed of 12 knots and a complement of thirty-five. They had the same three-furnace, Scotch-type boilers as the previous classes, bunkering 126.5 tons of coal in the cross bunker and a further 57.5 tons in the wings. The first of the class was *Hamlet* (T.167), from Cook, Welton & Gemmell on 24th July 1940. She was followed at almost monthly intervals by her sisters, the last ship being *Othello* (T.76), from Hall, Russell's on 7th October 1941. Three of the class were lost: *Laertes* (T.137) to *U201* off Freetown on 25th July 1942; *Horatio* (T.153) on 7th January 1943 in the Mediterranean, after being torpedoed by an Italian motor anti-submarine boat; and *Coriolanus* (T.140) on 5th May 1945, which sank after striking a mine in the Adriatic.

One of the luckier trawlers was *Fluellen* (T.157), launched by Cochranes on 1st November 1940. After war service she was purchased by the Scottish Home Department in 1947 and converted to *Scotia* (a fishery research vessel) in 1948, by George Brown & Sons of Leith (**Plan No. 63**). She had a more typical fishing arrangement, with a foremast stepped on the foredeck, starboard trawl gallows and a trawl winch. Initially, she retained the three deck superstructure but her casing abaft the engine room skylight was widened and lengthened to provide extra accommodation and laboratory space. A deckhouse was added on the casing, which contained both the Captain's and Chief Officer's cabin. Below deck, the crew space housed eighteen seamen in two-berth cabins, with mess rooms for both deck crew and firemen. The after cabin flat was fitted out with six separate cabins for officers and scientists, and the space below the wheelhouse housed both a main, and a plankton, laboratory (**Photo. 83**). A trial cruise was made from 16th to 23rd December 1948 and regular scientific operations began in January 1949. Early in 1951, she was converted to oil fuel by Clyde Fuel Oil Systems and during this refit, her top bridge was removed. She was later fitted with a diesel-powered generator, a heavier trawl winch and she had her laboratory spaces uprated. She worked continuously from Aberdeen for the Department of Agriculture & Fisheries for Scotland and the Torry Research Laboratory. In October 1971, she was renamed *Scarba*, when her own name was allotted to a new research ship. She continued to work for about a year under her new name, before switching to Fishery Protection duties until she was laid up in May 1973. She finally went to the breakers W.H. Arnott Young & Co. of Dalmuir, in November of that year.

Photo. 83: *Scotia* (ex-*Fluellen*) of the 'Shakespearian' Class, showing her conversion to research vessel. Extended accommodation has been fitted to house the laboratories and extra ship's complement, with a deckhouse abaft the funnel for officers. Pictured post-1951, after her conversion to oil firing.

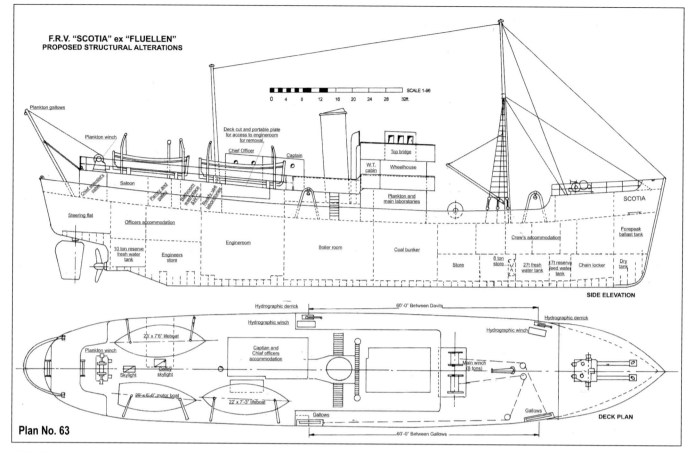

F.R.V. "SCOTIA" ex "FLUELLEN"
PROPOSED STRUCTURAL ALTERATIONS

Plan No. 63

'ISLES' CLASS

This was the most numerous of all the Admiralty trawler classes, the four-year build programme producing some 130 ships, most named after Scottish islands (164ft oa / 150ft bp x 27ft 6ins x 10ft 6ins, 545g, 850ihp). Nineteen ships were completed as dhan layers and four as controlled minelayers. These latter vessels had 'Bird' names: *Blackbird* (M.15 – ex-*Sheppey 1*), *Dabchick* (M.22 – ex-*Thorney*), *Stonechat* (M.25) and *Whitethroat* (M 03). All were built by Cook, Welton & Gemmell. Fifteen of the class were either lost in action or by stranding and one, *Colsay* (T.384), was sunk by an enemy human torpedo off Ostende on 2nd November 1944 (the only naval trawler sunk in this fashion). In addition to the British-built trawlers, a further sixteen were built in Canada, by yards such as Collingwoods, Kingston's, Davies and Midland Shipbuilding. Post war, fifty ships were sold out of service commercially, twenty-eight were transferred to other navies and forty-four were scrapped.

Benbecula (T.379) became *Vigilant* and served with the HM Customs & Excise fleet from 1946 until 1962. She was purchased for £10,000 (this was considered a bargain but it also had the proviso that she should be handed back to the Royal Navy should ever the need arise). However, she was not well liked by the Customs Service, because of her squarish shape and annual maintenance costs of around £7,500, coupled with running costs of nearly £30,000. She was retired in 1962. Another trawler, *Annet* (T.341) became the Fishery Protection vessel *Ulva* in 1958. Six other ships were transferred in 1947 to the War Department fleet (the Army's civilian navy) during the early 1950s; these Army trawlers acted as escorts to the landing craft tanks engaged in ammunition dumping from Cairnryan on the west coast of Scotland. *Mull* had the honour

of being the last of the class to serve with the Army. Her final tour of duty was at Singapore in 1951, after conversion to oil fuel but, as late as 1975, she was seen steaming up the Mersey.

The War Department had another three ex-Admiralty trawlers in its fleet: *Porcher* (T.281) and *Prospect* (T.282) were both Canadian built 'Isles'; and the 'Dance' Class *Foxtrot* (T.109), built by Cochranes in April 1940. By 1977, six of the class were still under naval control as tank cleaning ships, namely *Bern*, *Caldy*, *Graemsay*, *Lundy*, *Switha* and *Skomer*.

ADMIRALTY'S CIVILIAN DESIGNS

It was obvious, from the outset of hostilities, that the navy would desperately need large trawlers for both escort and anti-submarine duties, not to mention the replacement of those vessels lost in action. In order to speed up construction, their Lordships decided to use proven civilian types as the basis for placing the orders. This was a shrewd move, as the yards had all the information to hand and could commence work almost immediately. One necessary modification to the original designs had to be done before these vessels could enter service, however. This was to re-ballast them in order to allow for the extra topside weight of armaments and superstructure. The worst scenario was chosen, which was on return from duty when the fuel, stores and water would be almost all used up and the vessels be in their most tender stability condition. The Admiralty decided on a safe minimum metacentric height of around 12ins. This would ensure maximum stability when fully loaded, with the metacentric height in this condition being raised to nearly 24ins. To do this, the following extra ballast weight was recommended: vessels of 120-125ft – 20-30 tons; 125-150ft – 30-50 tons; 150ft and over – 50-80 tons. One advantage of the trawler

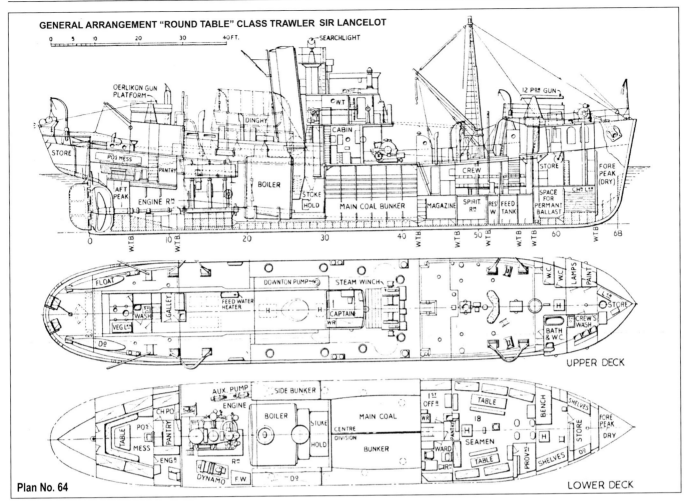

GENERAL ARRANGEMENT "ROUND TABLE" CLASS TRAWLER SIR LANCELOT

Plan No. 64

UPPER DECK

LOWER DECK

was their large rise of floor. This meant that a single bilge suction line could be run along the keelson, so when adding this extra ballast, it was not just a matter pouring more cement into the bilges. This would have cancelled out any advantage of the original design, as the cement would flatten out the bilge bottom and require more bilge suction lines to be fitted. The ballast was therefore loose blocks of concrete, securely stowed and carefully fitted around the bilge suctions, mainly in the fish room area. The trawlers were classed according to size and fell into four distinct types.

'ROUND TABLE' CLASS

This, the smallest class of trawler (137ft oa / 126ft bp x 23ft 9ins x 11ft 6ins, 440g, 600ihp), was based on Hall, Russell's *Star of Orkney*, built in 1936. The class comprised eight ships, all named after Arthurian Knights of the Round Table and costing £41,182 each. The first to join the fleet was *Sir Lancelot* (T.228), launched by John Lewis as Yard No. 160 on 4th December 1941. The remaining ships were completed in the following order: *Sir Galahad* (T.226) on 18th December 1941 by Hall, Russell as Yard No. 763; *Sir Tristam* (T.229) on 17th January 1942 by Lewis as Yard No. 161; *Sir Gareth* (T.227) on 19th January 1942 by Hall, Russell as Yard No. 764; *Sir Agravaine* (T.230) on 5th March 1942 by Lewis as Yard No. 162; *Sir Geraint* (T.240) on 15th April 1942 by Lewis as Yard No. 163; *Sir Kay* (T.241) on 26th October 1942 by Hall, Russell as Yard No. 768; and *Sir Lamorack* (T.242) on 23rd November 1942 by Hall, Russell as Yard No. 769.

They were designed solely as minesweepers for home waters. *Sir*

Galahad and *Sir Lancelot* were the only two ships of the class with Robertson's trawl winches and Oropesa sweeping gear for moored mines. The other six ships were designed to combat influence mines and had their trawl winches replaced by a deckhouse. This contained the powerful 50kw diesel generators and switchgear necessary for operating the Mark II 'LL' sweeps. This type of sweep had a Kango hammer, with an 'A' frame and bucket suspended over the bows. Their armament was a typical trawler 12 pounder 3ins gun on a Mark IX HA/LA mounting, one 20mm Oerlikon on a bandstand aft and either two or four machine guns on the bridge wings, plus four depth charges at the counter. All of the class survived the war and, after being sold, continued to give excellent service as commercial trawlers. *Sir Galahad* was converted to a dhan layer in 1944 and was sold in 1946 being renamed *Star of Freedom* (A.283), by Walker's. They sold her to Milford Fisheries in March 1956, who changed her name to *Robert Limbrick* (A.283). She was lost with all hands on 5th February the following year, after running aground at Quinish Point, off the Isle of Mull. *Sir Tristam* was sold out of service in 1947. *Sir Gareth* was sold on 11th April 1946 to Walker Steam Trawling & Fishing Co. Ltd, Aberdeen, as *Star of the East* (A.277). She changed hands again in 1958 as *Milford Star* (M.120), owned by Westward Trawlers Ltd who converted her to oil firing. They in turn sold her in 1964 as *Kudnais* and she was broken up two years later. *Sir Agravaine* was sold on 10th April 1946 to the Great Western Fishing Co. of Aberdeen as A.276. She was sold in 1954 to Norwegian owners Nils Uthiem as *Utheim* and converted to oil fuel in 1957. She was

1964. *Sir Kay* was purchased by Walkers in April 1946 as *Star of the North* (A.334). They sold her in 1956 to J. Croan & Co. Ltd, Granton, who changed her name to *Robert Croan* (LH.22) and she went to the breakers at Grangemouth on 26th December 1961; *Sir Lamorack* was sold on 10th April 1946 to the Don Fishing Co. Ltd, Aberdeen and renamed *Braconbank* (A.237). She went to Norwegian owners C. Rango in 1954, who fitted her with a five-cylinder Alpha diesel engine and renamed her *Bracon*. She was still in the register in 1980.

Sir Lancelot (**Plan 64**) gives a good impression of the class. She was fitted for contact sweeping and the deck plan shows the layout of the gear in detail. The layout of her trawl gallows, warp rollers, etc, is standard practice and ideal for working the Oropesa sweep. This gear was the Mark III, which used a serrated sweep wire, Type 8747 otter with a Type 8733 kite and a Type 8742 float, towed at 7.5 knots. She bunkered 158 tons, enough for eighteen to twenty days. In 1944 she was converted to a dhan layer (**Photo. 84a**).

After the war, she was purchased by the Ministry of Agriculture & Fisheries, Lowestoft and after a refit in early 1947 by Menzies & Co, Leith, she went to work as *Sir Lancelot* (LT.263 – **Plan No. 65, Photo. 84b**). This overhaul saw her converted to oil fuel

sold again in 1972 to Rolf Hansen Pardrederi, renamed *Federal* and was lost on 24th July the following year. *Sir Geraint* was sold to Walker's on 10th April 1946 and renamed *Star of the South* (A.398). She was sold again in 1959 to E.E. Carter of Milford Haven as *Haven Star* (M.144) and went to the breakers in July

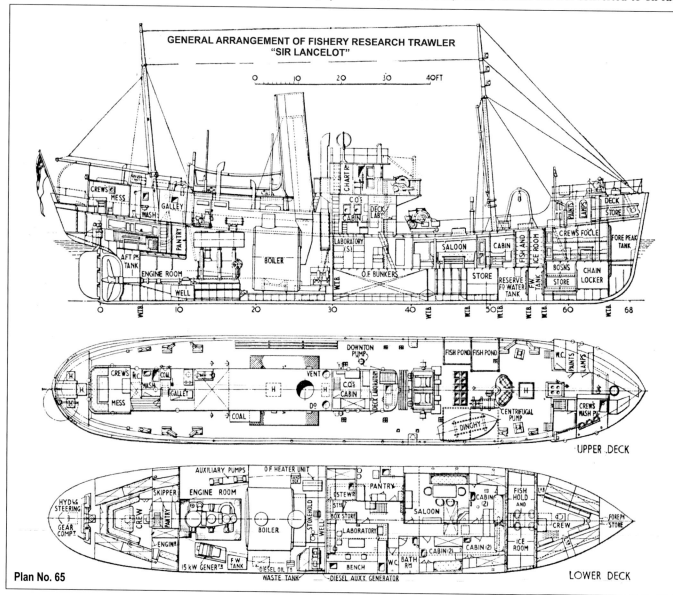

Plan No. 65

Photo. 84b: *Sir Lancelot*, ex-'Round Table' Class, as a research ship, with extended wheelhouse and twin lifeboat arrangement. Her forward fishing number is in a strange place and her funnel numbers are on either side rather than on the front.

and her steam steering gear in the wheelhouse was replaced by a Donkin steam/hydraulic system, installed aft in the tiller flat. The removal of her coal bunkers made space available for laboratories and accommodation for the extra scientific staff. Above deck, her casing was extended to incorporate a crew's mess on upper deck level and a mizzen mast was fitted, complete with a triangular steadying sail. Two boats were carried on sparred extensions either side of the casing, the starboard being an oared, transom sterned boat and the port a double-ended motor lifeboat. A 16ft workboat was stowed in the starboard pounds on the foredeck. Also on the foredeck is the petrol powered centrifugal pump, capable of delivering up to seven tons of water a minute, from any depth. The wheelhouse verandah was extended forward to accommodate the new Elliot & Garrood steam winch. This operated both the Petersen grab on the foremast and the geared Nansen Petterson bottle davit on the verandah. The former was used to collect live samples from the seabed and the latter collected samples of salinity, temperature and other observations necessary to the scientists. After a useful working life with the Ministry, she was sold in 1962 as *Hair-Ed-Din-Barbaross* and was still around in 1981.

'FISH' CLASS

The next size up from the 'Round Table' Class, ten 'Fish' Class ships were built as anti-submarine trawlers (162ft oa / 46ft 6ins bp x 25ft x 14ft, 153n, 358g), based on Cochrane's *Gulfoss* of 1929. Eight had engines of 700ihp from Amos & Smith and a service speed of 11 knots but *Bonito* and *Whiting* had C.D. Holmes' engines. They bunkered 197 tons of fuel oil and had a range of around 4,700 miles. *Gulfoss* (GY.146) was accepted from the builders in September 1929 by Consolidated Fisheries Ltd, Lowestoft, until she was requisitioned in September 1939. She served as a minesweeper, FY710, until she struck a mine in the English Channel on 9th March 1941.

The class were armed with the usual trawler 12 pounder forward and three 20mm Oerlikons, one aft on the galley roof and the others either side of the foredeck in bandstands. Twin Lewis machine guns were mounted either side of the upper bridge and her anti-submarine armament consisted of twin throwers aft of the casing and sixteen charges in two racks on the counter. They carried a crew of thirty-five who were housed in various 'messes', in typical naval fashion. A single 16ft transom sterned trawler boat was carried in radial davits on a boat deck abreast the funnel and two Carley floats were fitted port side. The helmsman was protected by a bullet proof (non-magnetic) shelter but the upper

bridge had no protection. Steering was steam/hydraulic, with the emergency wheel and hand pump placed on the casing top ahead of the main engine room skylight and protected by a waist-high steel plate on its forward side. The builders drawings (**Plans 66 a & b**) show smart, fine lined Distant Water ships, with whaleback fo'c'sles, raked stems and cruiser sterns. No mizzen mast is shown, as it would hamper the operation of the Oerlikon mounted on the galley roof but they are fitted with aerial masts on the foreside of the funnel and an ensign gaff on the after side. The main stokehold cowl vents have their trunks cranked aft to clear the extended verandah and the ash shoots can be clearly seen on the plan. They had the reputation of being coal gobblers when running at full speed, making them unpopular with the firemen. Being designed for anti-submarine work no trawl winch was fitted. This class had wood sheathed foredecks in keeping with commercial trawlers but the quarterdecks were bare steel and remained so until their demise. All the hands had bunks rather than the naval hammocks that had been crammed into the First World War ships.

During the war, they saw a lot of service as escorts in the Adriatic and around Sicily, with *Bonito*'s skipper receiving a decoration for towing a loaded ammunition ship out of Bari during an air raid, after another ammunition ship had blown up. Two of the class, *Mackerel* and *Turbot* were converted to controlled minelayers and renamed *Corncrake* (M55) and *Redshank* (M31) respectively, with their displacement increased to 700 tons. The former foundered in a gale on 25th January 1943 when in the north Atlantic. *Redshank* remained in Admiralty service until she went to the breakers at Sunderland on 9th May 1957.

The only other casualty was *Herring* (T.307), lost after a collision in the North Sea on 22nd April 1943. The remainder of the class were purchased by Consolidated Fisheries Ltd, Lowestoft, after the war and converted to force-draught firing (**Plan 67**). A typical example was *Grayling* (T.243), purchased for £45,666 and renamed *Barry Castle* (SA.33 – **Photo. 85**). She foundered in a gale off Iceland on 1st November 1955, with the loss of four of her eighteen man crew

'HILLS' CLASS.

Larger again than the 'Fishes' were the 'Hills' Class (181ft oa / 166ft bp x 28ft x 12ft, 750g, 970ihp). They were built by Cook, Welton & Gemmell and engined by Charles D. Holmes, with a service speed of 11 knots. They were based on the builder's *Barnett* (GY.454), launched on 26th July 1937 by the owner's wife Mrs Crampin and named in the firm's tradition after a British cricketer – Charles John Barnett was an accomplished player for both his home side Gloucestershire and England. On 29th September 1937, he and his wife were honoured guests on the ship as she ran acceptance trials before steaming into Grimsby. On her maiden trip to the White Sea in October, she landed 2,300 boxes of fish. She was requisitioned as an anti-submarine trawler but, as there already was an Admiralty trawler of that name, she was renamed *Blackfly* (FY117). She served on the Northern Patrol, in addition to escorting the Russian PQ convoys. Later, in May 1944, she assisted in the destruction of *U731* in the Straits of Gibraltar. After the war, she was purchased by the Hull Fishing & Ice Co. Ltd in March 1946 and Crampins bought her back as *Barnett* (GY.200) in the November. They ran her until October 1960, when they sold her to Belgium. The owners had suffered heavy losses throughout the

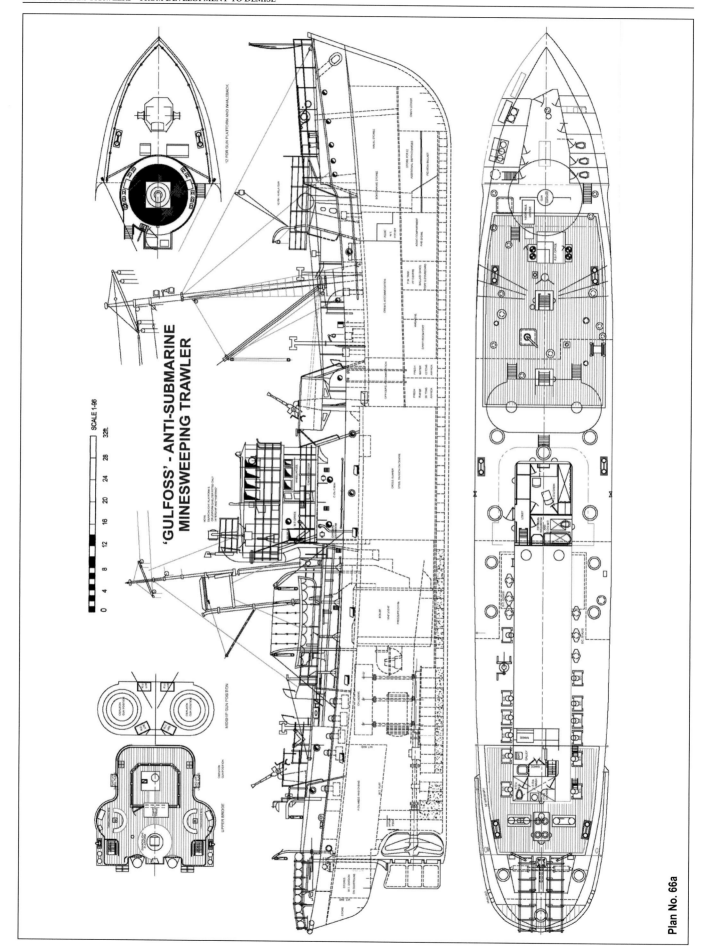

'GULFOSS' - ANTI-SUBMARINE
MINESWEEPING TRAWLER

SCALE 1-96

0   4   8   12   16   20   24   28   32ft.

Plan No. 66a

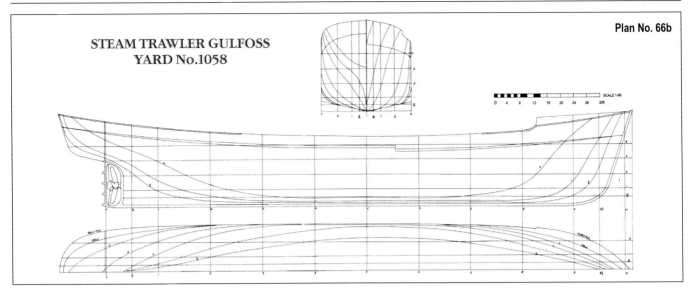

STEAM TRAWLER GULFOSS
YARD No.1058

Plan No. 66b

SCALE 1·96

war, with five of their fleet lost in action: *Bradman* (GY.358), *Hammond* (GY.284), *Jardine* (GY.301), *Larwood* (GY.255) and *Leyland* (GY.254). The 'Hills' Class of eight ships were fitted out as anti-submarine trawlers and were fitted with the same weapons as the 'Fish' Class.

Their average build time was nine months and they were launched in the following order in 1944:

Yard No. 681 *Birdlip* (T.218) launched on 9th September. She was lost on 13th June 1944 after being attacked by *U547* off West Africa.

Yard No. 683 *Butser* launched twenty days later. She survived the war and was sold in 1946 to Hellyers as *Balthazar* (H.359). In February 1952, she crossed the Humber to Grimsby as *Royal Marine* (GY.213), owned by the Loyal Steam Fishing Co. Ltd, Grimsby and she was sold again in March 1960 to Wyre Trawlers Ltd of Fleetwood as *Royal Marine* (FD.63 – **Photo. 86**). She went to the breakers at Troon in September 1963.

Yard No. 684 *Duncton* (T.220), launched on 6th September. She too survived and was sold in 1945 as *Colwyn Bay* (H.387), managed by the Marine Steam Fishing Co. Ltd, Hull (a subsidiary

Photo. 85: *Barry Castle* (ex-*Grayling*) showing her Swansea registration and the 'chessman' type Castle funnel motif adopted by Consolidated Fisheries Ltd of Grimsby for these ships.

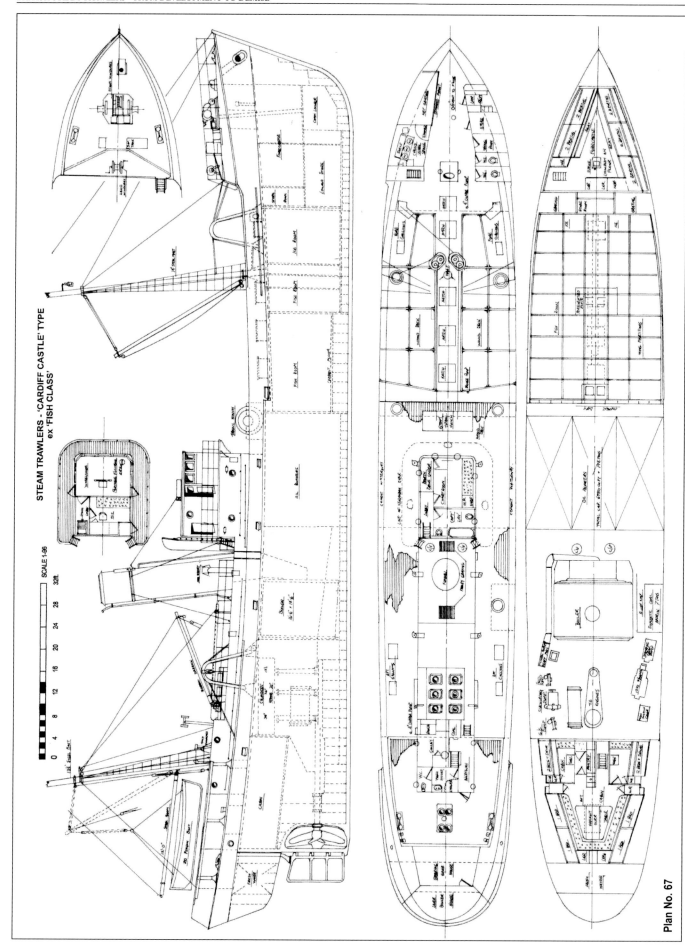

STEAM TRAWLERS - 'CARDIFF CASTLE' TYPE
ex 'FISH CLASS'

SCALE 1:96

Plan No. 67

Photo. 86: *Royal Marine* (ex-*Butser*) in Wyre Trawlers Ltd colours of black funnel with two white bands and quite unrecognisable from her wartime configuration.

of the Boston Deep Sea Fishing & Ice Co. Ltd). She was converted to oil fuel in March 1953 and went to the breakers in 1964

Yard No. 685 *Portsdown* (T.221), launched on 24th September and sold in 1946 to Hull Merchants Amalgamated Trawlers Ltd as *Sollum* (H.369). They sold her to Crampin's in February 1949 and she became another cricketer, *Hargood* (GY.8). They converted her to oil fuel in the December and she was sold again in June 1955, to Iago Steam Trawling Co. Ltd, Fleetwood as *Red Sabre* (LO.71), sporting their distinctive black funnel with a red band. She sailed for the scrap yard at Passage, West Cork on 2nd December 1964.

Yard No. 686 *Yestor* (T.222) launched on 21st October and decommissioned in 1946. She became *Cape Cleveland* (H.355), owned by Hudsons Brothers (Trawlers) Ltd. A year later she was sold to Charleston-Smith Trawlers Ltd, Hull as *Stella Carina* (H.355) and they converted her to oil firing in November. In 1951, she returned to Hudsons as *Cape Finisterre* and she went to the Great Grimsby & East Coast Steam Fishing Co. Ltd in January 1952 as *Cape Finisterre* (GY.222). They renamed her *Dragoon* a month later. In March 1960, she transferred to Wyre Trawlers Ltd at Fleetwood as *Dragoon* (FD.60) and went to the breakers at Troon on 18th December 1966.

Yard No. 682 *Bredon* (T.223), launched on 20th November and sunk by *U521* in the North Atlantic on 8th February 1943.

Yard No. 688 *Inkpen* (T.225) was the last of the class, launched on 22nd December. In 1946, she was bought by Charleston-Smith Trawlers Ltd, who renamed her *Stella Capella* (H.358) and they converted her to oil fuel in September 1947. She went to the scrap yard at Blyth on 24th October 1963.

They seemed to have been quite lucky ships, with only two being lost to hostilities and a third whilst fishing.

'MILITARY' CLASS

The 'Military' Class were the largest and most powerful of all the naval trawler classes. Although 10ft shorter, some 3 to 4 knots slower and with 20% less crew than the 'Flower' Class corvettes, they could keep the seas when these larger escorts were forced to

lay to or run before the weather. They were Distant Water trawlers of the latest design, based on Cook, Welton & Gemmell's Yard No. 651, launched in November 1939 as *Lady Madeleine* (H.243 – 193ft 7ins oa / 178ft 1in bp x 30ft x 15ft 2ins, 581g, 214n, 165nhp), for Jutland Amalgamated Trawlers Ltd, Hull, with engines supplied by C.D. Holmes and a service speed of 12.5 knots. She was hired as an anti-submarine trawler in February 1940 and returned in February 1946. In common with many hired trawlers, she changed hands during her wartime service, being bought by the Kingston Steam Trawling Co. Ltd in 1943. She was renamed *Kingston Diamond* (H.243 – **Photo. 87**) and they converted her to oil fuel in December 1949. In 1964, she was sold to Wyre Trawlers Ltd of Fleetwood, retaining her name and number but she went to the breakers at Port Glasgow in April 1965.

She was actually the third ship to carry the *Lady Madeleine* name. Her immediate predecessor was built by Cook, Welton & Gemmell in 1934 for Jutland's as *Lady Madeleine* (H.85 – 151ft bp, 390g) and she in turn replaced another *Lady Madeleine* (H.278), built and owned by the same two firms in 1926. This first *Lady Madeleine* was sold to Grant's of Grimsby as GY.65, after her successor was completed in June 1934. A month later, she was renamed *Cameron* (GY.65). In October 1935, she went to the Clan Steam Fishing Co. Ltd, Grimsby, who sold her back to the Hull owners Loch Line in April 1939 as *Loch Alsh* (H.73). Reserved as a fishing trawler during the war, she met her end on 30th January 1942, after being attacked by enemy bombers off the Humber.

The 'Military' Class were ordered in three programmes between 1941 and 1943, with the first six ships completed in 1943, the rest in 1944, and an average build time of around seven and a half months. The yard numbers were allocated at the time of order and are out of step with the launch dates. The builder's drawing (**Plan 68 a & b**) is for Yard No's 703 to 708, the first two batches.

The first, Yard No. 703 *Grenadier* (T.334), was launched on 26th September 1942 and completed on 10th February 1943 (listed on the builders drawings as *Grenardier*). She was refitted when in service to meet the later specification, at which time her

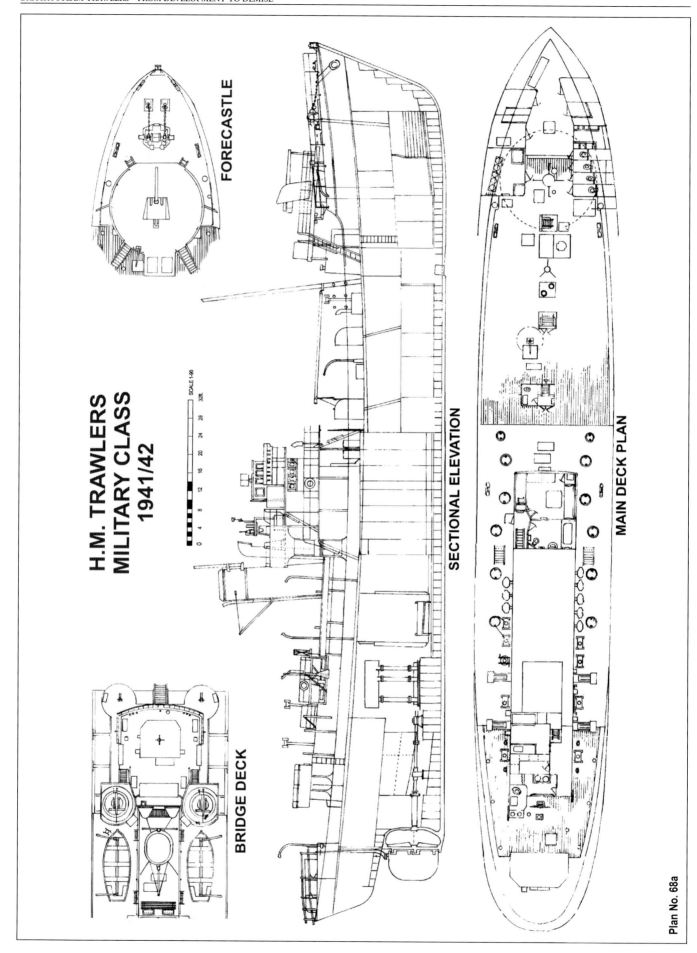

FORECASTLE

H.M. TRAWLERS
MILITARY CLASS
1941/42

SCALE 1=96

0   4   8   12   16   20   24   28   32ft.

SECTIONAL ELEVATION

MAIN DECK PLAN

BRIDGE DECK

Plan No. 68a

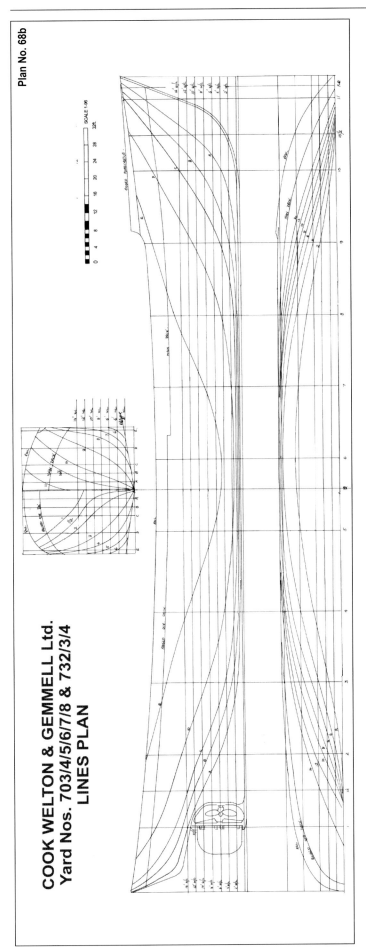

SCALE 1:96

0 4 8 12 16 20 24 28 32ft.

COOK WELTON & GEMMELL Ltd.
Yard Nos. 703/4/5/6/7/8 & 732/3/4
LINES PLAN

foremast was removed. She was sold to the Great Grimsby & East Coast Steam Fishing Co. Ltd in December 1946 as *Isernia* (GY.488) and was immediately converted to oil fuel. Post war she had her share of ill fortune. Posted as missing in February 1950, she limped home under tow following five days adrift, having been knocked down by terrible weather off Norway when homeward bound from the North Cape. The wheelhouse and radio cabin were gutted, wrecking her wireless equipment and trapping the radio operator. After being swept by numerous heavy seas, which had lain her on her beam ends, it was only the skill of her skipper Sid Farnley and the determination of her crew that brought her safely home. On 26th January 1955, she was again damaged by bad weather whilst dodging in a gale off the west coast of Iceland. One of her crew was badly smashed when washed about the deck and a large section of her headrails were carried away. She was lucky, however, as this was the gale that saw *Lorella* (H455) and *Roderigo* (H135) capsize with the loss of all hands. Misfortune hit the vessel again in October 1957, when four of her crew were dragged over the side by the net. Two were lost, the mate and a deckhand, but the other two were rescued by the skipper and other hands. In January 1966, after a serious fire on board, she was sold to Dutch owners.

Yard No. 704 *Lancer* (T.335) was launched on 26th October 1942 and completed on 25th February 1943. She was sold to Derwent Trawlers Ltd, Hull (part of Trawlers Grimsby), renamed *Stella Orion* (H.379) and converted to oil burning at the same time. Her career ended on 7th November 1955, when she was wrecked on the north west coast of Norway near Vestfjorden.

Yard No. 705 *Sapper* (T.336) was launched on 11th November 1942 and completed on 19th March 1943. After the war, she was sold to Hudson's as *Cape Gloucester* (H.395) and converted to oil burning. In 1957, she became *Admetus* (H.395 – the Prince of Thessay in Greek legend). She went for scrap in 1966.

Yard No. 708 *Bombardier* (T.304) was launched on 23rd January 1943 and completed on 19th May. Subsequently, she was modified to meet the specification of the later ships. Her foremast was removed and replaced by a tri-pod mast in front of the funnel, her bridge Oerlikons were moved to zareebas on the fore welldeck and she also carried a light tripod mizzen. However, it would seem that these changes were made sometime later in her career, as another photograph of her successor, *Coldstreamer*, shows the early arrangement. In 1946, she was bought by the Northern Fishing Co. Ltd, Hull, converted to oil burning and renamed *Norman* (H.289). Hull mourned her tragic loss on 4th October 1952, after she grounded in fog at Cape Farewell, Greenland. Of her twenty-one man crew, there was only one survivor.

Yard No. 706 *Coldstreamer* (T337) was launched on 10th December 1942 and completed on 10th April the following year. In 1946, Hellyer's purchased her as *Esquimaux* (H.297) and converted her to oil fuel. They sold her to the West Dock Steam Fishing Co. Ltd, Hull in 1956, who renamed her *Dunsley Wyke* (H.297) and she went to the breakers in 1967.

Yard No. 707 *Fusilier* (T.305) was launched on 23rd December 1942 and completed on 30th April 1943. She

Photo. 87: *Kingston Diamond* (ex-*Lady Madeleine*) in Kingston's colours of black topped white funnel, with the triple gold crown motif on a red circle.

was bought by the Standard Steam Fishing Co. Ltd, Grimsby in August 1946 as *Serron* (GY.309 – **Photo. 88**) and they converted her to oil fuel. She went for scrap in August 1965.

The three remaining ships that made up the 1943 programme (**Plan 68b**) had a more naval appearance than their predecessors but carried the same complement of forty and an identical weapons fit.

Yard No. 732 *Guardsman* (T.393) was launched on 7th June 1944 and completed on 22nd August. She was sold in August 1946 to the Great Grimsby & East Coast Steam Fishing Co. Ltd as *Thuringia* (GY.321) and converted to oil fuel in August 1947. In March 1966, she went to Northern Trawlers of Grimsby but, by that November, she was no longer viable and went to the scrap yard at Dunston.

Yard No. 733 *Home Guard* (T.394) was launched on 8th July 1944 and completed on 19th September. She became *Loyal* (GY.344) in October 1946, owned by the Loyal Steam Steam Fishing Co. Ltd, Grimsby, who converted her to oil firing in November the following year. In January 1966, she went to Northern Trawlers, who scrapped her at Antwerp on 2nd July that year.

Yard No. 708 *Royal Marine* (T.395), was launched on 22nd July 1944 and completed on 30th October. She was bought by the Standard Steam Fishing Co. Ltd, Grimsby in November 1946, renamed *Sisapon* (GY.381) and was later converted to burn oil. In April 1965, she went to Wyre Trawlers Ltd of Fleetwood as FD.92 and, in July 1967, she went to the breakers in Belgium.

According to the drawings, all these ships were built to the early specification. They carried the normal trawler foremast complete with derrick, open well deck and modified trawler superstructure. Their mizzens were replaced by a light wireless mast fitted to the fore side of the funnel, with an ensign gaff on its after side. Their main armament consisted of a 4ins Mark XIX gun on a Mark XXIII mounting. The mounting had a depression rail at its forward end, which gave a maximum depression of some 5 degrees clear of the bull ring. Their anti-aircraft weaponry comprised four, single, 20mm Oerlikons, two on the upper bridge and the others on the casing. A pair of twin Lewis guns were fitted on either side

of the wheelhouse verandah and a Holman steam projector was located on a light deck over the engine room skylight. However, this weapon was reckoned a complete waste of good steam. For anti-submarine work, they carried four throwers and racks at the counter. Mounted on the bridge roof was the parachute and cable rocket platform. These rockets were fired electrically and being classed as fireworks, could not be stowed below deck, hence the fireworks tanks on the maindeck at the break of the fo'c'sle.

These, then, were the trawlers that made up 'Harry Tate's Navy' of the Second World War. Manned by crews from all walks of life, they did sterling work in all theatres of the war. The RN Patrol Service began the war with 600 ships and 6,000 men but this had matured ten fold by the end of hostilities. The final cost was that 2,385 officers and men of the 'Silver Badge Fleet' perished, along with some 474 ships. These losses were far in excess of those suffered by the 'proper Navy'. Their sacrifice enabled the merchant ships to fight off the U-boats and ensured a safe channel for the convoys. Yes, theirs was a 'humdrum war', as so aptly stated by Ewart C. Brookes in his book *The Glory Passed Them By*.

Photo. 88 *Serron* (ex-*Fusilier*). Her lower shrouds are plated in to prevent damage by the cod end swinging inboard and her bulwarks have been raised. Note the pole compass on the starboard side of the wheelhouse, along with twin radars and binnacle. Her boats are carried in radial davits and she still carries her original bull ring. She wears Northern's colours of black hull with white band and brown superstructure, and a grey funnel with a black top separated by a white band.

Chapter 16: THE POST WAR YEARS

When the war finally ended, the Patrol Service was all but disbanded and the ships gradually returned from their stations for disarming and refitting prior to going back to their peace time roles. Some of the trawlers, such as the Admiralty types, had never fished commercially but, being based on proven fishing designs, they made attractive propositions as Distant Water ships and were soon sold out of naval service. There were other trawlers that had been taken over while on the stocks and finished off as minor war vessels. Almost all of the pre-war Arctic trawlers had been requisitioned, along with a large percentage of the Near and Middle Water ships. The ships that had remained fishing throughout the war were in a poor state of repair and had been kept going by the owners as best they could, hampered by the shortage of materials and spare parts. Peace had come at last and the trawling industry was in buoyant mood. It recalled that, after the 1914 war, fish were plentiful, having had time to rejuvenate stocks and so possibly it would be a bonanza time again for the fleet, after the lean days of the late 1930s. In fact, in the immediate post-war period, it was impossible not to fill the ships with fish. The net was only on the bottom a short time before it had to be hauled. Huge catches were taken from the Distant Waters of Bear Island, Iceland, the North Cape and the White Sea. To maximise fish room space, the catch was headed and only the bodies stowed. This process actually turned out to be an unsavoury one, as tens of thousands of rotting fish heads were left to fester on the grounds. The meshes of the trawl net were much smaller than post EEC regulations and many immature fish were taken, only to be thrown to the gulls to leave space for the larger cod. At Hull, some of the exceptional landings in 1946 included *Man O'War* (H.181) landing 4,102 kits grossing £16,996 on 12th March, *St. Bartholemew* (H.216) landing 4,225 kits grossing £17,302 on 19th March and, on 22nd May, *Northella* (H.244) landing 4,319 kits grossing £12,842 (one kit = 10 stones, 16 kits = 1 ton, thus 4,000 kits = 250 tons).

Germany at this time was screaming out for fish, as the nation was starving after the war and many Distant Water ships took their catches to these markets. Ironically, many of the ex-Bremerhaven built 'Northerns' landed their catches in the land of their birth. Landings averaging 4,500 kits were commonplace during this period. The Near and Middle Water ships were also doing very well, even with this sector of the fleet working with worn out vessels. Soon these ships, along with their larger sisters, were to be replaced by larger, more powerful trawlers. The industry welcomed the return of the requisitioned vessels but not all the ships returned to their original ports or owners. Ex-Grimsby trawlers were allotted to Hull and vice versa. The Hull Steam Fishing & Ice Co. Ltd became the registered keepers of those ships returned to the port. They were in turn managed by their various rightful owners until such time as they could afford to buy them back. Why this scheme was necessary at all seems rather strange, as the owners had all received either a cash payment for their ships from the government or alternatively a very good hire rate. Where this capital had gone when there were no ships to manage or other overheads, seems rather mysterious. As for losses, surely the insurance payments covered these and the older trawlers that worked commercially must have made some profit throughout the war rationing period but taxation was high and prices had increased.

OIL FIRING

Shipyards and engineering works were busy refitting trawlers for their peacetime role as fast as they were released, whilst new ships were being ordered as replacements for those lost. Lessons had been learned from the Navy and thoughts turned to phasing out the use of coal for firing and replacing it with heavy fuel oil. Commercially, this seemed an attractive proposition, as the price of coal was escalating dramatically and good quality was becoming harder to source. Low grade oil fuel was readily available, it was more thermally efficient and much cheaper than coal, with less bulk storage space required on board. The heavy oil, with a viscosity of some 3,500 seconds, had to be pumped daily from the bunkers into one of the two settling tanks. Here, the fuel, often contaminated by water from the double bottom tanks, would be heated for around twenty-four hours. The water would then be drained from the bottom of the tank and the clean oil could then be fed to the burners.

As with coal firing, oil firing required a high degree of skill on the part of the firemen, as badly set dampers or too low a fuel temperature resulted in poor combustion, clogged burner jets, and clouds of black smoke issuing from the funnel. It was essential, therefore, that the oil entered the burners at around $260°F$, otherwise it would not vapourise. These burners or sprayers were constructed from tool steel to close tolerances. The previously heated oil entered the sprayer body through a screwed connection and passed along an annular space to the outside of the cap. It then passed through tangential holes to the chamber in the centre of the cap, thus causing the oil to swirl around, before being forced through the hole in cap. It passes through the exit hole not as a jet but as a hollow swirling mass. As it exits this cap at around 150psi, it dissipates into a hollow conical spray before being ignited within the furnace. All this heating and pumping of the oil was done by steam driven auxiliaries, with two sets being fitted. With oil firing, the need for ash dumping would disappear and deckhands would no longer have to assist the firemen with trimming the coal from the fish room to the stokehold (in March 1947, the trawlermen of Hull went on strike demanding the cessation of deckhands doubling up as trimmers. The stoppage lasted a week and an agreement was reached whereby ships over 160ft would carry an extra dedicated trimmer.). Another advantage oil had over coal was that the firemen (on non-superheated ships) no longer had to physically clean out the soot deposits from the smokebox tubes, as only the burners themselves required cleaning. These ships would all be fitted with sea water evaporating plants, which supplied the boilers with a constant feed of fresh water.

EARLY RADAR SETS AND ECHO SOUNDERS

The electronics industry was beginning to look seriously at the fishing vessel market and much improved equipment for both fish-finding and navigation was on offer. Radar sets were being developed specifically for trawler use, with the first sighting being at

Photo. 89: *Ingolfur Arnarson* (RE.201) seem here adjusting her compass prior to sailing on her delivery trip. Note the radar scanner and absence of fishing numbers.

Hull in 1947, when the Icelandic *Ingolfur Arnarson* showed off her Cossor Mark 1 set (**Photo. 89**). This set when compared to modern radars was a massive affair, its bulk being in inverse proportions to its performance, the main 10kw, 12 mile range unit being housed in a wardrobe-sized cabinet, linked to a diminutive 9ins display. The Boston Company were among the first British owners to fit Cossor radar sets to their ships, the first in *Boston Seafire* (H.584), followed soon after by *Prince Phillip* (H.32). Other owners soon followed suit and sets were fitted to Marr's *Junella* (H.497), Kingston's *Kingston Sardius* (H.588) and the ill-fated *Kingston Peridot* (H.55). Thomas Hamling had an identical Cossor set fitted to *St. Apollo* (H.592) after he had attended a demonstration trip to the North Sea, organised by Cossor's. He later remarked "*Radar did for navigation what the sounder did for fishing*".

The price for these sets at the time was £3,750. As the decade drew to a close, owners and skippers were clamouring to have this new aid fitted to their ships but the sets were still in their infancy, with poor definition and very little in the way of technical back-up, either ashore or afloat. Icebergs would show up as solid targets, often being mistaken for other trawlers. Screen 'clutter' was also a problem, with ghost echoes being thrown back from masts and funnels. Before the introduction of the later 'head-up' displays, interpreting the bearings was problematical for untrained skippers.

By the end of 1947, other manufacturers were appearing on the scene. The echo sounder company Kelvin Hughes supplied their first radar set to *Rinovia* (GY.527). This was the Type 1 30kw set, costing around £3,350. It had a maximum range of twenty-four miles but a refinement allowed for the first one to five miles to be variable. The transmitter was fitted externally along with the scanner and the display consol was housed in a compact filing cabinet-sized unit. In January the following year, the company introduced their Mark 1A range, with the transmitter housed inside the ship well away from the elements. Cossor's immediately followed with their 1A set, with an increased range of thirty miles. Both firms had been awarded the Board of Trade Type Approval Certificate as far

back as August 1918. Marconi's first radar set did not appear until January 1949, when it was fitted to Marr's *Benella* (H.15). The set was a thirty mile unit with the unusual name of 'Radio-locator'. In December that year, the Boyd Line specified new Decca D159 radar sets for their existing vessels *Arctic Explorer* (H.287), *Arctic Ranger* (H.251) and *Arctic Viking* (H.452).

The Decca Company were already well known for their navigation receiver, the first of which had been fitted to the old non-standard 'Strath' Class trawler *John Gillman* (GY.273) in January 1948. Their D159 radar sets were well received by the industry, being very compact reliable units costing £1,500. No longer had technicians a problem with shoe-horning the equipment into older ships, as the brief case-sized receiver, along with its 7ins PPI screen in a 12ins cube casing, could easily be accommodated in the wheelhouse. This was the set that was to establish the standard for the future of fishing vessel radars. Kelvin Hughes introduced their Type 2A, 7kw, 24 mile set in 1950. This was fitted with the first parabolic scanner, which gave better performance than the earlier cheese type (**Fig. 46**). Trawler skippers were by now demanding better range and efficiency from manufacturers and, in response, Cossor unveiled their Mark 2 set, with its 12ins PPI and 40 mile range. Marconi soon followed with the 60kw, 40 mile range Radiolocator IV. Costing around £1,950, this was to be the trawlerman's favourite for the next fifteen years. Trawler radar development took three distinct phases, with 1947-1963 being the valve period, 1963-1970 the transistor period and finally from 1970 onwards we have the solid state period. Cossor, the first company to fit radar to steam trawlers, dropped out of the race in 1958.

The forerunner of the echo sounder or echometer, as we know it today, was totally unrelated to either navigation or fish-finding. The first experiments took place in Lake Geneva in 1827, by two scientists, Colladin and Sturm, who developed a means of accurately measuring the speed of sound through water. Later, in 1842, a Dr Joule discovered the principle of magneto-striction. His experiments proved that if a metal such as nickel was surrounded by the fluctuations of a magnetic field, it

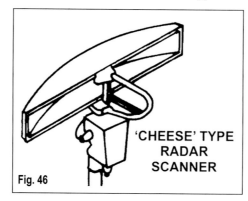

'CHEESE' TYPE RADAR SCANNER

Fig. 46

would expand and contract. This movement converted the electrical pulses into acoustic pulses, a phenomena which worked equally well when reversed. In the early 1900s, Pierre and Jacques had discovered a similar behaviour in the piezo-electric excitement of quartz, which led to Professor Paul Langevin's discovery that acoustic beams could be formed in water.

However, it was not until the mid-1920s that all these results came together and Henry Hughes & Son of London produced the world's first ultrasonic echo sounder, using the properties of magneto-striction. This gave the company's products the well known MS prefix, still in use today. They developed a series of 'sonic' echo-sounders (where the transmitted pulses were within the audible frequency range) for the Admiralty in 1926. These sets utilised a spring-loaded electro-magnetic hammer, which acted on a diaphragm under the ship's hull. The transmitted sound pulse would reverberate back from the sea bed, through a carbon microphone, to the operator's headset. He would then read off the moment of reception on a rotating dial, thus giving the depth of water. However, these low frequency sets suffered a great deal of interference from air bubbles passing under the bottom of the ship, so in order to arrive at an accurate figure, the ship had to be stopped. By 1930, Hughes had overcome this problem with the development of the ultrasonic MS oscillator. Used in conjunction with mechanical timing, accurate soundings could be taken at full speed.

The next step was the introduction of the Hughes Type MS3 starch iodide or 'wet' paper recorder in 1933. This gave a paper print out of the soundings. During this period, Marconi founded the Sounding Device Company to manufacture its 'Atlantic' and 'Pacific' sounders. These units used the principle of the piezo-electric quartz oscillator rather than the magneto-striction method favoured by their competitors (although Marconi did utilise the MS system after 1940). These two sounders produced their results in different ways. The former used a meter, while the latter reproduced the soundings by means of a pen working on dry paper. During the Second World War, the Royal Navy further developed the principles of the echo sounder into ASDIC, named after the Allied Submarine Detection Investigation Committee, which had been set up after the First World War to look at methods for detecting submerged U-boats.

The echo sounder first attracted the attention of fishermen in the early 1930s. Initially installed as a navigational aid, it soon became apparent that it had another important use as a fish finding tool. The first British skipper to use the sounder to locate fish shoals was Ronnie Balls of Yarmouth, in his steam drifter *Violet and Rose* (YH.757) in 1933. Ronnie used a Marconi echo sounder and he kept detailed records of his findings over a seven year period. The problem with these early sets was that the echo, a tiny spot of light flashing over the fathom scale, was momentary and could not be held or repeated. Once the echo had gone it was lost forever. Nevertheless, it was found that, by interpretation, these fleeting echoes could identify shoals of fish, wrecks, etc. The Norwegian scientist Oscar Sund used a Hughes Type MS3 echometer to locate shoals of cod from the research vessel *Johan Hjort*, off the Lofoten Islands in 1935, thus establishing the instrument as a definitive fish finding aid.

NEW BUILDS AND PLATE STEMS

After the war, trawler building became even more specialised and was concentrated at the Aberdeen and Yorkshire shipyards, very few post-war steam trawlers being built outside of these areas. Another development during this period was the introduction of the plate or 'soft nosed' stem. This replacement for the bar stem made for much drier ships. Its design allowed for wider fore ends, often incorporating a chine or knuckle at main deck level, which increased the flare. These designs threw the green water away from the ship when it crashed down into a heavy head sea.

Photo. 90: *Rinovia*, one of the first post war oil burners, sporting her new radar on the wheelhouse top. She is shown in Rinovia's colours of grey hull with a white band and red boot topping. The casing is wood grained, except the boat deck sides which are white, and the funnel is grey with a black top, and logo of a yellow cross on a blue flag.

The first Distant Water trawlers to leave the slips at Cochrane's after the cessation of hostilities were Yard No's 1309 and 1310 *St. Bartholemew* (H.216) and *St. Mark* (H.218), both for the St. Andrews Steam Fishing Co. Ltd, Hull and Yard No. 1311 *Northella* (H.244) for Marrs (all 175ft bp x 30ft x 16ft, 578g). The first two ships were engined by C.D. Holmes and the third by Amos & Smith. *St. Bartholemew's* first owners were associated with Boston Deep Sea Fishing & Ice Co. Ltd. They sold her in late 1946 to Charleston-Smith Trawlers Ltd (part of the Ross Group) as *Stella Arcturus* (H.216), her name being changed to *Ross Arcturus* in 1965. She was sold to the Boyd Line in 1967 as *Arctic Outlaw* and she went for scrap a year later, A year after her launch, *St. Mark* was sold to Hudson's as *Cape Trafalgar* (H.218). In 1955, she was sold again to the West Dock Steam Fishing Co. Ltd, Hull as *Auburn Wyke*. Four years later she was sold to Boyd's as *Arctic Hunter* and she went to Antwerp for scrap on 1st April 1968. *Northella* was sold by Marr's in 1948 to Charleston-Smith as *Stella Canopus* (H.244) and she went for scrap as *Ross Canopus* in 1967.

Grimsby's first new post-war trawler was Cochrane's Yard No. 1328 *Rinovia* (GY.527 – 188ft 6ins oa/170ft bp x 29ft 5ins x 15ft 5ins, 557g, 173nhp), in August 1945 for the Rinovia Steam Fishing Co. Ltd, Grimsby, with engines supplied by Amos & Smith (**Photo. 90**). She was a long time on the stocks, as a full workload (Cochrane's were completing an eight-ship, Distant Water trawler order for the Icelandic government) and a severe winter in 1947 delayed her completion. She eventually reached Grimsby in January 1948, heralding the start of the new generation of oil burners. She was revolutionary in other respects, as a Kelvin Hughes Type 1 radar was fitted to a trawler for the first time by the builders. Her crew were provided with showers and a public address system was linked to all areas of the vessel for summoning the men. Her outline was not too different from the Distant Water ships of the pre-war period but the lack of ash shoots confirmed her oil burning pedigree. Her lifeboats were carried in crescent-type mechanical davits supplied by Welin MacLachlin. In 1960, *Rinovia* was taken over by Ross Trawlers Ltd, Grimsby and renamed *Ross Stalker*. In 1964, she was fitted with a Ruston & Hornsby 4SA, seven cylinder diesel engine of 1,300bhp, which gave her a service speed of 12.5 knots.

By November 1966, she was owned by Ross Trawlers (a subsidiary of the Ross Group) as *Ross Resolution* (GY.527). She transferred to Hull in June 1970 under Hudson Brothers (Trawlers) Ltd management, retaining her name and registration, and she was eventually laid up after the decline of the Distant Water fleet. On 28th April 1978, she was sold to Richard Brooks who renamed her *Debut*. After a minimal conversion to a yacht, he sailed to Plymouth and thence to the Windward Isles in the West Indies on a salvage contract. She spent a further six years working and cruising around the Caribbean, picking up whatever was on offer in order to run the ship and, at some time during this venture, he married his Polynesian wife. They operated *Debut* by themselves, occasionally hiring local labour when required. She was not an economical vessel to run, as diesel oil was very costly and she was allowed to drift with the currents for long periods to conserve fuel. In the interests of economy, the vessel's auxiliaries were seldom run and this meant living on tinned meat and provisions for six months at a time. In December 1984, she made her way to Australia where she finished up at Cairns. In 1986, she was to be used as a stand-in for the ill-fated *Rainbow Warrior*. This filming work was to have been shot in Fiji in October 1986 but, by the following year, Richard Brooks seems to have fallen foul of the Australian government and he was told to leave their territorial waters. He took *Debut* out beyond the Great Barrier Reef where she lay at anchor but sometime later that year, she snapped her anchor cable in a gale and drifted onto the reef. Four years later she was still aground but by this time Mrs Brooks had left. He refused to leave the rapidly deteriorating trawler and the last reports said that he was even growing his own food aboard. A rather sad and ignominious end for the first post-war oil fired Arctic trawler – a vessel that was always registered at Great Grimsby.

Another of Rinovia's trawlers was *Sletnes* (GY.526 – 176ft bp x 27.5ft x 16ft, 524g) of 1947. Her engine was coupled to a Bauer Wach LP exhaust turbine, with double reduction gearing and hydraulic shaft coupling. Superheated steam was supplied at 227psi. She was the ninth new coal burner to arrive at Grimsby after the war but prior to this date, she had led a short, varied life. Built by Norderwerft Koser & Meyer at Hamburg in 1940, as *Larwot*, she was commandeered by the German Navy and rebuilt as a torpedo boat. Her armament comprised two bow and two midships tubes, a 37mm dual-purpose quick fire gun on the fo'c'sle and four 20mm anti-aircraft mounts. Her actual war service amounted to nothing and she was taken by the Allies at the end of the war, later being bought by Rinovia. She underwent another major conversion by Leake & Wilson at Grimsby in October 1948, which saw her converted to oil fuel and fitted out for Arctic trawling. This included fitting a new Robertson's 'Bear Island' trawl winch, and a cod-liver oil plant capable of producing 13 tons of oil and fed by an under deck conveyor from the foredeck. Her 14,680 cubic foot fish room could stow 3,800 kits of shelving quality fish and her navigational aids included radar, DF wireless telephony and telegraphy. Her crew still lived in the fo'c'sle but they did have a heated mess room on the upperdeck at the after end of the casing. Although not possessing the graceful lines of our own Distant Water ships, with her Maerform bow and heavy rounded cruiser stern, she was still a good sea ship with a top speed of 13 plus knots. She went for scrapping at Sunderland on 30th March 1960.

ABERDEEN YARDS

The first pair of post war steam trawlers from Lewis's Yard in Torry, Aberdeen were Yard No's 189 and 190, *Marinda* (FD.155) and *Braconvale* (A.14), launched on 6th October and 4th December 1946 respectively. The drawings (**Plans 69 a & b**) show sturdy well-proportioned coal burners (136ft, 342g). They would have looked exceptionally smart in their company colours, with the Marr ship sporting a cream hull with red band at the sheerline (**Fig. 46**), and her sister in her dark green and red hull. Both ships had beautifully grained and varnished superstructures but, unfortunately, they were not the most economical ships to run. The peacetime price of coal had rocketed and although fish were plentiful, they did not have the catching capacity to cover their running costs. Had they been oil burners and twenty feet longer, then probably things would have been different.

One noticeable difference when compared to other designs was their plate or 'soft nosed' stems. *Marinda* was also the first new Middle Water trawler ordered by J. Marr & Sons Ltd in peacetime

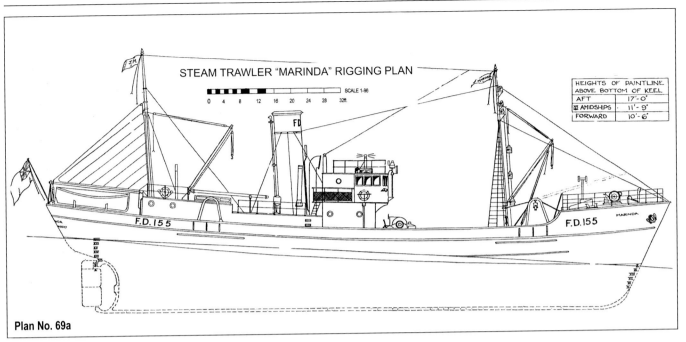

STEAM TRAWLER "MARINDA" RIGGING PLAN

SCALE 1-96

0 4 8 12 16 20 24 28 32ft.

HEIGHTS OF PAINTLINE ABOVE BOTTOM OF KEEL	
AFT	17'-0"
AMIDSHIPS	11'-9"
FORWARD	10'-6"

F.D.155

F.D.155

Plan No. 69a

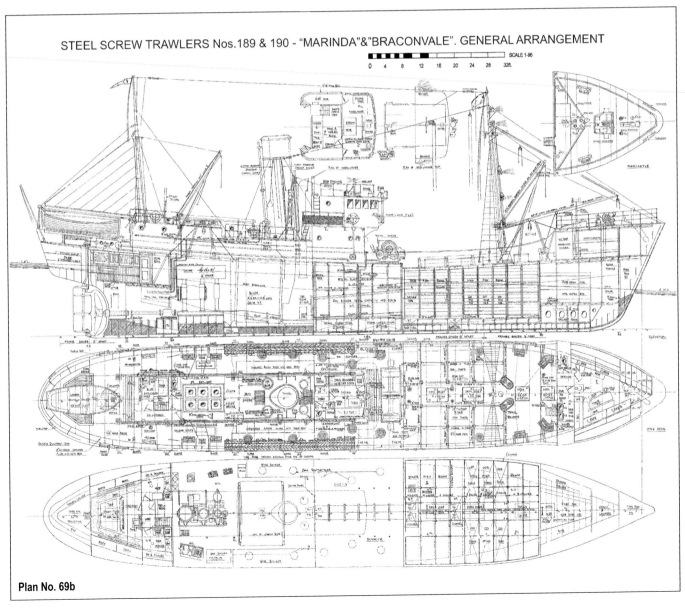

STEEL SCREW TRAWLERS Nos.189 & 190 - "MARINDA" & "BRACONVALE". GENERAL ARRANGEMENT

SCALE 1-96

0 4 8 12 16 20 24 28 32ft.

Plan No. 69b

Fig. 46: Paint scheme for *Marinda*.

SHIP No.189 PAINT SCHEME

	ITEM	COLOUR
1	TOPSIDES	STONE COLOUR PROTECTIVE PAINT
2	RIBBONS, NAMES & NUMBERS	"SUPER" MAROON PROTECTIVE PAINT
3	HULL BOTTOM	2 COATS ANTI CORROSIVE; 1 COAT ANTI FOULING*
4	ANCHOR	STONE COLOUR PROTECTIVE PAINT
5	BRIDGE - OUTSIDE	TO BE GRAINED LIGHT TEAK
6	CHART ROOM	TO BE GRAINED LIGHT TEAK
7	ENGINE ROOM	TO BE GRAINED LIGHT TEAK
8	GALLEY - OUTSIDE	TO BE GRAINED LIGHT TEAK
9	CASINGS – OUTSIDE	TO BE GRAINED LIGHT TEAK
10	BOAT – OUTSIDE	TO BE GRAINED LIGHT TEAK
11	FORWARD HOUSES – OUTSIDE	TO BE GRAINED LIGHT TEAK
12	HATCH COAMINGS	TO BE GRAINED LIGHT TEAK
13	BULWARKS – INSIDE	RED OXIDE PAINT
14	GALLOWS & GALLOWS BARS	RED OXIDE PAINT
15	FOREMAST	STONE COLOURED PROTECTIVE PAINT
16	MIZZEN MAST – BOTTOM HALF	STONE COLOURED PROTECTIVE PAINT
17	MIZZEN MAST – TOP HALF	BLACK
18	ENSIGN STAFF	WHITE
19	BOATS COVER	STONE COLOUR PROTECTIVE PAINT
20	ENGINE ROOM TOP & LIVER BOILER	BLACK
21	VENTILATORS & 2 STOVE FUNNELS	BLACK
22	COMPASS POLE	VARNISHED – NOT GRAINED
23	WINCH & WINDLASS	BLACK & GREEN
24	GALLEY STOVE	BLACK
25	FUNNEL	RED LEAD
26	FUNNEL TOP ABOVE BAND	BLACK
27	FORECASTLE RAILS	WHITE
28	BRIDGE RAILS	WHITE
29	CASING RAILS	WHITE
30	CAPPING	WHITE
31	STEEL WORK	BEST QUALITY OIL PAINT
32	CABINS, INSIDES & WASH PLACES	WHITE ENAMEL
33	UNDERSIDES OF DECK-ACCOMMODATION	FLAT WHITE
34	INSIDE SKYLIGHTS	FLAT WHITE
35	HEAD OF CAPTAIN'S CABIN	WHITE ENAMEL PAINT
36	FITINGS (CREW'S SPACES)	LIGHT OAK GRAINED
37	INSIDE FISHROOM'S & FITTINGS	WEBOLAC
38	TEAK WORK	VARNISHED

for their Fleetwood operations. They sold her on 3rd February 1947 to the Seddon Fishing Co. Ltd, Fleetwood, for £54,000. Two years later, on 2nd August 1949, Marrs bought her back for £35,000 but, in the October, they sold her again to the National Trawling & Fishing Co. Ltd, Capetown for £40,000 and she worked the Atlantic grounds until sunk as a gunnery target by the South African Navy in 1968. Her sister, *Braconvale*, was built for the Don Fishing Co. Ltd, Aberdeen and was also the first new trawler for the port to be built after the war. She left Aberdeen in 1947, renamed *Orion* and was broken up at Boom in August 1973.

The next two sisters from this yard, No's 191 and 192, were Aberdeen's first oil burners; *Dunkinty* (A.43) on 4th February and *Avondow* (A.122 – **Photo. 91**), on 6th March 1946 (144ft oa/125ft bp x 24ft x 13ft, 113n, 308g). Being very fine lined forward (**Plan 70**), they always appeared down by the head, even when light and were rumoured to have been very wet ships. Their design was a radical departure from anything the Aberdonians had previously seen, with their steeply raked stems, long whalebacks, funnel set well back from the superstructure and casings which extended almost to the stern. Below decks too they were different, with all

accommodation aft in a cabin fitted out with tubular steel bunks. The lines plan shows a soft nosed stem yet they were built with bar stems.

The North Star Steam Fishing Co. Ltd was to be one of the last operators of steam trawlers in Aberdeen and one of their stranger acquisitions was *Lord Sands* (GN.3 – 137ft oa/127ft 6ins bp x 24ft x 12ft 9ins, 113n, 266g – **Photo. 92**), built at Hamburg by A.G. Seebeck in 1935 as *Else Rykens*. Her engines had a Bauer Wach exhaust turbine, with double reduction gearing and hydraulic coupling, giving her 525ihp. Originally a coal burner, she was converted to oil fuel in November 1956. She came to Hull in 1948 as war reparations, renamed *Lord Sands* (H.503) and owned by the Lord Line Ltd, Hull. They sold her in 1952 to the Granton Trawling Co. Ltd and she became *Lord Sands* (GN.3). By 1959, she was owned by William Carnie Ltd, Granton, who sold her to the North Star Company around 1960. She eventually went for scrap at St. Davids on Forth on 4th November 1965. She had a sister, *Peter Henriks*, which also went to the Lord Line as *Lord Rivers* (H.485) and later to Granton as GN.4, before going to the breakers at Grangemouth on 2nd November 1963.

The shipyard of John Lewis, Torry, Aberdeen was relatively small but what it lacked in size, it more than made up for with innovative trawler designs. Their managers and naval architects endeavoured to give the trawling industry the very best, both in price and build quality. Not all their ships turned out as they had hoped – *e.g. Dunkinty* and *Avondow* – but even these two vessels gave their owners a good return on their investments, no matter that when doing so, they often gave their crews some very frightening experiences.

The yard had previously been the first to fit liver boilers to their vessels back in 1931 and, by 1945, they were experimenting with a conveyor system for moving the livers from the foredeck to the boilers at the stern; one of the priorities was that the livers remained whole until they were cooked. After unsuccessfully trying a coal conveyor, it became clear that an enclosed pipe running below deck was required. Initially they thought of using water pressure to push the livers through the pipe but this was also discarded as the implications of having water in the mixture were horrendous. Compressed air was considered, which would have been feasible on a diesel ship but not on a steamer unless a compressor was fitted. In the end, it was decided to pump the livers slowly through the pipe using their own oil as a lubricant. To achieve this, an electric pump would be needed and various types were tried, from toothpaste

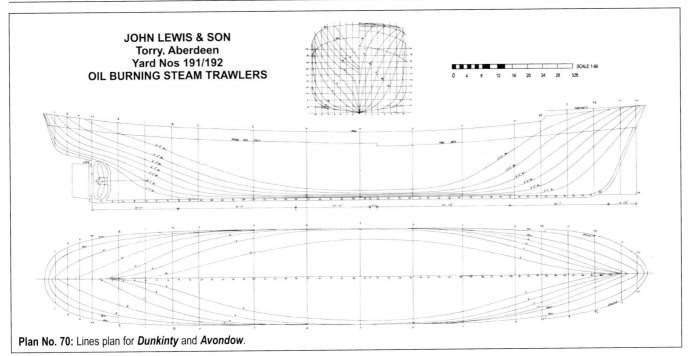

JOHN LEWIS & SON
Torry, Aberdeen
Yard Nos 191/192
OIL BURNING STEAM TRAWLERS

SCALE 1-96
0   4   8   12   16   20   24   28   32ft.

Plan No. 70: Lines plan for *Dunkinty* and *Avondow*.

pumps for filling tubes, pickling pumps and even a conserve pump from a jam factory. The eventual outcome was a 4ins bore mono pump running at 200rpm, using stainless steel rotors and synthetic rubber stators, with the internals chromium plated. The design was accepted by the vessels' owners and was the fore-runner of many similar systems which were fitted to our Distant Water fleet.

JOHN LEWIS'S STREAMLINERS

If there was ever a Distant Water ship was to make hard-bitten trawlermen sit up and take notice it was Yard No. 202 *Cordella*

(H.572 – 185ft 7ins x 29ft x 15ft 3ins, 604g, 930ihp), ordered by J. Marr & Sons Ltd, Hull in 1948 at a cost of £84,304. She was a radical departure from normal ships. Her superstructure was an exciting streamlined shape, with the conical funnel built in to it. Her service speed was 12.5 knots and she had a fish room capacity of 13,000 cubic feet. In order to produce as good a sea ship as possible, her model was rigorously tested at the Teddington tank, where her superstructure design was also wind tunnel tested at the same time. The mizzen mast was replaced by a pair of steel sampson posts, which served a double purpose as engine room

Photo. 91: *Avondow*, showing her 'bows down' appearance and tall radar mast. She has a black hull white band and red boot topping, a wood grained wheelhouse over a buff casing and a red oxide lower section to her black funnel. As an 'aftside job', there is strangely quite a gap between the funnel and the wheelhouse.

Photo. 92: *Lord Sands*. Note her peculiar bridge verandah and the plating on her foremast shrouds. She is seen in the same North Star colour scheme as *Avondow*. She is passing by Alexander Hall's shipyard, with the motor trawler *Aberdeen Merchant* A.134 (1957) nearing completion on the left.

ventilators and heel mounts for bobbin derricks.

The crew were still housed in the fo'c'sle but they were provided with a heated drying room and a bathroom with WCs under the whaleback. The streamlined superstructure housed the wheelhouse, chart room and wireless operator's cabin, with another drying room built into the funnel casing. Built as an oil burner using the Wallsend-Howden forced-draught system, her boiler delivered superheated steam at 22psi. The engines from Lewis's engine shop had high pressure and medium pressure cylinders fitted with piston valves and the low pressure with an Andrews & Cameron back balanced slide valve. She caused quite a stir when she arrived at Hull for the first time and served her owners well, until problems with the Distant Water grounds forced her into retirement. She was sold for scrapping at Antwerp in August 1965 for some £8,000.

She was followed by her sister ship, Yard No. 210 *Thornella* (H.582), launched on 8th June 1948 and sailing on 26th of October. In 1954, Marrs sold her to Hellyer Brothers Ltd, who renamed her *Banquo*. She transferred to Wyre Trawlers Ltd, Fleetwood, as FD.99 in 1967 but after one trip they sent her to the breakers at Ghent in the September. Marr's later had another two slightly larger sister ships built to this design, Yard No's 213 and 218, *Benella* (H.15) and *Primella* (H.103 – 180ft oa/175ft bp, 666g, 234n – **Plans 71 a, b & c**). They cost £114,000 and were the first Hull trawlers to come from the builders with radar fitted as part of the original specification. *Benella* was built for the Trident Steam Fishing Co. Ltd, Hull (a Marrs subsidiary) and was sold to the Newington Steam Trawling Co. Ltd, Hull in 1951 as *James Barrie* (**Photo. 93**). She came to grief while outward bound

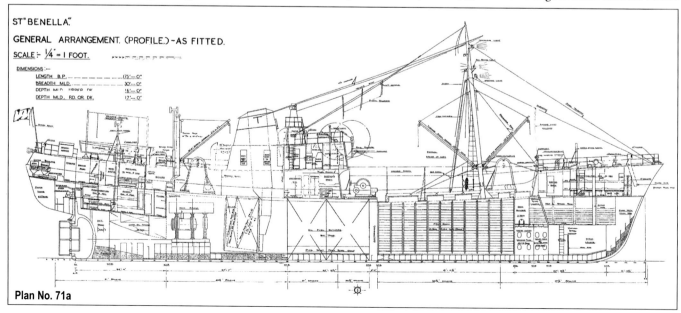

ST" BENELLA.

GENERAL ARRANGEMENT. (PROFILE.) - AS FITTED.

SCALE :- ¼" = 1 FOOT.

DIMENSIONS :-
LENGTH B.P. .... 175'—0"
BREADTH MLD. .... 30'—0"
DEPTH MLD UPPER DK .... 16'—0"
DEPTH MLD. RD. OR DK. .... 17'—0"

Plan No. 71a

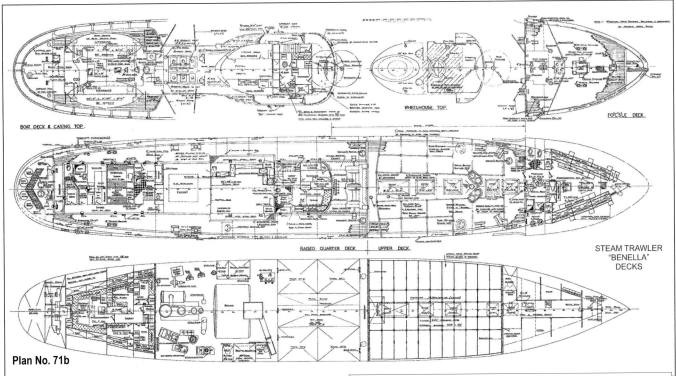

STEAM TRAWLER
"BENELLA"
DECKS

Plan No. 71b

on Louther Skerry in the Pentland Firth on 27th March 1969. but all her twenty-one men were rescued from their two inflatable rafts by the Wick lifeboat. This was a difficult situation for Coxswain Neil Stewart Jnr, as one of the lifeboat's propellers had been fouled by a rope but, by skilful use of one engine and in heavy broken surf, he effected the rescue. For his bravery he received the BEM in the New Years honours list. *Primella* was sold by Marrs in May 1951 to the Newington Steam Trawling Co. Ltd and renamed *Peter Scott*. She went to Spanish ship breakers in 1974.

Another two sisters built to the original *Cordella* design were *Stockham* (GY.19) and *Laforey* (GY.85). Both were ordered by Trawlers Grimsby Ltd and transferred to Derwent Trawlers Ltd in 1953. They were beautiful ships, with their light grey hulls, grained superstructures and varnished boats, and were to be Grimsby's first streamliners. Originally built without a mizzen, they were

Photo. 93: *James Barrie* (ex-*Benella*) showing the handsome appearance of these Lewis-built ships and in Newington's colours of black hull with a white band, bow flashes over red boot topping, wood grained superstructure and a grey, black topped funnel separated by a broad blue band.

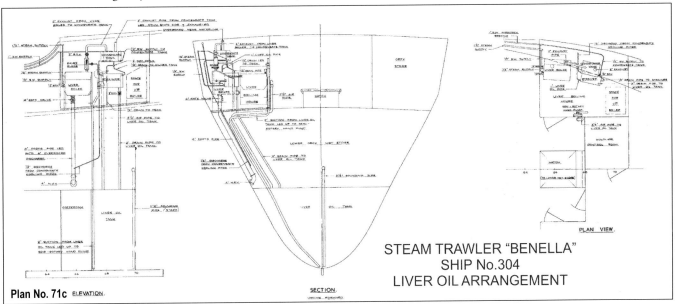

STEAM TRAWLER "BENELLA"
SHIP No.304
LIVER OIL ARRANGEMENT

Plan No. 71c ELEVATION.

SECTION.

both fitted with a steel mast later on, after the rules for steaming lights changed. Yard No. 214 *Stockham* was the first to leave the ways on 29th January 1949 and she sailed on 19th of May. In August 1961, when Derwents' were taken over by Ross Trawlers Ltd, her name was changed to *Ross Battler*. She sailed from Grimsby for the last time on 22nd December 1963 to the breakers at Blyth.

Laforey, which was launched on 28th April 1949 as Yard No. 217, sailed on 26th August for Grimsby but, six years later on 8th February 1955, the port town was stunned by the news of her loss. *Laforey* had been returning from the Norwegian grounds with a catch of some 1,500 kits, when she ran aground four miles SW of Kvalholmen Light near Floroe. She capsized almost immediately and her desperate radio messages were picked up by Floroe wireless station shortly after midnight on 7th: "*Mayday, Mayday, Mayday, Laforey, Laforey, we are ashore at Yttero, we are ashore at Yttero … we need immediate assistance*". Ten minutes later came the final message: "*Laforey, Laforey, Laforey … we are ashore at Yttero, Yttero … need help … we are heeling over …*". Then silence as twenty Grimsby trawlermen went to their deaths.

One of the ships that rushed to the rescue was her sister *Stockham*, skippered by Tom Evans, the son-in-law of *Laforey*'s skipper William Mogg. Other vessels searching included the salvage steamer *Hercules*, the Floroe and Kalvaag lifeboats, along with the Fleetwood trawler *Velia*. Next day the upturned hull of the stricken trawler was located by the Norwegian salvage vessel *Conrad Langaard*; unfortunately, there was no sign of survivors. She was the last Grimsby trawler to suffer such a fate and with a fishing number that added up to 13 (GY.85), many a superstitious fishermen murmured that it may "*have had a bearing on the tragedy*".

John Lewis built another ill-fated Distant Water trawler in 1949, *Cape Cleveland* (H.61 – 178ft 4ins x 30ft x 16ft, 659g – **Plans 72 a & b and Photo. 94**), which was part of a two-ship order for Hudson Brothers (Trawlers) Ltd, Hull, her sister being *Cape Spartel* (H.79). They were oil-burners, with streamlined superstructures and short conventional funnels. Radar was fitted by the builders but again a pair of sampson posts replaced the mizzen mast. They looked every inch a thoroughbred. The forced draught system necessary for the efficient combustion of the fuel resulted in a higher exhaust pressure at the base of the funnel and meant that shorter streamlined funnels became the order of the day. *Cape Cleveland* became *Ross Cleveland* in November 1965, nine months after the firm was sold to the Ross Group. It was under the latter name it sadly hit the national headlines on 4th February 1968, when it iced-up and capsized at Isafjord, north west Iceland, while dodging in an Arctic gale. She was actually seen to turn turtle but the weather was so bad that no other ship could render assistance. Her final radio message from skipper Phillip Gay bravely stated, "*I am going over …*

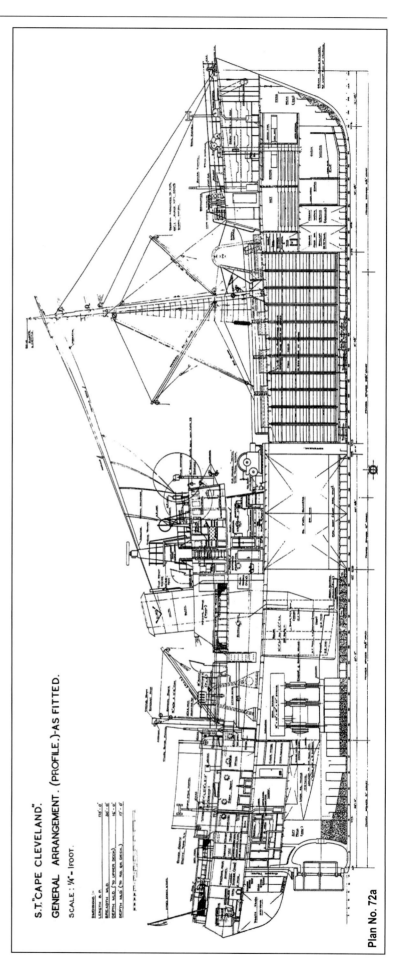

S.T. "CAPE CLEVELAND."
GENERAL ARRANGEMENT. (PROFILE.) - AS FITTED.

SCALE : ¼" = 1FOOT.

Plan No. 72a

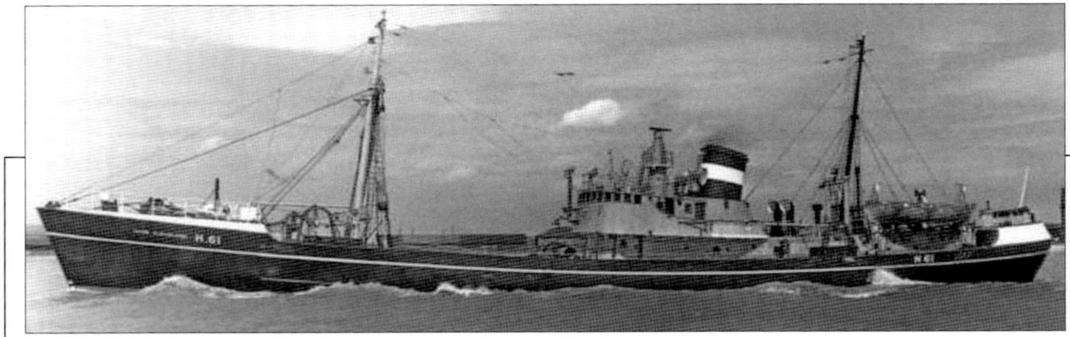

Photo. 94: ***Cape Cleveland*** in Hudson's colour scheme of black hull with a white line at deck level, wood grain casing and a black funnel with a broad white band

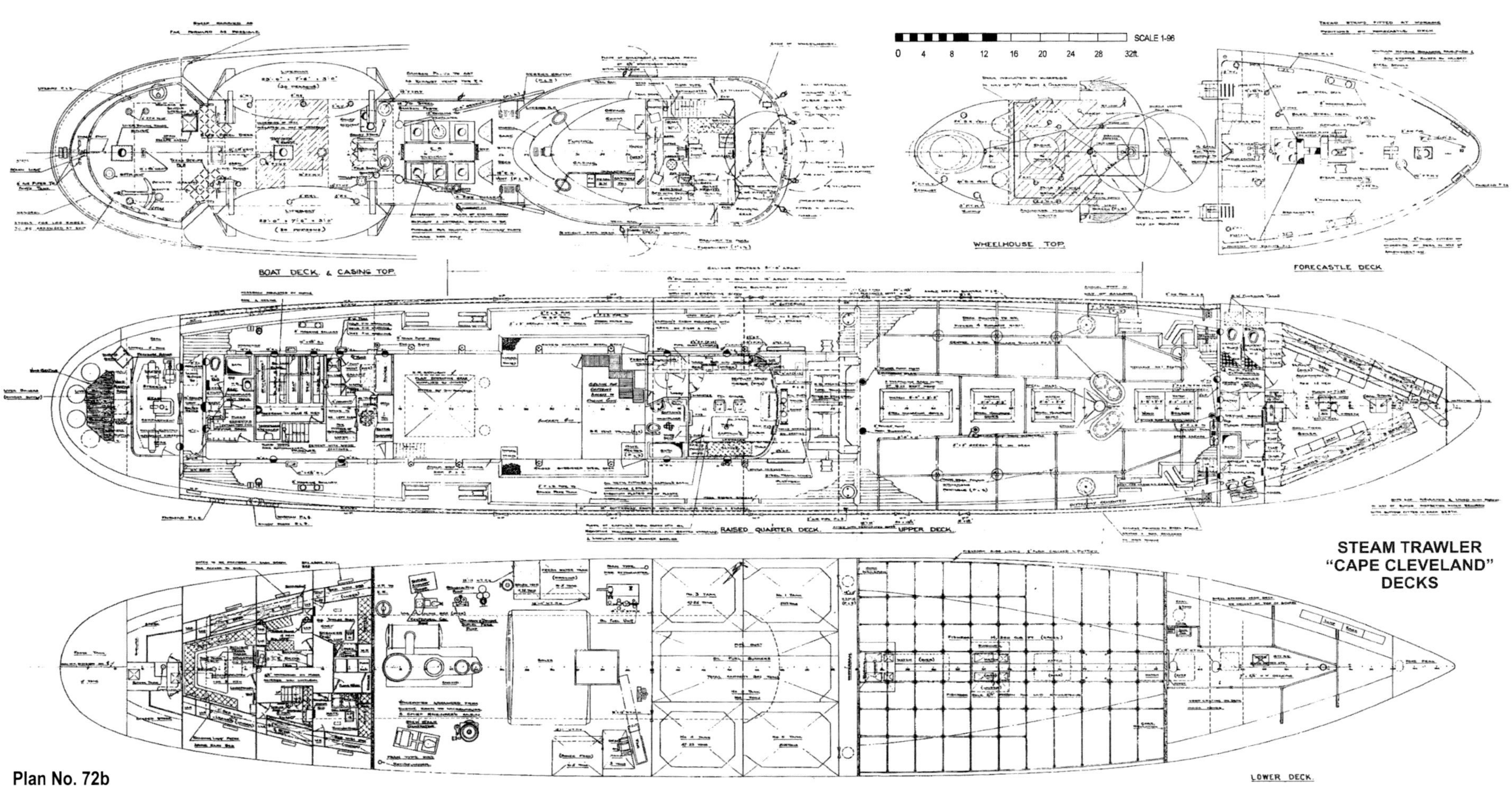

STEAM TRAWLER
"CAPE CLEVELAND"
DECKS
SCALE 1-96
0 4 8 12 16 20 24 28 32ft.
BOAT DECK & CASING TOP
WHEELHOUSE TOP
FORECASTLE DECK
RAISED QUARTER DECK
UPPER DECK
LOWER DECK

Plan No. 72b

Painting 9: The ill-fated *Kingston Peridot*. COURTESY S. FARROW

give my love and the crew's love to their wives and families". There was only one survivor, the mate Harry Eddom, who had been on the wheelhouse top in full foul weather gear chopping away the ice. He escaped in an inflatable raft with two others. Sadly his companions were clad only in singlets and pants and they succumbed to the sub zero temperatures.

In retrospect, the later fitting of the mizzen mast, although not directly responsible for her capsize, may have aggravated her tender condition. Tests later proved that such a mast accumulated some 4 to 5 tons of ice under the same conditions. Bearing in mind that this weight was high above the vessel's centre of gravity, it would have caused a large heeling lever and when added to about 140 tons of ice covering the ship, would have compromised her stability.

This was indeed a black time for the men of the northern trawl as, prior to the loss of *Ross Cleveland*, Hull lost twenty men when *St. Romanus* (H.223) foundered on 11th January 1968. A further twenty were drowned on 26th January, after *Kingston Peridot* (H.591) capsized after icing up off Iceland. Her last radio message stated, "*Vessel laying to for a couple of hours while the crew clear ice from the deck*". This was thirteen years to the day since the loss of the Hull trawlers *Roderigo* and *Lorella*.

After this triple tragedy, Hull was outraged and trawlermen's wives directed their bitterness at the trawler owners 'Couldn't care less attitude' towards their men. It also came to light that many Distant Water ships were sailing without qualified radio operators. The official Holland Martin Inquiry in July 1969 recommended that a new package of safeguards be implemented for Distant Water trawlers. These were quite far reaching and included:

1. The stationing of a support ship during winter months on the grounds to the north west of Iceland.

2. Meteorological forecasting information should be improved and the BBC should make extra time available for transmitting these forecasts.

3. Trawlers of 140 feet and over should carry radio-telephony equipment and to maintain a listening watch on the maritime distress frequency, and all trawlers operating beyond the UK R/T range should be fitted with radio telegraphy equipment plus a WT operator.

4. Life rafts which may be used in Arctic waters should be provided with survival clothing (**Plan 72b**).

5. That rigid lifeboats be replaced with inflatable rafts.

6. The Board of Trade to ensure that all safety equipment on trawlers be surveyed every two years, in addition to any spot checks that may be undertaken.

7. Distant Water trawlers to carry a third deck officer holding a statuary certificate of competency.

8. The government to seek powers to lay down statutory requirement on minimum rest periods aboard deep sea trawlers.

These were but a few of the eighty-three recommendations put forward in the report, which dealt with the whole spectrum of safety in the trawling industry.

THE ENGLISH YARDS

Icelandic/Middle Water ships were also being built at the Humber yards. Cook, Welton & Gemmell launched five coal-burning sister ships in 1946, as Yard No's 755 to 759 (all 148ft oa / 133ft bp x 25ft x 14ft, 139n, 369g – **Plan 73 a & b**). They were very handsome trawlers, well capable of fishing Faeroe and Iceland when required. A notable addition to trawlers of this type at the time was the Carley float, stowed on a platform abaft the funnel. All bar one were for J. Marr & Sons Ltd, Hull and their subsidiaries.

Aby (FD.138) was built for the Seddon Fishing Co. Ltd, Fleetwood (J. Marr). She became *Chaffcombe* (CF.18) owned by Neale & West of Cardiff in 1950. They later sold her to the Boston Deep Sea Fishing & Ice Co. Ltd, Fleetwood as *Boston Gannet* (FD.30) and she went for scrapping in October 1963 at Troon.

Bulby (FD.147) was launched in January 1946 for the Seddon Fishing Co. Ltd and was the second ship to carry the name, the first having been the wooden steam trawler FD.34, built in Quebec in 1917. The second *Bulby* was bought (on paper) by Marr's for around £40,000 in July 1949. In 1953, they sold her to the National Trawling & Fishing Co. Ltd, Cape Town, for £6,000 more than they had paid in 1949. In 1968, she was scuttled by the South African Government off Cape Town, to form part of an artificial reef.

Josena (H.207) was operated by Marrs for only a very short time before they sold her to Poland. She was renamed *Syriusz* and went to the breakers in 1969.

Navena (FD.149 – **Photo. 95**) was sold by Marrs in December 1946 to the Kingston Steam Trawling Co. Ltd, Hull and renamed *Iolite* (H.372). They bought her back again in August 1949 and sold her to Cape Town in 1951. She joined her sister on the artificial reef in 1969.

St. Boltoph (H.188) was completed in January 1946 for the St. Andrews Steam Fishing Co. Ltd, Hull who sold her later that year to Neale & West of Cardiff as CF.8. In 1958, she was sold to the Boston Deep Sea Fishing & Ice Co. Ltd of Fleetwood as FD.31. They in turn sold her to the St. Christopher Steam Fishing Co. Ltd, Fleetwood, in 1959 and she went to the breakers at Glasson Dock in September 1963.

Photo. 95: *Navena* running acceptance trials in the River Humber, resplendent in Marr's colours of cream hull with red band, wood grained casing and a red, black topped funnel.

These were followed in 1947 by *St. Crispin* (H.399) for the Boston Co. and *Lorella* (H.455) for Marrs, as Yard No's 778 and 785 respectively and both slightly larger ships (184ft 6ins x 29ft 2ins x 14ft 2ins, 559g). In 1951, *St. Crispin* was sold to Marrs for £108,412 and renamed *Junella*. She changed again, to *Farnella*, in 1961, after her name was given to a new stern trawler. She sailed to Bo'ness for scrapping on 3rd December 1965. Her sister *Lorella* unfortunately sailed into the history books on 26th January 1955 when, in company with *Roderigo* (H.135), she capsized and sank

Painting 10: *St. Boltoph* as depicted by Keith Sutton in the Boston Deep Sea Fishing & Ice Co. Ltd's colour scheme.

with the combined loss of forty men. The two vessels had battled against ferocious freezing weather for three days after leaving the shelter of Riter Huk, Iceland to go to the aid of *Kingston Garnet* (H.106), stricken with a fouled propeller. In the event, *Kingston Garnet* managed to free her propeller and ran for shelter but *Lorella* and *Roderigo* were too iced up to turn and seek safety. This manoeuvre would have meant turning the top heavy ships beam on to the heavy seas, so was not possible. By this time, *Lorella*'s radar had packed up and the two ships kept company until the very end. *Lorella* went first, her last desperate radio message sent by George Hobson: "*Have been thrown on side, need quick help*". Her companion, also in grave danger, could not help and soon George Leadley was sending out her SOS: "*We are overturning. Unable to abandon ship, conditions too bad.*". Then there was silence and forty fishermen died.

Before sailing on this fateful trip, second Engineer James Walker had stated of *Roderigo*, "*I would be happy to sail her round the world, she is such a good sea ship*". This incident probably highlights the fact that luck played a huge part in survival during these conditions. The two ships that foundered were 'double deckers', whereas the survivor, *Kingston Garnet*, was one of the first 'triple deckers' from Cook, Welton & Gemmell. With her larger, higher superstructure, it would have been thought that, in these conditions, her stability

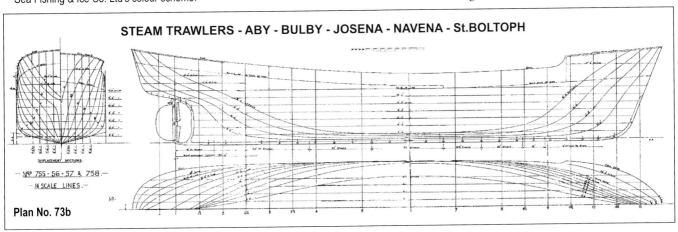

STEAM TRAWLERS - ABY - BULBY - JOSENA - NAVENA - St.BOLTOPH

Plan No. 73b

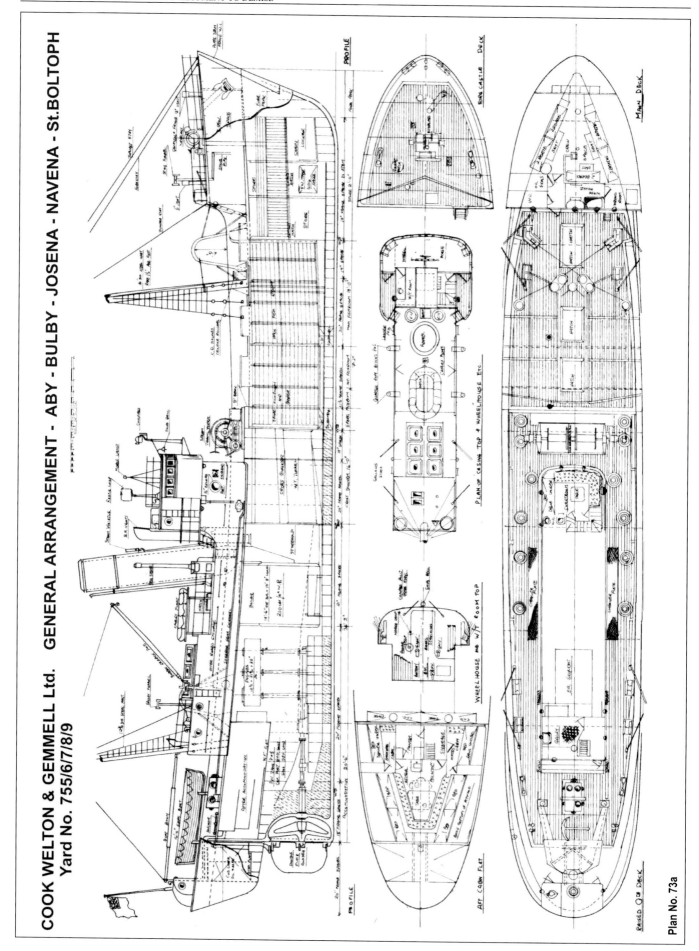

COOK WELTON & GEMMELL Ltd.   GENERAL ARRANGEMENT - ABY - BULBY - JOSENA - NAVENA - St.BOLTOPH
Yard No. 755/6/7/8/9

Plan No. 73a

Photo. 96: *Braconglen* is seen as repainted and ready to sail for Ceylon in 1950. Her two lifeboats are carried in Welin semi-rotary davits. Note Consolidated Fisheries Ltd's distinctive Lowestoft office building behind.

would have been compromised faster than that of the other two ships, yet she survived.

Fleetwood took delivery of its first oil burner in January 1948. *Margaret Wicks* (FD.265) was built as Yard No. 790 by Cook, Welton & Gemmell at Beverley, for the Clifton Steam Trawlers Ltd, Fleetwood (136ft 9in bp x 26ft x 13ft 6in, 366g). She was an easily recognised vessel, with her steeply raked masts and funnel, which was set well back from the superstructure. She later transferred to Boston's ownership and was broken up at Faslane on 12th February 1964, after running aground and becoming a constructive total loss.

Further south at Lowestoft, well known Richards Shipbuilders launched the only two steam trawlers ever built by the yard, in late 1948 and early 1949. The first, Yard No. 376, was *Boston Typhoon* (FD.272) for the Boston Deep Sea Fishing & Ice Co. Ltd, Fleetwood, with the second, Yard No. 377 *Braconglen* (FD.283), for the Don Fishing Co. Ltd, Aberdeen. Both were oil burning, Distant/ Middle Water ships (133ft 4in bp x 25ft 6in x 14ft,

338g). The former ship was sold in 1953 to Norwegian owners and renamed *Rollanes*, and was broken up in 1967. *Braconglen* was soon sold to Bostons but, in 1950, after being fitted with air conditioning and a refrigeration plant, she was sold to Ceylon. She eventually sank in Colombo harbour in 1971. This size of a ship proved to be of little use to Fleetwood, bearing in mind the distance to and from the Icelandic grounds, so they were quickly sold off as being uneconomical (**Photo. 96**).

MORE FROM ABERDEEN YARDS

A more successful trawler of this size was *David Ogilvie* (LO.363), built by J. Lewis in September 1948 as Yard No. 209 (136ft x 24ft 6ins x 13ft 1in, 341g) for Jenkerson's of London (*Photo 97 and Plan 74*). She was a sturdy looking oil burner, with a soft nosed plate stem and cruiser stern. No radar was originally supplied but this was fitted later. In 1957, she went to Aberdeen owners, North Star Steam Fishing Co. Ltd but retained her name and number. Considered by some to be a lucky ship, this was borne out on

Photo. 97: *David Ogilvie* was the only Aberdeen trawler registered in London. She is shown here in North Star colours.

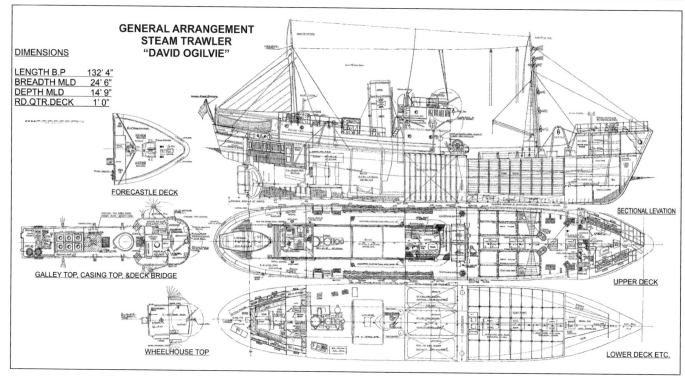

GENERAL ARRANGEMENT
STEAM TRAWLER
"DAVID OGILVIE"

DIMENSIONS

LENGTH B.P	132' 4"
BREADTH MLD	24' 6"
DEPTH MLD	14' 9"
RD.QTR.DECK	1' 0"

FORECASTLE DECK

GALLEY TOP, CASING TOP, &DECK BRIDGE

WHEELHOUSE TOP

SECTIONAL LEVATION

UPPER DECK

LOWER DECK ETC.

the early morning of 27th October 1959, when she was driven ashore in the navigation channel at Aberdeen during a severe gale. Refloated, she went back to fishing, eventually sailing for the last time on 16th November 1966 for the breakers at Blyth.

Alexander Hall's yard was more conservative with their post war designs. In 1948, they launched the oil burning sisters *St. Bartholemew* (H.516) and *St. Mark* (H.520) as Yard No's 722 and 723 (180ft 1in, 613g) for the St. Andrews Steam Fishing Co. Ltd, Hull. Both were sold in 1952. The former became *Arctic Buccaneer* (H.516) of the Boyd Line and went to the breakers in 1972. Her sister went to Kingston's as *Kingston Aquamarine* (H.520) but met an untimely end two years later. On 11th January 1954, she ran aground at Stainfjord, Norway after her radar had broken down (possibly by icing up) in a snowstorm. An identical ship followed in October, *Churchill* (GY.585) for Grimsby Merchants Amalgamated Trawlers Ltd (**Photo. 98**). In May 1952,

she transferred to Consolidated Fisheries Ltd, Grimsby and worked for them until going to the scrap yard in Belgium in 1968. She was the fleet's only surviving trawler not named after a football team. *Churchill* for a while fell into the unique category of a peacetime trawler having in its crew five members of the RNR, commanded by skipper Bill Hardie, an RNR Lieutenant. This entitled her to fly both the red and blue ensign.

The yard's next three sisters, No's 727, 728 and 729, *Loch Inver* (H.110), *Loch Leven* (H.82) and *Loch Doon* (H.101 – **Photo. 99**), were all built for the Loch Fishing Co. of Hull Ltd in 1949. They were the same overall size as the three previous ships but had a higher gross tonnage of 670, with a reputation of being excellent heavy weather trawlers. In 1953, *Loch Doon* had the honour of representing Hull at the Spithead Review. Although the owners sold out to Hellyer's in 1960, the ships kept their names but not their original colours. They sailed to the breakers in 1972.

ABOVE: Plan No. 74: *David Ogilvie*, showing Jenkersons funnel badge of a red Maltese cross on a broad white band.

LEFT: Photo. 98: *Churchill* when new from the builders in Consolidated Fisheries' colours. She is a typical example of Hall's Distant Water ships, built to withstand heavy weather.

Photo. 99: *Loch Doon* in later days wearing Hellyer colours of light grey hull with a white band and wood grained superstructure. The funnel is yellow with a black top and bears the company logo of a blue flag with a white 'H'.

Hall's first very moderate attempt at streamlining came in late 1949, with Yard No's 730 and 731, two ships for Bostons of Hull, *Boston Vampire* (H.94) and *Boston Meteor* (H.114 – **Plan 75 and Photo. 100**). Much smaller vessels (150ft, 386g), they had the traditional Hall's straight-fronted wheelhouse, with a funnel streamlined into the after end of the casing and drying rooms below. This casing differed from the usual design, as it faired out from the aft end of the engine room to the lower bridge accommodation. Designed for Icelandic fishing, they carried two Carley floats on the mizzen shrouds, in addition to a single lifeboat. Their size made them a poor proposition, so they were sold in 1952 to National Sea Products, Nova Scotia as *Carina* and *Zaroba* respectively, with the former being later renamed *Cape Fearless*. Both ships went to the breakers in 1969.

The adjacent yard of Hall, Russell's built their last commercial British steam trawler, *Star of Orkney*, in 1936-7. However, they did propose a new larger steam ship for the Walker Steam Trawl Fishing Co. Ltd, Aberdeen in October 1944. She was to be called *Star of Scotland*, Yard No. 801, but the design was not accepted and a motor trawler of the same name was built instead. After the war, the yard still built steam trawlers for foreign owners, including four ships for Irvin & Johnson Ltd's Cape Town operations. In fact, the yard's very first two post-war steam trawlers were No's 793 and 794, *Gilia* and *Godetia* (160ft bp, 515g) for this South African company. They were large, solid looking coal burners and carried thirty-two man crews. No liver boiling plants are shown but they have large insulated offal stores forward of the main fish room.

YORKSHIRE'S STREAMLINERS

The Yorkshire yards soon followed Aberdeen's lead by building streamlined superstructures into their ships. In 1948, Cook, Welton & Gemmell received an order for two such trawlers from the Boston Deep Sea Fishing & Ice Co. Ltd. They were Yard No's 794 and 795, *St. Chad* (H.575) and *Boston Seafire* (H.584 – 181ft 7ins x 30ft 6ins x 16ft, 689g – **Plan 76**). Their insulated, refrigerated fish room capacity was 16,000 cubic ft and thermometer repeaters were fitted in the wheelhouse so the watch keepers could monitor the temperature. They carried 300 tons of oil fuel, which gave them a range of around thirty days. The liver oil tanks had a capacity of 3,600 gallons and the foots tanks held a further 600 gallons. The drawing shows no mizzen mast (although one was fitted in 1953) and the aerials lead to short triangular frames either side of the funnel. This is the first general arrangement drawing that I have where cowl ventilators have been replaced by French types. They were designed for fishing off Bear Island and Greenland, with accommodation for thirty-one hands.

St. Chad was launched in August 1948 for the St. Andrews Steam Fishing Co. Ltd (associated to Boston Deep Sea Fishing & Ice Co. Ltd). She was sold in 1951 to Charleston-Smith Trawlers Ltd, Hull and renamed *Stella Polaris* (H.575), becoming the third ship to carry the name. She became *Ross Polaris* in November 1965 and transferred to Grimsby in 1967, going to Belgium for scrapping in April 1968. *Boston Seafire* was launched in October for Boston's, who sold her in 1952 to Hudson Brothers (Trawlers) Ltd, Hull as *Cape Tarifa* (H.584). She was renamed with the Ross

Photo. 100: *Boston Vampire.* She was quite a dumpy looking ship, with her streamlined funnel and flat fronted bridge. Note the two Carley floats on the mizzen shrouds, a single boat and the awning over the fish room. She is seen here in Boston Deep Sea Fisheries Ltd's colours of black hull with a white band, wood grained casing and a white, black topped funnel.

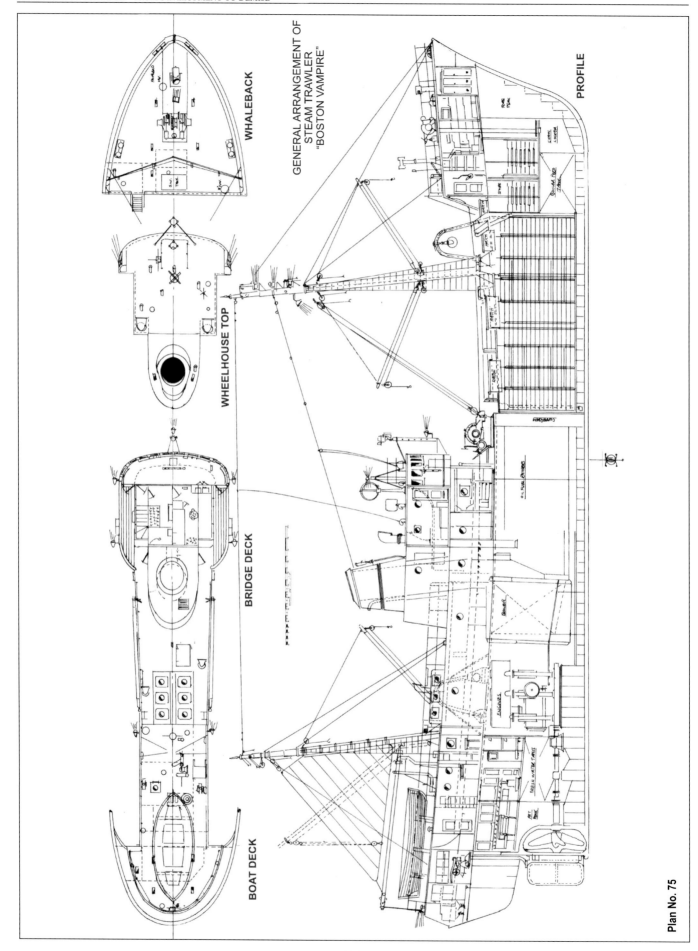

WHALEBACK

GENERAL ARRANGEMENT OF
STEAM TRAWLER
"BOSTON VAMPIRE"

PROFILE

WHEELHOUSE TOP

BRIDGE DECK

BOAT DECK

Plan No. 75

230

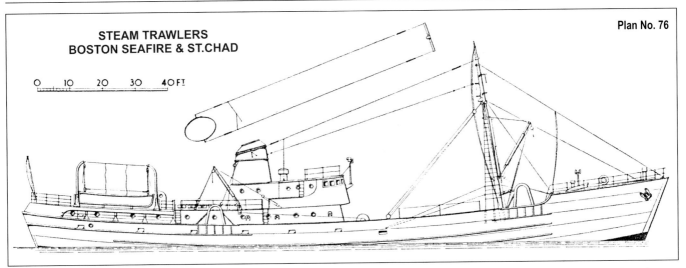

Plan No. 76

STEAM TRAWLERS
BOSTON SEAFIRE & ST.CHAD

0   10   20   30   40 FT

prefix in November 1965 and transferred to Grimsby in 1967. En route for Belgian breakers on 7th March 1968, she ran aground on the East Goodwin Sands and was declared a total loss.

Boston Deep Sea Fishing & Ice Co. Ltd, Grimsby took delivery of their first new Grimsby ship in December 1948, *Princess Elizabeth* (GY.590), Yard No. 800. She was almost a sister to the previous two ships, although shorter at 170ft and fitted with cowl stokehold vents. She was built to the order of the North Cape Steam Fishing Co. Ltd, Grimsby (a Boston Deep Sea Fishing & Ice Co. Ltd subsidiary) but Sir Basil Parkes, the company chairman, was unhappy with her performance and stability, so this necessitated many trial runs before she was accepted. On her maiden trip, she shipped a heavy sea over the stern as she rounded Spurn Point, which flooded the accommodation and engine room, and put back to Grimsby for new supplies to replace those damaged by seawater. She sailed again for the White Sea grounds but returned with a poor catch, after having to dodge about for days on end in bad weather.

A year later, she moved to Hull as *St. Ronan* (H.86), owned by Thomas Hamling & Co. Ltd, Hull. She was lost on 12th October 1952, after running aground at St. Johns Point, Caithness. She had a sister, *Prince Phillip* (H.32), built for Boston's Hull operations.

They transferred her to Grimsby in July 1955, selling her to Derwent Trawlers Ltd, who renamed her *Hargood* (GY.7). They in turn sold her in July 1958 to Charleston-Smith Trawlers Ltd, Hull, who changed her name to *Stella Rigel* (H.170). She met an untimely end on 21st December 1962, when she was wrecked north of Tromso, on the Norwegian coast.

FIRST ALUMINIUM FISH ROOM

Cayton Bay (H.72 – 171ft oa, 580g) ran trials in July 1949 and much interest was shown by the industry in the new ship. Built by Cook, Welton & Gemmell as Yard No. 807, for the Marine Steam Fishing Co. Ltd, Hull (**Photo. 101**), she was, strangely enough for the period, a coal burner and the last such trawler to be built for Hull owners. Her bunkers held some 350 tons, which gave her an operational range of some 3,000 miles and on trials she ran at 13.5 knots. She was a very attractive ship (almost identical to *Princess Elizabeth*), with a well raked and flared soft nosed plate stem, good sheer, and with a quarterdeck and cruiser stern. Her streamlined superstructure followed the sheerline from the stern deckhouse to the forward end of the casing. Her streamlined funnel housed the drying rooms for wet gear and was nicely faired into the after end of the upper superstructure. No mizzen mast was carried initially,

Photo. 101: *Cayton Bay.* No mizzen mast was fitted to this class and her two wooden boats are carried in Welin-type davits. Her colour scheme shows a light grey hull with white band, wood grained superstructure, light grey funnel with black top and two white bands.

the aerials leading to whisker booms on the funnel sides.

On top of the wheelhouse was a lattice radar tower, which carried the Marconi 'Radiolocator', with a maximum range of thirty miles. Below, in the wheelhouse, she had a whole host of up to the minute navigational and fish finding aids, such as 'Lodestone' DF, a Marconi 'Oceanspan' HF/MF 100 watt transmitter with two 'Lodestone' all waveband receivers, a Marconi 522 'Fishsnatcher' and a 'Visagraph' 600 fathom depth finder. For internal communications, an 'Oceanic' sound system was installed, which could relay commands and music to all parts of the vessel. The wheelhouse windows were fitted with steam defrosting and a Kent 'clear view' revolving screen was fitted to the forward facing windows. The steering pedestal was fitted with change over switches for either steam or hydraulic operation, a great improvement on the older system where these controls were down aft in the steering flat. She broke from tradition yet again, as most of her internal panelling was made up of plastic laminates instead of varnished wood. This was as a safeguard against rough usage and warping but the new material also helped brighten up the crew spaces, although its non-porous surfaces may have aggravated the condensation problems experienced aboard these ships.

However, it was in the fish room that the greatest improvements had been made. These were fully insulated with 'Isoflex', ranging from 7ins on the bulkheads to 3ins on the deckheads and completely lined in 'Birmabright' aluminium alloy. The shelf boards were also aluminium, along with all the lamp fittings. The advantages of using aluminium, as opposed to wood, were that it made for easier cleaning of the fish room, whilst there was no possibility of swelling or splintering. Under the deck and on the after bulkhead, cooling grids were installed, which maintained the 12,600 cubic ft space at a constant 34 degrees Fahrenheit. Two long distance Malone-type thermometers were fitted, with repeater recorders in the wheelhouse. For emergencies, two twenty-six man lifeboats were carried on the boat deck, in Welin-MacLachlan quadrantal davits. It may seem strange that this most up to date ship was coal fired but one should remember that many of these Distant Water

trawler owners, although turning more and more to oil firing, still may have had interests in coal mines, so it was not entirely to their own benefit to quickly phase out coal. In 1952, *Cayton Bay* became *Bayella*, transferring to Marrs' ownership. In September 1956, under skipper C. Drever, she successfully towed *Stella Arcturus* home from Spitzbergen. She was broken up in 1966.

Another three almost identical sisters, *Bombardier* (GY.30), *Lancer* (GY.65) and *Lifeguard* (GY.94), were launched by Cook, Welton & Gemmell in 1949, as Yard No's 805, 809 and 812. The first was for the Supreme Fish Curing Co. Ltd, Grimsby and the other two for Loyal Steam Fishing Co. Ltd, Grimsby. All three transferred to Northern Trawlers Ltd, Grimsby, in 1967. In 1954, after *Laforey* (GY.85) was lost with all hands off Norway, *Lifeguard* had her number changed to GY.395. This was a move to combat superstition, as her original registration number also added up to unlucky 13. *Lancer* was locally dubbed the 'spy trawler', as she often sailed with MoD personnel and their equipment on normal fishing trips (**Photo. 102**). All were broken up at Antwerp in 1968.

END OF THE 1940s

As the decade was coming to a close, new ships were swelling the ranks of the trawler fleets at the rate of almost one a month. The industry was still relatively optimistic. Although good catches were being taken, there were signs that the catching capability of the more modern ships was starting to deplete some of the Distant Water grounds. An international situation had arisen in the Barents Sea, so trawlers were advised to keep clear. This was a blow to the industry, as normally during the autumn months, our trawlers would bring home good catches from these grounds. Norway, too, was flexing her muscles by strictly imposing redefined fishing limits. These had originally been mooted in 1935 and differed quite considerably from any other limit then in operation. She identified forty fixed points offshore, such as rocks and islands, and linked them with straight lines termed baselines. From these extended the new four-mile limit, which meant that huge areas of fishing ground became inaccessible to foreign trawlers. Naturally the UK objected

Photo. 102: *Lancer*, seen leaving Grimsby for the Arctic grounds. She is in later Northern Tralwers Ltd colours of black hull, wood grained casing and a black topped grey funnel, separated by a white band. Her mizzen mast has been removed and replaced by a wireless mast fitted to the funnel and her original twin lifeboats have been replaced by a single boat launched by a single arm davit. Note the white name and port of registry on the black panel at the stern.

Photo. 103: The research trawler *Ernest Holt*. Note the tall radar mast, deckhouse at the stern and the lack of a mizzen mast. She has a black hull, with a white band over red boot topping and white upperworks and her cream black topped funnel carries the Ministry of Agriculture & Fisheries (MAF) logo.

to this but the war intervened and when peace came, our trawlers resumed their operations in the old areas. By 1948, however, Norway had begun arresting our trawlers, so the ships had to look to other grounds in order to supply the home market.

So bad was the shortage in September 1948, that many fish and chip shops were put out of business in and around Hull and Grimsby. In an effort to revitalise the market, Grimsby sent two ships on the 4,000 mile round trip to Greenland in late 1948; this was the first time since before the war that these grounds had been fished. It was slowly dawning on the trade that the lessons of history, with regard to over fishing, had not been learned and, indeed, they never would be. In order to assist with the research into Distant Water stocks, a new ship was ordered from Cochrane's of Selby as Yard No. 1342, for the Ministry of Agriculture & Fisheries, Grimsby. She was *Ernest Holt* (GY.591 – Photo. 103), named after the Victorian botanist E.W. Holt. Based on traditional Distant Water trawler lines, she was modelled on the builder's *St. Bartholemew* (H.216), Yard No. 1309 (193ft x 30ft x 16ft, 573g), with engines supplied by Amos & Smith. At first glance she could easily be mistaken for a commercial trawler, with fish and ice room hatches on the foredeck. On closer inspection, however, these were actually escape hatches for the accommodation below, in what would originally have been the main fish room. As this space was now used for laboratories, etc, her fish storage was confined to the forward end of this compartment, which was divided into three separate athwartship spaces, with a total capacity of 1,500 cubic ft. These comprised a main insulated fish room, with chilling grids for brine circulation to keep the ambient temperature at 0 degrees Centigrade, a pilot scale air/blast contact quick-freezing plant, of 5cwt capacity, and a low temperature store working at -10 degrees Centigrade. Her main trawl winch had a central barrel in addition to the two main ones. This was itself split into two, with each drum holding 600 fathoms of light wire used for the vessel's recording instruments. She worked out of the Royal Dock, Grimsby, until replaced in 1971 by a stern trawler. She sailed to Richards of Lowestoft for extensive upgrading and then to Leith where she took up new duties as a Fishery Patrol ship, being renamed *Switha* in June 1971. On 7th February 1980, she ran aground on a reef in the Firth of Forth, south east of the island of Inchkeith, her crew being rescued by helicopter.

Later, deemed to be a total loss, she was blown up by the Royal Navy as her fuel oil posed a threat to the area. *Switha* was in fact one of eight sister ships built by the yard, six for Lord Line of Hull (later Hellyer's) and one for the West Dock Steam Fishing Co. Ltd, Hull these being the last coal burners built for the port. Yard No. 1336 *Lord Wavell* (H.578) went to Grimsby in 1963 as GY.97. In March 1966, she was sold to Northern Trawlers Ltd and, in May the following year, she went to Fleetwood as FD.98, owned by Wyre Trawlers Ltd, going to the breakers in 1970. *Lord Ancaster* (H.583) Yard No. 1337, worked for the same company until going for scrap in 1967. *Lord Rowallan* (H.9), Yard No. 1338, was sold to Grimsby in 1963 as GY.98, transferring to Northern Trawlers Ltd in March 1966. They sold her to Belgium breakers in 1967. *Lord Willoughby* (H.36), Yard No. 1339, was transferred to Grimsby in 1963 as GY.102. Northern Trawlers Ltd took her over in March 1966 and ran her until she went for scrap in Belgium in October 1968. *Lord Fraser* (H.48), Yard No. 1340, worked out of Grimsby from April 1963 as GY.108, before being taken over by Northern Trawlers Ltd in March 1966. She joined her sisters in 1968 at the Belgian breakers. *Lord Cunningham* (H.69), Yard No. 1341, was the last of the Lord Line batch of ships and her history mirrors that of her sisters. She worked from Grimsby as GY.109, until going for scrap at Belgium in 1968. *Boynton Wyke* (H.74), Yard No. 1342, was built for the West Dock Steam Fishing Co. Ltd, Hull, who sold out later to Boyd Line Ltd and Lord Line Ltd. She was sold to Lord Line on 14th May 1959 and renamed *Arctic Crusader* (H.74) on 8th June. She went for scrapping in 1969.

One feature of all these ships was the absence of a boat deck and mizzen mast. This was originally seen on the pre-war Bremerhaven-built 'Northerns' and on Crampin Steam Fishing Co. Ltd's post-war ships *Paynter* (GY.480), *Barnett* (GY.200 – ex-GY.454) and *Wellard* (GY.300 – ex-GY.450). Mizzens were fitted later, because of changes to the rules regarding steaming lights. As the decade came to a close, big oil burning trawlers were still being built but they were not so prolific as the coal burners just after the war, as by now the fleets were up to strength and working to maximum efficiency. The motor trawler was beginning to find favour, especially with the Near and Middle Water fleet, and it was only to be a few years before they were to replace some of the Distant Water fleet's steamers.

Among the last deliveries, Grimsby's Northern Trawlers Ltd received three large, non-streamlined, oil-burning ships from Cook, Welton & Gemmell in January 1950, named *Northern Princess* (GY.110), *Northern Prince* (GY.121) and *Northern Queen* (GY.124 – all 181ft, 677g). They were to prove very well found ships and served the company well until they went for scrap, *Northern Princess* in 1971, with the other two following five years later. In 1950, the company took delivery from Cochrane's of *Northern Chief* (GY.128 – **Photo. 104**), *Northern Isles* (GY.149) and lastly *Northern Sea* (GY.142), Yard No's 1354, 1355 and 1356 respectively. This was actually the balance of a six-ship order placed in 1949, which included the three previous Beverley-built trawlers. The Cochrane-built ships had no boat decks, their lifeboats being carried in Schatt davits fitted to the casing side but, in all other respects, they were identical sisters to the earlier vessels built by Cook, Welton & Gemmell. All three went for scrap at Blyth in June 1976.

After 1945, Smith's Dock moved away from building trawlers to concentrate on other work. They did, however, build two Distant Water ships in 1949, Yard No's 1183 and 1184, *Brutus* (H.28) and *Benvolio* (H.22 – laid down as *Esmonde*). The former was to the order of the Devon Fishing Co. Ltd, Hull and the latter for Northern Fishing Co. Ltd, Hull (both companies were owned by Hellyer's). They must have served their owners well enough, as

Brutus went to the breakers in 1972 and her sister in 1975.

The eternal problems of supply and demand were again beginning to bite, after the food rationing for meat and eggs was gradually phased out in the late 1950s. The population, denied these more or less staple foods for more than a decade, moved away from eating fish. The market was being flooded with Distant Water fish, both from our own ships (whose catching power had risen some 11 per cent since before the war) and as foreign imports (these had risen 129 per cent in the same period), with the result that markets and prices were very depressed. In November 1949, a few months after the government abolished price controls, fish prices fell through the bottom, bringing despair and hardship to the Near and Middle Water fleets, with many fishermen unemployed. This brought about the setting up of the White Fish Authority (WFA), whose main task was to address the problem of ageing ships and falling stocks. The WFA brought in a series of grants, subsidies and loans to assist owners rebuild and modernise their fleets.

FOREIGN ORDERS FOR NEW SHIPS

In 1946, Belgium ordered from Cook, Welton & Gemmell its first British-built steam trawler for over forty years. The order was for four oil fired ships suitable for the White Sea and Bear Island grounds, for managers Motorvisscherj NV, Ostende. The first pair, *Breughel* and *Rubens* (181ft 2ins x 27ft 6ins x 15ft 3ins, 534g) achieved a trials speed of 13.5 knots. Their casings were extended right aft to meet the after deckhouse, enabling a mess room to be fitted next to the galley. Fish rooms were of 11,000 cu. ft and their cod liver oil plants were supplied by C.D. Holmes. The second pair delivered in 1947 were *Van Der Weyden* and *Van Orley*, similar but smaller (129ft bp x 25ft 7ins, 323g – **Photo. 105**).

ICELAND'S RENOVATION TRAWLERS

Early in 1945, Gisli Jonsson headed up an Icelandic Government mission to negotiate contracts for new builds. His remit was to provide Iceland with a fleet of steam trawlers comparable with, or superior to the best trawlers afloat. Under the chairmanship of A.L. Cochrane, five UK shipyards and engineers were involved in the tender process.

The ships incorporated numerous innovations in both accommodation and equipment not usually found in vessels of this type. In October 1945, a contract for thirty ships was signed, which was later increased to forty-four, comprising forty steamers and four motorships. Dubbed 'Renovation Trawlers' by the Icelanders, they were built by Cook, Welton & Gemmell, A.L. Cochrane, Alexander Hall, Hall, Russell and John Lewis. As the yards were heavily engaged in rebuilding the UK fleet, the final ship of the Icelandic order was not completed until 1952. During discussions it was realised that diesel powered ships would soon replace steamers, so the new fleet incorporated diesel and electric auxiliaries. Most vessels used steam for the main engine and winch, with auxiliary and deck

Photo. 104: *Northern Chief*. Note the absence of a boat deck. She carries Associated Fisheries funnel colours of a white lower section and black top, separated by an orange/yellow broad band over a similar size blue band, surmounted by a white 'A'.

Painting 11: *Northern Queen* (GY.124) in original Northern Trawlers Ltd colours. COURTESY OF S. FARROW

THE POST WAR YEARS

Photo. 105: *Van Der Weyden* showing her typical British outline.

machinery electrically powered. Traditionally the crew berthed forward in heated upper and lower fo'c'sles but with the added luxury of recreation rooms. Although built to the same outline specifications, there were minor differences as builders incorporated their own features, such as boat decks, etc. Some were built as wet fish ships, storing their catches in ice, whereas others were built with quick freeze facilities and cold stores. On these ships, the catch was cleaned and filleted, and wrapped in paper before being frozen ready for distribution ashore. Another feature fitted to some ships was a steam fish meal plant capable of handling 25 tons daily, where the processed offal was dried, ground down and bagged before being stored in a dedicated compartment. Most ships had five-boiler, cod liver oil plants aft and a storage capacity for 32 tons of liver oil. All the trawlers had the familiar two masts and outboard profile of a British owned Distant Water steam trawler.

Cook, Welton & Gemmell built *Akurey, Hvalfell, Nolsoyrar Pall, Joannes Patursson, Geir, Fylkir* and *Godanes*, followed in 1948 by *Rodull, Isborg, Gardar Thorsteinsson, Skuli Magnusson,* and *Jon Forseti*.

A.L. Cochrane's built *Ingolfur Arnarson, Helgafell, Kaldbakkur, Egill Skallagrimsson, Bjarni Riddari, Ellidi, Juli* and *Isolfur*.

Alexander Hall's Icelandic ships

were *Askur, Egill Raudi, Ellidaey, Hardbakur, Juni, Karlsefni, Keflvikingur, Solborg, Svalbakur* and *Uranus* – Yard No's 734, 735 and 736 being their last three commercial steam trawlers (**Photo. 106**).

Hall, Russells launched *Hrefna, Olafur Johannessen* (**Plan 77**) and *Drofin*, Yard No's 822, 823 and 824.

John Lewis built *Austfirdingur, Bjarnarey, Bjarni Olafsson, Martz, Neptunus, Petur Halldorsson* and *Surprise*. After 1950, very few new steam trawlers would leave Aberdeen's yards.

Photo.106: Launch of the Icelandic trawler *Solborg*, Yard No. 734 from A. Hall, Aberdeen in 1951. Note the bilge keels, davits rudder, propeller and the step in her rail.

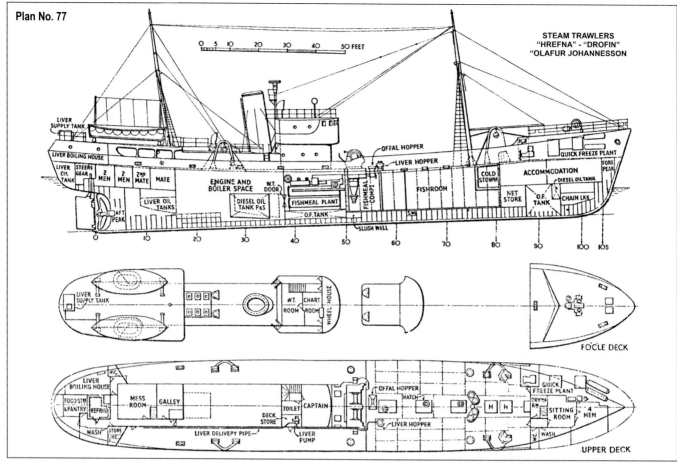

Plan No. 77

STEAM TRAWLERS
"HREFNA" - "DROFIN"
"OLAFUR JOHANNESSON

In 1946, French owners at Boulogne and La Rochelle ordered six new coal burners from John Lewis, as Yard No's 196 to 201 inclusive: *Cote D-Opale*, *Cote D-Argent* (later *Boston Valiant* (FD.214), sold again by Boston's to South Africa in 1957), *Poiton*, *Gascogne*, *Bearn* and *Guyenne* (all 137ft 6ins oa/124ft 8ins bp x 130ft wl x 26ft 7ins x 13ft 11ins, 116n, 296g). Rather heavy sterned vessels, their layout was pretty typical of the period, with the crew still housed in the fo'c'sle and the officers aft. The skipper's cabin, however, was not below the wheelhouse as was normal in British trawlers, as the space was occupied by the diesel engine for the Robertson 'Arctic' trawl winch. These were among the very first UK-built steam trawlers to have their trawl winches powered by anything other than steam. Another design difference was that all the frames were set perpendicular to the waterline and not to the keel as was the norm. The French classification society

maintained that this gave a much stronger ship. It was also adopted by Cook, Welton & Gemmell when they built another six identical ships for the Association Rochelaise de Peche a Vapeur in 1946, as Yard No's 769 to 774, with *Michel Bernard* (B.2360) being the lead ship. Her sisters were *Jacques Colin* (B.2366), *Aunis* (LR.4042), *Artois* (LR.4049), *Edmond Rene* (F.1053) and *Souvenir* (F.1038). *Artois* came to Fleetwood owners Grange Fishing Co. Ltd in 1951, as *Braconvale* (FD.80). They sold her in 1955 to Hammerfest Havfiske A/L, Norway, who renamed her *Masi* (F.29H) and she was broken up at Stavanger in March 1970.

Photo. 107: *Edmond-Rene* leaving Fécamp, Upper Normandy. She has a heavier appearance than British vessels.

Chapter 17: 1950s – THE BEGINNING OF THE END

Iceland followed Norway's lead in 1949 and declared that a similar four-mile limit would be imposed by 1951 (a two year notice of abrogation necessitated this wait). These new regulations came into force on 15th May 1952, only a few months after Iceland took delivery of the final three Distant Water trawlers from the UK. This drastically reduced the catching areas favoured by British Distant Water trawlers, including the much frequented Faxa Bay. The UK trawling industry threw up their hands in horror at this move and immediately called for a total ban on imports of Icelandic fish. This ban was met with mixed feelings by some of the fish merchants and by a few members of the British Trawler Federation, and it was only implemented fully after trawler crews held a three-day strike in November 1952. Unfortunately, by imposing this ban, the industry effectively shot themselves in the foot' Not only did it not have the desired effect of weakening the Icelandic economy, it forced that country to look elsewhere for new markets, in Brazil, Cuba, and West Africa, along with the USA and the USSR. Britain (as usual), eventually relented and *Ingolfur Arnarson* (RE.201) was the first Icelandic trawler permitted to land its 3,400 kit catch at Grimsby at the end of November 1956 (this was one the vessels built by Cochrane's in 1947).

The decade was to witness a totally unacceptable loss of human lives and vessels, plus a running down and scrapping of the old Near Water ships. Aberdeen was the first to lose a ship; *Kuvera* (A.384), the ex-'Strath' Class *John Heath*, was built by the Ouse Shipbuilding Co. Ltd, Goole in 1919. At the time of her loss on 26th January, she was Granton owned and crewed, and was working with *Chiltern* (GN.25), some 110 miles off Buchan Ness, when she started taking water. Her crew of thirteen were taken aboard the other ship. In the same year, Grimsby lost three Distant Water trawlers. The first was on 17th February, when *Pollard* (GY.244), built in 1930 by Cochranes and owned by Crampins, ran ashore on the Norwegian coast at Trannoy West Fjord. Two months later, on 14th April, *Preston North End* (GY.82), built by Smith's Dock in 1934 and owned by Consolidated Fisheries Ltd, went ashore at Saeberg, Iceland. Ten days later, *Ogano* (GY.69), owned by the Ogano Steam Fishing Co. Ltd, Grimsby, was wrecked on Brokur Reef, south Iceland. She was a non-standard 'Castle' Class, built by Cook, Welton & Gemmell in 1917. All the sixty-three trawlermen were rescued from the above ships but one later died of hypothermia. A year later, Grimsby lost the old North Sea trawler *Aucuba* (GY.117), built in 1906 by Cook, Welton & Gemmell and owned at the time by Derwent Trawlers Ltd, Grimsby. She collided with an Italian steamer in Robin Hood's Bay but, fortunately, all her crew were saved. Closer to home still, on 9th January 1951, *St. Leander* (H.19), built at Beverley in 1949 and owned by Thomas Hamling & Co. Ltd, Hull, foundered in the Humber after colliding with the anchored *Davy* (H.213).

The year 1952 saw seven East Coast trawlers lost, among them the Aberdeen trawler *Loch Lomond* on 23rd October. Built in 1930 by Smith's Dock as *Lune* (FD.59), Yard No. 910, for Wyre Trawlers Ltd, Fleetwood. In September 1938, she went to the Earl Steam Fishing Co. Ltd, Grimsby as GY.538. During her war service, she was sold to Malcolm Smith Ltd, Aberdeen

in September 1941. She moved north in April 1947 and was renamed *Loch Lomond* (A.299). I was only ten years old as I stood and watched from Victoria Road School (a glass covered stair case gave a clear view of the navigation channel) as she buffeted her way down-channel on that stormy morning. Ahead of her was another of Malcolm Smith's ships, *Loch Laggan* (A.82), which safely crossed the harbour bar to the open sea. Just as *Loch Lomond* approached the broken water at the bar, she was swept northwards and on to the concrete apron at the base of the North Pier. Within minutes, all her thirteen crewmen had been rescued by breeches buoy, assisted by the local life-saving apparatus team. By evening, her wheelhouse had been torn off and was later washed ashore at the Torry side of the channel. She became a total loss and was broken up where she lay. She had run ashore in the same spot that claimed *George Stroud* (A.88) on Christmas night 1935, when all her crew were swept to their deaths in sight of their homes. The same day that *Loch Lomond* came to grief, three other trawlers entered the casualty lists. Aberdeen's *Strathelliot* (A.46) ran ashore on the rocks of Selwick Hoy, Orkney but her crew were saved after a six hour ordeal. The Fleetwood trawler *Wyre Law* (FD 48) was wrecked in Broad Bay, Isle of Lewis in a 60mph gale. Her skipper, George Wood and his twelve man crew were rescued by *Charles Doran* (FD.275). Another Fleetwood ship had been in difficulties in the same place just a few days earlier. *Pern* (FD.983) had lost engine power and was drifting helplessly in a gale towards the rocky coast. Her radio message was picked up by *Boston Attacker* (FD.92) under skipper Jack Chard, who went to her assistance. After struggling for over twelve hours, she managed to tow the crippled trawler 20 miles to the safety of Loch Sheil. The worst disaster of the year was on 4th November, when the Hull trawler *Norman* (H.289) was wrecked off Cape Farewell, Greenland with the loss of twenty out of her crew of twenty one. Hull was to lose another nine ships by 1960 and over forty-five men would never see Hessle Road again. Her neighbour, Grimsby, lost twenty ships over the same ten year period and some 140 men, whilst Fleetwood lost ten trawlers, one of which, *Michael Griffiths* (FD. 249), foundered with all hands off Barra Head on 1st February 1953.

Amongst the lucky ones, were the twenty man crew of *Northern Crown* (GY.284. – **Photo. 108**). She ran ashore on the Isle of Eldey, a 226ft high rock some eight miles south west of Reykjanes Point, Iceland, on 11th October 1956. With her lifeboats smashed, the crew took to two inflatable rafts, which carried them to safety. This was one of the first instances of crews saved by these new rubber rafts and that year alone saw the crews of *Osako* (GY.100) and *St. Celestin* (H.233) saved by inflatables. In total, Aberdeen lost seventeen ships for the period and some twenty-four men perished.

The last disaster of the decade was that of *George Robb* (A.406), on the rocks of Duncansby Head during the night of 6th December 1959, when all her twelve man crew were drowned. She was built by Hall, Russell's as *Elsie I. Carnie* (GN.24), Yard No. 712, in 1930 at a cost of £9,725. In 1936, she was bought by George Robb & Sons Ltd, Aberdeen and re-registered A.406. She was requisitioned from 1939 until 1946 as a minesweeper. In October 1959, she was converted to diesel by Richards of

Photo. 108: *Northern Crown* (GY.284) in Northern Trawlers Ltd colours, with white wheelhouse over a light wood grained casing and a grey, white and black funnel. She is seen alongside the fitting out berth at Grimsby.

Lowestoft and was sailing on her second trip as a motor ship when disaster struck. At 22.50 hours, Caithness farmer William Ham picked up skipper Marshall Ryles distress call: *"Ashore south of Duncansby, making water rapidly, require immediate assistance"*. The Longhope Lifeboat was launched but could not get close enough to the stricken trawler to assist. The rocket teams were powerless to help in the howling onshore gale but several local folk managed to get down the treacherous cliffs, albeit to no avail as no survivors were located. So severe was the weather that winter's night that Station Officer Eric Campbell, of the Wick rescue team, collapsed and died on the cliff top.

In addition to all these losses, the end of the road had come for many of the older ships. The age analysis of the Scottish trawling fleet in 1948 showed that out of a total of 261 ships, some 223 were over twenty-five years old. This decade was one of full time employment for the cutting torch, as trawler after trawler made its final trip to the breaker's yards; forty-one ships alone were scrapped at Inverkeithing. Building costs for new ships were to escalate very considerably during this decade, with Distant Water ships increasing in price from around £100,000 in 1950, to some £300,000 by 1960.

SCRAP AND BUILD

All was not complete doom and gloom for the industry. The

Government was forced to introduce its 'Scrap and Build' scheme, in order to modernise the Near and Middle Water fleets, whose ships were all very long in the tooth. The favourably received grant and loan schemes, with their acceptable interest rates, allowed the owners to order new tonnage, with the result that the building yards were all working to full capacity. This scheme also made it cost effective to replace steamers with motor ships rather than convert them to diesel. By the end of the decade, the White Fish Authority had processed the following grants for new Near and Middle Water trawlers:

Port	New Ships
Aberdeen	66
Lowestoft	54
Fleetwood	47
Grimsby	45
Granton	19
Milford	6
Yarmouth	4
Hartlepool	2
Hull	2
North Shields	2
TOTAL	**247**

As well as supplying the home market, builders were still

receiving lucrative enquiries from abroad. In 1950, Cook, Welton & Gemmell completed a four-ship order for Motorvisserij NV, Ostend, Belgium. These were large (170ft oa, 600g), streamlined, oil burning Distant Water trawlers and all eventually came under Hamling's ownership in 1964: Yard No. 828 *Van Dyck*, later to become the ill-fated *St. Romanus* (H.223) lost without trace with all hands in the North Sea in January 1968; Yard No. 845 *Van Eyck*, later *St. Achilleus* (H.215), scrapped in 1969; Yard No. 847 *Van Orley*, which became *St. Andronicus* (H.241) and went for scrap in 1969; and Yard No. 848 *Van Oost*, renamed *St. Arcadius* (H.207) and scrapped in 1968

Another boost for the Yorkshire yards came in 1952, when Cochrane's secured a five-ship order for National Sea Products, Nova Scotia. Yard No's 1371, 1372, 1377, 1378 and 1379 (137ft bp, 399g), they were, in order of building, *Cape Beaver*, *Cape Brier*, *Cape Argo*, *Cape Bonnie* and *Cape Sambro*. All were oil fired steamers with streamlined single tier wheelhouses and small, streamlined, capped funnels sitting atop the superstructure. It appears that these trawlers were designed to work in even more hostile conditions than normal. All led quite short lives for trawlers, which was perhaps due to the harsh weather conditions of the region and they mostly went for scrapping in 1971-2, although the first to go was *Cape Argo* in 1967. They were in fact larger versions of Cook, Welton & Gemmell's motor trawler *Thorina* (H.318), Yard No. 766, built in 1946 for Marrs and had two features which set them apart from UK ships. Firstly, the windlass was fitted under the shelter of the whaleback, to help prevent the build up ice at the forward end of the vessel and, secondly, the winchman was protected by a shelter which jutted out from the front of the casing.

Two of Aberdeen's steam trawlers made the local news in January 1951, when they were sold to the Colonial Development Corporation to work out of Nigeria. They were *Strathalbyn* (A.48) and *Strathblair* (A.132 – both 117ft, 216g), previously owned by the Davidson Fishing Co. Ltd, Aberdeen. They were built by Hall, Russell in 1929 and 1930 as Yard No's 701 and 714 respectively, at a cost of £9,725 each. They were specially converted by the builders for their final trip from their home port to Lagos. The fish room was fitted with refrigeration plant and a racking system for storing metal fish boxes so that each received free air circulation. If required, the racks could be removed and the catch stored on shelves in the normal way. The crew's quarters were fully air-conditioned and a deck saloon was built on to the after end of the galley, with sliding windows. On the passage out to Africa, they were manned by transit crews of West Africans (who wished to work their passage home), under the command of British officers. *Strathalbyn* was skippered by James Flett of Findochty and her sister by Thomas Normandale from Scarborough (his grandfather was accredited with the use of the first otter trawl in the 1890s). These two trawlers formed the nucleus of Nigeria's trawling industry.

NEW NAVIGATION LIGHT RULES AND ICING PROBLEMS

In 1953, new legislation came into force regarding the Regulations for Preventing Collisions at Sea or, more especially, the rules concerning lights. Designed as an additional safety measure, it laid down that powered vessels over 150ft in length MUST carry an additional white light on the centre line of the keel. This, the after-most light, should be at least 15ft higher than the forward one, and be of similar construction:

'A BRIGHT WHITE LIGHT, so constructed as to show an unbroken light over an arc of the horizon of 20 points of the compass, so fixed as to throw the light 10 points on either side of the vessel, viz., from right ahead to 2 points abaft the beam on either side, and of such a character as to be visible at a distance of at least five miles.'

The vertical distance between the two lights had, at all times, to be less than the horizontal distance. Prior to this date, the rules merely stated that a vessel of this size MAY carry this extra steaming light, which explains the lack of mizzen masts on many post war Distant Water ships and their subsequent retro-fits after this change to the rules. On the surface and to most seamen, these new rules made good sense but, to the Arctic trawlerman, it was seen as a retrograde step. Unfortunately, a trawler is governed by the same rules as a merchant vessel of similar size but, unlike her counterpart, she spends almost all of her working life in the stormy ice-bound regions above 60 degrees north latitude. It is in these regions that the three elements mainly responsible for a trawler-icing up and losing stability are to be found:

1. Air and initial ship temperature of 20-25 degrees Fahrenheit
2. A wind speed of Force 6 and above
3. A mean sea temperature of 30-35 degrees Fahrenheit (sea water freezes around 28.4 degrees Fahrenheit). These conditions soon force the thermometer down to 0 degrees Fahrenheit and below, and the sea water striking the vessel freezes solid on impact. **(Photos 109 & 110)**

To maintain maximum stability, ice had to be constantly chopped away, which was bad enough at deck level but impossible on the masts. The new rules made the fitting of mizzens (previously phased out) compulsory, which only aggravated the situation. It was recommended that, whenever an icing situation was present, skippers should leave the area immediately and seek shelter. Basic, good seamanship but, unfortunately, this was not always possible, and ships were caught out.

ESTIMATED DISTRIBUTION OF ICE FOR FULL-SCALE, NORMALLY RIGGED TRAWLER DETERMINED FROM MODEL EXPERIMENTS
Topmast stay, forestay, two quarter stays, forward derrick and pivot, 'clutter' at joints, shrouds, bag ropes, etc, after mainmast derrick, fish tackles, landing span and aerials, mizzen shrouds and ratlines, boats and davits, forecastle rails, mast, radar tower rails and compass, mizzen mast = 45 tons
Add to this the forecastle deck, windlass etc, the superstructure, and main deck boat deck and rails = 100 tons
giving a total of 140 tons of ice for the complete ship.

All the above effects of icing at sea, can be summarised as follows:

Weight: Added weight results in loss of freeboard and will affect the range of stability.

Moment: Ice quickly forms on the masts, rigging and

ABOVE: Photo. 109: Attacking the build up of ice aboard *Ernest Holt*. Note how the radiated heat has kept her funnel free of ice.

LEFT: Photo.110: The build up of ice on the wheelhouse and winch. Note the crewman with his hammer clearing the wheelhouse windows

of aerials, radar, compass and boats is obvious, and calls for no further comment. Without any provision for its removal, ice will obviously build up on the ship for as long as the icing conditions prevail. It is also obvious that any worthwhile protection against the danger is out of the question in the case of the traditionally rigged trawler, as long as lengths of exposed rail, ropes, stays, shrouds, ratlines and derricks defy all practicable anti-icing measures. However, a high degree of protection could be afforded to

upperworks and, being placed high up on the ship, it has a large heeling lever and thus a most damaging affect on stability.

Area: The large area of ice build up, particularly around and ahead of the foremast, provides a large sail area to the wind. This would produce a large upsetting moment with the wind on the beam and the ship might have difficulty in answering her helm when heavily iced.

The decrease in the efficiency of the ship owing to the icing

a ship of refined design carrying only such essential elements of rigging as were necessary for her to earn her living at sea and to carry the navigation lights required by international law. There are two main requirements for the design of an iceworthy ship:

1. The elimation and suppression of as much of the rigging and superstructure excrescences as possible throughout the ship.

2. In revision of hull design, particular attention should be paid to freeboard and GM (Metacentric Height), and these increased

Photo. 111: *Avonriver* when new, before radar had been fitted and showing her shapely profile. She is wearing her original colour scheme of black topsides with white line at deck level, wood grained superstructure and a black topped red funnel with silver star motif. No mizzen mast is fitted but a triatic fish landing stay can be seen leading from the foremast head to the funnel. Note the anchor pocket, which was later removed.

where necessary in order that a greater weight of ice may be carried in safety. It is not thought that any major modification to the present fishing techniques would be necessary to meet these requirements. It is not practicable to provide a means of raising and maintaining the temperature of exposed surfaces of a ship above the freezing point of sea water to prevent icing. Accordingly, methods of protection are directed to removing, or rendering it easier to remove, ice already formed on the ship. There are a number of methods of de-icing and these may be divided into (a) Mechanical, (b) Chemical, and (c)Thermal.

Mechanical expedients such as chipping with axes and thermal methods such as steam hoses, were already in use on trawlers. These are the most practical but there are other possible methods, such as the use of silicones, Kilfrost and similar pastes. However, they are of limited application and relatively untried as far as marine conditions are concerned. A number of similar methods are employed in the aircraft industry but conditions are somewhat different with aeroplanes and whereas such protection as the Napier Spray Mat is now being tested for marine use, no method has been fully investigated, although sometime during the late 1960s and early 1970s, the Ministry of Defence sponsored anti-icing trials on the motor trawler **Boston Phantom**. She was fitted with PTFE (Polytetraflouroethylene) panels on her masts and wheelhouse and these panels were wired up electrically in order to displace the ice. Apparently it was only a very limited success and was not repeated.

Although it was now the beginning of the end of the British steam trawler, the fleet still totalled some 7,791 ships in the mid 1950s. The Middle and Near Water fleets were very gradually being replaced by modern diesel powered ships and it was only in the Distant Water sector that steamers still held sway. In the ten years since 1940, very few of the smaller home water ships had been built (seventy-four new trawlers for the whole of the UK) and the fleet consisted mainly of decrepit old pre-First World War ships and a handful of 1930s vessels. Aberdeen, in particular, had a very ancient fleet of around 200 Near Water 'scratchers', reinforced with a very few newer steamers; only four new ships were added to the city's steam trawler fleet after the war.

The last steam trawler for Aberdeen, *Avonriver* (A.660 – 149ft 3ins oa/145ft bp x 26ft x 14ft 3ins, 421g) was built by J. Lewis as Yard No. 224, for the North Star Steam Fishing Co. Ltd, Aberdeen; it was the largest steamer ever to work out of the port. She was a very handsome, streamlined, oil fired Distant Water ship, launched on 4th April 1951 and sailing on 21st June,

forming a fitting finale to Aberdeen's steam sidewinder fleet (**Plans 78 a, b & c**). She was another Distant Water ship to leave the builders without a mizzen, having two sampson post type engine room vents, with a stump aerial mast on the centre line. A taller steel topmast was fitted in 1953 to comply with the new rules. In early life with a pale cream hull, she was known affectionately as the 'Banana Boat'. She later reverted to the company's black hull with a white band (**Photo. 111**). After a full survey and refit in November 1962, her gross tonnage came down to 413. This was due to some modifications to the accommodation and by placing a limit on the capacity of the forward bosun's store. She was sold on 9th December 1966, to the Hubbard Explorational Co. Ltd, East Grinstead and re-registered at London as a steam yacht. On 28th February 1967, she underwent another reconstruction at Hull, in order to fit her out for her new role. The crew accommodation was again revamped and reduced from eighteen hands to nine. On 27th November 1967, she was sold to America and her British registry cancelled on 6th December.

It appears as a retrograde step to move the crew back to the fo'c'sle, after the company's earlier *Avondow* had them housed aft, but they did have a mess room at the after end of the casing on main deck level. As she was designed for Distant Water fishing and borderline with regards to length, a radio operator may have been a requirement, although one was never carried and the drawing shows the accommodation at the rear of the wheelhouse fitted out as a chartroom/radio cabin complete with bunk. She carried a full W/T and R/T fit, plus DF but, strangely enough, shows no radar installation, although this was fitted later. By this time it was common practice to fit two echo sounders to this class of ship and *Avonriver* was fitted with Marconi 'Sea Graph' and 'Sea Visa' types. Also shown on the plan are her Andanes fishing lights on the wheelhouse top, where she has her main, overhead inverted magnetic steering compass, supplemented by the pole compass in front of the bridge.

Her curved funnel casing housed a large drying room to port and a battery room to starboard. This latter space held the battery banks for the wireless equipment, as the regulations stipulated that if a radio installation was carried, a battery powered emergency transmitter/receiver must be fitted and kept in good working order. The main power for her electrics came from the 10kw steam generator and the 4.5kw stand by diesel set fitted in the engine room. Two wooden, double-ended lifeboats were carried in Schat davits, on the boat deck aft, and her liver oil plant could easily process the four tons required to fill the storage tanks.

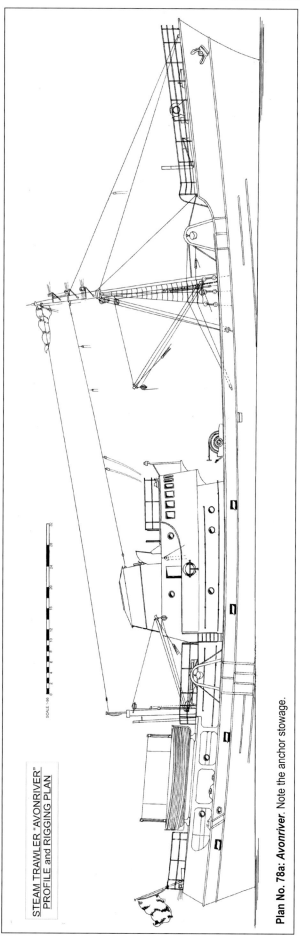

STEAM TRAWLER "AVONRIVER"
PROFILE and RIGGING PLAN

SCALE 1-96

Plan No. 78a: *Avonriver.* Note the anchor stowage.

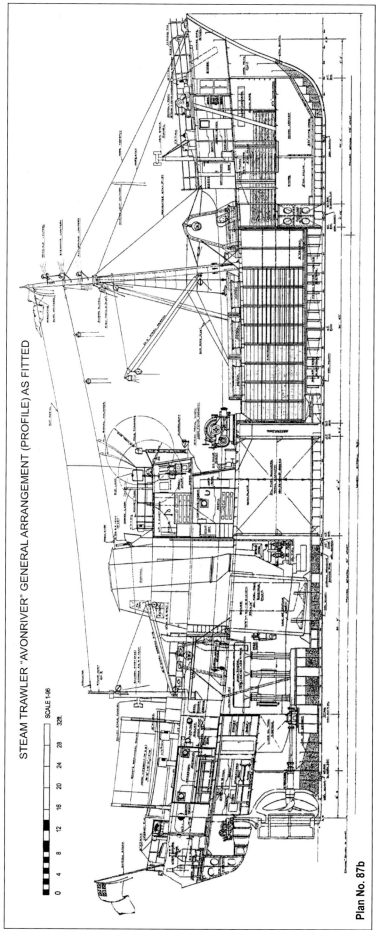

STEAM TRAWLER "AVONRIVER" GENERAL ARRANGEMENT (PROFILE) AS FITTED

SCALE 1-96

0 4 8 12 16 20 24 28 32ft.

Plan No. 87b

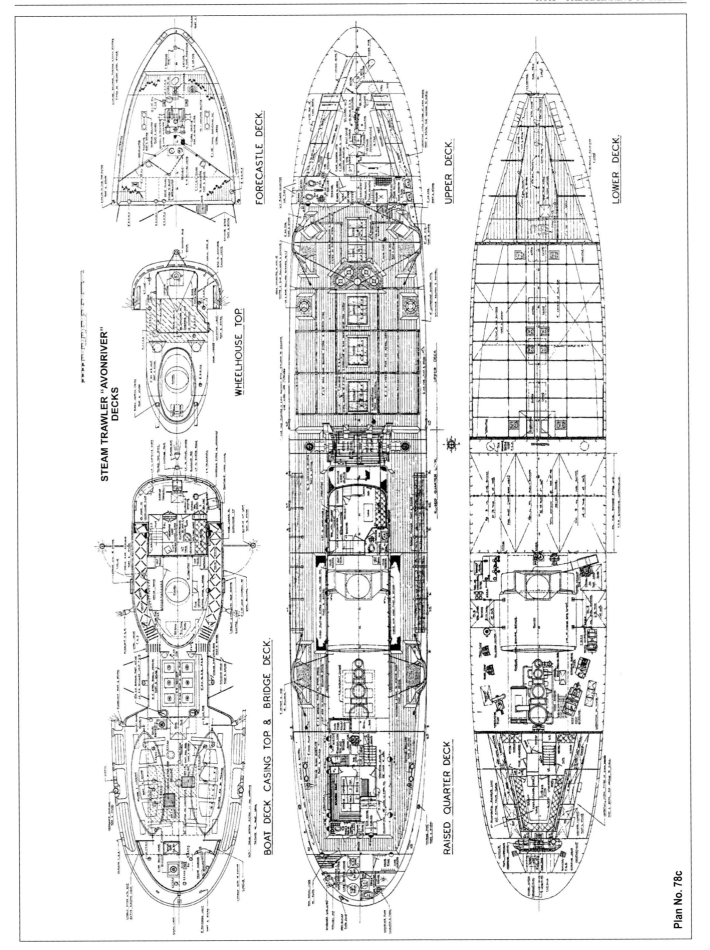

STEAM TRAWLER "AVONRIVER" DECKS

FORECASTLE DECK.

WHEELHOUSE TOP

BOAT DECK CASING TOP & BRIDGE DECK.

UPPER DECK.

UPPER DECK.

RAISED QUARTER DECK

LOWER DECK.

Plan No. 78c

243

Photo. 112: *Red Hackle*. Note the elliptical shaped wheelhouse, which gave better all round vision, and the goal post mizzen, which doubled as engine room ventilators. The ship is seen on trials in Iago colours of light mauve hull, wood grained super structure and black funnel with a red band. Her flared bow and knuckle line are evident in the picture, as well as the second bobbin derrick above the middle portlight on the casing

LEWIS'S TRIPLE DECKERS

Lewis's were still building large trawlers for English owners. They launched the world's first Doxford-engined diesel Distant Water trawler on 22nd October 1949, as Yard No. 220 *Lammermuir* (H.105 – 190ft 7ins oa/185ft bp x 32ft x 17ft 9ins, 729g). The first triple decker to come from an Aberdeen yard, she was built for a consortium which included Boston Deep Sea Fisheries Ltd, Hull. She was sold to Faeroese owners in 1956 and renamed *Jegvan Elias Thomsen*, going to the breakers in 1976. The company's next order was for two sister ships for the Iago Steam Trawling Co. Ltd, London, Yard No's 221 and 225, *Red Rose* (LO.85) and *Red Hackle* (LO.109 – 180ft oa/175ft 6ins bp x 30ft x 17ft, 674g – **Photo. 112**). The former left the ways on 22nd December 1949 and sailed on 13th April 1950, while her sister was launched on 14th August and sailed on 18th November (**Plan 79**). Her departure was quite an occasion for the city, with Vera Lynn present and the Regimental Pipe Band of the Black Watch playing her down-channel. All her crew were presented with a Red Hackle, which was the regimental

cap badge, and a celebratory bottle of Red Hackle whisky.

Beautiful, triple-decked, streamlined oil burners, with fuel for forty days steaming, they epitomised the new decade of Arctic trawlers. Even their colour scheme of lavender hulls and dark brown superstructures with red and black funnels made them stand apart from their classmates. They were in fact larger versions of *Avonriver*, with soft nosed clipper stems and a knuckle at the forward end of the sheerstrake, and with a large proportion of their hulls being electrically welded. They had aluminium superstructures and their wheelhouses were more streamlined than any on previous ships and oval in plan view, providing almost all-round vision. They were fitted with an inverted overhead magnetic compass, supplemented by a Sperry Minor Gyro compass, which replaced the external pole compass fitted to other ships of this type. Steering gear was the Donkins steam and hydraulic type, with hand emergency gear coupled up in the tiller flat. Incorporated in the wheelhouse was an enclosed chartroom/skipper's day cabin. On the lower bridge deck was the captains cabin running the full

Painting 12: *Red Hackle* by George Wiseman of Aberdeen.

width of the casing, with en-suite toilet facilities. Behind this to port was the radio room, where the operator lived and worked. He was supplied with the latest types of transmitting, receiving and DF equipment, and radar was fitted from the outset. Below, at the forward end of the casing, were single cabins for the mate, chief and second engineer. A cabin was also provided for a pilot, who was a compulsory addition to the crew when passing through the Norwegian Fjords. He would be a Norwegian national, who boarded and left the vessel at either end of the inshore passage. It seemed at last that the crew were berthed down aft. In the lower cabin there are bunks for twelve hands and behind this are a pair of two berth cabins. On the main deck above is another six berth cabin, with the officer's messroom to port and wash space aft. The crew took their meals in the fourteen place messroom adjacent to the galley and when going on or off watch, they no longer had to negotiate the open main deck, as they could access the wheelhouse from the casing top using the companionway escape ladder to the boat deck.

Another first for the builders was the fitting of all aluminium insulated fish rooms – 370 aluminium pound boards, to be scrubbed every trip! They were also among the earliest British steam trawlers to be fitted with automatic fish washers from new, two such washers being fitted, each with a capacity of 15 kits. The basic design was of a steel tank, open at the top with all four corners chamfered off and removable baffle bars or plates fitted to either end, which was fitted on stanchions over the fishroom hatch. The washer was kept full of sea water, pumped continuously by the donkey. As the gutted fish were thrown into the tank, the motion of the ship swilled them around and washed away the blood residue (a task that was usually done by the deckhands standing in a water filled pound and kicking the fish around with their feet). The cleaned fish would then overflow the chosen baffle plate, with gravity delivering them to the men in the fish room below. A sure sign that a trawler was almost full of fish was when her washer was reversed, with the fish filling the forward fish room. Although Lewis were the first to fit these washers from new, the original design was thought up by a Hull skipper, Wally Woods, who had

a wooden prototype fitted to his own trawler. They worked from Fleetwood with the rest of Iago's fleet, frequenting the White Sea, with odd runs to Greenland, etc, and *Red Hackle* landed her maiden trip on 12th December 1950. On returning from this trip to Fleetwood, all her crew received an invitation to see Vera Lynn's show at Blackpool. In 1953, she changed her number to FD.309 (the only Iago trawler ever to wear an FD registration) when she was chosen to represent the port at the Coronation Spithead Review, under her skipper at the time, Eric Littler. Both ships were sold to the Lord Line of Hull in April 1954, *Red Rose* being renamed *Lord Howe* (H.19) and her sister becoming *Lord Hawke* (H.39). They were later sold in March 1963 to Northern Trawlers Ltd, Grimsby, becoming GY.82, and GY.89 respectively. *Red Hackle* went for scrap in September 1968, and her sister followed in May 1971. By the end of their days, their overhanging boat decks had been cut back almost to the poop house wrapper plate and the twin lifeboats replaced by a single transom sterned type, with a Schat Single Arm davit. The Sampson post engine rom vents had been cut down and when fitted, a light steel mast was stepped on the after end of the funnel casing.

In between these two ships, Lewis built another very large trawler for Boston Deep Sea Fisheries Ltd's Grimsby operation. Launched on 1st June 1950 as Yard No. 222 *Boston Fury* (GY.153 – 206ft 4ins x 32ft 3ins x 16ft 3ins, 760g), she sailed on 6th September (**Photo. 113**). She was a larger version of Iago's ships and two foot wider in the beam and was to be the largest steamer to work from the port until the arrival of *Velinda* in 1956. She was also the first Grimsby trawler to be fitted with an automatic liver transfer system; no longer would the 'deckies' have to drag the baskets of cod livers along the open deck to the boilers aft, now they could dump them in the hopper fitted to the starboard fish pounds, from where they would be pumped to the storage tank at the stern of the boat deck.

Although their below deck accommodation was similar to the earlier ships, with all the crew aft, the superstructure quarters were a little different. No cabin was provided for a pilot, although a central berth for a navigator was provided at the fore end of the

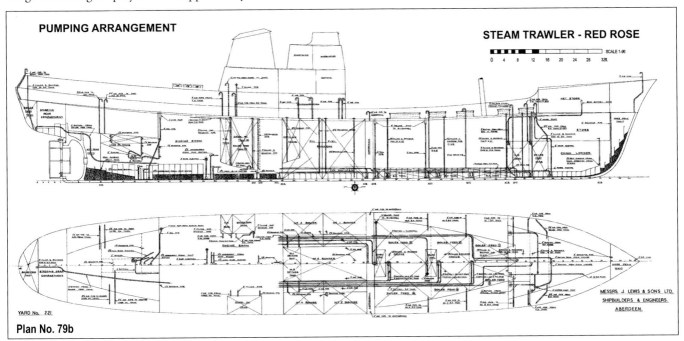

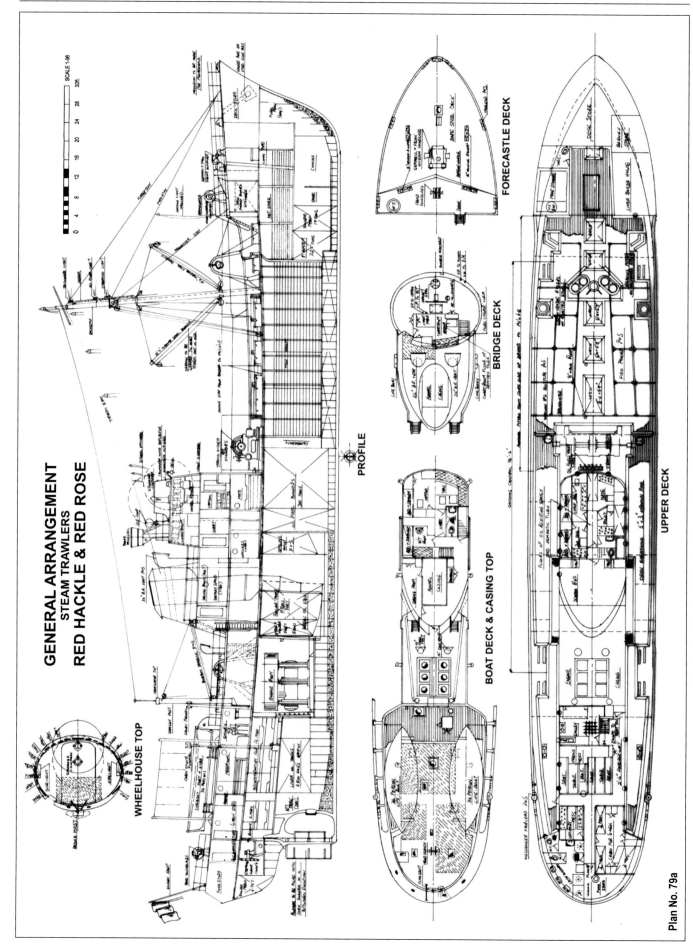

GENERAL ARRANGEMENT
STEAM TRAWLERS
RED HACKLE & RED ROSE

WHEELHOUSE TOP

PROFILE

FORECASTLE DECK

BRIDGE DECK

BOAT DECK & CASING TOP

UPPER DECK

Plan No. 79a

casing, below the lower bridge deck (a certificated navigator was required for trips to Greenland). This space also accommodated the mate, first and second engineers in single cabins, plus an officer's saloon. The lower bridge deck (casing top) above had a large skipper's cabin with en-suite bathroom. An athwartship lobby separated this from the radio room, with an adjacent berth for the operator (on Iago's ships, the operator shared his cabin with the radio equipment.) The funnel casing contained a spacious drying room to port and battery stowage on the other side. The upper bridge or wheelhouse had the same frontal profile as the previous vessels but instead of being completely oval in plan, with only a single door on the port side, it was more traditional, with wings and doors on either side and a squarish chartroom behind. This served as the skipper's working cabin and it also held the radar transmitter and screen. A pole compass was stayed to the wheelhouse front (which would appear to indicate that no gyro was fitted), with the inverted steering compass on the wheelhouse top. The radar tower was kept

short so the revolving scanner would not foul the aerials. Again, no mizzen mast was originally fitted, the aerials leading to the sampson posts on the casing.

It was not long before she was in the news. On 4th October 1950, while under skipper John Hobbs, she went to the aid of the merchant steamer *Fred Borchard* listing badly in a force nine gale off the Lofoten Islands after her deck cargo of timber shifted, the water being thick with plank of wood as the trawler approached. The crew managed to get a rocket line aboard the ship but this parted, so, in atrocious conditions, the steamer's crew took to the water as the trawler closed with her. She succeeded in saving twenty-seven out of her twenty-nine man crew. *Boston Fury* was sold to Faeroe in April 1955 and renamed *Fiskanes* (TN.50 – **Photo. 114**). Bostons bought her back in March 1965, moving her to Hull as *Boston Fury* (H.252) once more. They sold her a year later to Weelsby Trawlers Ltd, Grimsby as *Brandur* (GY.111). In April, one year later, she hit the headlines when, under the command of fiery skipper Bunny

ABOVE: Photo. 113: *Boston Fury* heads back in to harbour after trials – note no fishing number as yet – carrying the goalpost type mizzen mast. She is in Boston Deep Sea Fisheries Ltd's colours of black hull with a white band at deck level (strangely kicking down forward, possibly for her fishing number), grained casing with white wheelhouse and a black topped red funnel.

RIGHT: Photo. 114: *Fiskanes* (ex-*Boston Fury*) in the later 1950s, little changed from new except for the pole mizzen.

Photo. 115: *Explorer*, showing her large wood grained and panelled aluminium superstructure, and cream funnel. Note the binnacle, D/F loop and radar tower on the wheelhouse.

Newton, she was arrested on 25th for fishing illegally off Eldey, south west Iceland. Taken into Reykjavik by the gunboat *Thor*, she was interned and her skipper taken to court. Nothing more was heard from her until 29th April, when the news broke that she had made a dash for freedom, abducting two Icelandic policemen. The attempt was short-lived and eleven hours later, she was in custody again. The legal proceedings against her skipper dragged on and no matter how much the British Consul and her owners tried to resolve matters, the Icelanders were determined to make an example of the trawler. On the night of 2nd May, a fire swept through part of the accommodation, gutting a two berth cabin and badly water damaging others. The crew were allowed one night ashore in the local sailor's home, before returning to clear up the mess. The ship was eventually released on 6th May, after her

skipper had been fined £2,400 for the fishing offence and given a three month prison sentence for abducting the policemen. His freedom was only gained after Boston's put up a bond of £100,000 pending an appeal against the conviction. He took *Brandur* to Aberdeen, where she landed her catch on 9th May and grossed £2,500. The public health officials only condemned three boxes of haddock, although the remainder of her catch was naturally in poor condition. It was some months later that the result of the appeal was made public, and a shocked skipper Newton heard that his prison sentence had been doubled to six months and the fine increased to over £2,500. She sailed for the breakers yard at Troon on 25th April 1968 and on 1st December that year, skipper Bunny Newton received a free pardon from the Icelandic Government. It was one of a number of such pardons granted for the Icelandic Day of Independence. So ends the story of the last British steam trawler ordered from John Lewis, Torry, Aberdeen.

Alexander Hall did, however, draw up a proposal in 1957 for a class of Near Water ships for the port. They were never built, as by this time the motor trawler had proved itself.

Halls were to build one other steam trawler, Yard No. 747, the Fishery Research Ship *Explorer*, for the Scottish Home Department (**Photo. 115 and Plan 80**) and launched on 21st June 1955 by the wife of the Secretary of State for Scotland, Lady Rachel Stuart. *Explorer* (202ft 5ins oa/183ft 6ins bp x 32ft x 16ft, 862g) was based on a design for a Greenland ship, specially strengthened for ice and commissioned into the department's fleet a year later, at a cost of £313,000. She was a credit to her builders and reckoned by the fishing fraternity to be the most handsome steam 'trawler' ever built in the city. Her superstructure was all aluminium and she was fitted with the yard's very last triple expansion

Photo. 116: *Lorenzo* in later Hellyer colour scheme of light grey hull with white band and white wheelhouse over a wood grained casing. The black topped cream funnel carries the white 'H' logo on a blue flag. Note the flared bow so typical of these ships and the wooden transom sterned lifeboat.

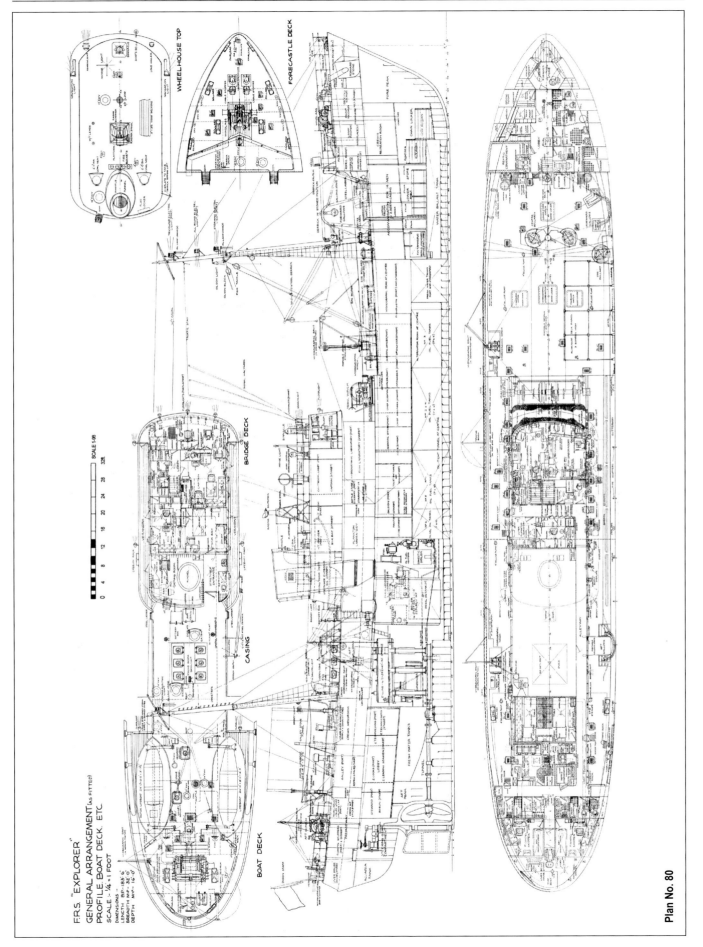

F.R.S. "EXPLORER"
GENERAL ARRANGEMENT (AS FITTED)
PROFILE, BOAT DECK, ETC.
SCALE :- ¼ = I FOOT

DIMENSIONS :-
LENGTH   B.P- 183'.6"
BREADTH MLD - 32'.0"
DEPTH   MLD - 16'.0"

WHEELHOUSE TOP

FORECASTLE DECK

BRIDGE DECK

CASING

BOAT DECK

SCALE 1-96

0   4   8   12   16   20   24   28   32ft.

Plan No. 80

Photo. 117: *Andanes* as new, in Rinovia's colours of grey hull with a white band, wood grained superstructure and white painted wooden lifeboats. Her grey, black topped funnel carries a red bordered white cross on a blue flag.

steam engine. After decommissioning, her engines were donated to the city of Aberdeen but the directors of the local Maritime Museum thought that they would be better served by preserving the complete vessel. Alas, the venture failed and the ship was eventually bought by the Explorer Preservation Society.

At Middlesborough, Smith's Dock launched their last two steam trawlers in 1952, Yard No's 1216 and 1128, *Caesar* (H.226) and *Lorenzo* (H.230 – 189ft 5ins x 32ft 2ins x 16ft, 830g – **Photo. 116**). Both were built for Hellyer Brothers Ltd, Hull but the second vessel was operated by Northern Fishing Co. Ltd, Hull who were a joint stock company of Hellyer's. They were powerful heavy weather triple deckers but without any streamlining. *Caesar* met her end some 40 miles off the Arkanes Lighthouse, north west Iceland, on 1st June 1971. She had previously run ashore near the lighthouse and was under tow when she foundered. Her sister led a relatively uneventful life and went to the breakers in 1975.

In February 1950, Cochrane's launched the last new steam

trawler ever to be delivered to the Andanes Steam Fishing Co. Ltd, Grimsby (a subsidiary of the Rinovia Company of Grimsby). She was Yard No. 1352 *Andanes* (GY53 – 198ft 6ins x 31ft x 16ft, 724g – **Plan 81 and Photo. 117**). She represented a good balance between full streamlining and traditional lines. Her moderate sheerline, nicely balanced cruiser stern, coupled to a rounded superstructure, streamlined funnel and twin masts, gave her a striking appearance. Her outline specification reads: fish room capacity – 16,400 cu ft; liver oil capacity – 5,400 gallons; fuel bunker capacity – 292 tons; fresh water capacity – 19 tons; feed water capacity – 48 tons; and trials speed – 14 knots.

The accommodation layout was quite standard, with the crew forward, mostly in single cabins, and the officers aft. A recreational crew room was provided below the whaleback, as well as a comfortable messroom aft. A pressurised domestic hot and cold fresh water system was piped to all compartments. The skipper's cabin was at the forward end of the casing on main deck level and

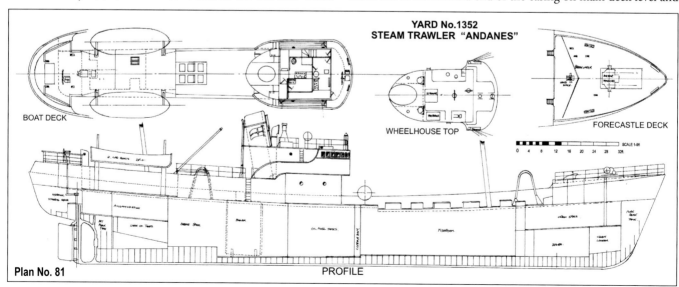

Plan No. 81

PROFILE

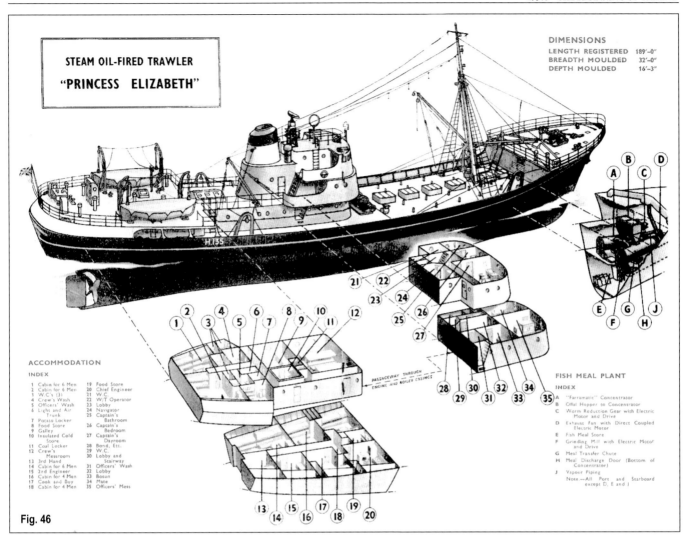

STEAM OIL-FIRED TRAWLER
"PRINCESS ELIZABETH"

DIMENSIONS
LENGTH REGISTERED 189'-0"
BREADTH MOULDED 32'-0"
DEPTH MOULDED 16'-3"

ACCOMMODATION

INDEX

1 Cabin for 6 Men	19 Food Store
2 Cabin for 6 Men	20 Chief Engineer
3 W.C.'s (3)	21 W.C.
4 Crew's Wash	22 W/T Operator
5 Officers' Wash	23 Lobby
6 Light and Air	24 Navigator
Trunk	25 Captain's
7 Potato Locker	Bathroom
8 Food Store	26 Captain's
9 Galley	Bedroom
10 Insulated Cold	27 Captain's
Store	Dayroom
11 Coal Locker	28 Bond, Etc.
12 Crew's	29 W.C.
Messroom	30 Lobby and
13 3rd Hand	Stairway
14 Cabin for 6 Men	31 Officers' Wash
15 2nd Engineer	32 Lobby
16 Cabin for 4 Men	33 Bosun
17 Cook and Boy	34 Mate
18 Cabin for 4 Men	35 Officers' Mess

FISH MEAL PLANT

INDEX

A "Farramatic" Concentrator
B Offal Hopper to Concentrator
C Worm Reduction Gear with Electric
   Motor and Drive
D Exhaust Fan with Direct Coupled
   Electric Motor
E Fish Meal Store
F Grinding Mill with Electric Motor
   and Drive
G Meal Transfer Chute
H Meal Discharge Door (Bottom of
   Concentrator)
J Vapour Piping
   Note—All Port and Starboard
        except D, E and J

Fig. 46

the deck above contained the radio room, with adjacent operator's cabin and wheelhouse. The latter compartment contained the very latest navigational equipment, including a Sperry Mark E1 Gyro compass and a Sperry single-unit Gyro Pilot, for automatic steering (the first to be fitted in a British trawler). In addition, she carried a Kelvin Hughes Projector Binnacle on the roof and an overhead inverted Olsen steering compass. The former was fitted with a series of lenses and mirrors, which allowed readings to be taken from inside the bridge using the built-in periscope. Two Chernikeef electric logs were fitted, one which could be withdrawn remotely and the other by the usual engine room controls. Steering was Donkin's hydraulic type, with full hand and power control in the wheelhouse. Two echo sounders were carried, a Kelvin & Hughes MS.21 recording set and a Hughes MS.24 X type. The windows were the Beclawat balanced type, with a Kent 'clear view' screen fitted to the central forward window. A Kelvin Hughes Type 1A radar was fitted, with the scanner on the wheelhouse top and the display consol in the chartroom. It was a high definition set with ranges of up to 40 miles.

The radio room was fully equipped with a Marconi Dolphin DF indicator, plus a longer range Lodestone set. Wireless gear comprised a dual telegraphy and telephony Marconi Transarctic TX/RX set, and three receivers of the Electra, Yeoman and Valiant types, which allowed the operator to monitor several frequencies simultaneously. To power this host of electrical equipment, she

had both steam and diesel generators of 15kw output, backed up by a 6kw stand-by diesel set. They were all interconnected through a switchboard, allowing them to be run separately or in tandem.

COOK, WELTON & GEMMELL'S LARGE TRIPLE DECKERS

Cook, Welton & Gemmell launched their largest steam trawler to date in 1950. She was Yard No. 824 *Princess Elizabeth* (H.135 – 205ft oa/189ft 1in bp x 32ft 2ins, 810g) for the St. Andrew's Steam Fishing Co. Ltd, Hull (**Fig. 46**). A 13 knot, oil fired triple decker, she was the lead ship for the largest steam trawlers ever to be sideways launched into the Hull River at Beverley and it required at least three full tides to float them down the river for final fitting out. Her three-tier, mainly aluminium superstructure gave a high degree of strength for a lower gross weight. On the lower level were single cabins for the mate and bosun, along with an officers messroom, wash space and bonded store. Above on the lower bridge deck were the skipper's quarters, which included a separate dayroom, bedroom and bathroom, plus those of the wireless operator and a spare cabin for a navigator. At the upper bridge deck level was the wheelhouse, chartroom and WT office. The funnel casing was fitted out with drying rooms and battery storage compartments. An aluminium tower on the wheelhouse top carried the radar scanner. Electronic equipment included, a Marconi radar, WT and RT, plus DF sets and two echo sounders,

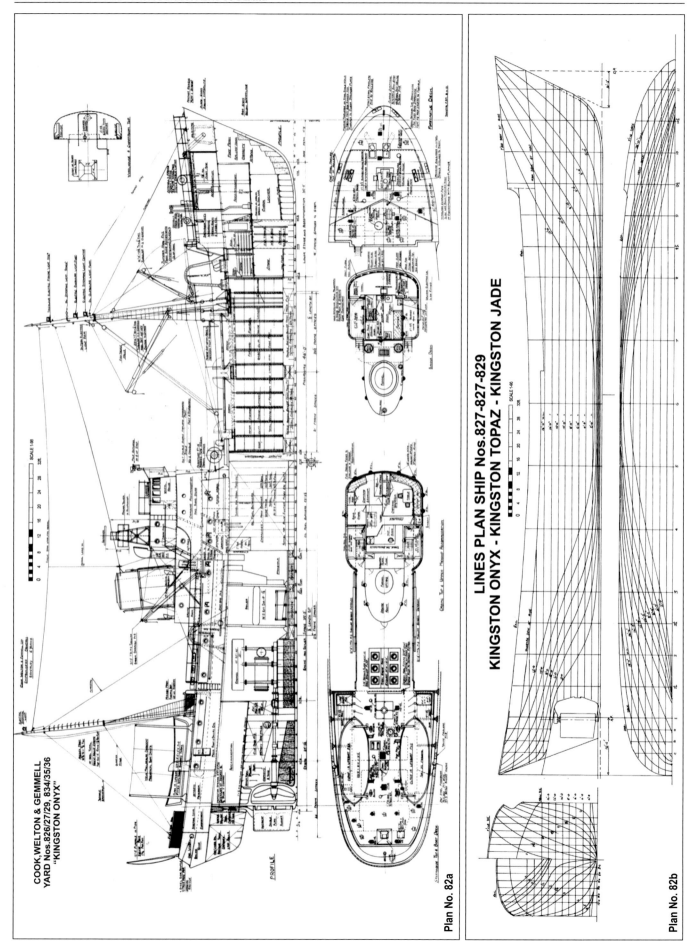

COOK, WELTON & GEMMELL
YARD Nos.826/27/29, 834/35/36
"KINGSTON ONYX"

Plan No. 82a

LINES PLAN SHIP Nos.827-827-829
KINGSTON ONYX - KINGSTON TOPAZ - KINGSTON JADE

Plan No. 82b

Photo. 118: *Lord Lovat* in Lord Line colours of black hull with white band and wood grained superstructure, with dark brown wheelhouse window frames. The funnel has a broad red band separating a red oxide lower from a black top.

of Seagraph and Seavisa types. Her steering was Donkin's hand/ steam/hydraulic, with the emergency wheel aft in the tiller flat. No mizzen mast was originally specified but one was fitted later and no gyro compass is apparent, as she carries a pole compass on the forward face of the wheelhouse. The crew were all housed aft, with the majority of the deckmen in two six berth cabins under the boat deck. The lower flat contained another six berth crew cabin, plus single and double cabins for the officers. In total, she was fitted out for thirty-seven hands. This arrangement meant that there was no longer any need for crewmen to cross the exposed main deck at watch change. For fishing, she had an Andanes steam trawl winch supplied by Robertson's of Fleetwood, a liver oil plant hopper fed from the pounds to holding tanks on the boat deck and a fish meal processing plant at the forward end of the fish room capable of turning 10 tons of offal into around 2.5 tons of meal daily. The main refrigerated fish room had a capacity of 17,000 cu ft.

Princess Elizabeth was sold to Hellyer's of Hull in 1951. Her name was changed to *Roderigo*, one of the names that will be forever remembered in the annals of trawler history, after her sudden loss on 21st June 1955, with all hands, whilst going to the assistance of the stricken Hull trawler *Lorella* (H.455), which was icing-up and about to capsize in fiercesome weather at Nord Cap, Iceland. Both ships were lost, along with forty men (*see description on page 225*).

The other six ships, although built to the same lines as *Princess*

Elizabeth, were fitted with a different style of superstructure. First to leave the yard was No. 826 *Kingston Onyx* (H.140 – **Plans 82 a & b**). Unlike *Princess Elizabeth*, their triple decked, streamlined superstructures were not faired into full height funnel casings. This stopped at lower bridge deck level and gave the ships a squatter, heavier profile. The mizzen was later replaced on all the ships by a much lighter aerial mast on the funnel casing. *Kingston Onyx* went for scrapping in 1975. Her sisters were: Yard No. 827 *Kingston Topaz* (H.145), delivered December 1950 and scrapped in June 1975 at Sittingbourne, Kent; Yard No. 829 *Kingston Jade* (H.159), delivered in January 1951 and scrapped at Drapers of Hull on 26th April 1975. These were followed by another three trawlers to the same design, the first two for Hamlings and the third for Kingstons: Yard No. 834 *St. Keverne* (H158) sailed in March 1951 and worked for Hamlings until going for scrap in 1974; Yard No. 835 *St. Leger* (H.178) sailed in June 1951 and went for scrapping in 1975; Yard No. 836 *Kingston Jacinth* (H198) was delivered in February 1952 and she was also scrapped in 1975.

The last three steam trawlers to be built for Kingstons by Cook, Welton & Gemmell were all basically to the same design as the earlier ships (205ft oa / 189ft 4ins bp x 32ft 1in. 811g): Yard No. 894 *Kingston Emerald* (H.49), delivered in December 1954 and scrapped in 1976; Yard No. 895 *Kingston Turquoise* (H.50) was delivered in February 1955 and wrecked off the Orkney Islands on 25th January 1965, some 14 miles north north west of Hoy

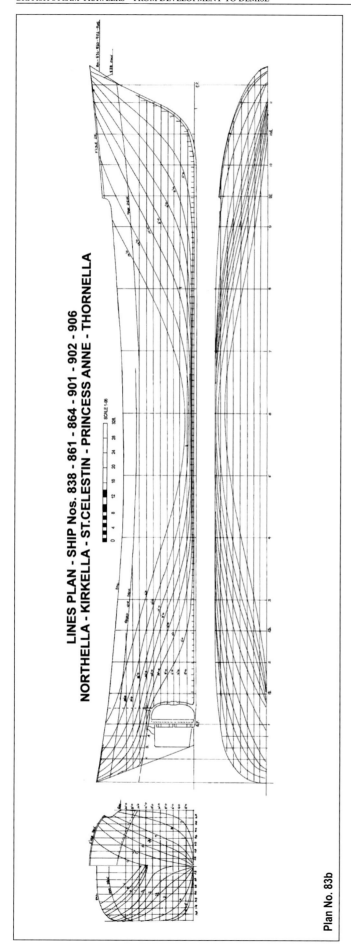

LINES PLAN - SHIP Nos. 838 - 861 - 864 - 901 - 902 - 906
NORTHELLA - KIRKELLA - ST.CELESTIN - PRINCESS ANNE - THORNELLA

Plan No. 83b

Head; the third ship, Yard No. 896 *Kingston Sapphire* (H.95), was delivered in November 1955 and scrapped in 1977.

TRAWLERS WITHOUT BOAT DECKS

In 1951, Cochrane's received an order for three sister ships from the Lord Line Ltd, Hull, Yard No's 1360, 1361 and 1362, all (181ft 3ins oa/178ft bp x 31ft x 16ft 3ins, 713g). In keeping with Lord Line's policy, no boat decks were fitted to these ships but they came from the builders fitted with radar. The first to enter service was *Lord Lovat* (H.148 – **Photo. 118**) and, apart from being boarded by an armed Russian Naval crew in 1974 for suspected spying activities, she led an uneventful life and was broken up at Cairnryan by Shipbreaking Queenborough Ltd on 14th July 1976. The next ship to join the Lord Line fleet was *Lord Tedder* (H.154). During her lifetime she was arrested twice by the Icelandic Coastguard for illegally fishing inside their territorial limit, in April and again in October, 1957. The scrapping records show that she was broken up at Cairnryan on 13th August 1975. The last of the trio was *Lord Mountevans* (H.169). In March 1966, she crossed the Humber to Grimsby as GY.79, to join Northern Trawlers Ltd and she recrossed the river for her last trip to Draper's slip for scrapping in November 1973.

MARRS' NEW SHIPS

During the period 1951 to early 1958, Cook, Welton & Gemmell built another six almost identical sister ships for Hull owners, five for Marrs and one for Thomas Hamling & Co. Ltd. They were in the main all large oil burners, with triple-decked superstructures and part-welded hulls. First off the stocks was Yard No. 838 *Northella* (H.159) at a cost of almost £136,000. She was the smallest of the class (188ft 5ins x 32.1ft x 16ft 6ins, 786g) and her stem, although steeply raked was straight. The other five ships had clipper type stems, which gave them additional length (190ft 2ins, 795g). *Northella* was sold to P.F. Sjornan A/S of the Faroe Islands in 1956 for around £178,000 and renamed *Gullberg*. In 1965, she came back to Hull as *Calydon* (H.253), of Henriksen's fleet. The third ship of the group was Yard No. 864, *St. Celestin* (H.233) and Hamling's took delivery on 25th August 1952. A short-lived ship, she was lost on 27th May 1956 near Bear Island, after colliding with *Arctic Viking* (H.452). Thankfully, all her crew were saved as death would have been instant in the freezing waters. *Arctic Viking* herself was later overwhelmed during a gale in the North Sea, some 16 miles off Flamborough Head, at about 20.30 hours on the night of 18th October 1961. Built originally as *Arctic Pioneer* (H.462) in 1937 by Cochrane's, she was returning home with a catch of 1,400 kits. The weather at the time was the worst in living memory, with the East Coast being battered by hurricane force winds. At the wheel of the trawler that night was David Cressey and the first freak wave struck her starboard quarter and forced her off course. He was slowly bringing her head round when the second and fatal wave hit her behind the wheelhouse, forcing her over on her port side. Two minutes later she capsized, taking five of her crew of nineteen with her. She remained upside down until 00.30, when she went down stern first. The survivor's distress flares were spotted an hour later by the Polish trawler *Derkacz*, which had been dodging nearby. So severe was the weather that the rescue ship was unable to turn round, so *Viking*'s families had another agonising wait of forty-eight hours before seeing their menfolk.

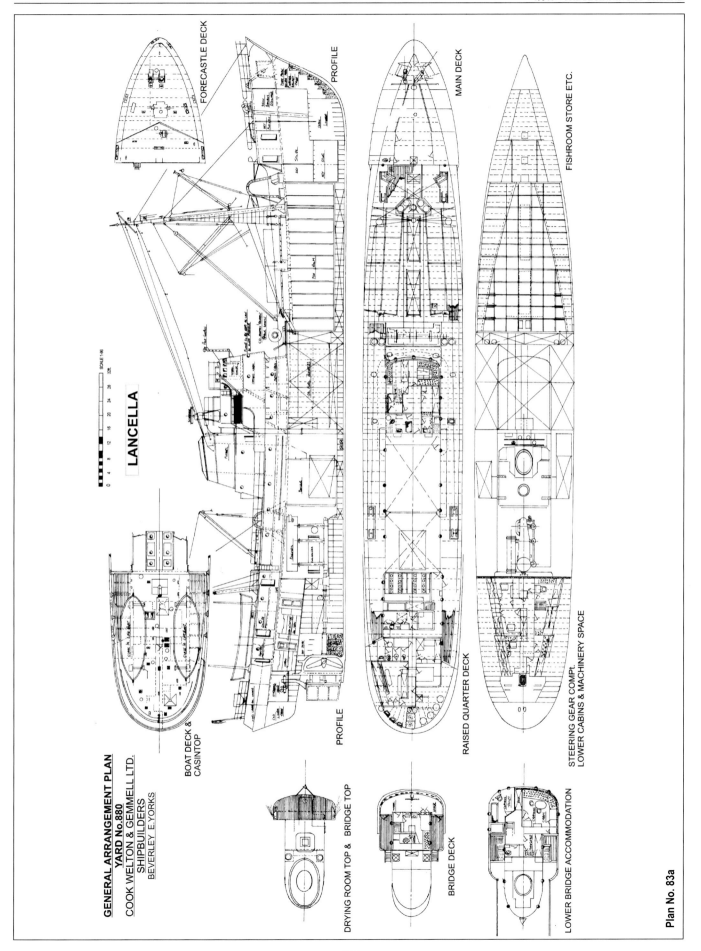

FORECASTLE DECK

PROFILE

MAIN DECK

FISHROOM STORE ETC.

SCALE 1:96

LANCELLA

BOAT DECK & CASINTOP

PROFILE

RAISED QUARTER DECK

STEERING GEAR COMPL. LOWER CABINS & MACHINERY SPACE

GENERAL ARRANGEMENT PLAN
YARD No.880
COOK WELTON & GEMMELL LTD.
SHIPBUILDERS
BEVERLEY E.YORKS

DRYING ROOM TOP & BRIDGE TOP

BRIDGE DECK

LOWER BRIDGE ACCOMMODATION

Plan No. 83a

The fourth of Marrs' ships to enter service, in July 1953, was Yard No. 880 *Lancella* (H.290 – **Plans 83 a & b**), built at a cost of £170,000. She was the first of the class to be fitted with a proper mizzen mast, in compliance with the new lighting rules. Another innovation was the provision of tanks to hold small fish and offal between the after fish room and the bunker space. They had a total capacity of 51 tons, were hopper fed from the pounds and discharged through four scuttles fitted to the side decks. Four liver boilers on the starboard side were hopper fed, with the livers being pumped directly from the pounds. The resulting oil was stored below in the 420 barrel capacity tanks. All the crew ate and berthed aft, two firemen and six hands in the poop house on the upper deck. The chief and second engineer, the cook with his assistant, the third hand and thirteen crew were below in the after cabin space. With the exception of a small single cabin for a navigator, the lower bridge deck was home to the skipper. Below this, at the forward end of the casing, were cabins for the mate and radio officer, along with the officer's mess.

In 1956, she won the coveted Silver Cod Trophy under the command of skipper Bill Turner. To win this award, she spent 340 days at sea, landing 45,936 ten stone kits of fish, with a market value of £131,633. This trophy was an annual event from 1954 until 1968 and was presented by the British Trawler Federation to the trawler with the highest total yearly catch. There was, however, a downside to this trophy. Being based on the total annual catch, skippers filled their trawlers with fish of all sizes. This had a disastrous knock on effect to already diminishing breeding stocks, as immature fish were swept up in the small meshed trawls by the Silver Cod Trophy hunters. The trophy was abandoned in 1969 after the tragic losses in ships and men during the previous year, and mounting pressure from the trawlermen's union.

ABOVE: Photo. 119: *Kirkella* when new, with streamlined superstructure in Marrs' colours of cream hull with a red band, wood grained superstructure and a black topped red funnel. Her lifeboats are hung in Welin MacLachlan mechanical davits.

LEFT: Photo. 120: *Northern Sceptre*. Note the steel plated lower shrouds and the Northern colour scheme of grey, white and black funnel, white wheelhouse over brown casings and black hull, with white line at deck level above red boot topping.

The penultimate ship, Yard No. 902 *Marbella* (H.52), joined Marrs in May 1955. They sold her in December 1965 to the Boyd Line as *Arctic Brigand*. Under her new name, she came runner up in the 1967 Silver Cod awards, spending some 328 days at sea and landing a total catch of 38,561 kits, valued at £134,482. Also that year, she won the Distant Water Challenge Shield under skipper Thresh, when she landed 38,806.5 kits, which grossed £134,462 10s and earned her 13,076.8 points for the year. She sailed from Hull to the breakers at Zeebrugge on 4th July 1975.

The last of the class to be registered was Yard No. 906 *Thornella* (H.84) in September 1955. In 1956, she became Britain's top earning trawler, grossing around £130,000. She worked for Marrs until going for scrapping on Tyneside in 1973.

COCHRANE'S TRIPLE DECKERS

At the end of 1953, Cochrane's received an order for three new ships from Northern Trawlers Ltd, Grimsby. They were large triple-deckers (183ft 4ins oa/180ft bp x 32ft x 16ft 6ins, 804g) and their well rounded superstructure was the only sign of streamlining. Designed to fish from both sides, their fish room capacity was 17,000 cu. ft and they had an offal compartment in either wing, between the fish room and bunker space. Cochrane's 1950s drawings were very basic and neither the liver blower chute nor the offal chutes are shown but in a vessel of this size and date, they would probably have been fitted.

The first of the trio was Yard No. 1386 *Northern Crown* (GY.284). She was delivered in November 1953 and lost off Iceland in the October three years later. She was followed in February 1954 by Yard No. 1387 *Northern Sceptre* (GY.297 – **Photo. 120**). She had the honour of being the very last oil burning steam trawler to leave Grimsby for the breakers in September 1977. Prior to her departure, she had lain derelict for nearly two years and moves were made to

preserve her as the last remaining example of her type. The venture failed but salt was rubbed into the wounds of the enthusiasts, for she lay at the scrap yard until February 1979, before finally being broken up. The third ship was ordered as Yard No. 1392 *Kopanes* but was cancelled and bought by Northern Trawlers Ltd as *Northern Jewel* (GY.1). She was handed over to the company in June 195 and worked for them until going for scrap in 1975 (**Plan 84**).

CONSOL'S LARGEST SHIPS

It was also in 1953 that Consolidated Fisheries of Grimsby took delivery of two of their largest steamers from Cochrane's. They were Yard No. 1384 *Grimsby Town* (GY.246) in July (**Photo. 121**) and Yard No. 1385 *Hull City* (GY.282 – 178ft x 31ft x 16ft 8ins, 711g), which was launched in August and ran her acceptance trials on 10th September. Both ships were engined by Amos & Smith. Their two tier superstructure made them very stable vessels, capable of withstanding a great deal of punishment from the Arctic weather, whilst no verandahs were fitted in an attempt to prevent the build up of ice. By 1974, *Grimsby Town* had been converted to starboard side trawling, her mizzen mast replaced by a light pole mast in front of the funnel and her twin boats swapped for inflatable rubber rafts. Both ships went to the breakers in 1975, *Grimsby Town* to Dublin, and her sister to Fleetwood.

A more traditional ship for the Lord Line of Hull was *Lord Alexander* (H.12 – 183.4ft oa x 32ft x 16ft 6ins, 790g), built by Cochrane's in April 1954 as Yard No. 1388 (**Photo. 122**). Her profile resembles a much earlier design (**Plans 85 a & b**). From new she carried both fore and mizzen masts, and her lower superstructure gave her a long sleek appearance. In common with many of the Lord Line ships, she was not fitted with a boat deck, her two lifeboats being carried in Schat gravity davits fitted to the casing side.

Photo. 121: *Grimsby Town* showing Consolidated Fisheries colours of a grey hull, with red line and red boot topping, wood grained superstructure and a black topped light blue funnel, with broad white band surmounted with the company's distinctive crown logo.

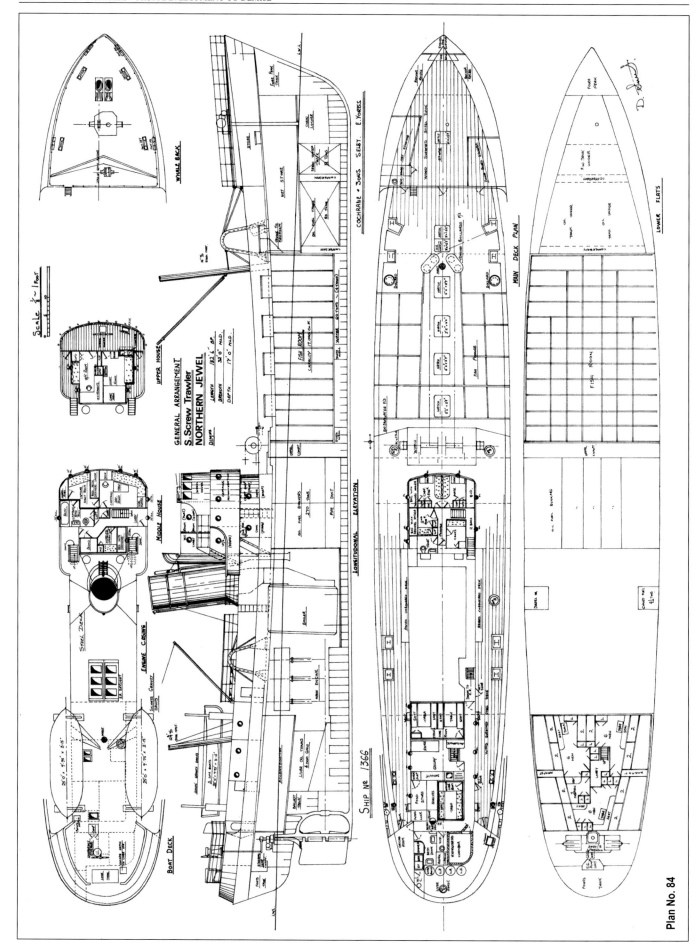

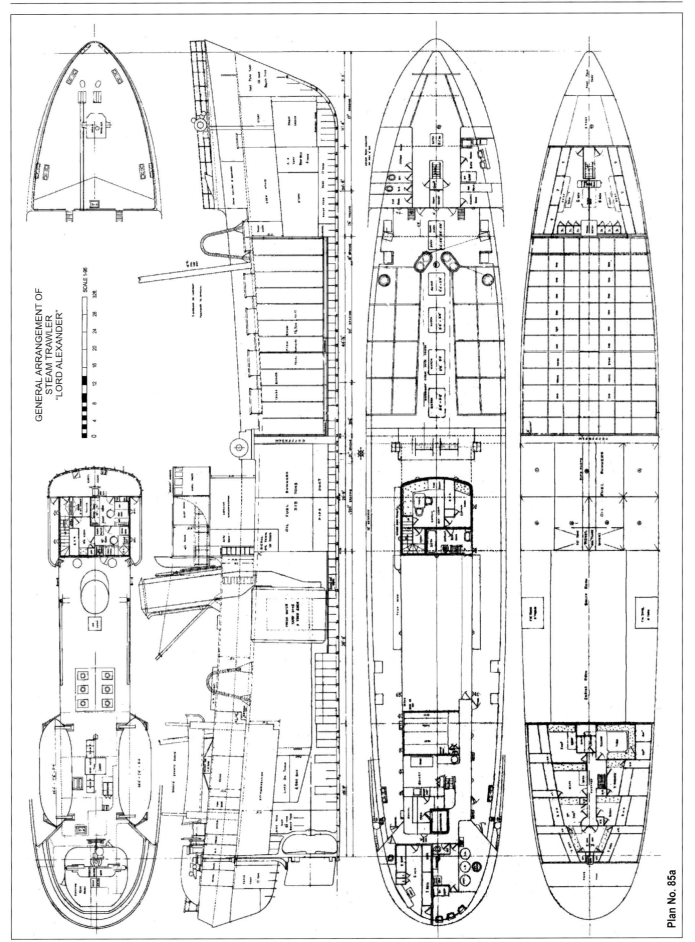

GENERAL ARRANGEMENT OF
STEAM TRAWLER
"LORD ALEXANDER"

Plan No. 85a

259

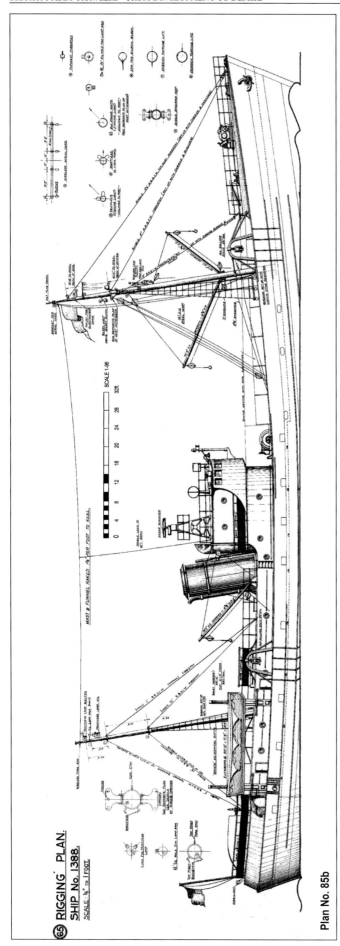

RIGGING PLAN.
SHIP No. 1388.
SCALE ¼" to 1 FOOT.

Plan No. 85b

Her crew, unfortunately for the time, were relegated to the fo'c'sle and had to negotiate the open deck when going for their meals or changing watches. The superstructure, being more compact than that of the triple decked ships, mirrored the layout of mid 1940 vessels, the only exception being that the radio operator's cabin was separate from his office.

The skipper's berth was below the wheelhouse and radar was fitted from new, along with the very latest navigational and fish-finding aids. No liver blowers are shown on the plan, so the full baskets were dragged the length of the starboard side deck to the boiling room aft. The emergency steering gear was enclosed in a turtle-backed house on the casing top, rather than in the tiller flat, which was the norm by this time.

In 1963, the parent company of Lord Line, Associated Fisheries, were amalgamated with Hellyer's, passing completely into their ownership in 1966 and she went to the breakers in 1975.

In 1956, Britain at last agreed to honour the Icelandic four mile limit, imposed some two years earlier. By this time, mutterings were heard in high places that Iceland was looking at a twelve mile limit. This did not bode well for our Distant Water ships, so alternative sources would need to be found. It was ironic that 1956 was also the centenary of Great Grimsby as a fishing port. Fortunately, the Lincolnshire centre did not depend solely on the Distant Water grounds as did her neighbour on the North bank of the Humber. Nevertheless, the viability of all their fishing grounds was fast disappearing.

FIRST WITHOUT PORT SIDE GALLOWS

One of the larger trawlers to join the Grimsby fleet at this time was *Velinda* (GY.29 – 205ft oa x 185ft bp x 32ft 6ins, 779g – **Plan 86**). She was built as Yard No. 916 by Cook, Welton & Gemmell in October 1956, at a cost of £189,380, for the Atlas Steam Fishing Co. Ltd, Hull. She was a development of the yard's *Princess Elizabeth* Class. From the starboard side, she looked identical to these earlier ships but when viewed from the other side, she was different entirely. No gallows were fitted to the port side and her casing ran full width from the back of the wheelhouse to the stern, giving ample room for a crew of forty plus. A larger crew was required to fish the Greenland cod grounds, salting a proportion of her catch in a similar fashion to the French ships. This port side accommodation held the twin berth cabins for two firemen, third and spare hands, a single berth for the cook, with another twin cabin for the boys. The living quarters in the superstructure were quite standard and the poop house held the bosun's cabin, with an eight-man cabin to port. The crew space in the after flat had a combination of one-, two-, four- and six-man cabins. On these new ships, the wooden hatch boards were replaced with MacGregor steel hatch covers to the fish room. They were in two sections and could be rolled fore and aft, from where they could tip vertically, clearing the opening. The fish room contained 17,000 cubic feet of stowage space and the wings were fitted out as salt cod pounds. In the space between this compartment and the bunker space were two wing offal tanks and two centre immature bulk fish tanks. These were filled from the pounds by means of a hopper and emptied through Woollens scuttles fitted in the side decks. Also in the starboard pounds was the steam blower for the cod livers. From here they went to a hopper on the boat deck, then into the boilers and finally into the oil storage tanks.

Photo. 122: *Lord Alexander* in later life, with port side gallows removed. Her lifeboat arrangement can be clearly seen. She is in Hellyer's colours of light grey hull with white band, wood grained casing and black topped yellow funnel with a white 'H' on a blue flag.

Two wooden thirty-person lifeboats were carried in Welin MacLachlan mechanical davits, which were raked forwards. This actually brought them to the vertical, for when in normal fully loaded condition, trawlers usually trimmed by the stern. Her 54ins diameter, teak, emergency steering wheel, offset to port, was directly connected to the steering flat. In December 1973, *Velinda* broke Grimsby's landing record, when she made £47,500 from her catch of 29,290 stones. She was in the news again in February 1975, after colliding with *Ross Canaveral* (H.267) off Spurn Point. Although not badly damaged, the state of the industry was such that repairs were uneconomic and she was laid up until August, when she went to the breakers (**Photo. 123**).

Photo. 123: *Velinda* undergoing a repaint, hence no fishing numbers but a fresh white wheelhouse over a mid brown casing. The funnel too is as yet unfinished in her full Atlas Steam Fishing Co. Ltd colours. Her mizzen has been replaced with a steel pole abaft the funnel and her bobbin derrick has been moved. Her twin lifeboats have also been replaced by rubber rafts, and a single boat and centre line davit.

FIRST WITH A BULBOUS BOW

The Beverley Shipyard's next vessel, Yard No. 914, was *Cape Columbia* (H.118 – 188ft 6ins oa/185ft bp, 806g), the first trawler ever to be launched with a bulbous bow (**Photo. 124**). Hudson Brothers (Trawlers) Ltd, Hull took delivery of their advanced ship in July 1956, running her successfully until they were taken over by Ross Trawlers Ltd, Grimsby, in 1960. In 1965, she was renamed *Ross Columbia* and her funnel bore the new company colours. They in turn sold her in 1967 to the Boyd Line as *Arctic Avenger* and she carried this name until she went to the breakers in 1976. By this time, the pace of building new steam trawlers had slowed

Photo. 124: *Cape Columbia* showing her bulbous bow. She is seen in Hudson's colours of black topsides with a white band over red boot topping, wood grained casing, white wheelhouse and has a black funnel with a broad white band.

261

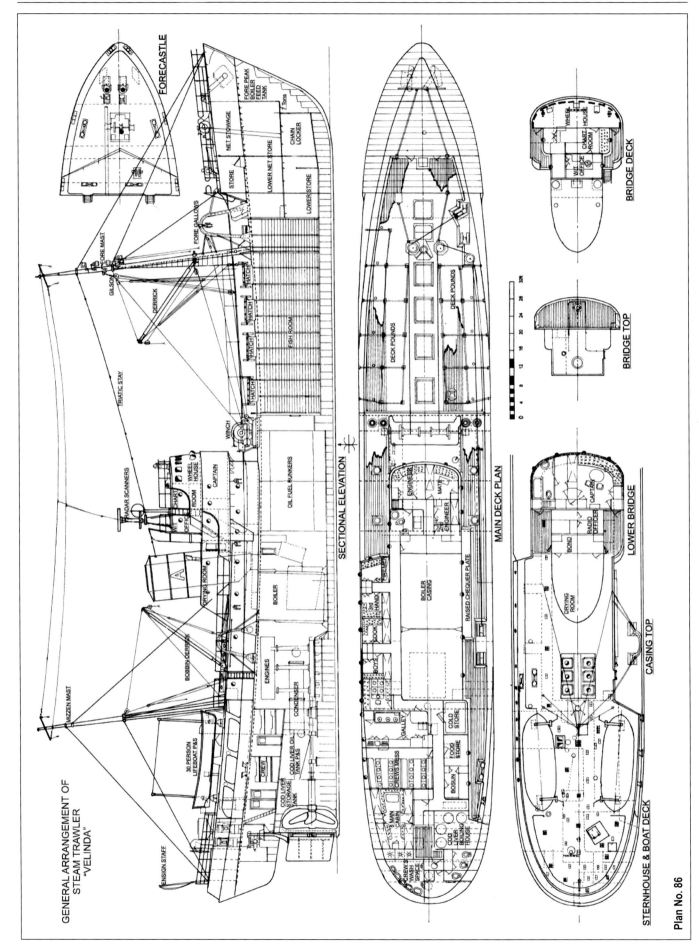

GENERAL ARRANGEMENT OF
STEAM TRAWLER
"VELINDA"

FORECASTLE

SECTIONAL ELEVATION

MAIN DECK PLAN

BRIDGE DECK

BRIDGE TOP

LOWER BRIDGE

STERNHOUSE & BOAT DECK

CASING TOP

Plan No. 86

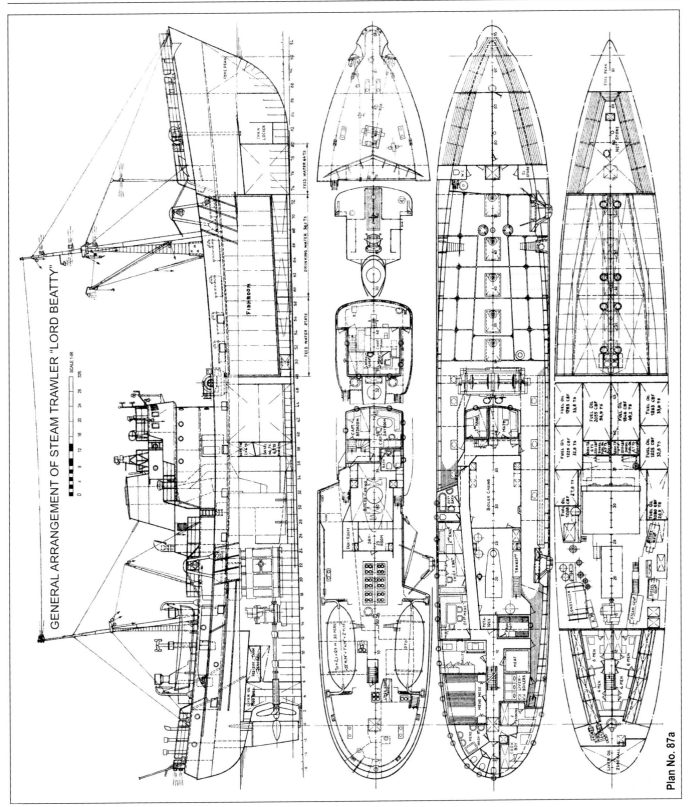

GENERAL ARRANGEMENT OF STEAM TRAWLER "LORD BEATTY"

Plan No. 87a

down very considerably, as more and more motor ships were being launched. The price of heavy fuel oil had been rising steadily and this, coupled with the need to make the industry 'leaner and meaner', meant that the days of the big steamers were numbered.

From 1950 to 1956, Grimsby took delivery of twenty-five large Distant Water ships and Hull received around sixty-two such ships but, from then on, it was downhill for the Distant Water steam trawler. New steamers would still be built but, where as once new

trawlers were so common that they were only news for a day or so, the last of the breed would be remembered for the sad fact that they were becoming oddities on the fast changing scene.

In 1956, the British Steam trawler fleet consisted of some 512 English and 222 Scottish vessels. The majority of the Scots trawlers sailed from Aberdeen, with 192 Near/Middle Water ships. Grimsby had 218, split 50/50 between Distant Water and Near Water ships, whilst Hull had 157, all Distant Water ships.

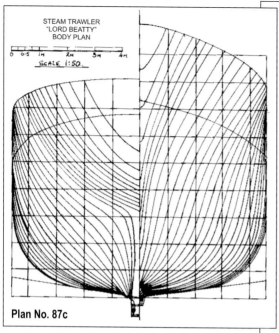

Plan No. 87c

BREMERHAVEN-BUILT STEAMERS

The largest influx of new ships were from the Rickmers Werft Yard in Bremerhaven in 1955-56. These were six large, powerful 14 knot trawlers (203.75ft, 700g) and although drawing slightly less water than British-built craft, they were reckoned by various skippers to be the finest sea ships ever built for the Distant Water grounds. They were powered by conventional engines (430mm, 700mm, 1130mm by 700mm stroke) supplemented by a low pressure exhaust turbine, double reduction gearing and hydraulic coupling, all supplied by Ottensener Eisenwerk of Hamburg. Their speed enabled them to steam home from Iceland in three days or less, thus ensuring that their shelved fish reached market in top condition. Another factor in the decision to build in Germany was that they were constructed to a guaranteed price and operating speed (**Plans 87 a, b & c**).

The first was Yard No. 273 *Coldstreamer* (GY10), registered on 25th July 1955 by the Standard Steam Fishing Co. Ltd, Grimsby. She was the first British trawler to be fitted with gallows only on the starboard side. When she arrived at Grimsby, she had on board the managing director of the shipyard, Bertram Rickmers, and her owners' representative stated:

'The ship will be fishing two years sooner than she would have been, if the order had been placed with a UK yard. Her machinery is more economical, and we shall probably save as much as a ton of fuel oil per day, in addition to a lot of lubricating oil.'

On her maiden trip to the White Sea Grounds under skipper Jasper Pigen, she landed some 3,000 kits. On 21st January 1957, he took her to the Newfoundland grounds but the trip was dogged by

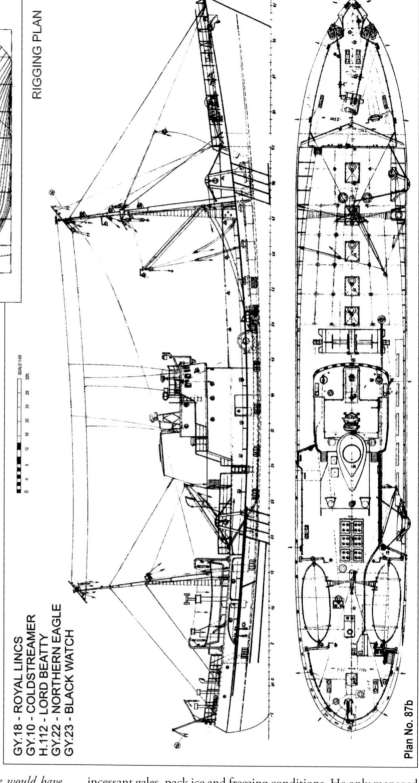

GY.18 - ROYAL LINCS
GY.10 - COLDSTREAMER
H.112 - LORD BEATTY
GY.22 - NORTHERN EAGLE
GY.23 - BLACK WATCH

RIGGING PLAN

Plan No. 87b

incessant gales, pack ice and freezing conditions. He only managed four and a half day's fishing, returning with 1,700 kits. In October 1973, she beat the world landings record with 2,300 kits of prime cod, which fetched £44,678. She averaged around £19 per kit and £2,030 a day. In August 1976, she went to Doig's slipway behind the Royal Dock, Grimsby for scrapping.

Next came Yard No. 274 *Royal Lincs* (GY.18), registered by the Great Grimsby & East Coast Steam Fishing Co. Ltd in September

Photo. 125: *Lord Beatty* pictured during the 1959 Cod War off Iceland, in Lord Lines' colours of dark green hull with white band and a white wheelhouse over a grained casing, whilst the funnel has a broad white band separating red oxide from the black top.

1955. In January the following year, she transferred to Northern Trawlers and worked under their colours, until following her predecessor to Doig's for scrapping in January 1976.

Yard No. 281 *Lord Beatty* (H.112) was the third ship from the Bremerhaven yard, launched in February 1956 for the Lord Line of Hull (**Photo. 125**). In 1957, under skipper W. Lewis, she won the coveted Silver Cod Trophy, spending 302 and 330 days at sea and landing catches of 38,873 and 40,563 kits, with a value of £114,927 and £155,903 respectively. In February 1961, they sold her to Northern Trawlers of Grimsby as GY.91, who ran her until December 1976, when she recrossed the Humber to Draper's yard for scrapping.

Northern Eagle (GY.22) was registered by Northern Trawlers Ltd in April 1956 and owned by them until going for scrap at Hull in January 1977.

Black Watch (GY.23) was built in July 1956 for the Loyal Steam Fishing Co. Ltd, Grimsby, who sold her to Northern Trawlers in January 1966. She went to the scrappers at Bruges in February 1979.

Statham (GY.25) went to Crampin Steam Fishing Co. Ltd, Grimsby in September 1956, as one of their fleet of 'English Cricketers', being the last of the group (**Photo. 126**). Transferred to Ross colours after the take over in 1965, she was renamed *Ross Repulse* (GY.25). They moved her to Hudson Trawlers Ltd, Hull (a Ross Group subsidiary) in October 1967 but she was then bought by Northern Trawlers in April 1968 as *Northern Sky*, giving the company final control of all these large German-built trawlers. She was scrapped at Draper's Yard, Hull in December 1976.

Although built to the same design, there was the odd difference between the ships, the most apparent being that some of them carried two stream anchors in chutes on the fo'c'sle head, whereas others, such as *Lord Beatty* and *Statham*, only had one on the starboard side. The latter's funnel also differed from that of her sisters, being straight, with a shallower top cowling.

Photo. 126: *Statham* off Iceland, in Crampin's colours of black hull with a white band, and white sides to the whaleback and poop deck. She also has a white wheelhouse over a grained casing, whilst her funnel colours are a yellow 'C' on a blue band between a lower bottom section and a black top. She has a windbreak rigged to shelter the crew while gutting.

In 1957, Thomas Hamling & Co. Ltd of Hull ordered *St. Loman* (H.156) from Cook, Welton & Gemmell as Yard No. 921 (190ft x 33ft 1in, 895g, 1600ihp), Britain's largest steam trawler by gross tonnage. C.D. Holmes supplied her engines, which gave a top speed of 13.5 knots. Laid down in July, she left the yard in November 1957. In 1965, she went to the Forth Steam Trawling Co. Ltd, Hull and was broken up at Milton Regis (Sittingbourne) on 25th March 1976 (**Photo. 127**).

COCHRANE'S 'K' CLASS

The last steamer to be ordered by H. Croft Baker & Sons of Grimsby (Derwent Trawlers Ltd, Ross Group) was *Joseph Knibb* (GY.2 – 139ft 7ins oa/137ft 6ins bp 28ft x 14ft 8ins, 442g) built as Yard No. 1400, by Cochrane's in March 1955 (**Photo. 128**). She was named after the famous clockmaker Joseph Knibb but was renamed *Kenilworth* in January 1959 on transfer to Richardson Trawlers Ltd, Grimsby; thus she is often confused with the later 'K' Class ships. One main feature which immediately set her apart from these was the boat launching gear. She rigged the mizzen

Photo. 127 *St. Loman* H.156 The largest steam trawler out of Hull, In the river Humber while adjusting her compass.

Photo.128 *Joseph Knibb* GY.2 running builders trials in Derwent Co. colours. She has a pole foremast and mizzen, with boat launching boom for the double ended boat.

boom for this, while the 'K' Class had Schat single arm davits. In January 1962, her name was given the Ross pre-fix, in keeping with company policy and in May that year, she was lost off Iceland, only three trips after her final name change.

The lead ship of the actual 'K' Class that followed was *Kelly* (GY.6), from Cochrane's as Yard No. 1408, for Derwent Trawlers in March 1956. In January 1959, she transferred to Ross Trawlers and later that year saw her owned by Yorkshire Trawlers Ltd. She became *Ross Kelly* in 1962 but changed hands again to G.F. Sleight in April of that year. In 1966, along with her two sisters, *Kipling* (GY.38) and *Kashmir* (GY.43), she was lengthened, fitted with a transom stern and converted to diesel. In 1967, she was owned in Newfoundland but she returned to Grimsby the following year as GY.125, owned by British United Trawlers Ltd. In March 1972, she transferred to Ross Trawlers Ltd but they sold her that July to the Colne Shipping Co. Ltd, Lowestoft who renamed her *Caicos* (LT.125). She operated as an oil rig stand-by vessel until she went to Spanish shipbreakers in 1987.

The fourth ship of the class, *Kelvin* (GY.60), Yard No. 1431, was delivered in October 1958. She was the last steam trawler to be launched from Cochrane's (the later two 'K' Class were built as motor ships) and the very last for British owners, whilst her steam engine, No. 865, was the very last manufactured by Amos & Smith; she was also the first side trawler built with a transom stern. She underwent the same ownership changes as *Kelly*, although remaining in the UK all her days. She, too, was lengthened in 1966 and re-engined. In July 1972, she was sold to Lowestoft as LT.60, owned by the Colne Shipping Co. Ltd and also used as an oil rig stand-by vessel.

THE LAST NEW STEAM TRAWLERS
Cochrane's penultimate steamer was *Everton* (GY.58), Yard No. 1429 for Consolidated Fisheries Ltd, Grimsby (Consol's). She was a repeat of the earlier *Grimsby Town* and *Hull City* of 1953, and the last Distant Water ship to be completed by Cochrane's, as well as the last for the owners. In addition, she was also the largest steam trawler ever to be registered at Grimsby. She was launched

on 20th February 1958 by Mrs Northcote, the wife of one of Consol's directors. The local schoolchildren were late for classes that morning, as no one wanted to miss the nine o' clock launch.

On her maiden trip she was commanded by William Balls Jnr, one of the firm's crack skippers who had been transferred from *Arsenal*. He was in command of her until she was handed over to skipper Donald Lister, who had her for most of her working life and was asked to take her on her last trip to the breakers but Lister refused, as he felt so much admiration for the vessel. She had her share of mishaps, such as having her mizzen mast broken, and her

Painting 15: *Kipling* by George Wiseman. Shown in Ross Trawlers' colours, she carries a single boat with a centreline davit and her short mizzen is topped with a radar repeater.

266

boat and rafts being swept overboard on the Viking Bank when homeward bound from the White Sea. On another occasion, she rammed an iceberg off Iceland sustaining sprung bow plates. Her engineer saved the day by plugging the worst of the leaks and running her pumps flat out to keep her afloat. On arrival at Grimsby, she had to be slipped and eleven new plates fitted. In 1971, she became Britain's top earning steamer, landing 2,714 kits which grossed £28,500. She was well known to the Icelandic Coastguard service, as in May 1972, they arrested her for illegal fishing within the twelve-mile limit and her skipper Barry Green was fined £3,100. She was thrown into the public spotlight again in May 1973, when she was attacked by *Aegir* and received eight hits from the patrol boat's gun. She returned to her home port and relieved relatives, with a gross catch of some £20,000. In February 1975, after rising oil prices and restricted fishing grounds, Consol's sold her for £27,000 to a Fleetwood scrap yard.

It was in 1956 that Fleetwood took delivery of its two last new steam trawlers. The first, and also the last to operate from the Lancashire port, was Yard No. 913 *Samuel Hewett* (LO.117 – 170ft oa/166ft 7ins bp x 29ft 3ins x 16ft, 589g) from Cook, Welton & Gemmell, with engines from C.D. Holmes which ran on superheated steam. She joined the fleet of Heward Trawlers Ltd, London in May and was a distinctive ship, her profile being typical of the smaller Distant Water ships (**Photo. 129**). Around this time, trawlers were experiencing ghosting problems with their higher definition radars, caused by the heavy steel mizzen masts. This was rectified by fitting repeater units at the hounds band, pointing forward. These can be identified on photographs as a square box, either mounted off to the port side or centrally in front of the mast. On the newer ships, the traditional mizzen mast was replaced by a slender pole type, which alleviated the ghosting problem. *Samuel Hewett* worked out of Fleetwood for some twelve years, before going for scrap in 1968.

She was followed in July by Yard No. 1412 *Wyre Mariner* (FD.34 – 172ft oa/169ft bp x 30ft 6ins x 16ft, 656g), built by Cochrane's for Wyre Trawlers Ltd, Fleetwood. She later went to Northern Trawlers Ltd of Grimsby, as *Northern Sun* (GY.2), and finally to the breakers in May 1976. Two years previously, she was instrumental in saving the crew of the stricken Aberdeen motor trawler *Dalewood*, after she had run aground below the cliffs at Dunnet Head. Assistance messages from the trawler were picked up by *Northern Sun* and relayed to Wick Radio. This

enabled rescuers to find the trawler, as she had previously given the wrong position in her original Mayday call.

January 1957 saw Cochrane's launch Yard No. 1415 *Rodney* (GY.34) for Ross Trawlers Ltd, Grimsby (182ft 6ins x 32ft x 17ft, 751g, 1,350ihp). She was the first British-built Distant Water trawler to be fitted with a Bauer Wach exhaust turbine, coupled to her Amos & Smith engine. Another first for this ship was her Schat single arm davit and single lifeboat. This and her tripod foremast were fitted to lessen the risk of her top-hamper icing up in Arctic waters. In 1962, she was renamed *Ross Rodney* and later, in 1967, converted to diesel power. She passed to British United Trawlers in 1969 and was scrapped at Hartlepool in 1980.

Another film star trawler was Boyd Line's *Arctic Ranger* (H.155 – 192ft 4ins x 32ft 6ins x 16ft 6ins, 867g), built by Cook, Welton & Gemmell in 1957 as Yard No. 920. She was a triple decker with full streamlining and starred as *Dynasty Neptune* in the Yorkshire Television serial 'Snacker', which dramatised the life of a deckie learner aboard a typical Distant Water trawler. In 1959, she came second in the Silver Cod Challenge Trophy, skippered by R. Bryant and landing some 37,480 kits worth £133,123. She featured in the league table for vessels competing in the Hull Distant Water Challenge Shield, both in 1970 and 1973, a trophy that was awarded annually from 1967 until 1977. The winners were the skipper and crew landing the highest catch value for the year. Points were allotted on the basis of number of kits landed, added to the Gross value, divided by the ships registered speed. She made her last short trip to Draper's Yard for breaking up on 26th October 1976.

The final two new steam trawlers to be built for the industry were *Joseph Conrad* (H.161) and *Arsenal* (GY.48), both by Cook, Welton & Gemmell as Yard No's 924 and 928. *Joseph Conrad* (190ft 7ins oa/185ft 2ins bp x 32ft 1in x 16ft 6ins, 823g) joined the fleet in January 1958. She made an impressive sight in the Humber, with her well-raked clipper stem, long graceful sheerline, three-decked streamlined superstructure and cruiser stern. She was designed for starboard side fishing only, with a full width casing on the port side, giving ample space for crew accommodation, a

Photo.129 *Samuel Hewett* in Heward colours of blue hull with a red line, white wheelhouse and funnel casing over a brown superstructure. Her black funnel carries the company motif of a blue flag. Another feature was her bow emblem of an owl set into a shield with it's piercing eyes staring straight ahead.

Painting 16: *Joseph Conrad* towing her gear in flat calm weather. Note the single ship's boat and single arm davit, and the tall pole mizzen mast behind the funnel casing. *COURTESY S. FARROW*

far cry from the early days of damp, cramped fo'c'sles. In 1972, she was converted to diesel in a Dutch yard and, on 15th August 1980, she went to Albert Draper's, Hull, where she was broken up.

No. 928 was Cook, Welton & Gemmell very last ever British steam trawler. *Arsenal* (GY.48 – 189ft 4ins oa/185ft bp x 32ft 5ins x 16ft 6ins, 744g), built for for Consolidated Fisheries (**Photo. 130 & Plan 88**), was a magnificent ship and a fitting end to a great line of steam sidewinders dating back to the 1880s. She was fitted with the very last set of engines supplied by Charles D. Holmes, a company who were 'in at the beginning' and who, in 1962, were to take over the Cook, Welton & Gemmell yard. *Arsenal* was some two feet longer, one foot narrower and 140 gross tons lighter than her counterpart, Cochrane's *Everton*, although as the last of the big 'footballers', they were often mistaken for sister ships.

The latter had a pronounced knuckle forward, where as *Arsenal* had a more usual flared bow section. The anchor recesses also differed, with that of the Beverley ship being angled forward, whilst those of the Selby vessel were perpendicular to the waterline. Both carried tri-pod foremasts designed to combat the effects of icing but, later, *Everton* had a tall pole mizzen, replacing the more conventional mast as carried by *Arsenal*, although both were fitted with radar repeater boxes. The introduction of tri-pod masts followed exhaustive tank tests, using a one twelfth scale model of a 180ft trawler in the Vickers-Armstrong climate chamber at Weybridge in 1957. These proved conclusively that, with the tri-pod mast, the centroid of the ice was some 5ft lower than would have been on a fully rigged mast, carrying the equivalent weight of ice. The loss of metacentric height was some two thirds of that with conventional rigging. Their wheelhouses also had differing window configurations, Cochrane's ship having all square windows, as opposed to the square, rectangular and circular type found on the other ship. This latter ship had her short bobbin derrick fitted to the forward end of the wheelhouse verandah, while that on *Everton* was fitted to the side of the funnel casing. Even the verandas were different, with that on *Arsenal* a wood capped open rail and the other being plated in.

Both trawlers were only fitted with one lifeboat and a centre-line davit. *Everton* carried a traditional wooden boat, whereas *Arsenal* was fitted with a new type of Glass Reinforced Plastic (GRP) lifeboat. This GRP boat was stronger and lighter than a wooden one, and did not suffer from the plank shrinkage which was inherent with timber construction. These boats were supplemented by inflatable life-rafts in GRP containers. Again, these had replaced the earlier

canvas valises and wooden containers, and afforded much better protection to the rafts from mildew. Another factor for replacing the davit carried lifeboats was the impossibility of launching them when the boat deck and its gear was frozen solid.

Apparently, *Everton* had a crew space forward fitted out for twenty extra hands. *Arsenal*, however, had no such outfit, having accommodation for thirty-nine hands in total, all berthed aft. The latter's Robertsons' Arctic-type trawl winch had a capacity for 1,200 fathoms of 3ins warp per drum. This type of steam winch was unusual by not having horizontal cylinders on the mainframes; instead, a separate high speed, three-cylinder, vertical steam engine was fitted inside the main casing below the wheelhouse, with a shaft drive to the winch. Although more costly than a conventional winch, the power unit was completely protected from the effects of weather where, often, frozen condensate could result in a cracked cylinder, putting paid to fishing operations. In February 1971, Consolidated Fisheries evaluated the possibility of converting her to diesel power, at a cost of some £4,500. The company decided against the scheme, favouring new motor ships instead of converting older steamers. *Arsenal* served Consol's well enough until escalating oil prices, along with diminishing fishing grounds, made her no longer viable, so she fell victim to the breaker's torch at Doig's slipway, Grimsby in June 1975.

By 1959, the state of Britain's steam trawler fleet looked like this: Aberdeen – 16; Fleetwood – 32; Glasgow – 5; Granton – 12; Grimsby – 154; Hull – 139; Leith – 4; London – 16; Milford – 20. In addition, Lowestoft had a few steam trawlers but most were dual purpose drifter/trawlers that worked the North Sea grounds.

OIL PRICE AND TERRITORIAL LIMITS

The problem of oil prices was one which, above all, was to sound the death knell for the steam trawler. In the two years from 1973 to 1975, oil fuel rose from 7 pence a gallon, to 21 pence and as a result, running costs went through the roof. By 1974, the bunkering costs for a Distant Water ship had risen to around £100,000 a year. There was also the 'knock on' effect of these price rises, in that all the nets, plastic boxes, oilskins, etc, being by-products of the petro-chemical industry, rose proportionally or, in some cases, disproportionally. In 1958, Iceland extended her territorial fishing limits to twelve miles, a move which was to drive yet another nail into the coffin of Britain's Distant Water fleet. The move was outlawed by the UK and Royal Navy frigates were sent north to prevent the Icelandic Coastguard enforcing these new regulations. In 1960, Britain pulled the Navy out after agreeing to abide by the decisions formulated by the UN at the second Conference on the Law of the Sea in Geneva. Agreement was reached in 1961, which permitted our trawlers to fish inside the twelve mile limit for a period of three years, after which any further extensions were to be taken to the International Court of Justice. For a time, the *status quo* was retained.

The British trawler owners were becoming increasingly perturbed by these reductions of our traditional fishing grounds. Their ships were having to steam further afield in order to bring home worthwhile catches. These longer trips meant higher running costs but as long as the price of fuel oil remained stable, they could survive. Unfortunately, things were rapidly changing for the worse on this front too. The Humber owners had previously banded together in order to secure a fixed annual price for fuel,

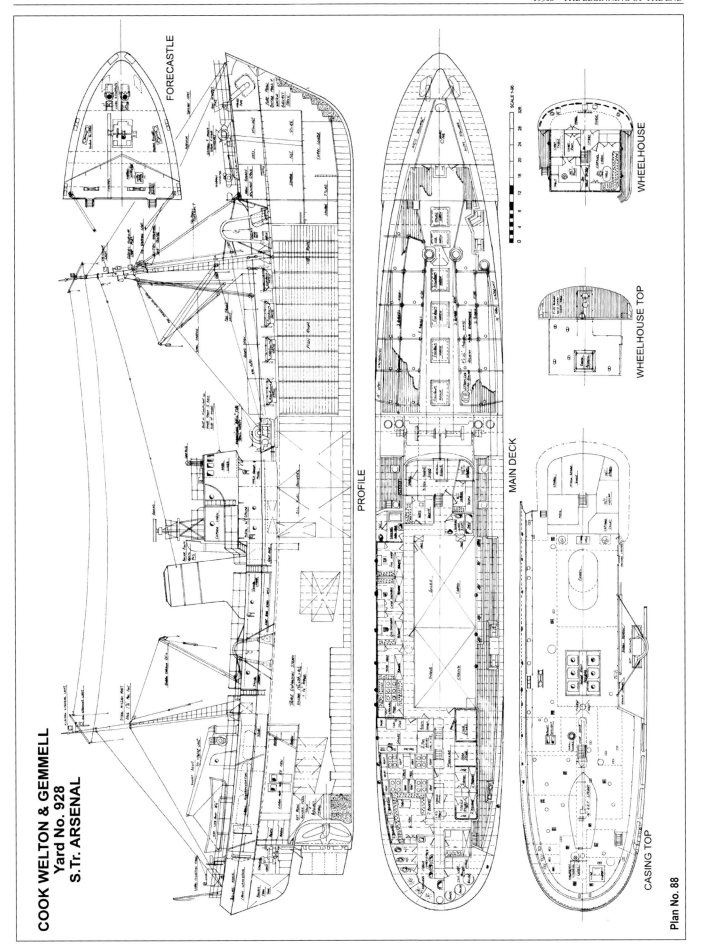

FORECASTLE

PROFILE

MAIN DECK

WHEELHOUSE

WHEELHOUSE TOP

CASING TOP

SCALE 1:96

COOK WELTON & GEMMELL
Yard No. 928
S.Tr. ARSENAL

Plan No. 88

Photo. 130: *Arsenal* adjusting her compass during her acceptance trials. Note her tri-pod foremast, the first Distant Water Grimsby steam trawler with this feature. The box at the mizzen mast head was a radar repeater. She is shown in Consolidated Fisheries colour scheme and note her bow shield, a standard feature of the company.

consumption of which, which averaged some 300,000 tons a year. This price suddenly rocketed from £10 to £30 a ton, which made the viability of Distant Water steamers that burned 10 tons daily a matter for grave concern. The average fuel consumption for both steam and diesel trawlers are given below, showing the advantages of the motor ship over the steamer:

TYPE	POWER	TONS PER DAY
Straight TE* (oil fired at full superheat)	1,250 ihp	10.5-12.5
Oil fired TE* (with Bauer Wach ex-turbine)	1,350 ihp	9.5
Ditto	1.600 ihp	10.5
Straight diesel	1,400 bhp	4
Ditto	1,700 bhp	5.5
Diesel Electric	1,500 shp	4.5-5.5

*TE – Triple Expansion

FISH TRANSFER AT SEA

In January 1961, the Ross Group and Christian Salvesen, in an endeavour to reverse this downturn on traditional fishing grounds, undertook a feasibility study into fish transfer at sea off the Newfoundland Grand Banks. *Ross Hunter* (GY.28 – ex-*Kinknes* (GY.28) in 1949, built as *Junella* (H.497) in 1948), under skipper Norman Cheater, paired up with Salvesen's stern factory trawler *Fairtry II* for this trial trip. The voyage lasted some three months but the limited endurance of *Ross Hunter* meant that she had to refuel and take on stores at St. Johns when the need arose. In all, a total of 3,300 basket (mainly cod) weighing some 100 tons were transferred during both day and night, and in all weathers. Although weather on the Grand Banks made the trial unrenumerative, enough was learned to convince Salvesen's of its virtues. Later that year, the Torry Research Station published a report on their own experiments with fish transfer at sea. They examined three methods:

• The SAUSAGE: A netting bag similar to a cod end, which could hold up to a ton of fish. It was kept afloat by a large seine net float.

• The FISH POT: A flexible rubber container, equipped with inflatable buoyancy pockets and a slush well for ice melt water; it could hold half a ton of fish and ice.

• The DETACHABLE COD END: This method was also explored by *Ross Hunter*.

Painting 17: *Everton*, also seen in Consolidated Fisheries colours. COURTESY S. FARROW

Chapter 18: THE 1960s AND '70s

By now, more and more steam trawlers were making their last trips to the breakers' yards. First to go were all the pre-1920 coal burners, followed in turn by their younger sisters. So many of these ships went for scrap after 1950 that they would require a book of their own to do them all justice but many have already been mentioned in the foregoing text. However, I will now study one or two ships that were either personally known to me or had an unusual history.

Two of Grimsby's old timers, *Alsatian* (GY.323) and *Bengal* (GY.103), sailed to the Forth in May 1955 for scrapping by the British Iron & Steel Corporation Ltd at Inverkeithing. They were sister ships (123ft oa / 115ft bp x 22ft x 12ft, 211g), both built in 1905 by Cook, Welton & Gemmell, as Yard No's 80 and 88 respectively, to the order of Grant & Baker Steam Fishing Co. Ltd, Grimsby, but latterly owned by Sir Thomas Robinson & Son (Grimsby) Ltd. *Alsatian* seems to have begun life as *Barbados* (GY.71) a vessel on which the register was closed on 30th May 1940. However, on the same day, a new entry was made for an identical vessel, namely *Alastian*. The owners were listed as Robinsons, so presumably, she was the self same trawler.

The next but one trawler to be scrapped at Inverkeithing was *Yorick* (A.247), sold for £2,525 by the Grateful Steam Fishing Co. Ltd, Aberdeen. She had been built in 1909 by Cook, Welton & Gemmell as Yard No. 180 for Hellyers of Hull, registered H.49 and named after a Shakespearian character, in common with all this company's ships. Hired for a year in 1918, she spent the remainder of the war as a fishery trawler. She came to Aberdeen in 1935 as *Yorick* (A.382), owned by Alex Hay but, by 1939, her owners were Andrew King and others. By 1941, she had returned to Hellyers as H.410 but, by 1945, they had sold her to the Ocean Steam Trawling Co. Ltd, Grimsby, who in turn sold her to Odafoam Ltd in 1947. She was back at Aberdeen again by 1948, as *Yorick* (A.247), owned by the Grateful Steam Fishing Co. Ltd.

Another Aberdeen old timer was *Morven* (A.567 – 123ft oa/115ft bp x 2ft 6ins x 12ft, 198g), powered by a Lidgerwood engine and built by J. Duthie & Sons in 1902, for the Grampian Fishing Co. Ltd, Aberdeen. In June 1915, she was requisitioned as a minesweeper, returning to her former owners in 1919. By 1933, she had been fitted with radio equipment and given the call sign MFMT but she still used acetylene gas for lighting; she was to be the very last of Aberdeen's trawlers to switch over to electricity, as late as the 1950s, while she was owned by T. Graham Ltd. She was sold to the scrap yard at Charleston for £2,277 in August 1960 (**Photo. 131**).

When *Woods* (A.330) left for the breakers at St. Davids on Forth in February 1960, it was reputed that she was in such a run-down state that her engineer put his hand through her plates after stumbling in the engine room. Fortunately, she was running up the navigation channel at the time, so the incident (if true) had little effect on her seaworthiness. She was built as the 'Strath' Class trawler *James Brodigan* by Hall, Russells in 1920 and after the

Photo. 131: *Morven* leaving Aberdeen for the fishing grounds in the 1950s. She has dark green topsides, a brown superstructure and a black funnel with two red bands separated by a white band. Her trawl net is hanging on the funnel to dry. No whaleback was fitted to this class of North Sea ship.

Photo. 132: *Athenian*, seen at the end of her working life but, with the exception of the DF loop on the wheelhouse, she is little changed from new. She is in T. Robinsons' colours of black hull over red boot topping, brown casing and wheelhouse, and a black funnel with red white and blue houseflag.

war, she went to Hull as H.142. By 1933, she was owned by A.S. Wilson of Edinburgh but he sold her in 1935 to John & Alexander Wood Ltd, Aberdeen, who renamed her *Woods*. Her last owners were the Looker Steam Fishing Co. Ltd, Aberdeen.

By the 1960s, only a few of Grimsby's old coal burners were still fishing, intrepid old timers previously owned by G.F. Sleight & Co. Ltd, Grimsby, who were almalgamated into Yorkshire Trawlers Ltd, Grimsby in 1960 (Ross Group); by 1964, they all had gone for scrap. One such trawler was *Regardo* (GY.623), built by Cook, Welton & Gemmell as Yard No. 330 in September 1915 (120ft 3ins, 248g), the second ship of a six vessel order. The others were, first, Yard No. 329 *Ronso* (GY.605, which sailed for Belgian breakers in March 1962, accompanied by the third vessel, Yard No. 331 *Recondo* (GY.626); Yard No. 332 *Riskato* (GY.914), which was scrapped in March 1957; Yard No. 333 *Resparko* (GY.926), which was sunk by German aircraft off Falmouth on 20th August 1940, whilst in Admiralty service; and, lastly, Yard No .334 *Royalo* (GY.941), which sank off Cornwall on 1st September 1940, after hitting a mine whilst on active service. These steamers were relics from a bygone age, when the only fishing aids were the compass and leadline, coupled to the skill of their skippers. *Regardo* left for a Bruges scrapyard on the afternoon tide of Monday 16th April 1962 (ironically, the same tide saw the return of the company's new flagship *Ross Renown* (GY.66) from her maiden trip.) On *Regardo*'s last fishing trip she was under skipper Harry Wilkins and engineer Mick Kennedy, both of whom had served their time in Sleight's coal burners. In her forty-seven years, she steamed some

one and a quarter million miles, or the equivalent of fifty round the world circumnavigations, not a bad record for a mere trawler.

LAST COAL BURNERS LEAVE THE HUMBER

The very last two coal firers to leave Grimsby, in November 1964, were Cook, Welton & Gemmell ships, *Sardinian* (GY.251 – 117ft bp, 226g) and *Athenian* (GY.357 – 117ft bp, 218g), both owned by Sir Thomas Robinson & Son (Grimsby) Ltd. *Athenian*, Yard No. 365, was launched in June 1919, to replace her namesake GY.1273, which had been sunk by a U-boat off Aberdeen in February 1917. This earlier ship (101ft oa, 171g) came from Cook, Welton & Gemmell as Yard No. 349 in August 1903. The latter trawler was requisitioned in November 1939 as an armed patrol vessel, being converted to a minesweeper in 1940, before her final conversion to an oiler in March 1944. Although their final trip was under tow, *Athenian* was the last to leave and not only was she the last coal burner, she was also the only remaining example of a 'handsom cab' or wheelhouse aft trawler, very little altered from the day she had slipped sideways into the River Hull at Beverley so many years before (**Photo. 132**).

Her partner that day in November 1964, *Sardinian*, had seen quite a few changes of name and ownership since leaving Cook, Welton & Gemmell's in 1916 as *War Wing* (GY.857), for the Pelham Steam Fishing Co. Ltd, Grimsby. By the end of 1916, she had been sold to T.W. Bascomb but prior to this had been requisitioned in the June as a minesweeper, returning in 1919. By 1935, she was under Dobson Steam Fishing Co. Ltd and F. Parkes colours. Called up again in November 1939 as a minesweeper, she was released in January 1946, having been sold the previous year to the Wembley Steam Fishing Co. Ltd, Grimsby. They in turn sold her to the Cramond Fishing Co. Ltd, Leith in December 1948, as *War Wing* (LH.26). They renamed her *Cramond Island* in 1949 and it was under this name that she returned to Grimsby in July 1953, and to her final owner, Thomas Robinson & Son Ltd. Her name was changed to *Sardinian* (GY.251) in August that year.

By 1960, only three coal burners were left at Hull, all Distant Water ships built in 1937 but which, unlike the majority of their counterparts, never underwent conversion to oil firing. They went to the breakers at Ghent in 1963. The first to go, on 2nd March, was *Loch Oskaig* (H.431 – 173ft 6in, 534g), built by Smith's Dock in 1937 as Yard No. 1026 for the Caledon Steam Fishing Co. Ltd, Hull (Loch Line). She was requisitioned as FY175, an anti-submarine trawler, in August 1939 and returned to her owners in November 1945, after which she continued to serve them well for another eighteen years. The next to leave, on 20th March, was Yard No. 622 *Kingston Ruby* (H.477), built by Cook, Welton & Gemmell at Beverley as *Lady Rosemary* (H.477) for Jutland Amalgamated Trawlers Ltd, Hull. Requisitioned in 1940 as an anti-submarine trawler, she was later refitted for armed patrol duties, as FY253, before being sold out of service in 1946. In 1947, she was sold to the Kingston Steam Trawling Co. Ltd, Hull and renamed *Kingston Ruby*. The very last coal burner to leave, on 19th April, was *Othello* (H.581 – 180ft oa/173ft 2ins bp x 28ft 6ins x 15ft 6ins, 516g), launched by Cochranes in 1937, Yard No. 1180, for the Earl Steam Fishing Co. Ltd, Grimsby as *Le Tiger* (GY.398). At the time of her launch, she was the fastest trawler sailing out of Grimsby, with a trials speed of 14 knots. So impressed was her owner Sir Alex Black, that he presented every Cochranes' employee with a shilling piece. She went to Hellyers for four months in 1938, before returning to her former owners and was purchased by the Admiralty in December 1939 as the anti-submarine trawler FY243. By 1942, she was under lease to the USA and, in June of that year, she was accredited with the destruction of *U215*. A year later saw her on the Durban station, where she remained until being returned in October 1945. After refitting, she returned to Grimsby on 29th July 1947 as *Regal* (GY.312), owned by the Loyal Steam Fishing Co Ltd. She was in the news on 29th September, after a piece of naval ordnance exploded in her net, fortunately without harming the vessel or her crew. In September 1948, she transferred to Hellyers of Hull again as *Othello* and on her last fishing trip she bunkered 234 tons of coal.

Another old Hull registered steamer was Cook, Welton & Gemmell's *Alexandrite* (H.7), built in 1934 as Yard No. 585. She was Aberdeen owned but Hull registered when she sailed for the scrap yard at Grangemouth on 2nd November 1963. This decade also saw Hull's last pre-war trawler sail in March 1967 for the breakers yard at Bo'ness. She was Cochrane's Yard No. 1176 *Arctic Explorer* (H.287 – 187ft oa/165ft 6ins bp x 27ft 6ins x 15ft, 501g), built in 1937 for the Boyd Line of Hull as H.445 and requisitioned in August 1939 for anti-submarine duties, Admiralty No. FY162. In 1942, she was working with the US Navy, being sold back to commercial owners in 1946. In 1947, she was sold to the Northern Fishing Co. Ltd, Hull and renamed *Captain Oates* (H.287). A year later she was back for good with Boyd's as *Arctic Explorer* (H.287).

Fleetwood, too, disposed of many older trawlers during this period. The port's last coal burner, *Lord Lloyd* (FD.52), left for the breakers at Troon in September 1963. Another of Fleetwood's more famous coal burners, *Red Charger* (LO.460), left for a Troon scrap yard on 3rd June 1955. Built in 1930 as Yard No. 550 *Arkwright* (H.314 – 143ft, 369g) by Cook, Welton & Gemmell for F.T. Ross & Co. Ltd, Hull, she was requisitioned in August 1939 as a minesweeper, Admiralty No. FY653. In December 1945, she was purchased by the Iago Steam Trawling Co. Ltd, London and renamed *Red Charger* in 1946. In common with most of Iago's vessels, she carried a London registration but worked out of Fleetwood. Her call to fame came in 1950, when she was immortalised in the book *Red Charger* by George Goldsmith Carter. On the trip recored in that book, she sailed on Wednesday 22nd January for the Andanes grounds, returning on 12th February with 14,000 stones of fish. A second book was written about a trip aboard a Fleetwood steam trawler in 1954, *The Steam Trawler Uganda* by B.J. Taylor, which is a complete contrast to Carter's book. The former used real names for ships and identified real people as crew members, whereas Taylor used fictitious titles, such as Holpool for Fleetwood and *Uganda* for the ship. The following year, 1956, saw no less than twelve steam trawlers leave the Lancashire port on their final trip to the breakers. Fleetwood's last working steamer was *Samuel Hewett* (LO.117), an oil fired ship, built by Cook, Welton & Gemmell as Yard No. 913 for Heward Trawlers of London. When she left for the breakers in 1968, she was only twelve years old, a sad end for such a young vessel. By the end of 1969, the steam trawler fleet had shrunk to ninety-five ships: Aberdeen – three, Fleetwood – three, Grimsby – thirty, Hull – fifty-eight and London – one.

ICELANDIC PROBLEMS RE-EMERGE

In 1971, Iceland declared that she would abrogate her earlier 1961 agreement and extend her limit to fifty miles, which angered the British trawling industry. The matter was thrashed out in the International Court of Justice but Iceland refused to abide by their ruling. By 1973, she warned that any trawlers caught fishing within the new fifty-mile limit would have their gear cut away by her Coastguard cutters. In fact, some sixty such incidents took place, forcing our Government to send Royal Navy frigates and deep sea tugs north to protect the trawlers. In 1974, our politicians rapidly back-pedalled and accepted a short-term agreement for two years. This allowed 139 British registered trawlers access to the restricted areas, with a maximum total annual catch of 130,000 tons. The very next year, 1975, saw the Icelanders further extend their limit to 200 miles, a move that really incensed our trawlermen, who could see their very livelihoods slipping away. Although they were angry at Iceland, they were bitterly realistic about the prospect of their own Government stabbing them in the back again. Admittedly, we sent the Navy in again to protect the fleets and many close skirmishes ensued, with vessels on both sides damaged by collisions. The strain on the warps is immense and should they be intentionally or accidentally severed, they will whip back aboard the vessel and kill by amputation anyone in their path. It was thus prudent in cases where the gear was threatened to clear the men off the decks. On top of the danger factor, the loss of a set of warps and gear often made further fishing impossible, and the trawler had to steam for home, to 'settle below the red line'. The Icelanders were determined and complained to the UN Security Council

Photo. 133: *Arsenal* being broken up, showing the 'Consol Crown' motif.

about the harassment of her Coastguard ships by the Royal Navy, and 1976 saw diplomatic relations severed again, with NATO chairing a meeting between the two sides in May. A short term palliative was agreed, which permitted twenty-four of our trawlers to fish in Icelandic waters for six months and take a maximum of 50,000 tons. The agreement expired on 1st December and was not renewed. Ironically, Britain introduced her own 200-mile limit some ten days later but this was later made worthless by the EEC Common Fisheries Policy, as it only outlawed non-member countries. This latest Cod War was hard for our trawlermen to understand. Politicians ignored their advisers from the industry, whilst the Navy dictated where and when the trawlers would fish but had scant knowledge of the fishing grounds. The results were poor catches, with trawlers landing in debt, thus being laid up and subsequently sold. Prime Minister Harold Wilson had decided that on no account would this country accept an annual Icelandic quota of less than 110,000 tons. This was stupidity, as the total catching power of the fleet was around 70,000 tons a year and it was common knowledge in the industry that Iceland would have allowed the 70,000 tons.

Even with these restrictions to the fishing grounds, the remaining steam trawlers could still manage to bring home some good catches. In October 1973, *Coldstreamer* (GY.10) set up a new national record, when she grossed £44,678 for a twenty-two day Icelandic trip, after landing 2,352 ten stone kits. Her next trip, under the same skipper, Bill Sate, grossed £38,438 for a twenty-one day trip to the Icelandic grounds.

November 1973 saw the oldest trawler in the Grimsby fleet, *Northern Chief* (GY.128 – 178ft x 31ft x 16ft, 692g), under the command of Alan Farmery, gross £43,533, for an Iceland trip of twenty-seven days. Built by Cochrane's as Yard No. 1354 in 1950, she went to the breakers in May 1976. Meanwhile at Hull, the Newington Steam Trawling Co. Ltd had recently bought *Rudyard Kipling* (H.141) and she was proving a worthwhile investment, landing two good catches in November under skipper Eddie Wooldridge Jnr. The first grossed £31,000, whilst on her second, she landed 1,767 kits, which grossed £37,623. She was previously named *Tarchon*, owned by Henriksen & Co. Ltd but prior to that, she had been launched as *Swanella* for Marr & Sons. She made her last trip to the breakers in 1974. In December 1973, *Coldstreamer's*

record was broken by *Velinda* (GY.29), when, under skipper E. Hall, she grossed over £47,000. Even this catch was beaten by the Hull steamer *Arctic Ranger* (H.115), when she grossed £51,377 from 2,410 kits.

Fleetwood was in the news during May 1974, when her trawlermen went on strike for the first time and brought the port to a standstill. The dispute was deep-seated but the bottom line was that the Lancashire men were being treated as second class by their Humber-based bosses and paid a lesser weekly wage. By this time, the port was operating many of the Humber's cast-offs, older Distant Water ships that found it hard to make a good living. Although sticking out for a £12 rise per week, in July they eventually agreed to an £8 rise, linked to an improvement in working conditions. September 1974 saw another two fine ships withdrawn and laid up for scrapping, *St. Apollo* (H. 592) built at Beverley in 1948 and *Vanessa* (GY.257), which came from the same yard in 1952. A strike by the repair and maintenance trades at Hull in October/November 1974 gave Fleetwood its first steam trawler arrival for almost ten years. British United Trawlers' (Hellyers) vessel *Lord Tedder* (H.154) was ordered to discharge her catch at the Lancashire port, which gave the shore staff a slight problem. No heavy fuel oil was available for rebunkering the trawler and she had to refuel from a coastal tanker, prior to sailing again. The year also saw the Faeroese grounds tied up in strict quota restrictions, which further depleted our accessible stocks and, in October, Norway threatened to establish trawl free zones, off the North Cape and the Lofoten Islands, with 1st January 1975 being the start date. In addition to these frustrations, the price of fuel oil trebled during the year but Humber owners had negotiated a fixed price contract for oil, which cushioned the impact somewhat. This agreement expired on 1st January 1975 and almost immediately steam trawlers were laid up. The later British-built vessels were notoriously heavy on fuel when compared to the German-built ships. Crewing was also becoming a problem, as skilled hands no longer wished to serve on board the older ships, preferring instead the more modern diesel powered vessels.

By February 1975, the following British United Trawlers had been laid up: *Arsenal* (GY.48 – **Photo. 133**), *Grimsby Town* (GY.246), *Hull City* (GY.282) and *Northern Sceptre* (GY.297). The first three went to Mayer-Newman of Fleetwood for scrapping in June.

At Hull, the picture was even grimmer, with the following laid-up prior to scrapping: *Arctic Brigand* (H.52), built as *Marbella* in 1955, sold to Boyds in 1965 and renamed *Arctic Brigand* (190ft 2ins, 793g); *Benvolio* (H.22 – 184ft 6ins, 722g), built by Smith's Dock in 1949 for Hellyers, who operated her all her life; *Kingston Jade* (H.149 – 205ft 5ins, 794g), built at Beverley in 1951 for Kingston and her sister *Kingston Topaz* (H.145); *Newby Wyke* (H.111 – 178ft 4ins x 30ft 6ins x 16ft, 672g), built by Cochrane's in 1950 for the West Dock Steam Fishing Co. Ltd, Hull; and *Ross*

Aquilla (H.114 – 188ft 7in, 780g) built in 1956 as *Stella Aquilla* for Charleston Smith Trawlers, who sold her to Hudson' in 1965.

THE FINAL EXODUS

By April 1975, the operational steam trawler fleet was confined to the Humber ports and comprised just fifteen ships, all Distant Water types, hanging on to the bitter end and still bringing home profitable catches. April saw *Kingston Sapphire* (H.95), under skipper Dave Spivey, land an Icelandic trip of 2,180 kits, which grossed £37,400, whilst Consolidated Fisheries' *Everton* (GY.58) landed a trip from the White Sea at Grimsby worth some £37,200 under skipper George Tyrell. This was to be a final hurrah for the latter, however. May 1975 saw the vessel, Grimsby's last British-built steam trawler, laid up. In the same month, *Arctic Avenger* at Hull, along with *Lord Tedder* and *Lord Lovat*, were also laid up. This left the port with only the six Bremerhaven-built steamers, owned by British United Trawlers. This company, by the end of the year, had also laid up their remaining Hull-registered ships. As the new year of 1976 dawned, with the Icelandic 200-mile limit imposed and the agreed quotas lost forever, Britain had only seven steam trawlers still operational, the six German-built ships at Grimsby and Boyds' *Arctic Ranger* out of Hull.

By May, the North Wall at Grimsby was to be the last resting place for these, her remaining steamers, after they had been withdrawn from service by British United Trawlers. *Black Watch* (GY.23 – 185ft 2ins, 697g), built in 1956 in Germany, was scrapped in March 1979 at Bruges. *Coldstreamer* (GY.10 – 183ft 7ins, 597g), built at Bremerhaven in 1955, was scrapped at Grimsby in November 1976. *Everton* (GY.58 – 184ft 5ins,

884g), built by Cochranes in 1958, was scrapped in December 1976 at Fleetwood. *Lord Beatty* (GY.91), another 1956 German-built ship, was scrapped in December 1976 by Drapers of Hull. *Northern Eagle* (GY.22 – 185ft 2in, 701g), built at Bremerhaven in 1956, was scrapped at Hull in January 1977. *Northern Sky* (GY.25), sister to *Northern Eagle*, went to the breakers at Hull in April 1976 and, finally, *Royal Lincs* (GY.18), Bremerhaven-built in 1955, went to the breakers in January 1977.

In 1975, Hull said farewell to *Kingston Jacinth* (H.198 – 205ft 2in, 794g), built by Cook, Welton & Gemmell in 1952. In 1976, the port scrapped *Arctic Avenger* (H.118 – 188ft 6ins, 806g), ex-*Cape Columbia*, built at Beverley in1956; *Kingston Emerald* (H.49 – 205ft 2ins, 811g), another Beverley-built ship from 1954; *Lord Lovat* (H.148 – 181ft 3ins oa/178ft bp x 31ft x 16ft, 713g), built by Cochranes in 1951 and scrapped on 10th April; *Lord Tedder* (H.154 – *Lord Lovat*'s sister), broken up on 22nd May; and *Macbeth* (H.201 – 188ft 8ins, 810g – ex-*St. Matthew*, ex-*Breughel*), built at Beverley in 1957. Finally, 1977 saw the scrapping of *Kingston Sapphire* (H.95 – 205ft 2in, 809g), built by Cook Welton & Gemmell in 1955.

The last operational Hull steam trawler was to be *Arctic Ranger* (H.155 – 192ft 4ins, 867g), skippered by C. Walker and finally laid up in 1976. Built in 1957 by Cook, Welton & Gemmell, she went to Drapers' Yard for scrapping on 26th October 1976, thus ending forever Hull's era of the steam trawler.

With Grimsby's redundant steamers soon to meet the same ultimate fate, the hands of time came full circle when the Cochrane-built *Northern Sceptre* (GY.297), the last British registered steam trawler, finally succumbed to the cutting torch in February 1979. By March it was all over. The steam trawler was born, matured and died in the span of a single human lifetime.

Steam trawlers had been the nation's main fish provider for almost one hundred years. They and their crews had been Britain's first line of defence during two world wars. They had escorted our convoys and swept the sea lanes, in order to make the waters a safer place for fellow seamen. Through no fault of their own, they had maimed, killed and drowned countless hundreds of fishermen. They had battled through the worst seas in the world to assist their fellow men in times of distress, often falling victims themselves (**Photos 134 and 135**). They had been good and faithful servants, and had been all things to all men. Let us never forget them.

Photo. 134: *Thornella* (H.582), showing damage to her wheelhouse after being struck by a heavy sea off Iceland.

EPILOGUE.

Steam trawlers were built to the highest Lloyds standards and although many were lost, many others led long eventful lives, as the following two examples show.

Viola (H.868 – 108ft 5ins x 21ft 5ins, 174g) was built in 1906 as Yard No. 96 by Cook, Welton & Gemmell at Beverley. Her 45nhp engine, supplied by Amos & Smith, gave her a top speed of 9 knots. She was part of a nine ship batch, which was itself part of a £320,000 order by Hellyer's Steam Fishing Co. Ltd, Hull for fifty such 'steam fleeters' (**Photos 136 and 137, and Plan 89**). Requisitioned in September 1914 and fitted initially with a 3 pounder gun but later with a 12 pounder, she saw service in the Shetlands and with the River Thames Patrol as a minesweeper, before being returned to her owners in 1919. By this time Hellyers had decided to sell off their 'boxing fleet' and concentrate on the Distant Water grounds off Iceland

She was sold by the UK brokers Massey & Sons of Hull for £11,000 in February 1920, to L. Thorsen of Sandefjord on behalf of A/S Sandefjord Trawlfiskeselskap, renamed *Kapduen* and formed the nucleus of Norway's trawling fleet. When the Sandefjord company were taken over in 1923 by Nils Torvald Nielsen of Alonso, Norway, she was converted to a whale catcher, her wheelhouse being moved forward of the funnel and her name changed to *Dias*. Sold again in 1927 to Compania Argentina de Pesca Anonima, which operated a fleet of sealers from

Photo. 136: *Viola* in early Hellyer colours of black hull, and cream and black funnel, with their house flag of a white 'H' on blue.

Grytviken in South Georgia, she worked from there chasing and catching elephant seals (closely regulated by the Falkland Islands government). She was a very useful vessel, taking part in many research expeditions around South Georgia including the Kohl-Larsen one in 1928-9, when they made the first cine film of the island. It was around this time that her Swedish skipper Johan Johannesson located a long forgotten sheltered harbour bay, which was thereafter named Dias Cove.

She was converted to oil in the 1950s but, in 1960, the company sold out to Albion Star and *Dias* once again became a British-flagged vessel. In 1965-6, the whaling station closed and she was laid up along with *Petrel* and *Albatross*, being looked after by a caretaker until 1970. Sometime later she sank, caused jointly

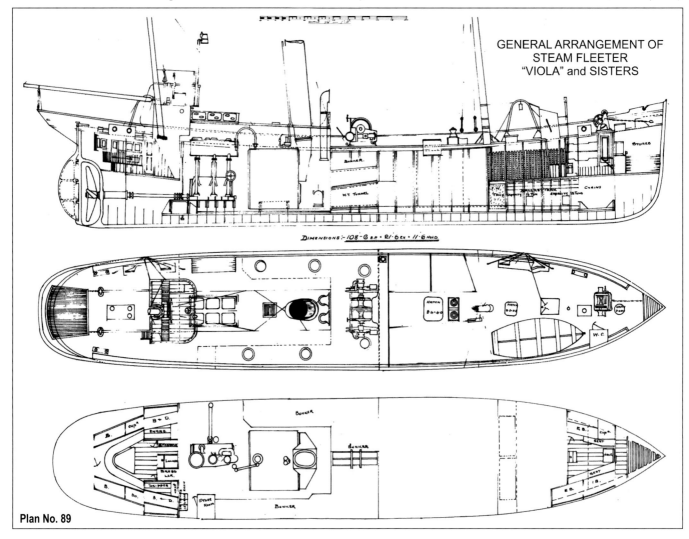

GENERAL ARRANGEMENT OF STEAM FLEETER "VIOLA" and SISTERS

Plan No. 89

by neglect and the accumulation of winter snow. Although now a derelict, she played an unwitting role at the start of the Falklands war, when a team of Argentinian scrap metal merchants landed on South Georgia tasked with the cutting up of the three ships. Given the subsequent action at nearby Cumberland Bay, she must be one of the very few vessels to have seen action in the First World War and the Falklands. In the late 1990s, a plan was formulated to raise her and bring her home to the National Fisheries Museum in Grimsby but to date this has not materialised. By the turn of the century, concerns were raised about the oil leaking from the tanks of the three ships and, in 2004, a decision was taken to raise *Viola/Dias*. This was successfully carried out and once again she is afloat, with her original steam engine still intact, although still a long way from home (courtesy www.viola-dias.org).

STEAM TRAWLER CONVERTED TO MOTOR YACHT

Another steam trawler that had an extended life was *Coot* (H897 – 110.2ft bp/120ft oa x 21ft 1in x 11ft 3in, 210g, 60nhp). She was completed as Yard No. 88 by Goole Shipbuilding & Repairing Co. in September 1906, for Messrs Kelsall Bros & Beeching and engined by Earle's of Hull. In November 1914, she was requisitioned as a minesweeper, Admiralty No. 420 and fitted with two 12 pounders and one 7.7ins anti-submarine howitzer. In March 1917, she was refitted as a Q-ship armed with one 12 pounder and one 6 pounder, going under the names *Burmah*, *Dorah Kia Ora* and *Lorne*, until returned to minesweeping in November 1918 as *Coot*. She was returned to her former owners in 1920 and transferred to Fleetwood in 1924. In March 196 Kelsall Bros & Beeching Ltd, Hull, went into voluntary liquidation and in 1937 she was sold to the Hewett Fishing Co. Ltd, London, (the Short Blue Fleet) who laid her up later that year and her Hull fishing registry was closed.

In August 1937, Joe and Edward Lumb were trying to order a new motor yacht but could not find an acceptable delivery date, so they looked at second hand tonnage. *Coot* was purchased and went to Nicholson's of Glasson Dock for conversion. She was completely gutted out and a number of hull plates and frames were replaced. Two fuel and two water tanks were built into the hull and four new bulkheads were fitted. New steel weather decks with teak planking and a new superstructure were constructed. Her two new 220hp National diesel engines were fitted with reverse-reduction gearing and supplemented by two auxiliary units; an 18hp National engine with a dynamo, general service pump and compressor,

Photo. 137: The newly converted *Manihine*. Her trawler hull is still recognisable but a raised fo'c'sle has been added.

and a similarly equipped 9.5hp unit were also fitted. Electrical equipment included a Marconi echo sounder, wireless direction finder and loudspeaker telephones from the wheelhouse to crew and engine rooms. On completion she was renamed *Dorade II*.

In September 1939, she was hired as a port examination vessel at £206 10s a month and was based in Reykjavik, Iceland under the command of skipper J.F. Nuttal RNR. On 2nd October 1941, she was compulsorily acquired by the Ministry of War Transport. After the war she was sold to Major H.W. Hall MA and registered as a yacht at Fleetwood. In 1945 he converted her to a research and survey vessel with the new name of *Manihine* (**Photo. 138**).

From 1955, when she was sold to the Government of the Colony of Singapore, she had many owners. The first was the East African Marine Fisheries Organisation, Zanzibar in 1961, then in 1964 she went to the East African Common Services Organisation, Mombasa and in 1965 her owners were the Southern Line Ltd, Mombasa. In 1976, she was back in Zanzibar owned by the Institute of Marine Sciences. It appears that they had little respect for the ship and by 1978 she was laid up through lack of maintenance. In June 1979, she was sold and used as a coaster until being abandoned at Dar es Salaam in the late 1980s. In 1992 breaking up commenced and by 1997, after ninety-one years of service, she was no more.

In complete contrast to these two trawlers was *Kathleen Anderson* (120ft x 22ft x 12ft 6ins, 219g), built as Yard No. 401 by A. Hall and completed in April 1903 for the Durban Steam Trawling & Fishing Co. Ltd, South Africa. A dual purpose tug/trawler, she was wrecked in November that same year.

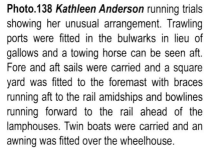

Photo.138 *Kathleen Anderson* running trials showing her unusual arrangement. Trawling ports were fitted in the bulwarks in lieu of gallows and a towing horse can be seen aft. Fore and aft sails were carried and a square yard was fitted to the foremast with braces running aft to the rail amidships and bowlines running forward to the rail ahead of the lamphouses. Twin boats were carried and an awning was fitted over the wheelhouse.

MOTOR YACHT DORADE II

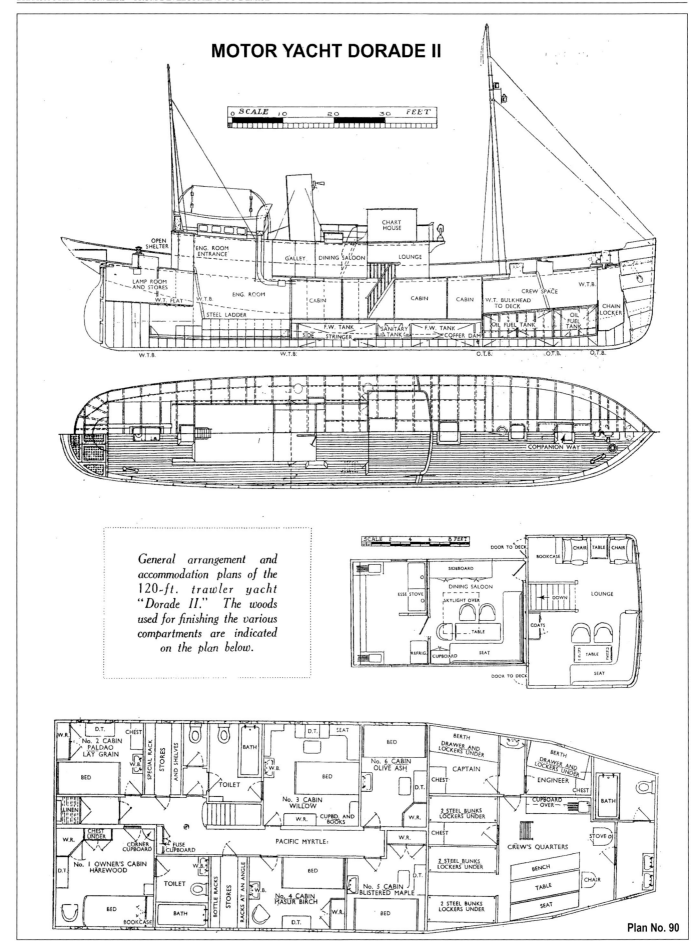

General arrangement and accommodation plans of the 120-ft. trawler yacht "Dorade II." The woods used for finishing the various compartments are indicated on the plan below.

Plan No. 90

Appendix I
Steam Trawler Specification 1883

Within these appendices, the reader will find full yard details of construction and outfit for typical steam trawlers. I realise that many people find such technical information a complete bore but, nevertheless, they will prove invaluable to the modelmaker when read in conjunction with the drawings produced throughout the book.

Description of one of the latest built steam trawlers:

A fine model of one of the most recently built trawlers of the Grimsby company's fleet, which differs somewhat from the *Zodiac*, was exhibited at London in 1883. The lines of this vessel are excellent for seaworthiness, carrying capacity, and for a reasonable turn of speed. She is moderately sharp forward, with a straight stem and nearly square fore-foot; rounding bilge, with medium dead-rise; a long, finely shaped run, and round stern. She has more sheer than average for this class of vessel, which, with the high bow chock forward, and quarter-deck aft, gives a gracefulness to her appearance, which is all the more pleasing because of its general absence in British steam fishing vessels. The main deck extends from the bow to within 25 feet of the stern, where the quarterdeck begins; the latter adds to the height of the after section, and gives more cabin room. The bridge, extending from side to side, and elevated seven to eight feet above the main deck, is placed just forward of the quarter, and over the after part of the engine-room. It is protected by a metal railing, and is reached by steps from the quarterdeck on the starboard side. The cabin companion is on the quarterdeck, just forward of the mizzen-mast, and a little to starboard of the latter. A large skylight abaft the mizzen-mast affords light and ventilation to the cabin. The entrance to the forecastle is aft of the windlass, while three hatches, one forward of the mainmast and two aft of it, on the main deck, lead to the hold and fish rooms. The trawl warp roller is on the port side (about five feet aft of the main rigging), and a capstan stands abreast of the roller in the middle of the deck. On the main-deck, a little forward of the smoke-stack, is a steam winch for winding in the trawl warp, hoisting sails etc., and the dandy winch or "wink", is on the port forward end of the quarter. The boat is carried on the davits aft of the starboard main rigging. The rig differs in no essential particular from that of the *Zodiac*.

She is 70.63 Tons, her length between perpendiculars, 95ft., beam, 20ft., and depth of hold, 10ft. 6 inches. She carries a 60 foot trawl beam, and has a capacity for 1,700 "trunks" of fish. Her speed under steam alone, is 10 Knots, and being so heavily rigged, she will often make 11 to 13 Knots under sail and steam. Often, when vessels of this class have a favourable wind, they disconnect the screw and run under sail alone.

Details of construction of a steam trawler:

The following are the details of dimensions, construction, etc., of one of the recent additions to the Grimsby company's fleet of steam trawlers. Length, and breadth as previously given. Spars; Pole foremast, 70 feet long, 26 feet from eyes of rigging to truck, diameter at deck 15 inches; pole mizzen-mast, 57 feet long, 21 feet form rigging to truck, 13 inches diameter at deck; bowsprit, full length, 33 feet, diameter at gammon hole, 11 inches; main boom, 40 feet long, diameter 10 inches; main-gaff, length, 32 feet; mizzen-boom, length, 25 feet; mizzen-gaff, length, 19 feet; two topsail yards, the forward one 12 feet long, and the after one, 15 feet.

The sails are made of canvas of the following weights; Mainsail and foresail are made of No. 1, extra G; small (or storm) jib, No. 0, extra G; second jib and mizzen, No. 1, ordinary; big jib, fore-topsail, and mizzen-staysail, No. 2; and mizzen-topsail of No. 3. The dimensions of the lower sails carried by these vessels are: Jib – luff, 49 feet; leach, 27 feet; foot, 27 feet. Stay-foresail – luff, 29 feet 3 inches; leach, 23 feet 6 inches; foot, 16 feet 6 inches. Mainsail – luff, 22 feet 6 inches; leach, 45 feet; foot, 32 feet 6 inches; head, 27 feet. Mizzen-staysail – luff (about), 22 feet 10 inches; leach, 20 feet; foot, 17 feet 3 inches. Mizzen – luff, 19 feet 6 inches; leach 32 feet; foot, 21 feet; head 20 feet.

These vessels are built to class 100A1 at Lloyds. They are provided with accommodation for eight men, there being four berths aft in the cabin for officers, and four berths forward. The cabin and forecastle are fitted in a comfortable and substantial manner, and are provided with side and deck lights, and each has a cooking stove of approved pattern.

Nothing but the best material of its respective class is used in the construction of these trawlers. The butts of all plating, the stringers and keel, are planed and drawn hard together. All butt straps are $^1/_{16}$ inch thicker than plates they connect, and all are double rivetted. The double lugs on the frames, for the attachment of stringers, are of the same scantlings as reverse bars, and fixed with at least three rivets.

The liners behind the frames, at alternate strakes of outside plating, and wherever required, are made in one piece, so that they accurately fill the space in length, breadth, and thickness. All stringers are continued fore and aft, the bulkheads and other obstructions being notched and made good up to them.

The keel and stem are made of bulb bar-iron 7 $^1/_2$ inches by 1$^1/_2$ inches. The stern frame is 7$^1/_2$ inches by 2$^1/_4$ inches. There are thee water-tight bulkheads, carried up to the deck, of $^4/_{16}$ inch plate iron, stiffened with 2$^1/_2$ inches by 2$^1/_2$ inches by $^4/_{16}$ inch angle iron, provided with valves to be worked from the deck.

The boiler is made of steel. There are two side bunkers, and one athwartship for coal, and the whole having sufficient capacity to hold fuel enough for fourteen days consumption.

The knight-heads are oak, 5$^1/_2$ inches thick, and extend five feet on each side of the stem; they are pierced with hawse pipes, and bowsprit hole. The forward warping chocks are also of oak, 6$^1/_2$ inches by 2$^1/_2$ inches, extending about 40 feet each side, and well rounded on top. There is also an iron bar fastened to the outer edge of the capping with a 6 inches by 2$^1/_2$ inches sheave at each side of the forward end of the towing chock.

The windlass is of the ordinary handspike form, and is provided with a lever ratchet purchase on the spindle outside of the bitts. The forward winch, similar to those on sailing trawlers is carried, and, by a peculiar arrangement, the winch and windlass can be combined on one set of bitts, if necessary.

The deck is pitch pine, the planks being 6 inches by 3$^1/_2$ inches. The space below deck under the capstan, is filled in solid with American elm chocks, and oak planking 14 inches wide is laid next to the gunwale bar, fore and aft, and also for capstan, windlass bitts, alongside the hatchways etc. The hatch coamings are iron, with round corners of plate iron,12 inches by $^6/_{16}$ inches, with half-round iron bar 2$^1/_2$ inches by 1$^1/_4$ inches, round top edges, and they are 9$^1/_2$ inches in height above deck. The bulwark stanchions are iron, 1$^5/_8$ inches in diameter. The rail bar is 4 inches by 3 inches by $^5/_{16}$

inches angle iron; and the beading iron is half-round bar, $2^1/_2$ inches by $^3/_4$ inch, this being fastened with $^3/_4$ inch rivets 12 inches apart.

The main rail is made of American elm, $7^1/_2$ inches by $3^1/_2$ inches inches, with a greenheart capping on top. There is a steam drum for winding in wire warp. This is provided with reversing gear and separate action of main barrel, and winch ends at the end of the drum, with brake power, separate pawls to the main barrel, and ends fitted with hand gear to treble purchase. There is also a capstan similar to those on a sailing trawler, which acts as a fairleader to the drum. The dandy winch, placed at the mizzen rigging on the port side, is the same as the improved forms used on other trawlers. The trawl warp gangway is provided with both horizontal and vertical iron rollers. There are two bollards aft for towing, and one revolving bollard or Sampson post on each side. At each bilge there is a rolling chock 30 feet long, made of bulb bar-iron $7^8/_{16}$ inches between two angle bars 3 inches by $3^1/_2$ inches by $^6/_{16}$ inch rivetted to the ships sides. The sheet of the stay-foresail works on an iron traveller, which extends from side to side of the bow. The chains are galvanised, and the anchors are of the ordinary short shanked pattern carried by other trawlers. The side of the vessel is made flush, the chain plates being rivetted to the bulwarks, so that boats may come alongside in a seaway without being damaged by projections.

Provision is made to pump the vessel out by steam, but she is also supplied with a 6 inches hand pump. There are two iron water tanks, having a total capacity of 500 gallons.

About 40 tons of ballast are carried, this being the best iron slag, it is grouted in with cement, and over the top of the ballast there is put a 3 inches face of Portland cement. The cement is rebated to take a wooden cover 2 inches thick, and a 9 inch gutter is left in the centre for drainage purposes. In the ice-room, a redwood floor $2^1/_2$ inches thick, is laid on top of the ballast and firmly secured.

Appendix II
Selected Ships Lines Plans

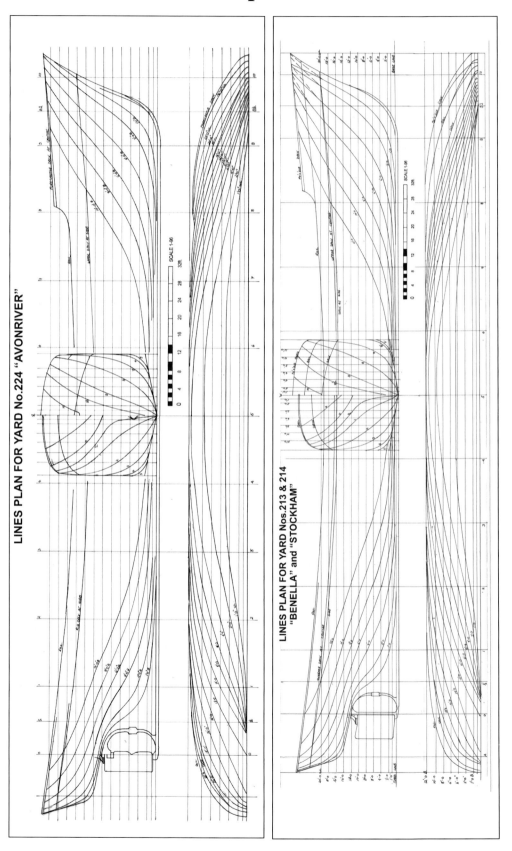

LINES PLAN FOR YARD No.224 "AVONRIVER"

LINES PLAN FOR YARD Nos.213 & 214 "BENELLA" and "STOCKHAM"

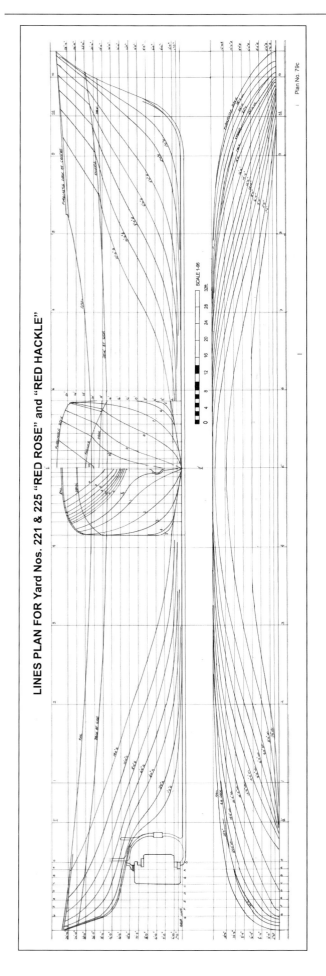

LINES PLAN FOR Yard Nos. 221 & 225 "RED ROSE" and "RED HACKLE"

Plan No. 79c

SCALE 1:95

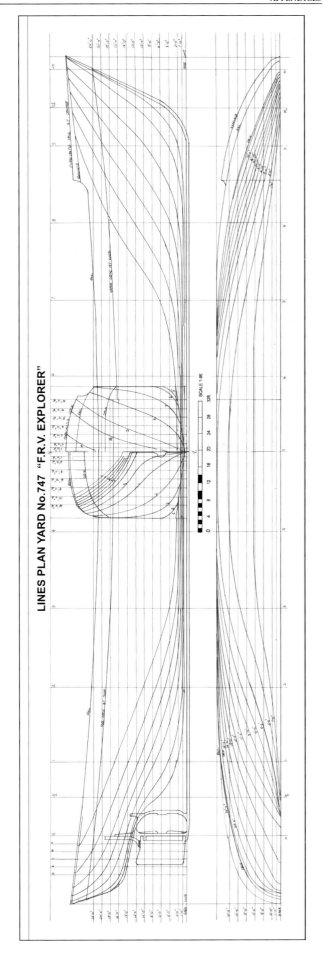

LINES PLAN YARD No.747 "F.R.V. EXPLORER"

SCALE 1:95

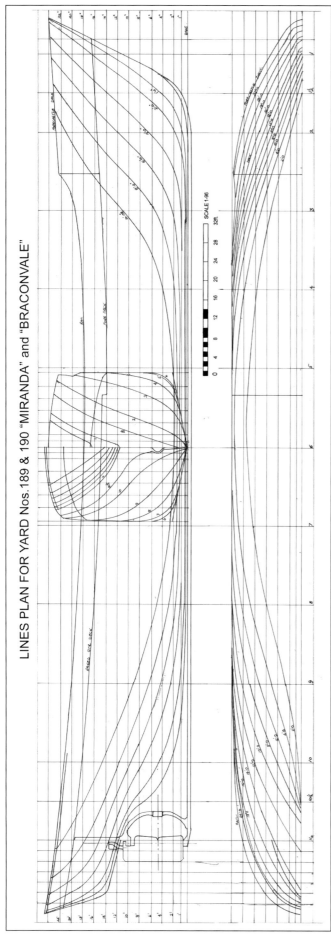

LINES PLAN FOR YARD Nos.189 & 190 "MIRANDA" and "BRACONVALE"

SCALE 1·96

Appendix III
Specification of Outfit for a Grimsby Steam Trawler (c1900)

ACETYLENE INSTALLATION: Fixed on board complete with all necessary piping etc: 1 "Comet" Generator, Oil Sealed, complete with 7 Lights comprising, 2 On Bridge, 1 on Boom, 2 on Galley Top, 1 in Engine Room, 1 across Casing (or approved positions).

ANCHORS and CHAINS: 90 Fathoms of 1 inch Stud Link Chain Cable, 1 Roger's Black Anchor, 5.5cwts., ex. Stock, 1 Roger's Black Anchor, 4.5cwts., ex. Stock, 1 Roger's Black Anchor, 2.5cwts., ex.Stock.

BOATSWAIN'S STORES: 2 1-Gallon Oil Tins, 1 Register Box, 1 Saw, 1 Pair Lamp Scissors, 2 Deep Sea Leads, 15 and 18 lbs, 1 Meat Saw, 2 2-Gallon Oil Tins, 1 Butter Dish, 1 Large Hammer, 1 Medicine Chest, 6 Assorted Gimlets, 1 Pair of Basket Hooks, Gin and Rope, 2 Ice Shovels, 2 Pairs of Rowlocks, 1 Spring Oil Feeder, 1 Box of Pins and Punches, 9 Life Jackets, 1 Each Seaming and Roping Palms, 2 Life Buoys with Ship's Name, 1 Dozen Sail Needles and Case, 2 Life Buoy Guards, 2 Deck Buckets, 2 Large Oil Feeders, 1 Water Funnel, 1 Claw Hammer, 2 6-Gallon Drums, 1 Buoy and Staff, 1 Water Can, 1 Tub for Washing Boards, 1 Chart Tin, 1 Mechanical Foghorn, 1 Clock for Wheelhouse, 3 Marline Spikes, 6 Paint Cans, 1 Walker's Cherub Log and Line, 4 Cork Fenders.

OUTFIT OF BLOCKS: 2 Double Fish Tackle Blocks (Iron, with Shackle), 2 Single Fish Tackle Blocks (Iron, with Shackle), 1 Iron Lazy Tackle Block (Iron, with Shackle), 2 Double Boat Tackle 7 inches Blocks (Wood, Iron bound), 2 Single Boat Tackle 7 inches Blocks (Wood, Iron bound), 1 Double Mizzen Sheet 7 inches Block (Wood, Iron bound), 1 Single Mizzen Sheet 7 inches Block (Wood, Iron bound), 2 Main Sheet Double 9 inches Blocks (Wood, Iron bound), 2 Double Handy Billy 6 inches Blocks (Wood, Iron bound), 2 Single Handy Billy 6 inches Blocks (Wood, Iron bound), 1 Double Mizzen Top lift Purchase 6 inches Block (Wood, Iron bound), 1 Single Mizzen Top lift Purchase 6 inches Block (Wood, Iron bound), 1 Double Mainsail Purchase 6 inches Block (Wood, Iron bound), 1 Single Mainsail Purchase 6 inches Block (Wood, Iron bound), 2 Single Foresail Halliard 7 inches Blocks (Wood, Iron bound), 2 Mizzen Sail Purchase 5 inches Blocks (Wood, Iron bound), 1 Double Main Top lift Purchase 6 inches Block (Wood, Iron bound), 1 Single 6 inches Block (Wood, Iron bound), 1 Main Top lift Block (Iron), 1 Mizzen Top lift Block (Iron), 2 Mizzen Halliard Blocks (Iron), 3 Mizzen Peak Halliard Blocks (Iron), 1 Main Halliard Block (Iron), 2 Pairs of Ash Oars, 2 Hand Spikes, 2 Short Hawks, 1 Boat Hook, 1 Main Boom, Mizzen Boom, and Mizzen Gaff, with all necessary Ironwork.

BRUSHES: 2 Blacklead Brushes, 2 Varnish Brushes, 2 Small Brushes, 6 Paint Brushes, 4 Deck Brushes, 3 Hand Brushes.

CABIN STORES: 1 Dozen Knives and Forks, 2 Fire Shovels, 1 Dozen Table Spoons, 1 Water Can, 1 Sugar Tin, 1 Pasteboard and Pin, 1 Flour Tin, 1 Pepper Tin, 1 Steel, 1 Almanack, 1 Meat Tin Opener, 1 Vinegar Jar, 1 Large Paraffin Feeder, 2 Wash Leathers, 1 Dozen Enamelled Plates, 1 Tea Tin, 1 Dozen Enamelled Mugs, 1 Coffee Tin, 2 Table Cloths, 3 Pokers, 1 Oil Baize Cloth for Table, 1 Candle Box, 1 Knife Board, 1 Coal Box for Cabin, 1 Carving Knife and Fork, 1 Rake, 1 Tea Pot, 1 Paraffin Tank,

25 to 30 Gallons, 1 Soup Tureen and Ladle, 1 Clock and Barometer, 1 Tin Saucepan, 1 Pair of Marine Glasses, 1 Coffee Pot, 1 1-Gallon Iron Saucepan, 3 Doormats.

COOKS STORES: 1 Beef Kettle and Steamer, 1 Pea Bowl, 2 False Bottoms, 1 Cooks Spoon, 1 Copper Boiler with Brass Tap, 1 Nutmeg Grater, 1 Iron Saucepan, 2 Large Iron Tea Kettles, 1 1-Gallon Treacle Tin, 1 Frying Pan, 2 Baking Tins, 2 Pudding Cloths, 1 Large Chopper, 2 Each Pepper and Salt Boxes, 1 Small Chopper, 2 Enamelled Pie Dishes, 1 Ship's Pot, 1 Flour Scoop, 4 Platters, 1 Grindstone in Trough, 2 Pudding Moulds, 1 Harness Cask, 1 Paste Cutter, 2 Bread Tins, 1 Cook's Ladle, 1 Cook's Knife, 1 Tormentor, 1 Cook's Fork, 1 Fish Slice, 1 Vegetable Cullender, 1 Large Bread Bowl.

DECK FITTINGS: 1 Double Barrelled Otter Trawling Winch, 1 Set of Triple Centre Bollards, 2 Side Rollers, 4 Patent Gallows complete with Blocks and Rollers, and Hutchinson's fairleads in foot, 1 Patent Towing Block.

FISHING GEAR: 2 Otter Trawls, fixed complete, 2 Spare Bellies, 2 Ground Ropes for same, 1 Spare Pair Lower Wings, 2 200-Fathoms Steel Wire Trawl Warp, 2 Spare 100 Mesh Pieces or Lower Ends marked and spliced, 1 Spare Full Trawl, fixed, 4 Pairs of Otter Boards 10ft 0ins by 4ft 6ins, 1 Spare Full Trawl in pieces, 1 Messenger complete, 18 fathoms.

FLAGS: 1 Burgee, 1 Red Ensign, 1 House Flag, 1 Set of Code Signals, with book, 1 Blue Peter, 1 Flag Bag, 1 Union Jack.

LAMPS: 1 Pair of Copper Dioptric Side Lights, 1 Lamp for Captain's Cabin, 1 Copper Dioptric Steaming, (or Masthead) Light, 1 Lamp for Engineer's Cabin, 1 Gimballed Brass Fo'c'sle Lamp and Shade, 1 Copper Dioptric Fishing Light, 1 Copper Dioptric Anchor Light, 2 Ruby Signal Lights, 1 Copper Plain Anchor Light, 1 Cage for Steaming Light, 1 Copper Deck Lantern, 2 Large Ducks, 1 Copper Stern Light, 1 Japanned Galley Lamp, 2 Japanned Buoy Lights, 1 Lamp for Chart Room, 1 Cabin Lamp, Stays, Brass Rail, and Shade, 1 Japanned Relieving Lamp, 2 Black Balls.

RIGGING, RUNNING GEAR, and WARPS: 1 Fore Stay and Stay Hanks, 1 Handy Billy, 1 Topmast Stay, 1 Set of Topsail Halliards, 1 Gang of Main Rigging, three Shrouds a side, 2 Main Reef Pennants, 2 Fish Tackle Strops, 2 Main Reef Lacings, 1 Pair of Lantern Stays, 2 Pairs of Lantern Halliards, 1 Main Tye, 1 Mizzen Sheet, 2 Bag Strops, 2 Mizzen Shackles, 4 Bag Ropes, 1 Mizzen Top lift Purchase, 1 Gang of Mizzen Rigging, two Shrouds a side, 1 Mizzen Tye Purchase, 2 Mizzen Stays, 1

Mizzen Reef Pennant, 2 Mizzen Strops, 2 Mizzen Reef Lacings, 1 Mizzen Top lift, 2 Pairs of Pennant Halliards, 1 Mizzen Tye, 1 White Manilla Hauling Line, 60 fathoms, 4.5 inches. 2 Fish Tackle Falls, 1 Main Sheet, 1 White Manilla Small Warp, 60 fathoms 5.5 inches. 1 Main Tye Purchase, 2 Small Fore Halliards, 1 Coil 3.5 inches White Manilla Rope, 1 Main Top lift and Purchase, 1 Stem Fender, 1 Lead Line, 60 fathoms.

OUTFIT FOR ENGINE-ROOM: 2 Pair Smith's tongs, 1 Ratchet Brace, 1 Drill Stand, 6 Drills assorted, 6 Cold Chisels, assorted, 6 Asst. Files and Handles, 1 Packing drawer for each size of gland, 1 Packing stick and 1 packing Knife, 1 Vice and Bench, 1 Pair copper Vice Grips, 1 Pair lead Vice Grips, 6 Steel Strake Wedges, 2 Hand Hammers, 1 Sledge or Quarter Hammer, 1 Flogging Hammer, 1 Copper Hammer, 1 Coal Hammer, 1 Lead Hammer, 1 Sealing Hammer, 2 Trimming Shovels, 2 Firing Shovels, 1 Back End Rake, 1 Rake, 3 Slices, 1 Long Rake, 2 Prickers, 6 Pricker Blades, 1 Large Ring Spanner for piston rod nuts, 1 Box Spanner for junk ring nuts, 1 Star spanner for Bottom End bolts, 1 Star spanner for Main Bearing bolts, 1 Spanner for Boiler manholes, 2 Brass wire Tube brushes, 2 Tube brush handles, 1 Tube Scraper and Handle, 3 Oil cans assorted, 2 Square Brass lamps, 1 Gauge Glass lamp, 3 Hand lamps, 1 Drip tray and strainer, of Tin, 1 Trimming can and scissors, 1 Gallon measure, 1 Iron Tallow Kettle, 1 Set of Eyebolts of different sizes, to lift different covers, 1 Brass Salinometer with case, 2 Tin Funnels, 1 Can for Salinometer, 1 Copper Thermometer of approved size, 2 Iron ash buckets, 2 Galvanised iron buckets, 1 Set of spanners to fit each nut, Shifting spanners, small and large, 1 Spanner rack, 1 Set of tubing tools for Condenser, 1 Soldering Iron, 2 lbs. of soft solder, with zinc and spirits of salt, 1 Screwdriver, 1 Pair of Tin Shears, 2 Caulking chisels, 1 Scraper, 1 Brass Engine-room clock, 1 Pair of pliers, 1 Sheet of tin, 1 Sheet of Muntz metal, 1 Crowfoot spanner for valve spindle nuts, 1 Securing tin, 1 Pair of 2 and 3 sheave rope blocks, 4 Tube stoppers, 1 Grindstone and trough, 1 Tube expander, 1 Set of Taps and Dies $1/4$ inch to $1\,1/4$ inch, 1 Rubber hose, 1 Brass Syringe, 2 Dozen asst. split pins, 1 Dozen asst. studs and nuts.

SPARE GEAR: 2 Main bearing bolts and nuts, 2 Top end bolts and nuts, 2 Bottom end bolts and nuts, 1 Set coupling bolts and nuts, 100 Asst. nuts and bolts, 20 Brass ferrules for condenser, 12 Gauge Glasses and 12 packing rings to suit mountings, 1 Set feed pump valves and seats, 1 Set bilge pump valves and seats, 6 Piston bolts and nuts, 1 Safety Valve spring, æ Set of Firebars and pattern, 6 Condenser Tubes, 1 Set of Air pump valves (Kinghorns), 3 Boiler tubes, 1 Spare Propeller, 1 Of each size spare springs.

Appendix IV
Radio Installations

As to the actual radio equipment carried on the early trawlers, I wish to thank the Marconi Company for allowing me to quote the following detailed description of their 1/2 kw Cargo Set, which was fitted to the trawlers (I trust the reader will bear with me, as my technical knowledge with regards to wireless sets is very scant indeed, so I have quoted the text in full).

THE MARCONI 1/2 KW CARGO SET
This is a small power installation designed to produce transmitting waves of 250 and 600 meters, or any intermediate wave with a simple change-over from one to the other. The working transmitting range depends upon the height, length, and shape of the aerial. The receiving apparatus provides for tuned reception of all waves between 250, and 1,600 meters. The working receiving range is also dependent on the aerial.

The transmitting plant consists of a rotary converter with its starter, field regulator, and guard lamps, driven by direct current from the ship's mains and supplying alternating current to the primary of the potential transformer. In series with the primary of this transformer is inserted the low frequency air core, adjustable inductance, and the manipulating key. The secondary coil of the potential transformer is connected through two air choking coils with the primary high frequency circuit. The primary coil of the oscillation transformer is connected in series with the transmitting condenser, and disc discharger, one end of the primary coil being connected to one terminal of the condenser, and the other to one of the electrodes of the disc discharger. The secondary of the oscillation transformer is connected at one end to an aerial, through an adjustable inductance, and an insulated lead-in, passing through the roof or side of the operating cabin. The other end of the secondary connects to the top plate of an arrester earth spark-gap, the bottom plate of the spark-gap being connected to earth bolts which are fastened to the plates of the iron shell of the ship. The receiving apparatus is connected across the arrester spark-gap, an arrangement which enables the receiving operator at a corresponding station to "break in" on the transmission in the event of erroneous reception, and thus avoid waste of time.

The rotary converter gives an alternating current output of 1/2 KW. It is of the vertical type, and occupies a minimum of floor space. The armature is of special design, and differs from the ordinary converter by giving at the slip rings a constant alternating current voltage, independent of the direct current impute voltage. The machine is designed to suit the direct supply available on the ship. It has eight poles, and runs at 2,250 revolutions per minute, thus giving a spark frequency of 300 per second.

The discharger box is made of aluminium, and is fitted on top of the converter, and contains an eight-stud disc, which is carried on the armature shaft by an insulating bush. The top of the box is made of ebonite, and carries the two electrodes. These electrodes are designed to be independently adjusted, and both electrodes can be moved so as to regulate the time of spark discharge in relation to the alternator. A scale of 180 degrees is fixed on top of the box discharger. The phase displacement is shown by an index mark on the ebonite disc carrying the electrodes. When this index mark is at 0 degrees on the scale, the discharge will take place at the moment of maximum volts on the alternator; at 10 degrees lag, the discharge will take place 10 degrees after the alternator has reached its maximum voltage, and so on. A small fan is fitted on the shaft at the bottom of the box discharger, and this carries away the gasses formed by the discharge. The switchboard consists of a black enamelled slate mounted on a cast iron frame, and fitted

with an ammeter of the spring controlled type, a double-pull switch, and two single-pull fuses, and is inserted between the alternating current side of the converter, and the primary of the potential transformer.

The low frequency primary inductance consists of several layers of No. 14 DCC copper wire wound on an ebonite tube. Tappings are made at various points, and connections made to the terminals mounted on top of the box. The function of the low frequency primary inductance is to regulate the power and assist in tuning the circuit. The low frequency potential transformer consists of a primary and secondary mounted on a closed laminated iron core, the complete transformer being enclosed in an aluminium frame. Being of the vertical type, it requires very little floor space. The ratio is about 95 to 1. The high frequency and air-core chokes consist of a number of turns of enamelled wire wound on porcelain bobbins and mounted on top of the potential transformer. They are inserted in the high tension circuit to prevent any rush of high frequency current into the transformer secondary.

The variable coupling oscillation transformer is of the air-core type, a sheet of ebonite, $1/8$ inch thick separating the primary coil from the secondary. The primary consists of about seven turns of copper strip mounted on ebonite; the secondary consists of twenty turns of stranded copper wire wound on a wooden former about twelve inches square. The secondary coil slides over the primary coil, and by this means a coupling between the wave-generating and the wave-radiating circuit is varied. Connection to the primary is made by means of easily detachable spring clips, which provide a ready method of altering the wave-length. The transmitting condenser consists of 34 glass plates interspaced with 17 zinc sheets, the whole supported in a galvanised iron cradle. The alternate zinc sheets are connected together, thus forming two sections. Each section is connected to an insulated terminal on top of the teak lead-lined container.

The two protecting lamps supplied are of the single straight filament carbon type suitable for the voltage of the converter, and mounted between spring clips on a board. One lamp is connected to a shunt to the armature, and the other to the field of the converter. These lamps protect the converter from the injurious effects of any high frequency currents which may be generated in the primary circuit by providing an alternative non-inductive path for them across the machine. The manipulating key is designed for fast sending, and is fitted with a side lever, which provides a ready method at the hand of the operator for breaking the primary circuit in an emergency. There are three terminals which have their connections marked on them. In addition there are two other terminals, which connect to the telephone terminals of the magnetic detector. These are mounted on the end of two insulated spring clips carrying contacts. The contacts touch when the key is depressed, and so short circuit the telephone and prevent it responding to impulses from the transmitting plant. The receiving circuit is always connected to the aerial, so that when the key is up signals can at once be received, and the operator interrupted in the middle of the message if necessary. The front and back upper contacts of the key, and the upper telephone short-circuiting contact are adjustable. The transmitting gear, with the exception of the oscillating transformer, the starter, the regulator, and manipulating key, are enclosed in a sound proof cabinet. The complete transmitting apparatus is mounted on a wooden base, which slides into the cabinet and provides an easy and efficient means for inspection and repairs.

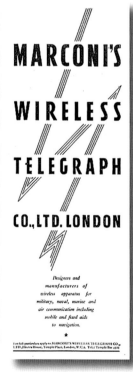

Appendix V
Ports and Owners

What follows is a very potted history of the subject, covering the era of steam trawling. For those readers wishing to further their research, local libraries and museums are an excellent source of material on the subject.

Aberdeen: Scotland's premier steam trawler port has been a fishing centre since the days of Alexander III. Trawling was introduced in the spring of 1882, with the fish market opening in 1889 and thereafter the trade grew and flourished until the 1960s. Aberdeen was favourably positioned for the North Sea grounds, such as the 'Great Fisher Bank' some 200 miles off. This bank was some 30-40 fathoms deep, 120 miles east to west, and 60-80 miles north to south. In later years, some ships were frequent visitors to the Icelandic grounds. The port was not so well placed for obtaining fuel for the ships, as the nearest coalfields were in Fife, which necessitated 'scratch crews' taking the ships to Methil for bunkering. The bulk of Aberdeen's fleet were 'Strath' Class Near Water ships and, by 1905, some 140 steam trawlers operated from the port. Also at this time, some fifty steam liners worked from here, fishing around Rockall and even as far as Greenland. It was reputed that line caught fish was better quality than the trawled variety. A North Sea trip lasted around five to six days and as fresh bread was not baked by the cook, the famous Aberdeen 'rowie' or 'buttery' was substituted, their high fat content meaning that they would stay reasonably fresh for the duration. Many of these early steam trawlers soldiered on until the1960s, when they were replaced by motor ships. Four of Aberdeen's former shipyards – John Duthie and John Lewis (Torry), Alexander Hall and Hall,

Russells (Footdee) – built many hundreds of steam trawlers for owners worldwide. Some of the better known owners were:

Aberdeen Pioneer Steam Fishing Co. Ltd

Aberdeen Steam Trawling & Fishing Co. Ltd (ships names prefixed 'Strath', hulls green topsides over red boot topping, black funnels with two white bands)

Alexander Hay Ltd (hulls green with white line over red boot topping, funnel yellow with black top separated by a silver band)

David Wood Ltd (hulls green over red boot topping, black funnels)

Derry Trawling Co. Ltd

Dodds Steam Fishing Co. Ltd

Don Fishing Co. Ltd, Aberdeen

Harrow Baxter Steam Fishing Co. Ltd

Iona Fishing Co. Ltd

Johnstone & Whyte Ltd

J.W. Johnstone Ltd

John Lewis Ltd (hulls green topsides over red boot topping, black funnel, names prefixed 'Fort'). By 1933 they operated the following trawlers: *Fort Dee* (A.34 – 115ft 6ins x 22ft1ins x 11ft 7ins, 212g, 65nhp), built by themselves as Yard No. 107 in 1929. Sold to Neale & West of Cardiff in 1942 as C.F.15. By 1950 she was back at Aberdeen as A.657, owned by North Eastern Fisheries Ltd (another company owned by J. Lewis). She was scrapped at Montrose on 3rd November 1960; *Fort Rona* (A.195), built by Scott & Sons at Bowling in 1918 as the 'Strath' Class trawler *John Gray*. By 1942, she was owned by United Trawlers Ltd at Milford and was lost in 1943; *Fort Royal* (A.171), built by Lewis in 1931.

An impressive line up of trawlers at Point Law, Aberdeen in 1923. Although the vessels have steam up, the crews were actually on strike against the landing and sale of fish caught by German trawlers in British waters, which was threatening their livelihood when they were prevented from fishing in the same areas due to the imposition of a 3-mile limit. The strike lasted for around a month and witnessed a number of violent confrontations.

She was hired (later purchased) as a minesweeper, No. FY711, in August 1939 and armed with a 12 pounder. She was sunk on 9th February 1940 after attack by two Heinkel III aircraft off Aberdeen. Her consorts that day were *Robert Bowen* (ex-M.269), also destroyed, *Ohm* (ex-H.128) and *Thomas Altoft* (ex-H.132); *Fort Ryan* (A.190 – 121ft x 22ft 6ins x 12ft 6ins, 255g, 68nhp) was built as Yard No. 126 by Lewis in 1932. She was requisitioned in 1939 as a boom defence vessel and returned in December 1944. She then came under North Eastern Fisheries Ltd's flag, until sold to the Binns Group (Trawlers) Ltd, Leeds in 1960. She went for scrap to Holland in October 1961; *Fortrose* (A.801), built as the 'Strath' Class trawler *Matthew Crooke* by Hall, Russell in 1917. Requisitioned in May 1940 as an armed patrol trawler and returned in 1945. She was sold to the Stephen Fishing Co. Ltd, Aberdeen, who sold her for scrap to Holland in June 1961.

A.W. King Ltd (hulls green over red boot topping, black funnels)

Looker Steam Fishing Co. Ltd

National Fishcuring Co. Ltd (hulls green over red boot topping, funnel black with white 'N' between narrow red and yellow bands)

North Eastern Fisheries Ltd

North Star Steam Fishing Co. Ltd (hull, black with white line, funnel black top half over red oxide bottom)

James Porter Ltd

George Robb & Sons Ltd (ships family named or pre-fixed 'Viking', hulls, green with red boot topping, funnels yellow with black top separated by silver over blue bands)

Joseph Craig (Craig Stores) Ltd

Malcolm Smith Ltd

Minerva Fishing Co. Ltd

National Steam Fishing Co. Ltd (black hulls, black topped red funnels, ships names ending in 'os'). In 1913-4, Duthies built the following for the company: *Semnos* (A.18), requisitioned March 1915 as a minesweeper, armed with a 3 pounder, returned 1920. Later GN.25, owned by R. Carnie, Newhaven, Edinburgh. Hired again in November 1939 as a dhan layer and later as an armed patrol vessel. Returned in October 1945 to the Regent Fishing Co. Ltd, Aberdeen as A.423. By 1953, she was owned by the Iver Fishing Co Ltd, Aberdeen. She went for scrap at Hamburg on 27th December 1958; *Sophos* (A.22), was called up in March 1915 as a minesweeper and returned in 1919. By 1937, she was owned and managed by John Craig, Aberdeen. She continued fishing throughout the Second World War and worked for the Southburn Fishing Co. Ltd, Aberdeen (managed by Craig's), until she went for scrap in March 1957 at Hamburg; *Leukos* (A.103), hired as a boom defence vessel from June 1915 until 1919. No entry after this date; *Lotos* (A.112), hired as a minesweeper in November 1914 and returned 1919. She became GN.92, owned by Carnie & Gibb Ltd. She worked for them until 1948, when she was sold back to Aberdeen owners the Lotus Fishing Co. Ltd, as A.21 and she went for scrap on 16th October 1959 at St. Davids on Forth)

Nigg Fishing Co. Ltd

Richard Irvin & Sons Ltd (ships named after Scottish 'Bens', pre-1950 hulls green over red boot topping but later black and black funnels with two red bands)

River Ness Fishing Co. Ltd

Stephen Fishing Co. Ltd (black hulls, black funnel with red band)

Horace E. Stroud Ltd

Walker Steam Trawling & Fishing Co. Ltd (hulls black, funnels grey with black top and white 'W' on red star on blue edged white disc, ship names pre-fixed with 'Star'. Name changed by 1920 to Walker Steam Trawl Fishing Co. Ltd)

William Brenner Ltd

Wood & Bruce Ltd

Granton: Steam trawling arrived here in the early 1880s, when the General Steam Fishing Co. Ltd, Granton was formed by R.W. Duff of Fetteresso (MP for Banffshire). By the turn of the century, some sixty trawlers worked from the port and trawling flourished until the 1960s. Granton was also the home port for ships from Newhaven and Leith. In the early days, trawlers fished from the Bell Rock to the Longstone grounds but later they worked the grounds some 180 to 340 miles off and round the west side off the Butt of Lewis. Some of the Granton owners were:

David Dow (Newhaven) Ltd

Edward Walker & Sons, Leith

Carnie & Gibb Ltd, Granton (hulls green with white line, funnels black with white 'C' on a white edged black disc on a grey band)

William Johnston (Newhaven) Ltd

Joe Croan Ltd, Granton (hulls green with white line over red boot topping. Funnels red with black top, green 'JC' on white disc)

Newhaven Trawling Co. Ltd, Granton (hulls green with white line and white whalemouth, funnels black with a blue 'L' in a white star inside a white ring)

Thomas L. Devlin & Sons Ltd, Granton (hulls green over red boot topping with white waterline, funnels yellow with black top, with yellow 'D' on blue disc)

Thomas Scales & Sons Ltd, Edinburgh

G.I. Ward Ltd, Leith (hulls dark red with white line, funnels red with black top separated by white ring, white 'W' within white ring on black star)

Glasgow and Dundee: Both had small fleets of steam trawlers but these ports were eclipsed by Aberdeen and Granton. They operated smaller Near Water ships supplying the local markets. Both cities had shipyards that built steam trawlers both for the Admiralty and commercial owners. Notable owners were:

Ardrossan Trawling Co. Ltd, Glasgow (hulls black over dark red divided by a white line, funnels houseflag on blue disc on yellow between maroon base and black top, ships names suffixed 'Paton')

Inch Steam Fishing Co. Ltd, Glasgow (Sir John Boyle Ltd – hulls dark red over red boot topping with yellow line, funnels white 'W' on red with black top)

North Shields: Often referred to as '*the birthplace of steam trawling*' after, in 1877, skipper James Kelly of the sailing smack *Zenith* (SN.944) requested a tow from the paddle tug *Messenger*, captained by William Purdy. The smack left her trawl down throughout the tow, managing to secure a good haul of fish. This spurred Purdy to fit out the tug for beam trawling and the end result was the birth of the steam trawler. Another 'Shield's' pioneer was Richard Irvin who, at the age of nineteen, had a part share in a sailing trawler and soon became the owner of the steam trawler *Enterprise*. Richard Irvin was a shrewd businessman and realised that Aberdeen was soon to become a major steam trawling centre, so he opened a branch office there in 1890. In 1901, he built the Shields Ice & Cold Storage Co. and, after seeing the huge

A typically crowded scene at the Fish Quay at Hartlepool in the later 1930s. There were a number of well known trawler operators established here but the vessels in this view are all Lowestoft registered steam drfiters: in the foreground is **Ocean Sunbeam** (LT658), renamed from **Conifer** circa 1935 and operated by R.H. Colby. Behind is **Peacemaker** (LT768) and **Familiar Friend** (LT1144), whilst the bow of **Lord Zetland** (LT777) can be identified behind LT1144's smoke stack.
NEIL PARKHOUSE COLLECTION

quantities of waste haddocks going for fish meal, built a cannery to preserve this fish for public consumption. This was a failure but, undeterred, he switched over to canning herring, which was a great success. North Shields owners favoured the 'Strath' Class trawler but one 'Castle' and one 'Mersey' Class were also registcred there. By 1904, the port had 135 steam trawlers and steam trawling was prevalent until 1964, when only one such vessel remained. A new fish quay was built in 1934, with an inner harbour where trawlers could shelter from the 'North Sea Range' a type of swell common to the port. Some notable trawler owners were:

T.B. Bilton & Sons Ltd, North Shields

R.H. Davidson & Co. Ltd, Hartlepool

J. Graham & Sons Ltd, Hartlepool (hulls black, funnels black with a red +)

Hartness Steam Fishing Co. Ltd, Hartlepool

R. Hastie & Sons Ltd, North Shields (hulls green with red boot topping, funnels black with white 'H' on red band)

Richard Irvin & Sons Ltd, North Shields (hulls black over red boot topping, black funnels with two red bands. Ships names pre-fixed 'Ben')

Walter Offard Ltd, North Shields

G.R. Purdy Trawlers Ltd, North Shields (hulls green, funnels black with narrow white band, ship's names suffixed 'Purdy')

S.H. Walker & Sons Ltd, North Shields

Vedra Steam Fishing Co. Ltd, Sunderland (hulls black, funnels black with single red band)

Warrior Steam Fishing Co. Ltd, Sunderland (hulls black, funnels black with white 'W' between two white bands)

Wear Steam Fishing Co. Ltd, Sunderland (hulls black, funnels black with single white band)

Hull: The River Humber and its close proximity to the 'Silver Pits' made it an ideal base for the 'boxing fleet' of the 1860s. These sailing smacks spent eight weeks on the grounds, transferring their catches daily to steam carriers that raced to Hull and Billingsgate markets. The operation was overseen by the 'Admiral', who was responsible to the owners for the smooth and safe operation of the

system – a system that, when steam trawlers replaced the smacks, continued in Hull until the 1930s. Hull steam trawlers started fishing the Icelandic grounds in 1891 and, from 1895, the larger vessels fished the White Sea. The neighbouring coalfields ensured a plentiful supply of fuel and the railways made for an efficient distribution network. The area was well served by shipyards that became highly specialised in trawler building: Cook, Welton & Gemmell, initially of Hull and later at Beverley; Cochranes of Selby; and Earles of Hull, all of which, along with engine builders Charles D. Holmes, helped construct many hundreds of ships and their names became synonomous with the steam trawler. In 1946, Cook, Welton & Gemmell built **St. John**, Hull's first oil burning steam trawler and her success gradually brought an end to the use of coal firing. Hull became the nation's main Distant Water trawling port, supplying thousands of fish and chip shops with cod, the staple diet of working class famillies. The trawlers required a huge support system for supplying nets, coal, ice, etc, efficient repair shops and fast fish landing facilities. After 1883, these industries were all based around St. Andrew's Dock. This dock contained the fish market – 'the wet side' – with the dry side opposite, where the trawlers were repaired, coaled, iced and made ready for sea, all within two days. The steam trawler reigned supreme at Hull until being replaced by the motor trawler, the last steamer **Arctic Ranger** leaving the port in October 1976 for scrapping. Hull was home to many companies with large fleets of steam trawlers and some of the better known were:

Anglo Norwegian Steam Fishing Co. Ltd (hulls black, black topped red funnel with a white five pointed star motif)

Boyd Line Ltd (hulls black with red line, funnels white with black top and two red bands, ships names prefixed 'Arctic')

Charleston-Smith Trawlers Ltd (hulls black with white line, bow emblem five pointed white star, funnels, white with black top and two white bands, ships name named after stars and prefixed 'Stella'). The company passed to Ross Group in 1948, who kept Charleston-Smith going as a subsidiary. The fleet ended up as part of British United Trawlers when Ross Group and Associated Fisheries merged in 1969. Previously, in 1965, all the ships became

Photo. 140: The steam trawler *Cairo* as originally built for fleeting. She is in the Hull Steam Fishing & Ice Co. Ltd's colours of black hull, brown superstructure and black funnel with white houseflag and red St. George's cross.

'Ross' prefixed (funnels grey with black top, with a white five pointed star on a green flag).

Great Northern Steamship Fishing Co. Ltd (hulls black, funnels black with broad yellow band with a red fish motif)

Thomas Hamling & Co. Ltd (hulls black with white line over red boot topping, funnels broad red band separating yellow from black top, ships names prefixed 'St')

Henriksen & Co. Ltd (hulls black, funnels yellow with blue maltese cross, in centre of cross was a red crown inside a white circle, ships all with seven letter Greek names);

Hellyer Bros Ltd (hulls light grey, funnels yellow with white 'H' on a blue flag, ships named after Shakesperian characters). Company founded as Hellyer's Steam Fishing Co. Ltd, Hull. Hellyers first *Imperialist* (H.2 – 130ft, 264g) was built by Cook, Welton & Gemmell in 1903 as Beverley Yard No. 39 for the Imperial Fishing Co. She was lost off Iceland in January 1907. The second *Imperialist* (H.250) was built by the same yard and lost at Tynemouth by a mine in September 1914. *Imperialist* (H.143) was another Beverley-built ship, Yard No. 457 of 1925, for Hellyers. Some time before 1937, she was sold to Newfoundland Trawling Co. Ltd of St. Johns (*Mercantile Navy List* for 1937). By 1938, she had transferred to French owners as *Administrateur De Bournat*, later *Bournat* in 1940. Later that year, her name changed to *White Nile* and, in 1947, she went to Poland as *Jupiter*.

Hudson Bros (Trawlers) Ltd (hulls black with white line, funnels black with broad white band, ships names prefixed 'Cape'). Some of Hudson's names were repeated on later vessels and two other ships carried the *Cape Barfleur* name. The first was originally *Quantock* (H.321 – 171ft, 441g) from Cochranes in 1936, as Yard No. 1166, for W.B. Willey, Hull. By 1939, she was under Hudsons' management. Her name was changed to *Cape Barfleur* (H.161) in 1946. In February 1949, she went to H. Croft Baker & Sons of Grimsby as GY.16 and a month later her name was changed to *Edward East*. January 1957 saw her as *Ashanti* (GY.16), owned by Roberts Fishing Co. Ltd, Grimsby and she went to Belgium in December 1960. The last trawler to carry the *Cape Barfleur* name was also a 1936-built ship, *Davy* (H.332 – 160ft x 27ft x 15ft, 449g), from Cook, Welton & Gemmell as Yard No. 612. She was launched on 8th July by Miss J. Ross, the owner's daughter, and ran her acceptance trials on 20th August. She was purchased by the

Admiralty in August 1939 as FY147, an anti-submarine trawler, and sold again in 1945, bought back by the Ross family as *Davy* (H.213). In 1951, she was sold to Hudson's as *Cape Barfleur*. In 1954, she went to Fleetwood as *Red Falcon* (LO.4), owned by the Iago Steam Trawling Co. Ltd, London, She was lost in 1959, off Skerryvore.

Hull Steam Fishing & Ice Co. Ltd (hulls black, funnels black with a white flag and red St. George's cross)

Jutland Almalgamated Trawlers Ltd (hulls black with white line, black topped white funnels, with a red maltese cross on a white flag, with blue top and bottom panels, ships names prefixed with 'Lady')

Kelsall Brothers & Beeching Ltd (hulls black, black topped red funnels with a red cockerel on a white flag)

Kingston Steam Trawling Co. Ltd (hulls black with white line, funnels red disc with three white crowns, on white with black top, ships names prefixed 'Kingston'). New ships were built for the company during the inter war period. In 1935, the company added the following five new ships from Cook, Welton & Gemmell: Yard No. 593 *Kingston Cornelian* (H.75), was the lead ship. Sold to the Royal Navy as the anti-submarine trawler FY121. On 5th January 1940, she was lost with all hands off Gibraltar after colliding with the French liner *Cheila*; Yard No. 599 *Kingston Chrysolite* (H.169), was purchased as the anti-submarine trawler FY184 in August 1939 and sold back to Kingston's in 1945. She went for scrap at Dunstan on 27th March 1956. She had the honour to represent Hull at the Royal Spithead Review in 1935, with her crew lining the rails to salute the Royal Yacht; Yard No. 600 *Kingston Ceylonite* (H.173). Also hired in September 1939 for anti-submarine duties as FY214. She was purchased in November of that year and loaned to the US in February 1942. Lost on 15th June that year by a mine off Chesapeake Bay; Yard No. 601 *Kingston Cairngorm* (H.175) was requisitioned in September 1939 as an anti-submarine trawler, lost in the Channel a year later after striking a mine; Yard No. 602 *Kingston Chrysobeyrl* (H.177) was an anti-submarine trawler, Admiralty No. FY236, from September 1939 until being returned in March 1945. Kingston's ran her until she went to the breakers at Bruges on 18th March 1955. In 1936, Cook, Welton & Gemmell built a further quartet of Arctic trawlers, all fitted with coupled Bauer Wach exhaust turbines (160ft 5ins x 26ft 6ins x 15ft 3ins, 432g) They were: Yard No. 607 *Kingston Cyanite* (H.254), launched 25th January by Sister K. Wyburn, and ran trials on 2nd March (built to replace her namesake H.237, purchased by the Admiralty). She was requisitioned in September 1939, as anti-submarine trawler FY217 and returned in September 1945. Kingstons ran her until she went for scrap in 1957; *Kingston Coral* (H.241) was launched on 10th February by Miss. N. Barker and ran her trials on 19th March (also built to replace her namesake purchased by the Admiralty). She was requisitioned as anti-submarine trawler FY215 and returned to Kingstons in September 1945. She fished for them until going to the breakers at Dunstan on 27th March 1956; Yard No. 609 *Kingston Cameo* (H.272) was launched on 27th February by Miss Wellstead and ran trials on 15th April. Almost a year to the day later, on 14th April 1936, she foundered 20 miles off Spurn Light after a collision with the SS *Faxfleet* of Goole; Yard No. 610 *Kingston Crystal* (H.281) was launched on 23rd March by Miss Dorothy Spring and ran trials on 4th May. She was also requisitioned in September 1939, as anti-submarine trawler FY216 and returned in March 1945. She worked for Kingstons until going for scrap in 1958. The first *Kingston Cyanite* (H.237) and *Kingston Coral* (H.241 – 140ft 3ins x 24ft 6ins x 14ft 3ins, 590g) were built by Cook, Welton & Gemmell in 1930, as Yard No's 541 and 540. The conversion drawing (**Plan 61**, page 198) shows them as HMS *Laurel* and HMS *Holly*, purchased by the Admiralty as 'Tree' Class minesweeping trawlers in 1935. The conversion was carried out by Amos & Smith of Hull in 1936. HMS *Laurel* (T.29) served firstly as a minesweeper, then as a dhan layer and finally as a wreck dispersal vessel. She was sold out of service in 1948, going to the Granton Trawling Co. Ltd as *Strathyre* (GN.46). HMS *Holly* (T.19) spent the war as a minesweeper and was sold in 1947 to Denmark as *Dragaberg* (KG.118), owned by P.J.F Kjolbro, Faeroe. In the 1960s, the loss of the homeward bound *Kingston Turquoise*, with the rescue of nineteen of her twenty man crew, could have been far worse but for the uprated rescue and co-ordination services. The timetable of events on that January day in 1965 reads thus:

17.10: *Kingston Turquoise* hits a sandbank some 14 miles NNW of Hoy Head in the Orkneys

17.13: Trawler clears the sandbank but engine room begins to fill with water

17.15: Skipper Colin Cross orders crew to abandon the trawler

17.16: Wick Radio receives Mayday from trawler giving her position and requesting immediate assistance

17.20: No further communication with trawler and 'Operation Playmate' is put into effect

17.25: An RAF Shackleton aircraft is scrambled from Ballykelly and Wick lifeboat is launched

20.00: Shackleton crew locate the life rafts and contact the lifeboat which is about a mile away

20.22: Wick lifeboat picks up nineteen survivors. Meanwhile, the Hull trawler *Stella Arcturus* (H.216), along with ships from Aberdeen and Grimsby, continue to search for the one missing man, Walter Denton

22.30: Search called off

24.00: Survivors landed at Aberdeen.

Loch Fishing Co. of Hull Ltd (hulls green, funnels black with black 'W' on white star, ships names prefixed 'Loch'). The Loch Line Trawling & Fishing Co. Ltd, Aberdeen was founded in 1935 by Harry Wright. In 1954, the company was taken over equally by Hudsons, Hamlings and Hellyers, and renamed Loch Fishing Co. of Hull Ltd. They then transferred the company to Kingston Steam Trawling Co. Ltd in exchange for forty per cent of Kingston's shares. The Loch Fishing Co. of Hull Ltd passed to Hellyer Bros in 1960, along with Kingstons. The fleet kept its identity until 1967, when the company's name was changed to Hellyers and the ships were repainted in their colours.

Lord Line Ltd (hulls black with white line, funnels, broad white band separating red oxide from black top, ships names prefixed 'Lord'). Formed as Pickering & Haldane in 1888 and renamed Lord Line in 1944, transferring to Associated Fisheries in 1950, becoming a limited company in 1953. When Hellyers amalgamated with Associated Fisheries in 1963, ten of Lord Line's ships went to Grimsby under Northern Trawlers, with Hellyers managing the rest. Hellyers eventually took over the Lord Line in 1966

J. Marr & Sons Ltd (hulls cream with red line over red boot topping. Funnels red with black top, ships names prefixed 'Mar');

National Steam Trawling Co. Ltd (hulls black with white line,

funnels broad red band separating black top from white bottom, with a white red centred circle bearing the lettering N S T Co. Ltd in blue)

Newington Steam Trawling Co. Ltd (hulls black with white line, funnels broad blue band separating grey from black top, ships usually named after British authors)

Pickering & Haldane's Steam Trawling Co. Ltd (hulls black, funnels black top separated from red bottom by a broad white band with a blue St. Andrew's cross and the lettering P H & Co in red)

Francis & Thomas Ross Ltd

St. Andrew's Steam Fishing Co. Ltd (hulls black with or without white line, funnels white with black top, ships names prefixed 'St')

West Dock Steam Fishing Co. Ltd (hulls black, funnels black with broad red band, ships names suffixed 'Wyke')

Yorkshire Trawlers Ltd (hulls black, funnels grey with black top and white Yorkshire rose badge).

Grimsby: In the year 875, the name 'Grimsby' arose from the old Scandinavian suffix 'by', meaning village or settlement, and a Dane named 'Grim'. Since then it has always been associated with fishing and records show of local boats fishing at Iceland in the 15th century. Modern Grimsby began in 1848, when the Manchester, Sheffield & Lincolnshire Railway arrived and the building of the Royal Dock commenced the following year. In 1854, the Deep Sea Fishing Co. Ltd, Grimsby introduced the steam liners *Pearl* and *George*, along with the auxiliary steam liners *Samuel Beale* and *Thomas*, thus beginning the port's long history with steam powered fishing vessels. In 1881, the Great Grimsby Coal, Salt & Tanning Co. Ltd operated four steam fish carriers and, in that first year, they ran 384,408 boxes of fish to Grimsby and 164,960 to London. The venture ran into trouble, however, and the ships were later sold for £19,500 to Robert Hewett & Co. Ltd, Barking. That same year, the Great Grimsby Steam Trawling Co. Ltd was formed and in December they launched Grimsby's first steam trawlers, *Zodiac* and *Aries*. By 1887, there were fifteen steam trawlers registered at the port and, by 1904, this number had risen to 483. Perhaps the most significant event was in 1896, when agreements were made between Britain and Iceland which allowed British vessels to shelter and use an Icelandic port provided their trawls were stowed. The new fish dock opened in 1934 at a cost of some £1,700,000. After both world wars, Grimsby's trawling fleet had to be rebuilt to make up for wartime losses but, in 1948, the National Coal Board almost brought the port's trawling industry to its knees, when it increased the price of bunker coal by 25s a ton. They exempted only coasters for whom the increase was restricted to 2s 6d a ton, classing trawlers as 'foreign going vessels'. Grimsby owners laid up their ships, putting over 1,000 men out of work, which forced the NCB to reconsider and trawlers were then classed as coasters for bunker coal (this change applied to all the fishing ports). Grimsby had a more varied fishing industry than Hull, with large Near and Distant Water fleets catching many species of both round and flat fish. The fish market, known locally as 'the Pontoon', covered an area of 314,750 sq. ft and the fish was landed by the 'lumpers' in 10 stone boxes or 'kits'. After being sold, the fish was filletted on the open dock ('Pneumonia Jetty'), before being sent off by rail to all parts of the UK. Grimsby's last steam trawler, *Northern Sceptre*, went to the breakers in 1979. Some of Grimsby's better known owners were:

Alsey Steam Fishing Co. Ltd (grey hulls with white line, black topped grey funnels bearing a Norwegian flag)

Associated Fisheries Ltd. This old established group gradually took over most of the better known Humber trawling companies including Hellyers. The core Grimsby company was the Shire Trawlers fleet owned by Markham Cook, whose ships merged with those of Northern Trawlers (managed by Markham Cook) in April 1950, (although Northern Trawlers Ltd was formed as a subsidiary in 1937 to acquire the fifteen German-built trawlers from the Lever Group company Macfisheries Ltd). At Hull in 1963, Associated Fisheries took over Hellyers, Kingstons, Loch Line and the Lord Line, and at Grimsby, the Great Grimsby & East Coast Steam Fishing Co. Ltd, Loyal Steam Fishing Co. Ltd, Standard Steam Fishing Co. Ltd and the Supreme Fish Curing Co. Ltd, whilst in 1966 they also took over the Atlas Steam Fishing Co. Ltd, Grimsby (Letten Bros). Associated Fisheries merged with the Ross Group in 1969, forming British United Trawlers Ltd, Grimsby, the largest British trawler fleet of the period.

Atlas Steam Fishing Co. Ltd (Letten Bros) (hulls black over red boot topping with white line, funnels black with white 'A' on yellow over blue bands, bordered by white rings; ships names had seven letters, 'V' being the first and 'A' the last)

E. Bacon & Co. Ltd (hulls, black, funnels, black with two red bands separated by a white band). Bacon later established the Lindsey Steam Fishing Co. Ltd, with similar ship colours.

Alfred Bannister (Trawlers) Ltd (hulls black and funnels bearing a red over blue flag with white diagonal stripe and a white 'A' on the red, and a white 'B' on the blue)

Boston Deep Sea Fisheries Ltd (hulls black with white line, funnels red with black top). Formed at a meeting held in Boston Guildhall in 1885, as the Boston Deep Sea Fishing & Ice Co. Ltd, with the company purchasing seven sailing smacks from Alfred Wheatley Ansell, who was the first managing director. Twenty days later, the company ordered two steam trawlers from Earles of Hull. With landing facilities restricted at Boston, the firm based their new ships at Hull but negotiations were in hand to have a new fish quay built, along with a new engineering workshop at Boston. In April 1886, the first four steam trawlers, *Withan*, *Holland*, *Kesteven* and *Lindsey*, moved to Boston. Three of the ships came from Hull carrying their crews, their famillies and furniture, while the fourth ship arrived home from the fishing grounds, her catch being sold the next morning. In 1897, Boston's amalgamated with the Steam Trawling Co. Ltd, Grimsby, thus increasing their fleet to twenty-four ships. By the outbreak of the First World War, the company was struggling financially and, in 1919, Fred Parkes took control and many of the old directors left the company. In 1922, Parkes began building up a new fleet to replace those trawlers lost in the war and the company prospered. All went well until relationships between the company and the Boston Harbour Commissioners soured after the steam collier *Lockwood* capsized, blocking the harbour channel. The company agreed with the Harbour Board to remove the stricken ship and free up the harbour. In short, the Commissioners failed to honour their agreement, with the result that Parkes decided to move the company to Fleetwood, having its headquarters there until 1962. In 1936, Boston's acquired the St. Andrew's Steam Fishing Co. Ltd of Hull (founded in 1897) and from then on Hull was to be their main east coast centre, with a new office block being built at the entrance to St. Andrew's Dock. From then on, Boston's bought out many well known companies,

and managed several more, until they had fifty-six companies on their books, making it the largest family owned fishing company in the world. In 1978, Sir Basil Parkes (Fred's son) retired and sold all his shares, thus ending this famous firm.

Consolidated Fisheries Ltd (grey hulls with red line and red boot topping, light blue funnels, with black tops with a yellow and red crown on a white band, this crown was also the bow badge. Up to the early 1930s, ships named after British Knights, having black hulls and funnels with a white crown, after this all named after football teams). Although the company Consolidated Steam Fishing & Ice Co. Ltd had been inaugurated back in 1906, by John D. Marsden (later knighted), it was not until September 1927 that the name was rationalised to Consolidated Fisheries Ltd. In 1911, Smith's Dock launched twelve steam trawlers for the Port of Blyth Steam Fishing & Ice Co. Ltd and, in August 1913, all were transferred to the Consolidated Steam Fishing & Ice Co. of Grimsby, some of them later transferring to Consolidated Fisheries Ltd in 1927. Their names reflected 'Consols' policy of using the titles of British knights and their fates were as follows: *Lord Allendale* (GY.891), requisitioned in February 1915 as a minesweeper, Admiralty No. 1351, armed with a single 12 pounder and returned in 1919. In April 1937, she was sold to Holland; *Lord Howick* (GY.882) went missing presumed lost with all hands on 14th September 1914; *Lord Tweedmouth* (GY.888). Ran aground at Keithinch, Peterhead, Aberdeenshire on 20th June 1914 and was declared a constructive total loss; *Lord Wolmer* (GY.917) was requisitioned in March 1915 as a minesweeper, Admiralty No. 1235, armed with a single 3 pounder, returned in 1919. She was sold to Holland in June 1926 and renamed *Clasina Luther* (IJM.136); *Lord Wimborne* (GY.916), requisitioned in November 1914 as a minesweeper, Admiralty No. 703 and armed with a 12 pounder, she was returned in 1919. In March 1937, she went to Aberdeen owners as *Lord Wimborne* (A.441), owned by J.S. Kelman, Aberdeen. By 1939 she was owned by Aggie B. Robb of Aberdeen. In January 1941, she went to Fleetwood to the Boston Deep Sea Fishing & Ice Co. Ltd and was lost on 27th March 1943, after stranding at Alftanes, Iceland; *Lord Durham* (GY.879), requisitioned in February 1915 as a minesweeper, Admiralty No. 460, armed with a 6 pounder and returned in 1919. In April 1917, 'Consols' sold her to Dutch owners; *Lord Percy* (GY.898), requisitioned in March 1915 as a minesweeper, Admiralty No. 1609, armed with a 6 pounder and returned in 1919. She ran ashore on the Island of Swona, in the Pentland Firth on 4th June 1930, becoming a total loss; *Lord Grey* (GY.904), requisitioned in March 1915 as a minesweeper, Admiralty No. 1605. She was wrecked on La Barrier Shoal, Cape Griz Nez on 2nd December 1917; *Lord Ashby* (GY.909), requisitioned in March 1915 as a minesweeper, Admiralty No. 1234, armed with a single 3 pounder and returned in 1919. She continued working for 'Consols' until going for scrap in March 1937; *Lord de Ramsay* (GY.911), requisitioned in February 1915 as a minesweeper, Admiralty No. 1144, armed with a 6 pounder and returned in 1919. She went for scrap in October 1924; *Lord Airedale* (GY.910), requisitioned in February 1915 as Admiralty No. 847, armed with a 3 pounder. She was lost on 29th November 1916, after hitting a mine off the Sunk Light Vessel; *Lord Ridley* (GY. 900), requisitioned in February 1915 as a minesweeper, Admiralty No. 850. She struck a mine off Whitby on 10th May 1917 and sank immediately. Sister trawlers *Lionheart* (GY.222) and *Black Prince* (GY.218 – 141ft bp

Steam trawlers alongside the North Quay in the Fish Dock at Grimsby in the 1930s. The identifiable vessels are all locally registered boats; nearest is *Framlingham* (GY1) and alongside it is *Exyahne* (GY150), completed in June 1914 by Cook, Welton & Gemmell for the Marshall Line Steam Fishing Co. Ltd of Grimsby and requisitioned in that September as a minesweeper (FY.264). She was sold in November 1915 to the Savoy Steam Fishing Co. Ltd and returned to them in 1919. She was again taken over by the Admiralty in April 1940 (becoming FY878), returned to her owner in December 1945 and scrapped at Krimpen, Netherlands in April 1961. The white painted stern just glimpsed beyond *Exyahne* is that of *Malayan* (GY322). NEIL PARKHOUSE COLLECTION

x 25ft 6ins x 13ft 6ins) were built by Smith's dock in 1930, as Yard No's 924 and 925. *Black Prince* was the lead ship of the 'Knights' but her life was short. She ran ashore on 12th May 1932 at the Westmann Isles. Her sister was sold to Trinity House in 1940 and later went to Holland. The 'Football Team' naming system did not appear until *Arsenal* in the early 1930s. Not all of 'Consols' ships were named after football teams, as they had interests in Cardiff, where the ships were suffixed 'Castle'. Cochranes fulfiled an order for five 'Castles' in 1928, Yard No's 1031-1035: *Picton Castle* (SA.32), *Pennard Castle* (SA.37), *Roche Castle* (SA.88), *Tenby Castle* (SA.89) and *Clyne Castle* (SA.1). 'Consols' also purchased some ex- 'Fish' Class trawlers, such as Yard No. 1239 *Bonito* (T.231). Launched as the lead ship of the 'Naval' Class on 8th October 1941, she became *Blaefell* (GY.456) in February 1947. In January 1955, she moved to Fleetwood as *Blaefell* (FD.40), owned by Clifton Steam Trawlers Ltd, Grimsby. They in turn sold her to South Africa in 1956 as *Benjamin Gelcer* and she was lost in 1967. As *Blaefell*, she was apparently the last coal burning trawler to work out of Grimsby; *Bream* (T.306) was launched on 10th December 1942, bought by 'Consols' in November 1946 and renamed *Vallafell* (GY.383). In 1952, she was arrested by the Russians for fishing inside their limit, her skipper at the time being Jimmy Hobson. Nothing was heard from the ship for three days and it was to be another month before the whole story came to light. After her arrest, she was escorted to Port Vladimir, where the crew were constantly interrogated. They were each fined the equivalent of £27, then released and the ship headed back to sea. After her release, news filtered through that five of her crew had been arrested at Honingsvaag for refusing to sail on the ship and she left for the grounds with five Norwegian replacements. The trawler eventually returned to her home port on 16th June. She was arrested again in July 1955, when under the command of Arthur Bruce, this time by the Icelandic authorities for alleged poaching and fined £1,600. She was in the news again in 1959, when she was saved from being arrested by the Icelandic gunboat *Thor* by the intervention of two Royal Navy 'Battle' Class destroyers, HMS *Agincourt* and HMS *Corunna*. She remained a coal burner to the end in June 1961, when she went to the breakers; *Grayling* (T.243) was launched on 4th March 1942, purchased by 'Consols' and registered at Swansea by the Rhondda Steam Fishing Co. Ltd as *Barry Castle* (SA.33 – **Photo. 85**). She foundered off

the north west of Iceland whilst under tow on 1st November 1955, when four of her crew were lost; *Grilse* (T.368) was launched on 6th April 1943. After the war, she went to Swansea as *Swansea Castle* (SA.27) in 1946. She was converted to oil fuel in August of the following year and went for scrap at Sunderland on 10th June 1960; *Mullet* (T.311) was launched on 14th August 1941 and was sold in 1946 to the Rhondda Steam Fishing Co. Ltd as *Neath Castle* (SA.49). In March 1958, she transferred to Grimsby as GY.52 and went to the breakers in June 1961; *Pollack* (T.347) was launched on 22nd April 1943 and became *Cardiff Castle* (SA.66) in 1946 (**Plan 67**). The following year she was converted for oil fuel. In 1952, she was purchased by Clifton Steam Trawlers Ltd, Fleetwood as *Julia Brierley* (FD.103) and she went for scrap in 1960; *Whiting* (T.232) was launched on 22nd October 1941. She later became *Burfell* (GY.346) and sailed on her last trip to the Sunderland breakers yard on 10th June 1960. Reports differ as to their sea-keeping qualities, though the majority complained of their wetness. They were reckoned by many to have been the worst sea ships in the Grimsby fleet. One ex-radio operator, Harry Hutson, stated: "*They were the only trawlers working out of Grimsby fitted with two echo sounders, one for measuring the water under the ship and the other for the depth above. So wet were they, that bungs should have been specified for the funnels.*".

Crampin Steam Fishing Co. Ltd (hulls black over red boot topping with white line at deck level, funnels yellow with black top separated by a red band with a white 'C', ships all named after English cricketers)

H. Croft Baker & Sons Ltd (hulls black with white line at deck level and red boot topping, funnels grey, black topped, bearing a five pointed white star on a green flag)

Crown Steam Fishing Co. Ltd (hulls black, funnels yellow, black topped, separated by a red band bearing a yellow and red crown)

Derwent Trawlers Ltd (part of Ross Group, same colour scheme)

Diamond Steam Fishing Co. Ltd (hulls black over red boot topping, funnels were yellow with black top separated by a broad red band edged by two blue rings and bearing a triple white diamond logo)

T.C.&F. Moss Ltd (hulls black and funnels yellow, black topped, bearing an inverted black horseshoe motif)

Northern Trawlers Ltd (hulls black with white line and red boot topping, funnels grey, black topped, separated by a white band. Ships names prefixed 'Northern'). The company took over the 1937 German-built ships from Fleetwood prior to 1939. They were as follows: *Northern Chief* (LO.165, later GY.445), scrapped 1957 at Hamburg; *Northern Dawn* (LO.136, later GY.289), scrapped 27th March 1963 at Dunstan; *Northern Duke* (LO.169 later GY.442), scrapped 30th October 1963 at Dunstan; *Northern Foam* (LO.153, later GY.490), scrapped 17th October 1963 at Dunstan; *Northern Gem* (LO.109 later, GY.204), scrapped 15th June 1966 at Antwerp; *Northern Gift* (LO.166, no GY number); *Northern Isles* (LO.172, no GY number), lost in 1945; *Northern Pride* (LO.104, later GY.169), the class leader, scrapped 7th March 1963 at Dunstan; *Northern Princess* (LO.170, no GY number) lost in 1942; *Northern Reward* (LO.168, later GY.431), sold to Iceland in 1947; *Northern Rover* (LO.164, no GY number), lost in 1939; *Northern Sky* (LO.162 later, GY.427), scrapped 27th July 1964 at Dunstan; *Northern Spray* (LO.140, later GY.190), wrecked NW Iceland on 23rd October 1963; *Northern Sun* (LO.161 later, GY.440), scrapped 2nd July 1966 at Antwerp; *Northern Wave* (LO.120, later GY.184), scrapped 30th October 1963 at Dunstan. *Northern Spray* led quite an eventful life after the war, rescuing the crew of the trawler *Red Gauntlet* in 1947, which had struck a reef off Spitzbergen. The survivors were saved from their lifeboats after the vessel had foundered. On 10th December 1950, *Northern Spray* herself was in trouble. Under skipper Sveri Ebernezersson, she ran aground at Iceland. The weather at the time was atrocious, gales and blinding snow, which knocked out her radar and she struck the rocks at Skutulsfjord at 15.50pm. After a struggle, she was refloated at 18.30pm but she ran aground again at Isafjoerdur some three hours later. She was not finally refloated until Christmas Day, after unsuccessful attempts by *Derby County* (GY.514) and *Frobisher* (LO.15) of Fleetwood. Her end came finally on 23rd October 1963 when, under skipper Peter Fenty, she was running for shelter in Isafjoerdur Fjord, West Iceland but struck fast on the rock bound coast. The Hull vessel *James Barrie* (H.15) came to her aid and eight of her crew were rescued after taking to their boat. The remaining twelve hands were taken off by the Icelandic Gunboat *Odin*. It was ironic that *Northern Spray* met her end in very close proximity to the spot where she grounded some thirteen years earlier. Another *Northern Gift* (GY.332) joined the fleet in April 1950. She was the second of a pair built by Smith's Dock as Yard No's 1007 and 1008 in 1936, for the Rutlandshire Fishing Co. Ltd, Grimsby. They were *Rutlandshire* (GY.335) and *Hertfordshire* (GY.332 – both 164ft 6ins bp x 27ft x 15ft, 458g). The lead ship, *Rutlandshire*, was requisitioned in 1939 as the anti-submarine trawler FY241. She took part in the Namsos raid and ran aground after being bombed by enemy aircraft on 20th April 1940. The enemy salvaged her a year later and put her to work as *Ubier*. She was sunk on 6th December 1942. *Hertfordshire* was also called up in 1939, as the anti-submarine trawler FY176. She was leased to the US in 1941 and returned in 1945. During her naval service she was bought by Shire Trawlers in April 1940 and by the time she joined Northern Trawlers in 1950, she had been converted to oil fuel. They in turn sold her to Fleetwood in August 1954, as *Wyre Gleaner* (FD.23), owned by Wyre Trawlers Ltd. She went to the breakers at Troon in September 1963.

Queen Steam Fishing Co. Ltd (hulls black, funnels black separated by a blue band with a red upper ring and white lower ring, with a white 'Q')

Rinovia Steam Fishing Co. Ltd (hulls grey or black with white line, funnels grey, black topped, bearing 'Norwegian flag' motif)

Sir Thomas Robinson & Son Ltd (hulls black, funnels black with red white and blue flag)

G.F. Sleight & Sons Ltd (hulls black, funnels black, two blue bands separated by a white band, ships names began with 'R' and ended with 'O')

H.L. Taylor Ltd

Vinur Steam Fishing Co. Ltd (hulls black with red boot topping, funnels black with white 'V' on broad blue band between narrow white and red rings)

Great Yarmouth: Once a port with a large fleet of sailing trawlers which used the fleeting system, transferring their catches at sea for fast shipment to the London market. Some of these sailing smacks were later converted to motor, with others sold abroad or eventually broken up. Eight such vessels were still working in 1939. Although Yarmouth was eclipsed as a steam trawling centre by neighbouring Lowestoft, it still had a few steam trawlers in the 1950s but none were registered at the port. Some steel drifter/trawlers were sold to Poland around this time and after renaming *Dal I, II, III*, etc, continued to work out of the River Yare. Few trawler owners were based here but some who operated out of Great Yarmouth were:

Hewett's Short Blue Fleet Ltd Ltd, London (black hulls, brown casings and black funnels with blue flag), which in the 1930s bought the Gamecock, Red Cross and Heward fleets to make them the major operator of LO registered steam trawlers.

Bloomfield's Ltd

Lowestoft: From the early 1870s, the port of Lowestoft differed from neighbouring Great Yarmouth in that the sailing trawlers worked independently, landing their catches here for rail distribution rather than operating the fleeting system, where the fish was transferred to fast steam carriers. At this time, the two ports were famous for their herring fishery, working huge fleets of sailing drifters. With herring being a seasonal catch, many of the drifters switched to trawling in the off-season and the 'converter smack' was born. This dual purpose vessel continued with the steam drifter/trawler until motor power was introduced. The first company to move into steam trawling was the Lowestoft Steam Trawling Co. Ltd, who in 1887 purchased three Scottish vessels, *Greencastle* (LT.101), *Dolphin* (LT.100) and *Bonito* (LT.106) but the venture was not a success and the ships were sold in 1888. Lowestoft developed slowly as a steam trawling port, even with the close proximity of the 'Silver Pits' area of the Dogger Bank. The main drawback was the distance from the nearest coalfields, which meant that coal transport costs were high. By 1900, the port had no local steam trawlers but operated some 300 sailing trawlers and these latter vessels dominated Lowestoft's trawling until 1939. The first steam trawler to be built for the port was *Lolist* (LT.427), from Smith's Dock in 1914. She joined two older iron steamers, *Adelaide* and *Labrador*, both purchased from the Hull Steam Fishing & Ice Co. Ltd. After the First World War, a few more steam trawlers arrived at the port, mostly ex- 'Straths' and, by 1930, Lowestoft had a mix of 325 steam drifters and trawlers, with many being the drifter/trawler type. The last of this type was *Merbreeze*,

A fleet of steam drifters entering the harbour at Lowestoft in the first decade of the 20th century. They are passing through the railway swing bridge which had to be opened to let ships enter. The nearest vessel is the Inverness registered **Annie Smith** (INS422), suggesting that the fleet seen here is probably Scottish. However, **Annie Smith** was fitted with a 25HP compound engine by local manufacturer Edgar C. Burrell & Sons when she was launched in 1907. Requistioned by the Admiralty in the First World War, she was lost off Lundy Island in 1918 whilst on minesweeping duties after a collision with another vessel. *NEIL PARKHOUSE COLLECTION*

STEAM DRIFTERS GOING THROUGH LOWESTOFT BRIDGE

built at Richards Ironworks in 1931. Two years later, one of the first motor trawlers arrived, *Purple Heather*, a wooden sailing smack fitted with a four cylinder Crossley two-stroke diesel engine. The last pure steam trawler to leave for the breakers in November 1959 was *Cairo* (LT.154 – 108ft 4ins x 21ft 3ins x 11ft 2ins, 172g), built at Beverley in 1902 as H.550 for the Hull Steam Fishing & Ice Co. Ltd. She came to George Mitchell, Lowestoft in 1945 (**Photo. 139**). A major boost came in 1935, when the East Anglian Ice & Cold Storage Co. Ltd placed an order with Richard's Ironworks for twelve new motor trawlers, heralding the beginning of the end for steam trawling at Lowestoft. Some of the port's better known owners were:

Boston Deep Sea Fisheries Ltd (colours as per Grimsby ships)

J.V. Breach & Co. Ltd

Breeze & Co. Ltd

F.E. Catchpole Ltd (black hulls with red boot topping, funnels yellow with black top, with a yellow star on a blue flag)

Colne Fishing Co. Ltd (hulls black, funnels blue with black top, bearing a blue 'C' on a white flag)

Drifter Trawlers Ltd

Hobson's Ltd

W.H. Kerr Ltd (black hulls and funnels with a white band between two blue bands)

Lowestoft Steam Herring Drifters Co. Ltd

Small & Co. Ltd (grey hulls over red boot topping, orange black topped funnels with houseflag)

West Hartlepool Steam Navigation Co. Ltd, Lowestoft (black hulls with white line, funnels yellow with a black 'G')

London: Although never a steam trawling port, it was the home to some large trawler owners who operated their fleets from other ports and of course, Billingsgate Fish Market is known world wide. Some London owners were:

Brandon Fishing Co. Ltd

Hewett Fishing Co. Ltd – 'The Short Blue Fleet' (hulls black with red boot topping, except those suffixed 'Hewett' which were blue with a red line. Funnels black with blue houseflag)

Heward Trawlers Ltd (a subsidiary of Hewetts)

Iago Steam Trawling Co. Ltd (hulls black with red boot topping, black funnels with red band, ships names prefixed 'Red');

Milford Steam Trawling Co. Ltd (black hulls and funnels with a red 'M' on broad white band);

Jenkersons Ltd (black hulls over red boot topping with white line, brown superstructures and black funnels with red Maltese cross on a white band)

Fleetwood: Britain's fourth steam trawling centre, it initially had a small jetty further up the River Wyre at Skippool. Fleetwood started as a commercial port in 1839, as an important ferry link for the Isle of Man and Scotland. The trawling industry began in 1889, when the steam trawler *Lark* (FD.120) was built for Moody & Kelly Ltd. This prompted Kelsall Brothers & Beeching Ltd, London to send some of their trawlers from Hull to the Lancashire port. A good rail service and the nearby Lancashire coalfields ensured a sound base for steam trawling. The trawler numbers grew with the addition of the ABC and Gamecock fleets but this did not last, as the latter company withdrew all thirty-two of its ships to Hull in 1897. In 1898, James H. Marr brought seven ships to Fleetwood and soon he began to revitalise the industry. He, along with other owners, saw that hake, abundant in the Irish Sea and the Scottish west coast, was treated as 'offal' and dumped at sea. Marrs began to aggressively market hake and soon this species was to be Fleetwood's main catch. By 1900, the port had fifteen steam trawlers and, by 1911, the fleet was valued at some half a million pounds. By 1913, the annual catch stood at some 37,000 tons. During the First World War, the port lost more than thirty steam trawlers but these were replaced in the post war period, when some ex- 'Castle' Class trawlers were purchased. The fleet continued to grow, with the smaller ships fishing for hake off St. Kilda, Muckle Flugga, Flannan Isle and Rockall, whilst the larger trawlers went to Iceland, Bear Island and north Norway for cod and haddock. Until the early 1930s, many of the ships had no electric light, calcium carbide being used instead which, when mixed with water, produced acetylene gas for lighting. As liver boilers did not arrive until after 1940, Fleetwood ships carried the fish livers in barrels. A major influx of new ships in the 1930s was Macfisheries' large Bremerhaven-built 'Northern' trawlers. However, these large London registered ships were unsuitable for the port and all moved to Grimsby in 1937. The Second World War cost Fleetwood dearly in lost ships and men but fishing was continued from here by Dutch, Belgian and Danish trawlers forced out of their home ports. After 1945, the fleet was reborn with both Iago and Hewett adding both new and older ships. Marrs too built a new generation of steam trawlers for the port, the first being *Miranda* from John Lewis in 1946, with *Navena* and *Josena* following from Cook, Welton & Gemmell. In the 1950s, coal firing gave way to oil; Fleetwood's last oil fired steam trawler, *Samuel Hewett*, was built in 1956 and went for scrapping in 1968, five years after the last coal burner, *Lord Lloyd*. Fleetwood was home to a great many owners, some having only one or two ships, whilst others operated large fleets. A few of the better known firms were:

R.H. Bagshaw Ltd

Boston Deep Sea Fishing & Ice Co. Ltd (ships wore standard 'Boston' colours)

Boston Deep Sea Fisheries Ltd

Brixham Trawlers Ltd (hulls black over red boot topping, funnels black with a red cockerel on a white flag)

Cevic Steam Fishing Co. Ltd (hulls black with or without white line, funnels black with two red bands)

Clifton Steam Trawlers Ltd (hulls black, funnels black topped red separated by a white band)

Dalby Steam Fishing Co. Ltd (hulls black with white line and red boot topping, funnels black)

Dinas Steam Trawling Co. Ltd (hulls either grey with red boot topping or black with white line, funnels black with broad red band)

H. Elliot & Sons Ltd

Filey United Steam Trawling Co. Ltd

Fleetwood Steam Fishing Co. Ltd (hulls black, funnels yellow, black topped bearing a black 'F')

Hewett Fishing Co. Ltd – 'The Short Blue Fleet' (hulls black, funnels bearing a square blue flag)

Iago Steam Trawling Co. Ltd (early hulls black over red boot topping, later hulls mauve; funnels black with single red band)

Alex Keay Ltd

Lancashire Steam Fishing Co. Ltd (hulls black over red boot topping, funnels yellow, black topped separated by a red band)

Lune Steam Fishing Co. Ltd (hulls black, funnels black with red band separated from lower section by a white ring with a white 'L' on the red)

Macline Ltd

J. Marr & Sons Ltd (hulls yellow with red line at deck level, funnels black topped red);

Mason Trawlers Ltd (hulls green with white line and red boot topping, funnels broad dark red band separating yellow from black top)

Melling Steam Trawling Co. Ltd (hulls black with white line and red boot topping, funnels had a broad white band separating pink from black top)

Mount Steam Fishing Co. Ltd

Parkhouse Trawlers Ltd

River Steam Fishing Co. Ltd

Rosalind Fishing Co. Ltd

Scarisbrook Steam Trawlers (Fleetwood) Ltd

Sun Steam Trawling Co. Ltd

Transvaal Steam Trawling Co. Ltd

John N. Ward & Son Ltd (hulls black, funnels white, black topped)

Wyre Steam Trawling Co. Ltd (hulls black with white line and red boot topping, funnels black with two white bands; early ships had a white funnel with a black top, ships names prefixed 'Wyre')

Plymouth: This was the main steam trawling port on the south west coast, based in Sutton Pool, one of Plymouth's six harbours. The first steam trawler, *Reginald* (PH.75), arrived in 1899 and, by 1906, there were twelve steam trawlers using the port, with seven ships being owned by Chant & Paddon. During the First World War, this owner lost six ships, the only survivor being *Condor* (PH.15), Yard No. 191 by Alexander Hall. After the war, six ex-'Castles' came to Plymouth: *James Laveney*, *Peter Cary*, *Thomas Alexander*, *Thomas Lawrie*, *William Carberry* and *William Keylon*. The inter-war years saw very little change, with no large fleet owners and no new tonnage being bought. One exception was a couple of ex-French trawlers, one taken over as payment for a bunkering debt and the other bought by a local rag and bone man who named it after himself, *George Turner*. The end of Plymouth's steam trawling came in 1954, when *Perverus* (PH.116) and *Roskeen* (A.81) left the port and through its history, the steam trawler fleet never numbered more than some thirty vessels. Plymouth had only a few owners:

Chant & Paddon Ltd (hulls black, funnels green with black top, ships named after seabirds)

O. Curphey & Sons Ltd

J.H. Luxton Ltd

Percy Turner Ltd

Milford Haven: The main catch here was hake. It dominated the trawling because of the closeness of the grounds, which meant fish were in prime condition when landed, thus fetching good prices. The port's first steam trawler, *Albatross* (M.2), was launched from the Castle Street Iron Works in 1883. *Sybil* (LT.77) was the first steam trawler to enter the new dock, on 27th September 1888 and, by 1891, some twenty-one steam trawlers were berthed at Milford. By the end of the century, the port became the fifth largest in the country, when some 18,245 tons of fish were landed, with the fleet expanding to sixty-six steamers by 1904. The port was hit hard by a coal strike in 1912, with all the ships laid up, causing a large part of the fleet to be transferred to Fleetwood. The First World War saw sixty Milford trawlers taken over by the Admiralty, with twenty-four Belgian vessels carrying some 700 refugees arriving. By 1915, the port had lost seven trawlers to enemy action. By 1925, the Milford fleet comprised 110 steam trawlers but this large fleet found it harder to remain profitable during the inter war period and, in 1930, the Iago Steam Trawling Co. Ltd transferred its ten trawlers to Fleetwood. In 1934, David Pettit sold his fleet of ten trawlers, also to Fleetwood but, in 1935, the Milford Docks Company formed the Milford Steam Trawling Co. Ltd. The Second World War saw the fleet reduced to fifty-one, as ships were requisitioned for war service, leaving around forty trawlers still fishing. The immediate post war period saw the fleet expand and, by 1946, it stood some ninety strong, with a record 59,000 tons of fish landed. The increase in coal prices by 1955 saw many older ships laid up for scrapping, with the remainder of the fleet depending heavily on subsidies. This situation was made worse by dwindling hake stocks and the phrase 'hake, hope and charity' was coined at Milford. The steamers cost on average £120 more for fuel per trip than a motor trawler and

Photo. 141: The Inner Dock, Milford Haven circa 1908, with up to a dozen steam trawlers in the picture. Bunkering coal was delivered here from local collieries in the railway wagons seen on both sides of the dock. Note the bow of a Lowestoft registered vessel on the extreme left of the picture, in front of which is Milford Haven Steam Trawling Co. Ltd's 1905-built **St. Bride** (M88). *NEIL PARKHOUSE COLLECTION*

The Inner Dock, Milford Haven

the only thing in their favour was that they had been written off for depreciation purposes, thus costing little for insurance. To replace them with motor trawlers was unthinkable, as a new £100,000 ship meant that higher earnings were essential but quite impossible with the state of the industry, although Milford Trawlers Ltd did convert six of their ships to diesel in an attempt to stem the tide. By 1957-8, only ten steam trawlers were operating out of Milford Haven. Over the years, some of the port's owners were:

Bricknell & Sons Ltd

E.E. Carter Ltd

Crescent Trawling Co. Ltd

The Don Trawling Co. (Milford Haven) Ltd

Drifter Trawlers Ltd

Hakin Trawling Co. Ltd

Haven Trawlers Ltd

S.J. Hellings & Son Ltd

Jenkersen & Jones Ltd (hulls black, funnels black with a blue band separated from two red bands by two white bands)

J.C. Llewellin Ltd

Milford Fisheries Ltd

Milford Haven Steam Trawling Co. Ltd (hulls black, funnels black with two blue rings on a red band)

G.R. Parsley Ltd

Pettit & Younds Ltd

Phoenix Trawling Co. Ltd (hulls black, funnels black topped red)

H.E. Rees & Co. Ltd

Ritchie & Davies Ltd

Southern Steam Trawling Co. Ltd (hulls black over red boot topping, funnels black topped white, with red flag bearing a white circle with blue centre)

Vanessa Fishing Co. Ltd (hulls black, funnels black with white band bearing a red and black butterfly motif)

Welsh Trawling Co. Ltd (hulls black, funnels black topped red)

Western Steam Trawling Co. Ltd (hulls black, funnels black topped white, with a blue flag bearing a white circle with red centre)

W. Wilox Ltd, Milford

Yolland Brothers Ltd, Milford

Swansea and Cardiff: Little has been recorded about the trawling operations of these two large ports on the south Wales coast. The largest trawler owner at Cardiff was Neale & West Ltd, who opened a fish merchants business in 1885. They bought their first trawler, *Lark*, from Hull in 1888, which was the forerunner of a large steam trawling fleet. Henry West left the firm in 1910 but it continued to operate under the former name. J.J. Neale befriended a Japanese businessman, with whose firm a training scheme was set up for Japanese trawlermen and from then on all the company's ships had Japanese names. The complete fleet was requisitioned in the First World War, with the majority being lost. To rebuild it, the firm entered into a long standing relationship with Smith's Dock, Middlesborough. The list of vessels built for Neale & West by Smith's Dock is shown in Table 1, overleaf (note that after their Yard No. 816, the company changed the numbers and the next vessel after that was No. 337). By the end of the 1940s, the company's main areas of operation, the south and west Irish coasts, were suffering from over fishing, which caused some difficulties. The Second World War again saw most of the fleet called up for war service, after which it had to be rebuilt with second hand ships from other ports. The firm's Cardiff base was at West Bute Dock but, by 1956, trawling from the port had ceased, with the company moving it's remaining vessels to Milford Haven. Company colours, were black hulls and black funnels with a white band bearing a red 'N'. The only two other Cardiff companies I have any details for are:

Gibb & Co. Ltd (hulls black, funnels black topped red)

Jenkins Brothers Ltd (hulls black, funnels black).

For Swansea, I only have details for the following:

Castle Steam Trawling Co. Ltd (hulls black, funnels black topped red bearing a white 'Castle' motif, ships names suffixed 'Castle')

Hector Steam Trawling Co. Ltd (hulls black, funnels black with two white bands)

Rhondda Fishing Co. Ltd (hulls black, funnels black with two narrow white bands and a white 'Bull' motif in between)

Liverpool: Little is known about trawling at this Mersey port, although records show that twenty steam trawlers worked from here in 1894. One of the main owners was J. Duncan & Co. Ltd (initially, hulls light grey but later black, funnels black with a yellow band bearing a blue flag, on which was a yellow over red diagonal panel with a red 'D' and yellow 'L').

TABLE 1: TRAWLERS BUILT BY SMITH'S DOCK FOR NEALE & WEST OF CARDIFF

YEAR	YARD NO.	NAME & NO.	RADIO	NOTES
1906	805	*Hirose* (CF.20)	HJKB	Sunk by a U-boat 130 miles W by S of Lundy on 2.6.1915
1908	371	*Oyama* (CF.23)	HMSR	Hired as minesweeper 1914-19
	372	*Nogi* (CF.24)	HMST	Hired as minesweeper 1915-19
1909	412	*Oku* (CF.25)		Hired as minesweeper 1916-19
	413	*Kuroki* (CF.8)		Hired as minesweeper 1915-19, again in 1940 as a boom defence vessel, returned 1945
1911	475	*Kodama* (CF.34)	MDSB	Hired as minesweeper 1915-19
	476	*Ijuin* (CF.35)		Hired as minesweeper 1915, sank by U-boat's guns on 22.7.1918
	481	*Miura* (CF.36)		Hired 1914, sunk by a U-boat off Great Yarmouth 23.08.1915
	482	*Nodzu* (CF.22)		Hired as minesweeper 1915, sank after hitting a submerged wreck in the Bristol Channel in January 1919. She was later raised and sold in 1920 to Australian owners as *Olive Cam*. She met her end a long way from home when she foundered off Eden NSW on 2.11.1954
1912	510	*Hatano* (CF.16)		Hired as minesweeper 1916-19
	511	*Fuji* (CF.17)		Hired as minesweeper 1915-19
1913	546	*Mikasa* (CF.41)		Lost 1914
	547	*Sasebo* (CF.27)		Hired as minesweeper 1915-19
1914	575	*Sunia* (CF.)		
	584	*Asama* (CF.18)		Sunk while serving as a decoy vessel by a U-boat on 16.7.1917
	585	*Kyoto* (CF.)		Sunk by gunfire from U-boat off Fastnet on 2.11.1916
	586	*Hatsuse* (CF.21)		Sunk by U-boat 86 miles SW of Fastnet on 14.11.1916
1915	604	*Hirose* (CF.44)		Hired as minesweeper 1915, sank after striking a mine off Aldborough, 29.6.1916
	605	*Mikasa* (CF.41)		Hired as minesweeper 1916-19, again from December 1939 to February 1940 and once more from April 1944 to October 1944 as an armed patrol vessel. After this she went to Milford as LO.4, under G. Jenkerson Milford & D.G. Jones of Pembroke Dock. All their ships carried a red Maltese cross on the funnel
1918	637	*Hirose* (CF.)		
	638	*Miura* (CF.)		
1923	775	*Nogi* (CF.)	GJSB	Sold to Jenkerson & Jones as LO.49. She was requisitioned as a minesweeper in August 1939 and was lost on 23.6.1941
	776	*Oyama* (CF.29)		
1924	786	*Chiyo* (CF.14)		
	787	*Yezo* (CF.)		Sold to Jenkerson & Jones as LO.74. Hired as a minesweeper 1939 and as a wreck dispersal vessel from February 1944 to 1946. She then returned to Jenkersons
	794	*Tamura* (CF.)	GKDM	Sold to Jenkersons as LO.63. Lost in 1940
	795	*Settsu* (CF.)		Sold to Jenkersons as LO.75. Hired in January 1940 as a boom defence vessel and returned in 1946. She was sold to the Milford Steam Trawling Co. in 1958
1925	806	*Hatano* (CF.16)		By 1939 she was owned by Jenkersons as LO.177. She was requisitioned as a minesweeper in September 1939, Admiralty No. FY662, and returned in May 1945. She went for scrap at Milford Haven on 14.5.1956
	807	*Fuji* (CF.17)		Sold to Holland in 1936, renamed *Maria Van Hattem* (IJM.1)
1927	829	*Kunishi* (CF.20)		Hired August 1939 as Admiralty No. FY692, for minesweeping duty. Sold out of service
	830	*Suma* (CF.19)	GMVX	Hired August 1939 as a minesweeper, FY618. Returned in March 1946
	834	*Hatsuse* (CF.21)		Listed above in description
1928	853	*Honjo* (CF.26)		Listed above
	854	*Sasebo* (CF.27)		Listed above
1929	882	*Oku* (CF.3)	GQKW	Requisitioned August 1939 as FY660, a minesweeper and returned February 1945. She went for scrapping on 20.2.1957
	883	*Yashima* (CF.6)	GQLM	Hired as a minesweeper in August 1939, Admiralty No. FY1894, returned in April 1946. She went for scrap on 9.4.1956 at Newport, Mon.
	894	*Asama* (CF.18)		Listed above in description
	895	*Nodzu* (CF.22)		Listed above
1931	913	*Naniwa* (CF.24)	GLMV	Built at the Stockton yard
	914	*Nuroto* (CF.28)	GLPY	Built at the Stockton yard. Hired as a minesweeper in August 1939, Admiralty No. FY611, returned in January 1944. Scrapped 14.5.1956 at Newport, Mon.
	926	*Oyama* (CF.29)	GPLK	Built at the Middlesborough yard. She went to Clifton Steam Trawlers Ltd of Fleetwood in 1940, as *Dorothy Lambert* (FD.122) and went for scrapping at Ghent on 25.11.1955
	927	*Sata* (CF.30)	GPLN	Built at the Middlesborough yard. Not hired during the war for naval duties. Fished for Neale & West until going for scrap at Newport, Mon. on 25.5.1956

Appendix VI
Trawler Insurance

Another side to trawler ownership was insurance. This was a very specialised form of marine insurance and, as such, tended to be left largely in the hands of mutual associations or 'Clubs'. Each owner entered their vessels, paying a small initial entrance fee and subsequently sharing all claims incurred by other vessels of the association in direct proportion to the listed tonnage or amount insured by each member. It may be fair to say that by far the greater number of British trawlers were insured through these associations and these in turn passed on most or all of their risks to underwriters in the open insurance market. There seems to have been three main reasons for the formation of the mutual associations. Firstly, small craft were notoriously difficult risks to assess. Thus the mutual basis by which claims were shared by a number of trawlers spread the risk and promised a more accurate method of assessment than was possible by direct rating. Secondly, trawler owning was a very specialised form of ship owning. Owners at different ports and even on different coasts tend to be very clannish and are subsequently in closer touch with each other than was the case in the carrying trades. And thirdly, the comparatively small values on which trawlers are insured assisted the associations to absorb the whole of these values direct, even when there was a subsequent resort to reinsurance. Thus the owners found it convenient to insure their fleets by one transaction, rather to partly insure their craft with an association and the balance in the open insurance market.

These mutual associations offered three main classes of cover to the owners. The first was for total loss, damage done by collision and general average. The second covers particular average, whilst the third covers loss of life and those risks excluded by the ordinary maritime policy, which became known as protecting the indemnity risks, such as the removal of wrecks, damage to jetties, plus claims under the Workmen's Compensation Acts. In the 'Damage Done' and 'Average' classes, the rules provided that the actual insurance contract was with the Club, and that all premiums were calculated according to the incurred losses, as if the insured were themselves mutual insurers.

Entries in this section are made by amounts insured, as distinct from entries in the Particular Average class, which are made on the basis of gross registered tonnage. The perils covered under the Total Loss, Damage Done and General Average classes speak for themselves, while the perils covered under the Average class are those of the ordinary marine policy but this policy is warranted free of capture, seizure, etc and free of claim for trade of contraband of war or breach or attempted breach of blockade. This class is also warranted free of claim for loss of life, personal injury and injury to livestock or cargo. It is further provided that claims incurred by a vessel when within a prohibited area shall be subjected to a deduction of from 10 to 30 per cent. In the Average class, the most noticeable feature is the franchise and the class is divided into four sub-classes. Class A has a franchise of £10.00, class B of £50.00, class C of £100.00 and class D of £200.00. In calculating these franchises, only the cost of repairs is taken into consideration and not the cost of surveys or other incidental expenses. The insurers will pay the full cost of sighting-the-bottom after a stranding when reasonably incurred.

Another point in favour of the Average class was that it worked on the principle of 'new for old', as compared with the ordinary marine policy's 'no thirds'. This was possibly one of the reasons for the success of the associations, permitting them to operate successfully when the open market was unable to do so. The definition of Average is given by the British Marine Mutual Insurance Co. as '... *GENERAL AVERAGE. Average is a partial loss. General average is a deliberate act, part of the cargo or ship being sacrificed to prevent total loss of the ship, cargo, and freight. All of these three interests pay towards the cost of the partial loss. PARTICULAR AVERAGE. A partial loss other than General Average.*'

With regards to war risks, some Clubs would offer cover for an extra premium. Article 56 of the North British Fishing Boat Insurance Co. Ltd rules of 1st January 1919, states:

For an extra premium the Company, although they shall not be under obligation to do so, may in addition to the risks here-in before mentioned agree to hold the vessel insured against all or any of the following risks or perils, namely - The risks or perils of capture, seizure or detainment by the King's enemies and the consequences thereof or any attempt there at, and all consequences of hostilities or warlike operations by or against the King's enemies, whether before or after declaration of war, and other like perils, and also as incidental thereto to relieve such insured of all losses, claims, and expenses incurred by him as owner of the vessel insured arising out of these risks and perils under and in respect of the Workmen's Compensation Acts, or any statuary modification thereof.

There were of course additional restraints issued by the insurers for war risks:

A. The vessel shall be employed only in sea fishing.
B. The vessel shall not be employed in any area prohibited by His Majesty's Government or by the Fishing Vessels War Risks Insurance Association, Limited, or by the company.
C. Vessels so insured must not approach, enter, or leave the harbours in England or Scotland or Ireland or Orkney or Shetland except during daylight.
D. The vessel shall comply with the orders of His Majesty's Government and the directions of the Association or Company, as to sailing routes, ports of call, stoppages, arrival, manning, equipment and otherwise.
E. The vessel shall leave an enemy's port within the days of grace allowed by the enemy, and shall comply with the terms of any pass granted by the enemy.
F. The vessel shall not enter or leave, or attempt to enter or leave any port which is known to be blockaded by the enemy.
G. It is recommended in order to minimise the risk both to the vessels and those on board, that vessels should be navigated as far as practicable only during daylight.
H. The vessel shall comply with the rules of the British Fishing Vessels War Risks Insurance Association Limited.

Although trawlers were insured without trading warranties, they were restricted to working within defined limits, such as the North Sea as far as Latitude 63, the English Channel, the Atlantic as far south as Bayonne, and as far west as Longitude 17, and the Sound as far as Copenhagen. Beyond these limits they were uninsured. All the claims were met out of the fund provided for by the entrance fees but, when this was used up, the directors would call on the owners for a further contribution based on the tonnage entered.

On 19th June 1922, the Aberdeen Mutual & General Insurance

Co. Ltd sent the following to their members: '*Sir, the following claims having been intimated, I have been instructed to make a call as under noted to meet the same. Duncan Rennie. Secretary*'.

A list of claims met by the association from October 1921 until 20th February 1922 followed and the owner of *Frigate Bird* (A.769) was asked for a premium based on the following classes:

CLASS 1. Total Loss, General Average and Salvage Charges. Insured at 4000 at £0.8.6 per cent = £17.0.0

CLASS 2. Particular Average. Insured at 4000 at £0.4.6 per cent = £9

CLASS 3. Workmen's Compensation, 7 men insured at £0.11.0 per man = £3.17.0.

CLASS 4. Protection and Indemnity, 99 Tons insured at 1s.6d. per ton = £7.8.6.

The total premium being £37.5.6d. The bill was received on 19th June and was paid by the owners on 20th (who pays their insurance bills as fast to-day?). The previous request for payment on 12th November 1921 covered the claims from 2nd July until 30th September, these were much heavier claims and the bill was made up thus:

CLASS 1. 4000 insured at £1.5.4d per cent. = £50.13.4d.

CLASS 2. 4000 insured at £0.1.3d per cent. = £2.10.0d.

CLASS 3. 7 Men insured at £0.4.0 per man. = £1.8.0d.

CLASS 4. 99 Tons insured at 9d. per Ton. = £3.14.3d.

A total premium of £58.5.7d. (Again paid the next day).

The main benefit of the Mutual Association was that, when collisions occurred, the insurers quickly and amicably settled the disputes. When the two trawlers belonged to the same association, there was a great incentive to the owners of keeping their claims to a minimum, since they were both contributing to the ultimate settlement. Even when the vessels belonged to different Clubs, the incentive was still there to keep the claims as small as possible. This could be described as an early form of 'No claims bonus', as practiced by present day motor insurers. Generally, claims for damage to trawlers differ quite considerably from those of merchant vessels, due not only to their trade but also to certain factors that are not really appreciated. At one time, trawlers working the Icelandic grounds could put into any of the island's ports. There they could obtain powerful, cheap liquor, often putting back to sea in a condition detrimental to good seamanship and navigation. This was believed to be the reason for the number of losses. Another system that prevailed at some ports was that of giving pre-sailing bonuses. These had to be worked off before they started earning money. This increased the risk to vessels, since they would hang on to their gear long after the weather dictated otherwise. Thankfully, these practices were discontinued, the trawlerman's job was risky enough without these added dangers. The main task of the deep sea trawler was to return to port safely with a catch of fish. Ironically this catch was not normally insured, as the policy was usually for a fixed amount which was payable after the vessel was totally lost (whether she had full holds or not). In the case of salvage, however, claims are settled with a percentage allowed for the value of any catch on board. Bearing in mind that the value of a 300 ton trawler in the mid thirties was around £25,000 and the fact that, in the winter of 1935, no less than eight Grimsby trawlers were lost with all hands, a total of sixty-three lives, the premiums demanded by outside marine insurers would have been way in excess of those levied by the mutual associations, hence the reason for their formation.

Appendix VII
Trawler Sales Brokers

Unlike coasters, which tended to stay with one or possibly two owners throughout their lifetime, trawlers would change hands frequently, sometimes to new owners but often to subsidiary companies operating under the main parent company. The trawler, like the coaster, was a specialist vessel, both built for a specific task but here the similarity ended. The coaster was designed to carry a stipulated cargo tonnage, from a port of lading to an agreed destination. Payment and profit on the trip depended on the cargo arriving safely and in good condition. Delivery times, although tight, still depended on the vagaries of the weather, with ships having to shelter sometimes for days on end before finally reaching their discharge ports. Unless the goods were of a very perishable nature or were livestock, then the cargo would suffer little from the delay and payment in full could be demanded at the end of the contract. The trawler had no such leeway with regards to her cargo. She had to reach the fishing grounds, get a catch of fish and return with it in prime condition to port. Should the quality of this catch suffer in any way from delays, no matter how they were caused, then the balance sheet would reflect this. At best, poor quality fish would be sold for fish meal at a fraction of the price it should have made were it for human consumption. At worst, the catch would be dumped overboard, with the trip making a total financial loss. This was indeed a bitter pill to swallow for both the crew and owners alike. The fishermen, who had grafted for up to eighteen hours a day, in some of the worst weather in the world, were left in debt and the owners had to subsidise the trip from the profits made by other vessels in their fleet. Such were the commercial risks allied to the fishing industry. This meant that as the nearer grounds were suffering from over fishing, trawlers had to travel longer distances to find fish, trips where the older, smaller and slower vessels just could not compete with their newer counterparts. So the ships were sold. Often to smaller companies, with smaller profit margins and fewer directors who all wanted their cut. Some ships were heavy on fuel, some were very wet, others were dogged by mechanical problems but these were all factors governing the viability of the vessel.

These changes of ownership would undoubtedly have been handled by brokers such as Thomas McLaren & Co. of Glasgow (established in 1867), H.E. Moss & Co. of Newcastle on Tyne, W.A. Massey of Hull and John Lister of Hartlepool; these firms were to act as sales brokers for the many thousands of vessels that moved around during the history of the sidewinder. Their drawing style was a prime example of austerity and absence of real detail, as was found on most of the shipyard drawings. No longer were deck fittings drawn in full detail, trawl winches became a rectangle in plan and, if shown at all in side elevation, were depicted by a circle. The after cabins, once so beautifully detailed, became little more than an empty shell; funnels, and masts became truncated, with no rigging shown whatsoever. It is fair to say that these drawings were done solely as a marketing tool, usually by skilled female tracers, working from the original plan and filling in only enough detail so as to provide a prospective purchaser with a general overview of the vessel. But, although they lacked detail, in many cases, these are the only records left of the many hundreds of vessels that passed through their hands. So if, as the saying goes, '*a picture is worth a thousand words*', then these sketchy drawings are priceless to the student.

Appendix VIII
Landing & Distribution

Trawlers were unloaded by 'porters' at Aberdeen, 'bobbers' at Hull and 'lumpers' at Fleetwood and Grimsby. They started in the early hours of the morning following the ship's return, working in teams or gangs, with one group below in the fish room sorting the different species into baskets. These were hauled aloft by the 'winchman' and swung onto the quay by the 'swinger'.

The fish were then weighed and placed into fresh baskets or 10 stone 'kits', before being placed on the market for sale. Prior to 1930, the baskets were hoisted manually from the holds using tackles fitted above on the 'landing span' but this method was later replaced by electric winches on the quay. Another team of men, the 'board scrubbers', thoroughly cleaned every pound board before they were stowed away again. Prior to the late 1920s, the fish, after being sold on the market, fetched up at two main retail outlets, the fishmonger or the fish-frier. Numbers of the former were always difficult to ascertain, as in addition to the listed fishmongers' shops, there were thousands of other grocery concerns that had a small fish counter, for the convenience of their customers. The fish-friers were predominantly found in the poorer areas of the industrial hinterland and their numbers rose by 175% from 1901 to 1931. In the same period, the number of fishmongers dropped slightly. As to figures, there were an estimated 16,000 fishmongers, and 30,000-plus fish-friers in 1935. In England, this could be further broken down to:

Northern England	Population	Fishmongers	Fish-Friers
Yorkshire	4,821,000	1,034	4,383
Lancashire	4,529,000	670	3,700
Southern England			
London	4,397,000	944	1,263
Home Counties	7,235,000	1,578	670

These figures were from a detailed report by the UK Sea Fish Commission in 1935. It also showed that, in the West Riding of Yorkshire, the number of fishmongers had decreased by 25%, whilst the fish-friers had increased by fully 100% in the smaller towns from 1901 to 1927. It was the fact that the fish and chip shops used only a few species of fish, such as cod, haddock and hake, which kept the Distant Water ships in employment. The fall in demand during the summer months allowed the owners to lay up their ships, until the market picked up again in the autumn, with the peak coming in the winter months when every ship would be working to capacity.

Bibliography

PERIODICALS

Commercial Fishing
Engineering
Fishing News
Marine News
Motor Boat and Yachting
Norwegian Maritime and Fishing News 1954-1962
Sea Breezes
Shipbuilding and Shipping Record
Ships Monthly
The Engineer
The Marine Engineer
The Shipbuilder

REGISTERS etc
British Trawlers, Ian Allan (ABC)
British Warships 1914-1919, Dittmar & Colledge
List of Fishing Boats in Scotland 1914
List of Vessels Belonging to the East Coast of Scotland 1894/95
Lloyds Register of Shipping
Mercantile Navy Lists
Olsens Fisherman's Nautical Almanacs
The British Fisheries Manual & Directory 1947
Warships of WW2, Lenton & Colledge

BUILDERS' LISTS
Alexander Hall, Aberdeen
Caledon Shipyard, Dundee
Charles D. Holmes, Hull
Cochrane's Shipbuilders, Beverley and Selby
Cook, Welton & Gemmell, Beverley
David Allan, Granton
Dundee Shipbuilding, Dundee
Earle's Shipbuilding, Hull
Fleming & Fergusson, Paisley
Hall, Russells, Aberdeen
John Duthie (Torry Shipyard)
John Lewis Sons, Torry Aberdeen
Ramage & Ferguson, Leith
Richards Shipbuilders, Lowestoft
Smith's Dock, Middlesborough

BREAKERS' LISTS
Albert Draper, Hull
Metal Industries, Inverkeithing

PUBLICATIONS
An Examination into the Present State of the Grimsby Trawl Fishery 1895
B.R.77 Machinery Handbook 1941, Admiralty
Brown's Trawlers and Fishermen's Guide, Brown Son & Ferguson 1937
Directory of Shipowners, Shipbuilders & Marine Eengineers 1949

Fisheries in Wartime, HMS.O 1944
Fishermen's Handy Billy, Hull Fishing Vessel Owners 1914/1924
Fish on the Spotline, R. Balls, Marconi International
Introduction to Trawling, Fishing News Books 1964
Notes on Trawl Fishing, D.B. Cunningham (J. Lewis & Sons) 1949
Practical Shipbuilding, G. De Rooij, MINA Holland 1953
Reports of the White Fish Industry, HMSO
Rules of the North British Fishing Boat Insurance Co. 1919
Seafood Ships, A.C. Hardy 1947
Steel Ships (their construction and maintenance), T. Walton & J. Baird 1944
The Design and Construction of Small Craft, R. Munro Smith 1924
Trawlerman's Handbook, Fishing News 1965
Trawler Safety – Final Report, HMSO 1969
Trawl Fishing, The British Trawlers Federation.
Verbal Questions & Answers for Trawler Engineers, James Munro & Co., Glasgow

Photo. 140: The homeward bound *Ben Screel* (A.121) ran ashore in thick fog on the Girdlestone Rock, Aberdeen on 18th January 1933. All her crew were rescued by breeches buoy but the trawler later broke up. Unfortunately, this was the fate of many fine vessels whose crews perished only yards from safety – such was the ultimate price paid in ships and men throughout the period of the steam trawler. The industry was slow to change, as such losses were treated as isolated incidents. Not until the multiple tragedies of the 1950s was legislation put in place to safeguard the lives of our trawlermen.

No more we'll round the old Spurn Light and greet the wind,
No more our pounding engines, sound their heartbeat through the night;
Our working lives were written in the stories men tell yet,
You may damn us and discard us, but do not quite forget.

JOHN CONOLLY

THE CIRCLE OF LIFE
The trawlers caught the cod, that fed the miners, that dug the coal, that fuelled the trawlers,
that caught the cod, that fed the miners, that dug the coal etc.,etc.

(A North Shields round)

Index of Ships Names

An interesting vessel which appears twice in the Index above. A view on the port quarter of the Cochrane-built 'Fish' Class armed trawler **Mullett** (T.311). Note the upper conning bridge (mount misery) and the ash shoots fitted to her funnel. New in 1941, after the war she was bought by the Rhondda Steam Fishing Co. Ltd, who renamed her **Neath Castle**. After transferring to Grimsby in 1958, her 20-year career ended when she was sent for scrapping in 1961.

Index of Engineers & Equipment Suppliers

Another hard and dirty task in what was, for the majority of the time, the hard and dirty career of a trawlerman. This is a typical scene on board a North Sea steam trawler in the 1930s. She is a 'hansom cab' ship with acetylene lighting. Note the twin barrel trawl winch, the centre bollards, tall cowl vents and the starboard trawl board hanging from the aft gallows. The port side light screen is empty, as the oil lamp would be stowed in the lamp room. Gutting the fish at sea prior to packing in ice is still a job that has to be carried out by hand by trawlermen today. *ARCHIVE IMAGES/SUNNYFIELD COLLECTION*

Index of Owners

Index of Builders

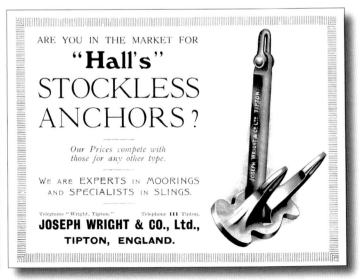

E. C. Grant, Grimsby.　　Loyal Steam Fishing Co., Ltd., Grimsby.　　W. & A. E. Lambert. Grimsby.　　Lindsey Steam Fishing Co., Ltd.

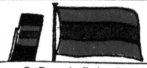

J. Grant, Grimsby.

W. Grant, Grimsby.

Grant & Baker, Grimsby.

J. L. Green, Grimsby.

Grimsby & East Coast Steam Fishing Co., Ltd.

Grimsby & North Sea Steam Trawling Co., Ltd.

Grimsby Steam Fishing Co., Ltd.

Letten Bros.,

FISH SALESMEN,
HERRING SALESMEN,
Fish & Ice Merchants,
Licensed Auctioneers,

AND

Steam Fishing Vessel Owners,
GRIMSBY.

Importers, Exporters, and Wholesale Dealers in

WET, SALTED & WIND-DRIED COD, LING, HADDOCKS, SAITHE, &c.

BROKERS

For the Sale and Purchase of

STEAM TRAWLERS, SMACKS, and FISHING VESSELS

OF EVERY DESCRIPTION.

W. S. LETTEN, Judge (by appointment of the Royal Commission,) on Fishery Exhibits at the World's Fair, Chicago, 1893.

Telegrams: "LETTEN, GRIMSBY."
National Telephone: No. 606 & 607.
Code: A B C 4th and 5th Editions, Lieber's Standard.

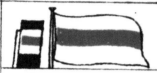

J. R. Mackrill & Sons, Grimsby.

Consolidated Steam Fishing & Ice Co. (Grimsby), Ltd.

Morris & Fisher, Grimsby.

T. C. & F. Moss, Grimsby

W. Mudd & Son, Grimsby.

North Eastern Steam Fishing Co., Ltd., Grimsby.

North Lincolnshire Steam Fishing Co., Ltd., Grimsby.

E. Bacon, Jr., Grimsby.　　Dolphin Steam Fishing Co., Grimsby.　　Premier Steam Fishing Co., Ltd., Grimsby.　　Northwold Steam Fishing Co., Ltd., Grimsby.

O. T. OLSEN, NAUTICAL BOOK PUBLISHER, GRIMSBY.